as a Percentage of Gross Domestic Product

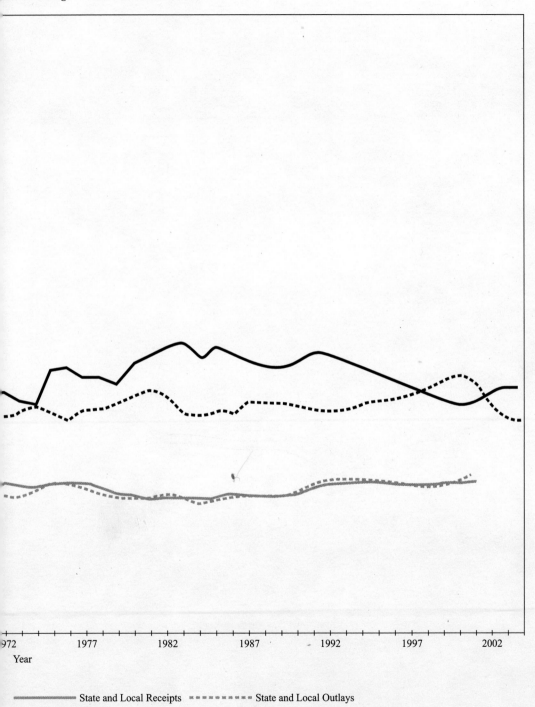

1972   1977   1982   1987   1992   1997   2002

Year

━━━━━━ State and Local Receipts   ▪▪▪▪▪▪▪▪▪ State and Local Outlays

Public Finance

SEVENTH EDITION

Harvey S. Rosen

Department of Economics
Princeton University

Boston   Burr Ridge, IL   Dubuque, IA   Madison, WI   New York
San Francisco   St. Louis   Bangkok   Bogotá   Caracas   Kuala Lumpur
Lisbon   London   Madrid   Mexico City   Milan   Montreal   New Delhi
Santiago   Seoul   Singapore   Sydney   Taipei   Toronto

PUBLIC FINANCE
International Edition 2005

Exclusive rights by McGraw-Hill Education (Asia), for manufacture and export. This book cannot be re-exported from the country to which it is sold by McGraw-Hill. The International Edition is not available in North America.

Published by McGraw-Hill/Irwin, a business unit of The McGraw-Hill Companies, Inc., 1221 Avenue of the Americas, New York, NY 10020. Copyright © 2005, 2002 by The McGraw-Hill Companies, Inc. All rights reserved. No part of this publication may be reproduced or distributed in any form or by any means, or stored in a database or retrieval system, without the prior written consent of The McGraw-Hill Companies, Inc., including, but not limited to, in any network or other electronic storage or transmission, or broadcast for distance learning.

Some ancillaries, including electronic and print components, may not be available to customers outside the United States.

10 09 08 07 06 05 04
20 09 08 07 06 05
CTF ANL

Library of Congress Cataloging-in Publication Data

Rosen, Harvey S.
    Public finance / Harvey S. Rosen.—7th ed.
      p. cm.
    Includes bibliographical references and index.
    ISBN 007-287648-4
      1.   Finance, Public—United States. I. Title.
HJ257.2.R67 2005
336.73—dc22   2003068851

When ordering this title, use ISBN 007-123842-5

Printed in Singapore

www.mhhe.com

To Marsha

About the Author

HARVEY S. ROSEN

Harvey S. Rosen is the John L. Weinberg Professor of Economics and Business Policy at Princeton University. Professor Rosen, a Fellow of the Econometric Society and a Research Associate of the National Bureau of Economic Research, is well known for his contributions to the fields of Public Finance, Labor Economics, and Applied Microeconomics. From 1989 to 1991, he served as Deputy Assistant Secretary (Tax Analysis) at the US Treasury. His articles have appeared in such journals as *Econometrica, American Economic Review,* and *Journal of Political Economy.* He is currently on the editorial boards of the *National Tax Journal, International Tax and Public Finance, Public Finance Review,* and *Regional Science and Urban Economics.*

Preface

"It is a foolish thing to make a long prologue" (II Maccabees 2:32). I shall once again follow this Biblical advice and be brief in describing the features of this seventh edition. The field of public finance is quite different than it was a generation ago. On the theoretical side, one of the main achievements has been to integrate the analysis of government spending and taxing more closely with basic economic theory. A prime example is the literature on optimal taxation, which attempts to *derive* prescriptions for government fiscal behavior using standard economic tools, rather than to annunciate a set of ad hoc "principles" for tax design. On the empirical side, the most exciting development is the widespread application of the tools of econometrics to understanding how expenditure and tax policies affect individual behavior and how the government itself sets policies.

The results of modern research have been slow to enter traditional texts. This book takes its readers to many of the frontiers of current research. The approach to the material, while accessible to undergraduates, is the same as the approach shared by most economists who are now active in the field.

The development of public finance has not proceeded free of controversy. In this book, disputes concerning both methodological and substantive issues are discussed at length. One reviewer of an early draft of the manuscript warned against displaying too much of the profession's dirty laundry in public. My feeling, however, is that "full disclosure" should apply not only in the market for securities, but in the market for ideas as well.

Economic analysis sometimes loses touch with the reality it is supposed to describe. I have tried to avoid this tendency. The relevant institutional and legal settings are described in ample detail. Moreover, the text constantly emphasizes the links between economic analysis and current political issues.

Organization

Part One now consists of three chapters that set the stage for the rest of the book. Chapter 1 consolidates two short chapters from the previous edition, and provides a broad perspective on the role of government in the economy. The next two chapters discuss the methodological tools used in the study of public finance. These include the methods of empirical analysis (Chapter 2) and the fundamentals of theoretical welfare economics (Chapter 3). The remainder of the book follows the conventional tactic of analyzing government expenditure and revenue-raising activities separately.

Part Two (Chapters 4 through 11) deals with the expenditure side of the budget. It describes and evaluates various government programs. Part Three (Chapters 12 through 14) presents a theoretical framework for discussing taxation. The major revenue-raising instruments are analyzed using this framework in Part Four (Chapters 15 through 19). Finally, Part Five deals with the special issues that arise under a federal system of government.

Some instructors may choose to do the tax side (Parts Three and Four) before the expenditure side (Part Two); the book is designed so this can be done easily. In the same way, the chapters within Parts Two, Three, and Four can generally be taken up in any order desired without serious loss of continuity.

This book is designed for use in undergraduate curricula as well as graduate programs in public administration. Readers should be familiar with microeconomic theory at the level of the standard introductory course. Because some use is made of indifference curve analysis, a topic not covered in all introductory courses, indifference curves are carefully explained in the appendix to the book. In addition, this appendix provides a brief review of other topics in basic microeconomics, including the supply and demand model, marginal analysis, and consumer and producer surplus. This review should be adequate to refresh the memories of readers who have been away from microeconomics for a while. A glossary of key terms appears after the appendix.

The British statesman Edmund Burke noted that "To read without reflecting, is like eating without digesting." To facilitate this digestive process, each chapter ends with a set of discussion questions. Their purpose is to encourage students to apply and extend the principles that they have learned. Several reviewers of the previous edition suggested that I both increase the number of discussion questions and include more computational exercises. It's a good idea, and instructors who like to assign problems will find a lot more selection than before.

I hope that *Public Finance* will whet readers' appetites to learn more about this field. To that end, a large number of articles and books are cited within the chapters. A typical citation consists of the author's name followed by the date of publication in brackets. Readers can find the full reference in the consolidated bibliography at the back of the book. The references vary considerably in technical difficulty; those who wish to pursue specialized topics further have to pick and choose. In addition, the end of each chapter has a short list of suggested readings. They are suitable for inclusion in undergraduate syllabi.

What's New in the Seventh Edition?

"Are you doing anything beside updating the tables?" That's the question many of my colleagues asked when they heard I was revising *Public Finance*. The answer is, "Quite a bit, actually." There are literally dozens of new examples of how the study of public finance can shed light on contemporary policy discussions. For example, the chapter on public goods uses the post-September 11 debate on airport security to frame the discussion of public versus private provision of public goods. Similarly, vaccinations against smallpox are used as an example of positive externalities in Chapter 5.

On the expenditure side, Chapter 8, "Expenditure Programs for the Poor", has been thoroughly revised to include new research on 1996 welfare reform. This research looks systematically at how the benefit reduction rates, time limits, and work requirements of the new system have affected labor supply and other economic decisions of welfare recipients. The section on Medicaid has been substantially augmented, and now discusses the impact of the recent Medicaid expansions on insurance coverage (the "crowding out" controversy) as well as the notch that the program induces in the leisure-income budget constraint.

Chapter 9 on Social Security has new explanations of the annuities market, the trust fund and its relationship to the federal budget, and the retirement effects of the system. It also discusses the recommendations of President Bush's Commission on Social Security Reform. Chapter 10 on Medicare analyzes one of the most prominent policy questions in this area, prescription drug coverage. In addition, there is a discussion of the intriguing conjectured relationship between health insurance coverage and the pace of technological change in medicine. Chapter 6, "Political Economy", now has a major new section on the rent-seeking model.

On the revenue side, Chapter 13, "Taxes and Efficiency", contains a new example that links excess burden to earlier material on externalities. This is the so-called "double-dividend hypothesis," which claims that efficiency would be enhanced by reducing marginal income tax rates and making up the shortfall in revenues with pollution taxes. The discussion of the personal income tax (Chapter 15) now includes a major section on the Alternative Minimum Tax (AMT). The material explains why the AMT is becoming so important as a policy issue and possible ways to deal with it. On the business tax side (Chapter 17), there is a discussion of the hypothesis that a link exists between the corporation tax and the Enron and other corporate accounting scandals. This chapter also covers the Bush administration's proposal for a dividend exclusion in the personal income tax. The discussion of the estate tax in Chapter 19 includes new research on its impact on saving. The chapter also discusses the peculiar status of the current law, according to which the estate tax is scheduled to be eliminated in 2010 and then brought back to life in 2011.

Despite these changes, the basic thrust of the book is unchanged. As in the previous editions, the goal is to interweave institutional, theoretical, and econometric material to provide students with a clear and coherent view of government spending and taxing.

Harvey S. Rosen

Acknowledgments

It is a pleasure to acknowledge all the people who have helped in the preparation of this book. As a graduate student, I was fortunate to be taught by two of the world's outstanding figures in public finance, Martin Feldstein and Richard Musgrave. Feldstein and Musgrave differed considerably in their approaches to the subject, but they shared a fundamental outlook—public finance is not a mere academic exercise; its goal is to help us understand and perhaps improve real-world situations. The intellectual influence of both these men is evident throughout the text.

Nearly 400 academic colleagues who teach public finance responded to a survey that provided useful material on how they focus their courses. The input afforded insights about their needs and those of the students who take their courses.

I have been the beneficiary of numerous suggestions for improvements over the previous edition. I am particularly grateful to Marco Bassetto (University of Minnesota, Minneapolis), Sewin Chan (New York University), Gary Galles (University of California, Los Angeles), Ted Gayer (Georgetown University), Malcolm Getz (Vanderbilt University), Gary Hoover (University of Alabama), Hilary Hoynes (University of California, Davis), Edward Lopez (University of North Texas), Stephen Rubb (Bentley College), Benjamin Scafidi (Georgia State University), John Sondey (South Dakota State University), John Straub (Texas A & M University), and Aaron Yelowitz (University of Kentucky), who reviewed the entire manuscript. I received detailed comments on entire chapters from Andrew Samwick (Dartmouth College), Amy K. Taylor (US Center for Health Services Research), and Janet Holtzblatt (US Treasury). Thanks are due to Ken Fortson (Princeton University) for assistance in preparing the manuscript. I am most appreciative and thankful to Sewin Chan (New York University) for examining the entire final manuscript and scrutinizing the page proofs to ensure this book's accuracy.

A number of scholars identified places for refinement and reorganization in this edition, or helped me out with particular issues. They include:

Rebecca Blank
University of Michigan

Kai Chan
Princeton University

Eric Engen
Federal Reserve Board

Lee Fennell
University of Texas

William Gale
Brookings Institution

Kevin Hassett
American Enterprise Institute

xiii

Wade Pfau
Princeton University

Eugene Steuerle
Urban Institute

Eytan Sheshinski
Hebrew University

Recognition of and an expression of appreciation to the people who reviewed and made useful suggestions for earlier editions of this text are also appropriate.

Roy D. Adams
Iowa State University

Eric Engen
Federal Reserve Board

James Alm
University of Colorado

O. Homer Erekson
Miami University, Ohio

Gary M. Anderson
California State University, Northridge

Allan M. Feldman
Brown University

Gerald Auten
US Treasury

John Fitzgerald
Bowdoin College

Charles L. Ballard
Michigan State University

Fred E. Foldvary
Virginia Tech

Thomas Barthold
Joint Committee on Taxation

Don Fullerton
University of Texas

Douglas Blair
Rutgers University

J. Fred Giertz
University of Illinois

David Bradford
Princeton University

Amihai Glazer
University of California, Irvine

Neil Bruce
Queens University

Roy T. Gobin
Loyola University of Chicago

Lawrence P. Brunner
Central Michigan University

Haynes Goddard
University of Cincinnati

Donald E. Campbell
College of William and Mary

Jane Gravelle
Congressional Research Office

Howard Chernick
Hunter College

Timothy J. Gronberg
Texas A & M University

John A. Christianson
University of San Diego

Jonathan H. Hamilton
University of Florida

Edward Coulson
Pennsylvania State University

Rich Hanson
University of California, Irvine

Bev Dahlby
University of Alberta

L. Jay Helms
University of California, Davis

Robert A. Dickler
Bowie State University

Roger S. Hewett
Drake University

Avinash Dixit
Princeton University

James Hines
University of Michigan

Kevin T. Duffy-Deno
Southeastern Massachusetts University

Douglas Holtz-Eakin
Syracuse University

Gary A. Hoover
University of Alabama

Paul Hughes-Cromwick
Henry Ford Health System

Robert Inman
University of Pennsylvania

Robert Kelly
Fairfield University

Edward Kienzle
Boston College

Bruce R. Kingman
SUNY, Albany

Jeffrey Kling
Princeton University

Helen Ladd
Duke University

Charles G. Leathers
University of Alabama

Gary D. Lemon
De Pauw University

Al Lerman
US Treasury

Steve Lile
Western Kentucky University

Alessandro Lizzeri
Princeton University

Bradley S. Loomis
Rochester Institute of Technology

Robin Lumsdaine
Brown University

Molly K. Macauley
Resources for the Future

Randall Mariger
University of Washington

Philip Meguire
University of Canterbury

Roger P. Mendels
University of Windsor

Fanus van der Merwe
Potchefstroom University for Christian Higher Education, South Africa

Olivia Mitchell
University of Pennsylvania

Robert Moore
Occidental College

John Murray
Bank of Canada

Susan Parks
University of Wisconsin, Whitewater

Anthony Pellechio
World Bank

Alfredo M. Pereira
University of California, San Diego

Paul Portney
Resources for the Future

James Poterba
Massachusetts Institute of Technology

B. Michael Pritchett
Brigham Young University

Uwe Reinhardt
Princeton University

Mark Rider
US Treasury

Robert Rider
University of Southern California

Steven R. Sachs
University of Connecticut

Efraim Sadka
Tel-Aviv University

Gian S. Sahota
Vanderbilt University

Ben Scafidi
Georgia State University

Albert J. Shamash
Trenton State College

Kenneth Small
University of California, Irvine

John L. Solow
University of Iowa

Richard Steinberg
Virginia Polytechnic Institute and State University

Thomas F. Stinson
University of Minnesota

Paul Styger
Potchefstroom University for Christian Higher Education, South Africa

Lennard van Vuren
*Potchefstroom University for Christian
  Higher Education, South Africa*

Marianne Vigneault
Bishop's University

Michael Wasylenko
Syracuse University

Kristen Willard
Columbia University

Clifford Winston
Brookings Institution

Aaron Yelowitz
University of Kentucky

James Young
Northern Illinois University

George Zodrow
Rice University

When I wrote the first edition of *Public Finance,* my children Lynne and Jonathan were babies. Now they are old enough to have friends who are using the book. To those friends I make a simple plea: Do not visit the sins of the father upon his children! Finally, I thank my family lawyer for technical advice and encouragement.

H. S. R.

Brief Table of Contents

Table of Contents

P A R T   Analysis of Public Expenditure

2

P A R T   A Framework for Tax Analysis

3

P A R T **Multigovernment Public Finance**

5

PART 1

Getting Started

People's views on how the government should conduct its financial operations are heavily influenced by their political philosophies. Some people's top priority is individual freedom, others place more emphasis on promoting other aspects of the well-being of the community as a whole. Philosophical differences can and do lead to disagreements as to the appropriate scope for government economic activity.

However, forming intelligent opinions about public policy requires not only a political philosophy but also an understanding of what government actually does. Where does the legal power to conduct economic policy reside? What does government spend money on, and how does it raise revenue? Chapter 1 discusses how political views affect attitudes toward public finance, and outlines the operation of the US system of public finance. It provides a broad framework for thinking about the details of the public finance system that are discussed in subsequent chapters.

Chapters 2 and 3 present the analytical tools used by public finance economists. Chapter 2 focuses on the tools of *positive analysis*, which deals with statements of cause and effect. The question here is how economists try to figure out the impacts of various government policies. However, we want to determine not only the effects of government policies, but whether or not they produce results that are in some sense good. This is the role of *normative analysis*, which requires an explicit ethical framework, because without one, it is impossible to say what is good. This ethical framework is covered in Chapter 3.

CHAPTER 1

Introduction

> *Public Finance is nothing else than a sophisticated discussion of the relationship between the individual and the state. There is no better school of training than public finance.*
>
> FORMER CZECH PRIME MINISTER VACLAV KLAUS

The year is 1030 BC. For decades, the Israelite tribes have been living without a central government. The Bible records that the people have asked the prophet Samuel to "make us a king to judge us like all the nations" [1 Samuel 8:5]. Samuel tries to discourage the Israelites by describing what life will be like under a monarchy:

> This will be the manner of the king that shall reign over you; he will take your sons, and appoint them unto him, for his chariots, and to be his horsemen; and they shall run before his chariots . . . And he will take your daughters to be perfumers, and to be cooks, and to be bakers. And he will take your fields, and your vineyards, and your oliveyards, even the best of them, and give them to his servants . . . He will take the tenth of your flocks; and ye shall be his servants. And ye shall cry out in that day because of your king whom ye shall have chosen. [1 Samuel 8:11–18]

The Israelites are undeterred by this depressing scenario: "The people refused to hearken unto the voice of Samuel; and they said: 'Nay; but there shall be a king over us; that we also may be like all the nations; and that our king may judge us, and go out before us, and fight our battles'" [1 Samuel 8:19–20].

This biblical episode illustrates an age-old ambivalence about government. Government is a necessity—"all the nations" have it, after all—but at the same time it has undesirable aspects. These mixed feelings toward government are inextricably bound up with its taxing and spending activities.

The king will provide things that the people want (in this case, an army), but only at a cost. The resources for all government expenditures ultimately must come from the private sector. As Samuel so graphically explains, taxes can be a serious burden.

Centuries have passed, mixed feelings about government remain, and much of the controversy still centers around its financial behavior. This book is about the taxing and spending activities of government, a subject usually called **public finance.** This term is something of a misnomer, because the fundamental issues are not financial (that is, relating to money). Rather, the key problems relate to the use of real resources. For this reason, some authors prefer the label **public sector economics** or simply **public economics.**

We focus on the microeconomic functions of government, the way government affects the allocation of resources and the distribution of income. Nowadays, the macroeconomic functions of government—the use of taxing, spending, and monetary policies to affect the overall level of unemployment and the price level—are usually taught in separate courses.

The scope of public finance is sometimes unclear. Governmental regulatory policies have important effects on resource allocation. Such policies have goals that sometimes can also be achieved by government spending or taxing measures. For example, if the government wishes to limit the size of corporations, one possible policy is to impose large taxes on big corporations. Another is to issue regulations making firms that exceed a particular size illegal. However, while corporate taxation is a subject of intense study in public finance, antitrust issues receive only tangential treatment in public finance texts and are covered instead in courses on industrial organization. While this practice seems arbitrary, it is necessary to limit the scope of the field. This book follows tradition by focusing on governmental spending and revenue-raising activities.

Public Finance and Ideology

Public finance economists analyze not only the effects of actual government taxing and spending activities but also what these activities ought to be. Views of how government should function in the economic sphere are influenced by ideological views concerning the relationship between the individual and the state. Political philosophers have distinguished two major approaches.

Organic View of Government

Society is conceived of as a natural organism. Each individual is a part of this organism, and the government can be thought of as its heart. Yang Chang-chi, Mao Tse-tung's ethics teacher in Peking, held that "a country is an organic whole, just as the human body is an organic whole. It is not like a machine which can be taken apart and put together again." (Quoted in Johnson [1983, p. 197].) The individual has significance only as part of the community, and the good of the individual is defined with respect to the good of the whole.

Thus, the community is stressed above the individual. For example, in the *Republic* of Plato, an activity of a citizen is desirable only if it leads to a just society. Perhaps the most infamous instance of an organic conception of government is provided by Nazism: "National Socialism does not recognize a separate individual sphere which, apart from the community, is to be painstakingly protected from any interference by the State . . . Every activity of daily life has meaning and value only as a service to the whole."[1]

The goals of the society are set by the state, which leads society toward their realization. Of course, the choice of goals differs considerably. Plato conceived of a state whose goal was the achievement of a golden age in which human activities would be guided by perfect rationality. On the other hand, Adolf Hitler [1971/1925, p. 393] viewed the state's purpose as the achievement of racial purity: "The state is a means to an end. Its end lies in the preservation and advancement of a community of physically and psychically homogeneous creatures." According to Lenin [1968/1917, p. 198], the proletarian state has the purpose of "*leading the whole people* to socialism, . . . of being the teacher, the guide, the leader of all the working and exploited people."

Because societal goals can differ, a crucial question is how they are to be selected. Proponents of the organic view usually argue that certain goals are *natural* for the societal organism to pursue. Pursuit of sovereignty over some geographical area is an example of such a natural goal. (Think of the Nazi drive for domination over Europe.) However, although philosophers have struggled for centuries to explain what natural means, the answer is far from clear.

Mechanistic View of Government

In this view, government is not an organic part of society. Rather, it is a contrivance created by individuals to better achieve their individual goals. As the American statesman Henry Clay suggested in 1829, "Government is a trust, and the officers of the government are trustees; and both the trust and the trustees are created for the benefit of the people." The individual rather than the group is at center stage.

Accepting that government exists for the good of the people, we are still left with the problem of defining just what *good* is and how the government should promote it. Virtually everyone agrees that it is good for individuals when government protects them from violence. To do so government must have a monopoly on coercive power. Otherwise, anarchy develops, and as the 17th-century philosopher Thomas Hobbes [1963/1651, p. 143] noted, "The life of man [becomes] solitary, poor, nasty, brutish and short." Recent events in Somalia, in which no effective national government exists and violence is widespread, confirm Hobbes's observation. Similarly, in *The Wealth of Nations,* Adam Smith argues that government should protect "the society from the violence and invasion of other independent

---

[1] Stuckart and Globke [1968, p. 330]. (Wilhelm Stuckart and Hans Globke were ranking members of the Nazi Ministry of the Interior.)

societies," and protect "as far as possible every member of the society from the injustice or oppression of every other member of it" [1977/1776, Book V, pp. 182, 198].

The most limited government, then, has but one function—to prevent its members from being subjected to physical coercion. Beyond that, Smith argued that government should have responsibility for "creating and maintaining certain public works and certain public institutions, which it can never be for the interest of any individual, or small number of individuals, to erect and maintain" [1977/1776, Book V, pp. 210–11]. Here one thinks of items such as roads, bridges, and sewers—the infrastructure required for society to function.[2]

At this point, opinions within the mechanistic tradition diverge. Libertarians, who believe in a very limited government, argue against any further economic role for the government. In Smith's words, "Every man, as long as he does not violate the laws of justice, is left perfectly free to pursue his own interest his own way" [1977/1776, Book V, p. 180]. Libertarians are extremely skeptical about the ability of governments to improve social welfare. As Thomas Jefferson pungently put it,

> Sometimes it is said that man cannot be trusted with the government of himself. Can he, then, be trusted with the government of others? Or have we found angels in the forms of kings to govern him? Let history answer this question.

In contrast, those whom we might call social democrats believe that substantial government intervention is required for the good of individuals. These interventions can take such diverse forms as safety regulations for the workplace, laws banning racial and sexual discrimination in housing, or welfare payments to the poor. When social democrats are confronted with the objection that such interventions impinge on individual freedom, they are apt to respond that freedom refers to more than the absence of physical coercion. An impoverished individual may be free to spend his income as he pleases, but the scope of that freedom is quite limited. Of course, between the libertarian and social democratic positions there is a continuum of views with respect to the appropriate amount of government intervention.

Viewpoint of This Book

The notion that the individual rather than the group is paramount is relatively new. Historian Lawrence Stone [1977, pp. 4–5] notes that before the modern period,

> It was generally agreed that the interests of the group, whether that of kin, the village, or later the state, took priority over the wishes of the individual and the achievement of his particular ends. "Life, liberty and the pursuit of happiness" were personal ideals which the average, educated 16th-century man would certainly have rejected as the prime goals of a good society.

---

[2] Some argue that even these items should be provided by private entrepreneurs. Problems that might arise in doing so are discussed in Chapter 4.

Since then, however, the mechanistic view of government has come to dominate Anglo-American political thought. However, its dominance is not total. Anyone who claims that something must be done in the "national interest," without reference to the welfare of some individual or group of individuals, is implicitly taking an organic point of view. More generally, even in highly individualistic societies, people sometimes feel it necessary to act on behalf of, or even sacrifice their lives for, the nation. As Kenneth Arrow [1974, p. 15] observes, "The tension between society and the individual is inevitable. Their claims compete within the individual conscience as well as in the arena of social conflict."

Not surprisingly, Anglo-American economic thought has also developed along individualistic lines. Individuals and their wants are the main focus in mainstream economics, a view reflected in this text. However, as stressed earlier, within the individualistic tradition there is much controversy with respect to how active government should be. Thus, adopting a mechanistic point of view does not by itself provide us with an ideology that tells us whether any particular economic intervention should be undertaken.[3]

This point is important because economic policy is not based on economic analysis alone. The desirability of a given course of government action (or inaction) inevitably depends in part on ethical and political judgments. As this country's ongoing debate over public finance illustrates, reasonable people can disagree on these matters. We attempt to reflect different points of view as fairly as possible.

Government at a Glance

We have shown how ideology can affect one's views with respect to the appropriate scope for governmental activity. However, to form sensible views about public policy requires more than ideology. One also needs information about how the government actually functions. What legal constraints are imposed on the public sector? What does the government spend money on, and how are these expenditures financed? Before delving into the details of the US system of public finance, we provide a brief overview of these issues.

The Legal Framework

The Founding Fathers' concerns about governmental intervention in the economy are reflected in the Constitution. We first discuss constitutional provisions relating to the spending and taxing activities of the federal government and then turn to the states.

Federal Government.   Article 1, Section 8, of the Constitution empowers Congress "to pay the Debts and provide for the common Defense and general

---

[3] This question really makes no sense in the context of an organic view of government in which the government is above the people, and there is an assumption that it should guide every aspect of life.

Welfare of the United States." Over the years, the notion of "general welfare" has been interpreted very broadly by Congress and the courts, and now this clause effectively puts no constraints on government spending.[4] The Constitution does not limit the size of federal expenditure, either absolutely or relative to the size of the economy. Bills to appropriate expenditures (like practically all other laws) can originate in either house of Congress. An appropriations bill becomes law when it receives a majority vote in both houses and the president signs it. If the president vetos an expenditure bill, it can still become law if it receives a two-thirds majority vote in each house.

How does Congress finance these expenditures? Federal taxing powers are authorized in Article 1, Section 8: "The Congress shall have Power to lay and collect Taxes, Duties, Imposts and Excises." Unlike expenditure bills, "All Bills for raising Revenue shall originate in the House of Representatives" (Article 1, Section 7).

In light of the enormous dissatisfaction with British tax policy during the colonial period, it is no surprise that considerable care was taken to constrain governmental taxing power, as described in the following paragraphs:

1. "[A]ll Duties, Imposts and Excises shall be uniform throughout the United States" (Article 1, Section 8). Congress cannot discriminate among states when it sets tax rates. If the federal government levies a tax on gasoline, the *rate* must be the same in every state. This does not imply that the per capita *amount* collected will be the same in each state. Presumably, states in which individuals drive more than average have higher tax liabilities, other things being the same. Thus, it is still possible (and indeed likely) that various taxes make some states worse off than others.[5]

2. "No . . . direct Tax shall be laid, unless in Proportion to the Census or Enumeration herein before directed to be taken" (Article 1, Section 9). A direct tax is a tax levied on a *person* as opposed to a *commodity*. Essentially, this provision says that if State A has twice the population of State B, then any direct tax levied by Congress must yield twice as much revenue from State A as from State B.

In the late 19th century, attempts to introduce a federal tax on income were declared unconstitutional by the Supreme Court because income taxation leads to state tax burdens that are not proportional to population. Given this decision, the only way to introduce an income tax was via a constitutional amendment. The 16th Amendment, ratified in 1913, states, "Congress shall have power to levy and collect taxes on incomes, from whatever source derived, without apportionment among the several states, and without regard

---

[4] Article 1 also mandates that certain specific expenditures be made. For example, Congress has to appropriate funds to maintain both an army and a court system.

[5] No tax law in history has ever been struck down for violating this clause. However, a close call occurred in the early 1980s. Congress passed a tax on oil that exempted oil from the North Slope of Alaska. A federal district court ruled that the tax was unconstitutional, but this decision was ultimately reversed by the Supreme Court.

to census or enumeration." Today the individual income tax is one of the mainstays of the federal revenue system.

3. "No person shall be . . . deprived of life, liberty, or property, without due process of law; nor shall private property be taken for public use, without just compensation" (Fifth Amendment). From the point of view of tax policy, this clause means distinctions created by the tax law must be reasonable. However, it is not always simple to determine which distinctions are "reasonable" and doing so is an ongoing part of the legislative and judicial processes.

4. "No Tax or Duty shall be laid on Articles exported from any State" (Article 1, Section 9). This provision was included to assure the southern states that their exports of tobacco and other commodities would not be jeopardized by the central government. It has had little impact on the development of the public finance system.

The federal government is not required to finance all its expenditures by taxation. If expenditures exceed revenues, it is empowered "to borrow Money on the credit of the United States" (Article 1, Section 8). Recently, a constitutional amendment to require a balanced federal budget has received some support, but so far it has not passed.

State and Local Governments. According to the 10th Amendment, "The powers not delegated to the United States by the Constitution, nor prohibited by it to the States, are reserved to the States respectively, or to the people." Thus, explicit authorization for states to spend and tax is not required. However, the Constitution does limit states' economic activities. Article 1, Section 10, states, "No State shall, without the Consent of the Congress, lay any Imposts or Duties on Imports or Exports." Thus, the federal government controls international economic policy. In addition, various constitutional provisions have been interpreted as requiring that the states not levy taxes arbitrarily, discriminate against outside residents, or levy taxes on imports from other states. For example, in 1986, the Supreme Court declared unconstitutional an Alaska law mandating that 95 percent of workers on public projects be Alaskans.

States can impose spending and taxing restrictions on themselves in their own constitutions. State constitutions differ substantially with respect to the types of economic issues with which they deal. In recent years, one of the most interesting developments in public finance has been the movement of some states to amend their constitutions to limit the size of public sector spending.

From a legal point of view, the power of local governments to tax and spend is granted by the states. As a 19th-century judge put it:

> Municipal corporations owe their origin to, and derive their powers and rights wholly from, the [state] legislature. It breathes into them the breath of life, without which they cannot exist. As it creates, so it may destroy. If it may destroy, it may abridge and control. [*City of Clinton* v. *Cedar Rapids,* 1868]

It would be a mistake, however, to view localities as lacking in fiscal autonomy. Many towns and cities have substantial political power and do not respond passively to the wishes of state and federal governments. An interesting development in recent years has been the competition of states and cities for federal funds. The cities often are more successful in their lobbying activities than the states!

The Size of Government

In a famous line from his State of the Union address in 1996, Bill Clinton declared: "The era of big government is over." Such a statement presupposes that there is some way to determine whether or not the government is "big." Just how does one measure the size of government?

One measure often used by politicians and journalists is the number of workers in the public sector. However, inferences about the size of government drawn from the number of workers it employs can be misleading. Imagine a country where a few public servants operate a powerful computer that guides all economic decisions. In this country, the number of government employees certainly underestimates the importance of government. Similarly, it would be easy to construct a scenario in which a large number of workers is associated with a relatively weak public sector. Although for many purposes the number of public sector employees is useful information, it does not cast light on the central issue—the extent to which society's resources are subject to control by government.

A more sensible (and common) approach is to measure the size of government by the volume of its annual expenditures, of which there are basically three types:

1. Purchases of goods and services. The government buys a wide variety of items, everything from missiles to services provided by forest rangers.

2. Transfers of income to people, businesses, or other governments. The government takes income from some individuals or organizations and gives it to others. Examples are welfare programs such as food stamps and subsidies paid to farmers for production (or nonproduction) of certain commodities.

3. Interest payments. The government often borrows to finance its activities and, like any borrower, must pay interest for the privilege of doing so.

The federal government itemizes its expenditures in a document referred to as the **unified budget.**[6] In 2001, federal expenditures (excluding grants made to state and local governments) were about $1,659 billion. Adding state and local government expenditures made that year gives us a total of

---

[6] The publication of some kind of budget document is constitutionally mandated: "a regular Statement and Account of the Receipts and Expenditures of all public Money shall be published from time to time" (Article 1, Section 9).

$2,952 billion [*Economic Report of the President, 2003,* p. 373].[7] Figures on government expenditures are easily available and widely quoted. Typically when expenditures go up, people conclude that government has grown and vice versa. However, some government activities have substantial effects on resource allocation even though they involve minimal explicit outlays. For example, issuing regulations per se is not very expensive, but compliance with the rules can be very costly. Air bag requirements raise the cost of cars. Various permit and inspection fees increase the price of housing. Labor market regulations such as the minimum wage may create unemployment, and regulation of the drug industry may slow the pace of scientific development.

Some have suggested that the costs imposed on the economy by government regulations be published in an annual **regulatory budget.** In this way, an explicit accounting for the costs of regulation would be available. Unfortunately, it is exceedingly difficult to compute such costs. For example, pharmaceutical experts disagree on what new cures would have been developed in the absence of drug regulation. Similarly, it is hard to estimate the impact of government-mandated safety procedures in the workplace on production costs. In view of such problems, it is unlikely there will ever be an official regulatory budget.[8] Unofficial estimates, however, suggest that the annual costs of federal regulations may be quite high, perhaps over $700 billion annually (Nivola 1998, p. 8).

Some Numbers.   We reluctantly conclude that it is infeasible to summarize in a single number the magnitude of government's impact on the economy. That said, we are still left with the practical problem of finding some reasonable indicator of the government's size that can be used to estimate trends in its growth. Most economists are willing to accept conventionally defined government expenditure as a rough but useful measure. Like many other imperfect measures, it yields useful insights as long as its limitations are understood.

With all the appropriate caveats in mind, we present in Table 1.1 data on expenditures made by all levels of US government over time. The first column indicates that annual expenditures have increased by a factor of over 290 since 1929. This figure is a misleading indicator of the growth of government for several reasons:

1. Because of inflation, the dollar has decreased in value over time. In column 2, the expenditure figures are expressed in 2001 dollars. In real terms, government expenditure in 2001 was about 25 times the level in 1929.

---

[7] Federal grants to state and local governments were $277 billion in 2001.

[8] Regulation is not necessarily a bad thing just because it creates costs. Like any other government activity, it can be evaluated only by assessing the benefits as well as the costs. (Problems in doing cost-benefit analysis are discussed in Chapter 11.)

Table 1.1   State, local, and federal government expenditures *(selected years)*

	(1) Total Expenditures (billions)	(2) 2001 Dollars (billions)*	(3) 2001 Dollars per Capita	(4) Percent of GDP
1929	$ 10	$ 118	$ 970	9.9%
1940	19	237	1,794	18.8
1950	61	428	2,812	20.7
1960	120	591	3,272	22.7
1970	286	1,080	5,268	27.6
1980	812	1,557	6,839	29.0
1990	1,778	2,249	8,991	30.6
2000	2,776	2,842	10,061	28.3
2001	2,951	2,951	10,335	29.3

*Conversion to 2001 dollars done using the GDP deflator.

SOURCE: Calculations based on *Economic Report of the President, 2003* (Washington, DC: US Government Printing Office, 2003), pp. 276, 280, 317, 373.

2. The population has also grown over time. An increasing population by itself creates demands for a larger public sector. (For example, more roads and sewers are required to accommodate more people.) Column 3 shows real government expenditure per capita. Now the increase from 1929 to 2001 is a factor of about 10.

3. It is sometimes useful to examine government expenditure compared to the size of the economy. If government doubles in size but at the same time the economy triples, then in a relative sense, government has shrunk. Column 4 shows government expenditure as a percentage of gross domestic product (GDP), the market value of goods and services produced by the economy during the year. In 1929, the figure was 9.6 percent, and in 2001, it was 29.3 percent.

In light of our previous discussion, the figures in Table 1.1 convey a false sense of precision. Still, there is no doubt that in the long run the economic role of government has grown enormously. With almost a third of GDP going through the public sector, government is an enormous economic force.

Some international comparisons can help put the US data in perspective. Table 1.2 shows figures on government expenditure relative to gross domestic product for several developed countries. The data indicate that the United States is not alone in having an important public sector. Indeed, compared to countries such as Sweden and France, the US public sector is quite small. While relative public-sector sizes differ across nations for many reasons, the ideological considerations discussed earlier in this chapter probably play an important role. One explanation for the large public

Table 1.2   **Government expenditures as a percentage of gross domestic product**
(*selected countries*)

Australia	31.0%	Japan	38.3%
Canada	37.4	Sweden	53.1
France	49.4	United Kingdom	38.8
Germany	44.5		

SOURCE: U.S. Census Bureau, *Statistical Abstract of the United States, 2002*, p. 838. Figures are for 2001.

sector in Sweden, for example, is that the government pays for most of health care, which is thought of as a community responsibility. In the United States, on the other hand, health care is viewed as more of an individual responsibility, so the bulk of health care expenditures are made in the private sector.

Expenditures

We now turn from the overall magnitude of government expenditures to their composition. It is impossible to reflect the enormous scope of government spending activity in a brief table. In the federal budget for fiscal year 2004, the list of programs and their descriptions required almost 1,100 pages! (Details are provided at the Web site: http://w3.access.gpo.gov/usbudget/index.html.)

The major categories of federal government expenditure in 1965 and the present are depicted in Figure 1.1; the state and local expenditure data are in Figure 1.2. The following aspects of the figures are noteworthy:

- National defense is an important component of government expenditure, but its relative importance has decreased over time. In 1965, it was 47 percent of the federal budget; this figure is now down to 17.3 percent.
- Social Security has grown enormously. Among other things, this program transfers income to individuals who are retired. It is now the single largest spending item in the federal budget.
- Medicare, a health insurance system for the elderly, did not even exist in 1965; it now absorbs 11.5 percent of the federal budget.
- Public welfare activities have increased. As shown in Figure 1.2, between 1965 and 1999, their share of state and local budgets roughly doubled from 8 to 15.7 percent. At the same time, the share of state and local spending devoted to highways has fallen considerably.
- Payments of interest on debt have remained roughly constant as a proportion of federal expenditures since 1965. They now account for about 8.5 percent of federal expenditures.

Note that fast-growing areas such as Social Security and interest payments are relatively fixed in the sense that they are determined by previous decisions.

FIGURE 1.1

Composition of federal expenditures

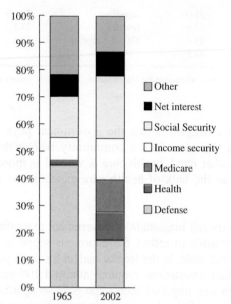

SOURCE: *Economic Report of the President, 2003*
(Washington, DC: US Government Printing Office,
2003), p. 371.

FIGURE 1.2

Composition of state and local expenditures

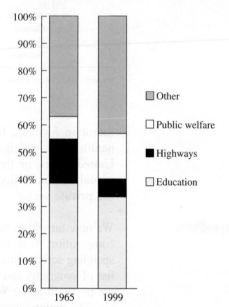

SOURCE: *Economic Report of the President, 2003*
(Washington, DC: US Government Printing Office, 2003),
p. 377.

Indeed, much of the government budget consists of so-called **entitlement programs**—programs with cost determined not by fixed dollar amounts but by the number of people who qualify. The laws governing Social Security, many public welfare programs, farm price supports, and so forth include rules that determine who is entitled to benefits and their magnitude. Expenditures on entitlement programs are, therefore, out of the hands of the current government, unless it changes the rules. Similarly, debt payments are determined by interest rates and previous deficits, again mostly out of the control of current decision makers. According to most estimates, about three-quarters of the federal budget is relatively uncontrollable. In Chapter 8, we discuss whether government spending is in fact out of control and if so, what can be done about it.

It is useful to break down total expenditures by level of government. The federal government accounts for about 51 percent of all direct expenditures, the states for 21 percent, and localities for 28 percent. State and local governments are clearly important players. They account for the bulk of spending on items such as police and fire protection, education, and transportation. Substantial public welfare expenditures are also made through the states. Chapter 20 discusses the complications that arise in coordinating the fiscal activities of different levels of government.

FIGURE 1.3

Composition of federal taxes

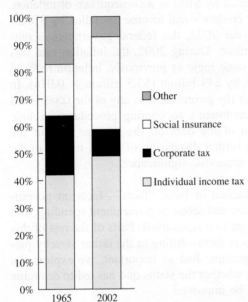

SOURCE: *Economic Report of the President, 2003* (Washington, DC: US Government Printing Office, 2003), p. 371.

FIGURE 1.4

Composition of state and local taxes

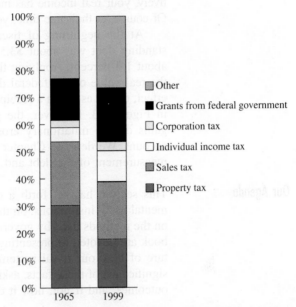

SOURCE: *Economic Report of the President, 2003* (Washington, DC: US Government Printing Office, 2003), p. 377.

Revenues

The principal components of the federal tax system are depicted in Figure 1.3; the state and local tax information is in Figure 1.4. At the federal level, personal income taxation is currently the single most important source of revenue, accounting for about 46 percent of tax collections. Note the importance of the "Social Insurance" category in Figure 1.3. These are payroll tax collections used to finance Social Security and Medicare. They now account for more than a third of federal revenue collections. The fall in the importance of the federal corporate income tax is also of some interest. In 1965 it accounted for about 22 percent of federal revenues; the figure is now only 8 percent. In the state and local sector, the two most striking changes over time are the decreased importance of the property tax and the increased reliance on individual income taxes.

Changes in the Real Value of Debt.   In popular discussions, taxes are usually viewed as the only source of government revenue. However, when the government is a debtor and the price level increases, changes in the real value of the debt may be an important source of revenue. To see why, suppose that at the beginning of the year you owe a creditor $1,000, which does not have to be repaid until the end of the year. Suppose further that during the year, prices rise by 10 percent. Then the dollars you use to repay your creditor are worth

10 percent less than those you borrowed from him. In effect, inflation has reduced the real value of your debt by $100 (10 percent of $1,000). Alternatively, your real income has increased by $100 as a consequence of inflation. Of course, at the same time, your creditor's real income has fallen by $100.[9]

At the beginning of fiscal year 2002, the federal government's outstanding debt was about $3.5 trillion. During 2002, the inflation rate was about 1.4 percent. Applying the same logic as previously, inflation reduced the real value of the federal debt by $49 billion ($3.5 trillion × 0.014). In effect, this is as much a receipt for the government as any of the taxes listed in Figure 1.3. However, the government's accounting procedures exclude gains due to inflationary erosion of the debt on the revenue side of the account. We defer to Chapter 18 further discussion of issues related to the measurement of the debt and its economic significance.

Our Agenda

This section has set forth a collection of basic "facts"—facts on governmental fiscal institutions, on the size and scope of government spending, and on the methods used by government to finance itself. Parts of the rest of this book are devoted to presenting more facts—filling in the rather sketchy picture of how our fiscal system operates. Just as important, we explore the significance of these facts, asking whether the status quo has led to desirable outcomes, and if not, how it can be improved.

Summary

- Public finance, also known as public sector economics or public economics, focuses on the taxing and spending activities of government and their influence on the allocation of resources and distribution of income.

- Public finance economists analyze both actual policies and develop guidelines for government activities. In the latter role, economists are influenced by their attitudes toward the role of government in society.

- In an organic view of society, individuals are valued only by their contribution to the realization of social goals. These goals are determined by the government.

- In a mechanistic view of society, government is a contrivance erected to further individual goals. It

is not clear how the government can reconcile sometimes conflicting individual goals.

- Individual decision making is the focus of much economics and is consistent with the mechanistic view of society adopted in this book. This does not eliminate much controversy over the appropriate role of the government in our economy.

- The Constitution embodies constraints on federal and state government economic activity.

- The federal government may effectively undertake any expenditures it wishes and may use debt and taxes to finance them. The federal government may not discriminate among states when choosing tax rates and may not place a levy on state exports. The 16th Amendment empowers the federal government to tax personal incomes.

---

[9] If the inflation is anticipated by borrowers and lenders, one expects that the interest rate will increase to take inflation into account. This phenomenon is discussed in Chapter 15 under "Taxation and Inflation."

- State governments are forbidden to levy tariffs on imports, discriminate against outside residents, or tax other states' products. Most states have balanced budget requirements.

- All common measures of the size of government—employees, expenditures, revenues, etc.—involve some deficiency. In particular, these items miss the impact of regulatory costs. Nonetheless, there is strong evidence that the impact of the government on the allocation of national resources has increased over time.

- The level of government expenditures has increased in both nominal and real absolute terms,

in per capita terms, and as a percentage of gross domestic product.

- The share of defense spending in federal expenditure has fallen over time, while Social Security, public welfare, and payments on outstanding debt have increased in importance. The combination of entitlement programs and interest payments reduces yearly control over the level of expenditures.

- Personal income and Social Security payroll taxes are currently the largest sources of government revenue.

Discussion Questions

1. Indicate whether each of the following statements is consistent with an organic or mechanistic view of government:

    a. "A strong state for Russians is not an anomaly, not something that must be fought against, but on the contrary is . . . the initiator and main driving force of all change." (Russian President Vladimir Putin.)

    b. "The highest end which the state can serve is to serve no end at all, but merely exist as a means for the individuals within it to realize their own ends." (Supreme Court Justice William Rehnquist, in his master's thesis for Stanford University.)

2. French law requires movie theaters to reserve 20 weeks of screen time per year for feature films produced in France. The putative purpose is to reduce the number of US films shown in France and hence reduce the US cultural influence there. How would you expect each of the following to react to such a law?

    a. someone with an organic conception of the state

    b. a libertarian

    c. a social democrat.

3. Obesity is perceived to be a national health problem in the United States. One suggestion to deal with this problem is a "fat tax." The idea is to levy a tax on foods containing more than a gov-

ernment prescribed percentage of the daily minimal fat intake. Is such a tax consistent with a mechanistic view of government?

4. In each of the following circumstances, decide whether the impact of government on the economy increases or decreases and why. In each case, how does your answer compare to that given by standard measures of the size of government?

    a. Normally, when employers offer health insurance benefits to their workers, these benefits extend to the spouses of the workers as well. Several years ago, San Francisco passed a law requiring firms that do business with the city to offer health and other benefits to both same- and opposite-sex unwed partners.

    b. The ratio of government purchases of goods and services to gross domestic product falls.

    c. The federal budget is brought into balance by reducing grants-in-aid to state and local governments.

5. During 2002, the inflation rate in the United Kingdom was about 2.1 percent. At the beginning of that year, the national debt of the United Kingdom was about £311 billion. Discuss the implications of these facts for measuring government revenues in that country during 2002.

6. As noted in the text, Bill Clinton declared that the era of big government is over. Did the size of

government fall during his administration? Provide an answer based on the following data: In 1993, federal government spending was $1.41 trillion and Gross Domestic Product (GDP) was $6.64 trillion. In 2001, federal spending was $1.86 trillion and GDP was $10.2 trillion.

During this period, prices increased by about 16 percent.

What additional data would you seek to provide a more complete answer to this question?

Selected References

Congressional Budget Office. *The Economic and Budget Outlook: Fiscal Years 2004–2013.* Washington, DC: US Government Printing Office, January 2003.

Smith, Adam. *The Wealth of Nations.* London: J.M. Dent and Sons, 1997 (1776) (book V, Chapter 1.)

APPENDIX

Doing Research in Public Finance

Throughout the text, we cite many books and articles. These references are useful for those who want to delve into the various subjects in more detail. Students interested in writing term papers or theses on subjects in public finance should also consult the following journals that specialize in the field:

International Tax and Public Finance

Journal of Public Economics

National Tax Journal

Public Finance

Public Finance Quarterly

In addition, all the major general-interest economics journals frequently publish articles that deal with public finance issues. These include, but are not limited to:

American Economic Review

Journal of Economic Perspectives

Journal of Political Economy

Quarterly Journal of Economics

Review of Economics and Statistics

Articles on public finance in these and many other journals are indexed in the *Journal of Economic Literature* and can be searched on the internet.

In addition, students should consult the volumes included in the Brookings Institution's series *Studies of Government Finance.* These books include careful and up-to-date discussions of important public finance issues. The Congressional Budget Office also provides useful reports on current policy controversies. A list of documents is provided at its Web site, http://www.cbo.gov.

The working paper series of the National Bureau of Economic Research, available in many university libraries, is another good source of recent research on public finance. The technical difficulty of these papers is sometimes considerable, however. Papers can be downloaded at its Web site, http://www.nber.org.

Vast amounts of data are available on government spending and taxing activities. The following useful sources of information are published by the US Government Printing Office and are available on line as indicated:

Statistical Abstract of the United States
(http://www.census.gov/prod/www/statistical-abstract-us.html)

Economic Report of the President (http://w3.access.gpo.gov/eop/)

Budget of the United States
(http://w3.access.gpo.gov/usbudget/index.html)

U.S. Census of Governments
(http://www.census.gov/govs/www/cog.html)

All the preceding are published annually, except for the *U.S. Census of Governments,* which appears every five years. *Facts and Figures on Government Finance,* published annually by the Tax Foundation, is another compendium of data on government taxing and spending activities. For those who desire a long-run perspective, data going back to the 18th century are available in *Historical Statistics of the United States from Colonial Times to 1970* (US Government Printing Office). Readers with a special interest in state and local public finance will want to read the reports issued by the US Advisory Commission on Intergovernmental Relations.

A great deal of public finance data is available on the Internet. A particularly useful site is *Resources for Economists on the Internet* (http://rfe.org). It lists and describes more than 900 Internet resources. The home page of the US Census Bureau (http://www.census.gov/econ/www/) is also very useful. Finally, for up-to-date information on tax policy issues, consult the Web site of the University of Michigan's Office of Tax Policy Research (http://otpr.org) and the Urban-Brookings Tax Policy Center (http://www.taxpolicycenter.org/).

CHAPTER 2

Tools of Positive Analysis

Numbers live. Numbers take on vitality.

JESSE JACKSON

A good subtitle for this chapter is "Why Is It So Hard to Tell What's Going On?" We constantly hear economists—and politicians—disagree vehemently about the likely consequences of various government actions. For example, when George W. Bush proposed reducing tax rates in 2003, conservatives argued that lower tax rates create incentives for people to work harder. Liberals were skeptical, arguing that taxes have little effect. Each side had economists testifying that its opinion was correct. Is the cynicism expressed in the cartoon on the following page really surprising?

An important reason for the lack of definitive answers is that economists are generally unable to perform carefully controlled experiments with the economy. To determine the effects of a fertilizer on cabbage growth, a botanist can treat one plot of ground with the fertilizer and compare the results with an otherwise identical unfertilized cabbage patch. The unfertilized patch serves as the control group. Economists do not have such opportunities. Although the government can change the economic environment, there is no control group with which to make comparisons. Therefore, we never know for certain the consequences of various policy changes.

Lacking controlled experiments, economists use other methods to analyze the impact of various government policies on economic behavior. One of the most exciting developments in public finance in recent decades has been the widespread use of modern statistical tools to study public policy issues.

We will use the debate over the effect of taxes on labor supply to illustrate how positive analysis is done in public finance. The general approach is applicable to any number of problems.

*"That's the gist of what I want to say. Now get me
some statistics to base it on."*

• • •

The Role of Theory

One often hears the assertion, "The numbers speak for themselves." What do the numbers say about income tax rates and labor supply? Table 2.1 provides information on how the proportion of the last dollar of earnings taken by the tax collector—the **marginal tax rate**—varied over the period 1955 to 2001. The table also shows how the average weekly hours per worker have changed. The figures indicate tax rates have generally (though not steadily) increased, and hours of work have decreased. The numbers appear to say that taxes have depressed labor supply.

Is this inference correct? At the same time that tax rates were changing, so were numerous other factors that might influence labor supply. If *nonlabor income*—income from dividends, interest, and so forth—rose over the period, people may have worked less because they were richer. Alternatively, changing attitudes—a decrease in the Protestant ethic—might have depressed labor supply. Neither of these effects, and you can certainly think of many more, is taken into account by the numbers given. Clearly, what we need to know is the *independent* effect of taxes on labor supply. This effect simply cannot be learned solely from examining the trends in the two variables over time. This situation is typical—when we turn to data for answers, *the numbers never speak for themselves.*

In a sense, this observation opens a Pandora's box. An unlimited number of variables change over time. How do we know which ones have to be

Table 2.1   **Income tax rates and labor supply**

Year	Marginal Federal Tax Rate* (percent)	Average Weekly Hours†
1955	20.00%	39.6
1960	20.00	38.6
1965	17.00	38.8
1970	19.48	37.1
1975	22.00	36.1
1980	30.13	35.3
1985	29.05	34.9
1990	22.65	34.5
1995	22.65	34.5
2001	22.65	34.5

*Tax Policy Center, "Historical Combined Income and Employee Tax Rates for a Family of Four," URL: http://www.taxpolicycenter.org/taxfacts/overview/combined_family.cfm, January 15, 2003.

†*Economic Report of the President, 2002.* (Washington, DC: US Government Printing Office, 2002), p. 376.

considered to find the tax effect? One major purpose of economic theory is to help isolate a small set of variables that are important influences on behavior. The taxes and labor supply example illustrates how basic economic theory plays this role.

The theory of labor supply posits that the work decision is based on the rational allocation of time.[1] Suppose Mr. Rogers has only a certain number of hours in the day: How many hours should he devote to work in the market, and how many hours to leisure? Rogers derives satisfaction ("utility") from leisure, but to earn income he must work and thereby surrender leisure time. Rogers's problem is to find the combination of income and leisure that maximizes his utility.

Suppose Rogers's wage rate is $10 per hour. The wage is the cost of Rogers's time. For every hour he spends at leisure, Rogers gives up $10 in wages—time is literally money. However, a "rational" individual generally does not work every possible hour, even though leisure is costly. People spend time on leisure to the extent that leisure's benefits exceed its costs.

This model may seem absurdly simple. It ignores the possibility that an individual's labor supply behavior may depend on the work decisions of other family members. Neither does the model consider whether the individual can work as many hours as desired. Indeed, the entire notion that people make their decisions by rationally considering costs and benefits may appear unrealistic.

However, the whole point of model building is to simplify as much as possible, so one can reduce a problem to its essentials. The literary critic

---

[1] The theory of labor supply is presented here verbally. A graphical exposition appears in Chapter 16 under "Labor Supply."

Lytton Strachey said, "Omission is the beginning of all art" [Lipton, 1977, p. 93]. Omission is also the beginning of all good economic analyses. A model should not be judged on the basis of whether or not it is true, but on whether it is plausible and informative. Most work in modern economics is based on the assumption that utility maximization is a good working hypothesis. This point of view is taken throughout the book.

Imagine that Mr. Rogers has found his utility-maximizing combination of income and leisure based on his wage rate of $10. Now the government imposes a tax on wage income of 20 percent. Then Rogers's after-tax or *net* wage is $8. How does a rational individual react—work more, work less, or not change? In public debate, arguments for all three possibilities are made with great assurance. In fact, however, the impact of an earnings tax on hours of work *cannot* be predicted on theoretical grounds.

To see why, first observe that the wage tax lowers the effective price of leisure. Before the tax, consumption of an hour of leisure cost Rogers $10. Under the earnings tax, Rogers's net wage is lower, and an hour of leisure costs him only $8. Since leisure has become cheaper, he will tend to consume more of it—to work less. This is called the *substitution effect.*

Another effect occurs simultaneously when the tax is imposed. Assume Rogers will work a certain number of hours regardless of all feasible changes in the net wage. After the tax, Rogers receives only $8 for each of these hours, while before it was $10. In a real sense, Rogers has suffered a loss of income. To the extent that leisure is a *normal good*—consumption increases when income increases and vice versa—this income loss leads to less consumption of leisure. But less leisure means more work. Because the earnings tax makes Rogers poorer, it induces him to work more. This is called the *income effect.*

Thus, the tax simultaneously produces two effects: It induces substitution toward the cheaper activity (leisure), and it reduces real income. Since the substitution and income effects work in opposite directions, the impact of an earnings tax cannot be determined by theorizing alone. Consider the following two statements:

1. "With these high taxes, it's really not worthwhile for me to work as much as I used to."
2. "With these high taxes, I have to work more to maintain my standard of living."

For a person making the first statement, the substitution effect dominates, while in the second statement the income effect dominates. Both statements can reflect perfectly rational behavior.

The importance of the ambiguity caused by the conflict of income and substitution effects cannot be overemphasized. Only **empirical work**—analysis based on observation and experience as opposed to theory—can answer the question of how labor force behavior is affected by changes in the tax system. Even intense armchair speculation on this matter must be regarded with considerable skepticism.

Although we have developed the argument with a labor supply example, the lesson is more general—one major purpose of theory is to make us aware of the areas of our ignorance.

Methods of Empirical Analysis

Theory helps us organize our thoughts about how people react to changes in their economic environment. But it usually cannot indicate the magnitude of such responses. Indeed, in the labor supply case just discussed, theory alone cannot even predict the *direction* of the likely changes. Empirical work is necessary. The three types of empirical strategies are personal interviews, experiments, and econometric estimation. With each technique, the connections to theory are vital. Theory influences how the study is organized, which questions are asked, and how the results are interpreted.

Interviews

The most straightforward way to find out whether some government activity influences people's behavior is simply to ask them. This is the kind of empirical "research" done by reporters. ("Tell me, are you going to delay your retirement if the government lowers your Social Security benefit?") A number of sophisticated interview studies have been done to assess the effect of taxes on labor supply. A group of British lawyers and accountants were carefully questioned as to how they determined their hours of work, whether they were aware of the tax rates they faced, and if these tax rates created any incentives or disincentives to work. The responses suggested that relatively few people were affected by taxes [Break, 1957, p. 549]. A later survey of a group of affluent Americans told much the same story. "Only one-eighth . . . said that they have actually curtailed their work effort because of the progressive income tax . . . Those facing the highest marginal tax rates reported work disincentives only a little more frequently than did those facing the lower rates" [Barlow, Brazer, & Morgan, 1966, p. 3].

Pitfalls of Interviews. Interpreting interview surveys requires caution. After all, just because an individual cannot recite her tax rate does not mean she is unaware of the discrepancy between before- and after-tax pay.

An old Chinese proverb counsels, "Listen to what a person says and then watch what he does." The fact that people *say* something about their behavior does not make it true. Some people are embarrassed to admit that financial considerations affect their labor supply decisions. ("I'd rather not talk about money. It's kind of gross," said actress Barbra Streisand.) Others complain about government just for the sheer fun of it, although their behavior is not really influenced by taxes. If you want to find out what radio station a family listens to, what makes more sense: to ask them, or to see where the radio dial is set?

Experiments

At the outset, we stressed that the basic problem in doing empirical work in economics is the inability to do controlled experiments with the economy. However, the government has funded several attempts to use experimental methodologies in the study of economic behavior. The idea underlying these social experiments is illustrated by some work done on the relative effectiveness of public and private schools in the early 1990s.

Currently, there is a raging debate over whether public funds should be used to send children to private schools. Central to this debate is the question of whether private schools are more effective than public schools, especially when it comes to educating children from inner cities. A natural way to answer this question is to compare the performance of students from similar backgrounds who are in the same types of schools. Such studies have tended to show that private schools do better. However, this result may be due to the fact that higher-achieving students are the ones who tend to select private schools in the first place. In 1990, Wisconsin designed a social experiment to address this problem.[2] Students from poor households in the city of Milwaukee were allowed to apply to a program that provided money for attending nonreligious private schools. Of the students who applied, a random sample was chosen to participate in the program. The applicants who were not selected served as a control group. Any differences between the subsequent school achievement of the two groups could then be attributed to relative effectiveness of the two types of schools.

Pitfalls of Social Experiments. Experiments are a promising way to learn about economic behavior, but they also have limitations. One reason is that classical experimental methodology requires that samples be truly random— the members of the sample must be representative of the population whose behavior is under consideration. In social experiments, it is virtually impossible to maintain a random sample, even if one is available initially. For example, in the Milwaukee experiment, some of the students who were admitted to the private schools did not attend them, or attended only for a short period of time. Because these students *self-selected* out of the private schools, the characteristics of the students left were no longer representative of the low-income population.

In addition, unlike plants or laboratory animals, human beings are aware they are participating in an experiment. This consciousness affects their behavior. A related point is that people within the group may react differently to a program when only a small number of participants are involved than they would when the program is universal. Or an experiment that lasts only a few months may produce different behavior from a program expected to be permanent.

---

[2] See Rouse [1998] for details.

One thing is certain. Social experiments are costly. For example, an experiment on the impact of rent subsidies on the housing decisions of the poor cost $163.3 million. (See Ingram [1985].) According to Burtless [1995], total spending on social experiments has exceeded a billion dollars since 1970. But such costs should be kept in perspective. It may be worthwhile to spend a few million dollars to determine the efficacy of a program that would involve spending billions of dollars.

Laboratory Experiments.   Certain kinds of economic behavior can also be studied in laboratory settings, an approach often used by psychologists. An investigator recruits a group of people (subjects) who perform various tasks. To study labor supply, an investigator might begin by noting from the theory of labor supply that a key variable is the net wage rate. A possible experimental strategy would be to offer subjects different rewards for completing various jobs and record how the amount of effort varies with the reward.

Laboratory experiments are subject to some of the pitfalls of social experiments. The main problem is that the environment in which behavior is observed is artificial. Moreover, the subjects, who are often college undergraduates, are unlikely to be representative of the population as a whole. However, laboratory experiments are much cheaper than social experiments and provide more flexibility. Their popularity has been growing in recent years, and as we see in later chapters, they have provided some interesting and important results.

Econometric Studies

Econometrics is the statistical analysis of economic data. It does not rely on asking people for their opinions or subjecting them to experiments. Rather, the effects of various policies are inferred from the analysis of observed behavior.[3] While economists are unable to control historical events, econometrics makes it possible to assess the importance of events that *did* occur.

The simple labor supply model suggested that annual hours of work (which we denote as L, for *l*abor supply) depend on the net wage rate (w_n). A bit of thought suggests that nonlabor income such as dividends and interest (A), age (X_1), and number of children (X_2) may also influence hours of work. The econometrician chooses a specific algebraic form to summarize the relationship between hours of work and these explanatory variables. A particularly simple form is

$$L = \alpha_0 + \alpha_1 w_n + \alpha_2 A + \alpha_3 X_1 + \alpha_4 X_2 + \varepsilon \qquad (2.1)$$

The α's are the **parameters** of the equation and ε is a **random error.** The parameters show how a change in a given right-hand side variable affects hours of work. If $\alpha_1 = 0$, the net wage has no impact on hours of work. If α_1 is greater than 0, increases in the net wage induce people to

---

[3] Note that econometric methods can also be applied to data generated by surveys and experiments.

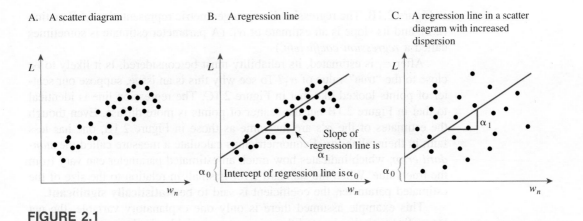

FIGURE 2.1

Multiple regression analysis

work more—the substitution effect dominates. If α_1 is less than 0, increases in the net wage induce people to work less—the income effect dominates.

The presence of the random error ε reflects the influences on labor supply that are unobservable to the investigator. No matter how many variables are included in the study, there is always some behavior that cannot be explained by the model.

Clearly, if we knew the α's, all debate over the effect of taxes on labor supply would be settled. The practical side of econometrics is to estimate the α's by application of various techniques. The most popular method is called **multiple regression analysis.** The heat of the debate over labor supply indicates that this technique does not always lead to conclusive results. To understand why, we consider its application to the labor supply example.

For this purpose, ignore for the moment all variables in Equation (2.1) other than the net wage, so the hours of work decision is simply

$$L = \alpha_0 + \alpha_1 w_n + \varepsilon \qquad (2.2)$$

Equation (2.2) is characterized as *linear* because if it is graphed with L and w_n on the axes, the result is a straight line.

Suppose information is obtained on hours of work and on after-tax wages for a sample of people. Plotting those observations gives a scatter of points like that in Figure 2.1A. Obviously, no single straight line can fit through all these points. The purpose of multiple regression analysis is to find the parameters of the line that fits best.[4] Such a **regression line** is illustrated

---

[4] The best line minimizes the sum of the squared vertical distances between the points on the line and the points in the scatter. See Wooldridge [2003].

in Figure 2.1B. The regression line is a geometric representation of Equation (2.2), and its slope is an estimate of α_1. (A parameter estimate is sometimes called a *regression coefficient.*)

After α_1 is estimated, its reliability must be considered. Is it likely to be close to the "true" value of α_1? To see why this is an issue, suppose our scatter of points looked like that in Figure 2.1C. The regression line is identical to that in Figure 2.1B but the scatter of points is more diffuse. Even though the estimates of the α's are the same as those in Figure 2.1B, one has less faith in their reliability. Econometricians calculate a measure called the *standard error,* which indicates how much an estimated parameter can vary from the true value. When the standard error is small in relation to the size of the estimated parameter, the coefficient is said to be **statistically significant.**

This example assumed there is only one explanatory variable, the net wage. Suppose that instead there were two variables in the equation: the net wage and nonlabor income. In analogy to fitting a regression *line* in a two-dimensional space, a regression *plane* can be fitted through a scatter of points in a three-dimensional space. For more than two variables, there is no convenient geometrical representation. Nevertheless, similar mathematical principles can be applied to produce estimates of the parameters for any number of explanatory variables (provided there are fewer variables than observations). The actual calculations are done with computers.

With estimates of the α's in hand, inferences can be made about the changes in L induced by changes in the net wage. Suppose $\alpha_1 = 100$. If a tax increase lowers the net wage by 50 cents, then an individual will work 50 hours (100 $\times$ \$.50) less per year.

Pitfalls of Econometric Analysis. There are difficulties involved in doing econometrics that explain why different investigators may reach contradictory conclusions. For example, implicit in Equation (2.1) is the assumption that the same equation describes everyone's behavior. However, different types of people may have different labor supply patterns. Married women may react differently than married men to changes in the net wage. Similarly, the young and the old have different behavioral patterns. Grouping together people with different behavior results in misleading parameter estimates. Investigators generally do not know beforehand along what lines their samples should be divided. Somewhat arbitrary decisions are required, and these may lead investigators to different results.

A related problem is that the parameters may change over time. A female labor supply equation using data from 1975 would very likely show different results from an equation using 2004 data. In part, this would be due to the impact of the women's movement on attitudes toward work and, hence, on the values of the α's. More generally, the reality that econometricians seek to understand is constantly changing. Estimates obtained from various data sets may differ even if the techniques used to obtain them are the same.

In addition, for an estimate of α_1 to be reliable, the regression equation must include all the relevant variables. Otherwise, some effects that are actually due to an omitted variable may be attributed to the net wage. Important variables are sometimes left out of an equation because information on them is simply not available. For example, it is very difficult to obtain accurate information on people's sources of nonlabor income. Suppose: (1) as nonlabor income increases (other things being the same), people tend to work less, and (2) there is a tendency for people with high wages also to have high nonlabor income. If nonlabor income is omitted from the equation, part of its effect on hours of work would be attributed to the wage, and the estimate of α_1 would be lower than its true value. In general, an estimate of α_1 is biased unless all the other variables that affect hours of work and that are also systematically related to the net wage are included.

A more severe version of this problem occurs when a potentially important variable is inherently unmeasurable. Attitudes such as aggressiveness may influence work decisions, but there is no satisfactory way to quantify these attitudes.

Investigators sometimes disagree over which variables should be included in a regression equation. Should an individual's educational level be included? Some argue that education affects attitudes toward work and therefore should be included as an explanatory variable. Others believe education affects work decisions only to the extent that it changes the wage, and therefore should not be included. While economic theory helps give some structure to the search for explanatory variables, it is rarely definitive. Different researchers make different judgments.

Difficulties in measuring variables can also make it hard to obtain reliable estimates. Consider problems in measuring hours of work. Superficially, this seems easy—just find out how much time elapses at the workplace. But a better measure would consider coffee breaks and "goofing off" time. These are obviously more difficult to measure. Calculating the wage rate also presents substantial problems. Ideally, the computation should include not only what a worker receives in the paycheck at the end of the week but also the value of fringe benefits—pension rights, health insurance, access to a company car, and so forth.

Finally, an important assumption is that variables on the right side of the equation affect the left-hand variable, but not vice versa. If this is not true, serious problems arise. Suppose that α_1 of Equation (2.1) is found to be positive. One interpretation is that when the net wage increases, people choose to work more. Another plausible interpretation is that employers pay higher wages to people who work longer hours. Indeed, wage rates might affect hours worked and *simultaneously* hours worked affect wages. If so, then the estimate of α_1 generated by multiple regression analysis does not correctly measure the effect of changes in the net wage on labor supply.

Several statistical techniques are available for dealing with this problem of simultaneous causation. They tend to be complicated, and different techniques can lead to different answers. This is another source of discrepancies in the results of econometric studies.

Concluding Remarks

Theory plays a crucial role for empirical researchers by helping to isolate a set of variables that may influence a particular kind of behavior. Empirical work then tests whether the theory is consistent with real-world phenomena. The most widespread method of empirical work in economics is econometric analysis, because economists tend to be most comfortable with results based on data from real-world environments. However, honest econometricians can come to very different conclusions, because the data and statistical techniques are imperfect. Reasonable people can disagree on the proper interpretation of a particular set of "facts":

> Facts are simple
> and facts are straight
> Facts are lazy
> and facts are late
> Facts all come with points of view
> Facts won't do what I want them to.[5]

Do we have to abandon all hope of learning about the factors that influence economic behavior? Definitely not. The economist researching an empirical question will doubtless come across a number of studies, each making somewhat different assumptions, each emphasizing a somewhat different aspect of the problem, and each therefore arriving at a somewhat different conclusion. In many cases one can reconcile the different studies and construct a coherent picture of the phenomenon under discussion. Feldstein [1982a, p. 830] has likened the economist who undertakes such a task to the maharajah in the children's fable about the five blind men who examined an elephant:

> The important lesson in that story is not the fact that each blind man came away with a partial and "incorrect" piece of evidence. The lesson is rather that an intelligent maharajah who studied the findings of these five men could probably piece together a good judgmental picture of an elephant, especially if he had previously seen some other four-footed animal.

On the numerous occasions throughout this book when we refer to the results of empirical studies, keep in mind the caveats presented here. In cases where the profession has failed to achieve consensus, the opposing views are discussed. More generally, it is hoped that this introduction to empirical methodology induces a healthy skepticism concerning claims about economic behavior that occur in public debate. Beware any argument that begins with the magic words "studies have proved."

---

[5] From "Cross-Eyed and Painless" © 1980 Bleu Disque Music Co., Inc., Index Music, Inc., and E. G. Music, Ltd. by permission of David Byrne and Brian Eno.

Summary

- Because economists generally cannot perform controlled experiments with the economy, the effects of economic policy are difficult to determine.

- Economic theory helps specify the factors that might affect a given kind of behavior. However, theory alone cannot say how important any particular factor is.

- Empirical research attempts to measure both the direction and size of the effect of government policy changes on behavior. Common types of empirical studies are interview studies, social and laboratory experiments, and econometric analysis.

- Interview studies consist of directly asking people how various policies affect their behavior. However, people may not actually react to policies in the way they say they do.

- Social experiments subject one group of people to some policy and compare their behavior with

that of a control group. Problems can arise because: the experiment itself may affect people's behavior; it is difficult to obtain a random sample; and social experiments are quite costly.

- Laboratory experiments are used to study some types of economic decisions.

- Econometrics is the statistical analysis of economic data. In econometrics, the effects of various policies are inferred from observed behavior.

- Multiple regression analysis is used to pick the "best" parameters for an econometric model. Knowing the parameters allows one to predict the effects of policy changes.

- Econometrics has some pitfalls. Misleading results occur if data from greatly dissimilar groups are combined; if important variables are omitted; if the wrong mathematical form is adopted; if variables are incorrectly measured; or if there is simultaneous causation between variables.

Discussion Questions

1. Like economists, astronomers are generally unable to perform controlled experiments. Yet astronomy is considered more of an exact science than economics. Why?

2. In 2003, George W. Bush proposed a cut in marginal income tax rates. Explain why it is difficult to predict the impact of such a tax cut upon labor supply on the basis of theory alone. What kind of empirical work might help you in making a prediction?

3. MDMA is an illegal recreational drug commonly known as Ecstasy. The conventional wisdom is that the use of Ecstasy leads to long-term problems such as nerve damage and brain impairment. Recently, a scientist challenged this view, arguing that previous studies had failed "to control for other factors, such as pre-existing psychological complaints or other drug use" (*The Economist,* September 7, 2002, p. 71). Relate the problems faced by medical researchers trying to determine the long-term

impact of Ecstasy to the problems faced by economists trying to determine the effects of economic policy.

4. In the 1970s, researchers at the RAND Corporation conducted a social experiment to investigate the relationship between health insurance coverage and health care utilization. In this experiment, samples of individuals were induced to trade their normal insurance policies for new RAND policies that offered various coinsurance rates (i.e., different rates at which the insurance would reimburse the individual for health care expenses). In 1993, the Clinton administration used the results of the RAND experiment to predict how health care utilization would increase if insurance coverage were made universal. What problems might arise in using the social experimentation results to predict the impact of universal coverage?

5. The budget proposal submitted by the Bush administration in 2003 projected increasing

deficits, that is, the gap between expenditures and revenues grew. A contentious debate ensued. On one side, critics of the administration argued that larger deficits would lead to higher interest rates, while supporters of the administration argued that it would have no impact on interest rates. The following table gives some historical data on deficits and interest rates. For each year, the deficit is the difference between revenues and expenditures measured in current dollars; a negative figure is a deficit and a positive figure is a surplus.

Year	Deficit	Interest rate
1980	−73.8	15.2%
1985	−212.3	9.9%
1990	−221.2	10.0%
1995	−164	8.8%
2000	236.4	9.2%

On the basis of these data, what inference would you make about the relationship between federal deficits and interest rates? Explain why inferences based on these data alone might be problematic.

Selected References

Burtless, Gary. "The Case for Randomized Field Trials in Economic and Policy Research." *Journal of Economic Perspectives* 9, no. 2 (Spring 1995), pp. 63–84.

Congressional Budget Office. *The Economic and Budget Outlook: Fiscal Years 1999–2008.* Washington, DC: US Government Printing Office, January 1998.

Smith, Vernon L. "Economics in the Laboratory." *Journal of Economic Perspectives* 8, no. 1 (Winter 1994), pp. 113–32.

Wooldridge, Jeffrey M. *Introductory Econometrics,* 2d ed. Cincinnati, OH: South-Western College Publishing, 2003.

CHAPTER 3

Tools of Normative Analysis

*The object of government is the welfare of the people. The
material progress and prosperity of a nation are desirable
chiefly so far as they lead to the moral and material welfare
of all good citizens.*

THEODORE ROOSEVELT

Pick up a newspaper any day and you are sure to find a story about a
debate concerning the government's role in the economy. Should
income taxes be cut? Do we need to subsidize the purchase of medicine for the elderly? Is it advisable to use public land in Alaska for oil
exploration? The list is virtually endless. Given the enormous diversity of
the government's economic activities, some kind of general framework is
needed to assess the desirability of various government actions. Without
such a systematic framework, each government program ends up being evaluated on an ad hoc basis, and achieving a coherent economic policy becomes
impossible.

Welfare Economics

The framework used by most public finance specialists is **welfare economics,** the branch of economic theory concerned with the social desirability of
alternative economic states.[1] This chapter sketches the fundamentals of welfare economics. The theory is used to distinguish the circumstances under
which markets can be expected to perform well from those under which
markets fail to produce desirable results.

---

[1] Welfare economics relies heavily on certain basic economic tools, particularly indifference curves. For a
review, see the appendix at the end of the book.

FIGURE 3.1

Edgeworth Box

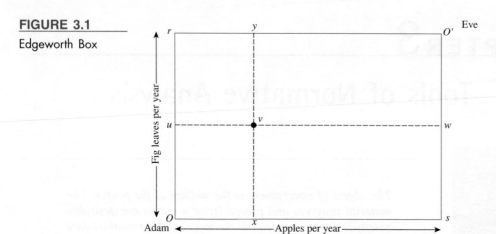

Pure Exchange Economy

We begin by considering a very simple economy. It consists of two people who consume two commodities with fixed supplies. The only economic problem here is to allocate amounts of the two goods between the two people. As simple as this model is, all the important results from the two good–two person case hold in economies with many people and commodities.[2] The two-by-two case is analyzed because of its simplicity.

The two people are Adam and Eve, and the two commodities are apples (food) and fig leaves (clothing). An analytical device known as the **Edgeworth Box** depicts the distribution of apples and fig leaves between Adam and Eve.[3] In Figure 3.1, the length of the Edgeworth Box, Os, represents the total number of apples available in the economy; the height, Or, is the total number of fig leaves. The amounts of the goods consumed by Adam are measured by distances from point O; the quantities consumed by Eve are measured by distances from O'. For example, at point v, Adam consumes Ou fig leaves and Ox apples, while Eve consumes $O'y$ apples and $O'w$ fig leaves. Thus, any point within the Edgeworth Box represents some allocation of apples and fig leaves between Adam and Eve.

Now assume Adam and Eve each have a set of conventionally shaped indifference curves that represent their preferences for apples and fig leaves. In Figure 3.2, both sets of indifference curves are superimposed onto the Edgeworth Box. Adam's are labeled with A's; Eve's are labeled with E's. Indifference curves with greater numbers represent higher levels of happiness (utility). Adam is happier on indifference curve A_3 than on A_2 or A_1, and Eve is happier on indifference curve E_3 than on E_2 or E_1. In general,

---

[2] See Chapter 11 of Henderson and Quandt [1980] where the results are derived using calculus.

[3] Named after the great 19th-century economist F. Y. Edgeworth.

FIGURE 3.2

Indifference curves in
an Edgeworth Box

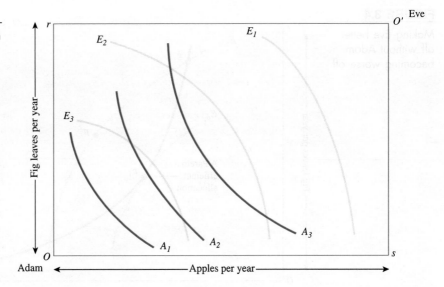

FIGURE 3.3

Making Adam better
off without Eve
becoming worse off

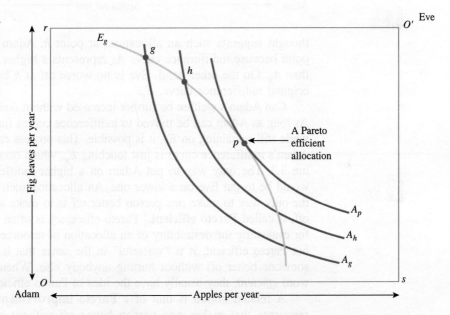

Eve's utility increases as her position moves toward the southwest, while
Adam's utility increases as he moves toward the northeast.

Suppose some arbitrary distribution of apples and fig leaves is selected—
say, point *g* in Figure 3.3. A_g is Adam's indifference curve that runs through
point *g*, and E_g is Eve's. Now pose the following question: Is it possible to
reallocate apples and fig leaves between Adam and Eve in such a way that
Adam is made better off, while Eve is made no worse off? A moment's

FIGURE 3.4

Making Eve better
off without Adam
becoming worse off

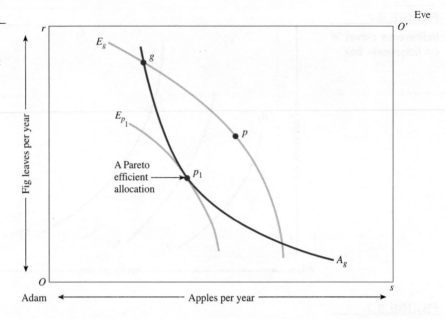

thought suggests such an allocation, at point h. Adam is better off at this point because indifference curve A_h represents a higher utility level for him than A_g. On the other hand, Eve is no worse off at h because she is on her original indifference curve, E_g.

Can Adam's welfare be further increased without doing any harm to Eve? As long as Adam can be moved to indifference curves further to the northeast while still remaining on E_g, it is possible. This process can be continued until Adam's indifference curve is just touching E_g, which occurs at point p in Figure 3.3. The only way to put Adam on a higher indifference curve than A_p would be to put Eve on a lower one. An allocation such as point p, at which the only way to make one person better off is to make another person worse off, is called **Pareto efficient**.[4] Pareto efficiency is often used as the standard for evaluating the desirability of an allocation of resources. If the allocation is not Pareto efficient, it is "wasteful" in the sense that it is possible to make someone better off without hurting anybody else. When economists use the word *efficient,* they usually have the idea of Pareto efficiency in mind.

A related notion is that of a **Pareto improvement**—a reallocation of resources that makes one person better off without making anyone else worse off. In Figure 3.3, the move from g to h is a Pareto improvement, as is the move from h to p.

Point p is not the only Pareto efficient allocation that could have been reached by starting at point g. Figure 3.4 examines whether we can make

---

[4] Named after the 19th-century economist Vilfredo Pareto.

FIGURE 3.5

Making both Adam and Eve better off

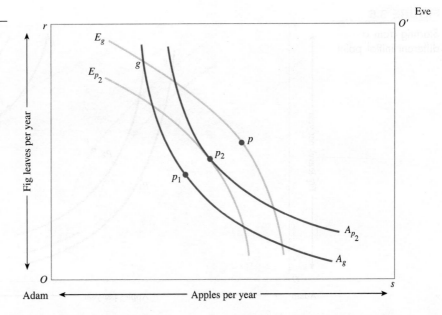

Eve better off without lowering the utility of Adam. Logic similar to that surrounding Figure 3.3 suggests moving Eve to indifference curves further to the southwest, provided that the allocation remains on A_g. In doing so, we isolate point p_1. At p_1, the only way to improve Eve's welfare is to move Adam to a lower indifference curve. Then, by definition, p_1 is a Pareto efficient allocation.

So far, we have been looking at moves that make one person better off and leave the other at the same level of utility. In Figure 3.5 we consider reallocations from point g that make *both* Adam and Eve better off. At p_2, for example, Adam is better off than at point g (A_{p_2} is further to the northeast than A_g) and so is Eve (E_{p_2} is further to the southwest than E_g). Point p_2 is Pareto efficient, because at that point it is impossible to make either individual better off without making the other worse off. It should now be clear that starting at point g, a whole set of Pareto efficient points can be found. They differ with respect to how much each of the parties gains from the reallocation of resources.

Recall that the initial point g was selected arbitrarily. We can repeat the procedure for finding Pareto efficient allocations with any starting point. Had point k in Figure 3.6 been the original allocation, Pareto efficient allocations p_3 and p_4 could have been isolated. This exercise reveals a whole set of Pareto efficient points in the Edgeworth Box. The locus of all the Pareto efficient points is called the **contract curve,** and is denoted mm in Figure 3.7. Note that for an allocation to be Pareto efficient (to be on mm), it must be a point at which the indifference curves of Adam and Eve are barely

FIGURE 3.6

Starting from a
different initial point

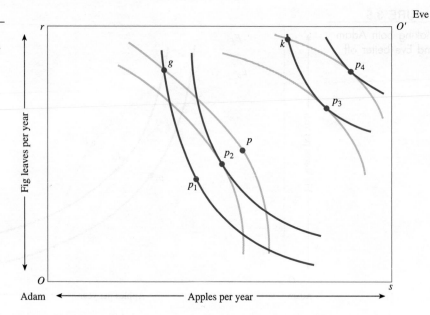

FIGURE 3.7

The contract curve

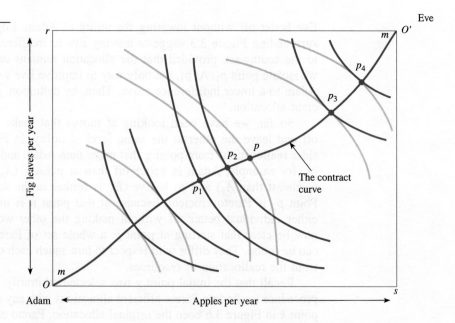

touching. In mathematical terms, the indifference curves are tangent—the
slopes of the indifference curves are equal.

In economic terms, the absolute value of the slope of the indifference
curve indicates the rate at which the individual is willing to trade one good

FIGURE 3.8

Production
possibilities curve

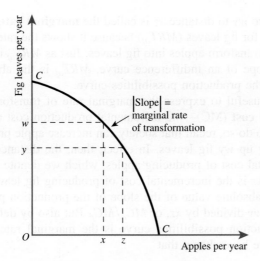

for an additional amount of another, called the *marginal rate of substitution*
(MRS).[5] Hence, Pareto efficiency requires that marginal rates of substitution
be equal for all consumers:

$$MRS_{af}^{Adam} = MRS_{af}^{Eve} \tag{3.1}$$

where MRS_{af}^{Adam} is Adam's marginal rate of substitution of apples for fig
leaves, and MRS_{af}^{Eve} is Eve's.

Production Economy **The Production Possibilities Curve.** So far we have assumed that supplies of
all the commodities are fixed. Consider what happens when productive
inputs can shift between the production of apples and fig leaves, so the quantities of the two goods can change. Provided the inputs are efficiently used,
if more apples are produced, then fig leaf production must necessarily fall
and vice versa. The **production possibilities curve** shows the maximum
quantity of fig leaves that can be produced along with any given quantity of
apples.[6] A typical production possibilities curve is depicted as *CC* in
Figure 3.8. As shown in Figure 3.8, one option available to the economy is
to produce *Ow* fig leaves and *Ox* apples. The economy can increase apple
production from *Ox* to *Oz*, distance *xz*. To do this, inputs have to be removed
from the production of fig leaves and devoted to apples. Fig leaf production
must fall by distance *wy* if apple production is to increase by *xz*. The ratio

---

[5] The marginal rate of substitution is defined more carefully in the appendix at the end of the book.

[6] The production possibilities curve can be derived from an Edgeworth Box whose dimensions represent
the quantities of inputs available for production.

of distance *wy* to distance *xz* is called the **marginal rate of transformation** of apples for fig leaves (MRT_{af}) because it shows the rate at which the economy can transform apples into fig leaves. Just as MRS_{af} is the absolute value of the slope of an indifference curve, MRT_{af} is the absolute value of the slope of the production possibilities curve.

It is useful to express the marginal rate of transformation in terms of **marginal cost** (MC)—the incremental production cost of one more unit of output. To do so, recall that society can increase apple production by *xz* only by giving up *wy* fig leaves. In effect, then, the distance *wy* represents the incremental cost of producing apples, which we denote MC_a. Similarly, the distance *xz* is the incremental cost of producing fig leaves, MC_f. By definition, the absolute value of the slope of the production possibilities curve is distance *wy* divided by *xz*, or MC_a/MC_f. But also by definition, the slope of the production possibilities curve is the marginal rate of transformation. Hence, we have shown that

$$MRT_{af} = \frac{MC_a}{MC_f} \tag{3.2}$$

Eficiency Conditions with Variable Production.   When the supplies of apples and fig leaves are variable, the condition for Pareto efficiency in Equation (3.1) must be extended. The condition becomes

$$MRT_{af} = MRS_{af}^{\text{Adam}} = MRS_{af}^{\text{Eve}} \tag{3.3}$$

To see why, we use an arithmetic example. Suppose that at a given allocation Adam's MRS_{af} is $\frac{1}{3}$, and the MRT_{af} is $\frac{2}{3}$. By the definition of MRT_{af}, at this allocation two additional fig leaves could be produced by giving up three apples. By the definition of MRS_{af}, if Adam lost three extra apples, he would require only *one* fig leaf to maintain his original utility level. Therefore, Adam could be made better off by giving up three apples and transforming them into *two* fig leaves, and no one else would be made worse off in the process. Such a trade is *always* possible as long as the marginal rate of substitution does not equal the marginal rate of transformation. Only when the slopes of the curves for each are equal is it impossible to make a Pareto improvement. Hence, $MRT_{af} = MRS_{af}$ is a necessary condition for Pareto efficiency. The rate at which apples can be transformed into fig leaves (MRT_{af}) must equal the rate at which consumers are willing to trade apples for fig leaves (MRS_{af}).

Using Equation (3.2), the conditions for Pareto efficiency can be reinterpreted in terms of marginal cost. Just substitute (3.2) into (3.3), which gives us

$$\frac{MC_a}{MC_f} = MRS_{af}^{\text{Adam}} = MRS_{af}^{\text{Eve}} \tag{3.4}$$

as a necessary condition for Pareto efficiency.

The First Fundamental Theorem of Welfare Economics

Now that we have described the necessary conditions for Pareto efficiency, we may ask whether a given economy will achieve this apparently desirable state. It depends on what assumptions we make about the operations of that economy. Assume that: 1) All producers and consumers act as perfect competitors; that is, no one has any market power. 2) A market exists for each and every commodity. Under these assumptions, the so-called *First Fundamental Theorem of Welfare Economics* states that a Pareto-efficient allocation of resources emerges. In effect, this stunning result tells us that a competitive economy "automatically" allocates resources efficiently, without any need for centralized direction (shades of Adam Smith's "invisible hand"). In a way, the First Welfare Theorem merely formalizes an insight that has long been recognized: When it comes to providing goods and services, free enterprise systems are amazingly productive.[7]

A rigorous proof of the theorem requires fairly sophisticated mathematics, but we can provide an intuitive justification. The essence of competition is that all people face the same prices—each consumer and producer is so small relative to the market that his or her actions alone cannot affect prices. In our example, this means Adam and Eve both pay the same prices for fig leaves (P_f) and apples (P_a). A basic result from the theory of consumer choice[8] is that a necessary condition for Adam to maximize utility is

$$MRS_{af}^{\text{Adam}} = \frac{P_a}{P_f} \qquad (3.5)$$

Similarly, Eve's utility-maximizing bundle satisfies

$$MRS_{af}^{\text{Eve}} = \frac{P_a}{P_f} \qquad (3.6)$$

Equations (3.5) and (3.6) together imply that

$$MRS_{af}^{\text{Adam}} = MRS_{af}^{\text{Eve}}$$

This condition, though, is identical to Equation (3.1), one of the necessary conditions for Pareto efficiency.

However, as emphasized in the preceding section, we must consider the production side as well. A basic result from economic theory is that a profit-maximizing competitive firm produces output up to the point at which marginal cost and price are equal. In our example, this means $P_a = MC_a$ and $P_f = MC_f$, or

$$\frac{MC_a}{MC_f} = \frac{P_a}{P_f} \qquad (3.7)$$

---

[7] "The bourgeoisie, during its rule of scarce 100 years, has created more massive and more colossal productive forces than have all preceding generations together," according to Karl Marx and Friedrich Engels in *The Communist Manifesto*, Part I [Tucker, 1978, p. 477].

[8] This result is derived in the appendix to this book.

But recall from Equation (3.2) that MC_a/MC_f is just the marginal rate of transformation. Thus, we can rewrite (3.7) as

$$MRT_{af} = \frac{P_a}{P_f} \qquad (3.8)$$

Now consider Equations (3.5), (3.6), and (3.8), and notice that P_a/P_f appears on the right-hand side of each. Hence, these three equations together imply that $MRS_{af}^{Adam} = MRS_{af}^{Eve} = MRT_{af}$, which is the necessary condition for Pareto efficiency. Competition, along with maximizing behavior on the part of all individuals, leads to an efficient outcome.

Finally, we can take advantage of Equation (3.4) to write the conditions for Pareto efficiency in terms of marginal cost. Simply substitute (3.5) or (3.6) into (3.4) to find

$$\frac{P_a}{P_f} = \frac{MC_a}{MC_f} \qquad (3.9)$$

Pareto efficiency requires that prices be in the same ratios as marginal costs, and competition guarantees this condition is met. The marginal cost of a commodity is the additional cost to society of providing it. According to Equation (3.9), efficiency requires that the additional cost of each commodity be reflected in its price.

Fairness and the Second Fundamental Theorem of Welfare Economics

If properly functioning competitive markets allocate resources efficiently, what role does the government have to play in the economy? Only a very small government would appear to be appropriate. Its main function would be to protect property rights so that markets can work. Government provides law and order, a court system, and national defense. Anything more is superfluous. However, such reasoning is based on a superficial understanding of the First Welfare Theorem. Things are really much more complicated. For one thing, it has implicitly been assumed that efficiency is the only criterion for deciding if a given allocation of resources is good. It is not obvious, however, that Pareto efficiency by itself is desirable.

To see why, let us return to the simple model in which the total quantity of each good is fixed. Consider Figure 3.9, which reproduces the contract curve mm derived in Figure 3.7. Compare the two allocations p_5 (at the lower left-hand corner of the box) and q (located near the center). Because p_5 lies on the contract curve, by definition it is Pareto efficient. On the other hand, q is inefficient. Is allocation p_5 therefore better? That depends on what is meant by better. To the extent that society prefers a relatively equal distribution of real income, q might be preferred to p_5, even though q is not Pareto efficient. On the other hand, society might not care about distribution at all, or perhaps care more about Eve than Adam. In this case, p_5 would be preferred to q.

FIGURE 3.9

Efficiency versus equity

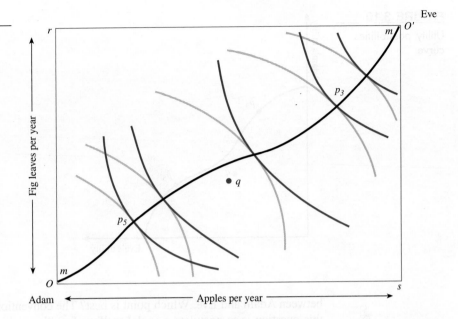

The key point is that the criterion of Pareto efficiency by itself is not enough to rank alternative allocations of resources. Rather, explicit value judgments are required on the fairness of the distribution of utility. To formalize this notion, note that the contract curve implicitly defines a relationship between the maximum amount of utility that Adam can attain for each level of Eve's utility. In Figure 3.10, Eve's utility is plotted on the horizontal axis, and Adam's utility is recorded on the vertical axis. Curve UU is the **utility possibilities curve** derived from the contract curve.[9] It shows the maximum amount of one person's utility given the other individual's utility level. Point $\tilde{p}_5$ corresponds to point p_5 on the contract curve in Figure 3.9. Here, Eve's utility is relatively high compared to Adam's. Point $\tilde{p}_3$ in Figure 3.10, which corresponds to p_3 in Figure 3.9, is just the opposite. Point $\tilde{q}$ corresponds to point q in Figure 3.9. Because q is off the contract curve, $\tilde{q}$ must be inside the utility possibilities curve, reflecting the fact that it is possible to increase one person's utility without decreasing the other's.

All points on or below the utility possibilities curve are attainable by society; all points above it are not attainable. By definition, all points on UU are Pareto efficient, but they represent very different distributions of real income

FIGURE 3.10

Utility possibilities
curve

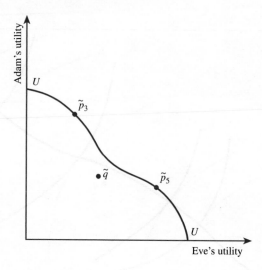

between Adam and Eve. Which point is best? The conventional way to answer this question is to postulate a **social welfare function,** which embodies society's views on the relative deservedness of Adam and Eve. A social welfare function is simply a statement of how society's well-being relates to the well-being of its members. Think of it this way: Just as an *individual's* welfare depends on the quantities of commodities she consumes, *society's* welfare depends on the utilities of each of its members. Algebraically, social welfare (W) is some function $F(\ )$ of each individual's utility:

$$W = F(U^{\text{Adam}}, U^{\text{Eve}}) \tag{3.10}$$

We assume the value of social welfare increases as either U^{Adam} or U^{Eve} increases—society is better off when any of its members becomes better off. Note that we have said nothing about how society manifests these preferences. Under some conditions, members of society may not be able to agree on how to rank each other's utilities, and the social welfare function does not even exist. For the moment, we simply assume it does exist.

Just as an individual's utility function for commodities leads to a set of indifference curves for those commodities, so does a social welfare function lead to a set of indifference curves between people's utilities. Figure 3.11 depicts a typical set of social indifference curves. Their downward slope indicates that if Eve's utility decreases, the only way to maintain a given level of social welfare is to increase Adam's utility, and vice versa. The level of social welfare increases as we move toward the northeast, reflecting the fact that an increase in any individual's utility increases social welfare, other things being the same.

In Figure 3.12, the social indifference curves are superimposed on the utility possibilities curve from Figure 3.10. Point *i* is not as desirable as point *ii* (point *ii* is on a higher social indifference curve than point *i*) even

FIGURE 3.11

Social indifference
curves

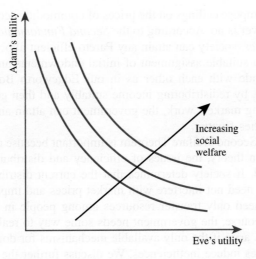

Adam's utility

Increasing
social
welfare

Eve's utility

FIGURE 3.12

Maximizing social
welfare

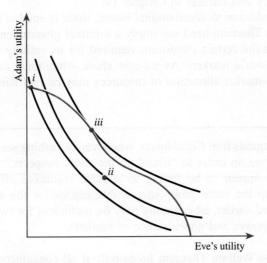

Adam's utility

i

iii

ii

Eve's utility

though point *i* is Pareto efficient and point *ii* is not. Here, society's value judgments, embodied in the social welfare function, favor a more equal distribution of real income, inefficient though it may be. Of course, point *iii* is preferred to either of these. It is both efficient and "fair."

Now, the First Welfare Theorem indicates that a properly working competitive system leads to some allocation on the utility possibilities curve. There is no reason, however, that it is the particular point that maximizes social welfare. We conclude that, even if the economy generates a Pareto efficient allocation of resources, government intervention may be necessary to achieve a "fair" distribution of utility.

Does the government have to intervene directly in markets in order to move the economy to the welfare-maximizing point? For example, does it have to impose ceilings on the prices of commodities consumed by the poor? The answer is no. According to the *Second Fundamental Theorem of Welfare Economics,* society can attain any Pareto-efficient allocation of resources by making a suitable assignment of initial endowments and then letting people freely trade with each other as in our Edgeworth Box Model.[10] Roughly speaking, by redistributing income suitably and then getting out of the way and letting markets work, the government can attain any point on the utility possibilities frontier.

The Second Welfare Theorem is important because of its implication that, at least in theory, the issues of efficiency and distributional fairness can be separated. If society determines that the current distribution of resources is unfair, it need not interfere with market prices and impair efficiency. Rather, society need only transfer resources among people in a way deemed to be fair. Of course, the government needs some way to reallocate resources, and problems arise if the only available mechanisms for doing so (such as taxes) themselves induce inefficiences. We discuss further the relationship between efficiency and fairness in Chapter 14.

In addition to distributional issues, there is another reason why the First Welfare Theorem need not imply a minimal government. This relates to the fact that the certain conditions required for its validity may not be satisfied by real-world markets. As we now show, when these conditions are absent, the free-market allocation of resources may be inefficient as well as unfair.

Market Failure

In the famous film *Casablanca,* whenever something seems amiss, the police chief gives an order to "round up the usual suspects." Similarly, whenever markets appear to be failing to allocate resources efficiently, economists round up the same group of possible causes for the supposed failure. As suggested earlier, an economy may be inefficient for two general reasons—market power and nonexistence of markets.

Market Power

The First Welfare Theorem holds only if all consumers and firms are price takers. If some individuals or firms are price makers (they have the power to affect prices), then the allocation of resources is generally inefficient. Why? A firm with market power may be able to raise price above marginal cost by supplying less output than a competitor would. Thus, Equation (3.9), one of the necessary conditions for Pareto efficiency, is violated. An insufficient quantity of resources is devoted to the commodity.

Price-making behavior can arise in several contexts. An extreme case is **monopoly,** where there is only one firm in the market, and entry is blocked.

---

[10] The proof requires that several technical conditions be satisfied. For example, all indifference curves have the standard (convex to the origin) shape.

Even in the less extreme case of oligopoly (a few sellers), the firms in an industry may be able to increase price above marginal cost. Finally, some industries have many firms, but each firm has some market power because the firms produce differentiated products. For example, a lot of firms produce running shoes, yet many consumers view Reeboks, Nikes, and Adidas as distinct commodities.

Nonexistence of Markets

The proof behind the First Welfare Theorem assumes a market exists for every commodity. After all, if a market for a commodity does not exist, then we can hardly expect the market to allocate it efficiently. In reality, markets for certain commodities may fail to emerge. Consider, for instance, insurance, a very important commodity in a world of uncertainty. Despite the existence of firms such as Aetna and Allstate, there are certain events for which insurance simply cannot be purchased on the private market. For example, suppose you wanted to purchase insurance against the possibility of becoming poor. Would a firm in a competitive market ever find it profitable to supply "poverty insurance"? The answer is no, because if you purchased such insurance, you might decide not to work very hard. To discourage such behavior, the insurance firm would have to monitor your behavior to determine whether your low income was due to bad luck or to goofing off. However, to perform such monitoring would be very difficult or impossible. Hence, there is no market for poverty insurance—it simply cannot be purchased.

Basically, the problem here is **asymmetric information**—one party in a transaction has information that is not available to another. One rationalization for governmental income support programs is that they provide poverty insurance that is unavailable privately. The premium on this "insurance policy" is the taxes you pay when you are able to earn income. In the event of poverty, your benefit comes in the form of welfare payments.

Another type of inefficiency that may arise due to the nonexistence of a market is an **externality,** a situation in which one person's behavior affects the welfare of another in a way that is outside existing markets. For example, suppose your roommate begins smoking large cigars, polluting the air and making you worse off. Why is this an efficiency problem? Your roommate consumes a scarce resource, clean air, when he smokes cigars. However, there is no market for clean air that forces him to pay for it. In effect, he pays a price of zero for the clean air and therefore "overuses" it. The price system fails to provide correct signals about the opportunity cost of a commodity.

Welfare economics provides a useful framework for thinking about externalities. The derivation of Equation (3.9) implicitly assumed marginal cost meant *social* marginal cost—it embodied the incremental value of all of society's resources used in production. In our cigar example, however, your roommate's private marginal cost of smoking is less than the social marginal cost because he does not have to pay for the clean air he uses. The price of a cigar, which reflects its private marginal cost, does not correctly reflect its social marginal cost. Hence, Equation (3.9) is not satisfied, and the allocation of resources is inefficient. Incidentally, an externality can be positive—confer a benefit—as well as negative. Think of a molecular biologist who publishes a paper about a novel gene-splicing technique that can be used by a pharmaceutical firm. In the case of a positive externality, the amount of the beneficial activity generated by the market is inefficiently small.

Closely related to an externality is a **public good,** a commodity that is *nonrival in consumption*—the fact that one person consumes it does not prevent anyone else from doing so as well. The classic example of a public good is a lighthouse. When the lighthouse turns on its beacon, all ships in the vicinity benefit. The fact that one person takes advantage of the lighthouse's services does not keep anyone else from doing so simultaneously.

People may have an incentive to hide how much they value a public good. Suppose that the lighthouse is beneficial to me. I know, however, that once the beacon is lit, I can enjoy its services, whether I pay for them or not. Therefore, I may claim the lighthouse means nothing to me, hoping that I can get a "free ride" after other people pay for it. Unfortunately, everyone has the same incentive, so the lighthouse may not get built, even though its construction could be very beneficial. The market mechanism may fail to force people to reveal their preferences for public goods, and possibly result in insufficient resources being devoted to them.

Overview

The First Welfare Theorem states that a properly working competitive economy generates a Pareto efficient allocation of resources without any government intervention. However, it is not obvious that an efficient allocation of resources is per se socially desirable; some argue that distributional fairness must also be considered. Moreover, we have just shown that in real-world economies, competition may not hold and not all markets may exist. Hence, the market-determined allocation of resources is unlikely to be efficient. There are, then, opportunities for government to intervene and enhance economic efficiency.

It must be emphasized that while efficiency problems provide opportunities for government intervention in the economy, they do not require it. The fact that the market-generated allocation of resources is imperfect does not mean the government is capable of doing better. For example, in certain cases, the costs of setting up a government agency to deal with an externality could exceed the cost of the externality itself. Moreover, governments, like people, can make mistakes. Some argue that government is inherently incapable of acting efficiently, so while in theory it can improve on the status quo, in practice it never will. While this argument is extreme, it highlights the fact that the fundamental theorem is helpful only in identifying situations in which intervention *may* lead to greater efficiency.

Buying into Welfare Economics

These days, the most vigorous debates over how to organize an economy are occurring in formerly Communist countries. Nevertheless, the same issues arise in Western nations as well: How much of national output should be devoted to the public sector, and how should public expenditures be financed? The theory of welfare economics introduced in this chapter provides the standard framework for thinking about these issues. There are, however, some controversies surrounding the theory.

First, the underlying outlook is highly individualistic, with a focus on people's utilities and how to maximize them. This is brought out starkly in the formulation of the social welfare function, Equation (3.10). The basic view expressed in that equation is that a good society is one whose members are happy. As suggested in Chapter 1, however, other societal goals are possible—to maximize the power of the state, to glorify God, and so on. Welfare economics does not have much to say to people with such goals. It is no surprise that Iran's Ayatollah Khomeini used to say that economics was for donkeys.

Because welfare economics puts people's preferences at center stage, it requires that these preferences be taken seriously. People know best what gives them satisfaction. A contrary view, once nicely summarized by Thomas O'Neill, former speaker of the House of Representatives, is, "Often what the American people want is not good for them." If one believes that individuals' preferences are ill formed or corrupt, a theory that shows how to maximize their utility is essentially irrelevant.

Musgrave [1959] developed the concept of **merit goods** to describe commodities that ought to be provided even if the members of society do not demand them. Government support of the fine arts is often justified on this basis. Operas and concerts should be provided publicly if individuals are unwilling to pay enough to meet their costs. But as Baumol and Baumol [1981] have noted,

> The term *merit good* merely becomes a formal designation for the unadorned value judgment that the arts are good for society and therefore deserve financial support . . . [the] merit good approach is not really a justification for support—it merely invents a bit of terminology to designate the desire to do so.
> [pp. 426–427]

Another possible problem with the welfare economics framework is its concern with *results*. Situations are evaluated in terms of the allocation of resources, and not of *how* the allocation was determined. Perhaps a society should be judged by the *processes* used to arrive at the allocation, not the actual results. Are people free to enter contracts? Are public processes democratic? If this view is taken, welfare economics loses its normative significance.

On the other hand, the great advantage of welfare economics is that it provides a coherent framework for assessing public policy. Every government intervention, after all, involves a reallocation of resources, and the whole purpose of welfare economics is to evaluate alternative allocations. The framework of welfare economics impels us to ask three key questions whenever a government activity is proposed:

- Will it have desirable distributional consequences?
- Will it enhance efficiency?
- Can it be done at a reasonable cost?

If the answer to these questions is no, the market should probably be left alone. Of course, to answer these questions may require substantial research and, in the case of the first question, value judgments as well. But just asking the right questions provides an invaluable structure for the decision-making process. It forces people to make their ethical values explicit, and facilitates the detection of frivolous or self-serving programs.

Summary

- Welfare economics is the study of the desirability of alternative economic states.

- A Pareto efficient allocation occurs when no person can be made better off without making another person worse off. Pareto efficiency requires that each person's marginal rate of substitution between two commodities equal the marginal rate of transformation. Pareto efficiency is the economist's benchmark of efficient performance for an economy.

- The First Fundamental Theorem of Welfare Economics states that, under certain conditions, competitive market mechanisms lead to Pareto efficient outcomes.

- Despite its appeal, Pareto efficiency has no obvious claim as an ethical norm. Society may prefer an inefficient allocation on the basis of equity or some other criterion. This provides one possible reason for government intervention in the economy.

- A social welfare function summarizes society's preferences concerning the utility of each of its members. It may be used to find the allocation of resources that maximizes social welfare.

- The Second Fundamental Theorem of Welfare Economics states that society can attain any Pareto-efficient allocation of resources by making a suitable assignment of initial endowments and then letting people freely trade with each other.

- A second reason for government intervention is market failure, which may occur in the presence of market power or when markets do not exist.

- The fact that the market does not allocate resources perfectly does not necessarily mean the government can do better. Each case must be evaluated on its own merits.

- Welfare economics is based on an individualistic social philosophy. It does not pay much attention to the processes used to achieve results. Thus, although it provides a coherent and useful framework for analyzing policy, welfare economics is not universally accepted.

Discussion Questions

1. In which of the following markets do you expect efficient outcomes? Why?

    a. Flood insurance for beach houses

    b. Medical care

    c. Stock market

    d. Personal computers

    e. Loans for students who wish to attend college

    f. Car insurance

2. Consider an economy with two people, Henry and Catherine, who consume two commodities, bread and water. Suppose that, due to a drought, the authorities decide to allocate exactly half the available water to each person. In order to prevent one person from "exploiting" the other, neither person may trade away any water to the other in exchange for more bread. Set up an Edgeworth Box to depict this situation and explain why it is unlikely to be Pareto efficient.

3. The government of France taxes movies that are produced outside of the country and subsidizes domestically produced movies. Is this policy consistent with a Pareto efficient allocation of resources? (Hint: Consider a model in which consumers choose between two goods, "foreign movies" and "domestic movies." How does the marginal rate of substitution between the goods compare to the marginal rate of transformation?)

4. Imagine a simple economy with only two people, Augustus and Livia.

   a. Let the social welfare function be

   $$W = U_L + U_A$$

   where U_L and U_A are the utilities of Livia and Augustus, respectively. Graph the social indifference curves. How would you describe the relative importance assigned to their respective well-being?

   b. Repeat a when

   $$W = U_L + 2U_A$$

   c. Assume that the utility possibility frontier is as follows:

   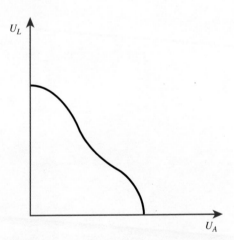

   Graphically show how the optimal solution differs between the welfare functions given in parts a and b.

5. From time to time, the city of Chicago provides free concerts. Can this program be rationalized on the basis of welfare economics?

Relate the program to the concept of merit goods.

6. In each case listed below, can you rationalize the government policy on the basis of welfare economics?

   a. In Los Angeles, the police respond to 127,000 burglar alarm calls per year. There is no charge. (97 percent of the alarms are false.)

   b. Honey production is subsidized by the federal government.

   c. The United States Department of Agriculture subsidizes crop insurance for farmers. Farmers pay no premiums for coverage against catastrophic production losses.

   d. In Washington, DC, you cannot become a hairdresser unless you have a license from the city government.

   e. The National Energy Policy Act requires that all new toilets flush with only 1.6 gallons of water. Most American homes have toilets that consume 5.5 to 7 gallons per flush.

   f. The federal government subsidizes the production of electricity from chicken manure. [Note: I am not making this up.]

7. Your airplane crashes in the Pacific Ocean. You land on a desert island with one other passenger. A box containing 100 little bags of peanuts also washes up on the island. The peanuts are the only thing to eat.

   In this economy with two people, one commodity, and no production, represent the possible allocations in a diagram, and explain why every allocation is Pareto efficient. Is every allocation fair?

8. According to Pope John Paul II, "The social order will be all the more stable, the more . . . it does not place in opposition personal interest and the interests of society as a whole, but rather seeks ways to bring them into fruitful harmony." Do markets constitute a good "social order" according to this criterion? What is the relevance of the First Welfare Theorem to your answer?

9. Consider an economy with two people, Victoria and Albert, and two commodities, tea and crumpets. Currently, Victoria and Albert

would both be willing to substitute two cups of tea for one crumpet. Further, if the economy were to produce one less cup of tea, the resources released from tea production could be used to produce three more crumpets. Is the allocation of resources in this economy Pareto efficient? If not, should there be more tea or more crumpets?

10. Indicate whether each of the following statements is true, false, or uncertain, and justify your answer.

a. If everyone has the same marginal rate of substitution, then the allocation of resources is Pareto efficient.

b. If the allocation of resources is Pareto efficient, then everyone has the same marginal rate of substitution.

c. When you get vaccinated against measles, you are producing a positive externality.

d. The Second Fundamental Theorem of Welfare Economics tells us that the competitive allocation of resources is socially desirable.

Selected References

Bator, F. M. "The Simple Analytics of Welfare Maximization." *American Economic Review* 47 (March 1957), pp. 22–59.

PART 2

Analysis of Public Expenditure

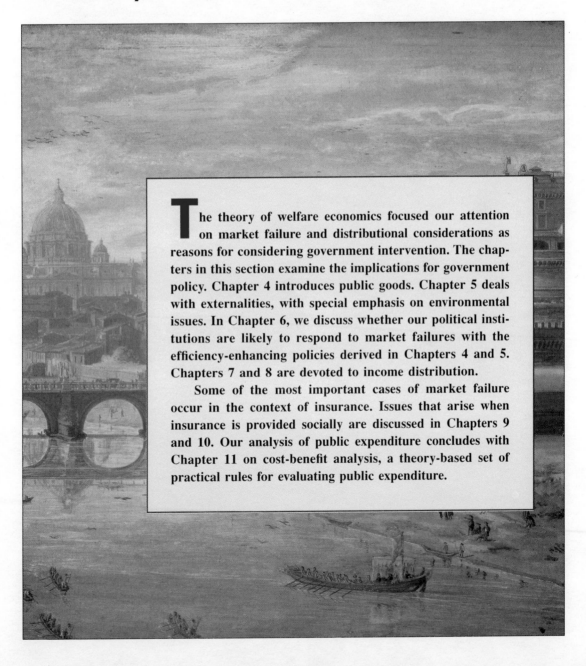

The theory of welfare economics focused our attention on market failure and distributional considerations as reasons for considering government intervention. The chapters in this section examine the implications for government policy. Chapter 4 introduces public goods. Chapter 5 deals with externalities, with special emphasis on environmental issues. In Chapter 6, we discuss whether our political institutions are likely to respond to market failures with the efficiency-enhancing policies derived in Chapters 4 and 5. Chapters 7 and 8 are devoted to income distribution.

Some of the most important cases of market failure occur in the context of insurance. Issues that arise when insurance is provided socially are discussed in Chapters 9 and 10. Our analysis of public expenditure concludes with Chapter 11 on cost-benefit analysis, a theory-based set of practical rules for evaluating public expenditure.

CHAPTER 4

Public Goods

There exists an intrinsic connection between the common good on the one hand and the structure and function of public authority on the other. The moral order, which needs public authority in order to promote the common good in human society, requires also that the authority be effective in attaining that end.

POPE JOHN XXIII

In the aftermath of the terrorist attacks on the United States on September 11, 2001, all Americans agreed that the government had to take steps to prevent future attacks. Although there was (and continues to be) a vigorous debate about just what those steps should be, everyone took for granted that providing defense was a proper function for government. What characteristic of national defense makes it an appropriate government responsibility? Are there other goods and services that partake of this characteristic, and should the government provide them as well? These questions lie at the heart of some of the most important controversies in public policy. In this chapter, we discuss the conditions under which public provision of commodities is appropriate. Special attention is devoted to understanding why markets may fail to provide particular goods at Pareto efficient levels.

Public Goods Defined

What's the difference between national defense and pizza? The question seems silly, but thinking about it leads to a useful framework for determining whether public or private provision of various commodities makes sense. To begin, one big difference between the two commodities is that two people cannot consume a pizza simultaneously—if I eat a piece, you can't. In contrast, your consumption of the protective services provided by the army does nothing to diminish my consumption of the same services. A second major difference arises because I can easily exclude you from consuming my pizza, but excluding you from the benefits of national defense is all but impossible. (It's hard to imagine a situation in which terrorists are allowed to overrun your home but not mine.)

National defense is an example of a **pure public good,** defined as follows:[1]

- Once it is provided, the additional resource cost of another person consuming the good is zero—consumption is *nonrival.*
- To prevent anyone from consuming the good is either very expensive or impossible—consumption is *nonexcludable.*

In contrast, a **private good** like pizza is rival and excludable.

Several aspects of our definition of public good are worth noting.

Even though everyone consumes the same quantity of the good, it need not be valued equally by all. Consider house cleaning in an apartment with many college roommates, which has a public good characteristic to it— everyone benefits from a clean bathroom, and it is hard to exclude anyone from these benefits. Yet some students care about cleanliness much more than others. Similarly, in our defense example, people who are deeply concerned about the intentions of hostile foreigners place a higher value on national defense than people who feel relatively safe, other things being the same. Indeed, people might differ over whether the value of certain public goods is positive or negative. Each person has no choice but to consume the services of a new missile system. For those who believe the system enhances their safety, the value is positive. Others think additional missiles only lead to arms races and decrease national security. Such individuals value an additional missile negatively. They would be willing to pay not to have it around.

Classification as a public good is not an absolute; it depends on market conditions and the state of technology. Think about a lighthouse. Once the beacon is lit, one ship can take advantage of it without impinging on another ship's ability to do the same. Moreover, no particular vessel can be excluded from taking advantage of the signal. Under these conditions, the lighthouse is a pure public good. But suppose that a jamming device were invented that made it possible to prevent ships from obtaining the lighthouse signal unless they purchased a special receiver. In this case, the nonexcludability criterion is no longer satisfied, and the lighthouse is no longer a pure public good. A scenic view is a pure public good when there is a small number of people involved. But as the number of

---

[1] There is some controversy in the literature with respect to the characteristics of a pure public good. Here we follow the treatment of Cornes and Sandler [1996].

sightseers increases, the area may become congested. The same "quantity" of the scenic view is being "consumed" by each person, but its quality decreases with the number of people. Hence, the nonrivalness criterion is no longer satisfied.

In many cases, then, it makes sense to think of "publicness" as a matter of degree. A pure public good satisfies the definition exactly. Consumption of an **impure public good** is to some extent rival or excludable. There are not many examples of really pure public goods. However, just as analysis of pure competition yields important insights into the operation of actual markets, so the analysis of pure public goods helps us to understand problems confronting public decision makers.

A commodity can satisfy one part of the definition of a public good and not the other. That is, nonexcludability and nonrivalness do not have to go together. Consider the streets of a downtown urban area during rush hour. In most cases, nonexcludability holds, because it is not feasible to set up enough toll booths to monitor traffic. But consumption is certainly rival, as anyone who has ever been caught in a traffic jam can testify. On the other hand, many people can enjoy a huge seashore area without diminishing the pleasure of others. Despite the fact that individuals do not rival each other in consumption, exclusion is quite possible if there are only a few access roads. Again, however the characterization of a commodity depends on the state of technology and on legal arrangements. The road congestion example is relevant here. E-ZPasses use radio waves to identify passing cars and automatically charge tolls to drivers' charge accounts. For example, State Route 91 near Los Angeles is a four-lane highway accessible only to drivers who buy the required devices for their cars. One can imagine someday using such technology to charge cars as they enter congested city streets—the streets would become excludable.

Some things that are not conventionally thought of as commodities have public good characteristics. An important example is honesty. If each citizen is honest in commercial transactions, all of society benefits due to the reduction of the costs of doing business. Such cost reductions are characterized both by nonexcludability and nonrivalness. Similarly, the income distribution is a public good. If income is distributed "fairly," each person gains satisfaction from living in a good society, and no one can be excluded from having that satisfaction. Of course, because of disagreements over notions of fairness, people may differ over how a given income distribution should be valued. Nevertheless, consumption of the income distribution is nonrival and nonexcludable, and therefore it is a public good. Certain types of information are also public goods. In Los Angeles, restaurants are now forced by the local government to display a hygiene rating—either "A" (clean), "B" (dirty), or "C" (disgusting). This information dissemination exhibits public good characteristics—it is nonrival in consumption in the sense that everyone can costlessly learn about the restaurant's hygiene by going to the Internet, newspaper, or simply glancing in the restaurant's window, and it is nonexcludable.

Private goods are not necessarily provided exclusively by the private sector. There are many **publicly provided private goods**—rival and excludable commodities that are provided by governments. Medical services and housing are two examples of private goods sometimes provided publicly. Similarly, as we see later, public goods can be provided privately. (Think of individuals donating money to maintain public spaces, which is how Central Park in New York City manages to have such beautiful flowers.) In short, the label *private* or *public* does not by itself tell us anything about which sector provides the item.

Public provision of a good does not necessarily mean that it is also *produced* by the public sector.   Consider refuse collection. Some communities produce this service themselves—public sector managers purchase garbage trucks, hire workers, and arrange schedules. In other communities, the local government hires a private firm for the job and does not organize production itself. In the United States, about 37 percent of fire protection services are contracted out to private firms. The figure is 23 percent for libraries and 48 percent for public transit [Lopez-de-Silanes, Shleifer, and Vishny, 1997].

Efficient Provision of Public Goods

What is the efficient amount of defense or any other public good? To derive the conditions for efficient provision of a public good, we begin by reexamining private goods from a slightly different perspective than that in Chapter 3. Assume again a society populated by two people, Adam and Eve. There are two private goods, apples and fig leaves. In Figure 4.1A, the quantity of fig leaves (f) is measured on the horizontal axis, and the price per fig leaf (P_f) is on the vertical. Adam's demand curve for fig leaves is denoted by D_f^A. The demand curve shows the quantity of fig leaves that Adam would be willing to consume at each price, other things being the same.[2] Similarly, D_f^E in Figure 4.1B is Eve's demand curve for fig leaves. At the same time, each person's demand curve shows how much he or she would be willing to pay for a particular quantity. (See the appendix at the end of the book.)

Suppose we want to derive the market demand curve for fig leaves. To do so, we simply add together the number of fig leaves each person demands at every price. In Figure 4.1A, at a price of $5, Adam demands one fig leaf, the horizontal distance between D_f^A and the vertical axis. Figure 4.1B indicates that at the same price, Eve demands two fig leaves. The

---

[2] Demand curves are explained in the appendix to this book.

FIGURE 4.1

Horizontal
summation of
demand curves

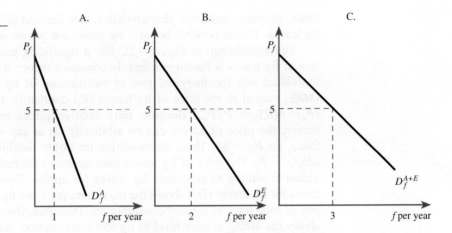

FIGURE 4.2

Efficient provision
of a private good

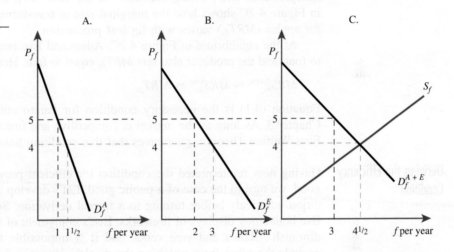

total quantity demanded at a price of $5 is therefore three leaves. The market demand curve for fig leaves is labeled D_f^{A+E} in Figure 4.1C. As we have just shown, the point at which price is $5 and quantity is three lies on the market demand curve. Similarly, finding the market demand at any given price involves summing the horizontal distance between each of the private demand curves and the vertical axis at that price. This process is called **horizontal summation.**

Figure 4.2 reproduces the information from Figure 4.1. Figure 4.2C then superimposes the market supply curve, labeled S_f, on the market demand curve D_f^{A+E}. Equilibrium in the market is found where supply and demand are equal. This occurs at a price of $4 in Figure 4.2C. At this price, Adam consumes one-and-one-half fig leaves and Eve consumes three. Note that there is no reason to expect Adam and Eve to consume the same amounts. Due to different tastes, incomes, and other characteristics, they demand different quantities of fig leaves. This is possible because fig leaves are private goods.

The equilibrium in Figure 4.2C has a significant property: The allocation of fig leaves is Pareto efficient. In consumer theory, a utility-maximizing individual sets the marginal rate of substitution of fig leaves for apples (MRS_{fa}) equal to the price of fig leaves (P_f) divided by the price of apples (P_a): $MRS_{fa} = P_f/P_a$.[3] Because only relative prices matter for rational choice, the price of apples can be arbitrarily set at any value. For convenience, set $Pa = \$1$. Thus, the condition for utility maximization reduces to $MRS_{fa} = P_f$. The price of fig leaves thus measures the rate at which an individual is willing to substitute fig leaves for apples. Now, Adam's demand curve for fig leaves (D_f^A) shows the maximum price per fig leaf that he would pay at each level of fig leaf consumption. Therefore, the demand curve also shows the MRS_{fa} at each level of fig leaf consumption. Similarly, D_f^E can be interpreted as Eve's MRS_{fa} schedule. In the same way, the supply curve S_f in Figure 4.2C shows how the marginal rate of transformation of fig leaves for apples (MRT_{fa}) varies with fig leaf production.[4]

At the equilibrium in Figure 4.2C, Adam and Eve both set MRS_{fa} equal to four, and the producer also sets MRT_{fa} equal to four. Hence, at equilibrium

$$MRS_{fa}^{Adam} = MRS_{fa}^{Eve} = MRT_{fa} \qquad (4.1)$$

Equation (4.1) is the necessary condition for Pareto efficiency derived in Chapter 3. As long as the market is competitive and functions properly, the First Welfare Theorem guarantees that this condition holds.

Deriving the Efficiency Condition

Having now reinterpreted the condition for efficient provision of a private good, we turn to the case of a public good. Let's develop the efficiency condition intuitively before turning to a formal derivation. Suppose Adam and Eve both enjoy displays of fireworks. Eve's enjoyment of fireworks does not diminish Adam's and vice versa, and it is impossible for one person to exclude the other from watching the display. Hence, a fireworks display is a public good. The size of the fireworks display can be varied, and both Adam and Eve prefer bigger to smaller shows, other things being the same. Suppose that the display currently consists of 19 rockets and can be expanded at a cost of $5 per rocket, that Adam would be willing to pay $6 to expand the display by another rocket, and that Eve would be willing to pay $4. Is it efficient to increase the size of the display by one rocket? As usual, we must compare the marginal benefit to the marginal cost. To

---

[3] See the appendix to the book for a proof.

[4] To demonstrate this, note that under competition, firms produce up to the point where price equals marginal cost. Hence, the supply curve S_f shows the marginal cost of each level of fig leaf production. As noted in Chapter 3 under "Welfare Economics," $MRT_{fa} = MC_f/MC_a$. Because $P_a = \$1$ and price equals marginal cost, then $MC_a = \$1$, and $MRT_{fa} = MC_f$. We can therefore identify the marginal rate of transformation with marginal cost, and hence with the supply curve.

compute the marginal benefit, note that because consumption of the display is nonrival, the 20th rocket can be consumed by *both* Adam and Eve. Hence, the marginal benefit of the 20th rocket is the *sum* of what they are willing to pay, which is $10. Because the marginal cost is only $5, it pays to acquire the 20th rocket. More generally, if the sum of individuals' willingness to pay for an additional unit of a public good exceeds its marginal cost, efficiency requires that the unit be purchased; otherwise, it should not. Hence, *efficiency requires that provision of a public good be expanded until the point at which the sum of each person's marginal valuation on the last unit just equals the marginal cost.*

To derive this result graphically, consider panel A of Figure 4.3 in which Adam's consumption of rockets (r) is measured on the horizontal axis, and the price per rocket (P_r) is on the vertical. Adam's demand curve for rockets is D_r^A. Similarly, Eve's demand curve for rockets is D_r^E in Figure 4.3B. How do we derive the group willingness to pay for rockets? To find the group demand curve for fig leaves—a private good—we horizontally summed the individual demand curves. That procedure allowed Adam and Eve to consume different quantities of fig leaves at the same price. For a private good, this is fine. However, the services produced by the rockets—a public good—*must* be consumed in *equal* amounts. If Adam consumes a 20-rocket fireworks display, Eve must also consume a 20-rocket fireworks display. It makes no sense to try to sum the quantities of a public good that the individuals would consume at a given price.

Instead, to find the group willingness to pay for rockets, we add the *prices* that each would be willing to pay for a given quantity. The demand curve in Figure 4.3A tells us that Adam is willing to pay $6 per rocket when he consumes 20 rockets. Eve is willing to pay $4 when she consumes 20 rockets. Their group willingness to pay for 20 rockets is therefore $10 per rocket. Thus, if we define D_r^{A+E} in Figure 4.3C to be the group willingness to pay schedule, the vertical distance between D_r^{A+E} and the point r = 20 must be 10.[5] Other points on D_r^{A+E} are determined by repeating this procedure for each output level. For a public good, then, the group willingness to pay is found by **vertical summation** of the individual demand curves.

Note the symmetry between private and public goods. With a private good, everyone has the same *MRS*, but people can consume different quantities. Therefore, demands are summed horizontally over the differing quantities. For public goods, everyone consumes the same quantity, but people can have different *MRS*s. Vertical summation is required to find the group willingness to pay. Put another way, for standard private goods, everyone sees the same price and then people decide what quantity they want. For public goods, everyone sees the same quantity and people decide what price they are willing to pay.

---

[5] D_r^{A+E} is not a conventional demand schedule because it does not show the quantity that would be demanded at each price. However, this notation highlights the similarities to the private good case.

FIGURE 4.3

Vertical summation of demand curves

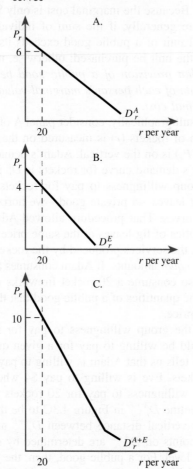

FIGURE 4.4

Efficient provision of a public good

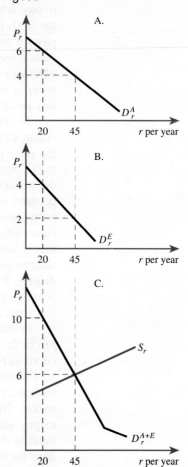

The efficient quantity of rockets is found where Adam's and Eve's willingness to pay for an additional unit just equals the marginal cost of producing a unit. In Figure 4.4C, the marginal cost schedule, S_r, is superimposed on the group willingness to pay curve D_r^{A+E}.[6] The intersection occurs at output 45, where the marginal cost is $6.

Once again, prices can be interpreted in terms of marginal rates of substitution. Reasoning as before, Adam's marginal willingness to pay for rockets

---

[6] This analysis does not consider explicitly the production possibilities frontier that lies behind this supply curve. See Samuelson [1955].

is his marginal rate of substitution (MRS_{ra}^{Adam}), and Eve's marginal willingness to pay for rockets is her marginal rate of substitution (MRS_{ra}^{Eve}). Therefore, the sum of the prices they are willing to pay equals $MRS_{ra}^{\text{Adam}} + MRS_{ra}^{\text{Eve}}$. From the production standpoint, price still represents the marginal rate of transformation, MRT_{ra}. Hence, the equilibrium in Figure 4.4C is characterized by the condition

$$MRS_{ra}^{\text{Adam}} + MRS_{ra}^{\text{Eve}} = MRT_{ra} \qquad (4.2)$$

Contrast this with the conditions for efficiently providing a private good described in Equation (4.1). For a private good, efficiency requires that each individual have the same marginal rate of substitution, and that this equal the marginal rate of transformation. For a pure public good, the sum of the marginal rates of substitution must equal the marginal rate of transformation.[7] Because everybody must consume the same amount of the public good, its efficient provision requires that the *total* valuation they place on the last unit provided—the sum of the *MRS*s—equal the incremental cost to society of providing it—the *MRT*.

Problems in Achieving Efficiency

As stressed in Chapter 3, under a reasonably general set of conditions, a decentralized market system provides private goods efficiently. Do market forces lead to the efficient level of public goods ($r = 45$) in Figure 4.4? The answer depends in part on the extent to which Adam and Eve reveal their true preferences for fireworks. When a private good is exchanged in a competitive market, an individual has no incentive to lie about how much he or she values it. If Eve is willing to pay the going price for a fig leaf, then she has nothing to gain by failing to buy one.

However, people may have incentives to hide their true preferences for a public good. Adam may falsely claim that fireworks mean nothing to him. If he can get Eve to foot the entire bill, he can still enjoy the show and yet have more money to spend on apples and fig leaves. Someone who lets other people pay while enjoying the benefits himself is known as a **free rider.** Of course, Eve also would like to be a free rider. Where there are public goods, "any one person can hope to snatch some selfish benefit in a way not possible under the self-policing competitive pricing of private goods" [Samuelson, 1955, p. 389]. Hence, the market may fall short of providing the efficient amount of the public good. No automatic tendency exists for markets to reach the efficient allocation in Figure 4.4.

Even if consumption is excludable, market provision of a nonrival good is likely to be inefficient. Suppose now that the fireworks display is excludable; people cannot see the show without purchasing an admission ticket to a very

---

[7] This analysis assumes the taxes required to finance the public good can be raised without distorting economic decisions in the private sector. When this is not the case, the efficiency condition changes. See Atkinson and Stern [1974].

large coliseum. A profit-maximizing entrepreneur sells tickets. For a fireworks display of a particular size, the additional cost of another person viewing it is zero (because the display is nonrival). Efficiency requires that every person be admitted who values the display at more than zero; that is, people should be admitted as long as the benefit to them exceeds the incremental cost of zero. Hence, efficiency requires a price of zero. But if the entrepreneur charges everyone a price of zero, then she cannot stay in business.

Is there a way out? Suppose the following two conditions hold: (1) the entrepreneur knows each person's demand curve for the public good; and (2) it is difficult or impossible to transfer the good from one person to another. Under these two conditions, the entrepreneur could charge each person an individual price based on willingness to pay, a procedure known as **perfect price discrimination.** People who valued the rocket display at only a penny would pay exactly that amount; even they would not be excluded. Thus, everyone who put any positive value on the show would attend, an efficient outcome.[8] However, because those who valued the display a lot would pay a very high price, the entrepreneur would be able to stay in business.

Perfect price discrimination may seem to be the solution until we recall that the first condition requires knowledge of everybody's preferences. But if individuals' demand curves were known, there would be no problem in determining the optimum provision in the first place.[9] We conclude that even if a nonrival commodity is excludable, private provision is likely to lead to efficiency problems.

The Free Rider Problem

Some suggest that the free rider problem necessarily leads to inefficient levels of public goods; therefore, efficiency requires government provision of such goods. The argument is that the government can somehow find out everyone's true preferences, and then, using its coercive power, force everybody to pay for public goods. If all this is possible, the government can avoid the free rider problem and ensure that public goods are optimally provided.

It must be emphasized that free ridership is not a *fact;* it is an implication of the *hypothesis* that people maximize a utility function that depends only on their own consumption of goods. To be sure, one can find examples in which public goods are not provided because people fail to reveal their preferences. On the other hand, in many instances individuals can and do act collectively without government coercion. Fund drives spearheaded by volunteers have led to the establishment and maintenance of churches, music halls, libraries, scientific laboratories, art museums, hospitals, and other such facilities. There is even some evidence of successful private provision of that

---

[8] The outcome is efficient because the price paid by the *marginal* consumer equals marginal cost.

[9] A number of mechanisms have been designed to induce people to reveal their true preferences to a government agency. See the appendix to this chapter.

classic public good, the lighthouse [Coase, 1974]. One prominent economist has argued, "I do not know of many historical records or other empirical evidence which show convincingly that the problem of correct revelation of preferences has been of any practical significance" [Johansen, 1977, p. 147].

These observations do not prove that free ridership is irrelevant. Although some goods that appear to have public characteristics are privately provided, others that "ought" to be provided (on grounds of efficiency) may not be. Moreover, the quantity of those public goods that are privately provided may be insufficient. The key point is that the importance of the free rider problem is an empirical question whose answer should not be taken for granted.

A number of laboratory experiments have been conducted to investigate the importance of free rider behavior. In a typical experiment, each of several subjects is given a number of tokens that they can either keep or donate to a "group exchange." For each token he keeps, a subject receives some payoff, say $4. Further, every time someone in the group donates to the group exchange, *everyone* in the group collects some amount of money, say $3, including the person who makes the donation. Clearly, all the subjects would be better off if everyone donated all their tokens to the group exchange. Note, however, that donations to the group exchange provide a nonrival and nonexcludable payoff. The free rider theory suggests that the subjects therefore might very well decide to make no contributions to the group exchange, so that they could benefit from everyone else's donations while putting nothing in themselves.

What do the results show? The findings vary from experiment to experiment, but the results from a study by Palfrey and Prisbrey [1997] seem fairly typical. On average, people contribute a *portion* of their resources to the provision of the public good. Some free riding therefore is present in the sense that the subjects fail to contribute all their tokens to the group exchange. On the other hand, the results contradict the notion that free riding leads to zero or trivial amounts of a public good. Two other important results are that the more people repeat the game, the less likely they are to contribute, and that the contribution rates decline when the opportunity cost of giving goes up (i.e., when the reward for keeping a token increases).

As was stressed in Chapter 2, caution must be exercised in interpreting the results of laboratory experiments. Still, the results suggest that people may derive a "warm-glow" from giving that works counter to the pursuit of narrow self-interest.

The Privatization Debate

Countries throughout the world are debating the virtues of privatizing governmental functions. **Privatization** means taking services that are supplied by the government and turning them over to the private sector for provision and/or production. In this section, we first discuss issues relating to *provision* and then turn to *production*.

Public versus Private Provision

Sometimes the services provided by publicly provided goods can be obtained privately. The commodity "protection" can be obtained from a publicly provided police force. Alternatively, to some extent, protection can also be gained by purchasing strong locks, burglar alarms, and bodyguards, which are obtained privately. Indeed, there are now three times as many privately hired policemen in the United States than public ones [*Economist,* 1997, p. 21]. A large backyard can serve many of the functions of a public park. Even substitutes for services provided by public courts of law can be obtained privately. For example, because of the enormous costs of using the government's judicial system, companies sometimes bypass the courts and instead settle their disputes before mutually agreed-upon neutral advisers. Annually, over 40,000 civil cases that traditionally would have been dealt with in the courts are now handled by private firms [Pollock, 1993, p. B1].

Over time, the mix between public and private modes of provision has changed substantially. During the 19th century, there was much greater private responsibility for education, police protection, libraries, and other functions than there is now. However, there appears to be a trend back to the private sector for provision of what we have come to consider publicly provided goods and services. For example, as a result of budget cuts that reduce sanitation collections, businesspeople in several cities band together and hire their own refuse collectors to keep their streets clean. In some communities, individual homeowners contract with private companies to provide protection against fires. Indeed, in Denmark about two-thirds of the country's fire service is provided by a private firm.

What is the right mix of public and private provision? To approach this question, think of publicly and privately provided goods as inputs into the production of some output that people desire. Teachers, classrooms, textbooks, and private tutors are inputs into the production of an output we might call educational quality. Assume that what ultimately matters to people is the level of output, educational quality, not the particular inputs used to produce it. What criteria should be used to select the amount of each input? There are several considerations.

Relative Wage and Materials Costs.   If the public and private sectors pay different amounts for labor and materials, then the less expensive sector is to be preferred on efficiency grounds, *ceteris paribus*. For example, the input costs faced by public schools exceed those in private schools when public sector teachers are unionized while their private sector counterparts are not.

Administrative Costs.   Under public provision, any fixed administrative costs can be spread over a large group of people. Instead of everyone spending time negotiating an arrangement for garbage collection, the negotiation is done by one office for everybody. The larger the community, the greater the advantage to being able to spread these costs. Similarly, a public school system that provides the same education in every school saves parents the time and effort involved in researching schools to figure out which are the good ones.

Diversity of Tastes.   Households with and without children have very different views about the desirability of high-quality education. People who store jewels in their homes may value property protection more than people who do not. To the extent such diversity is present, private provision is more efficient because people can tailor their consumption to their own tastes. As Ronald Reagan put it, "Such a strategy ensures production of services that are demanded by consumers, not those chosen by government bureaucrats" [*Economic Report of the President, 1986*, p. 9]. Clearly, the benefits to allowing for diversity must be weighed against any possible increases in administrative costs.

Distributional Issues.   The community's notions of fairness may require that some commodities be made available to everybody, an idea sometimes referred to as **commodity egalitarianism.** Commodity egalitarianism may help explain the wide appeal of publicly provided education—people believe everyone should have access to at least some minimum level of schooling. This notion also arises in the ongoing debate over medical care.

Public versus Private Production

Airport security became a major object of concern after September 11. While there was a consensus that the security system had failed miserably and had to be upgraded, there was a contentious debate on how to accomplish this. Some argued that airport security workers should be federalized; that is, they should be employees of the federal government. Others argued that while the government should pay for airport security, it would best be left to private firms, which would be monitored and held accountable for mistakes.

This debate highlights the fact that people can agree that certain items should be provided by the public sector, but still disagree over whether they should be produced publicly or privately. Part of the controversy stems from fundamental differences regarding the extent to which government should intervene in the economy. (See Chapter 1.) Part is due to differences of opinions about the relative costs of public and private production. Some argue that public sector managers, unlike their private sector counterparts, do not have to worry about making profits or becoming the victims of takeovers or bankruptcy. Hence, public sector managers have little incentive to monitor the activities of their enterprises carefully. This notion has an ancient pedigree. In 1776 Adam Smith argued

> In every great monarchy in Europe the sale of the crown lands would produce a very large sum of money which, if applied to the payments of the public debts, would deliver from mortgage a much greater revenue than any which those lands have ever afforded to the crown . . . When the crown lands had become private property, they would, in the course of a few years, become well improved and well cultivated.[10]

---

[10] Quoted in Sheshinski and Lopez-Calva [1999].

Anecdotal evidence for this viewpoint abounds. One celebrated case involved New York City, which spent $12 million attempting to rebuild the ice-skating rink in Central Park between 1980 and 1986. The main problem was that the contractors were trying to use a new technology for making ice, and it did not work. In 1986, after spending $200,000 on a study to find out what went wrong, city officials learned they would have to start all over. In June 1986, real estate developer Donald J. Trump offered to take over the project and have it completed by December of that year for about $2.5 million. Trump finished the rink three weeks ahead of schedule and $750,000 under projected cost. When Chicago replaced city crews with private towing companies to haul away abandoned cars, the net annual savings were estimated at $2.5 million. In 1998, a private company took over the South Florida State Psychiatric Hospital, which had long been viewed as a dumping ground where patients were treated poorly. While advocates for the mentally ill were initially horrified at this development, a year later they agreed that conditions at the hospital had improved. Further, the company said that it was making a profit. And in 2002, a US government study estimated that the Internal Revenue Service was failing to pursue at least $20 billion in unpaid taxes, and that these taxes could easily be collected if the task were turned over to private collection agencies [McKinnon, 2002, p. A1].

Opponents of privatization respond that these examples overstate the cost savings of private production. In fact, there is surprisingly little systematic evidence on the cost differences between private and public production. An important reason for this is that the *quality* of the services provided in the two modes may be different, which makes comparisons difficult. Perhaps, for example, private hospitals have lower costs than their public counterparts because the former refuse to admit patients with illnesses that are expensive to treat. This brings us to the central argument of opponents of private production: Private contractors produce inferior products.

Incomplete Contracts.   A possible response to this criticism is that the government can simply write a contract with the private provider, completely specifying the quality of the service that the government wants. However, as Hart, Shleifer, and Vishny [1997] note, it is sometimes impossible to write a contract that is anywhere near being complete because one cannot specify in advance every possible contingency. For example, a "government would not contract out the conduct of its foreign policy because unforeseen contingencies are a key part of foreign policy, and a private contractor would have enormous power to maximize its own wealth (by, for instance, refusing to send troops somewhere) without violating the letter of the contract" (p. 3). On the other hand, for certain relatively routine activities (garbage collection, snow removal), incomplete contracts are not a serious impediment to private production. In short, in cases where the private sector cost is lower than that in the public sector and relatively complete contracts can be written, a strong case can be made for private production.

Advocates of privatization believe that, even if it is impossible to write a complete contract, there are other mechanisms for getting private firms to refrain from engaging in inefficient cost reductions. To the extent consumers buy the good themselves and there are a number of suppliers, then they can switch if their current supplier provides shoddy service. Nursing homes are one example. In addition, reputation-building may be important—a private supplier who wants more contracts in the future has an incentive to avoid inefficient cost reductions in the present. Sheifer [1998] argues that the desire to build a good reputation has been of some importance among private producers of prisons.

The contracting framework provides a nice vehicle for thinking about airport security, the issue that was mentioned at the beginning of this section. Those who favored private production argued that it is quite possible to write complete contracts for routine tasks such as screening luggage. The government could set standards and monitor performance. Further, profit-maximizing private firms would have an incentive to take advantage of technology to keep labor costs down. They noted that Israel, which has some of the best airport security in the world, relies on private screeners. On the other hand, those who believed that airport security should be publicly produced argued that private firms would skimp on training for their workers to increase profits. Further, a privatized system would lead to different airports having different levels of security [Uchitelle, 2001, p. WK3]. Ultimately, the debate was won by those who favored having security screeners become members of the federal work force.

Market Environment. A final issue that is important in the privatization debate is the market environment in which the public or private enterprise operates. A privately owned monopoly may produce very inefficient results from society's standpoint, while a publicly owned operation that has a lot of competition may produce quite efficiently. With respect to this latter possibility, consider the case of Phoenix, Arizona. Dissatisfaction with the cost and performance of its public works department led Phoenix to allow private companies to bid for contracts to collect garbage in various neighborhoods. The public works department was allowed to bid as well. At first, the public works department was unsuccessful, because the private firms were able to do the job better and more cheaply. But over time, it tried various experiments such as having drivers redesign garbage collection routes, and eventually it was able to win back the contracts.

The Phoenix story suggests that public versus private ownership is less important than whether competition is present. Caves and Christensen [1980, p. 974] came to the same conclusion on the basis of a careful econometric study of public and private costs of railway operation in Canada: "The oft-noted inefficiency of government enterprises stems from isolation from effective *competition* rather than public ownership *per se*." Along the same lines, in their study of international data on privatization, Dewenter and Malatesta

[2001] found that while government firms are less profitable than private firms, there is not much evidence that privatization per se improves profitability. Rather, profitability begins improving a few years before privatization—substantial restructuring occurs before the firms are sold to the private sector. To explain this finding, Dewenter and Malatesta suggest that although governments are capable of improving efficiency, over time such gains can be dissipated because governments do not face competitive pressures to maintain them. If this is the case, then the real benefit of privatization is to perpetuate the gains.

Education

Education is one of the most important items in governments' budgets. In the United States, the combined spending of local, state, and federal governments exceeds $392 billion annually [US Census Bureau, 2002, p. 143]. As Table 4.1 indicates, since 1980, real per pupil expenditures on education have increased by about 55 percent. Let's use the theory of public goods to analyze government spending on education.

The framework of welfare economics suggests we begin with a fundamental question: Why does the government involve itself so extensively in education, rather than leave its provision to the market? As we saw in the last chapter, markets do not provide goods efficiently when those goods are public goods, they give rise to externalities, or they are provided monopolistically. Education is primarily a *private* good, improving students' welfare by enhancing their ability to earn a living and, more generally, to deal with life. Where transportation costs are high, local schools have an element of monopoly power, but this argument is not very persuasive, except perhaps in rural areas.

Others point to public good characteristics of education. Schools can be a powerful force for socialization. As the Greek historian Plutarch wrote in his *Morals,* "The very spring and root of honesty and virtue lie in good

Table 4.1   **Real expenditure per pupil in public elementary and secondary schools**

School Year	Expenditure per Pupil (2001 dollars)
1980	4,632
1985	5,537
1990	6,355
1995	6,452
2000	7,066
2001	7,161

SOURCE: Computed from US Census Bureau, *Statistical Abstract of the United States 2002.* Washington, DC, 2002, p. 146.

education." And in democratic governments, education gives voters background and perspective on which to base their political choices. As George Washington wrote, "In proportion as the structure of a government gives force to public opinion, it is essential that public opinion should be enlightened." A darker view is that education provides an avenue for political indoctrination that makes citizens more accepting of their governments, thus contributing to political stability.

These arguments in support of intervention in the market for education are concerned with economic efficiency. Welfare economics suggests that equity must also be considered, and here, too, arguments can be made for public education. Recall from earlier in this chapter the notion of commodity egalitarianism. Because access to education is arguably an important source of social mobility, it is an important good to be made available to all citizens.

If education gives rise to public goods, it follows that government may wish to subsidize it. We go beyond subsidization, however, when we make public elementary and secondary education both *free* (taxpayer financed) and *compulsory*. Such a system, which is common in many countries, cannot be rationalized on efficiency grounds alone. Furthermore, what is so special about education that leads the government not only to provide it but to *produce* it as well? One theory is that public education produces human capital while simultaneously inculcating belief in the existing political system. Because individuals care about their human capital but receive no private gains from belief in the political system, private schools in competition for students would devote all their resources to producing human capital. According to this view, the development of a common commitment to established democratic processes is more easily carried out in a system of public schools protected from competition.

Whatever the rationale for providing free public schools, a surprising result of economic theory is that such a system does not necessarily induce everyone to consume more schooling than they would have in a private market. Consider the case of Gepetto, who is deciding how much education his son Pinocchio should consume. In Figure 4.5, the amount of education is measured on the horizontal axis, and the quantity of all other goods consumed by the family on the vertical. (For simplicity, think of the amount of education as hours spent in the classroom. A more complicated model would also include aspects of the education that enhance its quality.) In the absence of a public school system, Gepetto can purchase as much education in the private market as he chooses at the going price, and his options are summarized by budget constraint AB. Subject to this constraint, he purchases e_o hours of education for Pinocchio; c_o is left over for expenditure on other goods.

Now suppose a public school opens. Gepetto can send Pinocchio to the public school for e_p hours per week at no additional cost to himself.[11] This

---

[11] We assume Gepetto's tax payments are independent of whether he has children enrolled in public school.

FIGURE 4.5

Free public schooling
and the amount of
education consumed

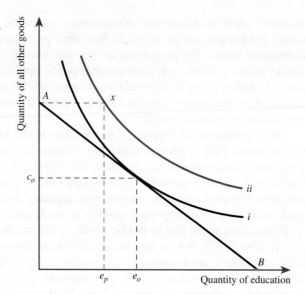

option is represented not by a line but by the single point x, where education consumption is e_p and Gepetto can spend his entire income on all other goods. Because indifference curve ii, which passes through x, is higher than indifference curve i, Gepetto takes Pinocchio out of private school and enrolls him in the public system. Importantly, e_p is less than e_o. Pinocchio's consumption of education falls. Intuitively, the existence of public education leads to a large increase in the opportunity cost of private education, inducing Gepetto to opt out of the private system, reducing Pinocchio's consumption of education as he does so.

Of course, for a different set of indifference curves, public education could have induced Gepetto to increase his household's consumption of education. Moreover, Figure 4.5 views public schooling as a "take-it-or-leave-it" option. To the extent that the amount of education offered through public schools can be supplemented by private lessons, it is less likely that public schooling would lead to reductions in the quantity of education consumed. Nevertheless, this analysis shows that one cannot take for granted that the government provision of free education (or any other commodity, for that matter) leads to an increase in its consumption.

What Do Expenditures for Public Education Accomplish?

One of the dominant issues in debates over public education is whether spending on it is high enough. Such debates force us to confront a crucial question: Do higher expenditures lead to better education?

Ultimately, we care about educational outcomes for students, not educational expenditures per se. Therefore, we need to know the relationship between inputs purchased and the amount of education produced. Attempts to measure the relationship between usage levels of various inputs to education, such as teachers' years of experience and the number of teachers available per student, face major difficulties. Part of the difficulty comes in defining, let alone measuring, the output "education."

Some measures that have been used to capture the increased human capital imparted through education are test scores, attendance records, dropout rates or continuation rates to higher levels of schooling, and labor market outcomes such as unemployment rates and earnings. Hanushek [2002] surveys 376 statistical estimates of the relationship between input usage and various measures of educational attainment. The inputs considered include the teacher/pupil ratio, teacher education, teacher experience, teacher salary, and expenditures per pupil. He reaches the startling conclusion that the data support virtually no correspondence between input usage per student and the quality of the educational experience. This conclusion is controversial, however [Sander, 1993]. One contentious question is how to account for expenditures on a relatively small group of disabled students—should the expenditure numbers be expressed only in terms of the money spent on "regular" students?

Even granting that inputs have little effect on achievement, the implications are not clear. As Hanushek [2002, p. 46] notes, "The evidence does not say that money and resources never matter. Nor does it say that money and resources could not matter. . . . Indeed, a plausible interpretation of the evidence is that some schools in fact use resources effectively but that these schools are counterbalanced by others that do not." However, the research does indicate that we cannot predict which schools will be effective simply by looking at data on their purchased inputs. The same is true of teachers; although principals can identify "good" teachers (those whose classes show educational gains), data on degrees held or years of teaching experience do not usefully discriminate between effective and ineffective teachers.

One particularly notable result emerges from the research on class size. It appears that, over a wide range, class size does not affect educational performance. Given the conventional methods of measuring educational output, teaching to a class of 20 appears no more effective than teaching to a class of 30. This research has tremendous policy implications given the enormous cost of class size reductions—for the United States overall, the cost per pupil of lowering class size by 10 percent would be about $615 [Hoxby, 2002b, p. 23]. If the research is correct, then, one cannot support the position that class sizes should be reduced in cost-benefit terms. Again, though, this does *not* mean all expenditures are futile. For example, there is some evidence that while classes of 20 are not measurably better than classes of 30, classes of three or fewer students are, especially if the students are in the early grades and are performing at below-average levels. Well-targeted class size reductions below the levels considered in the studies reviewed by Hanushek, such as tutoring sessions, might have payoffs.

The efficacy of expenditures on education also appears to depend on the ages of the students involved. In particular, the studies surveyed by Heckman

[1999] suggest that educational investments made in early childhood have a substantial payoff in terms of subsequent educational performance of children from low-income families. Well-designed programs for pre-kindergarten students involving frequent home visits with parents and intensive work with the children themselves can raise test scores for many years after participation in the program.This reinforces our earlier conclusion that targeted programs can be more effective than broad attempts to lower class size.

Finally, we note that although the impact of school expenditures on educational attainment is an important and interesting question, it doesn't give us direct evidence on another variable that is critical—earnings. That is, even if high educational expenditures do not increase test scores, we may not be very concerned if they increase people's earnings as adults. However, it appears that, on the margin, increases in educational expenditure have little impact on subsequent earnings. The most optimistic estimates suggest that a 10 percent increase in educational expenditures generates increases of only about 1 or 2 percent in subsequent earnings [Heckman, 1999]. But the same caveat as above applies—*some* programs (especially involving early interventions) have substantial effects on earnings.

New Directions for Public Education

The American public school system has been accused of producing a rising tide of mediocrity that puts our nation at economic and social risk. Like so much else in the area of education policy, this assertion is controversial. While SAT scores have been falling since the 1960s, this may be due to the fact that the composition of the students taking the exam has changed over time—as college has grown more popular, more students toward the lower end of the ability distribution have been taking the test. The National Assessment of Educational Progress, administered by the US Department of Education, is less subject to such composition biases, and suggests that over the past 30 years, there have been slight improvements in math and reading scores. Such modest increases do not mollify critics, who believe that there has not been enough improvement given the large increases in real per pupil spending over time (see Table 4.1).

Charter Schools. If simply spending more on education won't improve the situation, what will? Economists are often quick to consider whether any market in trouble might not benefit from an infusion of competition. This is true in the debate over what to do about the nation's schools. Some economists are convinced schools would improve if they were forced to compete with one another to attract students. This is part of the motivation for *charter schools,* which are public schools that operate under government charters that hold them to state standards, but have freedom to experiment and some independence in making their spending and hiring decisons. Anecdotal evidence from states like Arizona, which has the nation's most liberal charter law, suggests that charter schools increase diversity of choice and parental satisfaction. Some Arizona charter schools take a "back-to-basics" approach, some focus on the performing arts, some cater to pregnant students, and so on. Beyond anecdotal evidence, there is some econometric work suggesting that when public schools are thrown into competition with charter schools, the public schools improve. Hoxby [2002a] studied the impact of a charter school program that the state of Michigan introduced in 1994. Under the program, Michigan charter schools receive a certain fee for each student. Importantly, for each student that a public school district loses to a charter school, the district's budget is reduced by approximately the amount of the fee. Hoxby found that those public schools that faced competition from charters increased their students' achievement test scores relative to public schools that did not face such competition. And they appear to have done it without raising spending per pupil.

Vouchers.   Recently, much attention has been paid to plans to improve public school quality by increasing dramatically the scope of choice through a *voucher system.* The basic approach is to provide financial support to students rather than directly to schools. Each student could be given a tuition voucher, for example, that could be redeemed at whatever qualified school the student's family liked best. The theory is that the effects of competition would be as salutary in the education market as they are in other markets. Terrible schools would have few enrollees and would be forced to close. In effect, the parents' and students' perceptions of teacher quality, which are more or less ignored by the public school system, would become the basis for punishing bad teachers. Further, the availability of tuition monies would prompt entrepreneurs to establish new schools in areas where the existing schools were poor. This is a plausible scenario. A for-profit company, Edison Project, already manages 149 schools with 84,000 students, generally under contract with public school boards.

Many issues are involved in designing such a system. How much latitude can schools have in designing their curricula? Can schools hire teachers who are not credentialed? What criteria can oversubscribed schools use to choose which students will be enrolled? Can church-run schools be included in the program? Can parents donate extra resources to the schools of their choice, or would this violate standards of equal education? How will students' families be informed about the different schooling choices available to them?

Critics of market-oriented schemes offer a number of objections. Principal among them is that consumers in the education market are not well informed so the competitive outcome would be far from satisfactory. Supporters of this view point to the proliferation of vocational schools of dubious value that prey on students eligible for federal student loans and grants. Further, they argue that there would be a tendency for relatively good students to use vouchers to escape poorly performing public schools, leaving the weaker students behind. Because the quality of a student's education depends, in part, on the quality of his or her peers, the result would be an even worse education for the poor students than before the introduction of the vouchers. Indeed, when Chile introduced a voucher system several years ago, it appears that the higher ability students did in fact opt out of the public schools in disproportionately high numbers [Ladd, 2002, p. 19].

In response, supporters of choice note that the quality of public schools in the United States appears to be declining despite massive increases in spending. They argue that just because people are poor doesn't mean they are unwilling or unable to seek out the best opportunities available for their children.[12] A number of communities have recently begun experimenting with voucher schemes. In Milwaukee, for example, in 1990 about 1,000 low-income students began attending private schools using state-aid vouchers worth about $3,200 each. Rouse [1997] conducted an analysis of the results to date and found that students who attended the private schools had higher scores on mathematics achievement tests and about the same scores on reading tests.[13] The results of the Milwaukee and other experiments should help inform future debates over competition in the market for education.

Public Goods and Public Choice

The use of the word *public* to describe commodities that are nonrival and nonexcludable almost seems to prejudge the question of whether they ought to be provided by the public sector. Indeed, we have shown that private markets are unlikely to generate pure public goods in Pareto efficient quantities. Some collective decision must be made regarding the quantity to be supplied. Our discussion of education illustrated how, in contrast to a pure public good like national defense, sometimes there may be private substitutes for a publicly provided good. But community decision making is also needed in these cases, this time to choose the extent to which public provision will be used. Thus, the subjects of public goods and public choice are closely linked. In Chapter 6 we discuss and evaluate a number of mechanisms for making collective decisions.

Summary

- Public goods are characterized by nonrivalness and nonexcludability in consumption. Thus, each person consumes the same amount, but not necessarily the preferred amount, of the public good.

- Efficient provision of public goods requires that the sum of the individual MRSs equal the MRT, unlike private goods where each MRS equals the MRT.

[12] See Chubb and Moe [1990] for further arguments along these lines.

[13] The structure of Rouse's study is described in Chapter 2.

- Market mechanisms are unlikely to provide nonrival goods efficiently, even if they are excludable.

- Casual observation and laboratory studies indicate that people do not fully exploit free riding possibilities. Nonetheless, in certain cases, free riding is a significant problem.

- Public goods can be provided privately, and private goods can be provided publicly.

- Even in cases where public provision of a good is selected, a choice between public and private production must be made. A key factor in determining whether public or private production will be more efficient is the market environment. Another important question is the extent to which complete contracts can be written with private sector service providers.

- Although education is generally publicly provided, it is not clear that education is a public good. Moreover, statistical research suggests that the link between spending and educational outcomes is tenuous.

- Although general increases in educational expenditure to reduce classroom size seem unlikely to enhance educational performance, some targeted spending programs seem to be quite effective. In particular, well-designed early interventions appear to raise both future test scores and earnings.

- Some economists are convinced that public schools would improve if they were subjected to competition. One proposal in that direction is a voucher system, under which financial support for education goes to the family of the student, not directly to the school. The voucher could be redeemed at whatever qualified school was preferred by the family.

Discussion Questions

1. Which of the following do you consider pure public goods? Private goods? Why?

    a. Wilderness areas

    b. Municipal water supply

    c. Medical school education

    d. Public television programs

    e. An Internet site providing information on airplane schedules

2. Tarzan and Jane live alone in the jungle and have trained Cheetah both to patrol the perimeter of their clearing and to harvest tropical fruits. Cheetah can collect 3 pounds of fruit an hour and currently spends 6 hours patrolling, 8 hours picking, and 10 hours sleeping.

    a. What are the public and private goods in this example?

    b. If Tarzan and Jane are each currently willing to give up one hour of patrol for 2 pounds of fruit, is the current allocation of Cheetah's time Pareto efficient? Should he patrol more or less?

3. In Spain, private companies are finishing the beltway around Madrid. The companies make their money by charging tolls. Is a highway a public good? Is private provision of highways a sensible idea?

4. In 1997, the state of Texas invited bids from private companies to administer the state's entire welfare system. The Clinton administration told the Texans to halt the process, arguing that welfare must be administered by government employees. Is welfare a public good? Should it be publicly or privately produced? Relate your answer to the question of whether or not this is a situation in which a relatively "complete contract" could be written with a private sector firm.

5. It has been estimated that private prisons are about 10 percent cheaper, on a per prisoner basis, than public prisons [Hart, Shleifer, and Vishny, 1997]. On this basis, would you recommend that prisons be privatized? If not, what other information would you require?

6. Several years ago, some citizens of the town of Manchester, Vermont, decided to launch a school fundraising compaign. A private group of citizens decided how much every household and business should contribute, and there was a

good deal of social pressure to pay the full amount. One flier urged, "We cannot sit back and wait for our neighbors to carry the load" [Tomsho, 2001, p. A1]. Use the experimental results on free-riding discussed in this chapter to predict the outcome of this compaign.

7. Italy's great art treasures are owned and managed by the government. However, Italy's cultural institutions are in trouble because of inadequate government funding. (The Uffizi Gallery in Florence, one of the world's greatest museums, did not have enough cash to provide paper towels in the bathrooms.) In response, in 2002 the government set up a new state agency whose purpose was to value Italy's cultural treasures and decide what could be sold or leased to private firms [*Economist*, November 30, 2002, p. 55]. Is it appropriate for a nation to privatize its museums? Base your answer on the criteria for public versus private production discussed in the chapter.

8. The analysis surrounding Figure 4.5 assumes that public schooling is a "take-it-or-leave-it" option—individuals are not allowed to supplement public education with private lessons. Show how the diagram must be modified if, to the contrary, parents can purchase additional hours of education for their children who are enrolled in public school. Another assumption behind the model is that public education is "free" in the sense that parents do not pay any taxes for it. Show how the model must be modified if public school is financed by taxes levied on parents.

9. Rodolfo and Mimi share an apartment. The table below shows, for each temperature in the apartment, the marginal benefit (MB) to Rodolfo, the marginal benefit to Mimi, and the marginal cost (MC) of attaining that temperature:

Temperature (degrees)	MB to Rodolfo	MB to Mimi	MC
66	8	12	14
67	7	10	17
68	5	8	21
69	2	6	26
70	1	3	32

Explain why the apartment's temperature in this problem is a public good, and find the efficient temperature.

10. Thelma and Louise are neighbors. During the winter, it is impossible for a snowplow to clear the street in front of Thelma's house without clearing the front of Louise's. Thelma's marginal benefit from snowplowing services is $12 - Z$, where Z is the number of times the street is plowed. Louise's marginal benefit is $8 - 2Z$. The marginal cost of getting the street plowed is $16.

Sketch the two marginal benefit schedules and the aggregate marginal benefit schedule. Draw in the marginal cost schedule, and find the efficient level of provision for snowplowing services.

Selected References

Coase, Ronald H. "The Lighthouse in Economics." *Journal of Law and Economics* (October 1974), pp. 357–76.

Ladd, Helen F. "School Vouchers: A Critical View." *Journal of Economic Perspectives* 16 (Fall 2002), pp. 3–24.

Neal, Derek. "How Vouchers Could Change the Market for Education." *Journal of Economic Perspectives* 16 (Fall 2002), pp. 25–44.

Palfrey, Thomas R., and Jeffrey E. Prisbrey. "Anomalous Behavior in Public Goods Experiments: How Much and Why?" *American Economic Review* 87 (December 1997), pp. 829–46.

Samuelson, Paul A. "Diagrammatic Exposition of a Theory of Public Expenditure." *Review of Economics and Statistics* 37 (1955), pp. 350–56.

APPENDIX

Preference Revelation Mechanisms

Markets generally fail to induce individuals to reveal their true preferences for nonexcludable public goods, and, hence, a price system fails to provide them in efficient amounts. Is there some way, short of forcing everyone to take a lie detector test, to get people to tell the truth? Several procedures have been suggested for inducing people to reveal their true preferences. We now describe one based on the work of Groves and Loeb [1975].[14]

Imagine a government agent approaches Eve and says, "Please tell me your demand curve for rocket displays. I will use this information plus the information I receive from Adam to select a Pareto efficient quantity of rockets and to assign each of you a tax. But before you give me your answer, I want you to realize that you will be taxed in the following way: Whenever the level of public good provision increases by a unit, the change in your tax bill will be the incremental cost of that unit, minus the value that everyone else puts on the increase."

After the agent departs, the first thing Eve does is to represent the tax structure algebraically. If ΔT^{Eve} is the change in her tax bill when provision of the public good is expanded by one unit, MRT_{ra} is the incremental resource cost of the one unit, MRS_{ra}^{Total} is the marginal value of one more unit to Adam and Eve, and MRS_{ra}^{Eve} is the marginal value to Eve alone, then

$$\Delta T^{\text{Eve}} = MRT_{ra} - (MRS_{ra}^{\text{Total}} - MRS_{ra}^{\text{Eve}}) \tag{4A.1}$$

Faced with Equation (4A.1), Eve has to decide whether or not to tell the truth, that is, to reveal her true marginal valuation for every level of rocket display provision. She knows that from her selfish point of view, production should continue up to the point where the marginal benefit of consuming one more unit, MRS_{ra}^{Eve}, equals the marginal cost to her, which is just the increase in her tax bill. Thus, Eve would like to see the public good provided in an amount such that

$$\Delta T^{\text{Eve}} = MRS_{ra}^{\text{Eve}} \tag{4A.2}$$

Substituting from Equation (4A.1) for ΔT^{Eve} gives us

$$MRT_{ra} - (MRS_{ra}^{\text{Total}} - MRS_{ra}^{\text{Eve}}) = MRS_{ra}^{\text{Eve}}$$

Adding $(MRS_{ra}^{\text{Total}} - MRS_{ra}^{\text{Eve}})$ to both sides of the equation yields

$$MRT_{ra} = MRS_{ra}^{\text{Total}} \tag{4A.3}$$

---

[14] See also Tideman and Tullock [1976].

Because conditions (4A.2) and (4A.3) are equivalent, it would be in Eve's interest to tell the truth if she knew the government would use her information to achieve the allocation corresponding to Equation (4A.3).

But then she realizes this is exactly what the government agent will do. Why? Remember the agent promised to select a Pareto efficient provision given the information he receives. Such a provision is characterized by Equation (4.2) in the text. Since, by definition, $MRS_{ra}^{Total} = MRS_{ra}^{Adam} + MRS_{ra}^{Eve}$, Equations (4A.3) and (4.2) are identical. Thus, the government's provision of rocket displays will satisfy Equation (4A.3), and Eve has an incentive to tell the truth. Provided that Adam is confronted with the same kind of tax structure, he too has an incentive to be truthful. The free rider problem appears to have been solved.

To see intuitively why the system works, consider the right-hand side of Equation (4A.1), which shows how Eve's tax bill is determined. Note that $(MRS_{ra}^{Total} - MRS_{ra}^{Eve})$ is the sum of everyone's marginal benefit but Eve's. Hence, the increase in Eve's tax bill when output expands does not depend on her own marginal benefit, and therefore she has no incentive to lie about it.

There are several problems with this mechanism, many of which are shared by other devices to solve the free rider problem. First, taxpayers may not be able to understand the system. (If you don't think this is a problem, try to explain it to a friend who has not had any economics courses.) Second, even if the scheme can be made comprehensible, taxpayers have to be willing to make the effort to compute their entire demand curves and report them to the government. People may feel it is not worth their time. Third, given that millions of people are involved in governmental decisions, the costs of gathering and assimilating all the information would be prohibitive.[15] (For relatively small groups like social clubs, this would not be as much of a problem.) We conclude that although preference revelation mechanisms of this kind provide interesting insights into the structure of the free rider problem, they are not a practical way for resolving it, at least for public sector decision making.

---

[15] There are some additional technical problems. The taxes collected may not balance the budget, and it may be possible for coalitions to form and thwart the system. See Tideman and Tullock [1976].

CHAPTER 5

Externalities

We have always known that heedless self-interest was bad morals; we know now that it is bad economics.
FRANKLIN D. ROOSEVELT

As a by-product of their activities, paper mills produce the chemical dioxin. It forms when the chlorine used for bleaching wood pulp combines with a substance in the pulp. Once dioxin is released into the environment, it ends up in everyone's fat tissue and in the milk of nursing mothers. According to some scientists, dioxin is responsible for birth defects and cancer, among other health problems.

Economists often claim that markets allocate resources efficiently (see Chapter 3). Dioxin is the outcome of the operation of markets. Does this mean that having dioxin in the environment is efficient? To answer this question, it helps to begin by distinguishing different ways in which people can affect each other's welfare.

Suppose large numbers of suburbanites decide they want to live in an urban setting. As they move to the city, the price of urban land increases. Urban property owners are better off, but the welfare of tenants already there decreases. Merchants in the city benefit from increased demand for their products, while their suburban counterparts are worse off. By the time the economy settles into a new equilibrium, the distribution of real income has changed substantially.

In this migration example, all the effects are transmitted *via changes in market prices*. Suppose that before the change in tastes, the allocation of resources was Pareto efficient. The shifts in supply and demand curves change relative prices, but competition guarantees that these will be brought into equality with the relevant marginal rates of substitution. Thus, the fact that the behavior of some people affects the welfare of others does *not* necessarily cause market failure. As long as the effects are transmitted via prices, markets are efficient.[1]

The dioxin case embodies a different type of interaction from the urban land example. The decrease in welfare of the dioxin victims is not a result of price changes. Rather, the output choices of the paper mill factories directly affect the utilities of the neighboring people. When the activity of one entity (a person or a firm) directly affects the welfare of another in a way that is outside the market mechanism, that effect is called an **externality** (because one entity directly affects the welfare of another entity that is "external" to it). Unlike effects that are transmitted through market prices, externalities adversely affect economic efficiency.

In this chapter, we analyze these inefficiencies and possible remedies for them. One of the most important applications of externality theory is the debate over environmental quality, and much of the discussion focuses on this issue.

The Nature of Externalities

Suppose Bart operates a factory that dumps its garbage into a river nobody owns. Lisa makes her living by fishing from the river. Bart's activities make Lisa worse off in a direct way that is not the result of price changes. In this example, clean water is an input to Bart's production process. It gets used up just like all other inputs: land, labor, capital, and materials. Clean water is also a scarce resource with alternative uses, such as fishing by Lisa and swimming. As such, efficiency requires that for the water he uses, Bart should pay a price that reflects water's value as a scarce resource that can be used for other activities. Instead, Bart pays a zero price and, as a consequence, uses the water in inefficiently large quantities.

Posing the externality problem this way allows us to expose its source. Bart uses his other inputs efficiently because he must pay their owners prices that reflect their value in alternative uses. Otherwise, the owners of the inputs simply sell them elsewhere. However, if no one owns the river, everyone can use it for free. An externality, then, is a consequence of the failure or inability to establish property rights. If someone owned the river, people would have to pay for its use, and no externality would materialize.

Suppose Lisa owned the stream. She could charge Bart a fee for polluting that reflected the damage done to her catch. Bart would take these charges into account when making his production decisions and no longer use the water inefficiently. On the other hand, if Bart owned the stream, he

---

[1] Of course, the new pattern of prices may be more or less desirable from a distributional point of view, depending on one's ethical judgments as embodied in the social welfare function. Effects on welfare that are transmitted via prices are sometimes referred to as **pecuniary externalities.** Mishan [1971a] argues convincingly that because such effects are part of the normal functioning of a market, this is a confusing appellation. It is mentioned here only for the sake of completeness and is ignored henceforth.

could make money by charging Lisa for the privilege of fishing in it. The amount of money that Lisa would be willing to pay Bart for the right to fish in the stream would depend on the amount of pollution present. Hence, Bart would have an incentive not to pollute excessively. Otherwise, he could not make as much money from Lisa.

As long as someone owns a resource, its price reflects the value for alternative uses, and the resource is therefore used efficiently (at least in the absence of any other "market failures"). In contrast, resources that are owned in common are abused because no one has an incentive to economize in their use.

To expand on the subject, note the following characteristics of externalities:

They can be produced by consumers as well as firms.   Just think of the person who smokes a cigar in a crowded room, lowering others' welfare by using up the common resource, fresh air.

Externalities are reciprocal in nature.   In our example, it seems natural to refer to Bart as the "polluter." However, we could just as well think of Lisa as "polluting" the river with fishermen, increasing the social cost of Bart's production. As an alternative to fishing, using the river for waste disposal is not obviously worse from a social point of view. As we show later, it depends on the costs of alternatives for each of these two activities.

Externalities can be positive.   Suppose that in response to a terrorist threat you were to get yourself vaccinated against smallpox. You would incur some costs: the price of the vaccination, the associated discomfort, and the slight risk that it would induce a case of the disease. There would be a benefit to you in terms of a reduced probability of being stricken by the disease in the event of a bioterrorism attack. However, you simultaneously would benefit other members of your community, who would be less likely to come down with the disease if they could not catch it from you. But neither you nor other people take into account such external benefits when weighing the benefits and costs, and hence not enough people are vaccinated in the absence of some public intervention.

Public goods can be viewed as a special kind of externality.   Specifically, when an individual creates a positive externality with full effects felt by every person in the economy, the externality is a pure public good. At times, the boundary between public goods and externalities is a bit fuzzy. Suppose that I install in my backyard a device for electrocuting mosquitoes. If I kill the whole community's mosquitoes, then I have, in effect, created a pure public good. If only a few neighbors are affected, then it is an externality. Although positive externalities and public goods are quite similar from a formal point of view, in practice it is useful to distinguish between them.

FIGURE 5.1

An externality problem

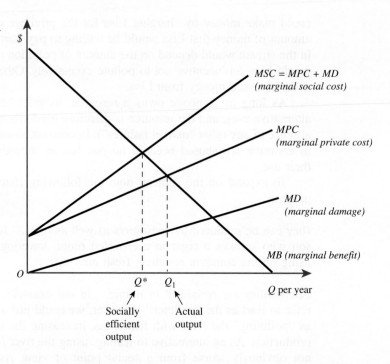

$MSC = MPC + MD$
(marginal social cost)

MPC
(marginal private cost)

MD
(marginal damage)

MB (marginal benefit)

O

Q^* Q_1

Q per year

Socially
efficient
output

Actual
output

Graphical Analysis

Figure 5.1 analyzes the Bart-Lisa example described earlier. The horizontal axis measures the amount of output, Q, produced by Bart's factory, and the vertical axis measures dollars. The curve labeled *MB* indicates the marginal benefit to Bart of each level of output; it is assumed to decline as output increases.[2] Also associated with each level of output is some marginal *private cost, MPC*. Marginal private cost reflects payments made by Bart for productive inputs and is assumed here to increase with output. As a by-product of its activities, the factory produces pollution that makes Lisa worse off. Assume that as the factory's output increases, so does the amount of pollution it creates. The marginal damage inflicted on Lisa by the pollution at each level of output is denoted by *MD*. *MD* is drawn sloping upward, reflecting the assumption that as Lisa is subjected to additional pollution, she becomes worse off at an increasing rate.

If Bart wants to maximize profits, how much output does he produce? Bart produces each unit of output for which the marginal benefit *to him* exceeds the marginal cost *to him*. In Figure 5.1, he produces all levels of output for which *MB* exceeds *MPC* but does not produce where *MPC* exceeds *MB*. Thus, he produces up to output level Q_1, at which *MPC* intersects *MB*.

---

[2] If Bart consumes all the output of his factory, then the declining *MB* reflects the diminishing marginal utility of the output. If Bart sells his output in a competitive market, *MB* is constant at the market price. Also, in this example, we assume a fixed amount of pollution per unit of output.

FIGURE 5.2

Gains and losses
from moving to an
efficient level of
output

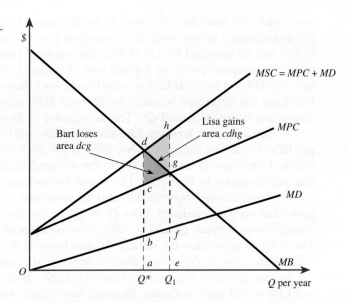

From society's point of view, production should occur as long as the marginal benefit *to society* exceeds the marginal cost *to society*. The marginal cost to society has two components: First are the inputs purchased by Bart. Their value is reflected in *MPC*. Second is the marginal damage done to Lisa as reflected in *MD*. Hence, marginal social cost is *MPC plus MD*. Graphically, the marginal social cost schedule is found by adding together the heights of *MPC* and *MD* at each level of output. It is depicted in Figure 5.1 as *MSC*. Note that, by construction, the vertical distance between *MSC* and *MPC* is *MD*. (Because $MSC = MPC + MD$, it follows that $MSC - MPC = MD$.)

Efficiency from a social point of view requires production of only those units of output for which *MB* exceeds *MSC*. Thus, output should be at Q^*, where the two schedules intersect.

Implications

This analysis suggests the following observations: First, unlike the case without externalities, private markets need not produce the socially efficient output level. In particular, when a good generates a negative externality, too much of it is produced relative to the efficient output.[3]

Second, the model not only shows that efficiency would be enhanced by a move from Q_1 to Q^* but also provides a way to measure the benefits from doing so. Figure 5.2 replicates from Figure 5.1 the marginal benefit (*MB*), marginal private cost (*MPC*), marginal damage (*MD*), and marginal social cost (*MSC*) schedules. When output is cut from Q_1 to Q^*, Bart loses profits. To calculate the precise size of his loss, recall that the marginal profit

---

[3] This model assumes the only way to reduce pollution is to reduce output. If antipollution technology is available, it may be possible to maintain output and still reduce pollution. However, the analysis is basically the same, because the adoption of the technology requires the use of resources.

associated with each unit of output is the difference between marginal benefit and marginal private cost. If the marginal private cost of the eighth unit is $10 and its marginal benefit is $12, the marginal profit is $2. Geometrically, the marginal profit on a given unit of output is the vertical distance between MB and MPC. If Bart is forced to cut back from Q_1 to Q^*, he therefore loses the difference between the MB and MPC curves for each unit of production between Q_1 and Q^*. This is area dcg in Figure 5.2.

At the same time, however, Lisa becomes better off because as Bart's output falls, so do the damages to her fishery. For each unit decline in Bart's output, Lisa gains an amount equal to the marginal damage associated with that unit of output. In Figure 5.2, Lisa's gain for each unit of output reduction is the vertical distance between MD and the horizontal axis. Therefore, Lisa's gain when output is reduced, from Q_1 to Q^* is the area under the marginal damage curve between Q^* and Q_1, $abfe$. Now note that $abfe$ equals area $cdhg$. This is by construction—the vertical distance between MSC and MPC is MD, which is the same as the vertical distance between MD and the horizontal axis.

In sum, if output were reduced from Q_1 to Q^*, Bart would lose area dcg and Lisa would gain area $cdhg$. Provided that society views a dollar to Bart as equivalent to a dollar to Lisa, then moving from Q_1 to Q^* yields a net gain to society equal to the difference between $cdhg$ and dcg, which is dhg.

Third, the analysis implies that, in general, zero pollution is not socially desirable. Finding the right amount of pollution requires trading off its benefits and costs, and the optimum generally occurs at some positive level of pollution. Because virtually all productive activity involves some pollution, requiring pollution to be set at zero is equivalent to banning all production, clearly an inefficient solution. If all this seems only like common sense, it is. But note that Congress once set as a national goal that "the discharge of pollutants into the navigable waters be eliminated by 1985." The adoption of such infeasible and inefficient objectives is not only silly but, as shall be argued later, may also actually hinder *any* movement away from points like Q_1.

Finally, implementing the framework of Figure 5.2 requires more than drawing hypothetical marginal damage and benefit curves. Their actual locations and shapes must be determined, at least approximately. However, difficult practical questions arise when it comes to identifying and valuing pollution damage.

What Activities Produce Pollutants?

The types and quantities of pollution associated with various production processes must be identified. Consider acid rain, a phenomenon of widespread concern. Scientists have shown that acid rain forms when sulfur oxides and nitrogen oxides emitted into the air react with water vapor to create acids. These acids fall to earth in rain and snow, increasing the general level of acidity with potentially harmful effects on plant and animal life.

However, it is not known just how much acid rain is associated with factory production and how much with natural activities such as plant decay and volcanic eruptions. Moreover, determining what amounts of nitrogen and sulfur emissions generated in a given region eventually become acid rain is difficult. It depends in part on local weather conditions and on the extent to which other pollutants such as nonmethane hydrocarbons are present.

Which Pollutants Do Harm?   The ability of scientists to conduct large-scale controlled experiments on the effects of pollution is severely limited. Hence, pinpointing a given pollutant's effect is difficult. Acid rain may be a case in point: Results from the federal government's 10-year, $500 million National Acid Precipitation Assessment Program "suggest that acid rain is having virtually no effect on agricultural output, and that its effects on forests are limited to mountain tops in the northeastern United States" [Portney, 1990, p. 175]. This finding has disrupted the scientific consensus that acid rain causes great damage in the United States. The difficulties associated with making policy in the absence of good scientific information about pollutants are well-illustrated by an episode in 1999, when the Environmental Protection Agency stopped requiring oil companies to add a chemical ingredient called M.T.B.E. to gasoline. M.T.B.E. had been mandated because it made gasoline burn more cleanly, reducing air pollution. Unfortunately, scientists discovered that, when it leaked, M.T.B.E. was a potentially dangerous source of *water* pollution. In this context, it is disconcerting to note that there is some evidence that certain chemicals that are unregulated by the US government pose a greater cancer risk than those that are regulated (see Viscusi [1995]).

What Is the Value of the Damage Done?   Once the physical damage a pollutant creates is determined, the dollar value of that damage must be calculated. When economists think about measuring the value of something, typically they think of people's willingness to pay for it. If you are willing to pay $162 for a bicycle, that is its value to you.

Unlike bicycles, pollution is generally not bought and sold in explicit markets. (Some exceptions are discussed shortly.) How, then, can people's marginal willingness to pay for pollution removal be measured? Some attempts have been made to infer it indirectly by studying housing prices. When people shop for houses, they consider both the quality of the house itself and the characteristics of the neighborhood, such as cleanliness of the streets and quality of schools. Suppose that families also care about the level of air pollution in the neighborhoods. Consider two identical houses situated in two identical neighborhoods, except that the first is in an unpolluted area and the second is in a polluted area. We expect the house in the unpolluted area to have a higher price. This price differential measures people's willingness to pay for clean air.

These observations suggest a natural strategy for estimating people's willingness to pay for clean air. Examine houses identical in all respects except for the surrounding air quality and compare their prices. The apparent problem is to find such houses. Luckily, the necessity of doing so can be avoided if the statistical technique of multiple regression analysis is used (see Chapter 2). The results of an econometric analysis by Chay and Greenstone [1998] imply that people would be willing to pay an amount equal to 0.7 to 1.5 percent of the value of their homes to obtain a one-unit reduction in the concentration of particulates (in micrograms per cubic meter). As stressed in Chapter 2, the validity of econometric analysis depends in part on the completeness with which the model is specified. If important determinants of housing prices are omitted, the estimate of the pollution effect may be unreliable. More fundamentally, the use of a willingness-to-pay measure can be questioned. People may be ignorant about the effects of air pollution on their health, and hence underestimate the value of reducing it. The econometric approach is promising, but it does definitively determine the value of damage done.

Conclusion

Implementing the framework of Figure 5.2 requires the skills of biologists, engineers, ecologists, and health practitioners, among others. Investigating a pollution problem requires a resolutely interdisciplinary approach. Having said this, however, we emphasize that even with superb engineering and biological data, one simply cannot make efficient decisions without applying the economist's tool of marginal analysis.

Private Responses

In the presence of externalities, an inefficient allocation of resources emerges if nothing is done about it. This section discusses the circumstances under which private individuals, acting on their own, can avoid externality problems.

Bargaining and the Coase Theorem

Recall our earlier argument that the root cause of the inefficiencies associated with externalities is the absence of property rights. When property rights are assigned, individuals may respond to the externality by bargaining with each other. To see how, suppose property rights to the river are assigned to Bart. Assume further that it is costless for Lisa and Bart to bargain with each other. Is it possible for the two parties to strike a bargain that results in output being reduced from Q_1?

Bart would be willing to not produce a given unit of output as long as he received a payment that exceeded his net incremental gain from producing that unit ($MB - MPC$). On the other hand, Lisa would be willing to pay Bart not to produce a given unit as long as the payment were less than the marginal damage done to her, MD. As long as the amount that Lisa is willing to pay Bart exceeds the cost to Bart of not producing, the opportunity for a bargain exists. Algebraically, the requirement is that $MD > (MB - MPC)$. Figure 5.3 (which reproduces the information from Figure 5.1) indicates that at output Q_1, $MB - MPC$ is zero, while MD is positive. Hence, MD exceeds $MB - MPC$, and there is scope for a bargain.

FIGURE 5.3

Coase theorem

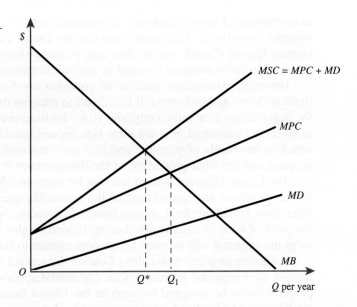

Similar reasoning indicates that the payment Lisa would be willing to make exceeds $MB - MPC$ at every output level to the right of Q^*. In contrast, to the left of Q^*, the amount of money Bart would demand to reduce his output would exceed what Lisa would be willing to pay. Hence, Lisa pays Bart to reduce output just to Q^*, the efficient level. We cannot tell without more information exactly how much Lisa ends up paying Bart. This depends on the relative bargaining strengths of the two parties. Regardless of how the gains from the bargain are divided, however, production ends up at Q^*.

Now suppose the shoe is on the other foot, and Lisa is assigned the property rights to the stream. The bargaining process now consists of Bart paying for Lisa's permission to pollute. Lisa is willing to accept some pollution as long as the payment is greater than the marginal damage (MD) to her fishing enterprise. Bart finds it worthwhile to pay for the privilege of producing as long as the amount is less than the value of $MB - MPC$ for that unit of output. Reasoning similar to the foregoing suggests that they have every incentive to reach an agreement whereby Lisa sells Bart the right to produce at Q^*.

Two important assumptions played a key role in the preceding analysis:

1. The costs to the parties of bargaining are low.
2. The owners of resources can identify the source of damages to their property and legally prevent damages.

A way to summarize the implications of the discussion surrounding Figure 5.3 is that, under these assumptions, the efficient solution will be achieved *independently* of who is assigned the property rights, as long as *someone* is assigned those rights. This result, known as the **Coase Theorem** (after Nobel laureate Ronald Coase), implies that once property rights are established, no government intervention is required to deal with externalities [Coase, 1960].

However, externalities such as air pollution involve millions of people (both polluters and pollutees). It is difficult to imagine them getting together for negotiations at a sufficiently low cost.[4] Further, even if property rights to air were established, it is not clear how owners would be able to identify which of thousands of potential polluters was responsible for dirtying their airspace and for what proportion of the damage each was liable.

The Coase Theorem is most relevant for cases in which only a few parties are involved and the sources of the externality are well defined. Even when these conditions hold, the assignment of property rights *is* relevant from the point of view of income distribution. Property rights are valuable; if Lisa owns the stream it will increase her income relative to Bart's, and vice versa.

Assigning property rights along Coasian lines could help solve some significant environmental problems. One commentator, for example, urged that property rights be assigned to rivers in the United States, pointing out that "in England and Scotland, private ownership of the rivers and waterways has successfully prevented overfishing and controlled water pollution for 800 years. The owners simply charge others for the right to fish in their section of the river. Consequently, the owners have an economic incentive to maintain the fish population and keep the waterway clean" [Conda, 1995, p. A18].

Another neat application of the Coase Theorem relates to wildlife preservation. In order to conserve elephant populations in Africa, one approach is simply to ban hunting. However, the local villagers have no incentive to obey the ban; they hunt anyway (the law is hard to enforce), and the marginal cost to them of each animal killed is effectively zero. A price of zero leads to substantial overhunting. Another approach is to assign property rights to the animals. In this case, the villagers have an incentive to conserve the herds, because they can make money by selling permission to hunt them. According to Sugg [1996], Kenya banned all hunting in 1977, and its elephant population fell from 167,000 to 16,000 by 1989. In contrast, in 1982, Zimbabwe granted landowners property rights over wildlife; between that time and 1995 its elephant population grew from 40,000 to 68,000. The idea of giving individuals property rights to wild animals on their land has apparently caught on. In southern Africa, many farmers have found it profitable to stop growing food, let their land revert to its natural state, and then charge tourists to view the animals. About 18 percent of the land in the southern third of Africa is now devoted to such ecotourism [Heal, 2001, p. 10].

---

[4] As we emphasized earlier, the transactions costs of implementing a government solution need not be less.

Mergers

One way to deal with an externality is to "internalize" it by combining the involved parties. For simplicity, imagine there is only one polluter and one pollutee, as in the Bart-Lisa scenario from earlier in the chapter. As stressed already, if Bart took into account the damages he imposed on Lisa's fishery, then a net gain would be possible. (Refer back to the discussion surrounding Figure 5.2.) In other words, if Bart and Lisa coordinated their activities, then the profit of the joint enterprise would be higher than the sum of their individual profits when they don't coordinate. In effect, by failing to act together, Bart and Lisa are just throwing away money! The market, then, provides a strong incentive for the two firms to merge—Lisa can buy the factory, Bart can buy the fishery, or some third party can buy them both. Once the two firms merge, the externality is internalized—it is taken into account by the party that generates the externality. For instance, if Bart purchased the fishery, he would willingly produce less output than before, because at the margin doing so would increase the profits of his fishery subsidiary more than

Irresponsible mountain goats

it decreased the profits from his factory subsidiary. Consequently, the external effects would not exist, and the market would not be inefficient. Put another way, an outside observer would not even characterize the situation as an "externality" because all decisions would be made within a single firm.

Social Conventions

Unlike firms, individuals cannot merge to internalize externalities. However, certain social conventions can be viewed as attempts to force people to take into account the externalities they generate. Schoolchildren are taught that littering is irresponsible and not "nice." If this teaching is effective, a child learns that even though he bears a small cost by holding on to a candy wrapper or a banana peel until he finds a garbage can, he should incur this cost because it is less than the cost imposed on other people by having to view his unsightly garbage. Think about the golden rule, "Do unto others as you would have others do unto you." A (much) less elegant way of expressing this sentiment is "Before you undertake some activity, take into account its external marginal benefits and costs." Some moral precepts, then, induce people to empathize with others, and hence internalize the externalities their behavior may create. In effect, these precepts correct for the absence of missing markets.

Public Responses to Externalities

In cases where individuals acting on their own cannot attain an efficient solution, government can intervene in several ways.[5]

Taxes

Bart produces inefficiently because the prices he faces for inputs incorrectly signal social costs. Specifically, because his input prices are too low, the price of his output is too low. A natural solution, suggested by the British economist A. C. Pigou in the 1930s, is to levy a tax on the polluter that makes up for the fact that some of his inputs are priced too low. A **Pigouvian tax** is a tax levied on each unit of a polluter's output in an amount just equal to the marginal damage it inflicts *at the efficient level of output*. Figure 5.4 reproduces the example of Figure 5.1. In this case, the marginal damage at the efficient output Q^* is distance cd. This is the Pigouvian tax. (Remember that the vertical distance between MSC and MPC is MD.)

How does Bart react if a tax of cd dollars per unit of output is imposed? The tax raises Bart's effective marginal cost. For each unit he produces, Bart has to make payments both to the suppliers of his inputs (measured by MPC) *and* to the tax collector (measured by cd). Geometrically, Bart's new marginal cost schedule is found by adding cd to MPC at each level of output. This involves shifting up MPC by the vertical distance cd.

---

[5] The list of possibilities considered here is by no means exhaustive. See Cropper and Oates [1992] for a careful discussion of several alternatives.

FIGURE 5.4

Analysis of a
Pigouvian tax

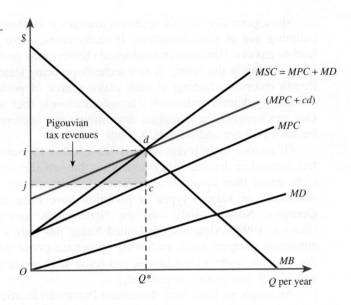

Profit maximization requires that Bart produce where marginal benefit equals his marginal cost. This now occurs at the intersection of *MB* and *MPC* + *cd*, which is at the efficient output *Q**. In effect, the tax forces Bart to take into account the costs of the externality that he generates and induces him to produce efficiently. Note that the tax generates revenue of *cd* dollars for each of the *id* units produced (*id* = *OQ**). Hence, tax revenue is *cd* × *id*, which is equal to the area of rectangle *ijcd* in Figure 5.4. It would be tempting to use these revenues to compensate Lisa, who still is being hurt by Bart's activities, although to a lesser extent than before the tax. However, caution must be exercised. If it becomes known that anyone who fishes along the river receives a payment, then some people may choose to fish there who otherwise would not have done so. The result is an inefficiently large amount of fishing done in the river. The key point is that compensation to the victim of the pollution is not necessary to achieve efficiency.

There are practical problems in implementing a Pigouvian tax system. In light of the previously mentioned difficulties in estimating the marginal damage function, finding the correct tax rate is bound to be hard. Still, sensible compromises can be made. Suppose a certain type of automobile produces noxious fumes. In theory, a tax based on the number of miles driven enhances efficiency. But a tax based on mileage might be prohibitively expensive to administer. The government might instead levy a special sales tax on the car, even though it is not ownership of the car per se that determines the size of the externality but the amount it is driven. The sales tax would not lead to the most efficient outcome, but it still might be a substantial improvement over the status quo.

More generally, the tax approach assumes it is known who is doing the polluting and in what quantities. In many cases, these questions are very hard to answer. However, technological changes may make it easier to monitor pollution in the future. A new technology being tested in Southern California involves attaching to each major source of pollution a sensor that continually detects emissions. The information is then sent to a computer. One can imagine the computer determining the appropriate Pigouvian tax for each polluter and sending it a bill.

Of course, the relevant issue is not whether Pigouvian taxes are a perfect method of dealing with externalities, but whether or not they are likely to be better than the other alternatives. In this context, it is useful to note that taxes on various types of pollution have been imposed in France, Germany, Norway, Italy, and the Netherlands, among other countries [Stavins, 1999]. Although the United States has only a modest system of emissions charges, taxes are levied on certain ozone depleting chemicals. For example, carbon tetrachloride and halon-1211 are taxed at rates of $9.84 and $26.85 per pound, respectively.

Although we have been discussing Pigouvian taxation in the context of environmental damage, it is equally relevant for dealing with other kinds of externalities. For example, on crowded roads and highways, every motorist imposes costs on other motorists by increasing congestion, but no one is forced to take these costs into account. A tax on driving equal to the marginal congestion cost would enhance efficiency. Winston and Shirley [1998] estimate that such a policy, called *congestion pricing,* would produce a welfare gain for the United States—the equivalent of area *dhg* in Figure 5.2— of at least $3.2 billion per year. Some cities are now experimenting with congestion pricing. London, for example, is dealing with its notorious traffic by levying a fee of £5 (about $7.80) for the privilege of driving into the center of the city during peak times. In a more high-tech version of the scheme, single drivers in San Diego can use the high-occupation-vehicle lanes on highways for a price that depends on how congested the highway is at the moment.

Subsidies

Assuming a fixed number of polluting firms, the efficient level of production can be obtained by paying the polluter not to pollute. Although this notion may at first seem peculiar, it works much like the tax scheme. This is because a subsidy for not polluting is simply another method of raising the polluter's effective production cost.

Suppose the government announces that it will pay Bart a subsidy of *cd* for each unit of output that he does *not* produce. What will Bart do? In Figure 5.5, Bart's marginal benefit at output level Q_1 is the distance between *MB* and the horizontal axis, *ge*. The marginal cost of producing at Q_1 is the sum of the amount Bart pays for his inputs (which we read off the *MPC* curve) *and* the subsidy of *cd* that he forgoes by producing. Once again, then, the perceived marginal cost schedule is *MPC* + *cd*. At output Q_1, this is

FIGURE 5.5

Analysis of a
Pigouvian subsidy

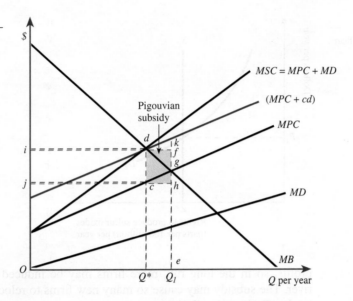

distance *ek* (= *eg* + *gk*). But *ek* exceeds the marginal benefit, *ge*. As long as the marginal cost exceeds the marginal benefit at Q_1, it does not make sense for Bart to produce this last unit of output. Instead, he should forgo its production and accept the subsidy. The same line of reasoning indicates that Bart chooses not to produce any output in excess of Q^*. At all output levels to the right of Q^*, the sum of the marginal private cost and the subsidy exceeds the marginal benefit. On the other hand, at all points to the left of Q^*, it is worthwhile for Bart to produce even though he has to give up the subsidy. For these output levels, the total opportunity cost, $MPC + cd$, is less than the marginal benefit. Hence, the subsidy induces Bart to produce just to Q^*, the efficient output.

The distributional consequences of the tax and subsidy schemes differ dramatically. Instead of having to pay the tax of *idcj*, Bart receives a payment equal to the number of units of forgone production, *ch*, times the subsidy per unit, *cd*, which equals rectangle *dfhc* in Figure 5.5.[6] That an efficient solution can be associated with different income distributions is no surprise. It is analogous to the result from Chapter 3—there are an infinite number of efficient allocations in the Edgeworth Box, each of which is associated with its own distribution of real income.

In addition to the problems associated with the Pigouvian tax scheme, the subsidy program has a few of its own. First, recall that the analysis of Figure 5.5 assumes a fixed number of firms. The subsidy leads to higher

---

[6] In Figure 5.5, Q_1 is the baseline from which Bart's reduction in output is measured. In principle, any baseline to the right of Q^* would do.

FIGURE 5.6

Market for pollution rights

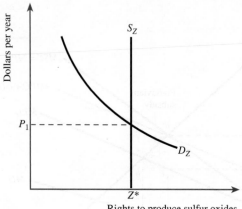

Rights to produce sulfur oxides
(parts per 100 million) per year

profits, so in the long run, more firms may be induced to locate along the river. The subsidy may cause so many new firms to relocate on the river that total pollution actually increases.

Second, subsidies may be ethically undesirable. As Mishan [1971a, p. 25] notes:

> It may be argued [that] the freedom to operate noisy vehicles, or pollutive plant, does incidentally damage the welfare of others, while the freedom desired by members of the public to live in clean and quiet surroundings does not, of itself, reduce the welfare of others. If such arguments can be sustained, there is a case . . . for making polluters legally liable.

Creating a Market

As we emphasized previously, the inefficiencies associated with externalities can be linked to the absence of a market for the relevant resource. This suggests another way for the government to enhance efficiency—sell producers permits to pollute. By doing so, the government in effect creates a market for clean air or water that otherwise would not have emerged. Under this scheme, the government announces it will sell permits to spew Z^* of pollutants into the environment (the quantity of pollutants associated with output Q^*). Firms bid for the right to own these permissions to pollute, and the permissions go to the firms with the highest bids. The fee charged is that which clears the market, so the amount of pollution equals the level set by the government. The price paid for permission to pollute measures the value to producers of being able to pollute.

Figure 5.6 illustrates the permit approach with a real-world example, the market for sulfur dioxide emissions. The horizontal axis measures the number of *rights to produce sulfur oxides,* and the vertical measures the price of these rights. The government announces it will auction off Z^* pollution rights. In effect, the supply of pollution rights is perfectly vertical at Z^*. The demand for pollution rights, D_Z, is downward sloping. The equilibrium price per unit is P_1. Those firms that are not willing to pay P_1 for each unit of pollution they produce must either reduce their output or adopt a cleaner technology.

Incidentally, the scheme also works if, instead of auctioning off the pollution rights, the government assigns them to various firms that are then free to sell them to other firms. The market supply is still perfectly vertical at Z^*, and the price is still P_1. Nothing changes because a given firm is willing to sell its pollution rights provided the firm values these rights at less than P_1. Even though the efficiency effects are the same as those of the auction, the distributional consequences are radically different. With the auction, the money goes to the government; with the other scheme, the money goes to the firms that were lucky enough to be assigned the pollution rights.

In any case, in this simple model, the permit and the Pigouvian tax both achieve the efficient level of pollution. Implementing either one requires knowledge of who is polluting and in what quantities. How is one to choose between them? Cropper and Oates [1992] argue that the permit has some practical advantages over the tax scheme. One of the most important is that the permit scheme reduces uncertainty about the ultimate level of pollution. If the government is certain about the shapes of the private marginal cost and marginal benefit schedules of Figure 5.4, then it can safely predict how a Pigouvian tax will affect behavior. But if information about these schedules is poor, it is hard to know how much a particular tax will reduce pollution. If lack of information forces policymakers to choose the pollution standard arbitrarily, it is more likely to be obtained with a system of pollution permits. In addition, assuming that firms are profit maximizers, they will find the cost-minimizing technology to attain the standard.

Moreover, when the economy is experiencing inflation, the market price of pollution rights would be expected to keep pace automatically, while changing the tax rate could require a lengthy administrative procedure. On the other hand, one possible problem with the auctioning scheme is that incumbent firms might be able to buy pollution licenses in excess of the firms' cost-minimizing requirements to deter other firms from entering the market. Whether such strategic behavior would occur is hard to predict.

Regulation

Under regulation, each polluter must reduce pollution by a certain amount or else face legal sanctions. In our model, Bart would simply be ordered to reduce output to Q^*.

Regulation is likely to be inefficient when there are multiple firms that differ from each other. To see this, consider two firms, X and Z, each of which emits carbon dioxide (CO_2), a chemical that is thought to contribute to global warming. In Figure 5.7, output of the firms is measured on the horizontal axis and dollars on the vertical. MB_X is the marginal benefit schedule for X and MB_Z the schedule for Z. For expositional ease only, X and Z are assumed to have identical MPC schedules and profit-maximizing outputs $X_1 = Z_1$.

FIGURE 5.7

Regulating two
polluters

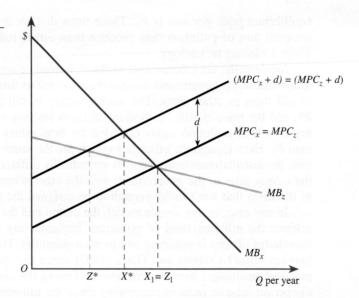

Suppose it is known that the marginal damage at the efficient level of total output is d dollars. Then efficiency requires that each firm produce where its marginal benefit curve intersects with the sum of its marginal private cost curve and d. The efficient outputs are denoted X^* and Z^* in Figure 5.7. The crucial observation is that efficiency does *not* require the firms to reduce their CO_2 emissions equally. The efficient reduction in production of Z exceeds that of X. Here this is due to different MB schedules, but in general, each firm's appropriate reduction in output depends on the shapes of its marginal benefit and marginal private cost curves. Hence, a regulation that mandates all firms to cut back by equal amounts (either in absolute or proportional terms) leads to some firms producing too much and others too little.

This analysis simply illustrates that the costs and benefits of pollution reduction are likely to differ from case to case. A car that operates in a relatively uninhabited area creates less damage than one that operates in a heavily populated area. What sense does it make for both cars to have exactly the same expensive emission abatement equipment or the same emissions standard? Under US policy, all cars must meet standards that were set to improve the air quality in just a half dozen heavily polluted cities. Clearly the policy is inefficient. Of course, the regulatory body could assign each polluter its specially designed production quota. But in the presence of a large number of polluters, this is administratively infeasible.

A number of empirical studies have sought to compare the costs of obtaining a given reduction in pollution using economic incentives and regulations. The particular results depend on the type of pollution being considered and the site of the pollution. In every case, though, economic incentives have been found to provide a much cheaper solution. (See Cropper and Oates [1992, p. 686].) A good example is provided by the federal government's corporate average fuel economy (CAFE) standards for all new passenger cars. These standards dictate the gasoline mileage that cars must attain (27.5 miles per gallon and 20.7 miles per gallon for SUVs). An alternative nonregulatory approach to reducing gasoline consumption and its attendant pollution would be to levy a tax on gasoline. According to Crandall [1992, p. 179], "CAFE costs about 7 to 10 times as much as a petroleum tax that would induce comparable reductions in oil consumption, because CAFE fails to equate the marginal costs of reducing fuel consumption across all uses, including usage of older vehicles and nonvehicular consumption."

Evaluation

The presence of externalities often requires some kind of intervention to achieve efficiency. Implementing any environmental policy entails a host of difficult technical issues. No policy is likely to do a perfect job. However, most economists prefer market-oriented solutions. They are more likely to achieve efficient outcomes than direct regulation.

The US Response

How do real-world responses to externality problems compare to the solutions suggested by theory? The main federal law dealing with air pollution is the Clean Air Act of 1963 and subsequent amendments.[7] In the clean air amendments passed in 1970, Congress set national air quality standards that were to be met independent of the costs of doing so. The Environmental Protection Agency (EPA) was established to set the standards and ensure the states attained the standards by 1975. Major additions to the Clean Air Act were introduced in 1990. One provision mandated that by 1995 all gasoline sold in the country's nine smoggiest cities had to be reformulated to cut emissions by 15 percent. In 1996, the EPA promulgated strict new ozone and particulate pollution standards, which were to be met by imposing controls on various sources of pollution.

These examples illustrate the US tendency to rely on regulation rather than market incentives. Indeed, important environmental legislation from the early 1970s explicitly prohibited policymakers from considering benefits and costs when setting environmental standards! As stressed above, this is a costly approach to correcting externalities. The EPA estimate of the annual cost of federal environmental regulations is about $135 billion. According to estimates by Portney [1990], as a consequence of the 1990 additions to the Clean Air Act, by the year 2005 the United States will increase its spending on pollution control by about $30 billion in return for benefits that range from $6 to $25 billion.

---

[7] Excellent summaries of the act's provisions are Portney [1990] and Cropper and Oates [1992].

Has clean air legislation accomplished its goals? Even ignoring the issue of costs, the record is mixed and difficult to interpret. Certain types of air pollution such as nitrogen oxides have actually increased since the original Clean Air Act passed. On the other hand, the presence of such dangerous substances as particulate matter has decreased. However, one must be cautious in attributing such decreases to environmental regulation. Perhaps, for example, the improvement was due to the decline in industrial activity associated with a generally sluggish manufacturing sector, and not to the EPA. EPA analyses of the data suggest that the Clean Air Act was, in fact, instrumental in reducing pollution below levels that otherwise would have occurred [Freeman, 2002, p. 127]. On the other hand, MacAvoy's [1992, p. 102] econometric analysis found just the opposite result. While there is no consensus, many analysts have concluded that the performance of regulation has been disappointing.

We have already shown why a regulatory approach like the Clean Air Act is likely to be inefficient. Why is it ineffectual as well? Baumol [1976] emphasizes how the efficacy of regulation depends on the vigilance of the regulator, that is:

> the promptness with which orders are issued, the severity of their provisions, the strength of the regulator's resistance to demands for modifications, his effectiveness in detecting and documenting violations, his vigor and success in prosecuting them, and the severity of the penalties imposed by the judicial mechanism. [p. 445]

This is a tall order, especially considering the political pressures under which the regulator is likely to be acting. In contrast, Pigouvian taxes "depend not on the watchfulness of the regulator but on the reliable tenacity of the tax collector. They work by inviting the polluter to avoid his payments through the loophole deliberately left to him—the reduction of his emissions" [Baumol, 1976, p. 446].

In addition, the "or else" approach of regulation often backfires. The ultimate threat is to close the polluting facility. In many cases, however, such closure would create major dislocations among workers and/or consumers and is therefore politically difficult. The Texas state legislature once decided that complying with EPA rules for testing cars and trucks for excessive emissions would be too costly. The legislature simply defied the EPA's orders to set up a new system. In the same spirit, when a court in India ordered authorities in Delhi to replace its fleet of 10,000 buses that run on diesel fuel with cleaner natural gas buses, nothing happened. The city authorities simply were not willing to go up against the bus owners, who promised, among other things, to protest by a hunger strike to the death. Indeed, two years after the court's decision, Delhi continued licensing new diesel buses [Dugger, 2001, p. A3].

This is not to say direct regulation is never useful. When very toxic substances are involved, it might be the best solution. But in general, the regulatory approach is probably the source of much of the failure in environmental policy. Why, then, is it so popular? Perhaps legislators like the immediate sense of doing something that enacting regulations gives them, even though more passive measures like creating a market would probably do the job more efficiently. A cynic would argue that the regulatory solution is the result of politicians' desire to have it both ways: Pass noble sounding legislation to please environmentalists, but make it unworkable to keep business happy.

Market-Oriented Approaches: Sulfur Dioxide

Although the regulatory approach has dominated US environmental policy, economists' arguments in favor of market-oriented approaches are beginning to have some influence. The 1990 Clean Air Act amendments created a market to control emissions of sulfur dioxide that works much along the lines illustrated in Figure 5.6. Each year the EPA sets a national cap on sulfur dioxide emissions. All electric utilities (the main producers of sulfur dioxide) must have an "emissions allowance" for each ton of sulfur dioxide they emit into the atmosphere. The total number of allowances equals the EPA cap. The allowances are initially distributed among existing electric generating units, after which they can be bought and sold. Currently, there are allowances for about 9 million tons per year [Burtraw, 2002, p. 140].

The market for the allowances is very active. The price per allowance ranges between $150 and $200. Interestingly, this is substantially below the price that was originally predicted, implying that hitting the target amount of sulfur dioxide emissions cost less than anyone guessed. Indeed, Stavins [1999] argues that the program saves about $1 billion per year relative to the costs of a conventional regulatory approach. One way in which emissions markets reduce costs is by providing financial incentives for firms to find new technologies for reducing pollution—a technology that lowers pollution saves the firm money on allowances. For example, some firms reduced their emissions by combining coals with various sulfur contents to attain intermediate results. Prior to the emissions trading program, such blending was not considered to be technologically practical, but the program gave firms incentives to figure out ways to make it work [Burtraw, 2002, p. 144].

In short, the SO_2 emissions trading experiment has been a success. Nevertheless, market-oriented approaches are far from replacing regulation as a means for dealing with environmental issues. As the costs of traditional environmental programs continue to increase—it is estimated they already amount to more than 2 percent of GDP—the efficiency of market-oriented approaches may make them more attractive to policymakers.

Implications for Income Distribution

Our main focus so far has been on the efficiency aspects of externalities. Welfare economics indicates that we must also take distributional considerations into account. However, attempts to assess the distributional implications of environmental improvement raise a number of difficult questions.

Who Benefits?

In our simple model, the distribution of benefits is a trivial issue because there is only one type of pollution and one pollution victim. In reality, individuals suffer differently from various externalities. Some evidence suggests that poor neighborhoods tend to have more exposure to air pollution than high-income neighborhoods [Cropper and Oates, 1992, p. 727]. If this is true, lowering the level of air pollution might make the distribution of real income more equal, other things being the same. On the other hand, the benefits of environmental programs that improve recreational areas such as national parks probably benefit mainly high-income families, who tend to be their main users.

Even knowing who suffers from some externality does not tell us the value to them of having it removed. Suppose a high-income family would be willing to pay more for a given improvement in air quality than a low-income family. Then even if a cleanup program reduces more of the *physical* amount of pollution for low- than for high-income families, in *dollar* terms the program can end up favoring those with high incomes.

Who Bears the Costs?

Suppose that large numbers of polluting firms are induced to reduce output by government policy. As these firms contract, the demand for the inputs they employ falls, making the owners of these inputs worse off.[8] Some of the polluters' former workers may suffer unemployment in the short run and be forced to work at lower wages in the long run. If these workers have low incomes, environmental cleanup increases income inequality.

The extent to which the poor bear the costs of environmental protection is a source of bitter controversy. Critics of environmentalism argue that efforts to prevent factories from operating in inner cities have "worsened the economic woes of the mostly poor" people who live there [Ross, 1999, p. A26]. Environmentalists label such assertions "job blackmail" and believe there is no good evidence that the poor are really hurt.

Another consideration is that if polluting firms are forced to take into account marginal social costs, their products tend to become more expensive. From an efficiency point of view, this is totally desirable, because otherwise prices give incorrect signals concerning full resource costs. Nevertheless, buyers of these commodities are generally made worse off. If the commodities so affected are consumed primarily by high-income groups, the distribution of real income becomes more equal, other things being the same, and vice versa. Thus, to assess the distributional implications of reducing pollution, we also need to know the demand patterns of the goods produced by polluting companies.

It is obviously a formidable task to determine the distribution of the costs of pollution control. In one study, Walls and Hanson [1999] found that

---

[8] More specifically, under certain conditions, those inputs used relatively intensively in the production of the polluting good fall in price. See Chapter 12 under "General Equilibrium Models."

the proportional costs of implementing a system of motor vehicle emissions fees would vary inversely with annual income. They calculated that for a family at the bottom of the income distribution, the policy would cost 2.65 percent of income, while for a family at the top, the figure was only 0.35 percent. To the extent such findings generalize to other environmental policies, they pose a dilemma for those who favor both a more equal income distribution and a cleaner environment.

Positive Externalities

Most of the focus so far has been on negative externalities. We did observe, however, that spillover effects could also be positive. The analysis of this case is symmetrical. Suppose that when a firm does research and development (R&D), the marginal private benefit (MPB) and marginal cost (MC) schedules are as depicted in Figure 5.8. The firm chooses R&D level R_1, where $MC = MPB$. Assume further that the firm's R&D enables other firms to produce their outputs more cheaply, but that these firms do not have to pay for using scientific results because they become part of general knowledge.[9] In Figure 5.8, the marginal benefit to other firms of each quantity of research is denoted MEB (for marginal external benefit). The marginal *social* benefit of research is the sum of MPB and MEB, and is denoted MSB.

Efficiency requires the equality of marginal cost and marginal *social* benefit, which occurs at R^*. Hence, R&D is underprovided. Just as a negative externality can be corrected by a Pigouvian tax, a positive externality can be corrected by a Pigouvian subsidy. Specifically, if the R&D–conducting firm is given a subsidy equal to the marginal external benefit at the optimum—distance ab in Figure 5.8—it will produce efficiently.[10] The lesson is clear: When an individual or firm produces positive externalities, the market underprovides the activity or good, but an appropriate subsidy can remedy the situation. Of course, all the difficulties in measuring the quantity and value of the externality still remain. Some research concludes that the private rate of return to R&D is about 10 percent, while the social rate of return is about 50 percent. If these figures are correct, then the positive externalities associated with R&D are substantial.

A Cautionary Note

Many people who have never heard the term *positive externality* nevertheless have a good intuitive grasp of the concept and its policy implications. They understand that if they can convince the government their activities create

---

[9] Sometimes this type of situation can partially be avoided by patent laws. But in many cases, the results of pure research are not patentable, even though they may be used for commercial purposes.

[10] Note that by construction, $ab = a'b'$.

FIGURE 5.8

Positive externality

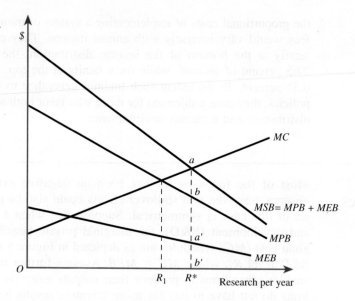

beneficial spillovers, they may be able to dip into the treasury for a subsidy. Requests for such subsidies must be viewed cautiously for two reasons:

- One way or another, the subsidy has to come from resources extracted from taxpayers. Hence, every subsidy embodies a redistribution of income from taxpayers as a whole to the recipients. Even if the subsidy has good efficiency consequences, its distributional implications may not be desirable. This depends on the value judgments embodied in the social welfare function.

- The fact that an activity is beneficial per se does *not* mean that a subsidy is required for efficiency. A subsidy is appropriate only if the market does not allow those performing the activity to capture the full marginal return. For example, a brilliant surgeon who does much good for humanity creates no positive externality as long as the surgeon's salary reflects the incremental value of his or her services.

We illustrate these points with two examples.

Owner-Occupied Housing.   Through a variety of provisions in the US federal income tax code, owner-occupied housing receives a substantial subsidy. (These provisions are detailed in Chapter 15.) This subsidy is worth about $96 billion annually [Joint Committee on Taxation, 2002, p. 22]. Can this subsidy be justified? Arguments usually boil down to an assertion that homeownership creates positive externalities. Homeowners take good care of their property and keep it clean, which makes their neighbors better off; hence, the externality. In addition, homeownership provides an individual with a stake in the nation. This increases social stability, another desirable spillover effect.

Careful maintenance of property certainly creates positive externalities, and homeowners are more likely than renters to take care of their property, to garden, and so on [Glaeser and Shapiro, 2002]. But is it homeownership as such that induces this desirable behavior? The beneficial side effects associated with homeownership might just as well be a consequence of the fact that the 66 percent of American families who are homeowners tend to have relatively high incomes. (The median income of homeowners is almost twice that of renters.) Neither is there any evidence that low ownership rates necessarily contribute to social instability. In Switzerland, a nation not known for its revolutionary tendencies, less than a third of the dwellings are owner occupied.

Of course, even if the subsidy does not contribute to correcting an inefficiency, it might be justifiable on equity grounds. But as just noted, homeowners tend to have higher incomes than renters. Thus, only if the distributional objective is to increase income inequality does a subsidy for homeownership make sense from this standpoint.

Higher Education.   The federal government has been supporting higher education on a large scale since the mid-1960s.[11] In 2002, direct grants, work study programs, and other forms of campus-based aid came to $12.8 billion. Student aid also came in the form of $39.2 billion worth of loans. More than 17 million awards of federal grants or loans were made in 2002 [US Census Bureau, 2002, p. 172]. In addition, several subsidies for higher education are included in the personal income tax system.

One rationalization for subsidizing higher education is that it produces externalities. As noted in Chapter 4, this argument is quite convincing for primary and secondary schooling. Such schooling not only increases an individual's earning capacity, but it also reduces crime and contributes to the literate and well-informed populace that is necessary for a smoothly functioning modern democracy. As John Adams argued in 1765,

> And the preservation of the means of knowledge, among the lowest ranks, is of more importance to the public, than all the property of the rich men in the country. It is even of more consequence to the rich themselves, and to their posterity (quoted in Krueger and Lindahl [1999]).

Some argue that college education should be subsidized because it increases productivity. Indeed, public colleges and universities receive about $50 billion annually in operating subsidies from state and local governments (Kane, 1998, p. 20). That college increases productivity may be true,[12] but

---

[11] For further details, see Kane [1998]. There is also substantial support for higher education from the states.

[12] Some argue that the higher incomes associated with more education are actually due to the fact that college is a screening device that identifies for prospective employers those individuals with high ability.

as long as the earnings of college graduates reflect their higher productivity, there is no externality. In fact, the earnings of college graduates are substantially higher than their counterparts who have not attended college. Labor economists estimate that other things being the same, each year of schooling increases annual earnings between 5 and 11 percent. For the externality argument to be convincing, one must show that the productivity gain *exceeds* this differential.

Even such evidence would not justify the form of current programs, which subsidize all eligible students at the same rate. Are the external benefits of all kinds of college training equal? Do art history, accounting, and premedical courses all produce the same externalities? If not, efficiency requires that they be subsidized differentially.

It is observed that if the subsidies were cut, fewer people would attend college. This may be true, but alone does not justify the subsidies. If subsidies were granted to young people who wanted to open auto repair shops and these were cut, then the number of auto repair shops would also decline. Why should a potential car mechanic be treated differently from a potential classicist?

Some argue that if government subsidies for college students were removed, students from poorer families would bear the brunt of the burden because they find it especially difficult to obtain loans from the private sector. It is very difficult to provide collateral for loans for "human capital" investments, so markets for these loans may not materialize. One possible remedy for this market failure is for the government to make loans available at the going rate of interest. Unless the existence of a positive externality can be established, there is no efficiency basis for subsidizing the interest rate. What about the problem of paying back the debt after graduation? As Passell [1985] notes, "The prospect of heavy debt after graduation would no doubt discourage some students from borrowing. But that may be the wisest form of restraint. Someone finally has to pay the bill, and it is hard to see why that should be the taxpayers rather than the direct beneficiary of the schooling."

The theory of welfare economics recognizes that an inefficient program can be justified if it produces "desirable" distributional effects. Subsidies for college students represent a transfer from taxpayers as a whole to college goers. Looking at the student as part of the family he or she has grown up in, it seems that educational aid programs do indeed enhance income equality. The likelihood of receiving federal aid decreases as family income increases. Remember, though, that most college students are individuals about to form their own households, and the lifetime incomes of college graduates are higher than those of the population as a whole. Such a transfer policy, by subsidizing individuals with college educations, could actually lead to greater inequality in the income distribution. Now, to the extent that the loan recipients would not otherwise have gone to college, the program may increase income equality. However, this argument is premised on the assumption that the reason why students from low-income families are less likely to attend college is that they don't have enough cash to cover tuition. A contrary (and controversial) view, expressed by Cameron and Heckman [1999] is that family income in itself does not affect college attendance. Rather, income is a measure of the long-term environment in which children are raised. When measures of ability are included in statistical analyses of college enrollment, tuition and family income diminish greatly in importance.

Subsidized loans and direct grants are a great deal for students and colleges, both of whom have lobbied intensely for their maintenance. In the absence of persuasive evidence on externalities, however, the benefit to society as a whole is less clear.

Summary

- An externality occurs when the activity of one person affects another person outside the market mechanism. Externalities may generally be traced to the absence of enforceable property rights.

- Externalities cause market price to diverge from social cost, bringing about an inefficient allocation of resources.

- The Coase Theorem indicates that private parties may bargain toward the efficient output if property rights are established. However, bargaining costs must be low and the source of the externality easily identified.

- A Pigouvian tax is a tax levied on pollution in an amount equal to the marginal social damage at the efficient level. Such a tax gives the producer a private incentive to pollute the efficient amount.

- A subsidy for pollution not produced can induce producers to pollute at the efficient level. How-

ever, subsidies can lead to too much production, are administratively difficult, and are regarded by some as ethically unappealing.

- Pollution rights may be traded in markets. This fixes the total level of pollution, an advantage when administrators are uncertain how polluters will respond to Pigouvian taxes.

- Regulation is likely to be inefficient because the social value of pollution reduction varies across firms, locations, and the populace. Nevertheless, this is the most widespread form of environmental policy—a source of dismay to economists. A prime example is the US Clean Air Act.

- Positive externalities generally lead to underprovision of an activity. A subsidy can correct the problem, but care must be taken to avoid wasteful subsidies.

Discussion Questions

1. According to former Vice President Al Gore, "Classical economics defines productivity narrowly and encourages us to equate gains in productivity with economic progress. But the Holy Grail of progress is so alluring that economists tend to overlook the bad side effects that often accompany improvements" [Miller, 1997, p. A22]. Discuss whether or not this is a fair characterization of "classical economics." Gore also stated that we need to take "bold and unequivocal action . . . [to] make the rescue of the environment the central organizing

principle for civilization." Suppose that you were a policymaker trying to decide what to do about automobile emissions. How might you use Gore's dictum as a framework for making your decision?

2. In the following figure, the number of parties that Cassanova gives per month is measured on the horizontal axis, and dollars are measured on the vertical. MC_p is the marginal cost of providing parties and MB_p is Cassanova's marginal benefit schedule from having parties.

   a. Graphically, show how many parties Cassanova will host.

   b. Suppose there is a fixed marginal external benefit, $b, per party to Cassanova's friends. Illustrate this on your graph.

   c. What is the socially (no pun intended) optimal level of parties? How could the Social Committee induce Cassanova to throw this number?

   d. On your graph, show the optimal subsidy per party and the total amount paid to Cassanova. Who gains and loses under this plan?

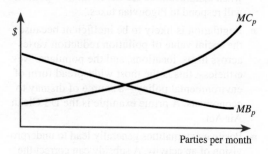

Parties per month

3. For each of the following situations, is the Coase Theorem applicable? Why or why not?

   a. A group of college students in a dormitory share a communal kitchen. Some of the users of the kitchen never clean up the messes they make when cooking.

   b. In Brazil it is illegal to catch and sell certain tropical fish. Nevertheless, in some remote parts of the Amazon River, hundreds of divers come to capture exotic fish for sale on the international black market. The presence of so many divers is depleting the stock of exotic fish.

   c. In the state of Washington, many farmers burn their fields to clear the wheat stubble and prepare for the next planting season. Nearby city-dwellers complain about the pollution.

   d. Users of the Internet generally incur a zero incremental cost for transmitting information. As a consequence, congestion occurs, and users are frustrated by delays.

4. Some observers have argued that importing oil makes the United States hostage to the policies of Saudi Arabia and other countries in the Middle East. This complicates U.S. foreign policy.

   a. Explain why an externality is present in this situation.

   b. Propose a Pigouvian tax to deal with the externality.

   c. Some economists want to curb domestic oil and gasoline consumption, but are wary of giving the government substantially more revenues than it already has. As an alternative, Feldstein [2001, p. A12] suggested a system of tradeable electronic Oil Conservation Vouchers:

   > If the government wanted to cut gasoline consumption from current annual levels of about 180 billion gallons to, say, 140 billion gallons, "it would distribute 140 billion Oil Conservation Vouchers to individuals and businesses. Those who buy gasoline would pay the cash price at the pump plus one such voucher for each gallon of gasoline. The vouchers would not be pieces of paper but would be credits available in a debit account. . . . Because the vouchers are needed to buy gasoline, they would have market value that is determined by the forces of supply and demand."

   Draw a diagram to illustrate how the price of the Oil Conservation Vouchers would be determined. Suppose that the market price per voucher were 75 cents. How would this change the opportunity cost of buying a gallon of gasoline?

5. The external costs of excessive alcohol consumption in the United States are estimated to be about $1.19 per ounce. These costs are associated mainly with fatalities resulting from drunk driving. Currently, taxes per ounce are about 27 cents for spirits, 13 cents for beer, and 12 cents for wine [Cutler, 2002, p. 20]. Use our model of Pigouvian taxation to assess the efficiency of this situation.

6. Discuss this excerpt from an editorial in the *Albuquerque Journal* [July 20, 1991]:

   It's one of the more odious examples of the amorality of the marketplace: The Chicago Board of Trade voted to create a private market for air pollution rights . . . It establishes a system by which the depth of your neighborhood polluter's pocket will determine the necessities of his cleanup, rather than the severity of his defiling of your air. The operation of this pollution futures market will soon demonstrate the moral bankruptcy of this particular market function [p. A7].

7. The Finger Lakes region of New York State attracts tourists who wish to sample its superb wines. In recent years, hog-raising farms—some with more than a thousand hogs—have taken root in the region. The smells emanating from the massive amounts of pig manure adversely affect the tourism. "Wine and swine, in other words, do not mix" [Chen, 2001, p. L1].

   Imagine that the Little Pigs (LP) hog farm is situated near the Tipsy vineyard. The table below shows, for each level of LP's output, the marginal cost of a hog, the marginal benefit to LP, and the marginal damage done to Tipsy:

Output	MC	MB	MD
1	3	13	5
2	6	13	7
3	10	13	9
4	13	13	11
5	19	13	13
6	21	13	15

   a. How many hogs does LP produce?

   b. What is the efficient number of hogs?

   c. The owner of LP gets tired of Tipsy's complaints about his hog farm, and he buys out Tipsy. After the merger, how many hogs does LP produce?

   d. How does the merger affect the sum of the profits earned by LP and Tipsy?

8. The private marginal benefit for commodity X is given by $10 - X$, where X is the number of units consumed. The private marginal cost of producing X is constant at $5. For each unit of X produced, an external cost of $2 is imposed on members of society. In the absence of any government intervention, how much X is produced? What is the efficient level of production of X? What is the gain to society involved in moving from the inefficient to the efficient level of production? Suggest a Pigouvian tax that would lead to the efficient level. How much revenue would the tax raise?

9. In 1997, the government of the United Kingdom announced that, for the first time, students would be required to pay part of the cost of their university education. A spokeswoman for the National Union of Students protested: "Free tuition is seen as a right. . . . We've always been told [that] if you choose to go on with your education, the state should pay because you'll give so much back to the state by getting a better job and paying more in taxes" (Lyall, 1997, p. A7). Comment on the validity of this assertion.

10. A country has decided to limit emissions of some pollutant to 50 units per year, and to organize a market in permissions to pollute. Each permission allows a firm to emit one unit of the pollutant per year. The market demand for the permissions is given by $Q = 100 - 10P$, where Q is the quantity of permissions demanded and P is the price per permission.

    a. What is the market price per permission?

    b. Suppose that it would cost the ACME company $8 to reduce its emissions by one unit. Will it buy a permission? What is the efficiency gain relative to a regulatory regime that simply orders ACME to reduce its emissions by one unit?

Selected References

Coase, Ronald H. "The Problem of Social Cost." *Journal of Law and Economics* (October 1960), pp. 1–44.

Cropper, Maureen L, and Wallace E Oates. "Environmental Economics: A Survey." *Journal of Economic Literature* 30 (June 1992), pp. 675–740.

Ellerman, A. Denny, Paul L. Joskow, Richard Schmalensee, Juan-Pablo Montero, and

Elizabeth M. Bailey. *Markets for Clean Air: The U.S. Acid Rain Program.* Cambridge, UK: Cambridge University Press, 2000.

Viscusi, Kip. "Carcinogen Regulation: Risk Characteristics and the Synthetic Risk Bias." *American Economic Review* 85 (May 1995), pp. 50–54.

CHAPTER 6

Political Economy

Monarchy is like a sleek craft, it sails along well until some bumbling captain runs it into the rocks; democracy, on the other hand, is like a raft. It never goes down but, dammit, your feet are always wet.

FISHER AMES

Textbook discussions of market failures and their remedies tend to convey a rather rosy view of government. With a tax here, an expenditure there, the state readily corrects all market imperfections, meanwhile seeing to it that incomes are distributed in an ethically desirable way. Such a view is at variance with apparent widespread public dissatisfaction with government performance. Public opinion polls, for example, consistently report that under 40 percent of the people have much confidence in Congress. Humorist P. J. O'Rourke probably summarized the sentiments of many when he quipped, "Giving money and power to government is like giving whiskey and car keys to teenage boys."

Perhaps this is merely gratuitous whining. As a matter of definition, in a democracy we get the government we want. Another possibility, however, is that it is inherently difficult for even democratically elected governments to respond to the national interest. This chapter applies economic principles to the analysis of political decision making, a field known as **political economy.** Political economy models assume that individuals view government as a mechanism for maximizing their self-interest. Two points are important regarding this assumption:

- Selfishness does not necessarily lead to inefficient outcomes. As we saw in Chapter 3, under certain conditions the marketplace harnesses self-interest to serve a social end. The question is what, if anything, performs that role in the "political market."

- While the maximization assumption may not be totally accurate, just as in more conventional settings, it provides a good starting point for analysis.

At the outset, we examine direct democracies and how well they translate the preferences of their members into collective action. We then turn to the complications that arise when decisions are made not by individuals themselves but by their elected representatives.

Direct Democracy

Democratic societies use various voting procedures to decide on public expenditures. This section looks at some of these procedures.

Unanimity Rules

Recall from Chapter 4 how the free rider problem can lead to a disturbing situation—because people are selfish, public goods are under-provided, even though everyone could be made better off if they were provided in efficient amounts. This suggests that in principle, if a vote were taken on whether to provide an efficient quantity of the good, consent would be unanimous as long as there was a suitable tax system to finance it. A procedure designed to elicit unanimous agreement was proposed in the early 20th century by Lindahl [1919/1958].

To understand Lindahl's procedure, assume again there are two individuals, Adam and Eve, and one public good, rockets for fireworks (r). Suppose Adam is told that his share of the cost of rocket provision will be 30 percent. Then if the market price per rocket is P_r, Adam's price per rocket is $.30 \times P_r$. Given this price, the prices of other goods, his tastes, and his income, there is some quantity of rockets that Adam wants to consume. More generally, let S^A denote Adam's share of the cost of rocket provision. For any particular value of S^A, Adam demands some quantity of rockets. As his tax share increases and rockets become more expensive for him, he demands a smaller quantity.

In Figure 6.1, the horizontal axis measures the quantity of rockets. Adam's tax share is measured by the vertical distance from point O. The curve D_r^A shows how the quantity of rockets demanded by Adam decreases as his tax share increases.

In the same way, define S^E as Eve's share of the cost of rockets. (By definition, $S^A + S^E = 1$.) When S^E goes up, the quantity demanded by Eve decreases. In Figure 6.1, Eve's tax share increases as we move down along the vertical axis from O'. (Thus; the distance OO' is 1.) Her demand schedule is denoted D_r^E. It slopes upward because upward movements along the vertical axis represent a lower price to her.

An obvious similarity exists between the role of tax shares in the Lindahl model and market prices in the usual theory of demand. But there is an important difference. Instead of each individual facing the same price,

FIGURE 6.1

Lindahl's model

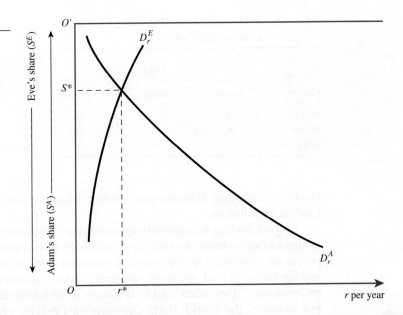

each faces a personalized price per unit of public good, which depends on his or her tax share. The tax shares are referred to as **Lindahl prices.**

An equilibrium is a set of Lindahl prices such that at those prices each person votes for the same quantity of the public good. In Figure 6.1, Adam's equilibrium tax share is OS^* and Eve's is $O'S^*$. At these Lindahl prices, both parties agree that r^* rockets should be provided.

Feasibility of Unanimity Rules.   The Lindahl model shows the tax shares and level of public good provision to which everyone agrees. The big question is how to reach the equilibrium. Imagine that an auctioneer announces some initial set of tax shares. On the basis of their respective demand schedules, Adam and Eve vote for the number of rockets they want. If agreement is not unanimous, the auctioneer announces another set of tax shares. The process continues until Adam and Eve unanimously agree on the quantity of rockets (r^* in Figure 6.1). The determination of the quantity of public goods, then, is quite similar to the market process. Like the market outcome, one can prove that the allocation is Pareto efficient.[1]

As a practical method for providing public goods, Lindahl's procedure has two main problems. First, it assumes people vote sincerely. If Adam can guess the maximum amount that Eve would spend for rockets rather than do without them, he can try to force her to that allocation. Eve has the same

---

[1] Intuitively, assume $P_r = 1$. Then Eve sets $S^E P_r = MRS_{ra}^{Eve}$, and Adam sets $S^A P_r = MRS_{ra}^{Adam}$. Therefore, $MRS_{ra}^{Eve} + MRS_{ra}^{Adam} = S^E P_r + S^A P_r = P_r(S^E + S^A) = P_r$. But P_r represents MRT_{ra}, so $MRS_{ra}^{Eve} + MRS_{ra}^{Adam} = MRT_{ra}$, which is the necessary condition for Pareto efficiency of Equation (4.2).

Table 6.1   **Voter preferences that lead to an equilibrium**

	Voter		
Choice	*Cosmo*	*Elaine*	*George*
First	A	C	B
Second	B	B	C
Third	C	A	A

incentives. Strategic behavior may prevent Adam and Eve from reaching the Lindahl equilibrium.

Second, finding the mutually agreeable tax shares may take a lot of time. In this example, there are only two parties. In most important cases, many people are involved. Getting everyone's consent involves enormous decision-making costs. Indeed, although unanimity rules guarantee that no one will be "exploited," they often lead to situations in which *no* decisions are made. For example, the World Trade Organization (WTO), which sets rules for coordinating trade among its 144 member nations, operates on a unanimity rule. A journalist reporting on a WTO meeting once noted that the only shocking thing that might happen would be "if they manage[d] to agree on anything at all" [Kahn, 2001, p. A3].

Majority Voting Rules

Because unanimity is difficult to attain, voting systems not requiring it may be desirable. With a **majority voting rule,** one more than half of the voters must favor a measure to gain approval.

Although the mechanics of majority voting are familiar, it is useful to review them carefully. Consider a community with three voters, Cosmo, Elaine, and George, who have to choose among three levels of missile provision, A, B, and C. Level A is small, level B is moderate, and level C is large. The voters' preferences are depicted in Table 6.1. Each column shows how the voter ranks the choices. For example, Elaine most prefers level C, but given a choice between B and A, would prefer B.

Suppose an election were held on whether to adopt A or B. Cosmo would vote for A while Elaine and George would vote for B. Hence, B would win by a vote of 2 to 1. Similarly, if an election were held between B and C, B would win by a vote of 2 to 1. Level B wins any election against its opposition, and thus is the option selected by majority rule. Note that the selection of B is independent of the order in which the votes are taken.

Majority decision rules do not always yield such clear-cut results. Consider the preferences depicted in Table 6.2. Again, imagine a series of paired elections to determine the most preferred level. In an election between A and B, A would win by a vote of 2 to 1. If an election were held between B and C, B would win by a vote of 2 to 1. Finally, in an election between

Table 6.2   **Voter preferences that lead to cycling**

	Voter		
Choice	Cosmo	Elaine	George
First	A	C	B
Second	B	A	C
Third	C	B	A

A and C, C would win by the same margin. This result is disconcerting. The first election suggests that A is preferred to B; the second that B is preferred to C. Conventional notions of consistency suggest that A should therefore be preferred to C. But in the third election, just the opposite occurs. Although each individual voter's preferences are consistent, the community's are not. This phenomenon is referred to as the **voting paradox.**

Moreover, with the preferences in Table 6.2, the ultimate outcome depends crucially on the order in which the votes are taken. If the first election is between propositions A and B and the winner (A) runs against C, then C is the ultimate choice. On the other hand, if the first election is B versus C, and the winner (B) runs against A, then A is chosen. Under such circumstances, the ability to control the order of voting—the agenda—confers great power. **Agenda manipulation** is the process of organizing the order of votes to assure a favorable outcome.

A related problem is that paired voting can go on forever without reaching a decision. After the election between A and B, A wins. If C challenges A, then C wins. If B then challenges C, B wins. The process can continue indefinitely, a phenomenon called **cycling.** A good historical example of cycling concerns the 17th Amendment to the US Constitution, which provides for direct election of US senators. Adoption "was delayed for 10 years by parliamentary maneuvers that depended on voting cycles involving the status quo (the appointment of senators by the state legislature) and two versions of the amendment" [Blair and Pollak, 1983, p. 88].

Clearly, majority voting need not lead to these problems. After all, the elections associated with Table 6.1 went smoothly. Why the difference? It turns on the structure of individual preferences for various levels of missile procurement. Consider again the people in Table 6.2. Because Cosmo prefers A to B to C, it follows that A gives Cosmo more utility than B, and B more than C. The schedule denoted Cosmo in Figure 6.2 depicts this relationship. The schedules labeled Elaine and George do the same for the other voters.

We define a **peak** in an individual's preferences as a point at which all the neighboring points are lower.[2] A voter has **single-peaked preferences** if,

---

[2] For this analysis, the absolute amount of utility associated with each alternative is irrelevant. The vertical distances could change, but as long as the pattern of peaks stays unchanged, so does the election's outcome.

FIGURE 6.2

Graphing the
preferences from
Table 6.2

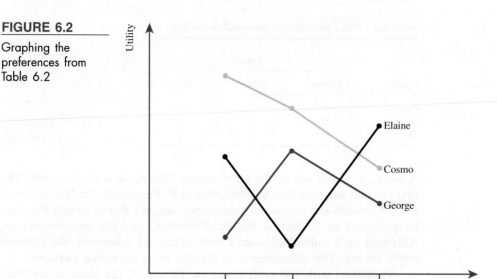

as she moves away from her most preferred outcome in any and all directions, her utility consistently falls. She has **double-peaked preferences** if, as she moves away from the most preferred outcome, utility goes down, but then goes up again. Thus, Cosmo has a single peak at point A; George has a single peak at point B; and Elaine has two peaks, one at A and one at C. It turns out that Elaine's preferences are the ones that lead to the voting paradox. If Elaine had *any* set of single-peaked preferences, majority voting would lead to a consistent decision. This is why no voting paradox emerges from Table 6.1. There, each voter has single-peaked preferences. More generally, if all voters' preferences are single peaked, no voting paradox occurs.

Because multipeaked preferences can throw a wrench into majority voting, it is important to know whether they are likely to be important as a practical matter. Consider again Elaine's two-peaked preferences in Table 6.2. She prefers either very large or very small missile expenditures to a quantity in the middle. Although such preferences are not necessarily irrational, they do seem a bit peculiar. Perhaps Elaine believes that moderate numbers of missiles provide little if any real protection, so that unless expenditures are large, they might as well be close to nothing.

Suppose, however, that instead of missiles, voters are choosing among expenditure levels for a public park—a good for which there are private substitutes. Assume that in the presence of small or medium public park expenditures, voter Jerry will join a private country club, but given large expenditures, he will use the public park. Provided that Jerry's tax burden increases with park expenditure, he prefers a small to a medium park—since neither of these options benefits Jerry, he prefers the one with the smaller tax burden. But his most preferred outcome might be the large expenditure public park. (This

Table 6.3   **Preferred level of party expenditure**

Voter	Expenditure
Donald	$ 5
Daisy	100
Huey	150
Dewey	160
Louie	700

depends in part on the associated tax burden compared to the country club membership fee.) In short, Jerry may prefer either the small or large public park to the medium-sized one. Thus, when there are private substitutes for a publicly provided good, a multipeaked pattern like Elaine's in Figure 6.2 can easily emerge.

Moreover, when issues cannot be ranked along a single dimension, multipeaked preferences are also a serious possibility.[3] Suppose that a community is trying to decide how to use a vacant building. Choice A is an abortion clinic, choice B is an adult book store, and choice C is an Army recruitment office. Unlike the choice among different levels of missile expenditure, here the alternatives do not represent more or less of a single characteristic. Multipeaked preferences can easily emerge.

The Median Voter Theorem.   Let us now return to the simple case in which all alternatives being considered represent smaller or greater amounts of a characteristic. People rank each alternative on the basis of this characteristic. An example is how much of some public good to acquire. Define the **median voter** as the voter whose preferences lie in the middle of the set of all voters' preferences; half the voters want more of the good than the median voter, and half want less. The **median voter theorem** states that as long as all preferences are single peaked, the outcome of majority voting reflects the preferences of the median voter. (With an even number of voters, there may be a tie between two median voters, which must be broken arbitrarily.)

To demonstrate the theorem, assume there are five voters: Donald, Daisy, Huey, Dewey, and Louie. They are deciding how large a party to give together, and each of them has single-peaked preferences over party sizes. The most preferred level for each voter is noted in Table 6.3. *Because preferences are single peaked, the closer an expenditure level is to a given voter's peak, the more he or she prefers it.* A movement from zero party expenditure to $5 would be preferred to no money by all voters. A movement from $5 to $100 would be approved by Daisy, Huey, Dewey, and Louie, and

---

[3] Atkinson and Stiglitz [1980, p. 306] explain how the notion of a "peak" is generalized to a multidimensional setting.

from $100 to $150 by Huey, Dewey, and Louie. Any increase beyond $150, however, would be blocked by at least three voters: Donald, Daisy, and Huey. Hence, the majority votes for $150. But this is just the amount preferred by Huey, the median voter. The election results mirror the median voter's preferences.

To summarize: When all preferences are single peaked, majority voting yields a stable result, and the choice selected reflects the preferences of the median voter. However, when some voters' preferences are multi-peaked, a voting paradox can emerge.[4] Because multipeaked preferences may be important in many realistic situations, majority voting cannot be depended on to yield consistent public choices. Moreover, as we shall discuss shortly, even when majority voting leads to consistent decisions, it may not be efficient in the sense that overall benefits exceed costs.

Logrolling

A possible problem with simple majority voting is that it does not allow people to register how strongly they feel about the issues. Whether a particular voter just barely prefers A to B or has an enormous preference for A has no influence on the outcome. **Logrolling** systems allow people to trade votes and hence register how strongly they feel about various issues. Suppose that voters Smith and Jones prefer not to have more missiles, but they don't care all that much. Brown, on the other hand, definitely wants more missiles. With a logrolling system, Brown may be able to convince Jones to vote for more missiles if Brown promises to vote for a new road to go by Jones's factory.

Vote trading is controversial. Its proponents argue that trading votes leads to efficient provision of public goods, just as trading commodities leads to efficient provision of private goods. Proponents also emphasize its potential for revealing the intensity of preferences and establishing a stable equilibrium. Moreover, the compromises implicit in vote trading are necessary for a democratic system to function. As sociologist James Q. Wilson [2000] has noted, "Vote trades are called pork barrels or logrolling, but such trades are essential to finding some way to balance competing interests, each of which is defended by a legislator who owes little to any other legislator. Vote trades and pork-barrel projects are an essential way of achieving what force and language cannot produce."

A numerical example helps illustrate these advantages. Suppose a community is considering three projects, a hospital, a library, and a swimming pool. The community has three voters, Melanie, Rhett, and Scarlet. Table 6.4 shows their benefits for each project. (A minus sign indicates a net loss; that is, the costs exceed the benefits.)

---

[4] The presence of one or more voters with multipeaked preferences does not *necessarily* lead to a voting paradox. It depends on the number of voters and the structure of their preferences. See Question 1 at the end of this chapter.

Table 6.4   **Logrolling can improve welfare**

| | Voter | | | |
Project	Melanie	Rhett	Scarlet	Total Net Benefits
Hospital	200	−50	−55	95
Library	−40	150	−30	80
Pool	−120	−60	400	220

The first thing to notice about the table is that the total net benefit for each project is positive. Thus, by definition, the community as a whole would be better off if each project were adopted.[5] But what happens if the projects are voted on *one at a time?* Melanie votes for the hospital because her net benefit is positive, but Rhett and Scarlet vote against it because their benefits are negative. The hospital therefore loses. Similarly, the library and the swimming pool go down in defeat.

Vote trading can remedy this situation. Suppose Melanie agrees to vote for the library if Rhett consents to vote for the hospital. Melanie comes out ahead by 160 (= 200 − 40) with the trade; Rhett comes out ahead by 100 (= 150 − 50). They therefore strike the deal, and the hospital and library pass. In the same way, Melanie and Scarlet can make a deal in which Melanie gives her support for the pool in return for Scarlet's vote for the hospital. Thus logrolling allows all three measures to pass, a desirable outcome.

On the other hand, opponents of logrolling stress that it is likely to result in special-interest gains not sufficient to outweigh general losses. Large amounts of waste can be incurred. For example, as part of the war against terrorism, the Transportation Security Administration was forced to spend "hundreds of millions of dollars to equip airports with a bomb-detection machine that has a history of breaking down and needing costly repairs" [Power, 2003, p. A9]. Why? The main reason is that the manufacturer was located in the district of the House Appropriations Chairman; his vote was important for the pet projects of other members of Congress.

Table 6.5 illustrates a situation in which logrolling leads to such undesirable outcomes. Here we have the same three voters and three projects under consideration as in Table 6.4, but with a different set of net benefits. Every project has a negative net benefit. Each should therefore be rejected, as would be the case if the projects were voted on one at a time.

However, with logrolling, some or all of these inefficient projects could pass. Suppose Melanie offers to support the library in return for Rhett's vote for the hospital. The deal is consummated because both of them come out

---

[5] We assume the absence of externalities or any other factors that would make private costs and benefits unequal to their social counterparts.

Table 6.5   **Logrolling can also lower welfare**

	Voter			
Project	*Melanie*	*Rhett*	*Scarlet*	*Total Net Benefits*
Hospital	200	−110	−105	−15
Library	−40	150	−120	−10
Pool	−270	−140	400	−10

ahead—Melanie by 160 (= 200 − 40) and Rhett by 40 (= 150 − 110). With the support of Melanie and Rhett together, both projects pass. In the same way, Rhett and Scarlet can trade votes for the pool and the library, so both of those projects are adopted.

To understand the source of this outcome, think about Melanie and Rhett's vote trading over the hospital and the library. Note that Scarlet comes out behind on both projects. This demonstrates how with logrolling, a majority of voters can form a coalition to vote for projects that serve their interests, but whose costs are borne mainly by the minority. Hence, although the benefits of the projects to the majority exceed the costs, this is not true for society as a whole. We conclude that while logrolling can sometimes improve on the results from simple majority voting, this is not necessarily the case.

Arrow's Impossibility Theorem

We have shown that neither simple majority voting nor logrolling has entirely desirable properties. Many other voting schemes have also been considered, and they, too, are flawed.[6] An important question is whether *any* ethically acceptable method for translating individual preferences into collective preferences is free of difficulties. It depends on what you mean by "ethically acceptable." Nobel laureate Kenneth Arrow [1951] proposed that in a democratic society, a collective decision-making rule should satisfy the following criteria:[7]

1. It can produce a decision whatever the configuration of voters' preferences. Thus, for example, the procedure must not fall apart if some people have multipeaked preferences.

2. It must be able to rank all possible outcomes.

3. It must be responsive to individuals' preferences. Specifically, if every individual prefers A to B, then society's ranking must prefer A to B.

---

[6] These include point voting (each person is given a fixed number of points that are cast for the different alternatives), plurality voting (the alternative with the most votes wins), Borda counts (each alternative is ranked by each voter, and the ranks are totaled to choose), Condorcet elections (the alternative that defeats the rest in paired elections wins), and exhaustive voting (the proposal favored least by the largest number of voters is repeatedly removed until only one remains). See Levin and Nalebuff [1995] for further details.

[7] Arrow's requirements have been stated in a number of different ways. This treatment follows Blair and Pollak [1983].

4. It must be consistent in the sense that if A is preferred to B and B is preferred to C, then A is preferred to C.[8]

5. Society's ranking of A and B depends only on individuals' rankings of A and B. Thus, the collective ranking of manned space travel and foreign aid does not depend on how individuals rank either of them relative to research on a cure for AIDS. This assumption is sometimes called the **independence of irrelevant alternatives.**

6. Dictatorship is ruled out. Social preferences must not reflect the preferences of only a single individual.

Taken together, these criteria seem quite reasonable. Basically, they say that society's choice mechanism should be logical and respect individuals' preferences. Unfortunately, the stunning conclusion of Arrow's analysis is that in general it is *impossible* to find a rule that satisfies all these criteria.[9] A democratic society cannot be expected to make consistent decisions.

This result, called Arrow's Impossibility Theorem, thus casts doubt on the very ability of democracies to function. Naturally, the theorem has generated debate, much of which has focused on whether other sets of criteria might allow formation of a social decision-making rule. It turns out that if any of the six criteria is dropped, a decision-making rule that satisfies the other five *can* be constructed. But whether or not it is permissible to drop any of the criteria depends on one's views of their ethical validity.

Arrow's theorem does not state that it is *necessarily* impossible to find a consistent decision-making rule. Rather, the theorem only says one cannot guarantee that society will be able to do so. For certain patterns of individual preferences, no problems arise. An obvious example is when members of society have identical preferences. Some have suggested that the real significance of Arrow's theorem is that it shows the need for a virtual uniformity of tastes if a democracy is to work. They then argue that many institutions have the express purpose of molding people's tastes to make sure that uniformity emerges. An example is mandatory public education. This observation is consistent with the view of the British statesman Benjamin Disraeli: "Whenever is found what is called a paternal government, there is found state education. It has been discovered that the best way to ensure implicit obedience is to commence tyranny in the nursery." Lott [1999] analyzed the pattern of expenditures on education across countries and found a result similar in spirit to Disraeli's assertion—more totalitarian governments tend to make greater investments in public education, other things being the same.

A very different view is that Arrow's theorem does not really have much to say about the viability of democratic processes. Another Nobel

---

[8] More precisely, in this context *preferred to* means *better than* or *just as good as*.

[9] The proof involves fairly sophisticated mathematics. The procedure of proof is to show that if all six conditions are imposed, phenomena like the voting paradox can arise.

prize winner, James Buchanan [1960], believes that the inconsistencies of majority voting have beneficial aspects:

> Majority rule is acceptable in a free society precisely because it allows a sort of jockeying back and forth among alternatives, upon none of which relative unanimity can be obtained . . . It serves to insure that competing alternatives may be experimentally and provisionally adopted, tested, and replaced by new compromise alternatives approved by a majority group of ever-changing composition. This is [the] democratic choice process. [p. 83]

Another important question raised by Arrow's theorem concerns the use of social welfare functions. Recall from Chapter 3 that a social welfare function is a rule that evaluates the desirability of any given set of individuals' utilities. In a democratic society, the social welfare function must be chosen collectively. But Arrow's theorem says that it may be impossible to make such decisions, and hence we cannot assume that a social welfare function really exists. However, if it does not exist, how can economists use the social welfare function to rank alternative states? Some economists therefore reject the function's use. They argue that it is merely a way of introducing value judgments and not a representation of "society's" preferences. As such, a social welfare function does not isolate the correct allocation of resources. However, most economists believe that the function is an important tool. It may not provide "the" answer, but it can be used to draw out the implications of alternative sets of value judgments. With this interpretation, the social welfare function provides valuable insights.

Representative Democracy

Although the discussion of public decision making thus far sheds light on some important questions, it is based on an unrealistic view of government. Government is essentially a big computer that elicits from citizens their preferences and uses this information to produce social decisions. The state has no interests of its own; it is neutral and benign.

In fact, of course, governing is done by people—politicians, judges, bureaucrats, and others. Realistic political economy models must study the goals and behavior of the people who govern. This section discusses a few such models. They assume that people in government, like other individuals, attempt to maximize their self-interest.

Elected Politicians

Our earlier discussion of direct democracy led to the median voter theorem: If individual preferences are single peaked and can be represented along a single dimension, the outcome of majority voting reflects the preferences of the median voter. In reality, direct referenda on fiscal matters are most unusual. More commonly, citizens elect representatives who make decisions on their behalf. Nevertheless, under certain assumptions, the median voter theorem helps explain how these representatives set their positions.

FIGURE 6.3

Median voter
theorem for elections

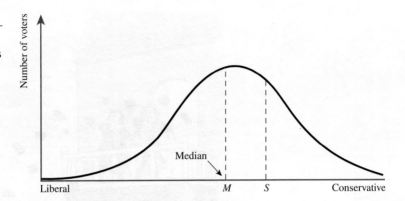

Consider an election between two candidates, Smith and Jones. Assume voters have single-peaked preferences along the spectrum of political views. Voters cast ballots to maximize their own utility, and candidates seek to maximize the number of votes received.

What happens? Downs [1957] shows that under these conditions, a vote-maximizing politician adopts the preferred program of the *median voter*—the voter whose preferences are exactly in the middle of the distribution of preferences. To see why, assume voters rank all positions on the basis of whether they are "conservative" or "liberal." Figure 6.3 shows a hypothetical distribution of voters who most prefer each point in the political spectrum. Suppose that Candidate Jones adopts position *M*, at the median, and Candidate Smith chooses position *S* to the right of center. Because all voters have single-peaked preferences and want to maximize utility, each supports the candidate whose views lie closest to his or her own. Smith will win all the votes to the right of *S*, as well as some of the votes between *S* and *M*. Because *M* is the median, one-half of the voters lie to the left of *M*. Jones will receive all of these votes and some of those to the right of *M*, guaranteeing him a majority. The only way for Smith to prevent himself from being "outflanked" is to move to position *M* himself. Therefore, it pays both candidates to place themselves as close as possible to the position of the median voter.

This model has two striking implications: First, two-party systems tend to be stable in the sense that both parties stake out positions near the "center." In some respects, this is a good description of American political life. It appears, for example, that presidential candidates who are perceived as too far from the middle-of-the-road (Barry Goldwater in 1964 and George McGovern in 1972) fare poorly with the electorate.[10] During

---

[10] One of Goldwater's campaign slogans was "A choice, not an echo." The median voter theorem helps to explain why echoes are so prevalent.

*"Perhaps Your Majesty should try governing
from the center."*

• •

the 2000 presidential election, a journalist characterized Al Gore and George W. Bush as "two candidates who hold surprisingly similar positions on a wide range of issues" [Farney 2000, p. A1]. According to the median voter model, there is nothing at all surprising about such a situation. As suggested by the cartoon, departing from the center can be hazardous for a politician!

Second, the replacement of direct referenda by a representative system has *no* effect on the outcome. Both simply mirror the preferences of the median voter. Thus, government spending cannot be "excessive" because political competition for votes leads to an expenditure level that coincides with the median voter's wishes.

Before taking these rather optimistic results too much to heart, however, several issues require careful examination.

Single-Dimensional Rankings.   If all political beliefs cannot be ranked along a single spectrum, the median voter theorem falls apart because the identity of the median voter depends on the issue being considered. The median voter with respect to affirmative action questions may not be the same person as the median voter on defense issues. Similarly, just as in the case of direct referenda, if preferences are not single peaked, there may not be a stable voting equilibrium at all.

Ideology. The model assumes that politicians are simple vote maximizers, but they may care about more than just winning elections. Ideology can play an important role. After all, in 1850 Henry Clay said, "Sir, I would rather be right than be president."

Personality. The assumption that voters' decisions depend only on issues may be unrealistic. Personalities may sometimes be more important. Some have argued, for example, that much of President Ronald Reagan's appeal was his fatherly personality.

Leadership. In the model, politicians passively respond to voters' preferences. But these preferences may be influenced by the politicians themselves. This is just another way of saying that politicians provide leadership. An interesting extreme case of how leadership can change election outcomes occurs when the actions of a politician actually change the composition of his or her constituency. For example, a mayor whose support comes primarily from the poor could implement policies that tend to drive high income people out of the jurisdiction, thus changing the identity of the median voter. There is some evidence that such a phenomenon occurred in Boston during the first half of the twentieth century and in Detroit during the second [Glaeser and Shleifer, 2002a].

Decision to Vote. The analysis assumes every eligible citizen chooses to exercise his or her franchise. If the candidates' positions are too close, however, some people may not vote out of boredom. Individuals with extreme views may feel too alienated to vote. The model also ignores the costs of acquiring information and voting. A fully informed voter makes a determination on the suitability of a candidate's platform, the probability that the candidate will be able and willing to keep his or her promises, and so forth. The fact that these costs may be high, together with the perception that a single vote will not influence the outcome anyway, may induce a self-interested citizen to abstain from voting. A free rider problem emerges—each individual has an incentive not to vote, but unless a sizable number of people do so, a democracy cannot function. Although low voter participation rates are often bemoaned (for example, in the 2000 presidential election, only 51 percent of the voting-age population cast a vote), the real puzzle may be why the percentage is so *high*. Part of the answer may be the success with which the educational system instills the idea that a citizen's obligation to vote transcends narrow self-interest.

Public Employees

The next group we consider is public employees, also referred to as bureaucrats. To understand their role, note that the legislation enacted by elected politicians is often vague. The precise way a program is run is in the hands of public employees. For example, the Clean Air Act stipulates that the government must set standards "requisite to protect the public health with an adequate margin of safety" [Epstein, 2001, p. A22]. How is health status to be measured? What scientific standard is to be used to determine what an "adequate margin" is? The law was silent on these issues. The task of filling these gaps fell to the bureaucrats in the Environmental Protection Agency, giving them enormous latitude and power.

Bureaucrats receive a lot of bitter criticism. They are blamed for being unresponsive, creating excessive red tape, and intruding too much into the private affairs of citizens. Even a new-wave rock group joined in the attack:

Red tape, I can see can't you see
Red tape, do'in to you, do'in to me
Red tape, bureaucracy in D.C.
Red tape, killing you and killing me.
Tax this, tax that, tax this, tax that.
NO MORE RED TAPE.[11]

However, a modern government simply cannot function without bureaucracy. Bureaucrats provide valuable technical expertise in the design and execution of programs. The fact that their tenures in office often exceed those of elected officials provides a vital "institutional memory." Another important function of bureaucrats is to provide accurate documentation of public sector transactions to ensure that all eligible citizens receive equal treatment from a particular publicly-provided service, and to prevent various forms of corruption.

On the other hand, it would be naive to assume a bureaucrat's only aim is to interpret and passively fulfill the wishes of the electorate and its representatives. Having said this, we are still left with the problem of specifying the bureaucrat's goals. Niskanen [1971] argued that in the market-oriented private sector, an individual who wants to "get ahead" does so by making his or her company as profitable as possible. The individual's salary rises with the firm's profits. In contrast, bureaucrats tend to focus on such items as perquisites of office, public reputation, power, and patronage because opportunities for monetary gains are minimal.[12] In the words of a student who was attempting to enter the civil service in India, becoming a bureaucrat "means a lot of power . . . power in the sense of whatever you feel like

---

[11] From "Red Tape," words and music by Keith Morris and Greg Hetson of the Circle Jerks. © 1980, Irving Music, Inc., and Plagued Music (BMI). All rights reserved. International copyright secured.

[12] Obviously, this distinction is blurred in the real world. Firm executives care about power and job perks as well as money. Nevertheless, the distinction is useful for analytical purposes.

FIGURE 6.4

Niskanen's model of bureaucracy

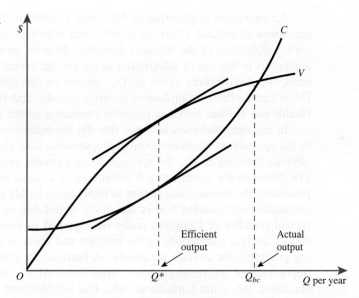

doing . . . They have a lot of hold over what the government does" [Gargan, 1993, p. A4]. Niskanen suggested that power, status, and so on are positively correlated with the size of the bureaucrat's budget and concluded that the bureaucrat's objective is to maximize his or her budget.

To assess the implications of this hypothesis, consider Figure 6.4. The output of a bureaucracy, Q, is measured on the horizontal axis. Q might represent the number of units of public housing managed by the Department of Housing and Urban Development or the quantity of Abrams tanks stockpiled by the Department of Defense. Dollars are measured on the vertical axis. The curve V represents the total value placed on each level of Q by the legislative sponsor who controls the budget. The slope of V is the marginal social benefit of the output; it is drawn on the reasonable assumption of diminishing marginal benefit. The total cost of providing each output level is C. Its slope measures the marginal cost of each unit of output. C is drawn on the assumption of increasing marginal cost.

Suppose the bureaucrat knows that the sponsor will accept any project whose total benefits exceed total costs. Then the bureaucrat (bc) proposes Q_{bc}, the output level that maximizes the size of the bureau subject to the constraint that C not be above V. Q_{bc}, however, is an inefficient level of output. Efficiency requires that a unit of output be produced only as long as the *additional* benefit from that output exceeds the *additional* cost. Hence, the efficient output is where marginal cost equals marginal benefit, *not* total cost equals total benefit. In Figure 6.4, the efficient level is Q^*, where the *slopes* of V and C are equal. Thus, the bureaucrat's desire to build as large an "empire" as possible leads to an inefficiently large bureaucracy.

An important implication of Niskanen's model is that bureaucrats have incentives to expend effort on promotional activities to increase the sponsor's perceptions of the bureau's benefits—to shift up the V curve. This is analogous to the use of advertising in the private sector. If such efforts succeed, the equilibrium value of Q_{bc} moves to the right. Hence, Defense Department officials emphasize security threats, and their counterparts in Health and Human Services promote awareness of the poverty problem.

In essence, Niskanen assumes that the bureaucrat can present his output to the sponsor as an all-or-nothing proposition: Take Q_{bc} or none at all. An obvious question is why the sponsor doesn't simply overrule the bureaucrat. The bureaucrat's informational advantage is critical here. The process of producing the bureaucratic output is likely to be highly complex and require specialized information that is not easily obtainable by the sponsor. Can a typical member of Congress really be expected to know about the intricacies of nuclear submarines or the benefits and costs of alternative job-training programs for welfare recipients? A particularly striking example of the importance of information comes from South Africa. Even after the fall of apartheid, the white bureaucrats who had administered that regime continued to play a predominant role in running the country. Why? "[T]he bureaucrats alone know the secrets of running the state" [Keller, 1994, p. A1].

Special Interests

We have been assuming so far that citizens who seek to influence government policy can act only as individual voters. In fact, people with common interests can exercise disproportionate power by acting together. The source of the group's power might be that its members tend to have higher voter participation rates than the population as a whole. Alternatively, members might be willing to make campaign contributions and/or pay bribes. As an example, over $950 million in campaign contributions were made during the House and Senate campaigns of 2002.

On what bases are these interest groups established? There are many possibilities.

Source of Income: Capital or Labor.   According to orthodox Marxism, people's political interests are determined by whether they are capitalists or laborers. This view is too simple to explain interest-group formation in the contemporary United States. Even though individuals with high incomes tend to receive a disproportionate share of their income from capital, much of the income of the rich is also derived from labor. Thus, it is difficult even to tell who is a "capitalist" and who a "laborer." Indeed, studies of the distribution of income in the United States and other Western nations indicate that the driving force behind inequality in total income is the inequality in labor income [Gottschalk and Smeeding,1997].

Size of Income.   The rich and the poor disagree on many economic policy issues. The poor favor redistributive spending programs and the rich oppose them. Similarly, each group supports implicit or explicit subsidies for goods they consume intensively. Hence, the rich support subsidies for owner-occupied housing, while the poor favor special treatment for rental housing.

Source of Income: Industry of Employment.   Both workers and owners have a common interest in government support for their industry. In the steel, textile and automobile industries, for example, unions and management work shoulder to shoulder in order to lobby the government for protection against foreign competition.

Region.   Residents of geographical regions often share common interests. Citizens of the Sun Belt are interested in favorable tax treatment of oil; midwesterners care about agricultural subsidies; and northeasterners lobby for expenditures on urban development.

Demographic and Personal Characteristics.   The elderly favor subsidized health care and generous retirement programs; young married couples are interested in good schools and low payroll taxes. Religious beliefs play a major role in debates over the funding of abortion and state aid to private schools. Ethnic groups differ on the propriety of government expenditure for bilingual education programs. Gender is an important basis for interest-group formation; in the 2000 elections, women voted in disproportionately large numbers for Democrats, and Republicans expressed much concern over the gender gap.

The list could go on indefinitely. Given the numerous bases on which interest groups can be established, it is no surprise that people who are in opposition on one issue may be in agreement on another; "politics makes strange bedfellows" is more or less the order of the day.

This discussion has ignored the question of how individuals with common interests actually manage to organize themselves. Belonging to a group may require membership fees, donation of time, and so forth. Each individual has an incentive to let others do the work while he or she reaps the benefits, becoming a free rider. The probability that a group will actually form increases when the number of individuals is small, and it is possible to levy sanctions against nonjoiners. But in some cases, rational financial self-interest is probably not the explanation. The debate over the public funding of abortion illustrates the influence of ideology and emotion on the decision to join a group.

Rent-Seeking.   We have noted that groups of citizens can manipulate the political system to redistribute income toward themselves. Generically, such activity is called **rent-seeking**—using the government to obtain higher than normal returns ("rents"). Rent-seeking takes a variety of forms. An important variant is when a group of producers induces the government to restrict

FIGURE 6.5

Rent-Seeking

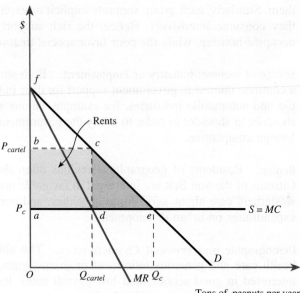

the output in their industry. Restricting output leads to higher prices for producers, allowing them to earn rents. For example, in the United States you can grow peanuts only if you have a government license, and the licenses allow for just 1.5 million acres of land to be devoted to peanut production. By restricting the amount of land that can be used to grow peanuts, the government reduces peanut production and generates rents for the producers.

To analyze rent-seeking, consider Figure 6.5, which depicts the peanut market. The demand curve is D. For simplicity, we assume that the supply of peanuts, S, is horizontal. In the absence of government intervention, the equilibrium is at the intersection of supply and demand, where output is Q_c and price is P_c. (The subscript c reminds us that it is the competitive outcome.) It would be in the peanut producers' interest if they could all agree to reduce their respective outputs and thereby force up the market price. More precisely, they would be better off if they jointly acted to maximize industry profits and split them up—in effect to form a **cartel,** an arrangement under which suppliers band together to restrict output and raise price.

Why don't they just do it? Because even though *collectively* they would benefit by being part of a cartel, this does not mean that it is any *individual's* self-interest. When the cartel raises its price, any individual farm has an incentive to cheat, that is, to increase its production beyond its agreed upon quota. But all farms face this incentive, and as they all increase their outputs, the price falls back to the competitive equilibrium. This is where the government comes in. If the producers can get the government to enforce the cartel, then they can maintain the high price without having to worry about cheating. In the case of the peanut industry, the government has a simple way to enforce the cartel—it makes growing peanuts without a license a federal crime! Further, even if you have a license, the quantity of peanuts you can grow is determined by a government quota. The rents associated with owning the licenses are huge—according to one estimate, the net rate of return is 51 percent [Bovard, 1995, p. A10].

What is the best price from the cartel's standpoint? To maximize industry profits, the cartel needs to produce the output at which industry marginal cost (the incremental cost of producing a ton of peanuts) equals industry marginal revenue (the incremental revenue from selling a ton of peanuts.) The supply curve represents the marginal cost (MC) of production, and the marginal revenue curve is depicted as MR. The cartel output, Q_{cartel}, is determined by their intersection, and the associated price is P_{cartel}. By virtue of the higher price they receive per ton of peanuts (distance ab) on each of the ad units they sell, the peanut farmers earn rents equal to area $abcd$.

It costs money for the producers to maintain the system of licenses. Presumably, they have to make campaign contributions to key members of Congress, hire lobbyists, and so on. What is the maximal amount that they would be willing to pay to maintain the system? Because rents are a payment above the ordinary return, the *most* that the firms would be willing to pay for their favored position is the total amount of the rents, $abcd$.

So far, it would seem that the rent-seeking behavior simply leads to a transfer from consumers (who pay a higher price) to the producers (who receive rents). But more is at stake. Recall that consumer surplus is the area above the price and below the demand curve. (See the Appendix at the end of this book.) Hence, prior to the licenses, consumer surplus was area fae. Similar reasoning suggests that consumer surplus after the licenses is area fbc. Hence, consumers are worse off by the difference between the two areas, $abce$. Recall that of this, $abcd$ goes to the producers. Who gets the rest of the lost surplus, dce? The answer is nobody—it is a deadweight loss to society, a pure waste with no accompanying gain. The deadweight loss occurs because the increase in peanut prices distorts consumers' choices between peanuts and all other goods.

In standard treatments of monopoly, area dce is the only deadweight loss. But in our rent-seeking model, the deadweight loss might actually be larger. As already suggested, rent-seeking can use up resources—lobbyists spend their time influencing legislators, consultants testify before regulatory panels, and advertisers conduct public relations campaigns. Such resources, which could have been used to produce new goods and services, are instead consumed in a struggle over the distribution of existing goods and services. Hence, area $abcd$ does not represent a mere lump-sum transfer; it is a measure of real resources used up to maintain a position of market power. In short, according to this view, the deadweight loss associated with rent-seeking is the *sum* of $abcd$ and dce, or $abce$.

We cannot conclude that area *abce* is always the loss, however. In many cases, this area may overstate the efficiency cost of rent-seeking. For example, some rent-seeking takes the form of campaign contributions and bribes, and these are simply transfers—they do not "use up" real resources Nevertheless, an important contribution of the rent-seeking model is that it focuses our attention on the potential size of the waste generated by the government's power to create rents.

A final question is why rent-seeking is allowed to exist. After all, Figure 6.5 shows that the losses to consumers are greater than the gains to the producers. Why don't the consumers insist on an end to the licenses?

One reason is that interest groups may be well organized and armed with information, while those who will bear the costs are not organized and may not even be aware of what is going on. Even if those citizens who will bear the costs are well informed, it may not be worth their while to fight back. Because the costs of the program are spread over the population as a whole, any given peanut consumer's share is low, and it is not worth the time and effort to organize opposition. In contrast, the benefits are relatively concentrated, making political organization worthwhile for potential beneficiaries.

Other Actors

Without attempting to be exhaustive, we list a few other parties that affect government fiscal decisions.

Through court decisions, the judiciary has major effects on government spending. Judges have mandated public expenditures on items as diverse as bilingual education in the public schools and prison remodeling. A striking example occured when a federal judge in Missouri ordered Kansas City to spend $1.2 billion in order to construct school facilities that he believed would attract white families into mostly minority districts. The judge ordered local governments to increase taxes to finance the plan [Blumstein, 1995, p. A13].

Journalists can affect fiscal outcomes by bringing certain issues to public attention. For example, the widespread publicity given to crumbling bridges and roads has induced a number of jurisdictions to increase spending on infrastructure.

Finally, given that information is potentially an important source of power, experts can influence public-sector decisions. Legislative aides who gain expertise on certain programs often play important roles in drafting statutes. There are also experts outside the government. Academic social scientists, environmental engineers, and others seek to use their expertise to influence economic policy. Economists love to quote John Maynard Keynes's [1965/1936, p. 383] famous dictum "the ideas of economists and political philosophers, both when they are right and when they are wrong, are more powerful than is commonly understood. Indeed, the world is ruled by little else." However, it is extremely difficult to determine whether social science research influences policy, and if so, through what channels this influence operates.

Table 6.6 **Ratio of government expenditures to GDP in selected countries**
(selected years)

Year	Canada	Switzerland	United Kingdom
1900	9.5	n.a.	14.4
1910	11.4	n.a.	12.7
1920	16.1	n.a.	26.2
1930	18.9	15.9	26.1
1940	23.1	19.2	30.0
1950	22.1	19.9	39.0
1960	29.7	17.7	31.9
1970	31.2	21.3	33.2
1980	37.8	29.3	41.8
1990	46.0	33.6	41.9
2001	37.4	n.a.	38.8

n.a.   Not available.

SOURCE: Years before 1970 from Pommerehne, "Quantitative Aspects of Federalism: A Study of Six Countries," in *The Political Economy of Fiscal Federalism*, ed. Wallace Oates (Lexington, MA: D C Heath, 1977), p. 310. Subsequent years computed from various editions of *National Accounts*, vol. 2 (Paris: Organization for Economic Cooperation and Development), except for 2001, which is from US Census Bureau, *Statistical Abstract of the United States 2002*, p. 838.

Explaining Government Growth

Much of the concern about political economy issues has been stimulated by the growth of government. As documented in Chapter 1, public expenditures in the United States have grown enormously over the long run, both in absolute terms and proportionately. A growing public sector is not unique to the United States, as the figures for a few other Western countries in Table 6.6 indicate. Thus, as we seek explanations for the growth of government, care must be taken not to rely too heavily on events and institutions that are peculiar to the US experience. Some of the most prominent theories follow. They are not necessarily mutually exclusive. No single theory accounts for the whole phenomenon. Indeed, even taken together, they still leave much unexplained.

Citizen Preferences.   Growth in government expenditure is an expression of the preferences of the citizenry. Suppose the median voter's demand for public sector goods and services (G) is some function (f) of the relative price of public sector goods and services (P) and income (I):

$$G = f(P,I) \tag{6.1}$$

There are many different ways such a demand function can lead to an increasing proportion of income devoted to the public sector. Suppose that when income increases by a given percentage, the quantity demanded of public goods and services increases by a greater percentage—the income elasticity of demand is greater than one. If so, the process of income growth by itself leads to an ever-increasing share of income going to the public sector, other things being the same.[13] Similarly, if the price elasticity of demand for *G* is less than one and *P* increases over time, the government's share of income can increase.

The important point is that the increase in the relative size of the public sector does not necessarily imply something is "wrong" with the political process. Government growth could well be a consequence of the wishes of voters, who rationally take into account its opportunity cost in terms of forgone consumption in the private sector. The question then becomes whether the actual changes in *P* and *I* over time could have accounted for the observed historical changes in *G*. To answer this question, Borcherding [1985] begins by computing the actual percentage changes in *P* and *I* that have occurred over time. He then multiplies the percentage change in *P* by an econometric estimate of the elasticity of *G* with respect to *P*, and the percentage change in *I* by the elasticity with respect to *I*. This calculation yields the percentage change in *G* attributable solely to changes in *P* and *I*. Borcherding then compares this figure with the actual change in *G* and finds that only about 38 percent of the growth in US public budgets can be explained by Equation (6.1). While this is an admittedly rough calculation, it does suggest that more is going on than a simple median voter story can explain.

Marxist View.   Some Marxist theories view the rise of state expenditure as inherent to the political-economic system. In the Marxist model, the private sector tends to overproduce, so the capitalist-controlled government must expand expenditures to absorb this production. Typically, this is accomplished by augmenting military spending. At the same time, the state attempts to decrease worker discontent by increasing spending for social services. Eventually, rising expenditures outpace tax revenue capacity, and the government collapses.

Musgrave [1980] argues that the historical facts contradict this analysis. "There is little evidence . . . [that] expenses directed at appeasing social unrest [have] continuously increased" [p. 388]. It is also noteworthy that in Western Europe, the enormous increase in the size and scope of government in the post–World War II era has been accompanied by anything but a resurgence in militarism. The main contribution of this Marxist analysis is its explicit recognition of the links between the economic and political systems as sources of government growth.

Chance Events.   In contrast to the theories that view government growth as inevitable are those that consider it to be the consequence of chance events. In "normal" periods there is only moderate growth in public expenditure.

---

[13] The hypothesis that government services rise at a faster rate than income is often called **Wagner's Law,** after Adolph Wagner, the 19th-century economist who formulated it.

Occasionally, however, external shocks to the economic and social system "require" higher levels of government expenditure and novel methods of financing. Even after the shock disappears, higher levels continue to prevail because of inertia. Peacock and Wiseman [1967] call this the *displacement effect*. Examples of shocks are the Great Depression, World War II, the Great Society, and the Vietnam War.

Changes in Social Attitudes.   Popular discussions sometimes suggest that social trends encouraging personal self-assertiveness lead people to make extravagant demands on the political system. At the same time, widespread television advertising creates unrealistically high expectations, leading to a "Santa Claus mentality" that causes people to lose track of the fact that government programs do have an opportunity cost.

However, one could just as well argue that people undervalue the benefits of government projects instead of their costs. In this case, the public sector is too small, not too big. More generally, although recent social phenomena might account for some movement in the growth of government expenditure, it has been going on for too many years and in too many places for this explanation to have much credibility.

Income Redistribution.   Government grows because low-income individuals use the political system to redistribute income toward themselves. The idea is that politicians can attract voters whose incomes are at or below the median by offering benefits that impose a net cost on those whose incomes are above the median. As long as average income exceeds the median, and the mechanisms used to bring about redistribution are not too detrimental to incentives, politicians can gain votes by increasing the scope of government-sponsored income distribution. Suppose, for example, that there are five voters whose incomes are $5,000; $10,000; $15,000; $25,000; and $40,000. The median income is $15,000 and the average income is $19,000. A politician who supports government programs that transfer income to those with less than $25,000 will win in majority voting. Consistent with this story is the notion that as the difference between the median and average income grows, so too does the amount of government sponsored redistribution—the more that income is concentrated at the top, the greater the potential benefits to the median voter of redistributive transfers. According to the literature surveyed by Persson and Tabellini [1999], this is indeed a reasonable characterization of income transfer policy in developed nations.

A possible problem with this theory is that it does not explain why the share of public expenditures increases *gradually* (as in Table 1.1). Why not a huge once-and-for-all transfer as the poor confiscate the incomes of the rich? Because in Western countries, property and/or status requirements for voting have *gradually* been abolished during the last century. In the United States, many of the remaining barriers to voting were removed by civil rights laws passed in the 1960s. Extension of the right to vote to those at the bottom of the income scale increases the proportion of voters likely to support politicians promising redistribution. Hence, the gradual extension of the franchise leads to continuous growth in government, rather than a once-and-for-all increase. This conjecture is consistent with Husted and Kenny's [1997] analysis of state spending patterns from 1950 to 1958. During this period, a number of states eliminated poll taxes and literacy tests, which led to higher voter turnout, particularly among the poor. In such states, there was "a sharp rise in welfare spending but no change in other spending" (p. 54).

A limitation of this theory is that it fails to explain the methods used by government to redistribute income. If it is correct, most income transfers should go to the poor and should take the form that would maximize their welfare, that is, direct cash transfers. Instead, as we see in Chapter 7, transfers in the United States are often given in kind and many benefit those in the middle- and upper-income classes.

An alternative view is that income redistribution favors primarily middle-income individuals: "Public expenditures are made for the benefit primarily of the middle classes, and financed by taxes which are borne in considerable part by the poor and the rich."[14] But there are also government transfer programs with rich beneficiaries; see, for example, the discussion of Medicare in Chapter 10.

Transfer programs that benefit different income classes can exist simultaneously, so these various views of government redistribution are not necessarily mutually exclusive. The important point here is their common theme. Politicians, rent-seeking special-interest groups, and bureaucrats vote themselves programs of ever-increasing size.

Controlling Government Growth

As already noted, substantial growth in the public sector need not imply that anything is wrong with the budgetary process. For those who believe that public sector fiscal behavior is more or less dictated by the preferences of the median voter, bringing government under control is a nonissue. On the other hand, for those who perceive growth in government as a symptom of flaws in the political process, constraining the government is very much a problem.

Two types of argument are made in the controllability debate. One view is that the basic problem results from commitments made by government in the past, so there is very little current politicians can do to change the rate of growth or composition of government expenditures. Entitlement programs that provide benefits to the retired, disabled, unemployed, sick, and others are the largest category of uncontrollable expenditures. When we add other items such as payments on the national debt, farm support programs, and certain defense expenditures, about 75 percent of the federal budget is uncontrollable.

---

[14] See Stigler [1970], who dubs this proposition **Director's Law,** after the economist Aaron Director.

Are these expenditures really uncontrollable? If legislation created entitlement programs, it can take them away. In theory, then, many of the programs can be reduced or even eliminated. In reality, both moral and political considerations work against reneging on past promises to various groups in the population. Any serious reductions are likely to be scheduled far in the future, so that people who have made commitments based on current programs will not be affected.

According to the second argument, our political institutions are fundamentally flawed, and bringing things under control is more than just a matter of changing the entitlement programs. A number of remedies have been proposed.

Change Bureaucratic Incentives. Niskanen, who views bureaucracy as a cause of unwarranted government growth, suggests that financial incentives be created to mitigate bureaucrats' empire-building tendencies. For example, the salary of a government manager could be made to depend negatively on changes in the size of his or her agency. A bureaucrat who cut the agency's budget would get a raise. (Similar rewards could be offered to budget-cutting legislators.) However, such a system could lead to undesirable results. To increase his or her salary, the bureaucrat might reduce the budget beyond the point at which marginal benefits equal marginal costs. Do we really want a social worker's salary to increase every time he cuts the number of families deemed eligible to receive welfare payments?

Niskanen also suggests expanding the use of private firms to produce public goods and services, although the public sector would continue to finance them. The issues surrounding privatization were already discussed in Chapter 4.

Change Fiscal Institutions. Most of the focus on bringing government spending under control has been on the budget-making process. Over the years, critics of the process have argued that federal budget making is undisciplined.

Beginning in the 1980s, Congress passed several pieces of legislation whose goal was to impose some discipline. The law now in effect, the **Budget Enforcement Act (BEA)** of 1990, focuses on spending and revenue targets. For example, the budget passed in 1997 put a cap on discretionary spending for each year from 1998 to 2002. (Discretionary spending refers to spending that Congress actually votes on, everything from building tanks to paying civil servants.) An elaborate set of parliamentary rules determines circumstances under which the cap can be exceeded.

The problem is that Congress has shown more than a little creativity when it comes to circumventing the rules. For example, spending does not count against the cap if it is for an unforeseen emergency. In 1999, $4.5 billion to pay for the decennial census was categorized this way. But given that the census is mandated by the Constitution, the need to pay for the year 2000 census arguably could have been predicted over 200 years ago!

Given such anecdotes, it is natural to ask whether fiscal institutions matter at all. If the President and Congress both want to spend a certain amount of money, won't they simply collude to get around whatever rules prevail? Indeed, in 2000 and 2001 discretionary spending exceeded the BEA limits by more than $200 billion. One observer characterized this as a "spending frenzy [that] made a mockery of the BEA" [Schick, 2002, p. 46]. In other words, the legislators didn't even bother with subterfuges; they simply ignored the rules. That said, it is hard to make a strong case one way or the other on the basis of our experience with BEA, because one doesn't know what spending would have looked like in the absence of the law.

Another way to try to study the importance of fiscal institutions is to look at the experience of the states, most of which have rules in their constitutions that forbid deficits in their operating budgets. (The operating budget pays for current expenses, as opposed to the capital budget, which finances long-term investments like roads and buildings.) Importantly, the rules differ in their scope and severity. In some states, the only requirement is for the governor to submit a balanced budget. If it turns out that the governor's projections are incorrect and a deficit results, there is no requirement that the state raise taxes or cut spending—the state can borrow to finance the deficit and carry it into the next year. Other states do not allow such behavior—deficits cannot be carried forward. Accounting tricks of the kind described above are sometimes used to deal with the presence of deficits in these states. For example, the governor of Colorado once reduced his state's deficit by $268 million by delaying payments of a month's worth of wages to state employees by one day, pushing them from the last day of the current fiscal year into the first day of the next. Nevertheless, such gambits are generally not employed.

A natural research strategy is to investigate whether states with strict budgetary rules have smaller deficits and react more quickly to unanticipated shortfalls in revenue than states with lenient rules. There is some evidence that, in fact, this is what happens. It is a bit tricky to interpret this evidence, because we do not know if the outcomes in the states with strict rules really are due to the rules themselves. It could be, for example, that strict rules are passed by fiscally conservative legislators, who would deal aggressively with deficits even without legal compulsion. Several econometric studies have concluded that, even after taking such complications into account, fiscal institutions matter. As Poterba [1997 p. 83] notes, "Although these findings cannot be carried over completely to analyzing the case of federal budget policy . . . , they create a presumption that altering the budget process can affect budget outcomes."

Institute Constitutional Limitations.   The problems with the BEA have been attributed to the fact that it is simply a piece of legislation and as such can readily be amended, suspended, or repealed by a majority vote of both houses of Congress. Some would go further and put budgetary rules into the

Constitution itself. Several constitutional amendments have been proposed; the provisions of the following variant are typical.

1. Congress must adopt a budget statement "in which total outlays are no greater than total receipts."
2. Total receipts may not increase "by a rate greater than the rate of increase in national income."
3. "The Congress and President shall . . . ensure that actual outlays do not exceed the outlays set forth in the budget statement."
4. The provisions can be overridden in times of war.

Most economists—both liberals and conservatives—believe a balanced budget amendment is an ill-conceived idea for several reasons.[15]

First, adopting a statement of outlays and revenues requires making forecasts about how the economy will perform. This problem is sufficiently difficult that forecasters with complete integrity can produce very different estimates. How does the Congress choose among forecasts? If an incorrect forecast is chosen, Congress may be in violation of the law without realizing it! Things become even murkier when one realizes that some forecasts will be biased by political considerations. Those who want to expand expenditures, for example, would encourage forecasts that overestimated tax revenues during the coming year and vice versa.

Second, the amendment fails to define "outlays" and "receipts." By using suitable accounting methods, Congress could easily circumvent the law. For example, the government could simply create various agencies and corporations that were authorized to make expenditures and borrow. Such off-budget activity is already an important way of concealing the actual size of the budget. Alternatively, legislators might try to accomplish with regulation goals they might otherwise have attained by increased expenditure. For example, instead of spending more on health care, Congress could mandate that employers provide insurance for their workers.

Finally, legal scholars have noted some important questions. What happens if there is a deficit? Is the entire Congress put in jail? Could Congress be sued for spending too much? Would federal judges wind up making economic policy? Could a single citizen go to court and obtain an injunction to stop all government activity in the event of a deficit? The BEA experience is informative. When the consequences of complying with the law seemed worse than ignoring the law, the law was ignored.

Nevertheless, constitutional limitations on spending and deficits remain popular. A balanced budget amendment was narrowly defeated in the Congress in 1997. But the proposal is likely to be raised again in the future.

---

[15] See Schultze [1995] for arguments against an amendment, and Buchanan [1995] for arguments in favor.

Conclusions

Public decision making is complicated and not well understood. Contrary to simple models of democracy, there appear to be forces pulling government expenditures away from levels that would be preferred by the median voter. However, critics of the current budgetary process have not come up with a satisfactory alternative. The formulation of meaningful rules and constraints for the budgetary process, either at the constitutional or statutory level, is an important item on both the academic and political agendas for the years ahead.

Finally, it should be stressed that a judgment that the current system of public finance is inequitable or inefficient does not necessarily imply that government as an institution is "bad." People who like market-oriented approaches to resource allocation can nevertheless seek to improve markets. The same goes for government.

Summary

Political economy applies economic principles to the analysis of political decision making.

- Economists have studied several methods for choosing levels of public goods in a direct democracy.

  Lindahl pricing results in a unanimous decision to provide an efficient quantity of public goods, but relies on honest revelation of preferences.

  Majority voting may lead to inconsistent decisions regarding public goods if some people's preferences are not single peaked.

  Logrolling allows voters to express the intensity of their preferences by trading votes. However, minority gains may come at the expense of greater general losses.

- Arrow's Impossibility Theorem states that, in general, it is impossible to find a decision-making rule that simultaneously satisfies a number of apparently reasonable criteria. The implication is that democracies are inherently prone to make inconsistent decisions.

- Explanations of government behavior in a representative democracy require studying the interaction of elected officials, public employees, and special-interest groups.

- Under restrictive assumptions, the actions of elected officials mimic the wishes of the median voter.

- Public employees have an important impact on the development and implementation of economic policy. One theory predicts that bureaucrats attempt to maximize the size of their agencies' budgets, resulting in oversupply of the service.

- Rent-seeking private citizens form groups to influence government activity. Special interests can form on the basis of income source, income size, industry, region, or personal characteristics.

- The growth of government has been rapid by any measure. Explanations of this phenomenon include:

  Citizens simply want a larger government.

  The public sector must expand to absorb private excess production.

  Random events (such as wars) increase the growth of government, while inertia prevents a return to previous levels.

  Unrealistic expectations have resulted in increasing demands that ignore the opportunity costs of public programs.

  Certain groups use the government to redistribute income to themselves.

- Proposals to control the growth in government include encouraging private sector competition, reforming the budget process, and constitutional amendments.

Discussion Questions

1. Suppose there are five people—1, 2, 3, 4, and 5—who rank projects A, B, C, and D as follows:

1	2	3	4	5
A	A	D	C	B
D	C	B	B	C
C	B	C	D	D
B	D	A	A	A

   a. Sketch the preferences, as in Figure 6.2.

   b. Will any project be chosen by a majority vote rule? If so, which one? If not, explain why.

2. In 2002 the US Senate passed an agriculture bill. Senators from the northeast voted to subsidize rice farmers in the south, and senators from the south voted to subsidize dairy farmers in the northeast. Which of our models of political decision-making best explains this behavior?

3. Industries in the country of Technologia invest in new equipment that annually increases productivity of private workers by 3 percent. Government employees do not benefit from similar technical advances.

   a. If wages in the private sector are set equal to the value of the marginal product, how much will they rise yearly?

   b. Government workers annually receive increases so that wages remain comparable to those in the private sector. What happens to the price of public services relative to privately produced goods?

   c. If the same quantity of public services is produced each year, what happens to the size of the government (measured by spending)?

4. The Free City of Christiania is a community of about 800 adults and 250 children within the city of Copenhagen. It was set up by "hippies and others" and is not subject to the same laws as the rest of Denmark. "There is no governing council or other administrative body, and everything is decided by consensus. . . . In practice, this means that many decisions are never made. . . . [T]ensions are rising among different groups of residents over how to share and pay for communal responsibilities" [Kinzer, 1996,

p. A3]. Is this outcome consistent with our theories of voting in a direct democracy? What voting procedures would you recommend for Christiania?

5. It is estimated that in the midterm elections of 2002, in the state of California white voters accounted for 76 percent of the voters although they comprised less than half of the state's population. If these figures are correct, what does it tell us about the validity of the predictions of the median voter theorem?

6. In 1998, the people of Puerto Rico held a referendum in which there were five choices—retain commonwealth status, become a state, become independent, "free association" (a type of independence that would delegate certain powers to the United States), and "none of the above." Discuss the problems that can arise when people vote over five options.

7. Members of the European Union (EU) are required to keep their deficits below 3 percent of Gross Domestic Product. Countries that violate the rule can face huge fines. On the basis of the U.S. experience with the Budget Enforcement Act of 1990, how effective would you predict the EU deficit limits to be? What kind of behavior would you expect to see EU countries exhibit?

8. The discussion of rent-seeking in this chapter noted that peanuts cannot be grown without licenses. The licenses can be sold to nonfarmers, and in fact, many of them are currently owned by firms that have nothing to do with farming, such as insurance companies. Does this fact affect your view of whether or not it would be fair to eliminate the system of licenses for peanut farming? Include in your answer a discussion of the price that owners of the licenses have to pay for them.

9. Assume that the demand curve for milk is given by $Q = 100 - 10P$, where P is the price per gallon and Q is the quantity demanded per year. The supply curve is horizontal at a price of 2.

   a. Assuming that the market is competitive, what is the price per gallon of milk and the number of gallons sold?

b. With the connivance of some politicians, the dairy farmers are able to form and maintain a cartel. (Such a cartel actually operates in the northeastern United States.) What is the cartel price, and how many gallons of milk are purchased? [Hint: The marginal revenue curve (MR) is given by $MR = 10 - Q/5$. Also, remember that the supply curve shows the marginal cost associated with each level of output.]

c. What are the rents associated with the cartel?

d. Suppose that in order to maintain the cartel, the dairy farmers simply give lump-sum campaign contributions to the relevant politicians. What is the maximum contribution they would be willing to make? What is the deadweight loss of the cartel?

e. Suppose that instead of lump-sum contributions to politicians, the diary farmers hire lobbyists and lawyers to make their case in Congress. How does this change your estimate of the deadweight loss associated with this rent-seeking activity?

10. In the aftermath of September 11 there were fears that terrorists would attempt to sabotage the country's food supply. Food safety is under the jurisdiction of the Food and Drug Administration (FDA). Use the Niskanen model of bureaucracy (Figure 6.4) to predict how new concerns over food safety would affect the optimal number of FDA employees and the actual number of employees.

11. According to *The Economist,* "One of the clearest lessons of recent American history is that in a relatively conservative country the Democrats flourish when they move towards the center" (November 16, 2002, p. 30). Which political economy model best explains this lesson?

Selected References

Borcherding, Thomas E. "The Causes of Government Expenditure Growth: A Survey of the U.S. Evidence." *Journal of Public Economics* 28, no. 3 (December 1985), pp. 359–82.

Levin, Jonathan, and Barry Nalebuff. "An Introduction to Vote-Counting Schemes." *Journal of Economic Perspectives* 9 (Winter 1995), pp. 3–26.

Persson, Torsten, and Guida Tabellini. "Political Economics and Public Finance." Working Paper 7097. Cambridge, MA: National Bureau of Economic Research, April 1999.

Poterba, James M. "Do Budget Rules Work?" In *Fiscal Policy: Lessons from Economic Research,* ed. Alan J Auerbach. Cambridge, MA: MIT Press, 1997.

CHAPTER 7

Income Redistribution: Conceptual Issues

A decent provision for the poor is the true test of civilization.
SAMUEL JOHNSON

"In general, the art of government consists in taking as much money as possible from one class of citizens to give to the other." While Voltaire's assertion is an overstatement, it is true that virtually every important political issue involves the distribution of income. Even when they are not explicit, questions of who will gain and who will lose lurk in the background of public policy debates. This chapter presents a framework for thinking about the normative and positive aspects of government income redistribution policy. The next chapter then uses this framework to analyze major government programs for maintaining the incomes of the poor.

Before proceeding, we must discuss whether economists should consider distributional issues at all. Not everyone thinks so. Notions concerning the "right" income distribution are value judgments and there is no "scientific" way to resolve differences on ethical matters. Therefore, some argue that discussion of distributional issues is detrimental to objectivity in economics and economists should restrict themselves to analyzing only the efficiency aspects of social issues.

This view has two problems. First, as emphasized in Chapter 3, the theory of welfare economics indicates that efficiency by itself is an inadequate normative standard. Criteria other than efficiency must be considered when comparing alternative allocations of resources. Of course, one can assert that only efficiency matters, but this in itself is a value judgment.

Second, decision makers care about the distributional implications of policy. If economists ignore distribution, then policymakers will ignore economists. Policymakers may then end up focusing only on distributional issues and pay no attention at all to efficiency. The economist who system-atically takes distribution into account can keep policymakers aware of both efficiency and distributional issues. Although training in economics certainly does not confer a superior ability to make ethical judgments, economists *are* skilled at drawing out the implications of alternative sets of values and mea-suring the costs of achieving various ethical goals.

A related question is whether government ought to be involved in chang-ing the income distribution. As noted in Chapter 1, some important traditions of political philosophy suggest that government should play no redistributive role. However, even the most minimal government conceivable influences the income distribution. For example, when the government purchases mate-rials for public goods, some firms receive contracts and others do not; pre-sumably the owners of the firms receiving the contracts enjoy increases in their relative incomes. More generally, the government's taxing and spending activities are bound to change the distribution of real income.

Distribution of Income

We begin by examining some information on the present distribution of income. Table 7.1 shows Census Bureau data on the US income distribution for selected years since the late 1960s. The table suggests the presence of a lot of inequality. In 2001, the richest fifth of the population received about 50 percent of total income, while the share of the poorest fifth was less than 4 percent. The table also suggests that inequality has increased over time. The share of income going to the poorest two-fifths of families is lower now than it was several decades ago. Interestingly, the increase in inequality has not been confined to the United States. It has occurred in all developed countries, although to a lesser degree [Topel, 1997].

Table 7.1   **The distribution of money income among households**   *(selected years)*

	Percentage Share					
Year	Lowest Fifth	Second Fifth	Middle Fifth	Fourth Fifth	Highest Fifth	Top 5 Percent
1967	4.0	10.8	17.3	24.2	43.8	17.5
1977	4.4	10.3	17.0	24.8	43.6	16.1
1982	4.1	10.1	16.6	24.7	44.5	16.2
1987	3.8	9.6	16.1	24.3	46.2	18.2
1992	3.8	9.4	15.8	24.2	46.9	18.6
1997	3.6	8.9	15.0	23.2	49.4	21.7
2001	3.5	8.7	14.6	23.0	50.1	22.4

SOURCE: US Bureau of the Census, *Current Population Reports*, series P60-209 (Washington, DC: US Govern-ment Printing Office), 2001, URL: http://www.census.gov/hhes/income/histinc/h02.html. These figures do not include the value of in-kind transfers.

Table 7.2 **Who is poor?**

Group	Poverty Rate	Group	Poverty Rate
All persons	11.7%	Under 18 years	16.3%
White	7.4	65 years and older	10.1
Black	20.7	Female households,	
Hispanic origin	19.4	no husband present	26.4

SOURCE: US Bureau of the Census, "Historical Poverty Tables." [WWW Document] URL: http://www.census.gov/prod/2002pubs/p60-219.pdf. Figures are for 2001.

Table 7.3 **Poverty rate** *(selected years)*

Year	Poverty Rate	Year	Poverty Rate
1959	22.4%	1980	13.0%
1960	22.2	1985	14.0
1965	17.3	1990	13.5
1970	12.6	1995	13.8
1975	12.3	2000	11.3
		2001	11.7

SOURCE: US Bureau of the Census, "Historical Poverty Tables." [WWW Document] URL: http://www.census.gov/hhes/poverty/histpov/perindex.html.

Another way to assess the income distribution is to compute the number of people below the **poverty line,** a fixed level of real income considered enough to provide a minimally adequate standard of living.[1] While there is clearly some arbitrariness in determining what is adequate, the notion of a poverty line still provides a useful benchmark. The poverty line for a family of four in 2001 was $18,244. During the same year, the median income—the level half the families were above and half below—was $42,228. In 2001, 32.9 million people were below the poverty line, 11.7 percent of the population.

Table 7.2 shows the proportion of people below the poverty line for various demographic groups. Poverty is particularly widespread among female-headed households in which no husband is present—26.4 percent of such families are below the poverty line. Blacks and individuals of Hispanic origin also have poverty rates substantially above that for the population as a whole.

Table 7.3 depicts changes in the poverty rate over time. The figures suggest that the incidence of poverty in the United States is considerably lower now than it was half a century ago. However, the trend has not been steadily downward.

---

[1] To compute the poverty line, the first step is to estimate the minimum cost of a diet that meets adequate nutritional standards. The second step is to find the proportion of income spent on food in families of different sizes. The poverty line is then found by multiplying the reciprocal of this proportion by the cost of the "adequate" diet.

The question of why there are large disparities in income has long occupied a central place in economics and is far from definitively settled.[2] In the United States and other Western countries, the most important reason for inequality in family incomes is differences in the wages of family heads. Differences in property income (interest, dividends, etc.) account for only a small portion of income inequality. While very important, this observation does not really explain income inequality—one must still account for the large differences in earnings. Earned income depends on items as diverse as physical strength, intelligence, effort, health, education, marriage decisions, the existence of race and sex discrimination, the presence of public welfare programs, and luck. Many economists believe that the key factor driving the increase in inequality in recent years is an increase in the financial returns to education—because of changes in technology such as the widespread introduction of computers into the workplace, workers with college educations are now earning relatively more than their low-education counterparts. But no single item can account for every case of poverty. As we see later, this fact has bedeviled attempts to formulate sensible policies for redistributing income.

Interpreting Distributional Data

The US Census data on the income distribution and the poverty rate receive an enormous amount of public discussion. It is therefore important to know the conventions used to construct these figures and their limitations.

Census Income Consists Only of the Family's Cash Receipts.   To understand the significance of this fact, we require a definition of *income*. A person's income during a given period is the sum of the amount consumed during that period and the amount saved. (A more detailed discussion of the definition of income is included in Chapter 15.) A family's income consists not only of the cash it receives but also **in-kind transfers**—payments in commodities or services as opposed to cash. The official definition's omission of in-kind income can lead to misleading estimates of the poverty rate. Imagine, for example, that your community provided poor people with vouchers that allowed them to live in the best hotel and eat in the fanciest restaurant in town. The official poverty rate would not change at all. While the government does not provide luxuries to the poor, it does provide food stamps, low-income housing programs, and subsidized medical care. According to one estimate, including various noncash benefits from the government would reduce the official poverty rate by more than 20 percent.[3]

One major form of in-kind income is the value of time adults devote to their households. The official data miss important differences in the levels

---

[2] Atkinson [1983] discusses alternative theories of the income distribution; Topel [1997] analyzes recent changes in the distribution.

[3] US Census Bureau, *CPS Annual Demographic Supplement.* Table available at http://www.census.gov/hhes/poverty/poverty01/r&dtable6.html.

of economic resources available to single-parent versus two-parent families and between two-parent families with both parents working versus those with one parent at home. In-kind income is also provided by durable goods. The most important example is a house, which provides its owner with a flow of housing services. The value of these services is the cost to the home-owner of renting a comparable dwelling. Thus, if a family owns a home that could rent for $5,000 per year, then this $5,000 should be included in its income. This observation is cogent given that more than 48 percent of house-holds with incomes below $15,000 are homeowners.

The Official Figures Ignore Taxes.   Specifically, all of the income data are *before*-tax. Hence, the fact that the income tax system takes a larger share of income from high- than from low-income families is not reflected in the numbers. One of the most important programs for redistributing income to the poor, the earned income tax credit (EITC), is run through the income tax. (The program is discussed in Chapter 8.) The EITC transfers over $31 billion annually to low-income families; these transfers are ignored in the poverty statistics.

Income Is Measured Annually.   The concept of income makes sense only if it is measured over some time period. But it is not obvious what the time frame should be. A daily or weekly measure would be absurd, because even rich individuals could have zero incomes during some short time periods. It makes much more sense to measure the flow of income over a year, as the official figures do. However, even annual measures may not reflect an individual's true economic position. After all, income can fluctuate substantially from year to year. From a theoretical point of view, lifetime income would be ideal, but the practical problems in estimating it are enormous.

Although distinguishing between different time periods may seem a mere academic quibble, it is really quite important. People tend to have low incomes when they are young, more when they are middle-aged, and less again when they are old and in retirement. Therefore, people who have *identical* lifetime incomes but are in different stages of the life cycle can show up in the annual data as having *unequal* incomes. Measures based on annual income, such as those in Tables 7.1 through 7.3, suggest more inequality than those constructed on the more appropriate lifetime basis. It has been estimated that using a longer-run measure of welfare than annual income would reduce the proportion of households in poverty by three or four percentage points [Jorgenson, 1998].

There Are Problems in Defining the Unit of Observation.   Most people live with others, and at least to some extent make their economic decisions jointly. Should income distribution be measured over individuals or house-holds? If economies are achieved by living together, should they be taken into account in computing an individual's income? For example, are the members of a two-person household with total income of $30,000 as well off as a single individual with $15,000? Although two may not be able to live as cheaply as one, they may be able to live as cheaply as 1.5. If so, the members of the couple are better off in real terms. But finding just the right adjustment factor is not easy. In this context, note from Table 7.2 that one of the categories is "female households, no husband present." However, according to Bauman's [1997] calculations, including the incomes of household members who are not legally members of a family (such as nonmarried cohabitors) would reclassify out of poverty about 55 percent of the people who are poor according to the official definition.

A related problem crops up when household structure changes over time. Consider what happens when increases in income allow a grandparent to move into an apartment of his or her own instead of sharing quarters with adult children. Now there is a new economic unit, with a fairly low level of income. As measured by the official statistics, things have gotten worse—average income falls and economic inequality rises. But presumably the new living arrangements are making all the individuals involved better off.

We conclude that while the standard measures of income distribution and poverty levels provide some useful information, they should be taken with a grain of salt. This is particularly true when making comparisons over time.

Rationales for Income Redistribution

While income is doubtless distributed unequally, people disagree about whether the government should undertake redistributional policies. This section discusses different views on this matter.

Simple Utilitarianism

Conventional welfare economics posits that society's welfare depends on the well-being of its members. Algebraically, if there are n individuals in society and the ith individual's utility is U_i, then social welfare, W, is some function $F(\cdot)$ of individuals' utilities:[4]

$$W = F(U_1, U_2, \ldots, U_n) \tag{7.1}$$

Equation (7.1) is sometimes referred to as a **utilitarian social welfare function** because of its association with the utilitarian social philosophers of the 19th century.[5] It is assumed that an increase in any of the U_is, other things

---

[4] This discussion ignores the problems that arise if the members of society cannot agree on a social welfare function. See Chapter 6 under "Direct Democracy."

[5] Actually, the utilitarians postulated that social welfare was the sum of utilities, Equation (7.2), but the label is now often used to describe the more general formulation of Equation (7.1).

being the same, increases W. A change that makes someone better off without making anyone worse off increases social welfare.

What does utilitarianism say about whether the government should redistribute income? The answer is straightforward but not terribly informative—redistribute income provided that it increases W. To obtain more specific guidance, let's consider an important special case of Equation (7.1):

$$W = U_1 + U_2 + \cdots + U_N \tag{7.2}$$

Here social welfare is simply the sum of individuals' utilities. This is referred to as an **additive social welfare function.**

Suppose that the government's goal is to maximize the value of W given in Equation (7.2). This social welfare function, together with a few assumptions, allows us to obtain strong results. Assume:

1. Individuals have identical utility functions that depend only on their incomes.
2. These utility functions exhibit diminishing marginal utility of income—as individuals' incomes increase, they become better off, but at a decreasing rate.
3. The total amount of income available is fixed.

With these assumptions and an additive social welfare function, the government should redistribute income so as to obtain *complete equality.*

To prove this, assume that the society consists of only two people, Peter and Paul. (It is easy to generalize the argument to cases where there are more people.) In Figure 7.1, the horizontal distance OO' measures the total amount of income available in society. Paul's income is measured by the distance to the right of point O; Peter's income is measured by the distance to the left of point O'. Thus, any point along OO' represents some distribution of income between Paul and Peter. The problem is to find the "best" point.

Paul's marginal utility of income is measured vertically, beginning at point O. Following assumption 2, the schedule relating Paul's marginal utility of income to his level of income slopes downward. It is labeled MU_{Paul}. Peter's marginal utility of income is measured vertically, beginning at point O'. His marginal utility of income schedule is denoted MU_{Peter}. (Remember that movements to the left on the horizontal axis represent *increases* in Peter's income.) Because Peter and Paul have identical utility functions, MU_{Peter} is a mirror image of MU_{Paul}.

Assume that initially Paul's income is Oa and Peter's is $O'a$. Is social welfare as high as possible, or could the sum of utilities be increased if income were somehow redistributed between Paul and Peter? Suppose that ab dollars are taken from Peter and given to Paul. Obviously, this makes Peter worse off and Paul better off. However, the crucial question is what happens to the *sum* of their utilities. Because Peter is richer than Paul, Peter's loss in utility is smaller than Paul's gain, so the sum of their utilities

FIGURE 7.1

Model of the
optimal distribution
of income

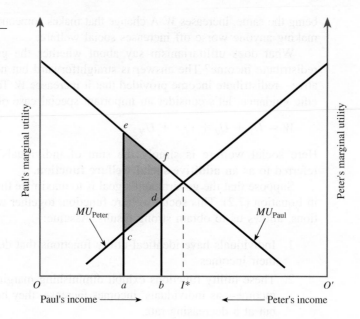

Paul's marginal utility

Peter's marginal utility

MU_{Peter}

MU_{Paul}

e

f

d

c

O a b I^* O'

Paul's income $\longrightarrow$ $\longleftarrow$ Peter's income

goes up. Geometrically, the area under each person's marginal utility of income schedule measures the change in his utility induced by the income change. Distributing *ab* dollars to Paul increases his utility by area *abfe*. Taking the *ab* dollars from Peter decreases his utility by area *abdc*. The sum of their utilities therefore increases by shaded area *cefd*.

Similar reasoning suggests that as long as incomes are unequal, marginal utilities are unequal, and the *sum* of utilities can be increased by distributing income to the poorer individual. Only at point *I**, where incomes and marginal utilities are equal, is social welfare maximized. Full income equality should be pursued.

The policy implications of this result are breathtaking, so the assumptions behind it require scrutiny.

Assumption 1. It is fundamentally impossible to determine whether individuals have identical utility functions. We simply cannot know whether individuals derive the same amount of satisfaction from the consumption of goods, because satisfaction cannot be objectively measured. There are, however, two possible defenses for the assumption.

First, although it cannot be *proved* that people derive the same utility from equal amounts of income, it is a reasonable guess. After all, if people generally do not vary wildly in their observable characteristics—weight, height, and so on—why should their utility functions differ? Further, as Nobel Prize winner Amartya Sen [1999, p. 358] argued, "it is difficult to see how people can understand anything much about other people's minds and feelings, without making some comparisons with their own minds and feelings. Such comparisons may not be extremely precise, but . . . very precise interpersonal comparisons may not be needed to make systematic use of interpersonal comparisons."

Second, one can interpret the assumption not as a psychological statement, but as an *ethical* one. Specifically, in designing a redistributional policy, government ought to act *as if* all people have the same utility functions, whether they do or not.

Clearly, neither of these defenses would convince a skeptic, and the assumption remains troublesome.

Assumption 2.   A more technical, but equally important, objection concerns the assumption of decreasing marginal utility of income. Although the marginal utility of any given *good* may decrease with its consumption, it is not clear that this is true for *income* as a whole. In Figure 7.1, the results change drastically if the marginal utility of income schedules fail to slope down. Suppose the marginal utility of income is instead constant at all levels of income. Then MU_{Peter} and MU_{Paul} are represented by an identical horizontal line. Whenever a dollar is taken from Peter, the loss in his utility is exactly equal to Paul's gain. Thus, the value of the sum of their utilities is independent of the income distribution. Government redistributive policy cannot change social welfare.

Assumption 3.   This assumption means that the total amount of income in the society, distance OO', is fixed. The size of the pie does not change as the government redistributes its pieces. Suppose, however, that individuals' utilities depend not only on income but also on leisure. Each individual chooses how much leisure to surrender (how much to work) to maximize her utility. The taxes and subsidies enacted to redistribute income generally change people's work decisions and diminish total real income. Thus, a society whose goal is to maximize the sum of utilities faces an inescapable dilemma. On one hand, it prefers to equalize the distribution of income. However, in doing so, it reduces the total amount of income available. The optimal income distribution must take into account the costs (in lost real income) of achieving more equality. Some studies suggest these costs may be substantial. Ballard [1996] analyzed a program of cash transfers from high- to low-income individuals, and estimated that the welfare losses for those who lose from the policy are from 1.28 to 2.14 times greater than the gains to the beneficiaries. However, research on this topic is still at a formative stage.

Thus, even the assumption of identical utility functions is not enough to guarantee that the goal of government distributional policy should be complete equality. The answer depends on the methods used to redistribute income and their effects on people's behavior.

The Maximin Criterion

In the utilitarian framework, the form of the social welfare function plays a crucial role in determining the appropriate governmental redistribution policy. So far, we have examined the simple additive social welfare function of Equation (7.2), according to which society is indifferent to the distribution of utilities.[6] If a unit of utility (or "util") is taken away from one individual and given to another, the sum of utilities is unchanged, and by definition, so is social welfare.

Other utilitarian social welfare functions do not carry this implication, and hence yield different policy prescriptions. Consider the following social welfare function:

$$W = \text{Minimum}(U_1, U_2, \cdots, U_n) \tag{7.3}$$

According to Equation (7.3), social welfare depends only on the utility of the person who has the lowest utility. This social objective is often called the **maximin criterion** because the objective is to maximize the utility of the person with the minimum utility. The maximin criterion implies that the income distribution should be perfectly equal, *except* to the extent that departures from equality increase the welfare of the worst-off person. Consider a society with a rich person, Peter, who employs a poor person, Paul. The government levies a tax on Peter, and distributes the proceeds to Paul. However, when Peter is taxed, he cuts production and fires Paul. Moreover, the income that Paul receives from the government is less than his job-related income loss. In this hypothetical economy, satisfaction of the maximin criterion would still allow for income disparities.

The maximin criterion has received considerable attention, principally because of philosopher John Rawls's [1971] assertion that it has a special claim to ethical validity. Rawls's argument relies on his notion of the **original position,** an imaginary situation in which people have no knowledge of what their place in society is to be. Because of this ignorance as to whether ultimately they will be rich or poor, Rawls believes that in the original position, people's opinions concerning distributional goals are impartial and fair. Rawls then argues that in the original position, people adopt the maximin social welfare function because of the insurance it provides against disastrous outcomes. People are frightened that they may end up at the bottom of the income distribution, and therefore want the level at the bottom as high as possible.

Rawls's analysis is controversial. One important issue is whether decisions that people would make in the original position have any superior claim to ethical validity. Why should individuals' amoral and selfish views in the original position be accorded special moral significance? Further, granted Rawls's view on the ethical validity of the original position, it is not obvious that rational self-interest would lead to the maximin criterion. Rawls's decision makers are so averse to risk that they are unwilling to take any chances. However, people might be willing to accept a small

---

[6] Equation (7.2) does *not* imply that society is indifferent to the distribution of *incomes,* as was proved in the preceding section.

probability of being very poor in return for a good chance of receiving a high income.

Finally, critics have noted that the maximin criterion has some peculiar implications. Feldstein [1976a, p. 84] considers the following scenario: "A new opportunity arises to raise the welfare of the least advantaged by a slight amount, but almost everyone else must be made substantially worse off, except for a few individuals who would become extremely wealthy." Because *all* that is relevant is the welfare of the worst-off person, the maximin criterion indicates that society should pursue this opportunity. Intuitively, however, such a course seems unappealing.

Pareto Efficient Income Redistribution

Our discussion of both additive and maximin social welfare functions assumed that redistribution makes some people better off and others worse off. Redistribution was never a Pareto improvement—a change that allowed all individuals to be at least as well off as under the status quo. This is a consequence of the assumption that each individual's utility depends on his or her income only. In contrast, imagine that high-income individuals are altruistic, so their utilities depend not only on their own incomes but those of the poor as well. Under such circumstances, redistribution can actually be a Pareto improvement.

Assume that if (rich) Peter were to give a dollar of income to (poor) Paul, then Peter's increase in satisfaction from doing a good deed would outweigh the loss of his own consumption. At the same time, assume that Paul's utility would increase if he received the dollar. Both individuals would be made better off by the transfer. Indeed, efficiency requires that income be redistributed until Peter's gain in utility from giving a dollar to Paul just equals the loss in Peter's utility caused by lower consumption. Suppose that it is difficult for Peter to bring about the income transfer on his own, perhaps because he lacks enough information to know just who is really poor. Then if the government costlessly does the transfer for Peter, efficiency is enhanced.

In a formal sense, this is just an externality problem. Paul's behavior (his consumption) affects Peter's welfare in a way that is external to the market. As usual in such cases, government may be able to increase efficiency. Pushing this line of reasoning to its logical extreme, one can regard the income distribution as a public good, because everyone's utility is affected by the degree of inequality. Suppose that each person would feel better off if the income distribution were more equal. No individual acting alone, however, is willing to transfer income to the poor. If the government uses its coercive power to force *everyone* who is wealthy to redistribute income to the poor, economic efficiency increases.

Although altruism doubtless plays an important part in human behavior, it does not follow that altruistic motives explain the majority of government income redistribution programs. This argument *assumes* that in the absence of coercion, people will contribute less than an efficient amount to the poor. Some argue, however, that if people really want to give to the poor, they do so—witness the billions of dollars in charitable contributions made each year.

There are other reasons self-interest might favor income redistribution. For one, there is always some chance that through circumstances beyond your control, you will become poor. An income distribution policy is a bit like insurance. When you are well off, you pay "premiums" in the form of tax payments to those who are currently poor. If bad times hit, the "policy" pays off, and you receive relief. The idea that government should provide a safety net is an old one. The 17th-century political philosopher Thomas Hobbes [1963/1651, pp. 303–4] noted, "And whereas many men, by *accident* become unable to maintain themselves by their labour; they ought not to be left to the charity of private persons; but to be provided for, as far forth as the necessities of nature require, by the laws of the Commonwealth" [emphasis added].

In addition, some believe that income distribution programs help purchase social stability. If poor people become *too* poor, they may engage in antisocial activities such as crime and rioting. A Norwegian businessman, commenting on his government's very large redistributional program, said, "It may be costly but there is social peace." The link between social stability and changes in income distribution is not totally clear, however. Some social commentators argue that in the United States, at least, the distribution of income has been of little political importance, perhaps because of an individualist strain in the characters of its citizens [Kristol, 1997].

Nonindividualistic Views

The views of income distribution discussed so far have quite different implications, but they share a utilitarian outlook. In each, social welfare is some function of individuals' utilities, and the properties of the optimal redistribution policy are *derived* from the social welfare function. Some thinkers have approached the problem by specifying what the income distribution should look like independent of individuals' tastes. As Fair [1971, p. 552] notes, Plato argued that in a good society the ratio of the richest to the poorest person's income should be at the most four to one. Closely related is the idea that inequality *per se* is undesirable. Suppose, for example, that the incomes of high-income individuals increase without low-income individuals becoming any worse off. Standard utilitarian considerations suggest that this would be a good thing for society, while those who are averse to inequality would consider it a bad thing. Many in the latter group believe that, as a first principle, incomes should be distributed equally.[7]

A less extreme proposal is that only special commodities should be distributed equally, a position sometimes called **commodity egalitarianism.** In

---

[7] This view is considerably stronger than that of Rawls, who allows inequality as long as it raises the welfare of the worst-off individual.

some cases, this view has considerable appeal. Most people believe that the right to vote should be distributed equally to all, as should the consumption of certain essential foodstuffs during times of war. Other types of commodity egalitarianism are more controversial. Should all American children consume the same quality of primary school education, or should some families be allowed to purchase more? Should everyone receive the same type of health care? Clearly, limiting the range of the "special" commodities is a difficult problem.

Interestingly, a position that bears at least a close resemblance to commodity egalitarianism can be rationalized on the basis of conventional welfare economics. Assume that Henry cares about Catherine's welfare. Specifically, Henry's utility depends on his own income as well as Catherine's level of *food consumption,* as opposed to her *income.* (This might be due to the fact that Henry does not approve of the other commodities Catherine might consume.) In effect, then, Catherine's food consumption generates a positive externality. Following the logic developed in Chapter 5, efficiency may be enhanced if Catherine's food consumption is subsidized, or perhaps if food is provided to her directly. In short, when donors care about recipients' consumption of certain commodities, a policy of redistributing income via these commodities can be viewed as an attempt to correct an externality.

Other Considerations

Processes versus Outcomes.   The positions discussed earlier take for granted that individuals' incomes are common property that can be redistributed as "society" sees fit. No attention is given to the fairness of either the processes by which the initial income distribution is determined or of the procedures used to redistribute it. In contrast, some argue that a just distribution of income is defined by the *process* that generated it. For example, it is a popular belief in the United States that if "equal opportunity" (somehow defined) were available to all, then the ensuing outcome would be fair, *regardless* of the particular income distribution it happened to entail. Hence, if the process generating income is fair, there is no scope for government-sponsored income redistribution.

Arguing along these lines, the philosopher Robert Nozick [1974] has attacked the use of utilitarian principles to justify changes in the distribution of income. He argues that how "society" should redistribute its income is a meaningless question because "society" per se has no income to distribute. Only *people* receive income, and the sole possible justification for government redistributive activity is when the pattern of property holdings is somehow improper. Nozick's approach shifts emphasis from the search for a "good" social welfare function to a "good" set of rules to govern society's operation. The problem is how to evaluate social processes. It is hard to judge a process independent of the results generated. If a "good" set of rules consistently generates outcomes that are undesirable, how can the rules be considered good? That said, some argue that the distribution of income generated by the market does, in fact, accord with conventional notions of justice: "The market does reward hard work, diligence, honesty, thrift, and so on, and this accords well with most concepts of justice. . . . The point . . . is not that the market distribution is totally just but that over a broad range, it is likely to be closer to most people's conception of justice than the alternatives" [Browning, 2002, p. 511].

Mobility.   An alternative argument against governmental redistributive policies is that, with sufficient social mobility, the distribution of income is of no particular ethical interest. Suppose that those at the bottom of the income distribution (or their children) will occupy higher rungs on the economic ladder in future years. At the same time, some other people will move down, at least in relative terms. Then, distributional statistics that remain relatively constant over time conceal quite a bit of churning *within* the income distribution. Even if people at the bottom are quite poor, it may not be a major social problem if the people who are there change over time. Interestingly, this notion seems to be consistent with survey information on people's attitudes toward income redistribution. To the extent they perceive that they have a chance to move upward in society, even relatively poor people say that they do not support income redistributive policies [Alesina and La Ferrara, 2001].

There have been several studies of income mobility. According to calculations by Gottschalk [1997, p. 37], of those who were in the lowest one-fifth of the earnings distribution in 1974, only 42 percent were there in 1991. Of those who were in the top one-fifth in 1974, only 54 percent were there in 1991. The United States is clearly not a stratified society. On the other hand, there is probably not sufficient mobility to convince utilitarians that income inequality is unimportant.

Corruption.   An argument in favor of redistribution is that extreme inequality can lead to the subversion of legal, political, and regulatory institutions. A society cannot flourish economically unless property rights are secure. This is because growth requires investment, and people will not invest if they fear that their property will be taken from them, either by other individuals or by the government. Extreme inequality enters the story because if some people are much richer than others, they may be able to use some of their money to corrupt the courts and the political process so that they can steal from others with impunity. Glaeser and Shleifer [2002b] find some evidence that in countries where the rule of law is relatively weak (such as the transition economies of Eastern Europe), inequality does have a detrimental effect on economic growth.

Expenditure Incidence

We turn now from a discussion of whether the government *ought* to redistribute income to analytical problems in assessing the effects of *actual* government redistributive programs. The impact of expenditure policy on the distribution of real income is referred to as **expenditure incidence.** The government influences income distribution through its taxation as well as its expenditure policies. (We defer a discussion of the tax side to Chapter 12.) Expenditure incidence is difficult to determine for several reasons, which follow.

Relative Prices Effects

Suppose that the government decides to subsidize the consumption of low-income housing. How does this affect the distribution of income? A first guess would be that the people who get the subsidy gain and those who pay the taxes lose. If those who pay the taxes have higher incomes than the subsidy recipients, the distribution of income becomes more equal.

Unfortunately, this simple story may be misleading. If the subsidy induces poor people to demand more housing, then the *pre*-subsidy cost of housing may rise. Therefore, the subsidy recipients do not benefit to the full extent of the subsidy; the landlords reap part of the gain. However, on theoretical grounds alone it cannot be determined how much, if at all, housing prices are bid up. As shown in Chapter 12, this depends on the shapes of the supply and demand curves for housing.

A housing subsidy program also affects the incomes of people who supply the inputs used in its construction. Thus, wages of workers in the building trades increase, as do prices of construction materials. If the owners of these inputs are middle and upper class, this will tend to make the distribution less equal.

More generally, any government program sets off a chain of price changes that affects the incomes of people both in their roles as consumers of goods and as suppliers of inputs. A spending program that raises the relative price of a good you consume intensively makes you worse off, other things being the same. Similarly, a program that raises the relative price of a factor you supply makes you better off. The problem is that it is very hard to trace all the price changes generated by a particular policy. As a practical matter, economists usually assume that a given policy benefits only the recipients and the effects of other price changes on income distribution are minor. In many cases, this is probably a good assumption.

Public Goods

Substantial government expenditure is for public goods—goods that may be consumed simultaneously by more than one person. As noted in Chapter 4, the market does not force people to reveal how much they value public goods. But if we do not know how much each family values a public good, how can we determine its impact on the income distribution? The government spent about $349 billion on defense in 2002. How much in dollar terms did this increase the real income of each family? Did each benefit by the same amount? If not, did the poor benefit less than the rich, or vice versa?

It is impossible to answer questions like these definitively. Unfortunately, alternative answers based on equally plausible assumptions have very different implications. Menchik [1991] examined the distributional implications of expenditures on public goods such as defense using two different assumptions: *(a)* a family's share of the benefit is in proportion to its income, and *(b)* its share is proportional to the number of people in it. Under assumption *(a),* the lowest one-fifth of the population would have its income increased by 3.8 percent of defense expenditures, while under assumption *(b),* its income would be increased by 14.6 percent of these expenditures. The results are clearly very sensitive to the assumptions.

Valuing In-Kind Transfers

Over the past several decades, the Agriculture Department has given away more than 3 billion pounds of surplus cheese, butter, and dried milk to poor Americans. The surplus food program is just one example of an in-kind transfer policy. We often think of in-kind transfers as being directed toward lower-income individuals: food stamps, Medicaid, and public housing come to mind. However, middle- and upper-income people also benefit from in-kind transfers. A prominent example is education.

Unlike pure public goods, in-kind transfers are not consumed by everyone. Nevertheless, estimating their value to beneficiaries is difficult. A convenient assumption is that a dollar spent by the government on an in-kind transfer is equivalent to a dollar increase in the recipient's income. Unfortunately, there is no reason to believe in-kind transfers are valued by beneficiaries on a dollar per dollar basis.

To see why, consider Jones, a typical welfare recipient who divides her monthly income of $300 between cheese and "all other goods." The market price of cheese is $2 per pound, and the units of "all other goods" are measured so that the price per unit is $1. In Figure 7.2, Jones's consumption of cheese is measured on the horizontal axis, and her consumption of all other goods on the vertical. Jones's budget constraint is line AB.[8] Assuming Jones maximizes her utility, she consumes bundle E_1, which consists of 260 units of all other goods and 20 pounds of cheese.

Now suppose the government provides Jones with 60 pounds of cheese per month, which she is prohibited from reselling on the market. How does introduction of the cheese program change her situation? At any level of consumption of all other goods, Jones can now consume 60 more pounds of cheese than previously. Geometrically, her new budget constraint is found by moving 60 units to the right of each point on AB, yielding AFD. The highest indifference curve that she can reach subject to constraint AFD is curve U in Figure 7.2. It touches the constraint at its "corner"—at point F, where Jones's consumption of cheese is 60 and her consumption of all other goods is 300.

Compared to her original consumption bundle, Jones's consumption of both cheese and all other goods has gone up. Because the government provides

---

[8] For details on how to construct budget lines, see the appendix at the end of the book.

FIGURE 7.2

An in-kind transfer
results in a lower
utility level than a
cash transfer

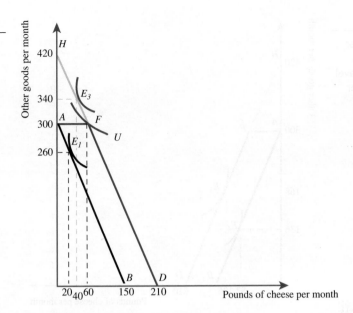

her with free cheese, Jones can use money that would have been spent on
cheese to buy more of all other goods.

Now suppose that instead of giving Jones 60 pounds of cheese, the
government gives her cash equal to its market value, $120 (= 60 pounds ×
$2 per pound). An increase in income of $120 leads to a budget line that
is exactly 120 units above *AB* at every point, represented in Figure 7.2
as line *HD*. Note that the cash transfer allows Jones to consume along segment *HF*. This opportunity was not available under the cheese program
because Jones was not allowed to trade government cheese for any other
goods.

Facing budget line *HD*, Jones maximizes utility at point E_3, where she
consumes 340 of all other goods and 40 pounds of cheese. Comparing points
E_3 and *F* we can conclude that (1) under the cash transfer program, Jones
consumes less cheese and more of all other goods than under the cheese
giveaway program; and (2) $120 worth of cheese does *not* make Jones as
well off as $120 of income. Because E_3 is on a higher indifference curve
than point *F*, the cash transfer makes her *better* off. Intuitively, the problem
with the cheese program is that it forces Jones to consume the full 60 pounds
of cheese. She would prefer to sell some of the cheese and spend the proceeds
on other goods.

Is an in-kind transfer always worse than the cash equivalent? Not necessarily. Figure 7.3 depicts the situation of Smith, whose income is identical to Jones's, and who therefore faces exactly the same budget constraints
(*AB* before the cheese program and *AFD* afterward). However, Smith has
different tastes and thus a different set of indifference curves. Before the

FIGURE 7.3

An in-kind transfer
can also result in
the same utility level
as a cash transfer

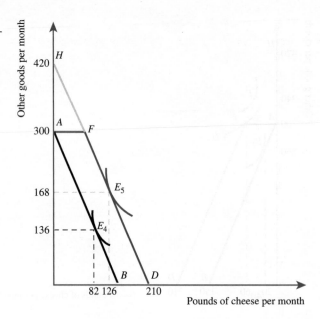

subsidy, he maximizes utility at point E_4, consuming 136 units of all other goods and 82 pounds of cheese. After the subsidy, he consumes 168 units of all other goods and 126 pounds of cheese. Smith would not be better off with a cash transfer because his most preferred point along HD is available under the cheese subsidy anyway. Because Smith is happy to consume more than 60 pounds of cheese, the restriction that he consume at least 60 pounds does him no harm.

Thus, we cannot know for certain whether an in-kind transfer is valued less than a direct income transfer. Ultimately, the answer has to be found by empirical analysis. For example, several studies of the consumption patterns of the poor suggest that a dollar received in housing subsidies is worth only about 90 cents received in cash [Crews, 1995].[9]

Another problem with in-kind transfer programs is that they often entail substantial administrative costs. In the cheese program just discussed, costs are incurred for storage, transportation, and distribution of the cheese. (The costs are so large that some communities choose not to participate.) Similarly, administrative costs of the food stamp program could be reduced if beneficiaries simply received checks instead of coupons redeemable for food.

Reasons for In-Kind Transfers

As we show in the next chapter, in-kind transfers involving food, housing, and medical care play an important role in US income maintenance policy.

---

[9] The structure of housing programs differs somewhat from the cheese program just analyzed because recipients have to pay some price for the housing. But the basic idea is the same. For further details, see the next chapter.

If in-kind transfers are less satisfactory than cash from the recipients' point of view *and* entail more administrative costs, how can we account for their presence? There are a number of possible explanations. Several relate to our earlier discussion of normative issues. In particular, commodity egalitarianism may play an important factor in distributional policy. For instance, the US Congress once explicitly set as a national goal "a decent home and a suitable living environment for every American family." Note the distinction between this goal and "enough income so that every American family can live in a decent home, if it chooses."

Moreover, in-kind transfers may also help curb welfare fraud. The discussion so far has assumed there are no problems in identifying who is eligible to receive a transfer and who is not. In reality, this is not the case, and people who do not qualify are sometimes able to obtain benefits. In-kind transfers may discourage ineligible persons from applying because some middle-class people may be quite willing to lie to receive cash, but less willing to lie to obtain a commodity they do not really want. This is especially true if the commodity is difficult to resell, like an apartment in a public housing project. In the same way, creating hassles for welfare recipients (waiting in line, filling out a lot of forms) may discourage those who are not "truly needy" from applying. Thus, there is a trade-off. On one hand, a poor person would prefer $500 in cash to $500 worth of public housing. But if the in-kind program leads to less fraud, more resources can be channeled to people who really need them. However, many would argue that the government has created far more than the optimal number of administrative hurdles for welfare recipients. For example, in 2003 the Bush administration proposed that to receive free school lunches, students would have to provide evidence, such as pay stubs, that their parents' incomes were sufficiently low. Some observers viewed this as an unfair burden on the children.

Finally, in-kind transfers are attractive politically because they help not only the beneficiary but also the producers of the favored commodity. A transfer program that increases the demand for housing benefits the building industry, which therefore is willing to lend its support to a political coalition in favor of the program. Similarly, the agricultural interests have always been avid supporters of food stamps. When the state of Oregon asked permission to convert food stamps into cash for welfare recipients several years ago, the idea was blocked by members of Congress from agricultural states. In the same way, the public employees who administer the various in-kind transfer programs put their political support behind them. For example, bureaucrats in the Department of Housing and Urban Development have traditionally registered vigorous opposition to proposals that subsidized housing be phased out and replaced with cash grants.

These explanations for in-kind transfers are not mutually exclusive, and they probably have all influenced policy design.

Conclusion

We have surveyed a wide range of opinions concerning the desirability of explicit governmental policies to redistribute income. The views run the gamut from engineering complete equality to doing nothing. The scope of disagreement is not surprising. Setting a distributional objective is no less than formalizing one's views of what a good society should look like, and this is bound to be controversial. Theories on the optimal income distribution are normative rather than positive. As we see in the next chapter, it is not clear whether any coherent normative theory is consistent with actual US income distribution practices.

We also stressed the difficulties involved in defining income and determining how government policy affects each person's income. Measures of income before intervention are calculated on an annual rather than a lifetime basis. Many important types of income are ignored because of measurement difficulties. Calculating the effect of government spending programs is no easier. These programs change relative prices and therefore real incomes in ways that are hard to discern. Transfers often take the form of public goods and in-kind payments on which it is difficult to put a dollar value. Thus, any evidence on how government programs change the distribution of income should be interpreted with caution.

Summary

- Measuring the extent of poverty is difficult to do. Problems with the government's official poverty figures include: a) they count only cash receipts; b) they ignore taxes; c) they are based on annual income measures; d) they ignore changes in household composition.

- If (1) social welfare is the sum of identical utility functions that depend only on income; (2) there is decreasing marginal utility of income; and (3) the total amount of income is fixed; then income should be equally distributed. These are strong assumptions and weakening them gives radically different results.

- The maximin criterion states that the best income distribution maximizes the utility of the person who has the lowest utility. The ethical validity of this proposition is controversial.

- The income distribution may be like a public good—everyone derives utility from the fact that income is equitably distributed, but government coercion is needed to accomplish

redistribution. Pareto efficient redistribution occurs when no one is made worse off as a result of a transfer.

- Other views of income distribution reject the utilitarian framework. Some believe it is a first principle that income, or at least certain goods, should be distributed equally. Others argue that the distribution of income is irrelevant as long as the distribution arises from a "fair" process.

- A government program can change relative prices, creating losses and gains for various individuals. It is difficult to trace all of these price changes, so economists generally focus only on the prices in the markets directly affected.

- Because people do not reveal how they value public goods, it is difficult to determine how these goods affect real incomes.

- Many government programs provide goods and services (in-kind transfers) instead of cash. Recipients are not legally allowed to sell the goods and services so received. If recipients would prefer to consume less, the value of the in-kind transfer is less than the market price.

■ The prevalence of in-kind transfer programs may be due to paternalism, commodity egalitarianism, administrative feasibility, or political attractiveness.

Discussion Questions

1. "I don't care how rich the very rich are. I care if they became rich in an unethical way, or if they use their riches in a particularly vulgar or revolting way. . . . I wouldn't mind if they lost [their wealth] or had it taxed away. But I don't mind if they keep it either. . . . But I do find poverty of the very poor unlovely. . . . That condition deserves, in my opinion, our most intensive care. I believe that the present focus on inequality of income diverts national attention from it" [Stein, 1996, p. A14]. Do you agree with this statement? Is it consistent with utilitarianism?

2. Suppose there are only two people, Simon and Charity, who must split a fixed income of $100. For Simon, the marginal utility of income is

   $$MU_s = 400 - 2I_s$$

   while for Charity, marginal utility is

   $$MU_c = 400 - 6I_c$$

   where I_c, I_s are the amounts of income to Charity and Simon, respectively.

   a. What is the optimal distribution of income if the social welfare function is additive?

   b. What is the optimal distribution if society values only the utility of Charity? What if the reverse is true? Comment on your answers.

   c. Finally, comment on how your answers change if the marginal utility of income for both Simon and Charity is constant:

   $$MU_c = 400$$

   $$MU_s = 400$$

3. A popular measure of the extent of the poverty problem is the **poverty gap,** which measures how much income would have to be transferred to the poverty population to lift every household's income to the poverty line. What are the conceptual difficulties in such a measure of poverty? [Hint: If the government were to give money to poor families to bring them up to the poverty line, what would happen to their supply of labor? What then would happen to their before-transfer income?]

4. Suppose that the government requires employers to provide day care centers for their workers. Suppose further that the market value of the day care center provided by a particular employer is $5,000 per year. Can we conclude that an employee who takes advantage of the day care center is better off by $5,000 per year? (Hint: Analyze a model in which the individual chooses between two commodities, "hours of day care" and "all other goods.")

5. Consider the following government programs:

   a. Giving a laptop computer to every seventh grader.

   b. Providing free after-school programs for children from impoverished families.

   How might each program affect the distribution of income?

6. An economy consists of two individuals, Lynne and Jonathan, whose utility levels are given by U_L and U_J, respectively.

   a. Suppose that the social welfare function is

   $$W = U_L + U_J.$$

   True or false: Society is indifferent between giving a dollar to Lynne and a dollar to Jonathan.

   b. Now suppose that, instead, the social welfare function is

   $$W = U_L + 8U_J.$$

   True or false: Society values Jonathan's happiness more than Lynne's.

c. Now suppose that, instead, the social welfare function is

$$W = \min[U_L, U_J].$$

True or false: In this society, the optimal distribution of income is complete equality.

7. Consider the model of an in-kind transfer in Figure 7.2. Suppose that it is illegal for a recipient of the cheese to sell it. Nevertheless, there is a black market, where cheese can be sold for $1 per pound. Show how the existence of the black market affects the individual's budget constraint. Does it make her better off?

8. Sherry's utility is U_S and her income is Y_S. Marsha's utility is U_M and her income is Y_M. Suppose it is the case that:

$$U_S = 100Y_S^{1/2}, \text{ and } U_M = 100Y_M^{1/2} + 0.8U_S.$$

Define the *Pareto efficient redistribution,* and explain why the concept is relevant in this situation. Suppose that initially Sherry and Marsha both have incomes of 100. Assuming that the social welfare function is additive, what happens to social welfare if 36 is taken away from Marsha and given to Sherry?

Selected References

Atkinson, A B. *The Economics of Inequality.* Oxford: Oxford University Press, 1983.

Browning, Edgar K. "The Case Against Income Redistribution." *Public Finance Review* 30 (November 2002) pp. 509–30.

Gottschalk, Peter. "Inequality, Income Growth, and Mobility: The Basic Facts." *Journal of Economic Perspectives* 11 (Spring 1997), pp. 21–40.

Jorgenson, Dale W. "Did We Lose the War on Poverty?" *Journal of Economic Perspectives* 12 (Winter 1998), pp. 79–96.

CHAPTER 8

Expenditure Programs for the Poor

And distribution was made to each as had need.

ACTS 4:35

W hile there is a strong consensus among Americans that government should help the poor, there is also enormous controversy over what form such help should take. This chapter discusses the major US expenditure programs aimed at helping the poor.

A Quick Look at Welfare Spending

"Welfare" in the United States is a patchwork of dozens of programs that provide benefits primarily to low-income individuals. These programs are **means-tested**—only individuals whose financial resources fall below a certain level can receive benefits. In 1968, government means-tested assistance accounted for about 1.8 percent of the gross domestic product (GDP). By 2000, the figure had grown to 4.1 percent. Most of the growth in government transfer programs has been in the form of in-kind assistance. In 1968, cash assistance was 48 percent of all means-tested benefits; it is now only about 21 percent of the total [Burke, 2001, pp. 1, 3].

The importance of in-kind transfers is reflected in Table 8.1, which lists various categories of welfare spending. Although the table provides an adequate overview, it is not a comprehensive "poverty budget." This is because some programs that are not explicitly redistributional end up transferring considerable sums to the poor. Social Security is usually considered an insurance program rather than a distributional program (see Chapter 9). Yet Social Security payments are the only source of income for 20 percent of the beneficiaries [www.ssa.gov]. Similarly, the poor receive some unemployment insurance payments and veterans' pensions. In addition, many families that are not below the poverty line receive some sort of assistance

Table 8.1   **Expenditures on major need-tested programs**   *(billions of dollars)*

Program	Federal	State and Local
Medical care	$131.4	$94.3
Cash aid	72.5	19.2
Food benefits	32.2	2.2
Housing benefits	29.3	5.6
Education	19.0	1.3
Services	14.2	6.5
Jobs/training	6.2	1.1
Energy aid	1.6	0.085

SOURCE: Burke [2001, pp. 7, 8]. Figures are for 2000.

from programs that are targeted to the poor. For example, about 11.6 percent of the households receiving food stamps are above the poverty level [US Department of Agriculture, 2003a].

TANF

From 1935 to 1996 the main government cash transfer program was **Aid to Families with Dependent Children (AFDC).** As the name implies, the program was focused on families with dependent children. Also, in general, only families in which one of the parents was missing were eligible. It was administered jointly by the federal government and the states. Each state determined its own benefit levels and eligibility standards, subject only to broad federal guidelines. Federal law required that an individual's AFDC grant be reduced by a dollar for each dollar she received in income, although certain small amounts of income were disregarded for this purpose.

In 1996 AFDC was superceded by the passage of the Personal Responsibility and Work Opportunity Reconciliation Act. This legislation created a new welfare program called **TANF—Temporary Assistance for Needy Families.** The major components of TANF are:[1]

- **No entitlement.** Under AFDC, anyone whose income was below a particular level and met certain other conditions was *entitled* to a cash benefit indefinitely. TANF ended AFDC and this cash entitlement. The *T* in TANF emphasizes that cash benefits are now available only on a *temporary* and provisional basis. About 6 million families receive TANF benefits each month.

- **Time limits.** In general, individuals cannot receive cash benefits for more than five years (although states can exempt up to 20 percent of their caseloads from this rule). States can set a shorter time limit if they choose.

[1] For additional details, see Burke [2001].

- **Work requirement.** At least 50 percent of single mother recipients and 90 percent of two-parent families must be working or in work preparation programs.

- **Block grants to states.** Under AFDC there was *no* fixed limit on federal spending. Under TANF each state is given a grant to finance welfare spending by the federal government; the size of the grant is fixed in advance. The state uses the grant (supplemented with its own funds) to run welfare as it sees fit, within broad limits. States now have virtually total control over the structure of their welfare systems, including which families to support. States can use their grants to pay for cash benefits, or job-training programs, or programs to eliminate teenage pregnancies and encourage marriage, etc. (But the states cannot loosen the work requirement and payment limits noted above.)

- **Benefit reduction rates.** As a corollary to the power to control the structure of their welfare programs, the states can decide how much to reduce benefits when welfare recipients earn income. Recall that, under AFDC, the reduction was (approximately) one-for-one—for each dollar of earnings, benefits were reduced by one dollar. Nine states and the District of Columbia have continued this policy. The other states have modified the rules.[2] Some have large benefit reduction rates. In Nebraska, for example, for each dollar of earnings, benefits are reduced by 80 cents. On the other hand, in Illinois, the reduction rate is only 33 cents on the dollar. California allows welfare recipients to earn $225 per month before reducing welfare payments, and then takes away 50 cents of benefits for each additional dollar of earnings. States vary not only in their effective tax rates, but also in the benefits they pay to a family with no earnings. For a single-parent family of three, for example, the figure is $164 in Alabama and $801 in Minnesota. In short, welfare recipients' earnings are now subjected to a wide variety of policies.

| Income Maintenance and Work Incentives | The question of whether welfare reduces work effort and increases dependence on the government has dominated discussions of welfare policy for years. In this section we discuss how TANF affects recipients' work decisions. |

The Basic Trade-offs

If we abstract from many of the complexities of TANF's rules, we can characterize a state's policy in terms of two variables. The first is a basic grant that the individual receives if she is not working, G. The second is the rate

---

[2] For details, see Moffitt [2002].

at which the grant is reduced when the recipient earns money, t. Suppose, for example, that a state provides \$300 a month to welfare recipients, but that benefit is reduced by 25 cents for each dollar the individual earns. Then $G = 300$ and $t = 0.25$. If an individual earns \$500, then her benefit is reduced by \$75 ($= 0.25 \times \$300$), leaving her with \$225. Note that the benefit reduction rate is in effect a tax on earnings, which is why we denote it with a t. Note also that at some point, the recipient's earnings become high enough that she no longer receives any welfare at all. In this example, when she earns \$1,200, the benefit reduction just equals her basic welfare payment. After that point, t no longer applies because her benefit is already zero.

Algebraically, the benefit received (B) is related to the basic grant, the tax rate, and level of earnings (E) by

$$B = G - tE$$

It follows that the benefit is zero ($B = 0$) when

$$E = G/t$$

or any higher level of E.

These two equations highlight the fundamental dilemmas involved in designing an income maintenance system. The first equation shows us that, for a given program cost, the larger the basic grant, the larger must be the tax rate. That is, a system with good work incentives (a low value of t) might provide little money for those who are unable to work. The second equation shows us that, for a given basic grant, the lower the tax rate, the higher the breakeven level of earnings. But as the breakeven level of earnings increases, so does the number of people who are eligible for welfare, which also increases the costs of the system.

Analysis of Work Incentives

Indifference curve analysis of the individual's choice between leisure and income provides a useful way to see how TANF affects labor supply decisions.[3] Consider Smith, who is deciding how much of her time to devote each month to work and how much to nonmarket activity, which we call *leisure*. In Figure 8.1, the horizontal axis measures the number of hours of leisure. Even if Smith does not work, there is an upper limit to the amount of leisure she can consume, because there are just so many hours in a month. This number of hours, referred to as the **time endowment,** is distance OT in Figure 8.1. We assume all time not spent on leisure is devoted to work in the market. Any point on the horizontal axis therefore simultaneously indicates hours of leisure and hours of work. For example, at point a, Oa hours are devoted to leisure, and the difference between that and the time endowment, OT, represents time spent at work, aT.

---

[3] A verbal discussion of the theory of labor supply was provided in Chapter 2 under "The Role of Theory." The reader may want to consult that discussion before proceeding with the graphical exposition provided here.

FIGURE 8.1

Budget constraint for the leisure/income choice

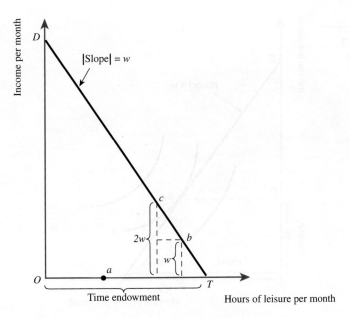

Our first problem is to illustrate how Smith's income, which is measured on the vertical axis, varies with her hours of work. Assume that she can earn a wage of w per hour. Also, for the moment, assume that no welfare is available. Then her income for any number of hours worked is just the product of w and the number of hours. Suppose, for example, Smith does not work at all. If labor is her only source of income, her income is simply zero. This option of zero work and zero income is represented by point T.

If Smith works one hour each week, her consumption of leisure equals her time endowment minus one hour. This point is one hour to the left of T on the horizontal axis. Working one hour gives her a total of w. The combination of one hour of work with a total income of w is labeled point b. If Smith works two hours—moves two hours to the left of T—her total income is $2 \times w$, which is labeled point c. Continuing to compute the income associated with each number of hours of work, we trace out all the leisure/income combinations available to Smith—straight line TD, whose slope, in absolute value, is the wage rate. TD is the analog of the budget constraint in the usual analysis of the choice between two goods. (See the appendix to the book.) Here, however, the goods are income and leisure. The price of an hour of leisure is its opportunity cost (the income forgone by not working that hour), which is just the wage.

To determine Smith's choice along TD, we need information on her tastes. In Figure 8.2 we reproduce the budget constraint TD. Assume that preferences for leisure and income can be represented by normal, convex-to-the-origin indifference curves. Three such curves are labeled i, ii, and iii

FIGURE 8.2

Utility-maximizing choice of leisure and income

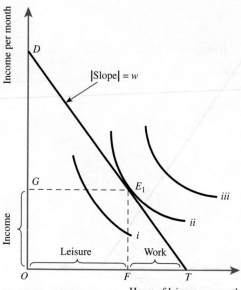

FIGURE 8.3

Budget constraint under TANF

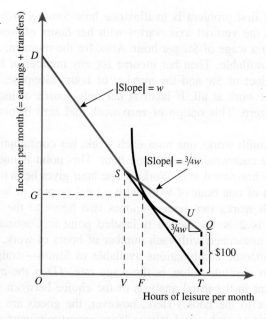

in Figure 8.2. Smith maximizes utility at point E_1, where she devotes OF hours to leisure, works FT hours, and earns income OG.

Suppose now that Smith is eligible to participate in TANF, and that in her state the basic grant is $100 per month and the implicit tax rate is 25 percent. How does TANF change her budget constraint? Figure 8.3 illustrates

FIGURE 8.4

Labor supply
decision under TANF

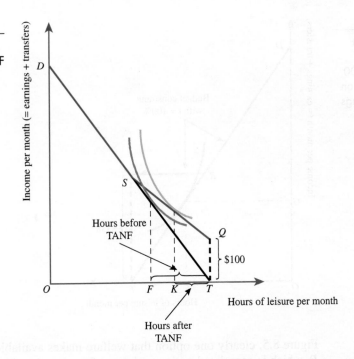

the situation. As before, in the absence of welfare, Smith works *FT* hours and earns *OG*. In the presence of TANF, one option is point *Q*, where no labor is supplied and Smith receives $100 from welfare. If Smith works one hour, she receives *w* from her employer. Simultaneously, her grant is reduced by ¼*w*, still leaving her ahead by ¾*w*. Thus, another point on the budget constraint is *U*, which is one hour to the left of *Q*, and ¾*w* above it. Similarly, Smith continues to receive an effective hourly wage of ¾*w* until she works *VT* hours, at which point her earnings are high enough that she receives no welfare. Thus, the budget constraint is the kinked line *QSD*. Segment *QS* has a slope in absolute value of ¾*w*, segment *SD* a slope of *w*.

As usual, the ultimate work decision depends on the shapes of the individual's indifference curves. As drawn in Figure 8.4, Smith works less than she did before TANF (*KT* hours, as opposed to *FT* before).

As already noted, nine states and the District of Columbia in effect impose a 100 percent tax rate on the earnings of welfare recipients. It is therefore of some interest to analyze the budget constraint and work incentives generated by this special case. Suppose, for concreteness, that an individual operating under such a system has a basic grant of $338.[4] In

---

[4] This was the monthly benefit in 1997 for a single parent with two children and no income in the state of Delaware.

FIGURE 8.5

Budget constraint under a welfare system with a 100 percent tax rate on additional earnings

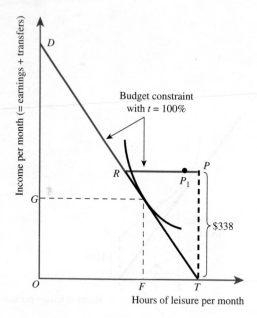

Hours of leisure per month

Figure 8.5, clearly one option that welfare makes available to Smith is point *P*, which is associated with zero hours of work and an income of $338 from welfare. Now suppose that Smith works one hour. Graphically, she moves one hour to the left from *P*. When Smith works one hour, she receives a wage of $*w* from her employer, *but* simultaneously her welfare is reduced by the same amount. The hour of work nets her nothing—her total income remains $338. This is represented by point P_1, where there is one hour of work and total income is $338. This continues until point *R*. Beyond *R*, each hour of work raises her income by $*w*.[5] Thus, the budget constraint is the kinked line *PRD*. Segment *PR* has zero slope, and segment *RD* has a slope whose absolute value is *w*.

How might Smith respond to such incentives? Figure 8.6 shows one distinct possibility: She maximizes utility at point *P*, where no labor is supplied. In no case will a rational person work between zero and *PR* hours. Why should someone work if she can receive the same income by not working?[6]

Of course, a welfare system with *t* = 100 percent does not necessarily induce an individual to stop working. Figure 8.7 depicts the leisure/income choice of Jones, who faces exactly the same budget constraint as Smith in Figure 8.5. However, Jones maximizes utility at point E_2, where she works *MT* hours per month.

---

[5] For simplicity, we ignore the fact that Smith's earnings may be subject to payroll and income taxes.

[6] In a more complicated model, an individual might select a point along segment *PR* to develop her skills or to signal her quality to future employers by maintaining a continuous work history.

FIGURE 8.6

Work decision under
a welfare system
with a 100 percent
tax rate on
additional earnings

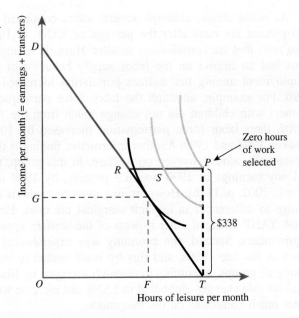

FIGURE 8.7

An individual
chooses to work in
the presence of a
100 percent tax rate

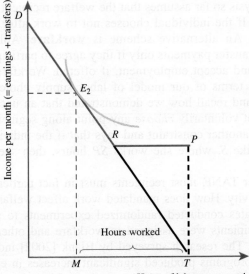

The negative effect on work incentives embodied in Figure 8.6 was one of the major criticisms of AFDC. Indeed, there is considerable evidence that AFDC substantially reduced the labor supply of recipients. In his survey of the research in this area, Moffitt [2002] concluded that AFDC reduced labor supply by 10 to 50 percent among welfare recipients.

As noted above, although several states continued to impose implicit 100 percent tax rates after the passage of TANF in 1996, a number now have rates that are considerably smaller. Have these implicit tax rate reductions had an impact on the labor supply behavior of welfare recipients? Employment among the welfare population increased substantially after 1996. For example, although the labor force participation rates of single mothers with children did not change much from the 1980s into the mid-1990s, their labor force participation increased by 10 percentage points between 1994 and 1999. Another informative finding is that work effort rose substantially among women on welfare. In this group, the proportion who had any earnings in 1990 was 6.7 percent; by 1999 it was 28.1 percent [Blank, 2002, p. 1116]. However, one must be cautious about ascribing this change to differences in implicit marginal tax rates. First, as already indicated, TANF changed other aspects of the welfare system, including work requirements. Second, the economy was experiencing an unprecedented boom in the late 1990s, and this by itself tended to increase employment among all groups. According to research surveyed by Blank [2002], the marginal tax rate changes embodied in TANF did increase work effort, but there is not much consensus on the magnitude.

Work Requirements

The analysis so far assumes that the welfare recipient can choose her hours of work. If the individual chooses not to work after she goes on welfare, so be it. An alternative scheme is **workfare.** Able-bodied individuals receive transfer payments only if they agree to participate in a work-related activity and accept employment, if offered. Workfare can be easily interpreted in terms of our model of labor supply choice. Turn back to Figure 8.6, and recall how we demonstrated that an unconstrained individual would not voluntarily *choose* any point along segment *RP*. Workfare simply adds another constraint and says that if the individual does not choose a point like *S*, where she works *SP* hours, then she receives no welfare at all.

Under TANF, most recipients must in fact participate in some kind of work activity. How does mandated work affect welfare recipients? A number of states conducted randomized experiments to answer this question. Some recipients were assigned to workfare and others, the control group, were not. The research surveyed by Blank [2002] indicates that almost all of these programs produced significant increases in employment and earnings, and decreases in welfare usage. Unfortunately, the mandatory work programs did little to increase income—the increases in earnings were just about offset by losses in welfare benefits. That is, the programs were really not effective at reducing poverty.

This observation forces us to confront the question of whether public concern over how much welfare recipients work is somewhat misplaced. True, an important aspect of any welfare system is the incentive structure it creates. And many people believe that special value should be placed upon work because it helps enhance individual dignity. That said, if the goal of welfare policy were only to maximize work effort, the government could simply force the poor into workhouses, as was done under the English Poor Law of 1834. Designing good transfer systems requires a careful balancing of incentive and equity considerations.

Time Limits

One of TANF's most dramatic innovations was the introduction of time limits—individuals can only receive five year's worth of benefits during their lifetimes. Did this policy succeed in getting people off of welfare? Any answer to this question must begin by noting perhaps the most dramatic statistic associated with TANF—the caseload dropped by over 50 percent between 1994 and 2000 [Blank, 2002, p. 1115]. We cannot attribute this drop in the caseload entirely to the time limits (or any other aspect of TANF) because during the 1990s, the economy was experiencing a boom, and this by itself tended to reduce the number of welfare recipients. Still, most analysts indicate that TANF and its time limits did play a role.

One interesting study along these lines was done by Grogger [2001], who noted that if time limits matter, they should have a bigger effect on welfare families having young children than families whose children are older. Why? Eligibility for TANF ends when the youngest child in the family turns 18. If your child is 13 or over, you may as well use up your benefits, because they will disappear in five years anyway. However, if your child is under 13, it makes sense to get off of welfare as soon as you can, so that you can "bank" your remaining quota of time and use it if you need the money at some later date. Grogger's analysis of the data suggests that time limits have, in fact, been important, accounting for about 12 percent of the decrease in welfare caseloads.

Family Structure

One of the main reasons for the passage of TANF in 1996 was the belief that AFDC had created incentives for low-income women to bear children out of wedlock. The basic idea was that an entitlement to welfare made it possible for low-income women to get by as single mothers. This tendency was reinforced by the fact that, in many states, women lost welfare benefits when they married. The hope was that the time limits on TANF would reverse this behavior. At the same time, a number of states developed specific programs to discourage teenage motherhood. An example is forcing a teen mother to live with her parents to be eligible for welfare.

Did TANF affect the structure of low-income families? The empirical results, unfortunately, are mixed. Some studies indicate positive effects of TANF (for example, more children were living with married parents after TANF than before), while others find no impact at all. It is unsurprising that the results are inconclusive. Marriage and childbearing patterns probably adjust only slowly over time. It is simply too soon to know if TANF has changed family structure.

National versus State Administration

During the debates over TANF, there was great concern that turning the system over to the states would lead to a "race to the bottom" because any state that enacted a generous welfare system would be flooded with poor individuals from other states, forcing it to reduce benefits. This is certainly possible, and there is indeed some statistical evidence that differences in TANF provisions have influenced the migration patterns of low-educated women across jurisdictions [Kaestner, Kaushal, and Ryzin, 2001]. The preliminary evidence, though, is that there has not been a race to the bottom under TANF. Most states kept their basic benefits at about the same level; some actually increased them [Gallagher *et al.,* 1998]. Of course, the usual caveats apply. In particular, TANF came into existence during a boom; during some future economic slowdown, the states might behave quite differently.

In any case, some commentators view the fact that the states can now design very different systems as a real advantage. "Any given state government may do no better than Washington, but the great variety of the former will make up for the deadening uniformity of the latter. And within the states, the operating agencies will be at the city and county level, where the task of improving lives . . . will be informed by the proximity of government to the voices of ordinary people" [Wilson, 1994, p. A10].

Of course, the well-being of the poor under TANF also depends on the other benefit programs that are available to them. We now turn to a discussion of these programs.

The Earned Income Tax Credit

You may be surprised to learn that the largest program for making *cash* transfers to low-income individuals is administered not through the welfare bureaucracy but through the tax system. The **earned income tax credit (EITC)** is a subsidy to the earnings of low-income families. Only the working poor are eligible for the EITC; in this sense, it is thoroughly in sync with TANF's emphasis on linking welfare with work. As its name implies, the subsidy comes in the form of a *tax credit,* which is simply a reduction in tax liability. For example, if you owe the government $1,000 in income taxes but you also have a tax credit of $600, then you only have to pay $400. Importantly, if the EITC exceeds your tax liability, the difference is refunded to you—the government sends you a check. In effect, then, the credit is as good as cash.

Although the EITC has been part of the tax system for a number of years, its scope was dramatically increased in 1993. The annual cost of the EITC is now about $31 billion.

The size of the subsidy depends on the number of children in the family; we consider here the case in which two or more children are present. In 2003, such a family is allowed a tax credit equal to 40 percent of all wage and salary income up to $10,510. Hence, the maximum credit is $4,204 (= 0.40 × $10,510). To help guarantee that only the poor benefit

FIGURE 8.8A

Relationship between earnings and the earned income tax credit*

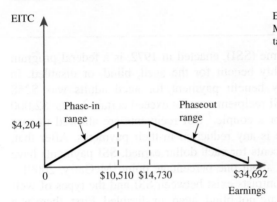

*2003 law for a family with two or more children.

FIGURE 8.8B

Implicit marginal tax rates under the EITC

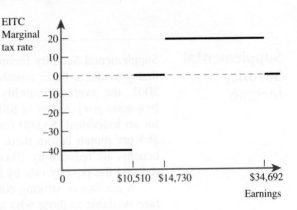

from the credit, it is phased out at incomes between $14,730 and $34,692. For each dollar of earnings in this phaseout range, the credit is reduced by 21.06 cents; at $34,692 of earnings, the credit is entirely exhausted. The system is summarized in Figure 8.8A, which shows the size of the credit for each level of earnings.

One justification for the EITC is to improve work incentives for the poor. In the phase-in range, the federal government adds 40 cents to each dollar of earnings; in effect this is a negative marginal tax rate of 40 percent on earnings. (The tax rate is "marginal" because it is the rate that applies to an additional dollar of earnings.) However, the fact that the credit is taken away creates an implicit positive marginal tax rate in the phaseout range—for each dollar of earnings, the credit goes down by 21.06 cents; in effect, this is a 21.06 percent marginal tax rate (see Figure 8.8B). This is higher than the ordinary income tax rate of 15 percent that applies to the lowest income bracket. Thus, at the same time that the EITC augments incomes of the poor, it can create substantial disincentives to work. This is a potentially serious issue because about 60 percent of the recipients have incomes that put them in the phaseout range of Figure 8.8A [Liebman, 2001a].

Recent research is virtually unanimous that the EITC has increased labor force participation rates. For example, Meyer and Rosenbaum [2001] analyzed data on the labor force behavior of single mothers between 1984 and 1996, a period of time during which several major expansions of the EITC took place. During that time period, the employment rate among single mothers increased from 58.5 percent to 64.5 percent. Meyer and Rosenbaum's estimates indicate that 60 percent of this increase was due to the EITC. On the other hand, there appears to be little evidence that, on net, the EITC affects hours of work for low-income people in the labor force. It is easy to explain this finding in terms of Figure 8.8B—hours of work are encouraged for individuals in the phase-in range but discouraged for those in the phaseout range, and the effects seem to about cancel.

Supplemental Security Income

Supplemental Security Income (SSI), enacted in 1972, is a federal program that provides a basic monthly benefit for the aged, blind, or disabled. In 2001, the average monthly benefit payment for aged adults was $258 [www.ssa.gov]. Assets of SSI recipients cannot exceed certain limits: $2,000 for an individual, $3,000 for a couple.[7] SSI recipients are allowed to earn $65 per month before there is any reduction in their payments. After that, benefits are reduced by 50 cents for each dollar earned. SSI payments have reduced the poverty rate by about one percentage point [McGarry, 2000].

A number of striking contrasts exist between SSI and the types of welfare available to those who are not blind, aged, or disabled. First, there is a uniform minimum federal guarantee for SSI and none for other programs.[8] Second, SSI benefits are considerably higher than the average in other programs. Third, work incentives under SSI are better than in many of the states. The implicit tax rate on additional earnings under SSI is only 50 percent. Further, there are no work mandates.

In recent years, there has been a perception that some recipients of SSI game the system, that is, they fake disabilities in order to receive payments. In response to these perceptions, the disability standards were tightened in 1996. At this point, there is not much evidence with respect to the impact of this change in eligibility rules.

Medicaid

Medicaid is by far the largest spending program for low-income individuals.[9] It was established in 1965 to provide health insurance for recipients of cash welfare programs. Eligibility has grown over time, however. The program, which is administered by the states and funded by both the federal government and the states, now covers children in families whose incomes are substantially above the poverty line, whether or not the parents are on welfare. It also includes low-income pregnant women. The expansion of eligibility has increased the number of recipients over time. In 1988, there were 22.9 million recipients; by 2002, this figure had almost doubled, to 40.1 million [Centers for Medicare and Medicaid Services, 2003]. The increase in the

---

[7] This excludes small amounts for the value of home, automobile, and life insurance policies.

[8] However, at their option, states can supplement the federal benefits.

[9] Medicaid should not be confused with Medicare, which provides health care insurance to the aged. Medicare is not means-tested. See Chapter 10 under "Medicare."

number of recipients has been accompanied by increased program costs. In 1975, the cost of Medicaid was $12.6 billion; by 2001 it was about $219 billion.

States have considerable flexibility in the administration of the program. In particular, states may institute **capitation fee** systems, under which medical care is provided for a particular individual or set of individuals for a fixed monthly fee. One reason for such systems is to hold down costs. The hope is that given that the fee per individual is fixed, health care providers will be careful about ordering medical tests and, in general, attempt to be efficient in the provision of health care services. However, it is not clear that this has been a successful cost containment strategy for Medicaid [Duggan, 2002].

In light of the previous chapter's discussion of cash versus in-kind payments, we might ask why society has chosen to make transfers in the form of medical services such an important component of the welfare system. One explanation is commodity egalitarianism. There appears to be a strong societal consensus that everyone should have access to basic medical services. Elements of paternalism may also be present. Some believe that even if affordable insurance policies were available to poor people, they would lack the foresight to purchase adequate coverage. The existence of Medicaid might also be explained by some of the special-interest-group theories introduced in Chapter 6. The health industry (hospitals, physicians, pharmaceutical firms, etc.) benefits from taxpayer-financed plans to provide medical services to the poor.

Crowding Out

We have noted how the number of Medicaid enrollees has increased over time. But this is not the same as saying how the number of low-income people with health insurance has increased. To the extent that people give up private insurance for themselves or their children when free (to them) Medicaid becomes available, the number of insured individuals does not increase. This phenomenon is referred to as *crowding out*—public insurance crowds out private insurance. Originally, this was not much of a concern for Medicaid, because the eligible were largely indigent and not likely to have insurance anyway. But with the changes in eligibility that allow coverage to those higher up on the income scale, crowding out has become a serious issue.

A number of studies have examined the various expansions of Medicaid and the extent to which they were accompanied by crowding out. Some estimate crowd-out rates as high as 50 percent, although other estimates are lower [McGarry, 2002]. While crowding out is certainly a phenomenon that policymakers should take into account if they contemplate further expansions of Medicaid, we should note that it is not necessarily a bad thing. For example, if families use the money they save on insurance for better nutrition or safer housing, child health might improve. There is, however, no evidence about this possibility one way or the other.

FIGURE 8.9

The Medicaid notch

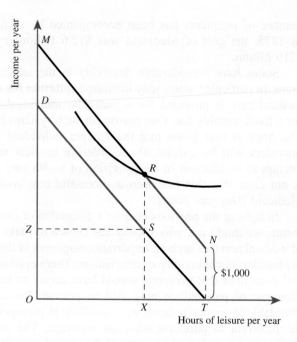

Hours of leisure per year

The Medicaid Notch

As already noted, historically, when families earned enough money to get out of welfare, they immediately lost their Medicaid benefits. The potential loss of these benefits could lead to implicit marginal tax rates of greater than 100 percent, and was a major disincentive to leaving welfare. However, under TANF, families that earn enough to leave welfare remain eligible for Medicaid for 12 months. Further, the Medicaid expansions of the 1980s and 1990s extended coverage to low-income children and pregnant women who have no other ties to the welfare system. For example, a child under the age of six is eligible for Medicaid until his or her family has earnings that are 33 percent above the poverty line.

The possible loss of Medicaid benefits can create work disincentives, which we analyze using our model of leisure-income choice. In Figure 8.9, *DT* is Smith's budget constraint before Medicaid. Now assume that Medicaid is introduced; Smith has a three-year-old child who is eligible for Medicaid; and the value of the Medicaid policy to Smith is $1,000 per year. Assume further than when her income reaches *Z* dollars, her child loses eligibility for Medicaid. Ignoring for simplicity any transfers that Smith receives or taxes that she pays, how does Medicaid affect her budget constraint? One point on the new budget constraint is exactly $1,000 above point *T*—at zero hours of work she has an in-kind income of $1,000. This is represented by point *N*. Moving to the left from *N*, Smith's income increases by her wage rate for each dollar she earns. Medicaid does not change her wage rate, so the slope as she moves away from *N* is the same as the slope of *DT*. At *XT* hours of work, her earnings are *Z*. At this point, her child loses Medicaid eligibility and, in effect, she has $1,000 taken away from her. That is, she moves from R to S. As she moves to the left of S, she again receives her wage rate for each hour of work and moves along segment DS.

Putting this all together, in the presence of Medicaid, Smith's budget constraint is NRSD. Looking at this constraint, you can see why the impact of Medicaid on work incentives is characterized as a "notch." How much does Smith work? A strong possibility is that the highest indifference curve she can attain touches the budget constraint right at the notch, point R. This makes perfect sense—she earns just short of Z dollars, because if she earns one more dollar, she loses a thousand! Thus, Medicaid creates incentives to keep one's earnings below the cutoff level.

Medicaid and Health

A primary reason for initiating Medicaid was to improve the health status of poor people. By all accounts, Medicaid has increased the access of the poor to health care. This information, though, reveals little about the quality of care received by the poor—does it improve their health? Some evidence does suggest that the health of the poor has improved since the start of Medicaid. Increasing the availability of Medicaid has reduced child mortality and led to a small but significant decline in the proportion of low-birthweight babies [McGarry, 2002, p. 818]. Of course, some of this improvement could be due to other factors, such as changes in lifestyle. Although it is difficult to sort out the contribution of various factors, the consensus is that Medicaid played an important role.

Food Stamps and Child Nutrition

A food stamp is a government-issued voucher that can be used only for the purchase of food. (Animal food, alcohol, tobacco, and imported food are not allowed.) In 2001, during an average month 17.3 million people received food stamps, and total benefits were about $16 billion [US Department of Agriculture, 2003b, p. xiii]. The direct cost of the food stamps is paid by the federal government. However, the administration of the program, including distribution of the stamps, is done by the states.

Virtually all poor people are eligible to receive food stamps, including poor families without children and childless single men and women. A household's monthly food stamp allotment is based on its size and income. In 2001, the average monthly food stamp allotment per person was about $75. The allotment is reduced when the household's income increases, but the implicit tax on food stamps is only 30 cents on the dollar.[10]

Because food stamps cannot be used to buy anything except food, we expect them to be worth less to individuals than the same amount of cash.

---

[10] In addition, the law allows certain deductions to be made before applying the 30 percent tax.

Some evidence that this is true comes from a set of social experiments that were conducted several years ago. A group of food stamp recipients were given checks instead of food stamps, while a control group continued to receive food stamps. When the two groups were compared, it was found that between 20 and 30 percent of food stamp recipients reduced their spending on food when they were given cash instead [Whitmore, 2002].

Is the fact that food stamps induce recipients to consume more food than a cash grant good news or bad news? Our analysis of in-kind transfers from the last chapter suggests that this is an indication that the food stamp program is inefficient—recipients could be made better off without any additional expense if the program were cashed out. Indeed, Whitmore calculated that food stamp recipients valued their total benefits at only 80 percent of the value of the food stamps. On the other hand, to the extent that "society" believes that the poor, left to themselves, would not consume enough food, then inducing them to consume more is desirable. Interestingly, however, on the basis of data from food diaries, Whitmore found that replacing food stamps with cash, while reducing food consumption, appears to have had no negative consequences for nutrition. Much of the reduction in food spending was due to reduced consumption of soda and junk food.

An interesting feature of the food stamp program is that only about 70 percent of eligible households actually participate. Why do people fail to take advantage of the program? One possibility is that individuals are unaware they are eligible. Another is that there is some stigma associated with participation in the program; that is, the process of participation per se causes some reduction in utility. Indeed, the presence of stigma may be one reason why the government does not cash out food stamps. If enrolling in the program embarrasses people, then they may be less likely to participate, which keeps down costs. Alternatively, from a political point of view, it may be easier to get support for a program to abolish hunger than simply to pay cash.

Housing Assistance

In the United States, subsidies for providing housing to the poor began in 1937. Until recently, the largest program was public housing. Public housing units are developed, owned, and run by local authorities that operate within a municipality, county, or several counties as a group. The federal government subsidizes both the costs of construction and a portion of the operating costs paid by the tenants. There are now about 1.3 million public housing units.

The average monthly value of public housing to a recipient has been estimated at about 90 percent of the cash value. The income limits for participation in public housing are locally established. Unlike other welfare programs, satisfying the means test does not automatically entitle a family to participate in public housing. As already noted, there are only 1.3 million public housing units, while there are about 33 million people whose incomes fall beneath the poverty line. Many more people want public housing than it is possible to accommodate. In short, public housing confers a relatively large value per recipient, but most poor people receive nothing from the program at all. Further, public housing has gained a reputation as a breeding ground for crime and other social pathologies. For this and other reasons, little federal public housing has been built since the early 1970s.

Many economists believe that if there are to be housing subsidies for the poor, their link to the public provision of housing should be broken. When subsidies are applied to private sector housing, the public sector no longer has to get involved in apartment construction and management. In addition, aid recipients are no longer geographically concentrated and marked publicly.

There are two federal housing programs organized somewhat along these lines, the so-called Section 8 certificate and voucher programs, founded in 1974 and 1983, respectively.[11] Under these programs, which serve about 1.4 million households, recipients search on the private market for housing units [www.hud.gov]. If the dwelling meets certain quality standards and the rent is deemed fair by the government, it subsidizes the rent with payments directly to the landlord. (The tenant's rent payment is a fixed proportion of family income, currently set at 30 percent.) Unlike traditional public housing, Section 8 attempts to give the poor access to the existing stock of housing, instead of trying to add to the stock. However, Section 8 recipients are limited in their choice of dwellings, and cannot spend more than 30 percent of their incomes on rent.

Does publicly provided and subsidized low-income housing actually increase the stock of housing? To the extent that such housing merely replaces equivalent low-income housing that would have been supplied privately, then the housing programs may have little real effect on housing consumption among the poor. This is another version of the crowding-out phenomenon that we confronted in our earlier discussion of Medicaid. Sinai and Waldfogel [2002] examined whether areas with more public and subsidized housing have more total housing, holding constant other variables that affect housing demand. They found that the government programs do increase the total stock of housing, but not on a one-for-one basis. Rather, for every three units of government subsidized housing there are two units less of housing that would have been provided by private markets. In short, some crowding out does occur. Sinai and Waldfogel find that crowding out is less important for programs such as Section 8 than for housing projects, which would seem to be another point in favor of the former.

_____

[11] Details on the operation of the programs are provided in Olsen [2001].

In recent years, questions about public housing have focused on its impact on the economic self-sufficiency of its inhabitants. We can imagine several ways in which such an impact might occur. Perhaps public housing is located so far away from employment opportunities that tenants have trouble getting jobs. To the extent that public housing is located in very poor neighborhoods, young people entering the labor force may lack role models and contacts for jobs. Or the physical environment provided by public housing may be detrimental to individuals' health, also limiting their ultimate ability to get along on their own.

If public housing generates such negative effects, then another benefit of voucher programs is simply getting low-income families into better environments. In an interesting social experiment, a randomized group of public housing residents were given Section 8 housing vouchers and their subsequent employment and earnings compared to those who stayed behind in public housing. There were no statistically significant differences between the two groups along these dimensions [Katz, Kling, and Liebman, 2001]. Hence, the notion that voucher plans enhance self-sufficiency remains speculative at this time.

Programs to Enhance Earnings

Most expenditures for the poor are designed to increase their current consumption levels. In contrast, some programs have been designed to enhance their ability to support themselves in the future. These include educational and job-training programs.

Education

A popular theory is that much poverty in the United States is due to lack of education. The argument is that with more and better education, individuals earn more money and are less likely to end up in poverty. Under legislation passed in 1965, the federal government provides funds to individual school districts for compensatory education at the elementary and secondary levels for disadvantaged students. The most famous example is the Head Start Program, which provides preschool activities for four- and five-year-old children from disadvantaged backgrounds. The idea is to assure that by the time they start kindergarten, they can achieve at the same level as children from more affluent families.

The available evidence suggests that Head Start has been successful in creating long-term improvements in outcomes such as schooling attainment, income, and law-abiding behavior [Garces, Thomas, and Currie, 2000]. One might wonder whether these findings are due to the fact that selection into Head Start is not random. For example, to the extent that the parents of children who enroll in Head Start are particularly supportive of education, then the positive outcomes may be due to family background rather than the program. Garces, Thomas, and Currie deal with this problem to some extent by comparing children who were in Head Start with siblings who were not. This goes a long way in controlling for differences in family background.

Employment and Job Training

Federal job-training programs address another possible cause of poverty—lack of job market skills. Suppose that poor people are not able to obtain jobs that provide good training because of discrimination, or because no such jobs are located in their neighborhoods. The goal of these programs is for the government to provide opportunities to develop marketable skills.

Do these programs work? According to the studies surveyed by Heckman [1999], they are not terribly effective. For adult females on welfare, the programs often produce earnings gains, and these gains exceed the costs of the programs. However, the impacts are not big enough to move many participants out of poverty. For males, programs that provide assistance with job search appear to be successful in the sense that the returns in terms of increased wages exceed the costs of the program, but these earnings increases are not large enough to make a significant difference in living standards. In short, "The best available evidence indicates that training programs are an inefficient transfer mechanism and an inefficient investment policy for low-skill adult workers" [Heckman, 1999, p. 31].

Overview

A reasonable way to begin an evaluation of the welfare system is to examine its impact on poverty rates. The impact is quite substantial. The various cash, food, and housing transfer programs reduce the poverty rate by about 48 percent.[12] This figure, of course, does not take into account the fact that in the absence of welfare, people's earnings might have been higher. Still, in terms of the popular metaphor of government welfare programs as a safety net, it appears that although many people have slipped through the holes, many others also have been caught. In this context, it is interesting to note that the introduction of TANF seems to have reduced the poverty rate among less-skilled women by about 2 percentage points [Blank, 2002, p. 1144]. This is significant because during the debate over TANF, there were many who feared that time limits and other provisions would lead to an increase in poverty.

An important question in this context is how work incentives have been affected in the process of redistributing all this income. It is a complicated question for several reasons. First, the Earned Income Tax Credit simultaneously subsidizes earnings for some workers and taxes them for others. Second, as stressed earlier, states have considerable autonomy in determining the implicit marginal tax rates associated with their programs, and these

---

[12] Personal communication from Dr. Wendell Primus, Joint Economic Committee, US Congress.

Table 8.2   **Estimated marginal tax rates for a one-parent, two-child household residing in a high-TANF benefit state**

Income range ($)	Marginal tax rate
0–1,650	–6.7%
1,650–9,800	24.5
9,800–12,850	61.7
12,850–14,350	81.3
14,350–14,700	50.1
14,700–15,050	33.4
15,050–19,550	50.6
19,550	notch of $1,000
19,550–25,000	50.6

SOURCE: Shaviro [1999]. Calculations take into account federal payroll and income taxes, EITC, state sales taxes, TANF benefit reduction rates, food stamps, and loss of Medicaid for one young child.

rates vary dramatically from state to state. Third, while our focus in this chapter has been on the implicit marginal tax rates associated with welfare, the explicit taxes levied on earnings by state and federal governments also affect incentives. In light of these considerations, the work incentives that confront an individual depend both on his or her state of residence and position in the earnings distribution.

While there is thus no "typical" welfare recipient, it is still useful to look at some illustrative calculations. Table 8.2 shows Shaviro's [1999] computations of marginal tax rates on earnings for a single parent with two children in a state with high TANF benefits. It takes into account all federal and state taxes, as well as TANF and Medicaid benefit reductions. The negative marginal tax rate at the very bottom of the income scale reflects, in part, the EITC subsidy. But the table makes clear that this is soon overwhelmed by the various implicit and explicit marginal tax rates. Indeed, TANF reductions in conjunction with the EITC phaseout contribute to marginal tax rates that, in some parts of the income distribution, exceed 80 percent! We conclude that the cumulative effect of the various welfare programs and the tax system is not encouraging to work effort.

The US welfare system has been unpopular for years for reasons that go beyond work incentive issues. Academic economists—both liberals and conservatives—have focused much of their criticism on the messiness of the current system. It certainly is a hodgepodge. Some programs give cash assistance, some are in-kind; some are entitlements, others are unavailable even to people with incomes far below the poverty line. Administrative responsibilities and financing are split haphazardly among federal, state, and local governments: "Every program or facility operates under its own idiosyncratic rules, and the poor . . . face exhausting rounds of visits and paper work to maintain benefits" [Salins, 1991, p. 54]. Why not replace the various programs with a single cash assistance program?

Some economists reject this position for several reasons. First, as suggested earlier in the chapter, it appears to be infeasible politically:

The American public has declared unmistakably that it is willing to provide those in need of aid such commodities as basic housing, food, and health care, but it is unwilling to give poor people the cash to buy these items themselves. This attitude has persisted long enough to be taken as a constant on the welfare scene. Further efforts to modify the welfare system should treat it as a reality rather than try to explain why it does not make sense. [Aaron, 1984, p. 16]

Second, from an efficiency point of view, a system of categorical programs may have some merit. If relatively large amounts of aid can be targeted at groups for whom labor supply incentives are not very important (for example, the disabled), then the overall efficiency of the system may be enhanced. Thus, while the current system is by no means ideal, its categorical structure is not necessarily a fatal flaw.

Perhaps the most controversial question associated with the current system is whether the benefits are high enough. Standard welfare economics indicates that the correct answer depends on the strength of one's preferences for income equality and the distortions in incentives induced by the system. A very different viewpoint is that poverty has moral and spiritual roots, and that conventional government programs are bound to fail because they fail to take this into account. In recent years, there has been some experimentation with faith-based social services, in which the government provides money to churches and other faith-based institutions, and they administer the programs. Indeed, increased federal support of faith-based programs is an important element of President George W. Bush's legislative agenda. There is some anecdotal evidence that such programs are effective, but not much in the way of systematic analysis.

An extreme critique of the current system, based in part on the fact that it ignores spiritual factors, is that "people cannot really be happy without self-respect, and it is difficult, if not impossible, to acquire self-respect living on the dole (at least if they are capable of supporting themselves)" [Browning, 2002, p. 527]. Proponents of transfers to the poor are quick to point out that they are not the only beneficiaries of public "charity." Numerous government expenditure and tax programs benefit middle- and upper-income people. Spending by the government on research and development increases the incomes of scientists [Goolsbee, 1998a]; subsidies for the production of energy increase the incomes of the owners of oil wells; and defense programs increase the incomes of munitions manufacturers. Sometimes programs that are ostensibly for other purposes are actually nothing more than income distribution programs favoring special interests. For example, most economists believe that import quotas on various commodities such as sugar and peanuts serve no efficiency purpose and are only a veiled way of transferring income to the politically powerful agricultural industry, particularly the wealthy owners of large farms. However, "welfare to the rich" does not carry that label. Perhaps that is why no one worries about them losing *their* self-respect.

Summary

- Means-tested programs transfer income to people whose resources fall below a certain level. Government means-tested programs are about 4.1 percent of GDP.

- The current program of cash assistance, Temporary Assistance for Needy Families (TANF), was enacted in 1996. It removed the entitlement to cash benefits. In general, recipients cannot receive cash transfers for more than five years, and after two years they must take part in some work-related activity.

- Under TANF, the states have virtually total control over the structure of their welfare systems. States vary considerably in the rates at which they reduce benefits when recipients earn income.

- Any income maintenance system must deal with several issues, including the conflict between adequate support and good work incentives, welfare dependence, work requirements, and state versus federal administration.

- The earned income tax credit (EITC) provides a subsidy to the wages of qualified low-income individuals. The phaseout of the EITC after earnings exceed a certain threshold imposes a high implicit marginal tax rate on earnings. Although

administered through the tax system, it is now the most important program for cash transfers to the poor.

- Supplemental Security Income (SSI) provides cash grants to the aged, blind, or disabled.

- Medicaid, the largest spending program for the poor, provides certain medical services at no charge. Medicaid partially crowds out private medical insurance.

- A food stamp is a voucher that can be used only for the purchase of food. Food stamps appear to induce more food consumption than an equivalent amount of cash.

- In the past, housing assistance in the United States focused on the creation of public housing for the poor. The Section 8 program now provides a small number of recipients with housing vouchers to pay the rent on dwellings of their choice.

- The goal of education and job-training programs is to enhance the ability of the poor to support themselves in the future. The efficacy of job-training programs does not appear to be very substantial. However, compensatory education for children, such as Head Start, leads to long-term improvements in educational attainment and education.

Discussion Questions

1. In California, a welfare recipient can earn $225 per month without having her benefits reduced. Beyond $225, benefits are reduced by 50 cents for every dollar of earnings. Consider Elizabeth, a resident of California, who can earn $10 per hour. If she does not work at all, she is eligible for welfare benefits of $645.

   a. If she works 10 hours, how much are her earnings; how much is her welfare benefit; and how much is her income?

   b. After Elizabeth works a certain number of hours, she does not receive any benefit at all. What is that number of hours?

   c. Use your answer to parts a and b to plot her budget constraint.

   d. Sketch a set of indifference curves consistent with Elizabeth's participating in the labor market.

2. Suppose you wanted to conduct an econometric study of the impact of job-training programs on

future earnings. What data would you need? Suggest a specific estimating equation.

3. Discuss: "Workfare is an efficient way to transfer income if the quantity of leisure consumed by the recipient appears in the utility function of the donor." [Hint: Consider the theory of externalities.]

4. Philip's demand curve for housing is shown in the following figure. (Assume that quantity of housing is measured simply by the number of square feet. Other aspects of quality are ignored.) The market price of housing is P_1; Philip can purchase as much housing as he desires at that price. Alternatively, Philip can live in public housing for a price of P_2 per square foot, but the only apartment available to him has H_2 square feet.

   Will Philip choose public housing or rent on the private market? Explain carefully. (Hint: Compare consumer surplus [appendix to the book] under both possibilities.)

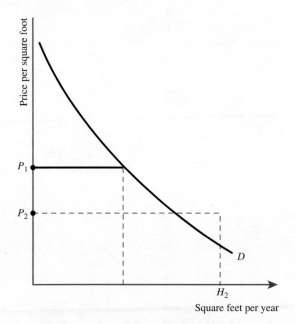

Square feet per year

5. Food stamp benefits are phased out in a complicated fashion that varies from state to state. However, at some point near the poverty line, food stamps worth about $1,250 are suddenly lost. Ignoring other aspects of the tax and transfer

systems, sketch the income-leisure budget constraint associated with this provision. (Don't worry about the specific slope and intercept of the constraint; just sketch the general shape.)

6. In the analysis of TANF's work incentives in Figure 8.4, the individual continues to work while receiving welfare. Reproduce the budget constraint from that figure, and sketch a set of indifference curves for an individual who would choose not to work while receiving welfare benefits.

7. The Section 8 program for housing assistance discussed in this chapter in effect shifts out the demand curve for low-income housing in a given community. Draw supply and demand diagrams that are consistent with the following outcomes:

   a. The price of low-income housing gets bid up, and there is no increase in the stock of low-income housing.

   b. There is no increase in the price of low-income housing, and there is an increase in the stock of low-income housing.

   c. There is an increase in the price of low-income housing, and there is an increase in the stock of low-income housing.

   Which of these scenarios is most consistent with the research by Sinai and Waldfogel that is discussed in the chapter?

8. Consider Eleanor, who qualifies for the Earned Income Tax Credit as depicted in Figure 8.8. Suppose that Eleanor can earn $8 per hour. Taking into account the EITC and ignoring other aspects of the tax and transfer systems:

   a. How much do her earnings increase when her labor supply increases from zero to 1,000 hours per year?

   b. How much do her earnings increase when her labor supply increases from 1,000 to 1,500 hours per year?

   c. How much do her earnings increase when her labor supply increases from 1,500 to 2,000 hours per year?

   In each case, compute the incremental amount of earnings associated with the increase in work effort. Relate your answer to the implicit marginal tax rates embodied in the EITC.

Selected References

Blank, Rebecca. "Evaluating Welfare Reform in the United States." *Journal of Economic Literature* 40 (December 2002), pp. 1105–66.

Currie, Janet. "Early Childhood Education Programs." *Journal of Economic Perspectives* 15 (Spring 2001), pp. 213–38.

McGarry, Kathleen. "Public Policy and the U.S. Health Insurance Market: Direct and Indirect

Provision of Insurance." *National Tax Journal* (December 2002), pp. 789–827.

Olsen, Edgar O. "Housing Programs for Low-Income Households." Working Paper No. 8208. Cambridge, MA: National Bureau of Economic Research, April 2001.

CHAPTER 9

Social Insurance I: Social Security and Unemployment Insurance

Will you still need me, will you still feed me, when I'm sixty-four?

JOHN LENNON AND PAUL McCARTNEY

Life is full of uncertainties. Unexpected events such as fires or illness can dramatically harm people. One way to gain some protection against such eventualities is to purchase insurance. In return for paying premiums to the insurance company, an individual receives benefits in the event of certain unlucky events. Several federal government programs also replace income losses that are consequences of events at least partly outside personal control. These programs, collectively referred to as **social insurance,** are listed in Table 9.1. As the table indicates, social insurance expenditures are a large proportion of both federal government expenditures and gross domestic product.

Although the various programs serve different functions, several share these characteristics:

- Participation is compulsory.
- Eligibility and benefit levels depend, in part, on past contributions made by the worker.
- Benefit payments begin with some identifiable occurrence such as unemployment, illness, or retirement.
- The programs are not means-tested—financial distress need not be established to receive benefits.

We begin by discussing possible rationales for social insurance. The rest of the chapter is devoted to two important social insurance programs, Social

Table 9.1   **Major social insurance programs**

Program	Date Enacted	2002
Social Security (OASDI)	1935	$453
Medicare	1965	254
Unemployment Insurance	1935	51
Veterans' Medical Care	1917	22
Total as percent of federal expenditure		37.9%
Total as percent of GDP		7.5%

SOURCE: First three items are from Congressional Budget Office, *The Economic and Budget Outlook: Fiscal Years 2004–2013* (Washington, DC: US Government Printing Office, 2003). Last item is from Executive Office of the President, Office of Management and Budget, *The Budget of the United States Government, for Fiscal Year 2004* (Washington, DC: US Government Printing Office, 2003).

Security and unemployment insurance. The next chapter takes up socially provided health insurance.

Why Have Social Insurance?

According to the First Welfare Theorem, private markets generally provide commodities in efficient quantities. What is special about the commodity "insurance"?

Adverse Selection

In our discussion of market failure in Chapter 3, we noted that *asymmetric information*—when one party in a transaction has information that is not available to another—can lead to inefficiencies in insurance markets. Let's briefly develop the argument, using life insurance as an example. The buyer characteristic that the insurance company cares about is the buyer's life expectancy. From the company's point of view, the ideal customer would never die. Since potential insurance buyers likely know more about their health than does the company, this is a situation of asymmetric information. When the insurer cannot observe the life expectancy of different people, it must offer the same policy to everyone. Who will find this insurance to be the most valuable? Those people who are most likely to collect benefits because they are in poor health. But these are the very people that the insurance company does not want as customers! Thus, the insurance company gets a selection of buyers that is adverse to its interests. And, adjusting the price upward to reflect this adverse selection may further drive out the "good" customers, making the problem worse. More generally, we can expect an individual who knows he is especially likely to collect benefits to have an especially high demand for insurance, a phenomenon known as **adverse selection.** In short, in the presence of asymmetric information, adverse selection can reduce the efficiency of a market—people who would have been willing to purchase life insurance if everyone were fully informed no longer purchase it.

Now consider a closely related kind of problem—insuring not against dying too soon, but against living too long. Why is this a problem? Think about the question of how long you will live after retirement. No one, including you, knows for sure. The average life expectancy after retirement is about 18 years, but about 25 percent of those alive at 65 will live into their 90s. While living to a ripe old age may be desirable, it's a problem if the money that you accumulated for retirement runs out before you die. How can you protect yourself against living longer than you anticipated? Insurance companies sell policies called **annuities,** which pay a fixed annual income for as long as the individual lives. In theory, the insurance company loses money on people who live longer than average, makes money on people who live shorter than average, and thus breaks even.

The problem, though, is that there is adverse selection in this market: People who expect to live longer than average will have a higher demand for annuities. This adverse selection raises the cost to insurance companies of providing annuities, so the price goes up. This, in turn, discourages still more potential annuity buyers, further shrinking the market. The market fails to provide an efficient amount of insurance against living too long. In essence, mandatory social insurance solves this adverse selection problem by forcing everyone to purchase the insurance. In fact, as we will see shortly, one way to view Social Security is as an annuity that everyone must purchase.

As stressed back in Chapter 3, just because asymmetric information can seriously impede efficiency doesn't mean that it will. Thus, we must ask whether adverse selection is empirically important enough to justify the provision of social insurance. It depends on the program being considered. Studies of the life insurance market suggest that adverse selection is not as important there. Buyers have to pass a medical examination and fill out a questionnaire about their health status; lying on the questionnaire renders the policy void. Apparently these provisions are sufficient to remove the informational asymmetry that can generate adverse selection [Hendel and Lizzeri, 2000]. There are well-developed markets for health insurance, and policies can be obtained by most people either as part of a group or on an individual basis. The case of the annuity market is controversial. It is certainly true that the US market for annuities is small and underdeveloped. Some see this fact and conclude that it is evidence of market failure. But others argue that the annuities market is small precisely because Social Security crowds out private annuities—many potential buyers don't go into the market because, in effect, they already own a publicly provided annuity.

Other Justifications

Several considerations other than adverse selection can be used to rationalize the compulsory nature of social insurance programs.

Lack of Foresight.   Some argue that individuals lack the foresight to buy sufficient insurance for their own good and therefore the government must force them to. For example, it is popularly believed that in the absence of the Social

Security program, most people would not accumulate enough assets to finance an adequate level of consumption during their retirement. This argument raises two issues. First, is it true that people would fail to provide for themselves adequately without Social Security? To find out requires estimating how people would behave in the absence of the program. As noted later, this is very difficult to do. Second, even if it is true, it does not necessarily follow that the government should step in. Those with a highly individualistic philosophical framework believe that people should be left to make their own decisions, even if this occasionally results in mistakes.

Moral Hazard.   A related consideration is that individuals who can opt out of a social insurance program may believe that if they put themselves in a sufficiently desperate situation, the government will feel obliged to come to their aid. For example, society may feel the presence of destitute elderly citizens to be intolerable. Some younger people may perceive this as a form of insurance, and allow themselves to become destitute. This is an example of *moral hazard,* the change in an individual's behavior induced by the fact that he or she has insurance. (See Chapter 3.) One justification for a compulsory system is to eliminate this type of moral hazard.

Economize on Decision-Making Costs.   Insurance and annuity markets are complicated, and it is likely to involve quite a bit of time and effort for an individual to choose the right policy. If public decision makers can select an appropriate program for everybody, individuals do not have to waste resources on making their own decisions. A clear criticism here is that there is no reason to believe the government would necessarily choose the right kind of policy. After all, different people have different needs, so it might be better to let people shop around on their own.

Income Distribution.   We noted earlier that benefits from social insurance programs are determined *in part* by past contributions. In fact, for some of the programs, the link between benefits and earlier contributions is quite weak. Some people do better than they would have if they had purchased private insurance, and some do worse. To an extent, then, social insurance programs are also income redistribution programs. This helps explain why the programs are compulsory. Otherwise, those who expect to lose might opt out of them. The social insurance program to which we now turn, Social Security, has important distributional aspects.

Structure of Social Security

Social Security—officially, Old Age, Survivors, and Disability Insurance (OASDI)—is the largest single domestic spending program. In brief, the system works as follows: During their working lives members of the system and their employers make contributions via a tax on payrolls. On retirement, members are eligible for payments based in part on their contributions. By providing a fixed annual benefit for as long as one lives, Social Security in effect provides insurance against the possibility that one will live longer than expected and hence prematurely use up all the assets one has accumulated for retirement. Social Security also provides benefits for disabled workers and for dependents and survivors of disabled and retired workers. In addition, as we will see below, Social Security also functions as a redistribution program. Today, virtually everyone who works is covered either by Social Security or some other government retirement program.

The system is rather complicated. The key provisions are set forth below; for more detail, consult the Social Security Web site (www.ssa.gov).

Basic Components

Pay-As-You-Go Financing.   When it was started in 1935, Social Security was broadly similar to a private insurance system. During their working lives, individuals deposited some portion of their salaries into a fund. Over time, the fund would accumulate interest, and on retirement, the principal and accrued interest would be used to pay benefits. Such a scheme is called **fully funded.** This plan was scrapped almost immediately. In 1939 the system was converted to a **pay-as-you-go** basis, meaning the benefits paid to current retirees come from payments made by those who are presently working. Each generation of retirees is supported by payments made by the current generation of workers, *not* by drawing down an accumulated fund. An important reason for the switch to pay-as-you-go was the perception that the savings of many of the elderly had been wiped out by the Great Depression, and they deserved to be supported at a level higher than possible with only a few years of contributions. Another reason for the switch was the fears of some politicians of the time that such a fund would be managed inefficiently by the government or simply spent.

As a consequence of changes in the system enacted in 1983, Social Security has accumulated some surpluses in a trust fund. However, as will be shown later, the trust fund is largely an accounting device without important real implications. Hence, it is still most accurate to characterize the system as pay-as-you-go.

The early Social Security recipients received very high returns on their contributions. An extreme case is that of Ida Fuller, the first beneficiary, who paid $24.85 in Social Security taxes. She lived until the age of 99 and collected $20,897 in benefits.

Explicit Transfers.   Another key change in the 1939 legislation was a broadening of the scope of the program. The 1935 act provided primarily for monthly retirement benefits for insured workers aged 65 and over. In 1939, monthly benefits for dependents and survivors of insured workers were introduced. Thus, Social Security not only provides insurance but it also transfers income among individuals. The transfer function has grown in importance over time and culminated in the enactment of **Supplemental**

Security Income (SSI) in 1972. SSI, although administered by the Social Security Administration, is not insurance by the conventional definition. It is a welfare program that provides a federal minimum income guarantee for the aged and disabled. SSI is discussed with other welfare programs in Chapter 8.

Benefit Structure.   An individual's Social Security benefits depend on his or her earnings history, age, and other personal circumstances. The first stage is to calculate the **average indexed monthly earnings (AIME).** This represents the individual's average wages in covered employment over the length of his or her working life.[1] Only annual wages up to a given ceiling are included in the calculation. This ceiling is the same as the maximum amount of wages subject to the Social Security payroll tax (discussed in the following section).

The next step is to substitute the AIME into a benefit formula to find the individual's **primary insurance amount (PIA),** which is the basic benefit payable to a worker who retires at the normal retirement age (currently about 65 years old; see below) or who becomes disabled. The benefits formula is structured so that the PIA increases with the AIME but at a slower rate. In 2003, the PIA was calculated as

90 percent of the first $600 of AIME, plus

32 percent of AIME between $600 and $3,653, plus

15 percent of AIME above $3,653.

Thus, for a retiree with an AIME of $200, the PIA was $180; while for a retiree with an AIME of $1,600, the PIA was about $863. Note that workers with low AIMEs are entitled to benefits that are a higher proportion of their earnings than those with high AIMEs.[2] In fact, for a typical low earner retiring at age 65 in 2003, Social Security was about 64 percent of AIME; for an average earner, 48 percent; and for a high earner, 40 percent [www.ssa.gov/OACT/COLA/examples.html].

An individual's actual benefit depends not only on the PIA but also on two factors.

Age at which benefit is drawn.   The age at which an individual qualifies for full Social Security retirement benefits is called the *normal retirement age.* The normal retirement age depends on the year in which a person was born. The normal retirement age is 66 for individuals who were born between 1944 and 1954. It then increases by two months per year, reaching 67 for workers born in 1960 or later. A worker can begin receiving benefits as early as age 62, but doing so results in a permanent reduction in monthly

---

[1] Wages earned over different years are not directly comparable because of changes in the price level over time. To correct for this, wages are indexed by the percentage increase in all workers' wages. For individuals who work at least 35 years, the best 35 years are counted for the computation.

[2] The law specifies a maximum PIA as well as a special minimum benefit that provides long-term low-paid workers with a higher benefit than the regular formula permits.

benefits. Once the normal retirement age is 67, this reduction will be 30 percent. In the same way, workers who don't start collecting benefits until after their normal retirement age receive a permanent increase in their benefits. Starting with workers born in 1943, each year delayed beyond the normal retirement age increases benefits by 8 percent.

Recipient's family status.   When a fully insured single worker retires at the normal retirement age, the actual monthly benefit is simply equal to the primary insurance amount. A worker with a dependent wife, husband, or child receives an additional 50 percent of the PIA. The average monthly benefit for a retired couple is about $1,460. [Office of the Chief Actuary, 2003].

Two additional rules have an important effect on the benefit structure. First, up to 85 percent of the benefits received by individuals whose incomes exceed certain base amounts are subject to the federal personal income tax. These base amounts are $25,000 for a single taxpayer and $32,000 for married taxpayers. Second, benefits are corrected for inflation. As already noted, the computation of AIME includes an adjustment of past earnings by an index of wage growth. Moreover, once a person becomes eligible for a Social Security benefit, the purchasing power of the benefit is maintained through annual cost-of-living increases based on the increase in prices as measured by the consumer price index. Very few financial assets offer this kind of protection against inflation.

The benefits of Social Security recipients who have not reached the normal retirement age are reduced by one dollar for each two dollars they earn above approximately $11,000. (The amount changes every year because it is indexed for increases in the average wage.) This provision is known as the **earnings test.** However, in some cases, individuals who lose benefits due to the earnings test may have their later benefits increased. Thus, "although the retirement earnings test is often portrayed as a tax on work, it is more accurately described as a means of deferring benefits until workers no longer have substantial earnings" [Congressional Budget Office, 2001, p. 24].

Financing.   The payroll tax is a flat percentage of an employee's annual gross wages up to a certain amount. Half the tax is paid by employers and half by employees. The legislative intention was apparently to split the cost of the program equally between workers and employers. However, employers may be able to "shift" part or all of their share to employees in the form of a lower pretax wage. Whether such shifting occurs is a complicated question discussed in Chapter 12. For now, we merely note that it is highly unlikely that the true division of the costs of the program is really 50–50.

As benefits have grown over time, so have payroll tax rates. The current tax rate, 6.2 percent (on the employer and employee *each*), is more than six times its original level. (See Table 9.2.) Legislation passed in 1977 mandated that maximum taxable earnings rise automatically with increases in average wages.

Table 9.2*   Social Security tax rates *(selected years)*

Year	Maximum Taxable Earnings (dollars)	Employer and Employee, Each (percent)
1937	$ 3,000	1.0%
1950	3,000	1.5
1960	4,800	3.0
1970	7,800	4.2
1980	29,700	5.08
1990	51,300	6.2
2000	76,200	6.2
2003	87,000	6.2

*These rates *do not* include the payroll tax used to finance Medicare, which is 1.45 percent each on employers and employees. There is no ceiling for that tax.

SOURCE: Office of the Chief Actuary, Social Security Administration. [URL: http://www.ssa.gov].

The figures in Table 9.2 do not include an additional payroll tax that finances the Medicare program, which is discussed in the next chapter. That tax is currently 1.45 percent on the employee and employer each and, with legislation passed in 1993, its base is *all* earnings. Thus, for an individual whose earnings are below the maximum taxed for Social Security, the combined payroll tax rate for both Social Security and Medicare is 15.3 [= 2 × (6.2 + 1.45)] percent.

A natural question to ask is why Social Security is financed through a special payroll tax rather than from general revenues. Indeed, in 1999, President Clinton unsuccessfully proposed using general revenues to extend Social Security's solvency, and the idea received little support. The reason for payroll tax finance appears to have more to do with politics than economics. The idea is that a link between taxes and benefits—no matter how tenuous—creates an obligation on the part of the government to maintain the system that promised the benefits. Franklin Roosevelt articulated this position with typical eloquence:

> Those taxes were never a problem of economics. They are politics all the way through. We put those payroll contributions there so as to give the contributors a legal, moral, and political right to collect their pensions. With these taxes in there, no damn politician can ever scrap my Social Security Program. ["Your Stake in the Fight," 1981, p. 504]

Distributional Issues   Our description of Social Security indicates that it is more than an insurance program. If providing insurance were the only objective, individuals would receive approximately the same return on their contributions. Specifically, each individual would receive an *actuarially fair return*—on average, the benefits received would equal the premiums paid. (The calculation must be made "on average" because total benefits depend on the individual's life

Table 9.3   **Estimated benefits and costs of Social Security**

Year of Retirement		Low Earner	Average Earner	High Earner
		\[*Earnings Level*\]		
1980	Social Security wealth	$ 67,048	$111,422	$139,186
	Lifetime payroll taxes	27,718	61,595	82,057
	Gain	39,330	49,827	57,130
1995	Social Security wealth	75,180	124,000	158,687
	Lifetime payroll taxes	54,516	121,146	171,658
	Gain	20,664	2,854	−12,971
2015	Social Security wealth	108,164	178,709	236,189
	Lifetime payroll taxes	89,311	198,468	314,610
	Gain	18,853	−19,759	−78,421

SOURCE: Updated tables, furnished by authors, 2002. See C. Eugene Steuerle and Jon M. Bakija, "Retooling Social Security for the 21st Century: Right and Wrong Approaches to Reform," Washington, DC: The Urban Institute Press, 1994, for original tables and methodology. All values expressed in 1993 dollars.

span, which cannot be known in advance with certainty.) In fact, some types of people systematically earn higher returns than others.

The complexity of the Social Security law makes it difficult to state who generally gains and who loses. The most straightforward way to explore distributional issues is actually to compute the expected lifetime net benefits from Social Security for several representative individuals and see which ones come out ahead. The first step in this computation is to estimate the expected lifetime value of the Social Security benefits to which the worker is entitled.[3] The value of expected future Social Security payments is referred to as **Social Security wealth.** Social Security wealth is an important part of people's assets—on average, it comprises about 38 percent of the liquid assets that individuals have at retirement [Baxter, 2001]. We should note, however, that although the present value of promised Social Security benefits is wealth from the individual's point of view, it is an unfunded liability of the government, and hence not net wealth from society's point of view.

The second step in the net benefit calculation is to find the expected lifetime value of the costs of being in the system—the payroll taxes paid by the individual. Of course, both Social Security wealth and future payroll taxes depend on wage growth over time. The calculations in Table 9.3 are for three "representative" individuals, a "low earner" who always earned

---

[3] Because Social Security benefits received depend on the length of life, the actual value is uncertain, and actuarial tables must be used to compute the value "on average," or the "expected" value. Because benefits and costs occur over time, lifetime magnitudes must be computed as "present values." Those unfamiliar with this concept should consult Chapter 11.

45 percent of the average wage, an "average earner" who earned the average wage in the economy, and a "high earner" who earned the maximum wage subject to the Social Security tax.

The computations are done for three different retirement years. Each cell of the table gives the following information: (1) Social Security wealth, (2) lifetime value of payroll taxes, and (3) the net gain from the Social Security system, calculated simply as (1) minus (2). Thus, an individual with average earnings who retired in 1995 can expect Social Security wealth of $124,000. Lifetime payroll taxes for this person are $121,146, so his net benefit from the system is $2,854.

Reading across Table 9.3 illustrates how Social Security redistributes income across income classes. For recent and future retirees, generally the higher the earnings, the smaller the gain from Social Security. Indeed, high-earnings individuals who retire in the year 2015 are expected to lose over $78,000 by virtue of their participation in Social Security. Reading down the table shows how Social Security redistributes income toward older generations. Consider two individuals with average earnings, one who retires in 1980, and the other in 2015. For the first, the net benefit of Social Security is $49,827, for the second, −$19,759. As suggested by the cartoon, Social Security is generally more generous to older than younger generations.

"By the way, Sam, as someday you'll be paying for my entitlements, I'd like to thank you in advance."

While Table 9.3 focuses our attention on how Social Security distributes income across generations, it also redistributes income within generations. In this context, it is important to note that much of the apparent redistribution embodied in the benefits formula is illusory when viewed from the context of *lifetime* earnings. This is simply because your lifetime social security benefit depends not only on the benefit per year, but also the number of years you receive it. Thus, for example, Liebman [2001b] calculates that among African-Americans who retired in the 1990s, the lifetime net benefit from Social Security was negative $2,514, as opposed to positive $250 for whites. However, if these African-Americans had the same expected lifespan and education as the rest of the population, their net benefit would have increased to a positive $18,259. Adopting a lifetime perspective also leads to some interesting differences by sex. Women live longer than men, so their lifetime benefits are greater. According to Liebman's calculations, among people who retired in the 1990s, on average men came out behind by about $43,000 while women came out ahead by $37,000.

Social Security also redistributes income based on people's choices about living arrangements. Other things being the same, married people with uncovered spouses gain more than single people. This is because the married person receives an extra benefit for his or her spouse equal to 50 percent of his or her own benefit. Moreover, if the married person dies, the surviving spouse becomes entitled to the entire benefit. Further, one-earner couples gain more than two-earner couples. Consider a family in which the wife has higher lifetime covered earnings than the husband. If the benefit the husband would receive on the basis of his earnings history turns out to be less than 50 percent of his wife's benefit, the husband is entitled to *no more* than the 50 percent of his wife's benefit, which he would have received even without working. If his benefit is more than 50 percent of hers, he gains only the difference between his benefit and 50 percent of hers. Thus, even though the spouse with lower earnings is subject to the payroll tax during his or her working life, he or she gains little in Social Security wealth.

Are these redistributive patterns desirable? As usual, the answer depends in part on value judgments. It could be argued, for example, that the people who suffered during the Great Depression and World War II were unfairly treated by fate, and therefore deserve to be compensated by younger generations. If so, the intergenerational transfers shown in Table 9.3 might be appropriate. On the other hand, it is not clear what principle of equity would justify the distributions across different family types that were just described.

Although there has been some public discussion of the transfers implicit in Social Security, one is struck by the relative lack of attention they have received. The sums involved are huge; if such amounts were being transferred via a direct expenditure program, there would probably be an ongoing major debate. However, the workings of the Social Security system are sufficiently obscure that public awareness of this situation is low.

The Trust Fund

When payroll tax revenues exceed payments to beneficiaries, the difference is used to buy government bonds, which are "deposited" in the Social Security trust fund. The reason for the quotation marks is that it is misleading to think of the trust fund as a gigantic savings account that can be drawn upon to pay benefits in the future. Instead, the trust fund is basically an accounting device for keeping track of the annual surpluses generated by the Social Security portion of the federal budget. By itself, the trust fund does not contribute to the government's ability to pay benefits in the future.

To see why, we must begin by recognizing a fundamental fact—in any year in the future, the consumption of both retirees and workers must come out of that year's production. Hence, the trust fund can help finance future retirees' consumption only to the extent that it allows future output to increase. And the only way it can increase output in the future is by increasing the capital stock in the present, because a larger capital stock increases the productivity of future workers. Put another way, unless the amounts accumulating in the trust fund are associated with more national saving, they do nothing to enhance the ability to pay future benefits.

Now, suppose that in the presence of Social Security surpluses, policymakers increase spending in the non-Social Security part of the budget. For example, the Social Security system runs a $10 billion surplus in a given year and Congress spends $10 billion more on other programs. There is still a $10 billion entry in the trust fund. This entry represents a $10 billion claim against the Treasury, which, when redeemed in the future, has to be financed by raising taxes, borrowing from the public, or reducing other expenditures. But this $10 billion has not increased national saving, so in a real sense, the ability of the society to pay benefits in the future has not increased. In fact, although Social Security has run large surpluses since the mid-1980s, these surpluses have been mostly offset by large deficits in the rest of the federal budget, implying that the value of the trust fund far exceeds the actual increase in saving [*Economic Report of the President,* 2002, p. 77]. We will return to this issue later in our discussion of proposals to reform Social Security.

Economic Status of the Aged

As we noted earlier, one of the main purposes of Social Security is to maintain the incomes of the elderly. Has the program achieved this goal? The numbers tell a pretty upbeat story. The elderly used to be a relatively disadvantaged group. In 1970, about one in four elderly households was below the poverty line. Not only has the poverty rate for the elderly fallen, but it is now below the rate for the population as a whole. In 2001, 10.1 percent of the population over 65 was poor, while for the population as a whole, the rate was 11.7 percent. In recent decades, the incomes of the elderly have increased at a faster rate than those of the rest of the population. Between 1974 and 2001, the real median income for all people over 15 increased by about 31 percent, while for the population over 65 the figure was 45 percent.[4] Currently, about 39 percent of all of the income going to elderly households is from Social Security. For the lowest fifth of the aged population, the figure is 82 percent [www.ssa.gov].

Two caveats are in order. First, although Social Security has doubtless reduced poverty among the elderly, it has not eliminated it. Elderly females, particularly widows, are especially likely to experience economic distress. Second, Social Security benefits do not necessarily represent a *net* addition to the resources available to retirees. Individuals may save less in anticipation of receiving Social Security, or they may leave the work force to qualify for benefits. The question of how Social Security influences individuals' decisions is thus central to assessing the system's impact. We turn now to this topic.

Effects on Economic Behavior

Some economists argue that the Social Security system distorts people's behavior and impairs economic efficiency. Most of the discussion has focused on saving behavior and labor supply decisions. As we shall see, all the difficulties in doing empirical work that were explained in Chapter 2 arise here with a vengeance. The impact of Social Security on behavior remains a controversial subject, so this section is best regarded as a report on research in progress, rather than a compendium of definitive conclusions.

Saving Behavior

The starting point for most work on Social Security and saving is the *life-cycle theory of savings,* which states that individuals' consumption and saving decisions are based on lifetime considerations. During their working lives, individuals save some portion of their incomes to accumulate wealth from which they can finance consumption during retirement.[5] Such funds are invested until they are needed, thus increasing society's capital stock. The introduction of a Social Security system can substantially alter the amount of lifetime saving. Such changes are the consequences of three effects:

Wealth Substitution Effect. Workers realize that in exchange for their Social Security contributions, they will receive a guaranteed retirement income. If they view Social Security taxes as a means of "saving" for these future benefits, they will tend to save less on their own. This phenomenon is referred to as the **wealth substitution effect.** As emphasized earlier, with a pay-as-you-go system, the contributions are paid out to current beneficiaries. Thus, public saving is less than the decrease in private saving, which means a reduction in the total amount of capital accumulation.

---

[4] Calculations based on www.census.gov/hhes/www/income.html.

[5] Of course, savings are also accumulated for other reasons as well: to finance the purchase of durables, to use in case of a rainy day, and so forth. For a more complete discussion of the life-cycle theory, see Modigliani [1986].

Retirement Effect.   Social Security may induce people to retire earlier than they would have, because to receive benefits, they have to withdraw from the labor force. However, if the length of retirement increases, the individual has more nonworking years during which consumption must be financed, but fewer working years to accumulate funds. This **retirement effect** tends to increase saving.

Bequest Effect.   Suppose an important reason for saving is the bequest motive—people want to leave inheritances for their children. Now recall from Table 9.3 that the Social Security system tends to shift income from children (worker/taxpayers) to parents (retiree/benefit recipients). Parents may therefore save more to increase bequests to their children so as to off-set the distributional effect of Social Security. In essence, people increase their saving to undo the impact of Social Security on their children's incomes. This is referred to as the **bequest effect.**

Econometric Analysis.   Given that the three effects work in different directions, theory alone cannot tell us how Social Security affects saving. Econometric analysis is necessary. The first step is to specify a mathematical relationship that shows how the amount of saving depends on Social Security wealth and other variables that might have an effect. Alternatively, an investigator can just as well posit a relation that explains the amount of *consumption* as a function of the same variables, because by definition, saving and consumption are opposite sides of the same coin—anything that raises consumption by a dollar must lower saving by the same amount.

In a controversial study, Feldstein [1974] assumed that consumption during a given year is a function of private wealth at the beginning of the year, disposable income during the year, and Social Security wealth, among other variables. Income and private wealth are included because they are measures of the individual's capacity to consume.

In an updated version of the paper, Feldstein [1996] estimated the regression equation with annual US data from 1930 to 1992, using statistical methods similar to those described in Chapter 2. For our purposes, the key question is the sign and magnitude of the parameter multiplying the Social Security wealth variable. Feldstein found a positive and statistically significant value of 0.028. This positive sign suggests that increases in Social Security wealth increase consumption and, hence, decrease saving. Thus, the wealth substitution effect dominates the retirement and bequest effects.

To assess the quantitative importance of the coefficient, consider a rough estimate of the value of Social Security wealth in 2002, $16,000 billion. A coefficient of 0.028 implies that Social Security reduced personal saving in 2002 by $448 billion (= 0.028 × $16,000). In comparison, during 2002 personal saving was about $296 billion. The $448 billion is 60 percent of the potential personal saving of $744 billion (the sum of $448 billion and $296 billion). Thus, if Feldstein's calculations are correct, Social Security's pay-as-you-go nature has had a huge negative impact on capital accumulation in the United States. Given that productivity depends importantly on the stock of capital, this is a serious matter.[6]

Feldstein's study spawned considerable controversy. Other studies using different data sets and methods of estimation have come up with rather different results. For example, Leimer and Lesnoy [1982] found evidence that Social Security might even have *increased* saving. Taking all the analyses together, though, it seems safe to say that Social Security has had a negative effect on saving, but the magnitude of the effect is unclear [Hurd, 1990].

Retirement Decisions

For people older than 62, Social Security provides incentives for partial or complete retirement. In 1930, 54 percent of the men over 65 participated in the labor force. By 1950, the participation rate for this group was 45.8 percent, and by 2001 it was about 18 percent.[7] Several factors have doubtless contributed to this phenomenon: rising incomes, changing life expectancies, and differences in occupations. Many investigators believe that Social Security has played a key role in this dramatic change in retirement patterns.

To understand the retirement incentives associated with Social Security, we must return to the concept of Social Security wealth—the expected present value of the benefits to which an individual is entitled. Suppose that a 66-year-old individual is deciding whether or not to work another year. A key issue is what happens to his Social Security wealth if he puts off retirement for a year and works. If the change in his Social Security wealth is positive, then it adds to the (after-tax) wages he gets from work, and increases the incentive to work. If the change in Social Security wealth is negative, then it reduces the incentive to work another year.

This immediately leads to another question: What determines the change in Social Security wealth for working another year? It depends on a variety of considerations, but the most important is the adjustment made to future benefits to compensate the individual for the fact that he hasn't drawn upon the system that year. One possibility is an *actuarially fair adjustment*, which means that if he gives up a year of benefits, his future benefits are increased by exactly enough so that in present value terms, his total Social Security benefits are unchanged. In this case, the change in Social Security wealth for working one more year is zero, and there is neither an incentive nor disincentive to retire. It turns out, however, that once a worker reaches 64, the adjustment is always worse than actuarially fair, which means that Social Security wealth falls if the individual works another year. Indeed, the ratio of the fall in the value of Social Security wealth to net earnings can

---

[6] Interestingly, when Social Security was introduced during the 1930s, the perception that it decreased saving was regarded as a virtue. Many believed that a major cause of the Great Depression was the failure of people to consume enough.

[7] See US Bureau of the Census [1975, p. 132] and www.bls.gov.

be quite high—about 23 percent for a 66 year old, according to Diamond and Gruber's [1999, p. 456] calculations.

How responsive are retirement decisions to this disincentive to work? Several econometric studies have assessed the impact of Social Security on retirement decisions. Many of them are consistent with the hypothesis that the system increases the likelihood of retirement and reduces the amount of labor supplied by those who continue to work. For example, in a study of the social security systems in eleven industrialized countries, Gruber and Wise [1999] found that the age at which benefits are first available has an important effect on the likelihood of retirement. However, as in the case of saving behavior, there is considerable uncertainty about the magnitude of the response. One important reason for the uncertainty is the fact that many of the variables influencing labor supply decisions of the aged are difficult to measure and sometimes unavailable altogether. These include health status, local labor market conditions, and the amount of wealth accumulated in private pensions.

Implications

Many economists believe that Social Security depresses both work effort and saving. However, the evidence is murky, and others are unconvinced. In any case, even if Social Security does distort economic decisions, this does not necessarily mean that it is a bad system. If society wants to achieve some level of income security for its elderly, then presumably it should be willing to pay for that security in terms of some loss of efficiency. On the other hand, if there are ways to obtain the same benefits to society with fewer inefficiencies, then reform of the system should be considered.

Long–Term Stresses on Social Security

Currently, Social Security payroll taxes exceed the benefits that are being paid out, and surpluses are expected to continue until the year 2016 or so. At that point, the government will either have to raise taxes, cut benefits or other expenditures, or borrow from the public. In short, given its current structure, Social Security is financially unstable.

A simple formula helps illuminate the sources of the problem. In a stable pay-as-you-go system, the benefits received by retirees equal the payments made by current workers. If N_b is the number of retirees and B is the benefit per retiree, then total benefits are $N_b \times B$. The taxes paid by current workers are the product of the tax rate (t), the number of workers (N_w), and the average covered wage per worker (w): $t \times N_w \times w$. Hence, equality between benefits received and taxes paid requires that

$$N_b \times B = t \times N_w \times w$$

Rearranging this equation gives us

$$t = (N_b/N_w) \times (B/w) \tag{9.1}$$

The first term on the right-hand side is the *dependency ratio,* the ratio of the number of retirees to the number of workers. The second term is the *replacement ratio,* the ratio of average benefits to average wages. The long-term problems with the Social Security system arise from the fact that the United States has an aging population, which implies that the dependency ratio is increasing over time. Currently it is about one-third, which means that there are about three workers per retiree. By 2030 (when the baby boom generation hits normal retirement age), the ratio will be 0.5—there will be only two workers supporting each retiree. Equation (9.1) tells us that, with an increasing dependency ratio, the only way for a pay-as-you-go system to maintain the same structure of benefits (i.e., a constant value of B/w) is to increase taxes on the workers. For example, today's combined employee-employer Social Security tax rate of 12.4 percent would have to be raised to roughly 20 percent in 2030. Alternatively, in order to keep from raising the tax rate, benefits would have to be cut by one-third. Many other countries are in the same boat. Dependency ratios are increasing in Canada, Australia, and most nations in Western Europe, Latin America, and Asia.

Social Security Reform

Social Security's financial problems have received widespread attention. Given that the status quo is not sustainable over the long term, there has been a vigorous debate over how it should be changed. We discuss a few of the options.

Maintain the Current System

One view is that Social Security is not really having a "crisis." As Aaron [1996, p. 1] notes, "The problems are real and certainly deserve attention, the sooner the better. Taxes will have to be increased, benefits cut, or both. But there is no need for political palpitations and heavy breathing." For example, if payroll tax rates were increased by 1.89 percentage points immediately and the revenues allowed to accumulate in the trust fund, then the system could be brought into balance over the next 75 years. Alternatively, we could lower the replacement ratio a bit by raising the eligibility age for benefits or subjecting benefits to higher rates of taxation. Proponents of this approach argue that Social Security is a popular and successful program and should therefore be left alone to the extent possible. Opponents point to problems mentioned earlier in this chapter—the system reduces national saving, brings about capricious redistributions of income, and so on. Further, the public does not seem to be in the mood for further tax increases at this time. Finally, to obtain *permanent* balance would require a substantially higher increase in payroll tax rates, about 4.7 percentage points.

Privatize the System

In recent years, both policymakers and academics have given serious thought to the possibility of privatizing Social Security. The term *privatization* refers to a variety of schemes that share a common feature: workers' and employers' compulsory contributions are earmarked for each individual's account. The workers then invest the funds in various financial assets, particularly mutual funds (which are collections of assorted stocks and bonds). At the end of their working lives, individuals finance their retirements out of the accumulations in their accounts. In principle, individuals could bequeath unused funds in their accounts to their heirs if they died prematurely.

The best-known privatized social security system is Chile's, which was implemented in 1981. The Chilean system has three main components: (1) Each covered worker must place 10 percent of his or her monthly earnings into an account that is managed by a government-approved financial services firm. (2) Upon retirement, benefits can be taken either as a series of phased withdrawals or as an annuity. (3) A guaranteed minimum pension is available for those who have been in the system a sufficient number of years; it is financed from general revenues [Edwards, 1998].

One attraction of moving to a Chilean-type system is that, over the long term, stocks have earned a substantially higher rate of return than the implicit rate of return that Social Security pays on individuals' contributions into the system. If Social Security taxes were invested in the private market, the argument goes, these substantial rates of return would allow retirees to enjoy large benefits without imposing huge taxes on the current workforce.

To evaluate this argument, recall our earlier observation that the consumption of both retirees and workers must come out of that year's production. Hence, privatization can help finance future retirees' consumption only to the extent that it allows future output to increase. And the only way it can do this is by increasing saving.

However, there is no reason to believe that privatization by itself would raise national saving. The government has to finance its deficit one way or another. Currently, the Social Security trust fund is held in government bonds. If Social Security surpluses are not held in government bonds, the government must sell its bonds to private investors. In order to induce private investors to accept government bonds that would have been bought by the trust fund, their yield has to go up (increasing the debt burden on taxpayers), or the yield on stocks must fall, or both. At the end of the day, all that takes place is a swap of public and private securities between the trust fund and private markets—no new saving is created.

This is why sophisticated schemes for moving to a privatized system always include some provision that would result in increased saving. For example, Feldstein and Samwick's [2001] proposal envisions the establishment of "personal retirement accounts" that would be funded by a portion of the individual's payroll tax equal to 1.5 percent of earnings *only if* the individual agreed to deposit an equal amount from her own pocket. They argue that the out-of-pocket contribution is likely to be new saving, and that this new saving would lead to substantial long-run increases in the capital stock and output.

Risk. The last several years have vividly demonstrated that stocks can go down as well as up. Thus, one possible drawback to privatization is that it would expose individuals to more financial risk. In response, proponents of privatization argue that the apparent certitude of the status quo is illusory—individuals face the possibility that future legislators, confronting the inexorable consequences of Equation (9.1), will reduce retirement benefits. In fact, a number of countries, including the United States, have already made changes in their systems whose effect is to reduce benefits available to the current generation of young and middle-aged workers when they retire [McHale, 1999]. In effect, proponents of privatization turn the risk argument on its head—by reducing political risk, privatization leads to a safer, not a riskier, system.

Administration. No pension system can be administered for free. It costs money to hire people to collect funds, keep records, manage assets, calculate benefits, and so on. Some fear that such costs would be very high under privatization. A natural way to get a sense of whether this would be a problem is to examine the costs of institutions that currently offer retirement savings accounts or provide income to retirees, for example, certain mutual funds. The result, not too surprisingly, is that the costs depend a lot on the details of the system. The more choices and services that are available to investors, the greater will be the administrative costs. For example, the more often people can change their investments, the more expensive the program. Plans can cut administrative costs by restricting how often people can reallocate their assets, but at the cost of reducing flexibility. The key point is that with reasonable compromises regarding the services it provides, it appears that a privatized system can be administered at a modest cost [Shoven, 2000].

Distribution. As already noted, although Social Security is called insurance, one of its important objectives is to redistribute income. The current system really has two distinct goals: to force individuals to insure themselves by reallocating income from their working years to their retirements, and to distribute income to those elderly citizens who would otherwise lack a "socially adequate" level of support. Many of the problems with Social Security stem from the fact that it attempts to meet both objectives through a single structure of benefits and taxes.

Most privatization schemes deal with these two objectives separately. The retirement finance objective is handled by the accumulations in individuals' retirement accounts. The redistribution objective is taken care of by a separate system of transfers to those whose retirement accounts would not provide a level of support considered adequate by society. Supplemental Security Income, which is funded out of general revenues, is a mechanism already in place for making such transfers. Presumably, it could be expanded to allow for as much redistribution to the elderly poor as society desired.

An important consequence of privatization is that family status would no longer have a major effect on the value of a person's Social Security wealth. If a one-earner couple and a two-earner couple paid the same amount into the same fund, they would receive the same benefits. The problem of supporting nonworking spouses could be dealt with by crediting each spouse with half of the total contributions made by the couple. In this way, even if a divorce occurred, each spouse would carry with him or her a given balance on which retirement payments would be based.

Of course, general financing of the transfer part of Social Security would require it to compete openly with other government priorities. Policymakers and the public would have to determine explicitly the value of transfers to the elderly relative to other social objectives. Opponents of privatization argue that this would ultimately undermine the entire program [Munnell, 1999], but proponents disagree.

Bush Commission   In 2001 President Bush formed a commission to devise proposals for privatizing Social Security. The commission came up with three alternatives. All three involved mixed public–private systems, in which individuals would be allowed to take some portion of their payroll taxes and deposit them into private accounts. Individuals who chose this option would have their pay-as-you-go benefits reduced commensurately. Under one of the plans, individuals would be allowed to divert 2.5 percent of their payroll taxes to a Personal Retirement Account (PRA), with the requirement that the worker contribute an additional one percent of her income to the PRA. (For low-income individuals, the 1 percent additional contribution would be subsidized.) This proposal, then, satisfied a key requirement for meaningful reform—it would likely involve new saving. However, many important details regarding administrative matters were not included in the proposal, so it is hard to evaluate it. In this context, however, it is important to note that public–private mixtures are not merely a theoretical possibility; they are used in a number of countries, including Sweden, Australia, Germany, and the United Kingdom. Whether the United States moves in this direction remains to be seen.

Unemployment Insurance

Congress passed the legislation that led states to establish unemployment insurance (UI) programs in 1935, the same year as Social Security. The purpose of the program is to replace income lost due to unemployment. Virtually all wage earners are covered, and in 2002, 10 million individuals received first payments. The average weekly UI benefit was $258 [www.doleta.gov].

Why should insurance against the possibility of unemployment be provided socially? Recall from Chapter 3 that private markets fail to provide adequate amounts of insurance in situations where adverse selection and moral hazard are important. Unemployment satisfies these conditions. Those workers who have the highest probability of becoming unemployed have the highest demand for unemployment insurance (adverse selection). Therefore, private firms that attempted to provide such insurance would have to charge relatively high premiums to make a profit, which would exclude many people from making purchases. At the same time, those workers who managed to obtain insurance might experience more unemployment than otherwise would have been the case (moral hazard). Because it is difficult for the insurer to determine whether or not a layoff is the fault of a worker, a private unemployment insurance company might find itself having to pay out large amounts of money for false claims. In short, it is hard to imagine that providing unemployment insurance would be a profitable venture for private insurance companies. Adverse selection would similarly discourage employers from providing UI benefits to their own employees, because offering UI as a fringe benefit might attract workers who were not interested in long-term employment relationships.

A compulsory government program avoids the adverse selection problem. Hence, government provision of UI has the potential to increase efficiency. However, government provision does *not* eliminate moral hazard. As we will see, this complicates the problem of designing a UI system. We now discuss how the UI program works.

Benefits

The number of weeks for which an individual can receive benefits is determined by a complicated formula that depends on work history and the state in which the person works. In most states, the regular maximum length of time is 26 weeks. However, this period can be extended if the state unemployment rate exceeds certain levels. For example, after September 11, it was extended by 13 weeks. In most states, the benefit formula is designed so that the **gross replacement rate**—the proportion of pretax earnings replaced by UI—is about 50 percent. (However, there is a maximum benefit level that cannot be exceeded.) UI benefits are subject to the federal personal income tax, but they are not subject to the Social Security payroll tax.

Financing

UI is financed by a payroll tax. Unlike the Social Security system, in most states this tax is paid by employers only, not jointly by employers and employees.[8] The employer's UI tax liability for a given worker is the product of the employer's UI tax rate, t_u, and the worker's annual earnings up to the UI tax ceiling. Federal law dictates that the UI tax base include at least the first $7,000 of each covered worker's annual earnings. Seventy-six percent of the states currently have UI tax bases above the federal base, with taxed earnings running as high as $29,300 in Hawaii [www.doleta.gov].

An important feature of the payroll tax is that t_u differs across employers because UI is **experience rated**—t_u depends on the firm's layoff experience. Firms that lay off relatively large numbers of employees generate a lot of

---

[8] As emphasized in Chapter 12, despite the fact that the statute requires the tax to be paid by employers, some or all of it may be shifted to employees.

demands on the UI system. Therefore, such firms are assigned a relatively high t_u. However, if a worker is laid off, generally the increased costs to the employer due to the higher value of t_u are less than the UI benefits received by the worker. For this reason, the experience rating system is described as "imperfect."

Effects on Unemployment

Since its inception, there have been concerns that UI increases unemployment. One possible reason is imperfect experience rating. To see why, suppose that the demand for a firm's product is temporarily slack, so the firm is considering temporary layoffs for some of its workers. With imperfect experience rating, the cost to the employer in increased UI taxes is less than the UI benefit to the worker. Hence, it may be mutually beneficial to lay the worker off temporarily. If the system were characterized by perfect experience rating, UI would provide no such incentive for temporary layoffs.

Much of the academic and political discussion of UI's incentives has focused on the impact of relatively high replacement rates on unemployment. As already suggested, an individual's employment status is often under his or her control. A worker's behavior on the job can influence the probability that he or she will lose it. Similarly, an unemployed worker can control the intensity with which he or she seeks a new job. The existence of UI may make workers more likely to accept employment in industries where the probability of future layoffs is great. In addition, UI may induce the unemployed to spend more time looking for work than they would have otherwise.

Is this moral hazard problem empirically important? This question has been the subject of many econometric studies. Typically, investigators estimate regressions in which the variable on the left-hand side is the number of weeks unemployment insurance is received. The explanatory variables include personal characteristics of the worker such as sex and marital status, as well as the UI weekly benefit amount. If UI encourages unemployment, the coefficient on the weekly benefit amount should be positive; higher benefits lead to a longer duration of unemployment. A typical finding is that a 10 percentage point increase in the net replacement rate of UI—increasing the ratio of weekly benefits to weekly wages from 45 percent to 55 percent, for instance—increases the duration of unemployment by about 1½ weeks [Meyer, 2002].

The fact that UI extends the duration of unemployment is not necessarily undesirable. If workers take more time to search, they may find jobs that are more appropriate for their skills, which enhances efficiency. This argument assumes that in the absence of UI, the amount of time devoted to search would be suboptimal. Such might be the case if unemployed workers could not borrow to maintain their consumption levels while looking for jobs. More generally, a society that believes it is worthwhile to maintain consumption levels for the involuntarily unemployed may be willing to pay the price in terms of some increased voluntary unemployment.

Having said this, we can still ask if there are other ways to provide security with fewer disincentives. Several fascinating social experiments have been conducted to explore this issue. In an experiment in Illinois, members of a randomly selected group of unemployed individuals were offered a bonus of $500 if they found a job within 11 weeks and kept that job for four months. On average, people who were offered the bonus received UI for one week less than members of the control group, and the program saved more on UI benefits than it spent on bonuses. While the experiment was subject to many of the usual problems involved in social experimentation (see Meyer [1995] for details), this is a fruitful approach to future research.

Conclusions

A thought suggested by this chapter is that social insurance programs have had unintended consequences. It is hard to imagine that the founders of Social Security really wanted to generate huge income redistributions based on marital status. Similarly, no one set out to design an unemployment insurance system that increased unemployment.

The extent to which social insurance actually causes economic problems is unknown. There does seem to be a widespread consensus, however, that US social insurance policy fails to operate fairly or efficiently. This is partly because our programs are an inheritance from earlier times when economic and demographic conditions were different than they are today. Part is also due to the failure of policymakers to think through fully the implications of their programs and to define their goals precisely. Reform is difficult because the current forms of social insurance have become almost sacrosanct.

Having said this, we should emphasize that designing "good" social insurance systems is not easy. As stressed throughout the chapter, moral hazard complicates the design of both private and social insurance plans. The presence of UI induces workers to spend "too much" time in between jobs, just as Social Security induces people to save "too little." Mitigating such incentives through lower replacement ratios and the like reduces the scope of the insurance provided. But a key reason for introducing the programs in the first place was to provide insurance. Finding the right trade-off between incentives and adequate insurance is a problem whose solution is not transparent.

Summary

- Social insurance may be justified on grounds of adverse selection, decision-making costs, income distribution, or paternalism.
- Social Security (OASDI) is the largest social insurance program, indeed the largest domestic

spending program. It provides retirement incomes for the aged.
- Social Security benefits are calculated in two steps. Average indexed monthly earnings (AIME) are derived from the worker's earnings history

and determine the primary insurance amount (PIA). To compute actual benefits, the PIA is adjusted by an amount depending on retirement age, family status, and other earnings.

- The Social Security system is pay-as-you-go. Current benefits are financed by taxes on current workers.

- The Social Security trust fund is essentially an accounting device, and by itself does not enhance society's ability to care for retirees in the future.

- Broadly speaking, Social Security redistributes incomes from high- to low-income individuals, from men to women, and from young to old. One-earner married couples tend to gain relative to either two-earner couples or individuals.

- Over time, the economic status of the elderly has improved. Social Security benefits have played an important role in this development.

- Social Security may reduce private saving—the *wealth substitution effect*—or increase saving—the *retirement and bequest* effects. A reasonable

conclusion on the basis of the econometric results is that saving has been reduced, but by how much is not clear.

- The percentage of retired older workers has increased dramatically since the introduction of Social Security. This is at least partially the result of work disincentives in the system.

- Social Security taxes are projected to fall short of benefits starting in about 2016. One possible response is to privatize the system—allow individuals to invest some or all of their contributions as they see fit. While such plans are worth considering, one must remember that unless a given proposal leads to increased saving in the present, it will not help ease the burden of providing for the elderly in the future.

- The unemployment insurance system has imperfect experience ratings for employers. Moreover, its benefits are frequently a substantial proportion of prior earnings. Both these factors increase unemployment.

Discussion Questions

1. In a test for asymmetric information in the French auto insurance market, Chiappori and Salanié [2000] look at the relationship between the comprehensiveness of an individual's policy and the cost per unit coverage. Their argument is that, in the presence of asymmetric information, the more comprehensive the coverage, the greater the cost per franc of coverage. Explain the reasoning behind this argument. (By the way, they find no evidence for asymmetric information on this basis.)

2. The current Social Security system requires mandatory participation; so do most privatization schemes. Arguing against such an approach, Milton Friedman [1999] states, "the fraction of a person's income that it is reasonable for him or her to set aside for retirement depends on that person's circumstances and values. It makes no more sense to specify a minimum fraction for all people than to man-

date a minimum fraction of income that must be spent on housing or transportation." What might be the implications of making participation in Social Security voluntary?

3. In 1990, the ratio of people age 65 or older to people ages 20 to 64 in the United Kingdom was 26.7 percent. In the year 2050, this ratio is expected to be 45.8 percent. Assuming a pay-as-you-go Social Security system, what change in the payroll tax rate between 1990 and 2050 would be needed to maintain the 1990 ratio of benefits to wages? If the tax rate were kept constant, what would happen to the ratio of benefits to wages?

4. Discuss the relationship between the following two statements: (*a*) Social Security benefits are partially subject to the personal income tax, but only for recipients whose other sources of income exceed certain limits. (*b*) Social Security is social insurance, not welfare; therefore it is not means-tested.

5. In her novel *Sense and Sensibility,* Jane Austen wrote, "If you observe, people always live forever when there is any annuity to be paid them." Relate this quotation to the issue of adverse selection in annuity markets.

6. The discussion surrounding Equation 9.1 noted that problems can arise in maintaining the same replacement ratio in a population in which the dependency ratio is growing. Suppose that instead of keeping the replacement ratio constant over time, the goal of public policy is to maintain a constant level of benefits. Explain how this changes one's views of the consequences of an increasing dependency ratio, especially if wages are increasing over time due to productivity gains.

7. Discuss: "Over the long term, the rate of return to stocks is greater than the rate of return to government bonds. Therefore, it would be easier to care for future retirees if the Social Security trust fund were invested in stocks rather than government bonds."

8. According to the calculations of Diamond and Gruber [2001, p. 456], if a male decides to work when he is 68 and then retire when he is 69, the effect of the extra year of work at age 68 is to change his Social Security wealth from $95,964 to $91,131. Is the adjustment to future benefits when an individual of this age defers retirement by a year actuarially fair? Explain.

9. It has been argued that the scheme for financing Social Security is unfair because people with low earnings are taxed at a higher rate than individuals with high earnings. Explain the basis for this contention. Opponents of this view argue that looking at the tax system by itself is misleading—when viewed as part of a tax-transfer system, Social Security gives proportionately larger increases to low-income individuals. Explain the basis for this contention as well.

10. Consider an individual whose earnings are taxed at a rate of 15 percent by the personal income tax and at a combined rate of 7.45 percent by the Social Security and Medicare payroll taxes. Suppose that if he becomes unemployed, unemployment insurance replaces 50 percent of his before-tax earnings. Recall that UI is subject to the income but not the payroll tax. What percent of the individual's *after*-tax income is replaced by UI? What are the implications for the effects of UI on unemployment?

Selected References

Congressional Budget Office. *Social Security: A Primer.* Washington, DC: US Government Printing Office, September 2001.

Feldstein, Martin, and Horst Siebert, eds. *Social Security Pension Reform in Europe.* Chicago: University of Chicago Press, 2002.

Meyer, Bruce D. "Comparing In-Work Benefits and the Reward to Work for Families with Children in the US and UK." *Fiscal Studies* 23 (March 2002), pp.1–49.

Meyer, Bruce D. "Lessons from the U.S. Unemployment Insurance Experiments." *Journal of Economic Literature* 33 (March 1995), pp. 91–131.

Munnell, Alicia H. "Reforming Social Security: The Case Against Individual Accounts." *National Tax Journal,* vol. LII, no. 4 (December 1999), pp. 783–802.

CHAPTER 10

Social Insurance II: Health Care

*I don't pretend to have all the answers, but I am absolutely
sure that this is a problem that America cannot let go.*

BILL CLINTON, ON HEALTH CARE

The view expressed in then President Clinton's statement is widespread—
many perceive the US health care system to be troubled. Much of the
debate over health care concerns the appropriate role for government.
This chapter uses the framework developed in earlier chapters to analyze
this issue. We begin by asking what is special about health care as a commodity, focusing on why private markets might not provide it optimally. We
then discuss the operation of the US health care sector and the government's
role in it.

What's Special About Health Care?

The uniqueness of health care appears obvious. After all, receiving it can be
a matter of life and death. But food and shelter are also crucial for survival,
and the nation is not debating whether private markets are a good way to
provide these commodities. Another possibly unique aspect of the health
care sector is the way it has been expanding in recent years. Health expenditures were 7.1 percent of gross domestic product in 1970, and they are
now about 13.2 percent [Centers for Disease Control and Prevention, 2003].
But by itself, the fact that people are spending disproportionately more on
a commodity is neither unique nor alarming. Expenditures on digital cam-
eras and DVD players have also grown dramatically in recent years, but no
one is terribly upset about it.

Why should the government be involved in this market? There are several possible reasons.

Poor Information.   We normally assume that consumers are fairly well informed about the commodities they purchase—when you buy an apple, you have a good idea of how it will taste and how much satisfaction it will give you. In contrast, when you are ill, you may not have much of a sense of what medical procedures are appropriate. To make things more complicated, the person on whom you are likely to rely for advice, your physician, is also the person who is selling you the commodity. True, there are other services whose purchase involve uncertainty and asymmetric information—think of home repair. However, in such situations there is generally more time to gather the relevant information than there is in the medical context.

Adverse Selection and Moral Hazard.   Health care costs can be unpredictable and very large. In such a situation, people will want insurance. Most of the previous chapter's general discussion about possible problems in private insurance markets applies to health insurance in particular.

- When a health insurance company sets a price for a policy for individuals in a given class (for example, middle-aged urban females), the policy tends to be purchased by those individuals with the highest risk. For example, if Monica believes that she is at high risk for a heart attack and Rachel does not, then if they are offered insurance at the same price, Monica is more likely to purchase it. This *adverse selection* problem causes the average buyer of insurance to have a higher risk than the average person in his or her class. But with a lot of its policyholders becoming ill, the insurance company finds itself losing money. To break even, the company must therefore raise premiums. With higher premiums, relatively low-risk individuals leave the market. (Facing the higher premium, Monica purchases the insurance only if she *really* believes that she is in danger of a heart attack.) Thus, the market may underprovide health insurance, other things being the same.

- Insurance may distort people's behavior. If people know that they have insurance, they may take less care to avoid risks. Thus, people with insurance may adopt more unhealthy lifestyles (eating a lot of junk food and not exercising much) because insurance reduces the negative consequences of doing so. Further, people have incentives to overconsume health care, because the insurance pays for some or all of the cost. These incentive problems are referred to as *moral hazard.*

Moral hazard can be analyzed using a conventional supply-and-demand diagram. In Figure 10.1, the market demand curve for medical services is labeled D_m. For simplicity, assume that the marginal cost of producing medical services is a constant, P_0. Hence, the supply curve, S_m, is a horizontal line at P_0. As usual, equilibrium is at the intersection of supply and demand; the price and quantity are P_0 and M_0, respectively. Total expenditure on medical

FIGURE 10.1

Moral hazard in the market for medical services

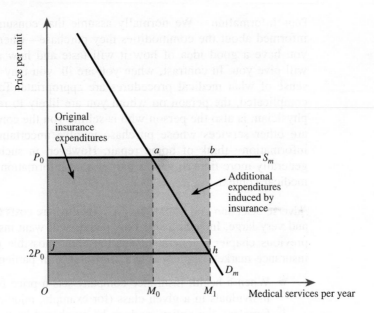

services is the product of the price per unit times number of units, that is, OP_0 times OM_0, or rectangle P_0OM_0a (the colored area in the diagram).

Before proceeding, we should note one possible objection to Figure 10.1—the downward sloping demand curve. When people are sick, don't they just follow the doctor's orders, regardless of price? Would you haggle with your surgeon in the midst of an appendicitis attack? The implication of this view is that the demand curve for medical services is perfectly vertical. Such reasoning ignores the fact that many medical procedures are discretionary. Patients make the initial decision whether to seek health care. And despite the conflict-of-interest issue referred to already, patients do not always comply with their doctor's advice.

How does the introduction of insurance affect the market? To keep things simple, assume that the policy pays for 80 percent of health costs. Then the proportion left for the patient to pay, referred to as the **coinsurance rate,** is 20 percent. The key to analyzing the impact of insurance is to realize that a 20 percent coinsurance rate is equivalent to an 80 percent reduction in the price facing the patient—if the incremental cost to the hospital for a day's stay is $800, the patient pays only $160. In Figure 10.1, the patient no longer confronts price P_0, but only .2 times P_0. Given this lower price, the quantity demanded increases to M_1, and the patient spends area $OjhM_1$ on medical services.

At the new equilibrium, although the patient is paying .2 P_0 per unit, the marginal cost of providing health services is still P_0; the difference (.8 P_0) is paid by the insurance. Hence, *total* expenditures are OP_0 times OM_1, or the rectangle P_0OM_1b, with the insurance company paying P_0bhj. Thus, because of the insurance, health care expenditures increase from P_0OM_0a to P_0OM_1b, or the gray area aM_0M_1b.

Of course, the actual amount by which expenditures increase depends on the shape of the demand curve. Estimating the shape was one of the goals of a famous randomized experiment conducted by the RAND Corporation in the 1970s. People were randomly assigned into insurance plans with different coinsurance rates to see how their spending on health care would be affected. The results suggested that a 10 percent increase in the price of medical services reduces the quantity demanded by about 2 percent [Newhouse *et al.*, 1993].

Externalities.   People's consumption of medical services can create externalities, both positive and negative. If you get a flu vaccination, there is a positive externality, because it reduces the probability that others will become infected by the disease. On the other hand, if you overuse antibiotics so that new strains of immune bacteria develop, then others become worse off. According to the usual arguments (see Chapter 5), in the presence of externalities, government intervention can enhance efficiency.

Paternalism.   People may not understand how insurance works, or they may lack the foresight to purchase it. Paternalistic arguments suggest that people should be forced into a medical insurance system for their own good. There does indeed appear to be a strong societal consensus that everyone should have access to at least basic medical services.

The US Health Care Market

The US health care industry is massive. It includes hospitals, nursing homes, doctors, nurses, and dentists, as well as producers of eyeglasses, prescription and nonprescription drugs, artificial limbs, and other equipment. It employs about 10 million people and accounts for about 13.2 percent of GDP. The two largest components of spending are on hospitals (about 32 percent) and physician services (about 22 percent). With the theory of health care markets from the previous section as background, we are now ready to discuss the key features of this market.

Private Insurance

Consumers pay only about 17 percent of health expenses out of pocket. The rest is paid for by "third parties"—private health insurance pays for 35 percent; the government pays for 43 percent; and the remainder is from philanthropy and other sources.[1] In short, consumers do not directly confront most of the costs for health care. In this section we discuss the provision of private health insurance.

---

[1] Computed from Centers for Medicare and Medicaid Services, *Data Compendium 2002*, www.cms.hhs.gov.

Employer-Provided Insurance.   An important peculiarity of private insurance in the United States is that most of it—about 93 percent for those under 65—is provided through employers as a benefit to their employees.[2] We don't purchase food or clothing through our employers, so why do we do it for health insurance? This phenomenon seems to be an inadvertent by-product of government wage and price controls instituted during World War II. Nonwage components of the compensation package such as health care were exempt from the controls. Predictably, employers started offering these nonwage benefits to attract workers. The popularity of employer-provided insurance has been fueled by certain provisions of the income tax law, which are discussed later.

An implication of employer-provided health insurance is that when you lose your job, you also lose your health insurance. However, in 1996, Congress enacted legislation to help people who change jobs hold onto their health insurance. Under the Health Insurance Portability and Accountability Act (known as the **Kennedy-Kassenbaum Act,** after its legislative sponsors), an employer must include a new employee (who previously had insurance) in the company's group insurance plan within 12 months, even if the employee has a preexisting medical condition that will be quite expensive to treat and thereby increase the firm's insurance premiums. Further, the law requires insurance companies to make coverage available (at a price) to individuals who leave group plans. One of the motivations for the Kennedy-Kassenbaum Act was to improve the efficiency of the labor market. Without such legislation, the argument goes, individuals who happened to be undergoing expensive medical treatment would be locked into their current jobs, because prospective employers would not want to incur the higher insurance costs associated with hiring them. Interestingly, although there were many anecdotal accounts of this "job-lock" phenomenon, the econometric evidence that it was important prior to the Kennedy-Kassenbaum Act is mixed [Holtz-Eakin, 1994]. In any case, some policymakers believe that the law has been stymied because insurers charge individuals very high prices for policies. This is not a very surprising outcome; because of both adverse selection issues and administrative costs one would expect policies sold to individuals to be quite expensive.

Another labor market issue also relates to adverse selection. It might appear that employer-provided insurance solves this problem—because insurance is purchased by the employer on behalf of a *group* of employees, the insurer knows that on average the costs of providing insurance should not be too high. However, this ignores the fact that the workers at a particular firm may not be a random group with respect to their health care needs. To see why, recall that health insurance is just one component of a worker's compensation. Other things being the same, a firm can pay

---

[2] Computed from Centers for Medicare and Medicaid Services, *Health United States 2002,* www.cms.hhs.gov.

its workers higher wages if it offers a less generous package of insurance benefits. Workers with lower than average risks of illness or who are covered through their spouses' insurance plans have incentives to select employers whose packages include a high proportion of wages and little or no insurance. The flip side of this phenomenon is that firms with relatively generous insurance benefits will find themselves with a work force that has higher risks than average. To pay the insurance premiums for this high-risk group, the employer has to lower the wage component of compensation, which makes the job appealing only to people with even higher risks, and so on. This is a typical adverse selection phenomenon, which may result in fewer firms offering insurance than is efficient, particularly smaller firms.

Diversity in Provision. Our discussion of employer-provided insurance has focused on the trade-off between the amount of health insurance and the level of wages. However, employers can also vary how health care is provided under the policies they offer. Until the early 1980s, most insurance policies provided for payments to health care providers on the basis of the actual costs of treating a patient, a system called **cost-based reimbursement** or **fee-for-service.** Cost-based systems provide little incentive to economize on methods for delivering health care; to the contrary, the more resources devoted to a patient, the more money the health care provider receives.

In response to high and growing health care costs, employers have turned to arrangements that limit utilization and keep prices down on the supply rather than demand side of the market. Under such arrangements, generically referred to as **managed care,** patients face little or no cost sharing, so there is no incentive to economize on health care on the demand side. Rather, health care suppliers are given incentives to keep costs down. One example of such an incentive is **capitation-based reimbursement,** under which providers receive annual payments for each patient in their care, regardless of the services used by that patient. There are a variety of managed care arrangements. With Health Maintenance Organizations (HMOs), a group of physicians work only for a particular plan and patients can see doctors only in that plan. With Preferred Provider Organizations (PPOs), a group of physicians accept lower fees for access to a network; patients can go outside the network but at a greater cost. There are many variations on these themes. Today about 95 percent of insured Americans are in some kind of managed care arrangement.

Has managed care helped to contain health costs? During much of the 1990s, this appeared to be the case—the rate of increase in health care costs and insurance premiums fell considerably. But this success at controlling costs turned out to be short-lived, and costs are on the rise again. The possible causes for this phenomenon are discussed later in this chapter.

The vexing problem with certain managed care arrangements is that they create incentives for health care providers to skimp on the quality of care.

After all, the same payment is received regardless of the services provided. However, while the evidence is mixed, the work surveyed by Cutler [2002] suggests that health is not worse for individuals in managed care arrangements, other things being the same.

The Role of Government

Government plays a large role in health care. It licenses physicians, monitors health threats in the environment, owns some hospitals, sponsors research on disease prevention, and runs childhood immunization programs, to name a few activities. Our focus here, however, is the federal government's role in providing health insurance. There are three key programs: Medicaid, Medicare, and the implicit subsidy for private insurance embodied in the federal income tax system. **Medicaid,** a federally supported health insurance program for certain low-income individuals and particularly children, was covered in Chapter 8. We now discuss the other two programs.

Medicare

The Medicare program, enacted in 1965, provides health insurance for people aged 65 and older and the disabled. Its purpose is to increase access to quality health care by the elderly without an undue financial burden. Expenditures for Medicare in 2002 were $254 billion. It is the second-largest domestic spending program; only Social Security is larger.

Before discussing the details of the Medicare program, we might ask why the government should be involved so extensively in the market for health insurance for the elderly. After all, it is foreseeable that eventually both earnings capacity and health are likely to decline. The discussion of the health care market at the beginning of this chapter is relevant here. Because of adverse selection, insurance may not be provided in efficient amounts. By forcing everyone to purchase insurance, this problem can be avoided. In addition, purchase of health insurance involves high administrative and sales costs. People have to search for the right policy, physical exams may be required, and so on. By forming the aged into a single group, a government program may economize on such costs. Of course, a drawback of this "one-size-fits-all" approach is that it ignores differences in individuals' preferences for insurance.

The Structure of Medicare.   Medicare covers nearly the entire population aged 65 and older. There are about 39.6 million enrollees. The program is administered by the federal government, and eligibility standards are uniform across the states. Unlike Medicaid, the program of health care for the poor, Medicare is *not* means-tested. Claimants do not need to establish that their incomes fall below a certain level to participate.

Benefits.   Once the government decides to become involved in the medical sector, it must make a fundamental decision: Will health care services be produced by the government or by the private sector? Different countries have made quite different decisions. In the United Kingdom, for example, the government owns and runs hospitals. In contrast, in the United States, health care is primarily provided by the private sector. Thus, Medicare is a system of government finance for health care, not government production of health care.

The Medicare program is divided into three parts, A, B, and C. Part A, which accounted for $131 billion in expenditures in 2000, is **hospital insurance (HI).** Participation in HI is compulsory. It covers 90 days of inpatient medical care per year and up to 100 days of care in a skilled nursing facility per lifetime. (In both cases, the patient is responsible for some portion of the costs.) HI does not cover long-term institutional services. Part B of Medicare is **supplementary medical insurance (SMI),** which pays for physicians, supplies ordered by physicians, and medical services rendered outside the hospital. Unlike HI, SMI is voluntary. Enrollees must pay a monthly premium that varies over time and is currently about $59. About 99 percent of the eligible population chooses to enroll in SMI. Part C, referred to as **Medicare+Choice,** allows individuals to enroll in certain managed care arrangements. All Medicare+Choice plans are required to provide the current Medicare benefit package, except for hospice services. The monthly premium for Medicare+Choice generally exceeds the Part B premium; in return, it may cover items such as prescription drugs, which are not covered by standard Medicare. Like conventional managed care, Medicare+Choice restricts individuals' choice of health care providers. Further details about Medicare premiums and benefits are available at the Web site of the Centers for Medicare and Medicaid Services, http://cms.hhs.gov/medicare/.

As just noted, Medicare generally provides no benefits for prescription drugs. This reflects the fact that Medicare was designed back in the 1960s, before the revolutionary developments in pharmaceutical technology that have made drugs central to the treatment of everything from heart disease to arthritis. Spending on prescription drugs is the fastest growing component of health care costs in the United States. Medicare beneficiaries spent almost $87 billion in outpatient prescription drugs in 2002, and this figure is expected to rise to $128 billion by 2005 [Congressional Budget Office, 2002, p. ix]. We will discuss later some issues involved in adding a prescription drug benefit to Medicare.

Financing.   HI is financed by a payroll tax on the earnings of current workers. The rate is 1.45 percent on the employer and employee each, for a total of 2.90 percent. The tax is applied to all earnings; there is no ceiling. The tax proceeds are deposited in the HI trust fund, from which disbursements to health care providers are made. Medicare runs on a pay-as-you-go basis. The medical bills of current retirees are paid by today's workers, not by drawing on money accumulated in the HI trust fund. Like the Social Security trust fund discussed in the last chapter, the HI

Table 10.1   **Federal government outlays for Medicare**   *(selected years)*

Year	Outlays (in billions)	Outlays as Percent of GDP
1967	$ 3.2	0.4%
1970	6.8	0.7
1975	14.1	0.9
1980	34.0	1.2
1985	69.6	1.7
1990	107.4	1.9
1995	177.1	2.4
2002	253.7	2.2

SOURCE: Congressional Budget Office [2003, pp. 156-57].

trust fund is primarily an accounting device, and does not increase the real ability of society to meet future health care bills.

Unlike HI, SMI relies on general revenues for financing, not on a payroll tax. In addition, SMI receives funds from the monthly premium mentioned earlier. Currently, about 82 percent of SMI financing is from general revenues and 18 percent from premiums, so the federal subsidy is heavy.

Putting Medicare on a Sounder Financial Footing.   Table 10.1 shows Medicare expenditures over time, both in dollars and as a proportion of GDP. In 1967, Medicare outlays were $3.2 billion, or about 0.4 percent of GDP. By 2002, the figure was $253 billion, or 2.2 percent of GDP. For the last decade or so, Medicare has grown at a faster rate than federal revenues, and there is now substantial policy interest in alleviating the stress that Medicare puts on the federal budget. As suggested by the cartoon on the next page, people are quite aware of Medicare's financial problems, and a substantial amount of thought has been given to dealing with them. The approaches include the following options.

Increase the burden on current beneficiaries.   Monthly premiums could be raised, the coinsurance rate could be increased, and the age of eligibility for benefits could be raised. Such proposals received serious consideration in 1997, but none survived the legislative process.

Price controls.   Since the early 1980s, the favored strategy for cutting Medicare costs has been controlling the prices received by service providers. In 1984, for example, Medicare Part A moved from cost-based reimbursement to prospective reimbursement, in which HI pays the hospital an amount per patient that depends on his or her illness and is determined *before* treatment is received. Medicare Part B has frozen physicians' fees for extended periods and put in place volume performance

*"You're in luck, in a way. Now is the time to be
sick—while Medicare still has some money."*

• • •

standards that set an acceptable growth rate for spending on doctors' services each year, with penalties if the target is breached. Price controls are always complicated to administer (there are over 100,000 pages of Medicare regulations), and tend to have undesirable side effects. In this context, one major concern is that the controls make health care providers less disposed to treat Medicare patients. For example, after Medicare announced a 5.4 percent across-the-board reduction in physician reimbursements in 2002, a substantial number of medical practices simply stopped taking Medicare patients, including the Mayo Clinic's branch in Jacksonville, Florida [Rosenberg, 2002, p. 11]. In any case, as Table 10.1 documents, Medicare has continued to grow rapidly despite the presence of the various controls.

Managed care.   As noted earlier in this chapter, there has been a virtual revolution in the way health care is provided in the US private sector. Managed-care options now dominate the traditional fee-for-service approach, and they are also of growing importance in the Medicaid program. Legislation passed in 1997 created new inducements for Medicare beneficiaries to enroll in managed care arrangements. However, this option does not seem to be very popular; only about 15 percent of the Medicare population has picked it up [Cutler, 2002, p. 11]. Further, a number of

HMOs have been dropping out of Medicare because of insufficiently high reimbursements. In any case, as noted earlier, it is not clear that, in the long run, managed care is effective at holding down the growth rate of health care costs.

Hospice and home health care.   Medicare beneficiaries tend to use relatively large amounts of health care as death approaches. Expenditures during the last year of life account for about 27 percent of Medicare costs. Some have suggested that, when patients are facing terminal illnesses, the goal of health care should be relief of suffering rather than possibly painful and expensive procedures to extend life. In this spirit, the Medicare rules allow terminal patients to obtain access to alternatives such as hospices. However, according to Garber, MaCurdy, and McClellan [1999], this change has not slowed the growth in expenditures at the end of life. They found that while use of hospitals for dying beneficiaries did decline, the associated increase in the use of hospices and other services rose enough to wipe out any expenditure savings.

Medical Savings Accounts (MSAs).   Most of the attempts to restrain Medicare costs have focused on the providers of health care. An alternative approach is to give the consumers stronger incentives to economize on purchases of health care. Most Medicare patients face little or no charge on the margin for covered expenses. In contrast, under a *catastrophic insurance policy,* individuals pay for their own health care expenses unless they are very large, at which point the insurer takes over. Thus, the individual has an incentive to control routine costs, but is covered in the event of a catastrophic illness.

Part C of Medicare allows a limited number of beneficiaries to enroll in a *Medical Savings Account,* which in effect is a catastrophic insurance policy. The government uses part of the money that would have been spent to enroll the individual in a managed care arrangement to purchase an insurance policy with a high deductible (about $6,000). The remainder of the money is deposited into an account. After the deductible is met, remaining payments come out of the account. Subject to certain requirements, any money left over in the account goes into the individual's pocket—it can be used for non-medical purchases. This provides an incentive to economize on health care spending.

In effect, MSAs are intended to deal with the moral hazard associated with insurance. They reduce the incentive to consume "excessive" medical care because the expenditure has an opportunity cost to the patient. However, we would expect adverse selection to be an important issue—a policy with a big deductible would be attractive primarily to people who are in good health and therefore anticipate low expenses. This would leave the other parts of Medicare to deal with the relatively ill (and expensive) patients. In any case, MSAs have been in effect only since 1997, and are currently available only to a limited number of participants, so at this time not much is known about their effects.

A perhaps depressing closing thought is that there may be no feasible policy that can stem the long-term increase in Medicare costs. As we will see later in this chapter, some believe that increases in the cost of health care are driven by forces that are beyond the control of conventional remedies.

The Implicit Subsidy for Health Insurance

One of the government's largest impacts on the health care market comes through a provision of the federal tax law. This provision states that an individual's wages are subject to the Social Security payroll and the personal income taxes, but employer contributions to medical insurance plans are not. For example, if your employer increases your wages by $2,000, you have to pay taxes on that amount. But if your employer uses the $2,000 to purchase health insurance for you, then your tax bill does not go up by a penny. To understand the implications of this provision, suppose that the combined tax rate on your wages is 38 percent. For each dollar your employer pays you, you can buy 62 cents worth of goods and services. In contrast, each dollar spent by your employer on insurance buys a full dollar's worth of insurance. In effect, then, this provision of the tax code subsidizes the purchase of health insurance by lowering its opportunity cost in terms of other commodities. In practical terms, the size of the subsidy is quite large. According to Gruber and Poterba [1996, p. 149], it reduces the relative cost of employer-provided health insurance by about 32 percent. The exclusion of health insurance benefits from the tax base costs the US Treasury about $75 billion per year in forgone tax revenues.

Because of the implicit subsidy, workers want a larger share of their compensation paid in the form of health insurance than otherwise would have been the case. Thus, health insurance packages become more generous. Similarly, the subsidy induces employers to expand insurance policies to include items such as vision and routine dental benefits.

Nothing is wrong with buying insurance; it fills an important need in people's lives. However, efficiency requires that when consumers purchase insurance, they make their decisions based on its marginal cost (see Chapter 3). The subsidy lowers the price to consumers below its marginal cost and induces them to consume insurance in more than efficient amounts. Consequently they consume too much medical care. Many analysts believe that this has contributed to the increase in medical costs and that employer-provided health benefits should be subject to taxation.

There is an important qualification to this argument that the tax subsidy leads to "too much" insurance. To some extent, technological change in the health care industry has been driven by the generosity of insurance—health insurance allows people to afford expensive new procedures, which gives producers the incentive to create them. But this just pushes the question back another level—perhaps the tax subsidy leads to too much innovation. The theory of public goods (Chapter 4) suggests that private markets underprovide innovation. Research on medical innovation produces valuable knowledge that has public-good characteristics—it is nonrival in consumption and nonexcludable. If that is so, then a subsidy may in fact be appropriate. In fact, some evidence suggests that the social return to medical innovation exceeds the private return [Cutler and McClellan, 2001]. In short, on balance it is not clear that the implicit tax subsidy does in fact reduce efficiency.

The Twin Issues: Access and Cost

Much of the current health care debate has been driven by two related concerns—access to health care and the costs of obtaining it. This section discusses these two key issues in more detail.

Access

Eighty-three percent of Americans under the age of 65 have some form of health insurance. This leaves 17 percent, or about 41 million people, uninsured. The percentage of the population under age 65 without insurance has been growing over time. In 1979, it was only 14.7 percent. Much of the anxiety over the state of US health care is due to concern for the uninsured.

The uninsured are a rather diverse group. For example, 31 percent of those with incomes below the poverty level are uninsured, but so are 7.7 percent of those whose incomes exceed $75,000. With respect to employment status, about 22 percent of part-time workers are uninsured, but so are 16 percent of full-time workers [US Census Bureau, 2002b]. Indeed, most of the uninsured are employed or the family member of someone who is employed. The probability of having health insurance rises with the size of the firm for which one works. Presumably, this difference is because the cost of insurance depends on firm size. As the number of employees increases, the per-employee administrative costs of running an insurance plan fall. Moreover, firms with many employees spread the risk of serious health care problems over a larger number of people, and hence can obtain better rates.

It is crucial to realize that the absence of health insurance and the absence of health care are not the same thing. Some people pay for their health care out-of-pocket, although on average, the uninsured pay for only 44 percent of the medical services they use. The free (to them) care is provided, primarily through hospitals. In 2001, US hospitals provided almost $24 billion worth of uncompensated care, which was financed by increasing the bills paid by other parties [Hadley and Holahan, 2003]. Nevertheless, people without health insurance generally consume fewer health care services than those with similar health problems who are insured. Surprisingly, it is not clear how this lack of care translates into health outcomes. As Meer and Rosen [2003] note, some studies find that extending insurance to the uninsured improves their health, but other studies do not.

Why has the proportion of people without insurance been increasing? Cost is the key factor. As health insurance becomes more expensive, people

Table 10.2   **National health expenditures**   *(selected years)*

Year	Total Expenditures (in billions of dollars)	Percent of GDP	Public Share as Percent of Total Health Expenditure†
1970	$ 73	7.0%	37.8%
1980	246	8.8	42.7
1990	696	12.0	40.6
1997	1,091	13.1	46.0
2000	1,300	13.2	45.2
2011*	2,800*	17.0*	—

*Projections.

†Includes federal, state, and local.

SOURCE: "Health United States 2002," Centers for Disease Control and Prevention [URL: www.cdc.gov]. Projections for 2011 from Centers for Medicare and Medicaid Services [URL: www.cms.hhs.gov].

Table 10.3   **Real health expenditures per capita in selected countries***

Canada	$2,535
Germany	2,748
Japan	2,012
United Kingdom	1,763
United States	4,631

*2000 US dollars.

SOURCE: Organization for Economic Cooperation and Development, *OECD Health Data 2002*, Table 9, [URL: www.oecd.org].

have to give up more of their wages in order to receive a given set of health benefits; at some point, obtaining the insurance just isn't worth it. Indeed, only about 89 percent of workers who have access to employment-related health insurance take up the option [Cooper and Schone, 1997]. Low-income workers are particularly likely not to take up employer-provided insurance. Their personal tax rates are low so that the benefit of excluding health benefits from taxation is relatively small. Hence, the issue of declining access to health care is intimately related to the problem of increasing costs.

Cost

Table 10.2 documents the breathtaking rate at which health care costs have been increasing in the United States. In 1970, health care expenditures were 7.1 percent of GDP. They are now about 13.2 percent, and according to government projections, they will be 17 percent by 2011. Table 10.3 puts US expenditures in an international context. It shows that the United States has much higher per capita expenditures on health care than Canada, Germany, Japan, or the United Kingdom. Interestingly, although the

FIGURE 10.2

Health expenditures
as a share of GDP

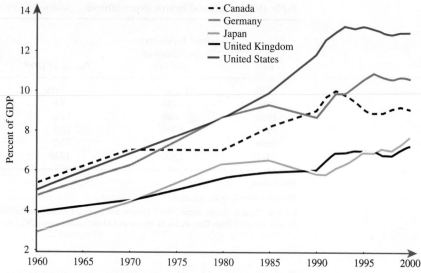

SOURCE: Organization for Economic Cooperation and Development, *OECD Health Data 2002*, Table 9. URL
[http://www.oecd.org].

United States has a higher *level* of expenditure than these countries, over
the long-term, its rate of *growth* in these expenditures has not been out of
line with theirs. This observation is documented in Figure 10.2, which
plots their health expenditures relative to GDP over time. These four countries have very different systems for financing health care than the United
States has. In particular, health care coverage is not provided by employers as it is in the United States, and the government plays a much larger
role in setting prices. Thus, as we seek explanations for the growth rate
of health care expenditures in the United States, we should not focus
exclusively on factors that are idiosyncratic to the US system. The following discussion is based on the work of Newhouse [1992a], who
attempted to calculate how much each of the following factors has contributed to this growth rate.

The Graying of America.   In 1980, 11.1 percent of the US population was
over 65; currently the figure is 12.4 percent. During the same period, the
proportion of the population over 85 increased from 1.0 percent to 1.5 percent [US Bureau of the Census, 2002, p. 13]. As the population ages, one
expects health care expenditures to increase as well. To what extent can this
phenomenon explain the rise in health care expenditures? To obtain a rough
answer to this question, Newhouse calculated how much total spending
would have changed if the per capita expenditures in each age group of the
population had stayed the same between 1950 and 1987 and only the proportions of the population in each age group changed. He found that the

change in age structure accounts for just a tiny fraction of the increase in expenditure.

Income Growth. To the extent that the demand for medical care increases with income, then income growth may drive the increase in health care expenditures. On the basis of econometric analyses of medical demand, Newhouse estimated that the income elasticity of demand for medical care is between 0.2 and 0.4—a 10 percent increase in income leads to a 2 to 4 percent increase in the demand for health care. Multiplying this elasticity by the actual percentage increase in income over time, Newhouse concluded that increases in income account for less than 10 percent of the growth in health care expenditures. Richer societies want more health care, but not enough more to explain the increase in health expenditures.

Third-Party Payments. We saw in Figure 10.1 how insurance increases the level of medical care demanded. Recall, however, that our task is to explain the continual *growth* in health expenditures over time. For third-party payments to be the reason for the growth in health care expenditures, it is necessary for insurance coverage to have been growing. The number of insured people has been increasing, but according to Newhouse's calculations, not by enough to account for more than about one-eighth of the growth of expenditures. Indeed, the average rate at which hospital expenditures were covered was essentially unchanged during the 1980s, while real expenditures on hospitals rose by over 50 percent [p. 7].

Improvements in Quality. Newhouse concluded that if all the preceding factors are considered, and a few others (such as the practice of defensive medicine, administrative costs, etc.) are thrown in as well, it explains less than half of the increase in expenditures. He argued that the rest of the increase is due to technological improvements. Physician training, medical techniques, and equipment have all improved over time. The last several decades have witnessed breathtaking developments in medical technology. As a result, the quality of health care has improved—diagnostic techniques, surgical procedures, and therapies for a wide range of medical problems get better all the time. Treatment of a heart attack today is simply not the same "commodity" as treatment of a heart attack in 1970. In fact, although innovations like coronary bypass surgery and cardiac catheterization have raised expenditures per heart patient, they have actually reduced the prices of obtaining various health outcomes, such as surviving hospitalization due to a heart attack [Newhouse, 2001].

Now, some improvements in medical technique are quite inexpensive. Prescribing aspirin for heart attack victims leads to a substantial improvement in their survival probabilities. But new medical technologies are often costly. For example, it costs about $2 million to acquire a PET (positron emission tomography) machine, which can detect changes in cells before they form a tumor large enough to be spotted by x-rays or MRI. Hence, even in the absence of the factors already noted, medical expenditures would be growing.

This technology-based theory also helps explain why countries with different health care financing and delivery systems have all experienced increases in health care expenditures. (See Figure 10.2.) These societies have at least one thing in common—they have all been exposed to the same expensive innovations in technology.

This technology-based explanation puts the debate over cost containment in a new light. If costs are rising mostly because of quality improvements, is it a bad thing? A key question in this context is whether people value these innovations at their marginal social cost. No one knows for sure, but Newhouse offers a provocative insight: "If many consumers felt that new technology wasn't worth the price, it seems odd that we do not observe some firms trying to enter and offer at least some aspects of 1960s medicine at 1960s prices" (p. 16).

Buttressing this argument is a calculation by Murphy and Topel [2000] that improvements in life expectancy added about $2.8 trillion (in 1992 dollars) per year to US national wealth between 1970 and 1990. Any such calculation must be regarded as just a rough approximation for several reasons. First, how does one put a dollar value on added years of life? Murphy and Topel use measures derived from statistical estimates of the increased wages that workers require in order to compensate them for taking jobs that require relatively high risks of dying on the job; this approach is described in the next chapter. Second, it is not clear that all the improvement in life expectancy was due to changes in health care. They note, though, that "about $1.5 trillion of the overall $2.8 trillion annual increase was due to the reduction in mortality from heart disease—an area in which medical advances in both prevention and acute care have been significant" (p. 24). Third, although increases in life expectancy are very important, advances in medical care have also improved the quality of life, and these are valuable as well. Just think of hip replacements, Viagra, Cox-2 inhibitors such as Vioxx to relieve arthritis pain, and arthroscopic surgery. While it is difficult or impossible to attach a dollar value to these improvements, the benefits must be substantial. Hence, even allowing for the roughness of the Murphy-Topel calculation, its basic message that there are enormous benefits to spending on health care is compelling.

The focus of this discussion has been on whether medical expenditure is driven by technological change. An intriguing possibility, however, is that at least to some extent, causation runs in the other direction—increases in spending increase the profitability of medical innovations and therefore encourage technological change. This is a difficult proposition to test, but some evidence suggests there is something to it. Finkelstein [2003] noted that in 1993, Medicare began covering the cost of flu vaccinations for all Medicare recipients, without any copayments or deductibles. She found that after this change in policy, pharmaceutical firms invested significantly more money on research and development for new flu vaccines.

In short, there is no reason to believe that all the growth in health care expenditures is a bad thing, or that there is some magic percentage of GDP that is the right percentage to devote to health care. Cost-containment measures that impede technological improvements may make society worse off.

New Directions for Government's Role in Health Care

Critics of the status quo believe it is simply impossible for costs to be brought down to an "acceptable" level without a more fundamental change in the system engineered by the federal government. Further, critics view intervention as imperative to reduce substantially the number of uninsured individuals.

A wide variety of proposals has been made for expanding the role of the government in the health care system. We now turn to a few of the prominent possibilities.

Individual Mandates

Most states require their residents to purchase automobile insurance. Why not, then, similarly require every person to buy basic health insurance? One version of this idea has been proposed by the Heritage Foundation, a public policy institute in Washington, DC. Under the Heritage plan, the Medicare and Medicaid programs would be kept in place. However, the exclusion from taxation of employer-provided health care benefits would be ended. Instead, employers would be required to provide to their employees vouchers for health insurance, which the employees would use to purchase insurance on their own, or through some other organization, such as a church or fraternal group. According to its proponents, "Costs would be controlled by using the best device ever found to hold down costs without sacrificing quality and efficiency: consumer choice within a competitive market" [Butler, 1992, p. 42–43]. The plan would require relatively little in the way of new bureaucracy, and it would preserve consumer choice. However, it is not clear that the vouchers would be large enough to induce most people to purchase insurance. Further, there might be adverse selection on the supply side of the market—insurers would have a tendency to reject high-risk customers. Either insurance companies would have to be allowed to charge higher premiums to such customers or some mechanism for forcing them to provide coverage would be needed. Finally, there are questions about how the mandate would be enforced. Would people who failed to buy insurance be thrown in jail? Is there any feasible financial penalty that would be large enough to force all people to buy health insurance?

Single Payer

One set of reforms would scrap the current health care insurance market and replace it with a single provider of health insurance. The single-payer system would be funded by taxes and provide all citizens, regardless of income or health status, with a determined set of health care services, at no direct cost to the insured. Forcing everyone into the system solves the adverse selection problem. Variants of this approach are used in Canada and several European countries. In Canada, health care services are produced by the private sector, with the reimbursements negotiated by the government. In the United Kingdom, health services are produced by the public sector through the National Health Service. In the US context, perhaps the easiest way to think about a single-payer system is extending Medicare to the entire population, not just the elderly.

The fact that single-payer systems do not confront individuals with the cost of their own care is a major virtue to its proponents and a major flaw to its critics. Proponents believe it is unethical to force sick people to have to make cost-benefit decisions about receiving health care and admire the universal access feature of the program. However, because patients pay little or nothing for care, critics note that there are no incentives to reduce costs in the system.

If prices are not used to ration health care, some other mechanism is needed. In single-payer countries, rationing is done by imposing constraints on the supply side of the system. A predetermined global budget for health care may be set and enforced by price controls and regulations with respect to what treatments can be used. In some cases, this may result in lengthy waits for some treatments and the denial of certain treatments. In the United Kingdom, for example, patients over 65 years of age are generally not permitted kidney dialysis.

Perhaps the major criticism of single-payer systems is that they take the choice about how much should be spent on health care out of the hands of individuals and throw it into the political arena. For example, in Canada all "medically necessary" health services are supposed to be publicly financed, but the definition of medical need differs across provinces depending, in part, on their political environments. Another critical issue is whether the introduction of new technologies takes longer in single-payer than in decentralized systems. Deaton and Paxson [2001] note that decreases in mortality in the United States are mirrored by decreases in mortality in the United Kingdom, but only after four years, and speculate that this is due to the fact that the centralized UK system impedes the adoption of expensive new technologies.

There now seems to be some anecdotal evidence that the single-payer systems of Canada and Western Europe may not be viable in the long run. As noted earlier, health care costs are increasing there as well as in the United States. A recent article about the health care system in Canada noted that "growing complaints about long lines for diagnosis and surgery . . . are eroding public confidence in Canada's national health care system." As a consequence, there are "growing moves toward privately managed medical services and user fees in return for quicker service" [Krauss, 2003, p. A3].

A critical question, of course, is the quality of care offered by the system. One biting critic of the Canadian health care observed, "The way things stand, Canada's boast should be that everyone is entitled to the same lousy health care." However, defenders point out that while Americans have easier access to physicians and do not have to put up with long waiting lines, life expectancy is about the same in the two countries. This suggests that health outcomes depend on factors in addition to health care spending, a theme to which we will return later.

Add a Prescription Drug Benefit

Both individual mandates and a single-payer system would represent radical changes in the US health care system. An alternative approach is to maintain the current system, but enrich it by adding a prescription drug benefit to Medicare. As noted earlier, prescription drugs are playing an ever-greater role in health care, but in general they are not covered by Medicare.

Designing a prescription drug program requires dealing with a number of difficult questions. One is how generous the program should be. That is, how large should the deductible and copayments be? Another is who should be eligible? Would all Medicare recipients be eligible, or just those with low incomes? As in any insurance program, adverse selection would be an issue. Presumably, those individuals who expected to have a high demand for prescription medicine would be the ones most likely to enroll, which would drive up the premiums. One could also expect adverse selection on the supply side of the market, with insurance companies trying to avoid enrolling people who are likely to have high drug costs. They could attempt this, for example, by advertising at health clubs instead of nursing homes.

These considerations raise the issue of costs. As we have already seen, Medicare is financially unstable; adding a drug benefit would presumably make the problem worse. While the costs obviously depend on the specific provisions, the Congressional Budget Office [2002] examined several variants, and found that the costs could easily exceed $200 billion over the period 2005–12. However, in this context it is interesting to note that some research suggests that increasing the use of prescription drugs might actually increase *overall* health costs less than one might expect. Lichtenberg [2002] studied the use of prescription medicines and other medical procedures in the Medicare population, and found that when patients use recently developed drugs, non-drug expenditures fall by eight times the amount that drug expenditures increase.

The Bush administration proposed a new drug benefit, but only for those Medicare beneficiaries who enrolled in managed care. However, as noted earlier, the Medicare population has not shown much enthusiasm for managed care options, so it is not clear whether or not this proposal is politically viable. In the years ahead, as drug expenses mount, there will surely be pressures on the government to deal with this issue in one way or another.

Final Thoughts

As one thinks about the debate over the future of health care reform, several points should be kept in mind:

- Coming up with a solution is bound to be difficult because of the same dilemma that arises in the design of *all* social insurance programs—the goal of providing security is likely to conflict with the goal of efficiency.

- There is no free lunch. The goals of universal coverage and cost containment are at odds with each other. We cannot bring 41 million people into the health care system and expect costs to go down. In the same way, we cannot expect to achieve universal coverage without an increase in regulation, because certain high-risk groups of people simply cannot obtain insurance in private markets. The only way one can imagine them getting insurance is a set of government rules that forces someone to insure them. This does not mean that universal coverage is an inappropriate goal, but one must be realistic about what is needed to achieve it.

- Although our focus has been primarily on health care expenditures, what we ultimately care about is people's health. The two are linked, although the statistical evidence on this matter is more tenuous than one might guess. Many commentators have argued that more spending on medical services in developed countries is unlikely to improve health, or at least the mortality rate. Lifestyle considerations such as smoking, diet, and exercise may be more important [Fuchs, 2000].

Summary

- Health markets may be inefficient because of poor information, and because of the adverse selection and moral hazard problems associated with health insurance.

- Most private medical insurance is provided through employers as a benefit to their employees.

- The Medicare program provides health insurance for people aged 65 and older. Benefits include hospital insurance (HI) and supplementary medical insurance (SMI), which pays for physicians and associated medical care.

- HI is financed by a payroll tax on the earnings of current workers at a rate of 1.45 percent on employers and employees each. SMI is financed out of general revenues. If current trends continue,

Medicare expenditures are likely to outpace revenues.

- Possible policies for restraining the growth of Medicare expenditures include placing more of the burden on current beneficiaries, price controls, managed care, greater use of hospice and home health care, and Medical Savings Accounts. It is not clear that any of these would be successful in the long run.

- Under federal tax law, employer-provided health insurance is not subject to taxation. This provides an implicit subsidy for health insurance.

- About 15 percent of the US population at any given time lacks health insurance. The proportion of the uninsured population under 65 years old has been growing over time.

- Health care costs have been increasing at a rapid rate. Possible reasons include the aging of the population, growth in income, the prevalence of third-party payments, and technological change. The evidence points to technological change as the primary factor.

- A number of proposals for changing the health care system have been made.

  Individual mandates would require all people to purchase health insurance.

  Single-payer systems would have all insurance provided by the government and financed by tax revenues.

  Add a prescription drug benefit to Medicare.

- Any attempts to increase access to health care to the uninsured are likely to involve both increased costs and increased government intervention in the health care market.

Discussion Questions

1. Consider carefully the following quotation: "[E]conomists seem always to talk about the cost of medical care, as if that kind of spending were a bad thing. After all, where does the money go? To doctors, nurses, and the makers of medical supplies. Don't they buy diapers and pasta and cars? Would the nation be better off with more boom boxes and less penicillin, more nail polish and less antibacterial ointment? What difference does it make how money is spent, as long as it changes hands and results in employment?" [*New York Times Magazine,* December 12, 1993, p. 28].

   a. Do economists view spending on health care as a "bad thing"?

   b. The last sentence in the quotation suggests a criterion for evaluating spending on health care. What criterion would an economist use?

2. "Opportunities for adverse selection can in theory destroy the insurance market although in practice the combination of the large individual gains from insurance, the use of large group purchases, and the tax subsidy has supported a thriving, perhaps too thriving, market for insurance" [Feldstein, 1995a, p. 3].

   a. Explain how adverse selection can destroy the insurance market.

   b. To what "tax subsidy" does the quotation refer?

   c. In what sense can the market for insurance be "too thriving"?

3. Suppose the annual number of doctor visits per year, D_d, is related to the price per doctor visit, P_d, by the relation $D_d = 4.22 - 0.0444\, P_d$.

   a. When the price is $50 per visit, how many visits are there per year? How much are expenditures on visits?

   b. Suppose the individual obtains insurance. There is no deductible, and the coinsurance rate is 10 percent. How many visits to the doctor occur now? What are the individual's out-of-pocket costs? How much does the insurance company pay? How much are total expenditures?

4. In 1994 the state of Tennessee created a program to provide health insurance to cover all people who could not afford health insurance or were too ill to qualify for private insurance. By 1999, the costs of the program had grown so much that the state began cutting benefits, tightening eligibility, and cutting its payments to physicians and HMOs. Use Figure 10.1 to explain why this outcome was predictable. Some observers suggest that a major miscalculation was the expectation that enrolling many of the beneficiaries would lead to major cost reductions, which did not materialize. What theory might explain the failure of HMOs to contain long-run health care costs?

5. Some have suggested that if a prescription drug benefit is made part of Medicare, then individuals must make a decision about whether or not to accept it when they enter the Medicare system, and stick to that decision permanently. That is, individuals either accept the prescription program and begin paying premiums as soon as they become eligible, or they can never enter the program. Explain the efficiency rationale behind this proposal.

6. So-called *Medigap insurance* fills the gap in coverage left by Medicare. This includes copayments, deductibles, and prescription drugs, among other things. Several years ago, the government enacted regulations that specify minimum standards for items that Medigap policies must cover. This made the policies more expensive, and as a consequence, about 25 percent of the elderly who would have purchased some Medigap insurance purchased none at all [Finkelstein, 2002].

   Consider an individual who consumes two goods, "insurance" and "all other goods." The cost of a unit of Medigap insurance is $1, as is the cost of a unit of all other goods. Sketch a budget constraint and set of indifference curves that are consistent with the following scenario: In an unregulated market, an individual with a $30,000 income purchases $5,000 worth of Medigap insurance. The government then puts mandates on Medigap policies that raise their minimum price to $8,000; that is, the individual must purchase at least 8,000 units of Medigap insurance or none at all. After considering the matter, she decides to go without Medigap insurance.

7. Connor's demand for insurance is given by $Q = 100 - 8P$, where P is the price per unit and Q is the number of units demanded. The current market price per unit of insurance is $2, and Connor can buy as much insurance as he wants at the going price. Purchases of insurance are excluded from income taxation, and Connor's income tax rate is 25 percent.

   a. How much insurance does Connor demand?

   b. Suppose that the law changes, and purchases of insurance are no longer excluded from taxation. How much insurance does Connor demand now?

   c. Explain how your answers to parts *a* and *b* illustrate the proposition that the exclusion of insurance expenditures from income taxation leads to over-consumption of insurance. What other factors must be considered to determine whether or not the exclusion is inefficient?

Selected References

Cutler, David. "Health Care and the Public Sector." Working Paper No. 8802. Cambridge, MA: National Bureau of Economic Research, February 2002.

McClellan, Mark. "Medicare Reform: Fundamental Problems, Incremental Steps." *Journal of Economic Perspectives* 14, no. 2 (Spring 2000), pp. 21–44.

Murphy, Kevin M, and Robert Topel. "Medical Research—What's It Worth?" *The Milken Institute Review,* First Quarter, 2000, pp. 23–30.

Newhouse, Joseph. "Medical Care Costs: How Much Welfare Loss?" *Journal of Economic Perspectives* 6, no. 3 (Summer 1992), pp. 3–22.

CHAPTER 11

Cost-Benefit Analysis

Paris is well worth a Mass.

ATTRIBUTED TO HENRI IV OF FRANCE

I f you visited Boston during the last decade, you probably noticed that traffic downtown was particularly congested. The reason was the "Big Dig," a massive $14.6 billion public works project that involved the construction of new roads and another tunnel to Logan Airport. Many people have doubts that it was worth the money. How would one go about thinking about this issue? Infrastructure projects like the Big Dig are just one variety of the thousands of public projects that are under consideration at any given time, everything from breast cancer screening programs to space exploration. How should the government decide whether or not to pursue a particular project? The theory of welfare economics provides a framework for deciding: Evaluate the social welfare function before and after the project, and see whether social welfare increases. If it does, then do the project.

This method is correct, but not very useful. The amount of information required to specify and evaluate a social welfare function is enormous. While social welfare functions are valuable for thinking through certain conceptual problems, they are generally not much help for the day-to-day problems of project evaluation. However, welfare economics does provide the basis for **cost-benefit analysis**—a set of practical procedures for guiding public expenditure decisions.[1]

Most government projects and policies result in the private sector having more of some scarce commodities and less of others. At the core of

---

[1] Boardman, Greenberg, Vining, and Weimer [1996] discuss the links between welfare economics and cost-benefit analysis.

cost-benefit analysis is a set of systematic procedures for valuing these commodities, which allows policy analysts to determine whether a project is, on balance, beneficial. Cost-benefit analysis allows policymakers to attempt to do what well-functioning markets do automatically—allocate resources to a project as long as the marginal social benefit exceeds the marginal social cost.

Present Value

Project evaluation usually requires comparing costs and benefits from different time periods. For example, preschool education for poor children requires substantial expenditures in the present and then yields returns in the future. In this section we discuss issues that arise in comparing dollar amounts from different time periods. Initially, we assume that no price inflation occurs. We show later how to take inflation into account.

Projecting Present Dollars into the Future

Suppose that you take $100 to the bank and deposit it in an account that yields 5 percent interest after taxes. At the end of one year, you will have $(1 + .05) \times \$100 = \$105$—the $100 initially deposited, plus $5 in interest. Suppose further that you let the money sit in the account for another year. At the end of the second year, you will have $(1 + .05) \times \$105 = \$110.25$. This can also be written as $(1 + .05) \times (1 + .05) \times 100 = (1 + .05)^2 \times 100$. Similarly, if the money is deposited for three years, it will be worth $(1 + .05)^3 \times \$100$ by the end of the third year. More generally, if $R are invested for T years at an interest rate of r, at the end of T years, it will be worth $R \times (1 + r)^T$. This formula shows the future value of money invested in the present.

Projecting Future Dollars into the Present

Now suppose that someone offers a contract that promises to pay you $100 *one year from now*. The person is trustworthy, so you do not have to worry about default. (Also, remember there is no inflation.) What is the maximum amount that you should be willing to pay *today* for this promise? It is tempting to say that a promise to pay $100 is worth $100. But this neglects the fact that the promised $100 is not payable for a year, and in the meantime you are forgoing the interest that could be earned on the money. Why should you pay $100 today to receive $100 a year from now, if you can receive $105 a year from now simply by putting the $100 in the bank today? Thus, the value today of $100 payable one year from now is *less* than $100. The **present value** of a future amount of money is the maximum amount you would be willing to pay today for the right to receive the money in the future.

To find the very most you would be willing to give up now in exchange for $100 payable one year in the future, you must find the number that, when multiplied by $(1 + .05)$, just equals $100. By definition, this is $100/(1 + .05)$, or approximately $95.24. Thus, when the interest rate is 5 percent, the present value of $100 payable one year from now is $100/(1 + .05). Note the symmetry with the familiar problem of projecting money into the future that we just discussed. To find the value of money today one year in the future, you *multiply* by one plus the interest rate; to find the value of money one year in the future today, you *divide* by one plus the interest rate.

Next consider a promise to pay $100 *two* years from now. In this case, the calculation has to take into account the fact that if you invested $100 yourself for two years, at the end it would be worth $100 \times (1 + .05)^2$. The most you would be willing to pay today for $100 in two years is the amount that when multiplied by $(1 + .05)^2$ yields exactly $100, that is, $100/(1 + .05)^2$, or about $90.70.

In general, when the interest rate is r, the present value of a promise to pay $$R$ in T years is simply $$R/(1 + r)^{T}$.[2] Thus, even in the absence of inflation, a dollar in the future is worth less than a dollar today and must be "discounted" by an amount that depends on the interest rate and when the money is receivable. For this reason, r is often referred to as the **discount rate.** Similarly, $(1 + r)^T$ is called the **discount factor** for money T periods into the future. Note that the further into the future the promise is payable (the larger is T), the smaller is the present value. Intuitively, the longer you have to wait for a sum to be paid, the less you are willing to pay for it today, other things being the same.

Finally, consider a promise to pay $$R_0$ today, *and* $$R_1$ one year from now, *and* $$R_2$ two years from now, and so on for T years. How much is this deal worth? By now, it is clear that the naive answer ($$R_0 + $R_1 + \cdots + R_T) is wrong because it assumes that a dollar in the future is exactly equivalent to a dollar in the present. Without dividing by the discount factor, adding up dollars from different points in time is like adding apples and oranges. The correct approach is to convert each year's amount to its present value and *then* add them.

Table 11.1 shows the present value of each year's payment. To find the present value (PV) of the income stream $$R_0$, $$R_1$, $$R_2$, . . . , $$R_T$, we simply add the figures in the last column:

$$PV = R_0 + \frac{R_1}{(1 + r)} + \frac{R_2}{(1 + r)^2} + \cdots + \frac{R_T}{(1 + r)^T} \tag{11.1}$$

The importance of computing present value is hard to overestimate. Ignoring it can lead to serious errors. In particular, failure to discount makes ventures that yield returns in the future appear more valuable than they really are. For example, consider a project that yields a return of $1 million 20 years from now. If the interest rate is 5 percent, the present value is

---

[2] This assumes the interest rate is constant at r. Suppose that the interest rate changes over time, so in year 1 it is r_1, in year 2, r_2, and so on. Then the present value of a sum $$R_T$ payable T years from now is $$R_T/[(1 + r_1) \times (1 + r_2) \times \cdots \times(1 + r_T)]$.

Table 11.1   Calculating present value

Dollars Payable	Years in Future	Discount Factor	Present Value
R_0	0	1	R_0
R_1	1	$(1 + r)$	$R_1/(1 + r)$
R_2	2	$(1 + r)^2$	$R_2/(1 + r)^2$
.	.	.	.
.	.	.	.
R_T	T	$(1 + r)^T$	$RT/(1 + r)^T$

$376,889 [= \$1,000,000/(1.05)^{20}]$. If $r = 10\%$, the present value is only $148,644 [= \$1,000,000/(1.10)^{20}]$.

Inflation

How do we modify the procedure when the price level is expected to increase in the future? To begin, consider a project that, in present prices, yields the same return each year. Call this return $\$R_0$. Now assume that inflation occurs at a rate of 7 percent per year, and the dollar value of the return increases along with all prices. Therefore, the dollar value of the return one year from now, $\$\widetilde{R}_1$, is $(1.07) \times \$R_0$. Similarly, two years into the future, the dollar value is $\$\widetilde{R}_2 = (1.07)^2 R_0$. In general, this same return has a dollar value in year T of $\$\widetilde{R}_T = (1 + .07)^T R_0$.

The dollar values $\$\widetilde{R}_0, \$\widetilde{R}_1, \$\widetilde{R}_2, \ldots, \$\widetilde{R}_T$ are referred to as **nominal amounts.** Nominal amounts are valued according to the level of prices in the year the return occurs. One can measure these returns in terms of the prices that exist in a single year. These are called **real amounts** because they do not reflect changes that are due merely to alterations in the price level. In our example, the real amount was assumed to be a constant $\$R_0$ measured in present prices. More generally, if the real returns in present year prices are $\$R_0, \$R_1, \$R_2, \ldots, \$R_T$, and inflation occurs at a rate of π per year, then the nominal returns are: $\$R_0, \$R_1 \times (1 + \pi), \$R_2 \times (1 + \pi)^2, \ldots, \$R_T \times (1 + \pi)^T$.

But this is not the end of the story. When prices are expected to rise, lenders are no longer willing to make loans at the interest rate r that prevailed when prices were stable. Lenders realize they are going to be paid back in depreciated dollars, and to keep even in real terms, their first year's payment must also be inflated by $(1 + \pi)$. Similarly, the second year's payment must be inflated by $(1 + \pi)^2$. In other words, the market interest rate increases by an amount approximately equal to the expected rate of inflation, from r percent to $r + \pi$ percent.[3]

---

[3] The product of $(1 + r)$ and $(1 + \pi)$ is $1 + r + \pi + r\pi$. Thus, the nominal rate actually exceeds the real rate by $\pi + r\pi$. However, for numbers of reasonable magnitude, $r\pi$ is negligible in size, so $r + \pi$ is a good approximation. Under some circumstances, nominal interest rates may fail to rise by exactly the rate of inflation. See Chapter 15 under "Taxes and Inflation."

We see, then, that when inflation is anticipated, *both* the stream of returns and the discount rate increase. When expressed in *nominal* terms, the present value of the income stream is thus

$$PV = R_0 + \frac{(1 + \pi)R_1}{(1 + \pi)(1 + r)} + \frac{(1 + \pi)^2 R_2}{(1 + \pi)^2 (1 + r)^2} + \cdots$$
$$+ \frac{(1 + \pi)^T R_T}{(1 + \pi)^T (1 + r)^T} \tag{11.2}$$

A glance at Equation (11.2) indicates that it is equivalent to Equation (11.1) because all the terms involving $(1 + \pi)$ cancel out. The moral of the story is that we obtain the *same* answer whether real or nominal magnitudes are used. It is crucial, however, that dollar magnitudes and discount rates be measured consistently. If real values are used for the Rs, the discount rate must also be measured in real terms—the market rate of interest *minus* the expected inflation rate. Alternatively, if we discount by the market rate of interest, returns should be measured in nominal terms.

Private Sector Project Evaluation

As we noted at the beginning of the chapter, the central problem in cost-benefit analysis is valuing the inputs and outputs of government projects. A useful starting point is to consider the same problem from a private firm's point of view.

Suppose a firm is considering two mutually exclusive projects, X and Y. The real benefits and costs of project X are B^X and C^X, respectively; and those for project Y are B^Y and C^Y. For both projects, the benefits and costs are realized immediately. The firm must answer two questions: First, should either project be done at all; are the projects *admissible?* (The firm has the option of doing neither project.) Second, if both projects are admissible, which is *preferable?* Because both benefits and costs occur immediately, answering these questions is simple. Compute the net return to project X, $B^X - C^X$, and compare it to the net return to Y, $B^Y - C^Y$. A project is admissible only if its net return is positive, that is, the benefits exceed the costs. If both projects are admissible and the firm can only adopt one of them, it should choose the project with the higher net return.

In reality, most projects involve a stream of real benefits and returns that occur over time rather than instantaneously. Suppose that the initial benefits and costs of project X are B_0^X and C_0^X, those at the end of the first year are B_1^X and C_1^X, and those at the end of the last year are B_T^X and C_T^X. We can characterize project X as a stream of net returns (some of which may be negative):

$$(B_0^X - C_0^X), (B_1^X - C_1^X), (B_2^X - C_2^X), \ldots, (B_T^X - C_T^X)$$

Table 11.2   **Comparing the present values of two projects**

Year	Annual Net Return		r =	PV	
	R&D	Advertising		R&D	Advertising
0	–$1,000	–$1,000	0	$150	$200
1	600	–0–	.01	128	165
2	–0–	–0–	.03	86	98
3	550	1,200	.05	46	37
			.07	10	–21

The present value of this income stream (PV^X) is

$$PV^X = B_0^X - C_0^X + \frac{B_1^X - C_1^X}{(1 + r)} + \frac{B_2^X - C_2^X}{(1 + r)^2} + \cdots + \frac{B_T^X - C_T^X}{(1 + r)^T}$$

where r is the discount rate that is appropriate for a private sector project. (Selection of a discount rate is discussed shortly).

Similarly, suppose that project Y generates streams of costs and benefits B^Y and C^Y over a period of T' years. (There is no reason for T and T' to be the same.) Project Y's present value is

$$PV^Y = B_0^Y - C_0^Y + \frac{B_1^Y - C_1^Y}{1 + r} + \frac{B_2^Y - C_2^Y}{(1 + r)^2} + \cdots + \frac{B_{T'}^Y - C_{T'}^Y}{(1 + r)^{T'}}$$

Since both projects are now evaluated in present value terms, we can use the same rules that were applied to the instantaneous project described earlier. The **present value criteria** for project evaluation are that:

- A project is admissible only if its present value is positive.
- When two projects are mutually exclusive, the preferred project is the one with the higher present value.

The discount rate plays a key role in the analysis. Different values of r can lead to very different conclusions concerning the admissibility and comparability of projects.

Consider the two projects shown in Table 11.2, a research and development program (R&D) and an advertising campaign. Both require an initial outlay of $1,000. The R&D program produces a return of $600 at the end of the first year and $550 at the end of the third year. The advertising campaign, on the other hand, has a single large payoff of $1,200 in three years.

The calculations show the discount rate chosen is important. For low values of r, the advertising is preferred to R&D. However, higher discount rates weigh against the advertising (where the returns are concentrated further into the future) and may even make the project inadmissible.

Thus, one must take considerable care that the value of r represents as closely as possible the firm's actual opportunity cost of funds. If the discount rate chosen is too high, it tends to discriminate against projects with returns that come in the relatively distant future and vice versa. The firm's tax situation is relevant in this context. If the going market rate of return is 10 percent, but the firm's tax rate is 25 percent, its after-tax return is only 7.5 percent. Because the after-tax return represents the firm's opportunity cost, it should be used for r.

Several criteria other than present value are often used for project evaluation. As we will see, they can sometimes give misleading answers, and therefore, the present value criteria are preferable. However, these other methods are popular, so it is necessary to understand them and to be aware of their problems.

Internal Rate of Return

A firm is considering the following project: It spends $1 million today on a new computer network and reaps a benefit of $1.04 million in increased profits a year from now. If you were asked to compute the computer network's "rate of return," you would probably respond, "4 percent." Implicitly, you calculated that figure by finding the value of ρ that solves the following equation:

$$-\$1,000,000 + \frac{\$1,040,000}{(1 + \rho)} = 0$$

We can generalize this procedure as follows: If a project yields a stream of benefits (B) and costs (C) over T periods, the **internal rate of return** (ρ) is defined as the ρ that solves the equation

$$B_0 - C_0 + \frac{B_1 - C_1}{1 + \rho} + \frac{B_2 - C_2}{(1 + \rho)^2} + \cdots + \frac{B_T - C_T}{(1 + \rho)^T} = 0 \qquad (11.3)$$

The internal rate of return is the discount rate that would make the present value of the project just equal to zero.

An obvious admissibility criterion is to accept a project if ρ exceeds the firm's opportunity cost of funds, r. For example, if the project earns 4 percent while the firm can obtain 3 percent on other investments, the project should be undertaken. The corresponding comparability criterion is that if two mutually exclusive projects are both admissible, choose the one with the higher value of ρ.

Project selection using the internal rate of return can, however, lead to bad decisions. Consider project X that requires the expenditure of $100 today and yields $110 a year from now, so that its internal rate of return is 10 percent. Project Y requires $1,000 today and yields $1,080 in a year, generating an internal rate of return of 8 percent. (Neither project can be duplicated.) Assume that the firm can borrow and lend freely at a 6 percent rate of interest.

On the basis of internal rate of return, X is clearly preferred to Y. However, the firm makes only $4 profit on X ($10 minus $6 in interest costs), while it makes a $20 profit on Y ($80 minus $60 in interest costs). Contrary to the conclusion implied by the internal rate of return, the firm should prefer Y, the project with the higher profit. In short, when projects differ in size, the internal rate of return can give poor guidance. In contrast, the present value rule gives correct answers even when the projects differ in scale. The present value of X is $-100 + 110/1.06 = 3.77$, while that of Y is $-1,000 + 1080/1.06 = 18.87$. The present value criterion says that Y is preferable, as it should.

Benefit-Cost Ratio

Suppose that a project yields a stream of benefits $B_0, B_1, B_2, \ldots, B_T$, and a stream of costs $C_0, C_1, C_2, \ldots, C_T$. Then the present value of the benefits, B, is

$$B = B_0 + \frac{B_1}{1 + r} + \frac{B_2}{(1 + r)^2} + \cdots + \frac{B_T}{(1 + r)^T}$$

and the present value of the costs, C, is

$$C = C_0 + \frac{C_1}{1 + r} + \frac{C_2}{(1 + r)^2} + \cdots + \frac{C_T}{(1 + r)^T} \tag{11.4}$$

The **benefit-cost ratio** is defined as B/C.

Admissibility requires that a project's benefit-cost ratio exceed one. Application of this rule always gives correct guidance. To see why, note simply that $B/C > 1$ implies that $B - C > 0$, which is just the present value criterion for admissibility.

As a basis for comparing admissible projects, however, the benefit-cost ratio is virtually useless. Consider a state that is studying two methods for disposing of toxic wastes. Method I is a toxic waste dump with $B = \$250$ million, $C = \$100$ million, and therefore a benefit-cost ratio of 2.5. Method II involves sending the wastes in a rocket to Saturn, which has $B = \$200$ million, $C = \$100$ million, and therefore a benefit-cost ratio of 2. The state's leaders choose the dump because it has the higher value of B/C. Now suppose that in their analysis of the dump, the analysts inadvertently neglected to take into account seepage-induced crop damage of \$40 million. If the \$40 million is viewed as a reduction in the dump's benefits, its B/C becomes $\$210/\$100 = 2.1$, and the dump is still preferred to the rocket. However, the \$40 million can just as well be viewed as an increase in costs, in which case $B/C = \$250/\$140 = 1.79$. Now the rocket looks better than the dump!

We have illustrated that there is an inherent ambiguity in computing benefit-cost ratios because benefits can always be counted as "negative costs" and vice versa. Thus, by judicious classification of benefits and costs, any admissible project's benefit-cost ratio can be made arbitrarily high. In contrast, a glance at Equation (11.1) indicates that such shenanigans have no effect whatsoever on the present value criterion because it is based on the *difference* between benefits and costs rather than their *ratio*.

▪ We conclude that the internal rate of return and the benefit-cost ratio can lead to incorrect inferences. The present value criterion is the most reliable guide.

Discount Rate for Government Projects

Sensible decision making by the government also requires present value calculations. However, the public sector should compute costs, benefits, and discount rates differently than the private sector. This section discusses problems in the selection of a public sector discount rate. We then turn to problems in evaluating costs and benefits.

As suggested previously, the discount rate chosen by private individuals should reflect the rate of return available on alternative investments. Although in practice pinpointing this rate may be difficult, from a conceptual point of view the firm's opportunity cost of funds gives the correct value of r.

There is less consensus on the conceptually appropriate discount rate for government projects. We now discuss several possibilities.[4]

Rates Based on Returns in the Private Sector

Suppose the last $1,000 of private investment in the economy yields an annual rate of return of 16 percent. If the government extracts $1,000 from the private sector for a project, and the $1,000 is entirely at the expense of private sector investment, society loses the $160 that would have been generated by the private sector project. Thus, the opportunity cost of the government project is the 16 percent rate of return in the private sector. Because it measures the opportunity cost, 16 percent is the appropriate discount rate. It is irrelevant whether or not this return is taxed. Whether it all stays with the investor or part goes to the government, the before-tax rate of return measures the value of output that the funds would have generated for society.

In practice, funds for a given project are collected from a variety of taxes, each of which has a different effect on consumption and investment. Hence, contrary to the assumption made earlier, it is likely that some of the funds for the government project would come at the expense of consumption as well as investment. What is the opportunity cost of funds that come at the expense of consumption? Consider Kenny, who is deciding how much to consume and how much to save this year. For each dollar Kenny consumes this year, he gives up one dollar of consumption next year *plus* the rate of return he would have earned on the dollar saved. Hence, the opportunity cost to Kenny of a dollar of consumption now is measured by the rate of return he would have received if he had saved the dollar. Suppose the before-tax yield on an investment opportunity available to Kenny is 16 percent, but he must pay 50 percent of the return to the government in the form of taxes. All that Kenny gives up when he consumes an additional dollar today is the *after*-tax rate of return of 8 percent. Because the after-tax rate of return measures what an *individual* loses when consumption is reduced, dollars that come at the expense of consumption should be discounted by the after-tax rate of return.

Because funds for the public sector reduce both private sector consumption and investment, a natural solution is to use a weighted average of the

---

[4] See Tresch [2002, Chapter 24] for further discussion of the alternative views.

before- and after-tax rates of return, with the weight on the before-tax rate equal to the proportion of funds that comes from investment, and that on the after-tax rate the proportion that comes from consumption. In the preceding example, if one-quarter of the funds come at the expense of investment and three-quarters at the expense of consumption, then the public sector discount rate is 10 percent ($\frac{1}{4} \times 16$ percent $+ \frac{3}{4} \times 8$ percent). Unfortunately, in practice it is hard to determine what the proportions of sacrificed consumption and investment actually are for a given government project. And even with information on the impact of each tax on consumption and investment, it is difficult in practice to determine which tax is used to finance which project. The inability to determine reliably a set of weights lessens the usefulness of this approach as a practical guide to determining discount rates.

Social Discount Rate

An alternative view is that public expenditure evaluation should involve a **social rate of discount,** which measures the valuation *society* places on consumption that is sacrificed in the present. But why should society's view of the opportunity cost of forgoing consumption differ from the opportunity cost revealed in market rates of return? The social discount rate may be lower for several reasons.

Concern for Future Generations.   It is the duty of public sector decision makers to care about the welfare not only of the current generation of citizens but of future generations as well. The private sector, on the other hand, is concerned only with its own welfare. Hence, from a social point of view, the private sector devotes too few resources to saving—it applies too high a discount rate to future returns. However, the idea of government as the unselfish guardian of the interests of future generations assumes an unrealistic degree of omniscience and benevolence. Moreover, even totally selfish individuals often engage in projects that benefit future generations. If future generations are expected to benefit from some project, the anticipated profitability is high, which encourages investment today. Private firms plant trees today in return for profits on wood sales that may not be realized for many years.[5]

Paternalism.   Even from the point of view of their own narrow self-interest, people may not be farsighted enough to weigh adequately benefits in the future; they therefore discount such benefits at too high a rate. Pigou [1932, Chapter 2] described this problem as a "defective telescopic faculty." The government should use the discount rate that individuals *would* use if they knew their own good. This is a paternalistic argument—government forces citizens to consume less in the present, and in return, they have more in the

---

[5] Why should people invest in a project whose returns may not be realized until after they are dead? Investors can always sell the rights to future profits to members of the younger generation and hence consume their share of the anticipated profits during their lifetimes.

future, at which time they presumably thank the government for its fore-sight. Like all paternalistic arguments, it raises the fundamental philosoph-ical question of when the government's preferences should be imposed on individuals.

Market Inefficiency.   When a firm undertakes an investment, it generates knowledge and technological know-how that can benefit other firms. In a sense, then, investment creates positive externalities, and by the usual kinds of arguments, investment is underprovided by private markets (see Chap-ter 5 under "Positive Externalities"). By applying a discount rate lower than the market's, the government can correct this inefficiency. The enormous practical problem here is measuring the actual size of the externality. More-over, the theory of externalities suggests that a more appropriate remedy would be to determine the size of the marginal external benefit at the optimum and grant a subsidy of that amount (see again Chapter 5).

It appears, then, that none of the arguments against using market rates provides much specific guidance with respect to the choice of a public sec-tor discount rate. Where does this leave us? It would be difficult to argue very strongly against any public rate of discount in a range between the before- and after-tax rates of return in the private sector. One practical pro-cedure is to evaluate the present value of a project over a range of discount rates and see whether or not the present value stays positive for all reason-able values of r. If it does, the analyst can feel some confidence that the conclusion is not sensitive to the discount rate. *Sensitivity analysis* is the process of conducting a cost-benefit analysis under a set of alternative rea-sonable assumptions and seeing whether the substantive results change.

**Government
Discounting in Practice**

The federal government uses a variety of discount rates, depending on the agency and the type of project [Bazelon and Smetters, 1999]. According to rules issued by the Office of Management and Budget, federal agencies are required to use a real rate of return of 7 percent, on the assumption that this well measures the before-tax rate of return on private-sector projects. Despite this rule, for many projects involving costs and benefits that come in over long periods of time, a real rate of return of 2 percent is used; this is supposed to be an approximation to the consumption rate of time preference, that is, the after-tax rate of return.

Even greater inconsistencies arise in the context of federal budget plan-ning. When a new tax or expenditure program is introduced, its effects over a five-year period must be reported to determine whether or not they will put the budget out of balance.[6] For these purposes, all that matters are the sums of the relevant taxes or expenditures; future flows are discounted at a

---

[6] For some purposes, the Senate requires flows over a 10-year period.

rate of zero. Thus, for example, a policy that increased spending by a billion dollars today and was financed by a tax of a billion dollars five years from now would be viewed as having no effect on the deficit, while in present value terms, the package would lose money.

Beyond the five-year window, the fiscal consequences of fiscal proposals are ignored; in effect, they are discounted at a rate of infinity! Consider a policy that raises $5 billion within the first five years, but after 10 years loses $20 billion. Under current budgetary rules, such a policy is scored as creating a surplus, while with any reasonable discount rate, its long-run effect is to lose money for the government. There is, in fact, some evidence that this peculiar fashion of discounting has biased government decision making in favor of policies that increase revenue in the short term but reduce it in the long term [Bazelon and Smetters, 1999].

Valuing Public Benefits and Costs

The next step in project evaluation is computing benefits and costs. From a private firm's point of view, their computation is relatively straightforward. The benefits from a project are the revenues received; the costs are the firm's payments for inputs; and both are measured by market prices. The evaluation problem is more complicated for the government because market prices may not reflect *social* benefits and costs. Consider, for example, a highway expansion that might do some damage to the environment. One can imagine both the private and public sectors undertaking this project, but the private and public cost-benefit analyses would be rather different, because the public sector should take into account social costs, which include externalities.

We now discuss several ways for measuring the benefits and costs of public sector projects.

Market Prices

As noted in Chapter 3, in a properly functioning competitive economy, the price of a good simultaneously reflects its marginal social cost of production and its marginal value to consumers. It would appear that if the government uses inputs and/or produces outputs that are traded in private markets, then market prices should be used for valuation.

The problem is that real-world markets have many imperfections, such as monopoly, externalities, and so on. Therefore, prices do not necessarily reflect marginal social costs and benefits. The relevant question, however, is not whether market prices are perfect, but whether they are likely to be superior to alternative measures of value. Such measures would either have to be made up or derived from highly complicated—and questionable—models of the economy. And, whatever their problems, market prices provide plenty of information at a low cost. Most economists believe that in the absence of any glaring imperfections, market prices should be used to compute public benefits and costs.

Adjusted Market Prices   The prices of goods traded in imperfect markets generally do not reflect their marginal social cost.[7] The **shadow price** of such a commodity is its underlying social marginal cost. Although market prices of goods in imperfect markets diverge from shadow prices, in some cases the market prices can be used to *estimate* the shadow prices. We discuss the relevant circumstances next. In each case, the key insight is that the shadow price depends on how the economy responds to the government intervention.

Monopoly.   In the nation of South Africa, the production of beer is monopolized by the company South African Breweries, Ltd. Imagine that the Education Ministry is contemplating the purchase of some beer for a controlled experiment to determine the impact of beer consumption on the performance of college students. How should the project's cost-benefit analysis take into account the fact that this input is monopolistically produced?

In contrast to perfect competition, under which price is equal to marginal cost, a monopolist's price is above marginal cost (see Chapter 3). Should the government value the beer at its market price (which measures its value to consumers) or at its marginal production cost (which measures the incremental value of the resources used in its production)?

The answer depends on the impact of the government purchase on the market. If production of beer is expected to increase by the exact amount used by the project, the social opportunity cost is the value of the resources used in the extra production—the marginal production cost. On the other hand, if no more beer will be produced, the government's use comes at the expense of private consumers, who value the beer at its demand price. If some combination of the two responses is expected, a weighted average of price and marginal cost is appropriate. (Note the similarity to the previous discount rate problem.)

Taxes.   If an input is subject to a sales tax, the price received by the producer of the input is less than the price paid by the purchaser. This is because some portion of the purchase price goes to the tax collector. When the government purchases an input subject to sales tax, should the producer's or purchaser's price be used in the cost calculations? The basic principle is the same as that for the monopoly case. If production is expected to expand, then the producer's supply price is appropriate. If production is expected to stay constant, the consumer's price should be used. A combination of responses requires a weighted average.

Unemployment.   If a worker for a public sector project is hired away from a private job, then this worker's opportunity cost is the wage rate that she was earning in the private sector. Things get trickier when the project employs someone who is currently involuntarily unemployed. Because hiring

---

[7] For further details, see Boardman, Greenberg, Vining, and Weimer [1996].

FIGURE 11.1

Measuring the
change in consumer
surplus

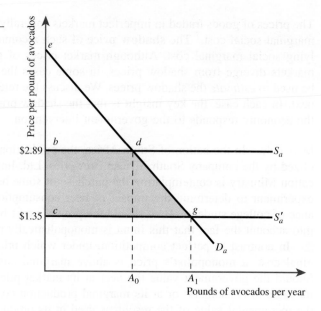

an unemployed worker does not lower output elsewhere in the economy, the wage the worker is paid does not represent an opportunity cost. All that is forgone when the worker is hired is the leisure he or she was consuming, the value of which is presumably low if the unemployment is involuntary. There are two complications, however: (1) If the government is running its stabilization policy to maintain a constant rate of employment, hiring an unemployed worker may mean reducing employment and output elsewhere in the economy. In this case, the social cost of the worker is his or her wage. (2) Even if the worker is involuntarily unemployed when the project begins, she may not necessarily be so during its entire duration. But forecasting an individual's future employment prospects is difficult. In light of the current lack of consensus on the causes and nature of unemployment, the pricing of unemployed resources remains a problem with no agreed-on solution. In the absence of a major depression, valuation of unemployed labor at the going wage is probably a good approximation for practical purposes.

Consumer Surplus

A private firm is generally small relative to the economy, so that changes in its output do not affect the market price of its product. In contrast, public sector projects can be so large that they change market prices. For example, a government irrigation project could lower the marginal cost of agricultural production so much that the market price of food falls. But if the market price changes, how should the additional amount of food be valued—at its original price, at its price after the project, or at some price in between?

The situation for a hypothetical avocado-growing region is depicted in Figure 11.1. Pounds of avocados are measured on the horizontal axis, the price per pound is measured on the vertical, and D_a is the demand schedule for avocados. Before the irrigation project, the supply curve is labeled S_a, and market price and quantity are $2.89 and A_0, respectively. (The supply curve is drawn horizontally for convenience. The main points would still hold even if it sloped upward.)

Suppose that after more land is brought into production by the irrigation project, the supply curve for avocados shifts to S_a'. At the new equilibrium, the price falls to $1.35, and avocado consumption increases to A_1. How much better off are consumers? Another way of stating this question is, "How much would consumers be willing to pay for the privilege of consuming A_1 pounds of avocados at price $1.35 rather than A_0 pounds at price $2.89?"

The economic tool for answering this question is consumer surplus—the amount by which the sum that individuals would have been willing to pay exceeds the sum they actually have to pay. As shown in the appendix to the book, consumer surplus is measured by the area under the demand curve and above a horizontal line at the market price. Thus, when price is $2.89, consumer surplus is *ebd*.

When the price of avocados falls to $1.35 because of the irrigation project, consumer surplus is still the area under the demand curve and above a horizontal line at the going price, but because the price is now $1.35, the relevant area is *ecg*. Consumer surplus has increased by the difference between areas *ecg* and *ebd*—area *bcgd*. Thus, the area behind the demand curve between the two prices measures the value to consumers of being able to purchase avocados at the lower price. Provided the planner can estimate the shape of the demand curve, the project's benefit can be measured.

If the supply curve of the commodity under consideration is upward sloping, then changes in producer surplus (also explained in the appendix) can be brought into play. For example, in the cost-benefit analysis of rent controls, the change in landlords' surplus could be estimated given information on the shape of the supply curve of rental housing.

Inferences from Economic Behavior

So far we have been dealing with cases in which market data can serve as a starting point for valuing social costs and benefits. Sometimes the good in question is not explicitly traded, so no market price exists. We discuss two examples of how people's willingness to pay for such commodities can be estimated.

The Value of Time.   One important component of Boston's Big Dig project mentioned at the beginning of this chapter was a 3.5 mile stretch of highway that cost $6.5 billion. It was estimated that with the new highway in place, the ride from downtown to the airport would be reduced from 45 minutes to 8 minutes. Was this a good deal? While it is true that "time is money," to do cost-benefit analysis we need to know *how much* money. A common way to estimate the value of time is to take advantage of the theory of leisure-income choice. People who have control over the amount they work do so up to the point where the subjective value of leisure is equal to the income they gain from one more hour of work—the after-tax wage rate. Thus, the after-tax wage can be used to value the time that is saved.[8]

Although this approach is useful, it has two major problems: (1) Some people cannot choose their hours of work. Involuntary unemployment represents an extreme case. (2) Not all uses of time away from the job are equivalent. For example, to avoid spending time on the road, a person who hated driving might be willing to pay at a rate exceeding his wage. On the other hand, a person who used the road for pleasure drives on weekends might not care very much about the opportunity cost of time, particularly if she could not work on weekends anyway.

Several investigators have estimated the value of time by looking at people's choices between modes of transportation that involve different traveling times. Suppose that in a given community people can commute to work either by bus or by train. The train takes less time, but it is more expensive. By seeing how much extra money people are willing to pay for the train, we can infer how much they are willing to pay to reduce their commuting time, and hence how they value that time. Of course, other characteristics of people, such as their incomes, affect their choice of travel mode. Statistical techniques like those described in Chapter 2 can be used to take these variables into account. On the basis of several such studies, a reasonable estimate of the effective cost of traveling time is about 50 percent of the before-tax wage rate. (See Small [1992, pp. 43–45].)

The Value of Life.   In the wake of September 11, a fund was set up to compensate the families of the victims. A journalist asked the man in charge of the fund, "What is a life worth?" He responded, "You'd have to be a rabbi or a priest to try to answer that" [Henriques, 2001, p. WK10]. Indeed, our religious and cultural values suggest that life is priceless. Consider the events that transpired several years ago when a scientist working at the South Pole, one Jerri Nielsen, discovered a lump in her breast and needed treatment. An air force jet was immediately dispatched to airdrop medical supplies for Dr. Nielsen (weather conditions made it impossible for the jet to land). Several months later, when it was determined that Dr. Nielsen required hospitalization, another jet was sent in, this time to land and fly her home to the United States. In all the news accounts of this story, no one questioned the cost of the rescue effort to the government or whether saving Dr. Nielsen's life was worth the cost. Arguing that any price was too high for saving her life would have been unthinkable. Similarly, if you were asked to value your own life, it would not be surprising if only the sky was the limit.

---

[8] For further details, see Chapter 16 under "Labor Supply."

Such a position presents obvious difficulties for cost-benefit analysis. If the value of life is infinite, any project that leads even to a single life being saved has an infinitely high present value. *This leaves no sensible way to determine the admissibility of projects.* If *every* road in America were a divided four-lane highway, traffic fatalities would doubtless decrease. Would this be a good project? Similarly, any project that cost even one life would have an infinitely low value. In this context, consider the fact that to meet government mandated fuel efficiency standards, automobile manufacturers produce lighter cars than would otherwise be the case. But lighter cars are associated with higher fatality rates in accidents. Do fuel standards therefore automatically fail cost-benefit tests?

Economists have considered two methods for assigning finite values to human life, one based on lost earnings and the other on the probability of death.

Lost earnings.   The value of life is the present value of the individual's net earnings over a lifetime. If an individual dies as a consequence of a given project, the cost to society is just the expected present value of the output that person would have produced. This approach is often used in law courts to determine how much compensation the relatives of accident fatalities should receive. However, taken literally, this approach means that society would suffer no loss if the aged, infirm, or severely handicapped were summarily executed. This implication is sufficiently bizarre that the method is rejected by most economists.

Probability of death.   A second approach has as its starting point the notion that most projects do not actually affect with *certainty* a given individual's prospects for living. Rather, it is more typical for a change in the *probability* of a person's death to be involved. For example, you do not know that cancer research will save *your* life. All that can be determined is that it may reduce the probability of your death. The reason this distinction is so important is that even if people view their lives as having infinite value, they continually accept increases in the probability of death for finite amounts of money. An individual driving a light car is subject to a greater probability of death in an auto accident than someone in a heavy car, other things being the same. People are willing to accept the increased risk of death because of the money they save by purchasing lighter cars.

Another way that people reveal their risk preferences is by their occupational choices. Some jobs involve a higher probability of death than others. Suppose we compare two workers who have identical job qualifications (education, experience, etc.), but one has a riskier job than the other. The individual in the riskier job is expected to have a higher wage to compensate for the higher probability of death. The difference between the two wages provides an estimate of the value that people place on a decreased probability of death. Garen [1988] estimated that increasing by one the number of fatalities per 100,000 workers in an occupation increases the yearly earnings in the occupation by about 0.55 percent.[9]

In the same spirit, there have been many studies of the amounts that people are willing to pay for safety devices, such as smoke alarms, that reduce the probability of death by a given amount. Different studies come up with quite different results, but a rough guess on the basis of such research is that the value of a life is between $4 million and $9 million [Viscusi and Aldy, 2003]. Now, you might think that this range is so great as to be useless. However, these estimates can be very useful in weeding out senseless projects. For example, the regulations relating to the emergency floor lights on commercial planes cost about $900,000 per life saved. These regulations clearly pass the admissibility criterion. On the other hand, governmental asbestos removal rules cost more than $100 million per life saved.

An appealing aspect of this approach to valuing life is that it puts the analysis on the same willingness-to-pay basis that is so fruitful in other contexts. It remains highly controversial, however. Broome [1978] has argued that the probabilistic approach is irrelevant once it is conceded that *some* people's lives are *certainly* going to be at stake. The fact that we happen to be ignorant of just who will die is beside the point. This position leads us back to where we started, with no way to value projects that involve human life.

This academic controversy has become a matter of public concern because of various proposals to subject government safety and environmental regulations to cost-benefit analysis. In an attack on one proposal, an environmental lobbyist stated that one simply could not "put a price on saving lives" [Wetstone, 1995]. Unfortunately, in a world of scarce resources, we have no choice in the matter. The only question is whether or not sensible ways for setting the price are used.

Valuing Intangibles

No matter how ingenious the investigator, some benefits and costs are impossible to value: One of the benefits of the space shuttle program is increased national prestige. Indeed, President George W. Bush argued that space exploration "is a desire written in the human heart." Creating national parks gives people the thrill of enjoying beautiful scenery. The mind boggles at putting a dollar value on these "commodities." Three points must be kept in mind when intangible items might be important.

First, intangibles can subvert the entire cost-benefit exercise. By claiming that they are large enough, *any* project can be made admissible. A journalist commenting on Britain's deliberations about whether to construct a

---

[9] See Viscusi [2003] for further discussion of such estimates. The cost-benefit analyst should also consider the psychological cost of bereavement to families and friends as well as changes in their financial status.

tunnel below the English channel gave this advice: "Build it, not because dreary cost-benefit analysis says it will pay but because Britain needs a big project to arouse it" [Will, 1985a]. However, presumably anyone who favors a particular project can make a case on the basis of its ability to "arouse." How does one then choose among projects? (The channel tunnel, of course, was ultimately built. When completed in 1994, it cost $15 billion, more than twice the original estimate.)

Second, the tools of cost-benefit analysis can be used to force planners to reveal limits on how they value intangibles. Suppose the space shuttle's measurable costs and benefits are C and B, respectively, and its intangible benefits, such as national prestige, are an unknown amount X. Then if the measured costs are greater than measured benefits, X must exceed $(C - B)$ for the program to be admissible. Such information may reveal that the intangible is not valuable enough to merit doing the project. If $(C - B)$ for the space shuttle were $10 million per year, people might agree that its contribution to national prestige was worth it. But if the figure were $10 billion, a different conclusion might emerge.

Finally, even if measuring certain benefits is impossible, there may be alternative methods of attaining them. If so, systematic study of the costs of the various alternatives should be done to find the cheapest way possible. This is sometimes called **cost-effectiveness analysis.** Thus, while one cannot put a dollar value on national security, it still may be feasible to subject the costs of alternative weapons systems to scrutiny.

Games Cost–Benefit Analysts Play

In addition to the problems we have already discussed, Tresch [2002] has noted a number of common errors in cost-benefit analysis.

The Chain-Reaction Game

An advocate for a proposal can make it look especially attractive by counting secondary profits arising from it as part of the benefits. If the government builds a road, the primary benefits are the reductions in transportation costs for individuals and firms. At the same time, though, profits of local restaurants, motels, and gas stations increase. This leads to increased profits in the local food, bed-linen, and gasoline-production industries. If enough secondary effects are added to the benefit side, eventually a positive present value can be obtained for practically any project.

This procedure ignores the fact that the project may induce losses as well as profits. After the road is built, the profits of train operators decrease as some of their customers turn to cars for transportation. Increased auto use may bid up the price of gasoline, decreasing the welfare of many gasoline consumers.

In short, the problem with the chain-reaction game is that it counts as benefits changes that are merely transfers. The increase in the price of gasoline, for example, transfers income from gasoline consumers to gasoline producers, but it does not represent a net benefit of the project. As noted later, distributional considerations may indeed be relevant to the decision maker. But if so, consistency requires that if secondary benefits are counted, so should secondary losses.

The Labor Game

Several years ago, the Congress was debating whether to keep alive the B-2 Stealth bomber program. The Department of Defense did *not* want to spend its money on this project. But California's Senator Dianne Feinstein definitely wanted it. The bomber, she declared, "can deliver a large payroll, precision or carpet." In the *Congressional Record* the next day, her remarks were amended to read "payload" [Ricks, 1994, p.A14].

The senator's Freudian slip is a typical example of the argument that some project should be implemented because of all the employment it "creates." Essentially, the wages of the workers employed are viewed as *benefits* of the project. This is absurd, because wages belong on the cost, not the benefit, side of the calculation. Of course, as already suggested, it is true that if workers are involuntarily unemployed, their social cost is less than their wage. Even in an area with high unemployment, it is unlikely that all the labor used in the project would have been unemployed, or that all those who were unemployed would have remained so for a long time.

The Double-Counting Game

Suppose that the government is considering irrigating some land that currently cannot be cultivated. It counts as the project's benefits the sum of (1) the increase in value of the land, *and* (2) the present value of the stream of net income obtained from farming it. The problem here is that a farmer can *either* farm the land and take as gains the net income stream *or* sell the land to someone else. Under competition, the sale price of the land just equals the present value of the net income from farming it. Because the farmer cannot do both simultaneously, counting both (1) and (2) represents a doubling of the true benefits.

This error may seem so silly that no one would ever commit it. However, Tresch [2002, p. 825] points out that at one time double counting was the official policy of the Bureau of Reclamation within the US Department of the Interior. The bureau's instructions for cost-benefit analysts stipulated that the benefits of land irrigation be computed as the *sum* of the increase in land value and the present value of the net income from farming it.

Distributional Considerations

In the private sector, normally no consideration is given to the question of who receives the benefits and bears the costs of a project. A dollar is a dollar, regardless of who is involved. Some economists argue that the same view be taken in public project analysis. If the present value of a project is positive, it should be undertaken regardless of who gains and loses. This is because as long as the present value is positive, the gainers *could* compensate the losers and still enjoy a net increase in utility. This notion, sometimes called the **Hicks-Kaldor criterion,**[10] thus bases project selection on whether there is a *potential* Pareto improvement. The actual compensation does not have to take place. That is, it is permissible to impose costs on some members of society if that provides greater net benefits to other individuals.

Others believe that because the goal of government is to maximize social welfare (not profit), the distributional implications of a project should be taken into account. Moreover, because it is the actual pattern of benefits and costs that really matters, the Hicks-Kaldor criterion does not provide a satisfactory escape from grappling with distributional issues.

One way to avoid the distributional problem is to assume the government can and will costlessly correct any undesirable distributional aspects of a project by making the appropriate transfers between gainers and losers.[11] The government works continually in the background to ensure that income stays optimally distributed, so the cost-benefit analyst need be concerned only with computing present values. Again, reality gets in the way. The government may have neither the power nor the ability to distribute income optimally.[12] (See Chapter 7.)

Suppose the policymaker believes that some group in the population is especially deserving. This distributional preference can be taken into account by assuming that a dollar benefit to a member of this group is worth more than a dollar going to others in the population. This, of course, tends to bias the selection of projects in favor of those that especially benefit the preferred group. Although much of the discussion of distributional issues has focused on income as the basis for classifying people, presumably characteristics such as race, ethnicity, and gender can be used, as well.

After the analyst is given the criteria for membership in the preferred group, she must face the question of precisely how to weight benefits to members of that group relative to the rest of society. Is a dollar to a poor person counted twice as much as a dollar to a rich person, or 50 times as much? The resolution of such issues depends on value judgments. All the analyst can do is induce the policymaker to state explicitly his or her value judgments and understand their implications.

A potential hazard of introducing distributional considerations is that political concerns may come to dominate the cost-benefit exercise.

---

[10] Named after the economists John Hicks and Nicholas Kaldor.

[11] *Costlessly* in this context means that the transfer system costs nothing to administer, and the transfers are done in such a way that they do not distort people's behavior (see Chapter 13).

[12] Moreover, as the government works behind the scenes to modify the income distribution, relative prices probably change. But as relative prices change, so do the benefit and cost calculations. Hence, efficiency and equity issues cannot be separated as neatly as suggested here.

Depending on how weights are chosen, any project can generate a positive present value, regardless of how inefficient it is. In addition, incorporating distributional considerations substantially increases the information requirements of cost-benefit analysis. The analyst needs to estimate not only benefits and costs but also how they are distributed across the population. As noted in Chapter 7, it is difficult to assess the distributional implications of government fiscal activities.

Uncertainty

In early 2003, the space shuttle Columbia disintegrated upon re-entry into the atmosphere. This disaster serves as a grim reminder of the fact that the outcomes of public projects are uncertain. Many important debates over project proposals center around the fact that no one knows how they will turn out. How much will a job-training program increase the earnings of welfare recipients? Will a high-tech weapons system function properly under combat conditions?

Suppose that two projects are being considered. They have identical costs, and both affect only one citizen, Kyle. Project X guarantees a benefit of $1,000 with certainty. Project Y creates a benefit of zero dollars with a probability of one-half, and a benefit of $2,000 with a probability of one-half. Which project does Kyle prefer?

Note that *on average*, X and Y have the same benefit. This is because the expected benefit from Y is ½ × $0 + ½ × $2,000 = $1,000. Nevertheless, if Kyle is risk averse, he prefers X to Y. This is because project Y subjects Kyle to risk, while X is a sure thing. In other words, if Kyle is risk averse, he would be willing to trade project Y for a *certain* amount of money less than $1,000—he would give up some income in return for gaining some security. The most obvious evidence that people are in fact willing to pay to avoid risk is the widespread holding of insurance policies of various kinds.

Therefore, when the benefits or costs of a project are risky, they must be converted into **certainty equivalents**—the amount of *certain* income the individual would be willing to trade for the set of uncertain outcomes generated by the project. The computation of certainty equivalents requires information on both the distribution of returns from the project and how risk averse the people involved are. The method of calculation is described in the appendix to this chapter.

The calculation of certainty equivalents presupposes that the random distribution of costs and benefits is known in advance. In some cases, this is a reasonable assumption. For example, engineering and weather data could be used to estimate how a proposed dam would reduce the probability of flood destruction. In many important cases, however, it is hard to assign probabilities to various outcomes. There is not enough experience with nuclear reactors to gauge the likelihood of various malfunctions. Similarly, how do you estimate the probability that a new AIDS vaccine will be effective? As usual, the best the analyst can do is to make explicit his or her assumptions and determine the extent to which substantive findings change when these assumptions are modified.

| An Application: Are Reductions in Class Size Worth It? | We saw in Chapter 4 that the efficacy of reducing class sizes in public schools is a hotly debated issue. Although much of the focus of this debate has been on the relationship between class size and educational performance, it is at least as important to examine the impact of class size on future earnings. Do children in relatively small classes have higher earnings as adults, other things being the same? In one econometric analysis of the relationship between class size and earnings, Card and Krueger [1996] estimated that a 10 percent reduction in class size is associated with future annual earnings increases of 0.4 to 1.1 percent. If it is correct, this estimate suggests that decreasing class size does produce monetary benefits. |

By itself, though, this does not tell us whether implementing reductions in class size would be a sensible policy. After all, making classes smaller is costly—more teachers need to be hired, additional classrooms built, and so on. Do the benefits outweigh the costs? Peltzman [1997] employs the tools of cost-benefit analysis to answer this question. His analysis illustrates several of the key issues raised in this chapter.

Cost-benefit analysis entails selecting a discount rate and specifying the costs and benefits for each year. We now discuss in turn how Peltzman deals with each of these problems.

Discount Rate

Theoretical considerations do not pin down a particular discount rate, so Peltzman follows the sensible practice of selecting a couple and seeing whether the substantive results are sensitive to the difference. The (real) rates he chooses are 3 percent and 7 percent.

Costs

Peltzman assumes that a 10 percent reduction in class size would require 10 percent more of all inputs used in public school education—teachers, classroom space, equipment, and so on. Thus, a permanent reduction in class size of 10 percent would increase yearly costs by 10 percent. In 1994, the average cost per student in US public schools was about $6,500, so a 10 percent increase is $650. This cost is incurred for each of the 13 years that the student is in school. Because these costs are incurred over time, they must be discounted. Row (1) of Table 11.3 shows the present value of $650 over a 13 year period for both $r = 3$ percent and $r = 7$ percent. In our earlier notation, these figures represent C, the present value of the project's costs, at each discount rate.

Table 11.3   **Costs and benefits of reducing class sizes by 10 percent**

	Present Value	
	r = 7%	*r = 3%*
(1) Costs ($650 annually for 1994 through 2006)	$5,813	$7,120
(2) Benefits ($225 annually for 2007 through 2056)	$1,379	$4,060
(3) Benefits minus costs	−$4,434	−$3,060

SOURCE: Computations based on Peltzman [1997].

This calculation of *C* involves a variety of simplifications; one of the most important is that the costs per year of schooling are constant. In fact, per student costs are typically higher in high school than in elementary school. Allocating a greater proportion of the costs to future years would tend to reduce their present value.

Benefits

As noted above, Card and Krueger estimate that the range of returns to an increase in class size is 0.4 to 1.1 percent. Peltzman takes the midpoint of this range, 0.75 percent. He assumes that individuals go to work immediately upon leaving school, and work for the next 50 years. Hence, earnings are increased by 0.75 percent for each of the next 50 years. In 1994 median annual earnings for male workers 25 and older were $30,000; increasing this sum by 0.75 percent implies a raise of $225 per year over a 50-year period. Just like the costs, the benefits must be discounted. Note that the first of these $225 flows occurs 13 years in the future; hence its present value is $225/(1 + r)^{13}$. The present values of the benefits (*B*) for both interest rates are recorded in row (2) of the table.

Just as was true on the cost side, the calculation of benefits involves a number of important simplifications. Men generally earn more than women, so that using median earnings for males imparts an upward bias to the estimate of the benefits. On the other hand, earnings typically increase over time instead of staying constant. Further, the analysis ignores non-monetary returns to education, which might include a reduced likelihood to commit crime, better informed choices in elections, and so on. To the extent that such effects are present, Peltzman's estimates of the social benefits to education are too low.

The Bottom Line and Evaluation

Computation of the net present value of this project is now straightforward. For each discount rate, take the benefit figure in row (2) of Table 11.3 and subtract from it the cost in row (1). These computations, recorded in row (3), reveal that when *r* is 7 percent, costs exceed benefits by $4,434, and when *r* is 3 percent, costs exceed benefits by $3,060. Thus, with either discount rate, (*B* − *C*) is less than zero, and reducing class size by 10 percent fails the admissibility criterion. On this basis, Peltzman concludes, tongue-in-cheek, that students would be better off if class size were *raised* by 10 percent, and the savings used to give each student a bond that paid the market rate of interest (p. 226).

This analysis of class-size reductions illustrates some important aspects of practical cost-benefit analysis:

- The analysis is often interdisciplinary because economists alone do not have the expertise to evaluate all costs and benefits. Thus, for example, engineering studies would be required to determine what expenditures really would be needed to expand classroom capacity by 10 percent. Similarly, if one wanted to include crime reduction in the benefits, one would want to consult sociologists who study criminal behavior.

- Evaluation of costs and benefits, especially those arising in the future, is likely to require ad hoc assumptions. We noted above, for example, that Peltzman's simplifying assumption that earnings are constant over time is certainly not correct. But in order to do better, one needs an alternative assumption of how earnings will rise (or fall) over time, and it is not obvious how to do that.

- In situations characterized by so much uncertainty, it may overburden the analysis to include distributional considerations. For example, an investigator who cannot predict with much precision how class size affects earnings overall can hardly be expected to estimate the distribution of the benefits by income group.

- For all its limitations, cost-benefit analysis is a remarkably useful way to summarize information. It also forces analysts to make explicit their assumptions so that the reasons for their ultimate recommendation are clear. In the case of Peltzman's examination of class size reductions, for example, because some of the assumptions are questionable, the conclusions may ultimately be proven incorrect. Nevertheless, it is an extremely valuable exercise because it establishes a rational framework within which to conduct future discussions of this important issue.

Use (and Nonuse) by Government

This chapter clearly indicates that cost-benefit analysis is not a panacea that provides a definitive "scientific" answer to every question. Nevertheless, it helps to ensure consistent decision making that focuses on the right issues. Have these methods been put to work by the government? The federal government has been ordering that various kinds of projects be subjected to cost-benefit analysis ever since the 1930s. Presidents Reagan, Bush, and Clinton each issued executive orders requiring cost-benefit analyses for all major regulations.

That said, both Democratic and Republican administrations often ignore or fudge orders to perform cost-benefit analyses, and the Congress has not been enthusiastic about getting them done either. Indeed, Hahn et al. [2000] studied 48 major federal health, safety, and environmental regulations issued in the late 1990s, and found that agencies quantified net benefits in less than a third of them. The agencies simply do not comply with the directives that require them to perform cost-benefit analyses. Why hasn't cost-benefit analysis had more effect on the style of government decision making? Part of the answer lies in the many practical difficulties in implementing cost-benefit analysis, especially when there is no consensus as to what the government's objectives are. In addition, many bureaucrats lack either the ability or the temperament to perform the analysis—particularly when it comes to their own programs. And neither are politicians particularly interested in seeing their pet projects subjected to scrutiny.

The story gets even worse when we consider the fact that, in certain vital areas, cost-benefit analysis has actually been expressly forbidden:

- The Clean Air Act prohibits costs from being considered when air quality standards are being set. In 1997, when the president's chief environmental aide was confronted with the fact that the costs of some new environmental regulations would exceed the benefits by hundreds of billions of dollars, she replied, "It is not at all about the money. . . . These are health standards" [Cushman, 1997, p. 28]. Any other stance would have been illegal!

- The same act requires companies to install equipment that reduces pollution as much as is feasible, regardless of how small the benefits of the incremental reduction or how large the incremental costs of the equipment.

- The Endangered Species Act requires the Fish and Wildlife Service to protect every endangered species in the United States, regardless of the cost.

- The Food, Drug, and Cosmetic Act requires the Food and Drug Administration to ban any additive to food that may induce cancer in animals or humans, regardless of how tiny the risk or how important the benefits of the substance.

A 1995 attempt by several members of Congress to change some of these laws was defeated. Moreover, in 2001 the Supreme Court upheld the constitutionality of the Clean Air Act's prohibition of cost-benefit analysis. While this may have been the right decision from a legal perspective, it was unfortunate from a policy standpoint. Although cost-benefit analysis is surely an imperfect tool, it is the only analytical framework available for making consistent decisions. Forbidding cost-benefit analysis amounts to outlawing sensible decision making.

Summary

- Cost-benefit analysis is the practical use of welfare economics to evaluate potential projects.
- To make net benefits from different years comparable, their present value must be computed.
- Other methods—internal rate of return, benefit-cost ratio—can lead to incorrect decisions.
- Choosing the discount rate is critical in cost-benefit analyses. In public sector analyses, three possible measures are the before-tax private rate of return, a weighted average of before- and after-tax private rates of return, and the social discount rate. Choosing among them depends on the type of private activity displaced—investment or consumption—and the extent to which private markets reflect society's preferences.
- In practice, the US government applies discount rates inconsistently.
- The benefits and costs of public projects may be measured in several ways:

  Market prices serve well if there is no strong reason to believe they depart from social marginal costs.

  Shadow prices adjust market prices for deviations from social marginal costs due to market imperfections.

  If labor is currently unemployed and will remain so for the duration of the project, the opportunity cost is small.

  If large government projects change equilibrium prices, consumer surplus can be used to measure benefits.

- For nonmarketed commodities, the values can sometimes be inferred by observing people's behavior. Two examples are computing the benefits of saving time and the benefits of reducing the probability of death.
- Certain intangible benefits and costs simply cannot be measured. The safest approach is to exclude them in a cost-benefit analysis and then calculate how large they must be to reverse the decision.
- Cost-benefit analyses sometimes fall prey to several pitfalls:

  Chain-reaction game—secondary benefits are included to make a proposal appear more favorable, without including the corresponding secondary costs.

  Labor game—wages are viewed as *benefits* rather than *costs* of the project.

  Double-counting game—benefits are erroneously counted twice.

- Including distributional considerations in cost-benefit analysis is controversial. Some analysts count dollars equally for all persons, while others apply weights that favor projects for selected population groups.
- In uncertain situations, individuals favor less risky projects, other things being the same. In general, the costs and benefits of uncertain projects must be converted to certainty equivalents.

Discussion Questions

1. "If you were running the government, would you ask whether it would be cost-effective to make children's pajamas flame-resistant, or would you just order the manufacturers to do it? Would you be moved by the pleas of crib manufacturers who told you it would cost them a bundle to move those slats closer together?" [Herbert, 1995]. How would you respond to these questions?

2. New Jersey recently instituted an enhanced auto emissions testing system at inspection sites throughout the state. According to news reports, the new tests increased waiting times from about 15 minutes to 2 hours. How should this observation be factored into a cost-benefit analysis of the emissions testing program?

3. A project yields an annual benefit of $25 a year, starting next year and continuing forever. What is the present value of the benefits if the interest rate is 10 percent? [Hint: The infinite sum $x + x^2 + x^3 + \ldots$ is equal to $x/(1 - x)$,

where x is a number less than 1.] Generalize your answer to show that if the perpetual annual benefit is B and the interest rate is r, then the present value is B/r.

4. An outlay of $1,000 today yields an annual benefit of $80 beginning next year and continuing forever. There is no inflation and the market interest rate is 10 percent before taxes and 5 percent after taxes.

 a. What is the internal rate of return?

 b. Taxes levied to fund the project come entirely from consumer spending. Is the project admissible? Why? Suppose instead that taxes are collected by reducing private firms' investments. Is the project admissible in this case? Finally, suppose consumers spend 60 cents of their last dollar and save 40 cents. Is the project admissible now? Explain your calculations.

 c. Suppose the social discount rate is 4 percent. What is the present value of the project?

 d. Now suppose 10 percent annual inflation is anticipated over the next 10 years. How are your answers to (a), (b), and (c) affected?

5. Bill rides the subway at a cost of 75 cents per trip, but would switch if the price were any higher. His only alternative is a bus that takes five minutes longer, but costs only 50 cents. He makes 10 trips per year. The city is considering renovations of the subway system that would reduce the trip by 10 minutes, but fares would rise by 40 cents per trip to cover the costs. The fare increase and reduced travel time both take effect in one year and last forever. The interest rate is 25 percent.

 a. As far as Bill is concerned, what are the present values of the project's benefits and costs?

 b. The city's population consists of 55,000 middle-class people, all of whom are identical to Bill, and 5,000 poor people. Poor people are either unemployed or have jobs close to their homes, so they do not use any form of public transportation. What are the total benefits and costs of the project for the city as a whole? What is the net present value of the project?

 c. Some members of the city council propose an alternative project that consists of an immediate tax of $1.25 per middle-class person to provide "free" legal services for the poor in both of the following two years. The legal services are valued by the poor at a total of $62,500 per year. (Assume this amount is received at the end of each of the two years.) What is the present value of the project?

 d. If the city must choose between the subway project and the legal services project, which should it select?

 *e. What is the "distributional weight" of each dollar received by a poor person that would make the present values of the two projects just equal? That is, how much must each dollar of income to a poor person be weighted relative to that of a middle-class person? Interpret your answer.

6. The consulting firm Arthur D. Little International recently prepared for the Czech government a cost-benefit analysis of smoking in that country. The report concluded that the net benefit of smoking was positive, in part because smoking causes premature death, which saves the government money on the care of retirees. Evaluate this approach to the problem, focusing on issues relating to the value of life.

7. In a journalist's discussion of the costs and benefits of recycling in New York, the first benefit he listed was that recycling created about 1,000 jobs in the private sector [Johnson, 2001, p. L23]. Discuss the logic of this statement.

8. According to Currie and Gruber [1996], the expansions of Medicaid in the 1980s led to a decline in child mortality of 5.1 percent. They calculate that the cost of the expansion per life saved was about $1.6 million. How would you determine whether or not the Medicaid expansion passed a cost-benefit test?

—————————————

*Difficult.

Selected References

Bazelon, Coleman, and Kent Smetters. "Discounting Inside the Washington, D.C., Beltway." *Journal of Economic Perspectives* (Fall 1999), pp. 213–28.

Boardman, Anthony E; David H Greenberg; Aidan R Vining; and David L Weimer. *Cost Benefit Analysis: Concepts and Practice.* New York: Prentice Hall, 1996.

Viscusi, W Kip, and Joseph E Aldy. "The Value of a Statistical Life: A Critical Review of Market Estimates Throughout the World." Working Paper No. 9487. Cambridge, MA: National Bureau of Economic Research, February 2003.

APPENDIX

Calculating the Certainty Equivalent Value

This appendix shows how to calculate the certainty equivalent value of an uncertain project.

Consider Jones, who currently earns E dollars. He enters a job-training program with an unpredictable effect on his future earnings. The program will leave his annual earnings unchanged with a probability of ½, or it will increase his earnings by y dollars, also with a probability of ½.[13] The benefit of the program is the amount that Jones would be willing to pay for it, so the key problem here is to determine that amount. A natural answer is $y/2$ dollars, the expected increase in his earnings.[14] However, this value is too high, because it neglects the fact that the outcome is uncertain and therefore subjects Jones to risk. As long as Jones dislikes risk, he would give up some income in return for gaining some security. When the benefits or costs of a project are risky, they must be converted into **certainty equivalents,** the amounts of *certain* income that the individual would be willing to trade for the set of uncertain outcomes generated by the project.

The notion of certainty equivalence is illustrated in Figure 11.A. The horizontal axis measures Jones's income, and the vertical axis indicates the amount of his utility. Schedule OU is Jones's utility function, which shows the total amount of utility associated with each income level. Algebraically, the amount of utility associated with a given income level, I, is $U(I)$. The shape of the schedule reflects the plausible assumption that as income

---

[13] Probabilities of ½ are used for simplicity. The general results hold regardless of the probabilities chosen.

[14] Expected earnings are found by multiplying each possible outcome by the associated probability and then adding: $(½ \times 0) + (½ \times y) = y/2$.

FIGURE 11.A

Computing the certainty equivalent of a risky project

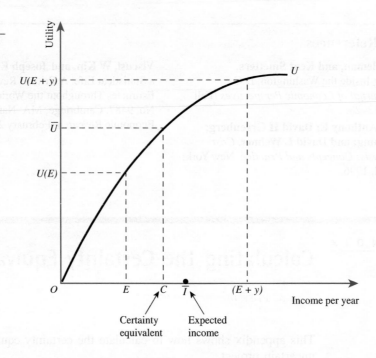

increases, utility also increases, but at a declining rate—there is diminishing marginal utility of income.

To find the utility associated with any income level, simply go from the horizontal axis up to OU, and then off to the vertical axis. For example, if the training project yields no return so that Jones's income is E, then his utility is $U(E)$, as indicated on the vertical axis. Similarly, if the project succeeds so that Jones's income increases by y, his total income is $(E + y)$, and his utility is $U(E + y)$.

Because each outcome occurs with a probability of ½, Jones's average or expected *income* is $E + y/2$, which lies halfway between E and $(E + y)$ and is denoted $\bar{I}$. However, what Jones really cares about is not expected income, but expected *utility*.[15] Expected utility is just the average of the utilities of the two outcomes, or $½U(E) + ½U(E + y)$. Geometrically, expected utility is halfway between $U(E)$ and $U(E + y)$ and is denoted by $\bar{U}$.

We are now in a position to find out exactly how much certain money the job-training program is worth to Jones. All we have to do is find the amount of income that corresponds to utility level $\bar{U}$. This is shown on the horizontal axis as C, which is by definition the certainty equivalent. It is crucial to note that C is less than $\bar{I}$—the certainty equivalent of the job-training

_____

[15] Those who are familiar with the theory of uncertainty will recognize the implicit assumption that individuals have "Von Neumann-Morgenstern utility functions."

program is *less* than the expected income. This is consistent with the intuition developed earlier. Jones is willing to pay a premium of $(\bar{I} - C)$ in exchange for the security of a sure thing. We have shown, then, that proper evaluation of the costs and benefits of an uncertain project requires that the project's expected value be reduced by a risk premium that depends on the shape of the individual's utility function.

In a way, this is a disappointing outcome, because it is much simpler to compute an expected value than a certainty equivalent. Fortunately, it turns out that in many cases the expected value is enough. Suppose a new bomber is being considered, and because the technology is not completely understood, analysts are unsure of its eventual cost. The cost will be either $15 per family or $25, each with probability $\frac{1}{2}$. Although in the aggregate a large amount of money is at stake, on a per-*family* basis, the sums involved are quite small compared to income. In terms of Figure 11.A, the two outcomes are very close to each other on curve OU. As points on OU get closer and closer together, the expected value and certainty equivalent become virtually identical, other things being the same. Intuitively, people do not require a risk premium to accept a gamble that involves only a small amount of income.

Thus, for projects that spread risk over large numbers of people, expected values can provide good measures of uncertain benefits and costs. But for cases in which risks are large relative to individuals' incomes, certainty equivalents must be computed.

PART 3

A Framework for Tax Analysis

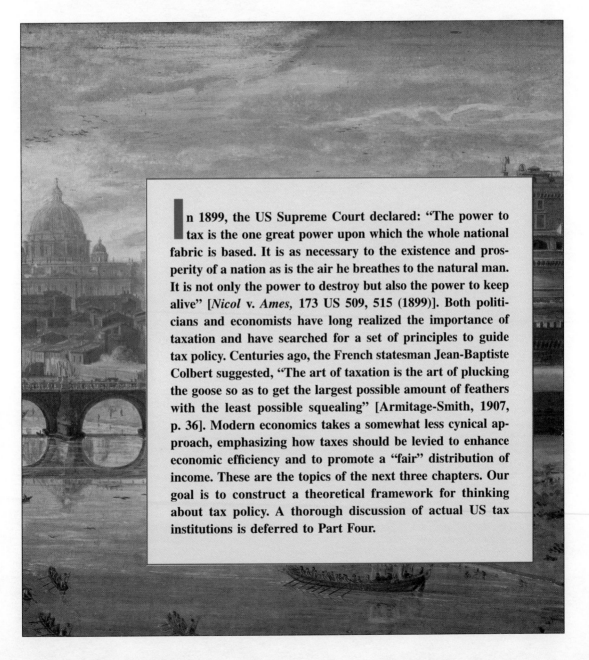

In 1899, the US Supreme Court declared: "The power to tax is the one great power upon which the whole national fabric is based. It is as necessary to the existence and prosperity of a nation as is the air he breathes to the natural man. It is not only the power to destroy but also the power to keep alive" [*Nicol* v. *Ames,* 173 US 509, 515 (1899)]. Both politicians and economists have long realized the importance of taxation and have searched for a set of principles to guide tax policy. Centuries ago, the French statesman Jean-Baptiste Colbert suggested, "The art of taxation is the art of plucking the goose so as to get the largest possible amount of feathers with the least possible squealing" [Armitage-Smith, 1907, p. 36]. Modern economics takes a somewhat less cynical approach, emphasizing how taxes should be levied to enhance economic efficiency and to promote a "fair" distribution of income. These are the topics of the next three chapters. Our goal is to construct a theoretical framework for thinking about tax policy. A thorough discussion of actual US tax institutions is deferred to Part Four.

CHAPTER 12

Taxation and Income Distribution

> *Struggle and contrive as you will, lay your taxes as you please, the traders will shift it off from their own gain.*
>
> JOHN LOCKE

merican policy debates about the tax system are dominated by the question of whether its burden is distributed fairly. A sensible discussion of this normative issue requires some understanding of the positive question of how taxes affect the distribution of income. A simple way to determine how taxes change the income distribution would be to conduct a survey in which each person is asked how many dollars he or she pays to the tax collector each year. Simple—but usually wrong. An example demonstrates that assessing correctly the burden of taxation is much more complicated.

Suppose the price of a bottle of wine is $10. The government imposes a tax of $1 per bottle, to be collected in the following way: Every time a bottle is purchased, the tax collector (who is lurking about the store) takes a dollar out of the wine seller's hand before the money is put into the cash register. A casual observer might conclude that the wine seller is paying the tax.

However, suppose that a few weeks after its imposition, the tax induces a price rise to $11 per bottle. Clearly, the proprietor receives the same amount per bottle as he did before the tax. The tax has apparently made him no worse off. Consumers pay the entire tax in the form of higher prices. On the other hand, suppose that after the tax the price increases to only $10.30. In this case, the proprietor keeps only $9.30 for each bottle sold; he is worse off by 70 cents per bottle. Consumers are also worse off, however, because they have to pay 30 cents more per bottle.[1] In this case, producers and consumers

---

[1] Actually, the change in the prices faced by consumers and producers is only part of the story. There is also a burden due to the tax-induced distortion of choice. See Chapter 13.

share the burden of the tax. Yet another possibility is that after the tax is imposed, the price stays at $10. If this happens, the consumer is no worse off, while the seller bears the full burden of the tax.

The **statutory incidence** of a tax indicates who is legally responsible for the tax. All three cases in the preceding paragraph are identical in the sense that the statutory incidence is on the seller. But the situations differ drastically with respect to who really bears the burden. Because prices may change in response to the tax, knowledge of statutory incidence tells us *essentially nothing* about who really pays the tax. In contrast, the **economic incidence** of a tax is the change in the distribution of private real income induced by a tax. Our focus in this chapter is on the forces that determine the extent to which statutory and economic incidence differ—the amount of **tax shifting.**

Tax Incidence: General Remarks

Several observations should be kept in mind in any discussion of how taxes affect the distribution of income.

Only People Can Bear Taxes

A *New York Times* editorialist once criticized a study of the distribution of the tax burden because the study assumed "that all money taken in by the Federal, state and local governments came from individuals, whether payments were made by people [or] companies" [Norris, 1999]. The statement reflects a common fallacy—that businesses have an independent ability to bear a tax. True, the US legal system treats certain institutions such as corporations as if they were people. Although for many purposes this is a convenient fiction, it sometimes creates confusion. From an economist's point of view, people—stockholders, workers, landlords, consumers—bear taxes. A corporation cannot.

Given that only people can bear taxes, how should they be classified for purposes of incidence analysis? Often their role in production—what inputs they supply to the production process—is used. (Inputs are often referred to as *factors of production.*) The focus is on how the tax system changes the distribution of income among capitalists, laborers, and landlords. This is referred to as the **functional distribution of income.**

Framing the analysis this way seems a bit old-fashioned. Perhaps in 18th-century England property owners never worked and workers owned no property. But in the contemporary United States, many people who derive most of their income from labor also have savings accounts and/or common stocks. (Often, these assets are held for individuals in pensions.) Similarly, some people own huge amounts of capital and also work full time. Thus, it seems more relevant to study how taxes affect the way in which total income is distributed among people: the **size distribution of income.** Given information on what proportion of people's income is from capital, land, and labor, changes in the functional distribution can be translated into changes in the size distribution. For example, a tax that lowers the relative return on capital tends to hurt those at the top of the income distribution because a relatively high proportion of the incomes of the rich is from capital.[2]

Other classification schemes might be interesting for particular problems. When increases in the federal tax on cigarettes are proposed, the incidence by region receives a great deal of attention. (Are people from tobacco-growing states going to suffer disproportionate harm?) Alternatively, when proposals are made to change the taxation of land in urban areas, analysts often look at incidence by race. It is easy to think of further examples based on sex, age, and so forth.

Both Sources and Uses of Income Should Be Considered

In the previous wine tax example, it is natural to assume that the distributional effects of the tax depend crucially on people's spending patterns. To the extent that the price of wine increases, the people who tend to consume a lot of wine are made worse off. However, if the tax reduces the demand for wine, the factors employed in wine production may suffer income losses. Thus, the tax can also change the income distribution by affecting the sources of income. Suppose that poor people spend a relatively large proportion of their incomes on wine, but that vineyards tend to be owned by the rich. Then on the uses of income side, the tax redistributes income away from the poor, but on the sources side, it redistributes income away from the rich. The overall incidence depends on how both the sources and uses of income are affected. This distinction is important for understanding the debate over former Vice President Gore's proposal to clean up the Florida Everglades. Because the ecology of the Everglades is harmed by the runoff from sugar fields, he argued that sugar products be subjected to a special tax and the proceeds used to finance a cleanup. Opposition came not only from consumer groups who were concerned about the price of products using sugar but also from Florida *workers,* who realized that by reducing the demand for sugar, such a tax would hurt their incomes.

In practice, economists commonly ignore effects on the sources side when considering a tax on a commodity and ignore the uses side when analyzing a tax on an input. This procedure is appropriate if the most *systematic* effects of a commodity tax are on the uses of income and those of a factor tax on the sources of income. The assumption simplifies analyses, but its correctness must be considered for each case. (See Fullerton and Rogers [1997].)

Incidence Depends on How Prices Are Determined

We have emphasized that the incidence problem is fundamentally one of determining how taxes change prices. Clearly, different models of price determination may give quite different answers to the question of who really bears a tax. This chapter considers several different models and compares the results.

---

[2] However, some low-income retirees also derive the bulk of their income from capital.

A closely related issue is the time dimension of the analysis. Incidence depends on changes in prices, but change takes time. In most cases, responses are larger in the long run than the short run. Thus, the short- and long-run incidence of a tax may differ, and the time frame that is relevant for a given policy question must be specified.

Incidence Depends on the Disposition of Tax Revenues

Balanced-budget incidence computes the combined effects of levying taxes *and* government spending financed by those taxes. In general, the distributional effect of a tax depends on how the government spends the money. Expenditures on AIDS research have a very different distributional impact than spending on hot lunches for schoolchildren. Some studies assume the government spends the tax revenue exactly as the consumers would if they had received the money. This is equivalent to returning the revenue as a lump sum and letting consumers spend it.

Tax revenues are usually not earmarked for particular expenditures. It is then desirable to be able to abstract from the question of how the government spends the money. The idea is to examine how incidence differs when one tax is replaced with another, holding the government budget constant. This is called *differential tax incidence*. Because differential incidence looks at changes in taxes, a reference point is needed. The hypothetical "other tax" used as the basis of comparison is often assumed to be a **lump sum tax**—a tax for which the individual's liability does not depend upon behavior. (For example, a 10 percent income tax is *not* a lump sum tax because it depends on how much the individual earns. But a head tax of $500 independent of earnings *is* a lump sum tax.)

Finally, *absolute tax incidence* examines the effects of a tax when there is no change in either other taxes or government expenditure. Absolute incidence is of most interest for macroeconomic models in which tax levels are changed to achieve some stabilization goal.

Tax Progressiveness Can Be Measured in Several Ways

Suppose that an investigator has managed to calculate every person's real share of a particular tax—the economic incidence as defined previously. The bottom line of such an exercise is often a characterization of the tax as proportional, progressive, or regressive. The definition of **proportional** is straightforward; it describes a situation in which the ratio of taxes paid to income is constant regardless of income level.[3]

Defining progressive and regressive is not easy and, unfortunately, ambiguities in definition sometimes confuse public debate. A natural way to define these words is in terms of the **average tax rate,** the ratio of taxes paid to income. If the average tax rate increases with income, the system is **progressive;** if it falls, the tax is **regressive.**

---

[3] However, the definition of income is not straightforward; see Chapter 15.

Table 12.1   **Tax liabilities under a hypothetical tax system**

Income	Tax Liability	Average Tax Rate	Marginal Tax Rate
$ 2,000	$-200	-0.10	0.2
3,000	0	0	0.2
5,000	400	0.08	0.2
10,000	1,400	0.14	0.2
30,000	5,400	0.18	0.2

Confusion arises because some people think of progressiveness in terms of the **marginal tax rate**—the *change* in taxes paid with respect to a change in income. To illustrate the distinction, consider the following very simple income tax structure. Each individual computes her tax bill by subtracting $3,000 from income and paying an amount equal to 20 percent of the remainder. (If the difference is negative, the individual gets a subsidy equal to 20 percent of the figure.) Table 12.1 shows the amount of tax paid, the average tax rate, and the marginal tax rate for each of several income levels. The average rates increase with income. However, the marginal tax rate is constant at 0.2 because for each additional dollar earned, the individual pays an additional 20 cents, regardless of income level. People could disagree about the progressiveness of this tax system and each be right according to their own definitions. It is therefore very important to make the definition clear when using the terms *regressive* and *progressive*. From here on, we assume they are defined in terms of average tax rates.

Measuring *how* progressive a tax system is presents an even harder task than defining progressiveness. Many reasonable alternatives have been proposed, and we consider two simple ones.[4] The first says that the greater the increase in average tax rates as income increases, the more progressive the system. Algebraically, let T_0 and T_1 be the true (as opposed to statutory) tax liabilities at income levels I_0 and I_1, respectively (I_1 is greater than I_0). The measurement of progressiveness, v_1, is

$$v_1 = \frac{\dfrac{T_1}{I_1} - \dfrac{T_0}{I_0}}{I_1 - I_0} \tag{12.1}$$

Once the analyst computes the values of T_1 and T_0 and substitutes into Equation (12.1), the tax system with the higher value of v_1 is said to be more progressive.

---

[4] See Formby, Smith, and Sykes [1986].

The second possibility is to say that one tax system is more progressive than another if its elasticity of tax revenues with respect to income (i.e., the percentage change in tax revenues divided by percentage change in income) is higher. Here the expression to be evaluated is v_2, defined as

$$v_2 = \frac{(T_1 - T_0)}{T_0} \div \frac{(I_1 - I_0)}{I_0} \tag{12.2}$$

Now consider the following proposal: Everyone's tax liability is to be increased by 20 percent of the amount of tax he or she currently pays. This proposal would increase the tax liability of a person who formerly paid T_0 to $1.2 \times T_0$, and the liability that was formerly T_1 to $1.2 \times T_1$. Member of Congress A says the proposal will make the tax system more progressive, while member of Congress B says it has no effect on progressiveness whatsoever. Who is right? It depends on the progressivity measure. Substituting the expressions $1.2 \times T_0$ and $1.2 \times T_1$ for T_0 and T_1, respectively, in Equation (12.1), v_1 increases by 20 percent. The proposal thus increases progressiveness. On the other hand, if the same substitution is done in Equation (12.2), the value of v_2 is unchanged. (Both the numerator and denominator are multiplied by 1.2, which cancels out the effect.) The lesson here is that even very intuitively appealing measures of progressiveness can give different answers.[5] Again, intelligent public debate requires that people make their definitions clear.

Partial Equilibrium Models

With preliminaries out of the way, we turn now to the fundamental issue of this chapter: how taxes affect the income distribution. Recall that the essence of the problem is that taxes induce changes in relative prices. Knowing how prices are determined is therefore critical to the analysis. In this section we analyze **partial equilibrium models** of price determination—models that look only at the market in which the tax is imposed and ignore the ramifications in other markets. This kind of analysis is most appropriate when the market for the taxed commodity is relatively small compared to the economy as a whole. The vehicle for our analysis is the supply and demand model of perfect competition.

Unit Taxes on Commodities

We study first the incidence of a **unit tax,** so named because it is levied as a fixed amount per unit of a commodity sold. For example, the federal government imposes a tax on champagne of $3.40 per wine gallon and a tax on cigarettes of 39 cents per pack. Suppose that the price and quantity of champagne are determined competitively by supply (S_c) and demand (D_c)

---

[5] Note also that v_1 and v_2, in general, depend on the level of income. That is, even a single tax system does not usually have a constant v_1 and v_2. This further complicates discussions of the degree of progressiveness.

FIGURE 12.1

Price and quantity before taxation

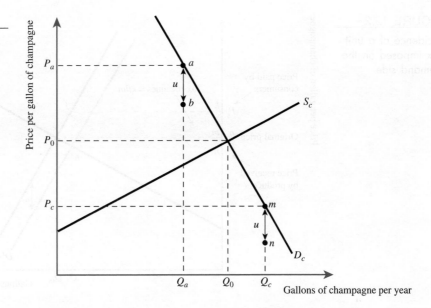

as in Figure 12.1. Before imposition of the tax, the quantity demanded and price are Q_0 and P_0, respectively.

Now suppose that a unit tax of $\$u$ per gallon is imposed on each purchase, and the statutory incidence is on buyers. A key step in incidence analysis is to recognize that in the presence of a tax, the price paid by consumers and the price received by suppliers differ. Previously, we could use a supply-demand analysis to determine the *single* market price. Now, this analysis must be modified to accommodate two different prices, one for buyers and one for sellers.

We begin by determining how the tax affects the demand schedule. Consider an arbitrary point a on the demand curve. This point indicates that the *maximum* price per gallon that people would be willing to pay for Q_a gallons is P_a. After the unit tax of u is imposed, the most that people would be willing to spend for Q_a is *still* P_a. There is no reason to believe the tax affects the underlying valuation people place on champagne. However, when people pay P_a per gallon, producers no longer receive the whole amount. Instead, they receive only $(P_a - u)$, an amount that is labeled point b in Figure 12.1. In other words, after the unit tax is imposed, a is no longer a point on the demand curve *as perceived by suppliers*. Point b is on the demand curve as perceived by suppliers, because they realize that if Q_a is supplied, they receive only $(P_a - u)$ per gallon. It is irrelevant to the suppliers how much consumers pay per gallon; all that matters to suppliers is the amount they receive per gallon.

Of course, point a was chosen arbitrarily. At any other point on the demand curve, the story is just the same. Thus, for example, after the tax is

FIGURE 12.2

Incidence of a unit
tax imposed on the
demand side

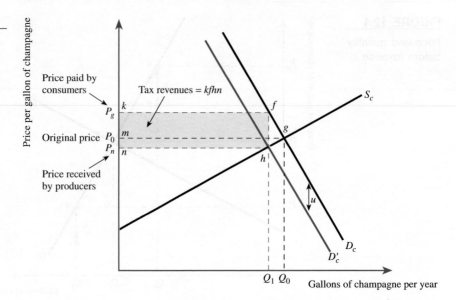

imposed, the price received by suppliers for output Q_c is at point n, which
is found by subtracting the distance u from point m. Repeating this process
at every point along the demand curve, we generate a new demand curve
located exactly u dollars below the old one. In Figure 12.2, the demand
curve so constructed is labeled D'_c. Schedule D'_c is relevant to suppliers
because it shows how much they receive for each unit sold.

We are now in a position to find the equilibrium quantity of champagne
after the unit tax is imposed. The equilibrium is where the supply equals
demand as perceived by suppliers, output Q_1 in Figure 12.2. Thus, the tax
lowers the quantity sold from Q_0 to Q_1.

The next step is to find the new equilibrium price. As noted earlier, there
are really two prices at the new equilibrium: the price received by producers, and the price paid by consumers. The price received by producers is at
the intersection of their effective demand and supply curves, which occurs
at P_n. The price paid by consumers is P_n *plus* u, the unit tax. To find this
price geometrically, we must go up from P_n a vertical distance exactly equal
to u. But by construction, the distance between schedules D_c and D'_c is equal
to u. Hence, to find the price paid by consumers, we simply go up from the
intersection of D'_c and S_c to the original demand curve D_c. The price so determined is P_g. Because P_g includes the tax, it is often referred to as the price
gross of tax. On the other hand, P_n is the price *net* of tax.

The tax makes consumers worse off because P_g, the new price they face,
is higher than the original price P_0. But the consumers' price does not
increase by the full amount of the tax—$(P_g - P_0)$ is less than u. Producers
also pay part of the tax in the form of a lower price received per gallon.
Producers now receive only P_n, while before the tax they received P_0. Thus,

FIGURE 12.3

Incidence of a unit tax imposed on the supply side

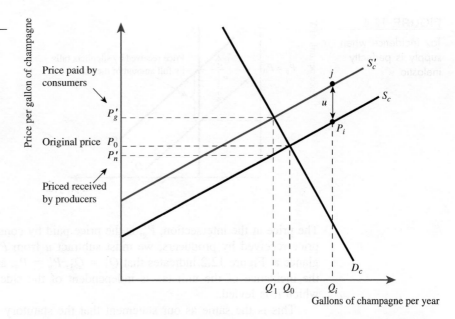

the tax makes both producers and consumers worse off.[6] Notice that consumers and producers "split" the tax in the sense that the increase in the consumer price ($P_g - P_0$) and the decrease in the producer price ($P_0 - P_n$) just add up to $u.

By definition, revenues collected are the product of the number of units purchased, Q_1, and the tax per unit, u. Geometrically, Q_1 is the width of rectangle *kfhn* and u is its height, so tax revenues are the area of this rectangle.

This analysis has two important implications:

The incidence of a unit tax is independent of whether it is levied on consumers or producers.   Suppose the same tax u had been levied on the suppliers of champagne instead of the consumers. Consider an arbitrary price P_i on the original supply curve in Figure 12.3. The supply curve indicates that for suppliers to produce Q_i units, they must receive at least P_i per unit. After the unit tax, suppliers still need to receive P_i per unit. For them to do so, however, consumers must pay price $P_i + u$ per unit, which is shown geometrically as point j. It should now be clear where the argument is heading. To find the supply curve as it is perceived by consumers, S_c must be shifted up by the amount of the unit tax. This new supply curve is labeled S'_c. The posttax equilibrium is at Q'_1, where the schedules S'_c and D_c intersect.

---

[6] In terms of surplus measures, consumers are worse off by area *mkfg* and producers are worse off by *mghn*. The loss of total surplus exceeds the tax revenues by triangle *fhg*; this is the *excess burden* of the tax, as explained in Chapter 13. For a review of consumer and producer surplus, see the appendix to Chapter 3.

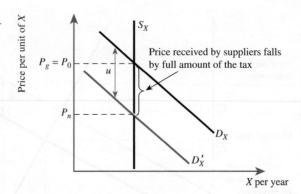

FIGURE 12.4

Tax incidence when supply is perfectly inelastic

(Figure labels: Price per unit of X; S_X; Price received by suppliers falls by full amount of the tax; $P_g = P_0$; u; P_n; D_X; D'_X; X per year)

The price at the intersection, P'_g, is the price paid by consumers. To find the price received by producers, we must subtract u from P'_g, giving us P'_n. A glance at Figure 12.2 indicates that $Q'_1 = Q_1$, $P'_g = P_g$, and $P'_n = P_n$. Thus, the incidence of the unit tax is independent of the side of the market on which it is levied.

This is the same as our statement that the statutory incidence of a tax tells us nothing of the economic incidence of the tax. It is irrelevant whether the tax collector (figuratively) stands next to consumers and takes u dollars every time they pay for a gallon of champagne or stands next to sellers and collects u dollars from them whenever they sell a gallon. Figures 12.2 and 12.3 prove that what matters is the size of the disparity the tax introduces between the price paid by consumers and the price received by producers, and not on which side of the market the disparity is introduced. The tax-induced difference between the price paid by consumers and the price received by producers is referred to as the **tax wedge**.

The incidence of a unit tax depends on the elasticities of supply and demand. In Figure 12.2, consumers bear the brunt of the tax—the amount they pay goes up much more than the amount received by producers goes down. This result is strictly determined by the shapes of the demand and supply curves. In general, the more elastic the demand curve, the less the tax borne by consumers, *ceteris paribus*. Similarly, the more elastic the supply curve, the less the tax borne by producers, *ceteris paribus*. Intuitively, elasticity provides a rough measure of an economic agent's ability to escape the tax. The more elastic the demand, the easier it is for consumers to turn to other products when the price goes up, and therefore more of the tax must be borne by suppliers. Conversely, if consumers purchase the same amount regardless of price, the whole burden can be shifted to them. Similar considerations apply to the supply side.

Illustrations of extreme cases are provided in Figures 12.4 and 12.5. In Figure 12.4, commodity X is supplied perfectly inelastically. When a unit tax is imposed, the effective demand curve becomes D'_X. As before, the price

FIGURE 12.5

Tax incidence when supply is perfectly elastic

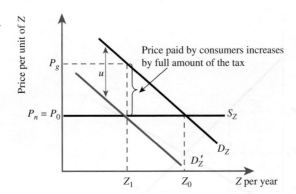

received by producers (P_n) is at the intersection of S_X and D'_X. Note that P_n is exactly u less than P_0. Thus, the price received by producers falls by exactly the amount of the tax. At the same time, the price paid by consumers, P_g ($= P_n + u$), remains at P_0. When supply is perfectly inelastic, producers bear the entire burden. Figure 12.5 represents an opposite extreme. The supply of commodity Z is perfectly elastic. Imposition of a unit tax leads to demand curve D'_Z. At the new equilibrium, quantity demanded is Z_1 and the price received by producers, P_n, is still P_0. The price paid by consumers, P_g, is therefore $P_0 + u$. In this case, consumers bear the entire burden of the tax.[7]

The Cigarette Tax Debate.   Recently, the United States has been engaging in a major policy debate regarding cigarette taxation. In 2000, the 24-cent-per-pack federal tax was raised to 34 cents, and it is now 39 cents. But certain legislators would like to go further and increase the tax to $1 or more. Some proponents of the higher tax seem to be interested primarily in discouraging smoking, and others care more about punishing tobacco producers. Those who want to discourage smoking are implicitly assuming that the tax will drive up the price paid by consumers, and those who want to punish the tobacco producers expect the price they receive to go down. How can one determine which effect would prevail? Our model of tax incidence tells us what we need to find out: the supply and demand elasticities in the cigarette market.

Ad Valorem Taxes

We now turn to the incidence of an **ad valorem tax,** a tax with a rate given as a *proportion* of the price. For example, the state of Tennessee levies a 6 percent tax on purchases of food. Virtually all state and local taxes on restaurant meals and clothing are ad valorem.

---

[7] Note that as long as input costs are constant, the *long-run* supply curve for a competitive market is horizontal as in Figure 12.5. Hence, under these conditions, in the long run consumers bear the entire burden of the tax.

FIGURE 12.6

Introducing an ad
valorem tax

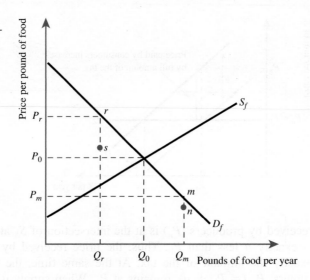

Luckily, the analysis of ad valorem taxes is very similar to that of unit taxes. The basic strategy is still to find out how the tax changes the effective demand curve and compute the new equilibrium. However, instead of moving the curve down by the same absolute amount for each quantity, the ad valorem tax lowers it by the same *proportion*. To show this, consider the demand (D_f) and supply (S_f) curves for food in Figure 12.6. In the absence of taxation, the equilibrium price and quantity are P_0 and Q_0, respectively. Now suppose that a tax of 25 percent of the gross price is levied on the consumption of food.[8] Consider point m on D_f. After the tax is imposed, P_m is still the most that consumers will pay for Q_m pounds of food; the amount producers will receive is 75 percent of the vertical distance between point m and the horizontal axis, which is labeled point n. Hence, point n is one point on the demand curve perceived by producers. Similarly, the price at point r migrates down one quarter of the way between it and the horizontal axis to point s. Repeating this exercise for every point on D_f, the effective demand curve facing suppliers is determined as D_f' in Figure 12.7. From here, the analysis proceeds exactly as for a unit tax: The equilibrium is where S_f and D_f' intersect, with the quantity exchanged Q_1, the price received by food producers P_n, and the price paid by consumers P_g. As before, the incidence of the tax is determined by the elasticities of supply and demand.

---

[8] Measuring ad valorem tax rates involves a fundamental ambiguity. Is the tax measured as a percentage of the net or gross price? In this example, the tax is 25 percent of the gross price, which is equivalent to a rate of 33 percent of net price. If the price paid by the consumer were $1, the tax paid would be 25 cents, and the price received by producers would be 75 cents. Expressing the 25 cent tax bill as a fraction of 75 cents gives us a 33 percent rate as a proportion of the net price.

FIGURE 12.7

Incidence of an ad
valorem tax

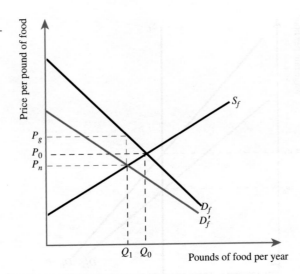

This analysis is applicable to any number of situations. Suppose that Figure 12.7 were relabeled so that it represented the market for rental housing instead of the food market. Then we could show that the burden of the property tax doesn't depend on whether landlords or tenants pay the property tax. This is counter to the usual perception that landlords bear the burden simply because they write the check.

Taxes on Factors

So far we have discussed taxes on goods, but the analysis can also be applied to factors of production.

The Payroll Tax.   Consider the payroll tax used to finance the Social Security system. As noted in Chapter 9, a tax equal to 7.65 percent of workers' earnings must be paid by their employers and a tax at the same rate paid by the workers themselves—a total of 15.3 percent.[9] This division has a long history and is a consequence of our lawmakers' belief that the payroll tax should be shared equally by employers and employees. But the *statutory distinction between workers and bosses is irrelevant.* As suggested earlier, the incidence of this labor tax is determined only by the wedge the tax puts between what employees receive and employers pay.

This point is illustrated in Figure 12.8, where D_L is the demand for labor and S_L is the supply of labor. For purposes of illustration, assume S_L to be perfectly inelastic. Before taxation, the wage is w_0. The ad valorem tax on labor moves the effective demand curve to D_L'. As usual, the distance between D_L' and D_L is the wedge between what is paid for an item and what

---

[9] After earnings exceed a certain level, the payroll tax rate falls. See Chapter 9.

FIGURE 12.8

Incidence of a
payroll tax with an
inelastic supply of
labor

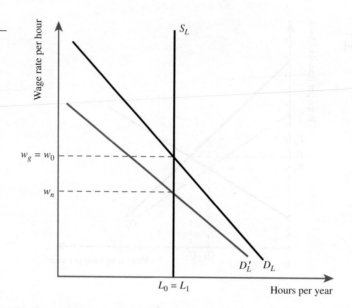

is received by those who supply it. After the tax is imposed, the wage received by workers falls to w_n. On the other hand, w_g, the price paid by employers, stays at w_0. In this example, despite the statutory division of the tax, the wage rate received by workers falls by exactly the amount of the tax—they bear the entire burden.

Of course, we could have gotten just the opposite result by drawing the supply curve as perfectly elastic. The key point to remember is that nothing about the incidence of a tax can be known without information on the relevant behavioral elasticities. In fact, there is some evidence that the elasticity of the total supply of hours of work in the United States is about zero [Heckman, 1993]. At least in the short run, labor probably bears most of the payroll tax, despite the congressional attempt to split the burden evenly.

Capital Taxation in a Global Economy.   The strategy for analyzing a tax on capital is essentially the same as that for analyzing a tax on labor—draw the supply and demand curves, shift or pivot the relevant curve by an amount depending on the tax rate, and see how the after-tax equilibrium compares with the original one. In an economy that is closed to trade, it is reasonable to assume that the demand curve slopes down (firms demand less capital when its price goes up), and that the supply of capital slopes up (people supply more capital (i.e., save more) when the return to saving increases).[10] In this case, the owners of capital bear some of the burden of the tax, the precise amount depending on the supply and demand elasticities.

---

[10] However, saving need not increase with the rate of return. See Chapter 16.

Suppose now that the economy is open and capital is perfectly mobile across countries. In effect, there is a single global market for capital, and if suppliers of capital cannot earn the going world rate of return in a particular country, they will take it out of that country and put it in another. In terms of a supply and demand diagram, the supply of capital to a particular country is perfectly elastic—its citizens can purchase all the capital they want at the going rate of return, but none whatsoever at a lower rate. The implications for the incidence of a tax on capital are striking. As in Figure 12.5, the before-tax price paid by the users of capital rises by exactly the amount of the tax, and the suppliers of capital bear no burden whatsoever. Intuitively, capital simply moves abroad if it has to bear any of the tax; hence, the before-tax rate of return has to rise.

Now, even in today's highly integrated world economy, capital is not perfectly mobile across countries. Moreover, for a country like the United States whose capital market is large relative to the world market, it is doubtful that the supply curve is perfectly horizontal. Nevertheless, policymakers who ignore globalization will tend to overestimate their ability to place the burden of taxation on owners of capital. To the extent that capital is internationally mobile, taxes on capitalists are shifted to others, and the apparent progressivity of taxes on capital is illusory.

Commodity Taxation without Competition

The assumption of competitive markets has played a major role in our analysis. We now discuss how the results might change under alternative market structures.

Monopoly.   The polar opposite of competition is monopoly—one seller. Figure 12.9 depicts a monopolist that produces commodity X. Before any taxation, the demand curve facing the monopolist is D_X, and the associated marginal revenue curve is MR_X. The marginal cost curve for the production of X is MC_X, and the average total cost curve, ATC_X. As usual, the condition for profit maximization is that production be carried to the point where marginal revenue equals marginal cost, at output X_0 where the price charged is P_0. Economic profit per unit is the difference between average revenue and average total cost, distance ab. The number of units sold is db. Hence, total profit is ab times db, which is the area of rectangle $abdc$.

Now suppose that a unit tax of u is levied on X. For exactly the same reasons as before, the effective demand curve facing the producer shifts down by a vertical distance equal to u.[11] In Figure 12.10, this demand curve is labeled D'_X. At the same time, the marginal revenue curve facing the firm also shifts down by distance u because the tax reduces the firm's incremental revenue for each unit sold. The new effective marginal revenue curve is labeled MR'_X.

---

[11] Alternatively, we could shift the marginal cost curve *up* by *u*. The final outcomes are identical.

FIGURE 12.9

Equilibrium of a monopolist

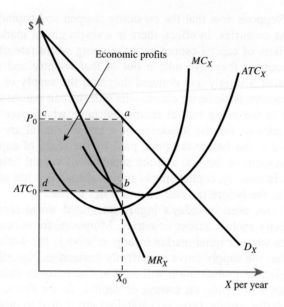

FIGURE 12.10

Imposition of a unit tax on a monopolist

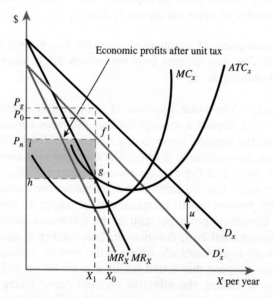

The profit-maximizing output, X_1, is found at the intersection of MR_X' and MC_X. Using output X_1, we find the price received by the monopolist by going up to D_X', the demand curve facing him, and locate price P_n. The price paid by consumers is determined by adding u to P_n, which is shown as price P_g on the diagram. After-tax profit per unit is the difference between the price *received by the monopolist* and average total cost, distance fg. Number of units sold is *if*. Therefore, monopoly economic profits after tax are measured by area *fghi*.

What are the effects of the tax? Quantity demanded goes down ($X_1 < X_0$); the price paid by consumers goes up ($P_g > P_0$); and the price received by the monopolist goes down ($P_n < P_0$). Note that monopoly profits are lower under the tax—area *fghi* in Figure 12.10 is smaller than area *abdc* in Figure 12.9. Despite its market power, a monopolist is generally made worse off by a unit tax on the product it sells. Public debates often assume that a firm with market power can simply pass on all taxes to consumers. This analysis shows that even a completely greedy and grasping monopolist must bear some of the burden. As before, the precise share of the burden borne by consumers depends on the elasticity of the demand schedule.

It is straightforward to repeat the exercise for an ad valorem tax on the monopolist (D_X and MR_X pivot instead of moving down in a parallel fashion); this is left as an exercise for the reader.

Oligopoly.   Between the polar extremes of perfect competition and monopoly is the oligopoly market structure in which there are a "few" sellers. Unfortunately, there is no well-developed theory of tax incidence in oligopoly. The reason for this embarrassing fact is simple: Incidence depends primarily on how relative prices change when taxes are imposed, but there is no generally accepted theory of oligopolistic price determination.

Still, we can get a sense of the issues involved by imagining the problem faced by the firms in an oligopolistic market. From the firms' point of view, the ideal situation would be for them to collude and jointly produce the output that maximizes the profits of the entire industry. This output level is referred to as the *cartel solution*. (A cartel is just a group of producers that act together to maximize profits. The international oil cartel OPEC is the most famous example.) The cartel solution requires each firm to cut its output to force up the market price. The problem for the firms is that the cartel solution is very difficult to obtain. Why? Once an agreement about how much each firm should produce is reached, each firm has an incentive to cheat on that agreement—to take advantage of the higher price and produce more than its quota of output. (Again, think about OPEC, and the problems it has in keeping its members from producing "too much" oil.) Consequently, output in an oligopolistic market is typically higher than the cartel solution. The firms would all be better off if there were some mechanism to force all of them to reduce their output.

What happens when this industry's output is subjected to a tax? As is the case both for competition and monopoly, the firms contract their output. However, unlike the other market structures, this is not necessarily bad for the oligopolistic firms. To be sure, for any given level of before-tax profits, the firms are worse off, because they have to pay the tax. However, as the firms contract their outputs, they move closer to the cartel solution, so their before-tax profits increase. It is theoretically possible for before-tax profits to increase by so much that even after paying the tax, the firms are better off [Delipalla and Keen, 1992]. Of course, it is also possible for the firms to be worse off. One needs more information on just how much the firms cut back their output to obtain a definitive answer.

As economic behavior under oligopoly becomes better understood, improved models of incidence will be developed. In the meantime, most economists feel fairly comfortable in relying on the predictions produced by competitive models, although they realize these are only approximations.

Profits Taxes

So far we have been discussing taxes based on sales. Firms can also be taxed on their **economic profits,** defined as the return to owners of the firm in excess of the opportunity costs of the factors used in production. (Economic profits are also referred to as *supranormal* or *excess* profits.) We now show that for profit-maximizing firms, a tax on economic profits cannot be shifted—it is borne only by the owners of the firm.

Consider first a perfectly competitive firm in short-run equilibrium. The firm's output is determined by the intersection of its marginal cost and marginal revenue schedules. A proportional tax on economic profits changes neither marginal cost nor marginal revenue. Therefore, no firm has the incentive to change its output decision. Because output does not change, neither does the price paid by consumers, so they are no worse off. The tax is completely absorbed by the firms. Here's another way to get to the same result: If the tax rate on economic profits is t_p, the firm's objective is to maximize after-tax profits, $(1 - t_p)\Pi$, where Π is the pretax level of economic profits. But it is just a matter of arithmetic that whatever strategy maximizes Π is identical to the one that maximizes $(1 - t_p)\Pi$. Hence, output and price faced by consumers stay the same, and the firm bears the whole tax.

In long-run competitive equilibrium, a tax on economic profits has no yield, because economic profits are zero—they are all competed away. For a monopolist, there may be economic profits even in the long run. But for the same reasons given in the preceding paragraph, the tax is borne by the owners of the monopoly. If a firm is maximizing profits before the profits tax is imposed, the tax cannot be shifted.[12]

Because they distort no economic decisions, taxes on economic profits might appear to be very attractive policy alternatives. In 1993, for example, certain members of the Clinton administration called for a "profits tax" on hospitals. However, profits taxes receive very little support from public finance specialists. The main reason is the tremendous problems in making the theoretical notion of economic profits operational. Economic profits are often computed by examining the rate of return that a firm makes on its capital stock and comparing it to some "basic" rate of return set by the government. Clearly, how the capital stock is measured is important. Should the

---

[12] On the other hand, if the firm is following some other goal, it may raise the price in response to a profits tax. One alternative to profit maximization is revenue maximization; firms try to make their sales as large as possible, subject to the constraint that they earn a "reasonable" rate of return.

original cost be used, or the cost of replacing it? And what if the rate of return is high not because of excess profits, but because the enterprise is very risky and investors have to be compensated for this risk? Considerations like these lead to major difficulties in administration and compliance.[13]

Tax Incidence and Capitalization

Several years ago the coastal city of Port Hueneme, California, levied a special tax on beach properties. The tax was determined in part by how close the properties were to the ocean. For owners close to the water, the extra tax was $192 per year. Owners of beachfront property complained vociferously.

This episode leads us to consider the special issues that arise when land is taxed. For these purposes, the distinctive characteristics of land are that it is fixed in supply and it is durable. Suppose the annual rental rate on land is R_0 this year. It is known that the rental will be R_1 next year, R_2 two years from now, and so on. How much should someone be willing to pay for the land? If the market for land is competitive, its price is just equal to the present discounted value of the stream of the rents. Thus, if the interest rate is r, the price of land (P_R) is

$$P_R = \$R_0 + \frac{\$R_1}{(1+r)} + \frac{\$R_2}{(1+r)^2} + \cdots + \frac{\$R_T}{(1+r)^T} \quad (12.3)$$

where T is the last year the land yields its services (possibly infinity).

Now it is announced that a tax of u_0 will be imposed on land now, u_1 next year, u_2 two years from now, and so forth. From Figure 12.4 we know that because land is fixed in supply, the annual rental received by the owner falls by the full amount of the tax. Thus, the landlord's return initially falls to $(R_0 - u_0)$, in year 1 to $(R_1 - u_1)$, in year 2 to $(R_2 - u_2)$, and so on. Prospective purchasers of the land take into account the fact that if they purchase the land, they buy a future stream of tax liabilities as well as a future stream of returns. Therefore, the most a purchaser is willing to pay for the land after the tax is announced (P_R') is

$$P_R' = \$(R_0 - u_0) + \frac{\$(R_1 - u_1)}{1+r} + \frac{\$(R_2 - u_2)}{(1+r)^2} + \cdots$$
$$+ \frac{\$(R_T - u_T)}{(1+r)^T} \quad (12.4)$$

Comparing Equations (12.4) and (12.3), we see that as a consequence of the tax, the price of land falls by

$$u_0 + \frac{u_1}{1+r} + \frac{u_2}{(1+r)^2} + \cdots + \frac{u_T}{(1+r)^T}$$

---

[13] See Gillis and McLure [1979] for further details.

Thus, at the time the tax is imposed, the price of the land falls by the present value of *all future tax payments*. This process by which a stream of taxes becomes incorporated into the price of an asset is referred to as **capitalization.** Because of capitalization, the person who bears the full burden of the tax *forever* is the landlord at the time the tax is levied. To be sure, *future* landlords write checks to the tax authorities, but such payments are not really a "burden" because they just balance the lower price paid at purchase. Capitalization complicates attempts to assess the incidence of a tax on any durable item that is fixed in supply. Knowing the identities of current owners is not sufficient—one must know who the landlords *were* at the time the tax was imposed. It's no wonder the owners of beach property in Port Hueneme were so upset![14]

General Equilibrium Models

A great attraction of partial equilibrium models is their simplicity—examining only one market at a time is relatively uncomplicated. In some cases, however, ignoring feedback into other markets leads to an incomplete picture of a tax's incidence. Suppose, for example, that the tax rate on cigarettes is increased. To the extent that the demand for cigarettes decreases, so does the demand for tobacco. Farmers who formerly raised tobacco on their land may turn to other crops, perhaps cotton. As the supply of cotton increases, its price falls, harming the individuals who were already producing cotton. Thus, cotton producers end up bearing part of the burden of a cigarette tax.

More generally, when a tax is imposed on a sector that is "large" relative to the economy, looking only at that particular market may not be enough. **General equilibrium analysis** takes into account the ways in which various markets are interrelated.

Another problem with partial equilibrium analysis is that it gives insufficient attention to the question of just who the "producers" of a taxed commodity are. Think again of the cigarette tax and the desire of some policymakers to use it as an instrument to punish "the tobacco industry." Only people can pay taxes, and the producers of tobacco include the shareholders who finance the purchase of machinery, farmers who own the land on which the tobacco is grown, the workers in the factories, and so on. The division of the tax burden among these groups is often important. General equilibrium analysis provides a framework for investigating it.

Before turning to the specifics of general equilibrium analysis, note that the fundamental lesson from partial equilibrium models still holds: Because

[14] When a land tax is anticipated before it is levied, presumably it is borne at least in part by the owner at the time the anticipation becomes widespread. If so, even finding out the identity of the landowner at the time the tax was imposed may not be enough.

of relative price adjustments, the statutory incidence of a tax generally tells *nothing* about who really bears its burden.

Tax Equivalence Relations

The idea of dealing with tax incidence in a general equilibrium framework at first appears daunting. After all, thousands of different commodities and inputs are traded in the economy. How can we keep track of all their complicated interrelations? Luckily, for many purposes, useful general equilibrium results can be obtained from models in which there are only two commodities, two factors of production, and no savings. For illustration, call the two commodities food (F) and manufactures (M), and the two factors capital (K) and labor (L). There are nine possible ad valorem taxes in such a model:

t_{KF} = a tax on capital used in the production of food

t_{KM} = a tax on capital used in the production of manufactures

t_{LF} = a tax on labor used in the production of food

t_{LM} = a tax on labor used in the production of manufactures

t_F = a tax on the consumption of food

t_M = a tax on consumption of manufactures

t_K = a tax on capital in both sectors

t_L = a tax on labor in both sectors

t = a general income tax

The first four taxes, which are levied on a factor in only some of its uses, are referred to as **partial factor taxes.**

Certain combinations of these taxes are equivalent to others. One of these equivalences is already familiar from the theory of the consumer.[15] Taxes on food (t_F) and manufactures (t_M) at the same rate are equivalent to an income tax (t).[16] To see this, just note that equiproportional taxes on all commodities have the same effect on the consumer's budget constraint as a proportional income tax. Both create a parallel shift inward.

Now consider a proportional tax on both capital (t_K) and labor (t_L). Because in this model all income is derived from either capital or labor, it is a simple matter of arithmetic that taxing both factors at the same rate is also equivalent to an income tax (t).

Perhaps not so obvious is the fact that partial taxes on both capital and labor in the food sector at a given rate ($t_{KF} = t_{LF}$) are equivalent to a tax on food (t_F) at the same rate. Because capital and labor are the only inputs to the production of food, making each of them more expensive by a certain proportion is equivalent to making the food itself more expensive in the same proportion.

---

[15] The theory of the consumer is outlined in the appendix at the end of the book.

[16] Note that given the assumption that all income is consumed, an income tax is also equivalent to a tax on consumption expenditure.

Table 12.2   **Tax equivalence relations**

t_{KF}	and		t_{LF}		are equivalent to	t_F
and			and			and
t_{KM}	and		t_{LM}		are equivalent to	t_M
are			are			are
equivalent			equivalent			equivalent
to			to			to
t_K	and		t_L		are equivalent to	t

SOURCE: Charles E. McLure, Jr., "The Theory of Tax Incidence with Imperfect Factor Mobility," *Finanzarchiv* 30 (1971), p. 29.

More generally, any two sets of taxes that generate the same changes in relative prices have equivalent incidence effects. All the equivalence relations that can be derived using similar logic are summarized in Table 12.2. For a given ad valorem tax rate, the equivalences are shown by reading across the rows or down the columns. To determine the incidence of all three taxes in any row or column, only two have to be analyzed in detail. The third can be determined by addition or subtraction. For example, from the third row, if we know the incidence of taxes on capital and labor, then we also know the incidence of a tax on income.

In the next section, we discuss the incidence of four taxes: a food tax (t_F), an income tax (t), a general tax on labor (t_L), and a partial tax on capital in manufacturing (t_{KM}). With results on these four taxes in hand, the incidence of the other five can be determined by using Table 12.2.

The Harberger Model

Harberger [1974c] pioneered in applying general equilibrium models to tax incidence. The principal assumptions of his model are as follows:

1. *Technology.* Firms in each sector use capital and labor to produce their outputs. In each sector, a simultaneous doubling of both inputs leads to a doubling of output, *constant returns to scale.* However, the production technologies may differ across sectors. In general, the production technologies differ with respect to the ease with which capital can be substituted for labor (the **elasticity of substitution**) and the ratios in which capital and labor are employed. For example, the capital-labor ratio in the production of food is about twice that used in the production of textiles [Congressional Budget Office, 1997d, p. 42]. The industry in which the capital-labor ratio is relatively high is characterized as **capital intensive;** the other is **labor intensive.**

2. *Behavior of factor suppliers.* Suppliers of both capital and labor maximize total returns. Moreover, capital and labor are perfectly mobile—they can freely move across sectors according to the wishes of their owners. Consequently, the net marginal return to capital must be the same in each sector, and so must the net

marginal return to labor. Otherwise, it would be possible to reallocate capital and labor in such a way that total net returns could be increased.[17]

3. *Market structure.* Firms are competitive and maximize profits, and all prices (including the wage rate) are perfectly flexible. Therefore, factors are fully employed, and the return paid to each factor of production is the value of its marginal product—the value to the firm of the output produced by the last unit of the input.

4. *Total factor supplies.* The total amounts of capital and labor in the economy are fixed. But, as noted above, both factors are perfectly free to move between sectors.

5. *Consumer preferences.* All consumers have identical preferences. A tax therefore cannot generate any distributional effects by affecting people's uses of income. This assumption allows us to concentrate on the effect of taxes on the sources of income.

6. *Tax incidence framework.* The framework for the analysis is differential tax incidence: We consider the substitution of one tax for another. Therefore, approximately the same amount of income is available before and after the tax, so it is unnecessary to consider how changes in aggregate income may change demand and factor prices.

Clearly, these assumptions are somewhat restrictive, but they simplify the analysis considerably. Later in this chapter, we consider the consequences of dropping some of them. We now employ Harberger's model to analyze several different taxes.

Analysis of Various Taxes

A Commodity Tax (t_F). When a tax on food is imposed, its relative price increases (although not necessarily by the amount of the tax). Consumers therefore substitute manufactures for food. Consequently, less food and more manufactures are produced. As food production falls, some of the capital and labor formerly used in food production are forced to find employment in manufacturing. Because the capital-labor ratios probably differ between the two sectors, the relative prices of capital and labor have to change for manufacturing to be willing to absorb the unemployed factors from food production. For example, assume that food is the capital-intensive sector. (US agriculture does, in fact, use relatively more capital equipment—tractors, combines, and so forth—than many types of manufacturing.) Therefore, relatively large amounts of capital must be absorbed in manufacturing. The only way for all this capital to find employment in the manufacturing sector is for the relative price of capital to fall—including capital already in use in

---

[17] The appendix to this book explains why maximizing behavior results in an allocation in which marginal returns are equal.

the manufacturing sector. In the new equilibrium, then, *all* capital is relatively worse off, not just capital in the food sector. More generally, a tax on the *output* of a particular sector induces a decline in the relative price of the *input* used intensively in that sector.

To go beyond such qualitative statements, additional information is needed. The greater the elasticity of demand for food, the more dramatic will be the change in consumption from food to manufactures, which ultimately induces a greater decline in the return to capital. The greater the difference in factor proportions between food and manufactures, the greater must be the decrease in capital's price for it to be absorbed into the manufacturing sector. (If the capital-labor ratios for food and manufactured goods were identical, neither factor would suffer relative to the other.) Finally, the harder it is to substitute capital for labor in the production of manufactures, the greater the decline in the rate of return to capital needed to absorb the additional capital.

Thus, on the sources side of the budget, the food tax tends to hurt people who receive a proportionately large share of their incomes from capital. Given that all individuals are identical (assumption 5), there are no interesting effects on the uses side. However, were we to drop this assumption, then clearly those people who consumed proportionately large amounts of food would tend to bear relatively larger burdens. The total incidence of the food tax then depends on both the sources and uses sides. For example, a capitalist who eats a lot of food is worse off on both counts. On the other hand, a laborer who eats a lot of food is better off from the point of view of the sources of income, but worse off on the uses side.

An Income Tax (t). As already noted, an income tax is equivalent to a set of taxes on capital and labor at the same rate. Since factor supplies are completely fixed (assumption 4), this tax cannot be shifted. It is borne in proportion to people's initial incomes. The intuition behind this result is similar to the analogous case in the partial equilibrium model; since the factors cannot "escape" the tax (by opting out of production), they bear the full burden.

A General Tax on Labor (t_L). A general tax on labor is a tax on labor in *all* its uses, in the production of both food and manufactures. As a result, there are no incentives to switch labor use between sectors. Further, the assumption of fixed factor supplies implies labor must bear the entire burden.

A Partial Factor Tax (t_{KM}). When capital used in the manufacturing sector *only* is taxed, there are two initial effects:

1. *Output effect.* The price of manufactures tends to rise, which decreases the quantity demanded by consumers.
2. *Factor substitution effect.* As capital becomes more expensive in the manufacturing sector, producers there use less capital and more labor.

FIGURE 12.11

Incidence of a
partial factor tax
(t_{KM}) in a general
equilibrium model

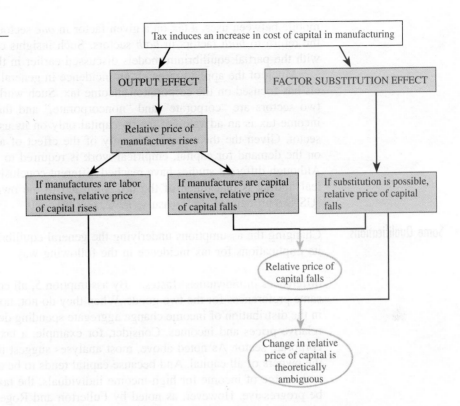

The flowchart in Figure 12.11 traces the consequences of these two effects. The output effect is described on the left side. As its name suggests, the output effect arises from reducing production in manufacturing. When the price of manufactures increases and demand falls, capital and labor are released from manufacturing and must find employment in the production of food. If the manufacturing sector is labor intensive, then (relatively) large amounts of labor have to be absorbed in the food sector, and the relative price of capital increases. If, on the other hand, the manufacturing sector is capital intensive, the relative price of capital falls. Thus, the output effect is ambiguous with respect to the final effect on the relative prices of capital and labor.

This ambiguity is not present with the factor substitution effect, as depicted in the right-hand side of Figure 12.11. As long as substitution between capital and labor is possible, an increase in the price of capital induces manufacturers to use less capital and more labor, tending to decrease the demand for capital and its relative price.

Putting the two effects together, we see that if manufacturing is capital intensive, both effects work in the same direction, and the relative price of capital must fall. But if the manufacturing sector is labor intensive, the final outcome is theoretically ambiguous. Even though the tax is levied on capital, it can make labor worse off! More generally, as long as factors are mobile between uses, a tax on a given factor in *one* sector ultimately affects the return to *both* factors in *both* sectors. Such insights cannot be obtained with the partial equilibrium models discussed earlier in this chapter.

Much of the applied research on incidence in general equilibrium models has focused on the corporation income tax. Such work assumes that the two sectors are "corporate" and "noncorporate," and that the corporation income tax is an ad valorem tax on capital only on its use in the corporate sector. Given the theoretical ambiguity of the effect of a partial factor tax on the demand for capital, empirical work is required to find its incidence. Although different studies have reached different conclusions, the most typical finding is that much of the tax is shifted to the owners of all capital [US Department of the Treasury, 1992, p. 146].

Some Qualifications   Changing the assumptions underlying the general equilibrium model affects its implications for tax incidence in the following ways:

Differences in Individuals' Tastes.   By assumption 5, all consumers have the same preferences for the two goods. When they do not, tax-induced changes in the distribution of income change aggregate spending decisions and hence relative prices and incomes. Consider, for example, a tax on capital in the corporate sector. As noted above, most analyses suggest that it is shifted to the owners of all capital. And because capital tends to be a relatively important source of income for high-income individuals, the tax would appear to be progressive. However, as noted by Fullerton and Rogers [1997], the tax also raises the relative prices of goods produced in capital-intensive industries such as agriculture and petroleum refining, whose outputs (food and gasoline) are purchased in high proportions by families at the low end of the income scale. Thus, when we allow for differences in uses between high- and low-income families, the tax becomes less progressive than it first appears.

Immobile Factors.   By assumption 2, resources are free to flow between sectors, seeking the highest rate of return possible. However, for institutional or technological reasons, some factors may be immobile. For example, if certain land is zoned for residential use, it cannot be used in manufacturing, no matter what the rate of return. Abandoning perfect mobility can dramatically affect the incidence of a tax. For example, earlier we showed that if factors are mobile, the incidence of a partial factor tax is ambiguous, depending on the outcome of several conflicting effects. If the factor is immobile, however, the incidence result is clear-cut: The taxed factor bears the whole burden. Intuitively, this is because the factor cannot "escape" taxation by migrating to the other sector. Note also that because the return to the taxed immobile factor falls by just the amount of the tax, the prices of capital and labor in the untaxed sectors are unchanged, as is the price of the good in the taxed sector.

Variable Factor Supplies.   By assumption 4, the total supplies of both factors are fixed. In the long run, however, the supplies of both capital and labor to the economy are variable. Allowing for growth can turn conclusions from the static model completely on their heads. Consider a general factor tax on capital. When the capital stock is fixed, this tax is borne entirely by the capital's owners. In the long run, however, less capital may be supplied due to the tax.[18] To the extent this occurs, the economy's capital-labor ratio decreases, and the return to labor falls. (The wage falls because labor has less capital with which to work, and hence is less productive, *ceteris paribus*.) Thus, a general tax on capital can hurt labor.

Because the amount of calendar time that must elapse before the long run is reached may be substantial, short-run effects matter. On the other hand, intelligent policy also requires consideration of the long-run consequences of taxation.

An Applied Incidence Study

The theory of tax incidence has served as a framework for a number of attempts to estimate how the US tax system affects the distribution of income. Table 12.3 reports the findings of a recent study by Gale and Potter [2002]. The study focuses on federal income, payroll, corporate, estate, and commodity taxes. The average tax rate ranges from 8.4 percent on families in the lowest quintile (under $15,000) to 31.3 percent in the top one percent of the population. This top 1 percent pays about 25 percent of all federal taxes. These figures suggest that the federal tax system is quite progressive.

However, it should be clear by now that all incidence results depend crucially on the underlying assumptions. This study assumes that there is no shifting of the personal income and payroll taxes and that commodity taxes are borne by consumers in proportion to their consumption of the taxed items. These assumptions help simplify the problem considerably. But the theory of tax incidence suggests that they are questionable, especially in the long run.

Another limitation of the analysis is that it is based on individuals' annual incomes. Using some measure of lifetime income would be more appropriate and could change the results importantly. To see why, we begin by noting that a substantial amount of empirical research suggests people's consumption decisions are more closely related to some lifetime income measure than the value of income in any particular year. Just because a person's income is *temporarily* high or low in a year does not have that great an impact on how much she consumes.

Assume that the consumption of commodity X is proportional to lifetime income. Assume further that the supply curve for X is horizontal, so that consumers bear the entire burden of any tax on X. Then a tax on X would be proportional with respect to lifetime income. However, in any particular year, some

---

[18] However, the supply of capital does not necessarily decrease. See Chapter 16.

Table 12.3   **An applied incidence study**

Income Category	Average Federal Tax Rate	Share of Federal Taxes
Lowest Quintile	8.4%	1.1%
Second Quintile	14.0	4.1
Third Quintile	18.8	9.2
Fourth Quintile	22.3	17.9
Top 1%	31.3	24.9

SOURCE: Gale and Potter [2002]. These figures include the tax changes embodied in the Economic Growth and Tax Relief Reconciliation Act of 2001.

people have incomes that are temporarily higher than their permanent values and some lower. A person with a temporarily high income spends a relatively small proportion of his annual income on X because he does not increase his consumption of X due to the temporary increase in income. Similarly, a person with a temporarily low income devotes a relatively high proportion of her income to good X. In short, based on annual income, good X's budget share appears to fall with income, and a tax on X looks regressive. Consistent with this theory, several investigators have found that incidence results are very sensitive to whether lifetime or annual measures are employed. For example, in his analysis of US state and local sales taxes, Metcalf [1993] finds that sales taxes are 1.90 percent of the *annual* incomes of the lowest income decile, and 1.07 percent in the highest decile—a decidedly regressive pattern. Using lifetime income, however, the pattern is actually reversed, with sales taxes taking 1.03 percent of lifetime income in the lowest decile, and 1.74 percent in the highest decile. We conclude that even though studies based on annual income are suggestive, the results should be viewed with some caution.

Conclusions

We began this chapter with an innocent question: Who bears the burden of a tax? We saw that price changes are the key to finding the burden of a tax, but that price changes depend on a lot of things: market structure, elasticities of supply and demand, mobility of factors of production, and so on. At this stage, an obvious question is: What do we really know?

For taxes that may reasonably be analyzed in isolation, the answer is "Quite a bit." A partial equilibrium incidence analysis requires only information on the market structure and the shapes of the supply and demand curves. In cases other than a clear-cut monopoly, the competitive market paradigm provides a sensible starting point. Estimates of supply and demand curves can be obtained using the empirical methods discussed in Chapter 2. Incidence analysis is on firm ground.

Even in general equilibrium models, incidence analysis is straightforward for a tax on an immobile factor—the incidence is entirely on the taxed factor. More generally, though, if a tax affects many markets, incidence depends on the reactions of numerous supply and demand curves for goods and inputs. The answers are correspondingly less clear.

Unfortunately, it seems that many important taxes such as the corporate tax fall into the last category. Why is this? It may be for the very reason that the incidence is hard to find. (What are the political chances of a tax that clearly hurts some important group in the population?) Complicated taxes may actually be simpler for a politician because no one is sure who actually ends up paying them.

In any case, the models in this chapter tell us what information is needed to understand the incidence even of very complex taxes. To the extent that this information is currently unavailable, the models serve as a measure of our ignorance. This is not altogether undesirable. As St. Jerome noted, "It is worse still to be ignorant of your ignorance."

Summary

- Statutory incidence is the legal liability for a tax, while economic incidence is the actual burden of the tax. Knowing the legal incidence usually tells us little about economic incidence.

- Economic incidence is determined by the price changes induced by a tax, and depends on both individuals' sources and uses of income.

- Depending on the policy being considered, it may be appropriate to examine balanced budget, differential, or absolute incidence.

- In partial equilibrium competitive models, tax incidence depends on the elasticities of supply and demand. The same general approach can be used to study incidence in a monopolized market. For oligopoly, however, there is no single accepted framework for tax analysis.

- Due to capitalization, the burden of future taxes may be borne by *current* owners of an inelastically supplied durable commodity such as land.

- General equilibrium incidence analysis often employs a two-sector, two-factor model. This framework allows for nine possible taxes. Certain combinations of these taxes are equivalent to others.

- In a general equilibrium model, a tax on a single factor in its use only in a particular sector can affect the returns to all factors in all sectors.

- Applied tax incidence studies indicate that the federal tax system is quite progressive. But such studies rest upon possibly problematic assumptions.

Discussion Questions

1. The federal government subsidizes the oil and gas industries. In defense of the subsidies, a spokesman for the industry observed "some alleged subsidies don't even go to the industry. For example, the government provides money to low-income families to help pay heating bills" [Cavaney, 1998]. Use a supply and demand model to analyze the incidence of a subsidy to consumers of oil and gas, and use your analysis to evaluate the claim that the subsidies to low-income families do not benefit the industry. [Note: To construct the model, note that a subsidy is just a negative tax.]

2. According to estimates by Goolsbee [1998], purchases on the Internet are highly sensitive to tax rates, and applying existing sales taxes to such purchases would substantially reduce the number of online buyers and the amount of on-line spending. What are the implications for the incidence of a tax levied on Internet sales?

3. For commodity X, average cost is equal to marginal cost at every level of output. Assuming that the market for X is competitive and the demand curve is linear, analyze the effects when a unit tax of u dollars is imposed. Now analyze the effects of the same tax assuming that the market for X is a monopoly. Discuss the differences.

4. Use a general equilibrium framework to discuss the possible incidence of a tax on cigarettes.

5. Suppose that the demand for cigarettes in a hypothetical country is given by $Q_c^D = 2000 - 200P_c$, where Q_c^D is the number of packs demanded and P_c is the price per pack. The supply of cigarettes is $Q_c^S = P_c \times 200$.

   a. Find the price and quantity of cigarettes, assuming the market is competitive.

   b. In an effort to reduce smoking, the government levies a tax of $2 per pack. Compute the quantity of cigarettes after the tax, the price paid by consumers, and the price received by producers. How much revenue does the tax raise for the government?

6. Suppose that the demand curve for a particular commodity is $Q^D = a - bP$, where Q^D is the quantity demanded, P is the price, and a and b are constants. The supply curve for the commodity is $Q^S = c + dP$, where Q^S is quantity supplied and c and d are constants. Find the equilibrium price and output as functions of the constants a, b, c, and d.

   Suppose now that a unit tax of u dollars is imposed on the commodity. Show that the new equilibrium is the same regardless of whether the tax is imposed on producers or buyers of the commodity.

7. In 2003, Senate Democrats proposed a tax reform that would reduce taxes for all workers by $300. For simplicity, assume that there is one earner per family, so each family would get a $300 reduction in its taxes. Use Equations (12.1)

and (12.2) to discuss how this proposal would affect the progressiveness of the tax system.

8. Assume that in a given country, tax revenues, T, depend on income, I, according to the formula

   $$T = -4,000 + 0.2I.$$

   Thus, for example, when a household has an income of $50,000, its tax burden is $-4,000 + 0.2 \times 50,000$, or $6,000. Is this a progressive tax schedule? [Hint: Compute average tax rates at several different levels of income.]

9. Now let's generalize the tax schedule from the last problem:

   $$T = a + tI,$$

   where a and t are numbers. (For example, in the previous problem $a = -4,000$ and $t = 0.2$.) Write down a formula for the average tax rate as a function of the level of income. Show that the tax system is progressive if a is negative, and regressive if a is positive. [Hint: The average tax rate is T/I.]

10. In 2002, New York City increased the tax rate on cigarettes from 8 cents a pack to $1.50 a pack. A month after the increase, a spokesman for the mayor noted that "fewer cigarettes are being sold, and the city is making more money" [Cooper, 2002, p. B7]. Assume for simplicity that the supply of cigarettes to New York City is perfectly elastic.

    a. Assuming that the spokesman's facts are correct, what must be true of the elasticity of the demand for cigarettes in New York City?

    b. Recall that the spokesman's comment was made just one month after the tax increase was enacted. As more time passes, what do you expect to happen to the elasticity of the demand curve, and how will this affect tax revenues for New York City?

11. In 2003, Hong Kong levied a tax of $51 per month on employers of domestic helpers from other nations. Many of these workers were from the Philipines, and President Arroyo of that country called the tax "unjust and unfair." Given that the tax was levied on *employers,* was President Arroyo correct in being disturbed? Sketch a model that is consistent with her concerns being justified.

Selected References

Fullerton, Don, and Diane Lim Rogers. "Neglected Effects on the Uses Side: Even a Uniform Tax Would Change Relative Goods Prices." *American Economic Review* 87 (May 1997), pp. 120–25.

Fullerton, Don, and Gilbert Metcalf. "Tax Incidence." Working Paper No. 8829, National Bureau of Economic Research, March 2002.

Gale, William G, and Samara R Potter. "An Economic Evaluation of the Economic Growth and Tax Relief Reconciliation Act of 2001." *National Tax Journal* 55 (March 2002), pp. 133–186.

CHAPTER 13

Taxation and Efficiency

Waste always makes me angry.
RHETT BUTLER IN *GONE WITH THE WIND*

axes impose a cost on the taxpayer. It is tempting to view the cost as simply the amount of money that he or she hands over to the tax collector. However, an example indicates that this is just part of the story.

Consider Breyer Dazs, a citizen who typically consumes 10 ice cream cones each week, at a price of $1 per cone. The government levies a 25 percent tax on his consumption of ice cream cones, so now Dazs faces a price of $1.25.[1] In response to the price hike, Dazs reduces his ice cream cone consumption to zero, and he spends the $10 per week on other goods and services. Obviously, because Dazs consumes no ice cream cones, the ice cream tax yields zero revenue. Do we want to say that Dazs is unaffected by the tax? The answer is no. Dazs is worse off because the tax has induced him to consume a less desirable bundle of goods than previously. We know that the after-tax bundle is less desirable because, before tax, Dazs had the option of consuming no ice cream cones. Since he chose to buy 10 cones weekly, this must have been preferred to spending the money on other items. Thus, despite the fact that the tax raised zero revenue, it made Dazs worse off.

This example is a bit extreme. Normally, we expect that an increase in price to diminish the quantity demanded but not drive it all the way to zero. Nevertheless, the basic result holds: Because a tax distorts economic decisions, it creates an **excess burden**—a loss of welfare above and beyond the tax revenues collected. Excess burden is sometimes referred to as *welfare cost* or *deadweight loss*. In this chapter we discuss the theory and measurement of excess burden, and explain its importance for evaluating actual tax systems.

---

[1] As emphasized in Chapter 12, the price paid by the consumer generally does not rise by the full amount of the tax. This assumption, which is correct if the supply curve is horizontal, is made here only for convenience.

FIGURE 13.1

Effect of a tax on
the budget constraint

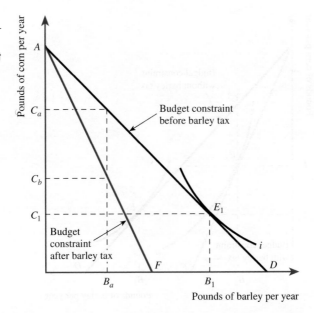

Excess Burden Defined

Ruth has a fixed income of I dollars, which she spends on only two commodities: barley and corn. The price per pound of barley is P_b and the price per pound of corn is P_c. There are no taxes or "distortions" such as externalities or monopoly in the economy, so the prices of the goods reflect their social marginal costs. For convenience, these social marginal costs are assumed to be constant with respect to output. In Figure 13.1, Ruth's consumption of barley is measured on the horizontal axis and her consumption of corn on the vertical axis. Her budget constraint is line AD, which has slope $-P_b/P_c$ and horizontal intercept I/P_b.[2] Assuming Ruth wants to maximize her utility, she chooses a point like E_1 on indifference curve i, where she consumes B_1 pounds of barley and C_1 pounds of corn.

Now suppose the government levies a tax at a percentage rate of t_b on barley so the price Ruth faces becomes $(1 + t_b)P_b$. (The before-tax price is unchanged because of our assumption of constant marginal social costs.) Imposition of the tax changes Ruth's budget constraint. It now has a slope of $-[(1 + t_b)P_b/P_c]$ and horizontal intercept $I/[(1 + t_b)P_b]$. This is represented in Figure 13.1 as line AF. (Because the price of corn is still P_c, lines AF and AD have the same vertical intercept.)

---

[2] The construction of budget constraints and the interpretation of their slopes and intercepts are discussed in the appendix at the end of the book.

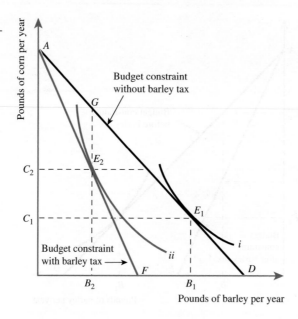

FIGURE 13.2

Effect of a tax on the consumption bundle

Note that at each consumption level of barley, the vertical distance between AD and AF shows Ruth's tax payments measured in corn. To see this, consider an arbitrary quantity of barley B_a on the horizontal axis. Before the tax was imposed, Ruth could have both B_a pounds of barley and C_a pounds of corn. After the tax, however, if she consumed B_a pounds of barley, the most corn she could afford would be C_b pounds. The difference (distance) between C_a and C_b must therefore represent the amount of tax collected by the government measured in pounds of corn. We can convert tax receipts to dollars by multiplying distance C_aC_b by the price per pound of corn, P_c. For convenience, we measure corn in units such that $P_c = 1$. In this case, the distance C_aC_b measures tax receipts in corn *or* dollars.

So far, we have not indicated Ruth's choice on her new budget constraint, AF. Figure 13.2 shows that her most preferred bundle is at E_2 on indifference curve *ii*, where her consumption of barley is B_2, her consumption of corn is C_2, and her tax bill is the associated vertical distance between AD and AF, GE_2. Clearly, Ruth is worse off at E_2 than she was at E_1. However, *any* tax would have put her on a lower indifference curve.[3] The important question is whether the barley tax inflicts a greater utility loss than is necessary to raise revenue GE_2. Alternatively, is there some other way of raising

---

[3] This ignores benefits that might be obtained from the expenditures financed by the tax.

FIGURE 13.3

Excess burden of the barley tax

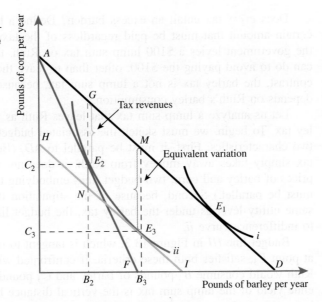

revenue GE_2 that would cause a smaller utility loss to Ruth? If so, the barley tax has an excess burden.

To investigate this issue, we need to find a dollar equivalent of the loss that Ruth suffers by having to move from indifference curve i to ii. One way to measure this is the **equivalent variation**—the amount of income we would have to take away from Ruth (before the barley tax was levied) to induce her to move from i and ii. The equivalent variation measures the loss inflicted by the tax as the size of the reduction in income that would cause the same decrease in utility as the tax.

To depict the equivalent variation graphically, recall that taking away income from an individual leads to a parallel movement inward of her budget line. Hence, to find the equivalent variation, all we have to do is shift AD inward, until it is tangent to indifference curve ii. The amount by which we have to shift AD is the equivalent variation. In Figure 13.3, budget line HI is parallel to AD and tangent to indifference curve ii. Hence, the vertical distance between AD and HI, ME_3, is the equivalent variation. Ruth is indifferent between losing ME_3 dollars and facing the barley tax.

Note that the equivalent variation ME_3 exceeds the barley tax revenues of GE_2. To see why, just observe that ME_3 equals GN, because both measure the distance between the parallel lines AD and HI. Hence, ME_3 exceeds GE_2 by distance E_2N. This is really quite a remarkable result. It means that the barley tax makes Ruth worse off by an amount that actually exceeds the revenues it generates. In Figure 13.3, the amount by which the loss in welfare (measured by the equivalent variation) exceeds the taxes collected—the excess burden—is distance E_2N.

Does *every* tax entail an excess burden? Define a **lump sum tax** as a certain amount that must be paid regardless of the taxpayer's behavior. If the government levies a $100 lump sum tax on Ruth, there is nothing she can do to avoid paying the $100, other than to leave the country or die. In contrast, the barley tax is not a lump sum tax, because the revenue yield depends on Ruth's barley consumption.

Let us analyze a lump sum tax that leaves Ruth as well off as the barley tax. To begin, we must sketch the associated budget line. It must have two characteristics. First, it must be parallel to *AD*. (Because a lump sum tax simply takes away money from Ruth, it does not change the relative prices of barley and corn; two budget lines embodying the same price ratio must be parallel.) Second, because of the stipulation that Ruth attain the same utility level as under the barley tax, the budget line must be tangent to indifference curve *ii*.

Budget line *HI* in Figure 13.3, which is tangent to indifference curve *ii* at point E_3, satisfies both these criteria. If confronted with this budget line, Ruth would consume B_3 pounds of barley and C_3 pounds of corn. The revenue yield of the lump sum tax is the vertical distance between E_3 and the before-tax budget constraint, or distance ME_3. But we showed earlier that ME_3 is also the equivalent variation of the move from indifference curve *i* to *ii*. This comes as no surprise, since a lump sum tax is just a parallel shift of the budget line. Because the revenue yield of a lump sum tax equals its equivalent variation, *a lump sum tax has no excess burden.*

In short, a lump sum tax that leaves Ruth on the *same indifference curve* as the barley tax generates more revenue for the government. Alternatively, if we compared a lump sum tax and a barley tax that raised the *same revenue*, the lump sum tax would leave Ruth on a higher indifference curve.

The skeptical reader may suspect that this result is merely an artifact of the particular way the indifference curves are drawn in Figure 13.3. This is not the case. One can prove that as long as the indifference curves have the usual shape, a tax that changes relative prices generates an excess burden.[4] Alternatively, a tax that changes relative prices is inefficient in the sense that it lowers individual utility more than is necessary to raise a given amount of revenue.

Questions and Answers

The previous section's discussion of excess burden raises some important questions.

If lump sum taxes are so efficient, why aren't they widely used?   Lump sum taxation is an unattractive policy tool for several reasons. Suppose the

---

[4] As noted, this assumes there are no other distortions in the economy. For a proof, see Hines [1999].

government announced that every person's tax liability was \$2,000 per year. This is a lump sum tax, but most people would consider it unfair because the loss of \$2,000 presumably hurts a poor family more than a rich family. In 1990, the government of British Prime Minister Margaret Thatcher implemented a tax that in some ways resembled a lump sum tax. The property tax that had financed local government was replaced by a head tax; in each local jurisdiction the amount depended on that jurisdiction's per capita revenue needs. The tax was lump sum in the sense that a person's tax liability did not vary with the amount of income earned or property owned; it did vary, however, with a person's choice of where to live. The perceived unfairness of that tax was one of the factors that led to Mrs. Thatcher's downfall in 1990, and it was repealed in 1991 by her successor, John Major.

As a way of producing more equitable results, one might consider making people pay different lump sum taxes based on their incomes. A rich person might be required to pay \$20,000 annually, independent of his or her economic decisions, while a poor person would pay only \$500. The problem is that people entering the work force would soon realize that their eventual tax burden depended on their incomes, and adjust their work and savings decisions accordingly. In short, because the amount of income individuals earn is at least in part under their control, the income-based tax is not a lump sum tax.

Ultimately, to achieve an equitable system of lump sum taxes, it would be necessary to base the tax on some underlying "ability" characteristic that measured individuals' *potential* to earn income. In this way, high- and low-potential people could be taxed differently. Because the base is potential, an individual's tax burden would not depend on behavior. Even if such an ability measure existed, however, it could not possibly be observed by the taxing authority. Thus, individual lump sum taxes are best viewed as standards of efficiency, not as major policy options in a modern economy.

Are there any results from welfare economics that would help us understand why excess burdens arise?   Recall from Chapter 3 that a necessary condition for a Pareto efficient allocation of resources is that the marginal rate of substitution of barley for corn in consumption (MRS_{bc}) equals the marginal rate of transformation of barley for corn in production (MRT_{bc}). Under the barley tax, consumers face a price of barley of $(1 + t_b)P_b$. Therefore, they set

$$MRS_{bc} = \frac{(1 + t_b)P_b}{P_c} \tag{13.1}$$

Equation (13.1) is the algebraic representation of the equilibrium point E_2 in Figure 13.3.

Producers make their decisions by setting the marginal rate of transformation equal to the ratio of the prices *they receive*. Even though Ruth pays

$(1 + t_b)P_b$ per pound of barley, the barley producers receive only P_b—the difference goes to the tax collector. Hence, profit-maximizing producers set

$$MRT_{bc} = \frac{P_b}{P_c}$$ (13.2)

Clearly, as long as t_b is not zero, MRS_{bc} exceeds MRT_{bc}, and the necessary condition for an efficient allocation of resources is violated.

Intuitively, when MRS_{bc} is greater than MRT_{bc}, the marginal utility of substituting barley consumption for corn consumption exceeds the change in production costs necessary to do so. Thus, utility would be raised if such an adjustment were made. However, in the presence of the barley tax there is no *financial* incentive to do so. The excess burden is just a measure of the utility loss. The loss arises because the barley tax creates a wedge between what the consumer pays and what the producer receives. In contrast, under a lump sum tax, the price ratios faced by consumers and producers are equal. There is no wedge, so the necessary conditions for Pareto efficiency are satisfied.

Does an income tax entail an excess burden?   The answer is generally yes, but it takes a little thinking to see why. Figure 13.3 showed the imposition of a lump sum tax as a downward parallel movement from *AD* to *HI*. This movement could just as well have arisen via a tax that took some proportion of Ruth's income. Like the lump sum tax, an income reduction moves the intercepts of the budget constraint closer to the origin but leaves its slope unchanged. Perhaps, then, lump sum taxation and income taxation are equivalent. In fact, if income were fixed, an income tax *would* be a lump sum tax. However, when people's choices affect their incomes, an income tax is *not* generally equivalent to a lump sum tax.

Think of Ruth as consuming *three* commodities, barley, corn, and leisure time, *l*. Ruth gives up leisure (supplies labor) to earn income that she spends on barley and corn. In the production sector, Ruth's leisure is an input to the production of the two goods. The rate at which her leisure time can be transformed into barley is MRT_{lb} and into corn MRT_{lc}. Just as a utility-maximizing individual sets the marginal rate of substitution between two commodities equal to their price ratio, the *MRS* between leisure and a given commodity is set equal to the ratio of the wage (the price of leisure) and the price of that commodity.

Again appealing to the theory of welfare economics, the necessary conditions for a Pareto efficient allocation of resources in this three-commodity case are

$$MRS_{lb} = MRT_{lb}$$

$$MRS_{lc} = MRT_{lc}$$

$$MRS_{bc} = MRT_{bc}$$

A proportional income tax, which is equivalent to a tax at the same rate on barley and corn, leaves the third equality unchanged, because producers and consumers still face the same *relative* prices for barley and corn. (The tax increases both prices by the same proportion, so their ratio is unchanged.) However, it introduces a tax wedge in the first two conditions. To see why, suppose that Ruth's employer pays her a before-tax wage of w, and the income tax rate is t. Ruth's decisions depend on her after-tax wage, $(1 - t)w$. Hence, she sets $MRS_{lb} = (1 - t)w/P_b$. On the other hand, the producer's decisions are based on the wage rate he or she pays, the before-tax wage, w. Hence, the producer sets $MRT_{lb} = w/P_b$. Consequently, $MRS_{lb} \neq MRT_{lb}$. Similarly, $MRS_{lc} \neq MRT_{lc}$. In contrast, a lump sum tax leaves all three equalities intact. Thus, income and lump sum taxation are generally not equivalent.

The fact that the income tax breaks up two equalities while taxes on barley and corn at different rates break up all three is irrelevant for determining which system is more efficient. Once *any* of the equalities fails to hold, a loss of efficiency results, and the sizes of the welfare losses cannot be compared merely by counting wedges. Rather, the excess burdens associated with each tax regime must be computed and then compared. There is no presumption that income taxation is more efficient than a system of commodity taxes at different rates, which is referred to as *differential commodity taxation*. It *may* be true, but this is an empirical question that cannot be answered on the basis of theory alone.

If the demand for a commodity does not change when it is taxed, does this mean that there is no excess burden?   The intuition behind excess burden is that it results from distorted decisions. If there is no change in the demand for the good being taxed, one might conclude there is no excess burden. This conjecture is examined in Figure 13.4. Naomi, the individual under consideration, begins with the same income as Ruth and faces the same prices and taxes. Hence, her initial budget constraint is AD, and after the barley tax, it is AF. However, unlike Ruth, Naomi does not change her barley consumption after the barley tax; that is, $B_1 = B_2$. The barley tax revenues are E_1E_2. Is there an excess burden? The equivalent variation of the barley tax is RE_3. This exceeds the barley tax revenues of E_1E_2 by E_2S. Hence, even though Naomi's barley consumption is unchanged by the barley tax, it still creates an excess burden of E_2S.

The explanation of this paradox begins with the observation that even though Naomi's barley consumption doesn't change, her corn consumption does (from C_1 to C_2). When the barley tax changes barley's relative price, the marginal rate of substitution is affected, and the composition of the commodity *bundle* is distorted.

A more rigorous explanation requires that we distinguish between two types of responses to the barley tax. The movement from E_1 to E_2 is the *uncompensated response*. It shows how consumption changes because of the tax and incorporates effects due to both losing income and the tax-induced change in relative prices. Now, we can imagine decomposing the move from E_1 to E_2 into a move from E_1 to E_3, and then from E_3 to E_2. The movement from E_1 to E_3 shows the effect on consumption of a lump

FIGURE 13.4

Excess burden of a
tax on a commodity
whose ordinary
demand curve is
perfectly inelastic

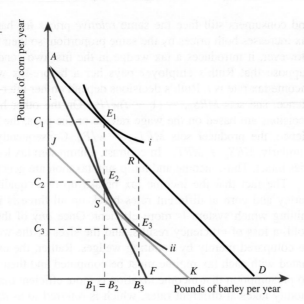

sum tax. This change, called the **income effect,** is due solely to the loss of income because relative prices are unaffected. In effect, then, the movement from E_3 to E_2 is strictly due to the change in relative prices. It is generated by giving Naomi enough income to remain on indifference curve *ii* even as barley's price rises due to the tax. Because Naomi is compensated for the rising price of barley with additional income, the movement from E_3 to E_2 is called the *compensated response,* also sometimes referred to as the **substitution effect.**[5]

The compensated response is the important one for calculating excess burden. Why? By construction, the computation of excess burden involves comparing tax collections at points E_2 and E_3 on indifference curve *ii*. But the movement from E_3 to E_2 along indifference curve *ii* is precisely the compensated response. Note also that it is only in moving from E_3 to E_2 that the marginal rate of substitution is affected. As shown earlier, this change violates the necessary conditions for a Pareto efficient allocation of commodities.

An ordinary demand curve depicts the uncompensated change in the quantity of a commodity demanded when price changes. A **compensated demand curve** shows how the quantity demanded changes when price changes *and* simultaneously income is compensated so that the individual's commodity bundle stays on the same indifference curve. A way of summarizing this discussion is to say that excess burden depends on movements along the compensated rather than the ordinary demand curve.

---

[5] See the appendix to the book for further discussion of income and substitution effects and compensated demand curves.

Although these observations may seem like theoretical nit-picking, they are actually quite important. Policy discussions often focus on whether or not a given tax influences observed behavior, with the assumption that if it does not, no serious efficiency problem is present. For example, some argue that if hours of work do not change when an income tax is imposed, then the tax has no adverse efficiency consequences. We have shown that such a notion is fallacious. A substantial excess burden may be incurred even if the uncompensated response of the taxed commodity is zero.

Excess Burden Measurement with Demand Curves

The concept of excess burden can be reinterpreted using (compensated) demand curves. This interpretation relies heavily on the notion of consumer surplus—the difference between what people would be *willing* to pay for a commodity and the amount they actually have to pay. As shown in the appendix at the end of the book, consumer surplus is measured by the area between the demand curve and the horizontal line at the market price. Assume that the compensated demand curve for barley is straight line D_b in Figure 13.5. For convenience, we continue to assume that the social marginal cost of barley is constant at P_b, so that the supply curve is the horizontal line marked S_b.[6] In equilibrium, q_1 pounds of barley are consumed. Consumer surplus, the area between the price and the demand curve, is *aih*.

Again suppose that a tax at percentage rate t_b is levied on barley, so the new price, $(1 + t_b)P_b$, is associated with supply curve S_b'. Supply and demand now intersect at output q_2. Observe the following characteristics of the new equilibrium:

- Consumer surplus falls to the area between the demand curve and S_b', *agf*.
- The revenue yield of the barley tax is rectangle *gfdh*. This is because tax revenues are equal to the product of the number of units purchased (*hd*) and the tax paid on each unit: $(1 + t_b)P_b - P_b = gh$. But *hd* and *gh* are just the base and height, respectively, of rectangle *gfdh*, and hence their product is its area.
- The sum of posttax consumer surplus and tax revenues collected (area *hafd*) is less than the original consumer surplus (*ahi*) by area *fid*. In effect, even if we returned the tax revenues to barley consumers as a lump sum, they would still be worse off by triangle *fid*. The triangle, then, is the excess burden of the tax.

This analysis provides a convenient framework for computing an actual dollar measure of excess burden. The area of triangle *fid* is one-half the product

---

[6] The analysis is easily generalized to the case when the supply curve slopes upward. See footnote 7.

FIGURE 13.5

Excess burden of a
commodity tax

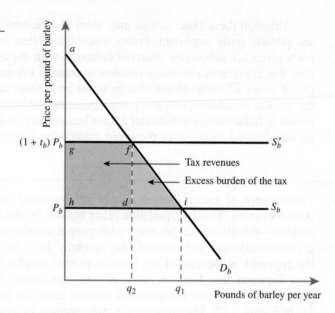

of its base (the tax-induced change in the quantity of barley) and height (the tax per pound). Some simple algebra shows that this product is equivalent to

$$\tfrac{1}{2}\eta P_b q_1 t_b^2 \tag{13.3}$$

where η (Greek *eta*) is the absolute value of the compensated price elasticity of demand for barley.[7] (A proof is provided in Appendix A at the end of the chapter.)

A high (absolute) value of η indicates that the compensated quantity demanded is quite sensitive to changes in price. Thus, the presence of η in Equation (13.3) makes intuitive sense—the more the tax distorts the (compensated) consumption decision, the higher the excess burden. $P_b \times q_1$ is the total revenue expended on barley initially. Its inclusion in the formula shows that the greater the initial expenditure on the taxed commodity, the greater the excess burden.

Finally, the presence of t_b^2 suggests that as the tax rate increases, excess burden goes up with its square. Doubling a tax quadruples its excess burden,

---

[7] The formula is an approximation that holds strictly only for an infinitesimally small tax levied in the absence of any other distortions. When the supply curve is upward sloping rather than horizontal, the excess-burden triangle contains some producer surplus as well as consumer surplus. The formula for excess burden then depends on the elasticity of supply as well as the elasticity of demand. In this case, the excess burden is

$$\tfrac{1}{2}\frac{P_b q}{\dfrac{1}{\eta}+\dfrac{1}{\varepsilon}}t_b^2$$

where ε is the elasticity of supply. Note that as ε approaches infinity, this expression collapses to Equation (13.3). This is because an ε of infinity corresponds to a horizontal supply curve as in Figure 13.5.

other things being the same. Because excess burden increases with the square of the tax rate, the *marginal* excess burden from raising one more dollar of revenue exceeds the *average* excess burden. That is, the incremental excess burden of raising one *more* dollar of revenue exceeds the ratio of total excess burden to total revenues. This fact has important implications for cost-benefit analysis. Suppose, for example, that the average excess burden per dollar of tax revenue is 12 cents, but the marginal excess burden per additional dollar of tax revenue is 27 cents [Jorgenson and Yun, 2001, p. 302]. The social cost of each dollar raised for a given public project is the dollar *plus* the incremental excess burden of 27 cents. Thus, a public project must produce marginal benefits of more than $1.27 per dollar of explicit cost if it is to improve welfare.

Airline-Ticket Taxation.   Let's illustrate Equation (13.3) with a real-world example. Airplane tickets are taxed by the federal government at a rate of 10 percent. What is the excess burden of this tax? The equation tells us that we have to know the price elasticity of demand. According to the survey of Oum, Waters, and Yong [1992], a reasonable estimate is about 1.0. We also need the product of price per ticket and number of tickets sold—airline-ticket revenues. This figure is roughly $94 billion annually [US Bureau of the Census, 2002, p. 661]. Substituting all of this information into Equation (13.3) tells us that the airline ticket tax imposes an annual excess burden of $\frac{1}{2} \times 94 \times (0.10)^2$ billion, or $470 million.

Preexisting Distortions   This analysis has assumed no distortions in the economy other than the tax under consideration. In reality, when a new tax is introduced, there are already other distortions: monopolies, externalities, and preexisting taxes. This complicates the analysis of excess burden.

Suppose that consumers regard gin and rum as substitutes. Suppose further that rum is currently being taxed, creating an excess burden "triangle" like that in Figure 13.5. Now the government decides to impose a tax on gin. What is the excess burden of the gin tax? In the gin market, the gin tax creates a wedge between what gin consumers pay and gin producers receive. As usual, this creates an excess burden. But the story is not over. If gin and rum are substitutes, the rise in the consumers' price of gin induced by the gin tax increases the demand for rum. Consequently, the quantity of rum demanded increases. Now, because rum was taxed under the status quo, "too little" of it was being consumed. The increase in rum consumption induced by the gin tax helps move rum consumption back toward its efficient level. There is thus an efficiency gain in the rum market that helps offset the excess burden imposed in the gin market. In theory, the gin tax could actually lower the overall excess burden. (Appendix B at the end of the chapter has a graphical demonstration of this phenomenon.)

We have shown, then, that the efficiency impact of a tax or subsidy cannot be considered in isolation. To the extent that there are other markets with distortions, and the goods in these markets are related (either substitutes or complements), the overall efficiency impact depends on what is going on in all the markets. To compute the overall efficiency impact of a set of taxes and subsidies, it is generally incorrect to calculate separately the excess burdens in each market and then add them up. The aggregate efficiency loss is not equal to the "sum of its parts."

This result can be quite discomfiting because strictly speaking, it means that *every* market in the economy must be studied to assess the efficiency implications of *any* tax or subsidy. In most cases, practitioners simply assume that the amount of interrelatedness between the market of their concern and other markets is sufficiently small that cross-effects can safely be ignored.[8] Although this is clearly a convenient assumption, its reasonableness must be evaluated in each particular case.

A controversy from the field of environmental economics provides an instance where accounting for preexisting distortions is important. Recall from Chapter 5 that in the presence of an externality, a tax can enhance efficiency. A Pigouvian tax in effect forces a polluter to take into account the costs that he imposes on other people and induces him to reduce output. Now, recall also that the US income tax system is highly inefficient. By distorting labor supply and other decisions, the income tax creates large excess burdens. Linking these two observations together, some have proposed that we increase reliance on environmental taxes and use the revenues to reduce income tax rates. This idea is called the **double-dividend hypothesis** because the scheme increases efficiency both in the market with the polluter and in the markets that are distorted by the income tax.

However, there is a possible flaw in this logic. To see why, note that the pollution taxes drive up the prices of the goods that are produced using polluting technology. However, when commodity prices go up, in effect this is a decrease in the real wage rate—a given dollar amount of wages buys you fewer goods and services. Put another way, the environmental taxes are, to some extent, also taxes on earnings. So if the labor market is already distorted because of an income tax, the environmental tax exacerbates the problem. It turns out that the added excess burden in the labor market can actually outweigh the efficiency gains from correcting the externality [Parry and Oates, 2000]. Put another way, the efficient pollution tax can be lower than in a situation in which there is not a preexisting income tax. This is not to say that Pigouvian taxation is a bad idea, only that its consequences for efficiency depend on the extent to which existing taxes already distort the labor market.

The Excess Burden of a Subsidy

Commodity subsidies are important components of the fiscal systems of many countries. In effect, a subsidy is just a negative tax, and like a tax, it is associated with an excess burden. To illustrate the calculation of the

---

[8] For an exception, see Fullerton and Rogers [1997].

FIGURE 13.6

Excess burden of a housing subsidy

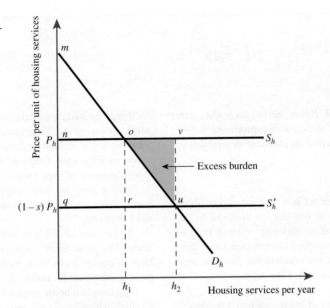

excess burden of a subsidy, we consider the subsidy for owner-occupied housing provided by the federal government via certain provisions of the personal income tax. (See Chapter 16 for details of the law.)

Assume that the demand for owner-occupied housing services is the straight line D_h in Figure 13.6. Supply is horizontal at price P_h, which measures the marginal social cost of producing housing services. Initially, the equilibrium quantity is h_1. Now suppose that the government provides a subsidy of s percent to housing producers. The new price for housing services is then $(1 - s)P_h$ and the associated supply curve is S_h'. The subsidy increases the quantity of housing services consumed to h_2. If the purpose of the subsidy was to increase housing consumption, then it has succeeded. But if its goal was to maximize social welfare, is it an appropriate policy?

Before the subsidy, consumer surplus was area *mno*. After the subsidy, consumer surplus is *mqu*. The benefit to housing consumers is the increase in their surplus, area *nouq*. But at what cost is this benefit obtained? The cost of the subsidy program is the quantity of housing services consumed, *qu*, times the subsidy per unit, *nq*, or rectangle *nvuq*. Thus, the cost of the subsidy actually exceeds the benefit—there is an excess burden equal to the difference between areas *nvuq* and *nouq*, which is the shaded area *ovu*. Estimates by Poterba [1992] imply that for someone who owns a $200,000 home, the excess burden is about $1,200 annually.

How can subsidizing a good thing like housing be inefficient? Recall that any point on the demand curve for housing services measures how much people value that particular level of consumption. To the right of h_1, although individuals do derive utility from consuming more housing, its value is less

American Way of Tax*

Humorist Russell Baker never uses the term excess burden *in the column reproduced below. Nevertheless, he gives an excellent description of the phenomenon.*

NEW YORK—The tax man was very cross about Figg. Figg's way of life did not conform to the way of life several governments wanted Figg to pursue. Nothing inflamed the tax man more than insolent and capricious disdain for governmental desires. He summoned Figg to the temple of taxation.

"What's the idea of living in a rental apartment over a delicatessen in the city, Figg?" he inquired. Figg explained that he liked urban life. In that case, said the tax man, he was raising Figg's city sales and income taxes. "If you want them cut, you'll have to move out to the suburbs," he said.

To satisfy his local government, Figg gave up the city and rented a suburban house. The tax man summoned him back to the temple.

"Figg," he said, "you have made me sore wroth with your way of life. Therefore, I am going to soak you for more federal income taxes." And he squeezed Figg until beads of blood popped out along the seams of Figg's wallet.

"Mercy, good tax man," Figg gasped. "Tell me how to live so that I may please my government, and I shall obey."

The tax man told Figg to quit renting and buy a house. The government wanted everyone to accept large mortgage loans from bankers. If Figg complied, it would cut his taxes.

Figg bought a house, which he did not want, in a suburb where he did not want to live, and he invited his friends and relatives to attend a party celebrating his surrender to a way of life that pleased his government.

The tax man was so furious that he showed up at the party with bloodshot eyes. "I have had enough of this, Figg," he declared. "Your government doesn't want you entertaining friends and relatives. This will cost you plenty."

than P_h, the marginal cost to society of providing it. In other words, the subsidy induces people to consume housing services that are valued at less than their cost—hence, the inefficiency.[9]

A very important policy implication follows from this analysis. One often hears proposals to help some group of individuals by subsidizing a commodity that they consume heavily. We have shown that this is an inefficient way to aid people. Less money could make them as well off if it were given to them as a direct grant. In Figure 13.6, people would be indifferent between a housing subsidy program costing *nvuq* and a direct grant of *nouq*, even though the subsidy program costs the government more money.[10] This is one

---

[9] Alternatively, after the subsidy the marginal rate of substitution in consumption depends on $(1 - s)P_h$, while the marginal rate of transformation in production depends on P_h. Hence, the marginal rate of transformation is not equal to the marginal rate of substitution, and the allocation of resources cannot be efficient.

[10] This result is very similar to that obtained when we examined in-kind subsidy programs in Chapter 7. That chapter also discusses why commodity subsidies nevertheless remain politically popular.

Figg immediately threw out all his friends and relatives, then asked the tax man what sort of people his government wished him to entertain. "Business associates," said the tax man. "Entertain plenty of business associates, and I shall cut your taxes."

To make the tax man and his government happy, Figg began entertaining people he didn't like in the house he didn't want in the suburb where he didn't want to live.

Then was the tax man enraged indeed. "Figg," he thundered, "I will not cut your taxes for entertaining straw bosses, truck drivers, and pothole fillers."

"Why not?" said Figg. "These are the people I associate with in my business."

"Which is what?" asked the tax man.

"Earning my pay by the sweat of my brow," said Figg.

"Your government is not going to bribe you for performing salaried labor," said the tax man. "Don't you know, you imbecile, that tax rates on salaried income are higher than on any other kind?"

And he taxed the sweat of Figg's brow at a rate that drew exquisite shrieks of agony from Figg and little cries of joy from Washington, which already had more sweated brows than it needed to sustain the federally approved way of life.

"Get into business, or minerals, or international oil," warned the tax man, "or I shall make your taxes as the taxes of 10."

Figg went into business, which he hated, and entertained people he didn't like in the house he didn't want in the suburb where he did not want to live.

At length the tax man summoned Figg for an angry lecture. He demanded to know why Figg had not bought a new plastic factory to replace his old metal and wooden plant. "I hate plastic," said Figg. "Your government is sick and tired of metal, wood, and everything else that smacks of the real stuff, Figg," roared the tax man, seizing Figg's purse. "Your depreciation is all used up."

There was nothing for Figg to do but go to plastic, and the tax man rewarded him with a brand new depreciation schedule plus an investment credit deduction from the bottom line.

*By Russell Baker, *International Herald Tribune*, April 13, 1977, page 14. © 1977 by The New York Times Company. Reprinted by permission.

of the reasons many economists prefer direct income transfers to commodity subsidies.

The Excess Burden of Income Taxation

The theory of excess burden applies just as well to factors of production as it does to commodities. In Figure 13.7, Jacob's hours of work are plotted on the horizontal axis and his hourly wage on the vertical. Jacob's compensated labor supply curve, which shows the smallest wage that would be required to induce him to work each additional hour, is labeled S_L. Initially, Jacob's wage is w and the associated hours of work L_1. In the same way that consumer surplus is the area between the demand curve and the market price, worker surplus is the area between the supply curve and the market wage rate. When the wage is w, Jacob's surplus is therefore area adf.

Now assume that an income tax at a rate t is imposed. The after-tax wage is then $(1 - t)w$, and given supply curve S_L, the quantity of labor supplied falls to L_2 hours. Jacob's surplus after the tax is agh, and the government collects revenues equal to $fihg$. The excess burden due to the tax-induced

FIGURE 13.7

Excess burden of a
tax on labor

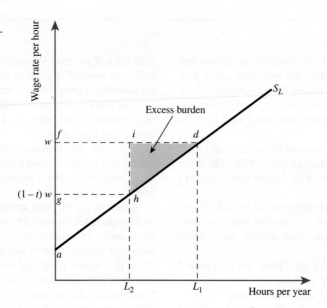

distortion of the work choice is the amount by which Jacob's loss of welfare (*fdhg*) exceeds the tax collected: area *hid* (= *fdhg* − *fihg*). In analogy to Equation (13.3), area *hid* is approximately

$$\tfrac{1}{2}\,\varepsilon w L_1 t^2 \tag{13.4}$$

where ε is the compensated elasticity of hours of work with respect to the wage.

A reasonable estimate of ε for an American male is about 0.2. For illustrative purposes, suppose that before taxation, Jacob works 2,000 hours per year at a wage of $20 per hour. A tax on earnings of 40 percent is then imposed. Substituting these figures into Equation (13.4), the excess burden of the tax is about $640 annually. One way to put this figure into perspective is to note that it is approximately 4 percent of tax revenues. Thus, on average, each dollar of tax collected creates an excess burden of 4 cents.

Of course, wage rates, tax rates, and elasticities vary across members of the population, so different people are subject to different excess burdens. Moreover, the excess burden of taxing labor also depends on tax rates levied on other factors of production. Jorgenson and Yun [2001] estimated that for plausible values of the relevant elasticities, the excess burden of labor income taxation in the United States is about 27 percent of the revenues raised. As we show in Chapter 16, however, there is considerable uncertainty about the values of some of the key elasticities. Hence, this particular estimate must be regarded cautiously. Still, it probably provides a good sense of the magnitudes involved.

FIGURE 13.8

The allocation of
time between
housework and
market work

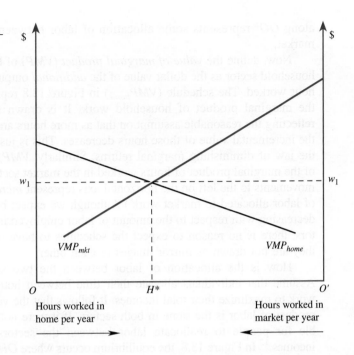

VMP$_{mkt}$ VMP$_{home}$

O H^* O'

Hours worked in
home per year

Hours worked in
market per year

Differential Taxation of Inputs

In the income tax example just discussed, we assumed that labor income was taxed at the same rate regardless of where the labor was supplied. But sometimes the tax on an input depends on where it is employed. For instance, because of the corporate income tax, capital employed in the corporate sector faces a higher rate than capital in the noncorporate sector. Another example is the differential taxation of labor in the household and market sectors. If an individual does housework, valuable services are produced but not taxed.[11] On the other hand, if the same individual works in the market, the services are subject to the income and payroll taxes. The fact that labor is taxed in one sector and untaxed in another distorts people's choices between them.

To measure the efficiency cost, consider Figure 13.8. The horizontal distance OO' measures the total amount of labor available in society. The amount of labor devoted to work in the home is measured by the distance to the right of point O; the amount of labor devoted to work in the market is measured by the distance to the left of point O'. Thus, any point

---

[11] The value of housework was expressed nicely by a biblical author who wrote at a time when it was assumed homes were managed only by females. In Proverbs 31, he discusses in detail the many tasks performed by the woman who "looketh well to the ways of her household" (v. 27). His general conclusion is that "her price is far above rubies" (v. 10). Unfortunately, price data on rubies during the biblical era are unavailable.

along OO' represents some allocation of labor between the home and the market.

Now, define the *value of marginal product (VMP)* of hours worked in the household sector as the dollar value of the *additional* output produced for each hour worked. The schedule (VMP_{home}) in Figure 13.8 represents the value of the marginal product of household work. It is drawn sloping downward, reflecting the reasonable assumption that as more hours are spent in the home, the incremental value of those hours decreases. This is just a manifestation of the law of diminishing marginal returns. Similarly, VMP_{mkt} shows the value of the marginal product of hours worked in the market sector. (Remember that movements to the left on the horizontal axis represent *increases* in the amount of labor allocated to market work.) Although we expect both schedules to be decreasing with respect to the amount of labor employed in the respective sectors, there is no reason to expect the schedules to have the same shapes, so they are not drawn as mirror images of each other.

How is the allocation of labor between the two sectors determined? Assume that individuals allocate their time between housework and market work to maximize their total incomes. It follows that the value of the marginal product of labor is the same in both sectors. If it were not, it would be possible for people to reallocate labor between the sectors to increase their incomes.[12] In Figure 13.8, the equilibrium occurs where OH^* hours are devoted to housework and $O'H^*$ hours to market work. The value of the marginal product of labor in both sectors is w_1 dollars. Competitive pricing ensures that the wage in the market sector is equal to the value of the marginal product.

Now assume that a tax of t is levied on income from market work, but the return to housework is untaxed. At any amount of labor employed in the market, the tax creates a wedge between the *VMP* and the associated wage rate. For example, if the value of the marginal product is $10 and the tax rate is 25 percent, then the wage rate will only be $7.50. More generally, the imposition of a tax on market wages at rate t lowers the wage rate from VMP_{mkt} to $(1 - t)VMP_{mkt}$. Geometrically, this amounts to moving every point on VMP_{mkt} down by t percent, as illustrated in Figure 13.9. Clearly, the original allocation is no longer an equilibrium, because at H^* the return to working in the household exceeds the rate in the market. That is, at H^*, VMP_{home} is greater than $(1 - t)VMP_{mkt}$. As a result, people begin working less in the market and more at home, which moves the economy rightward from H^*. Equilibrium is reached when the *after-tax* value of marginal product in the market sector equals the value of marginal product in the household sector. In Figure 13.9, this occurs when people work OH_t hours in the home and $O'H_t$ hours in the market.

At the new equilibrium, the after-tax *VMP*s in the two sectors are both equal to $(1 - t)w_2$. However, the *before-tax VMP* in the market sector, w_2, is greater than the *VMP* in the household sector, $(1 - t)w_2$. This means that if

---

[12] For further discussion of why this must be true, see the appendix at the end of the book.

FIGURE 13.9

Excess burden of
differential taxation
of inputs

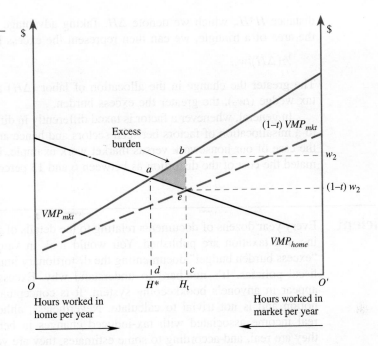

more labor were supplied to the market sector, the increase in income there (w_2) would exceed the loss of income in the household sector, $(1 - t)w_2$. But there is no incentive for this reallocation to occur, because individuals are sensitive to the returns they receive *after tax,* and these are already equal. The tax thus creates a situation in which there is "too much" housework and "not enough" work in the market. In short, the tax leads to an inefficient allocation of resources in the sense that it distorts incentives to employ inputs in their most productive uses. The resulting decrease in real income is the excess burden of the tax.

To measure the excess burden, we must analyze Figure 13.9 closely. Begin by observing that as a result of the exodus of labor from the market, the value of output there goes down by *abcd,* the area under VMP_{mkt} between H^* and H_t.[13] On the other hand, as labor enters the household sector, the value of output increases by *aecd,* the area under the VMP_{home} curve between H^* and H_t. Therefore, society comes out behind by area *abcd* minus area *aecd,* or triangle *abe,* which is the excess burden of the tax. The base of this triangle is just the size of the tax wedge, $w_2 - [(1 - t)w_2]$ or tw_2. Its height is the increase in the amount of time devoted to work at home,

---

[13] The vertical distance between *VMP* and the horizontal axis at any level of input gives the value of *marginal* product for that level of input. Adding up all these distances gives the value of the *total* product. Thus, the area under *VMP* gives the value of total product.

distance H^*H_t, which we denote ΔH. Taking advantage of the formula for the area of a triangle, we can then represent the excess burden as

$$\tfrac{1}{2}(\Delta H)tw_2.$$

The greater the change in the allocation of labor (ΔH) and the greater the tax wedge (tw_2), the greater the excess burden.

In general, whenever a factor is taxed differently in different uses, it leads to a misallocation of factors between sectors and hence an excess burden. In the case of our housework versus market work example, Boskin [1975] estimated the cost of the distortion as between 6 and 13 percent of tax revenues.

Does Efficient Taxation Matter?

Every year dozens of documents relating to the details of government spending and taxation are published. You would look in vain, however, for an "excess burden budget" documenting the distortionary impact of government fiscal policies. It's not hard to understand why. Excess burden does not appear in anyone's bookkeeping system. It is conceptually a rather subtle notion and is not trivial to calculate. Nevertheless, although the losses in real income associated with tax-induced changes in behavior are hidden, they are real, and according to some estimates, they are very large. We have emphasized repeatedly that efficiency considerations alone are never enough to determine policy. As Chief Justice Warren Burger remarked in a different context, "Convenience and efficiency are not the primary objectives—or the hallmarks—of democratic government." Still, it is unfortunate that policymakers often ignore efficiency altogether.

The fact that a tax generates an excess burden does not mean that the tax is bad. One hopes, after all, that it will be used to obtain something beneficial for society either in terms of enhanced efficiency or fairness. But to determine whether or not the supposed benefits are large enough to justify the costs, intelligent policy requires that excess burden be included in the calculation as a social cost. Moreover, as we see in the next chapter, excess burden is extremely useful in comparing alternative tax systems. Providing estimates of excess burden is an important task for economists.

Summary

- Taxes generally impose an excess burden—a cost beyond the tax revenue collected.
- Excess burden is caused by tax-induced distortions in behavior. It may be examined using either indifference curves or compensated demand curves.
- Lump sum taxes do not distort behavior but are unattractive as policy tools. Nevertheless, they are an important standard against which to compare the excess burdens of other taxes.
- Excess burden may result even if observed behavior is unaffected, because it is the compensated response to a tax that determines its excess burden.
- When a single tax is imposed, the excess burden is proportional to the compensated

elasticity of demand, and to the square of the tax rate.

- Excess-burden calculations typically assume no other distortions. If other distortions exist, the incremental excess burden of a new tax depends on its effects in other markets.

- Subsidies also create excess burdens because they encourage people to consume goods valued less than the marginal social cost of production.

- The differential taxation of inputs creates an excess burden. Such inputs are used "too little" in taxed activities and "too much" in untaxed activities.

Discussion Questions

1. Which of the following is likely to impose a large excess burden?

   a. A tax on land.

   b. A tax of 24 percent on the use of cellular phones. (This is the approximate sum of federal and state tax rates in California, New York, and Florida.)

   c. A subsidy for investment in "high-tech" companies.

   d. A tax on economic profits.

   e. A 10 percent tax on all computer software.

   f. A 10 percent tax only on the Excel spreadsheet program.

2. Under legislation passed in 2001, the marginal tax rate on the wages of individuals in the highest income category (over a million dollars annually) will decrease from 39.9 percent to 34.0 percent. Use Equation (13.4) to approximate the proportion by which this change will reduce the excess burden on individuals in this income group.

3. "In the formula for excess burden given in Equation (13.3), the tax is less than one. When it is squared, the result is smaller, not bigger. Thus, having t^2 instead of t in the formula makes the tax less important." Comment.

4. Some countries rely relatively heavily on taxes that distort economic behavior, and others do not. A recent econometric study found that countries in the latter category tend to grow faster than countries in the former [Kneller, Bleaney, and Gemmell, 1999]. Use the discussion surrounding Figure 13.9 to explain this phenomenon.

5. In the United Kingdom, each household that owns a television pays a compulsory levy that is equivalent to $160 per year. Do you think that

such a tax is likely to have a substantial excess burden relative to the revenues collected?

6. Because of federal subsidies, "the price of corn ($2.25 a bushel) is 50 cents less than the cost of growing it" [Pollan, 2002, p. 50]. Use a model along the lines of Figure 13.6 to model this situation, and show the excess burden of the subsidy.

7. Under the US tax system, capital that is employed in the corporate sector is taxed at a higher rate than capital in the noncorporate sector. This problem will analyze the excess burden of the differential taxation of capital.

   Assume that there are two sectors, corporate and noncorporate. The value of marginal product of capital in the corporate sector, VMP_c, is given by $VMP_c = 100 - K_c$, where K_c is the amount of capital in the corporate sector, and the value of the marginal product of capital in the noncorporate sector, K_n, is given by $VMP_n = 80 - 2 K_n$, where K_n is the amount of capital in the noncorporate sector. Altogether there are 50 units of capital in society.

   a. In the absence of any taxes, how much capital is in the corporate sector and how much in the noncorporate sector? (Hint: Draw a sketch along the lines of Figure 13.9 to organize your thoughts.)

   b. Suppose that a unit tax of 6 is levied on capital employed in the corporate sector. After the tax, how much capital is employed in each sector? What is the excess burden of the tax?

8. Consider a conventional supply and demand model in which the supply curve slopes up and the demand curve slopes down. Show graphically the excess burden when a unit tax is imposed. (Hint: Compare the losses of both consumer and producer surplus to tax revenues.)

Selected References

Auerbach, Alan, and James R Hines. "Taxation and Economic Efficiency." Working Paper No. 8181, National Bureau of Economic Research, March 2001.

Feldstein, Martin. "Tax Avoidance and the Deadweight Loss of the Income Tax." Working Paper No. 5055, National Bureau of Economic Research, Cambridge, MA, March 1995.

Jorgenson, Dale W, and Kun-Young Yun. *Investment, Volume 3, Lifting the Burden.* Cambridge, MA, MIT Press: 2001.

A P P E N D I X

Formula for Excess Burden

This appendix shows how the excess burden triangle *fdi* of Figure 13.5 may be written in terms of the compensated demand elasticity. The triangle's area, A, is given by the formula

$$A = \frac{1}{2} \times \text{base} \times \text{height}$$
$$= \frac{1}{2} \times (di) \times (fd) \tag{13A.1}$$

fd is just the difference between the gross and net prices (ΔP_b):

$$fd = \Delta P_b = (1 + t_b) \times P_b - P_b = t_b \times P_b \tag{13A.2}$$

di is the change in the quantity (Δq) induced by the price rise:

$$di = \Delta q \tag{13A.3}$$

Now, note that the definition of the price elasticity, η, is

$$\eta \equiv \frac{\Delta q}{\Delta P_b} \frac{P_b}{q}$$

so that

$$\Delta q = \eta \left(\frac{q}{P_b} \right) \Delta P_b \tag{13A.4}$$

We saw in (13A.2) that $\Delta P_b = t_b \times P_b$, so that (13A.4) yields

$$\Delta q = \eta \times \frac{q}{P_b} \times (t_b P_b) = \eta \times q \times t_b \tag{13A.5}$$

Finally, recall that $di = \Delta q$ and substitute both (13A.5) and (13A.2) into (13A.1) to obtain

$$A = \frac{1}{2}(di)(fd)$$
$$= \frac{1}{2}(\eta q t_b) \times (t_b P_b)$$
$$= \frac{1}{2} \times \eta \times P_b \times q \times (t_b)^2$$

as in the text.

APPENDIX

B

Multiple Taxes and the Theory of the Second Best

This appendix discusses the measurement of excess burden when a tax is imposed in the presence of a preexisting distortion.

In Figure 13.B, we consider two goods, gin and rum, whose demand schedules are D_g and D_r, and whose before-tax prices are P_g and P_r, respectively. (The prices represent marginal social costs and are assumed to be constant.) Rum is currently taxed at a percentage rate t_r, so its price is $(1 + t_r)P_r$.

FIGURE 13.B

Excess burden of a tax in the presence of an existing tax

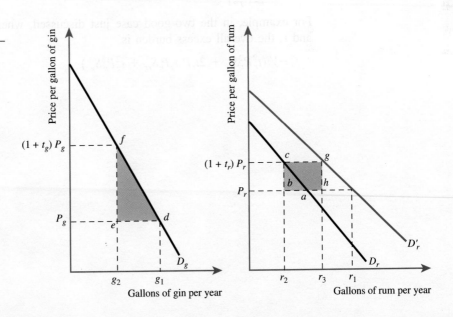

This creates an excess burden in the rum market, triangle *abc*. Now suppose that a tax on gin at rate t_g is introduced, creating a wedge between what gin consumers pay and gin producers receive. This creates an excess burden in the gin market of *efd*. But this is not the end of the story. If gin and rum are substitutes, the increase in the consumers' price of gin induced by the gin tax shifts the demand curve for rum to the right, say to D'_r. Consequently, the quantity of rum demanded increases from r_2 to r_3, distance *cg*. For each bottle of rum purchased between r_2 and r_3, the amount that people pay $[(1 + t_r)P_r]$ exceeds the social cost (P_r) by distance *cb*. Hence, there is a social gain of *cb* per bottle of rum times *cg* bottles, or area *cbhg*.

To summarize: Given that the tax on rum was already in place, the tax on gin creates an excess burden of *efd* in the gin market *and* simultaneously decreases excess burden by *cbhg* in the rum market. If *cbhg* is sufficiently large, the tax can actually reduce overall excess burden. This is an example of the **theory of the second best:** In the presence of existing distortions, policies that in isolation would increase efficiency can decrease it and vice versa.

This discussion is a special case of the result that the excess burden of a *set* of taxes generally depends on the whole set of tax rates, as well as on the degree of substitutability and complementarity among the various commodities. Specifically, suppose that n commodities are subject to taxation. Let P_i be the before-tax price of the ith commodity; t_i the ad valorem tax on the ith commodity; and S_{ij}, the compensated response in the demand of the ith good with respect to a change in the price of the jth good. Then the overall excess burden is

$$-\tfrac{1}{2} \sum_{i=1}^{n} \sum_{j=1}^{n} t_i P_i t_j P_j S_{ij}$$

For example, in the two-good case just discussed, where the goods are g and r, the overall excess burden is

$$-\tfrac{1}{2}(t_r^2 P_r^2 S_{rr} + 2t_r P_r t_g P_g S_{rg} + t_g^2 P_g^2 S_{gg})$$

CHAPTER 14

Efficient and Equitable Taxation

> A nation may fall into decay through taxation in two ways. In the first case, when the amount of the taxes exceeds the powers of the nation and is not proportioned to the general wealth. In the second case, when an amount of taxation, proportioned on the whole to the powers of the nation, is viciously distributed.
>
> PIETRO VERRI

The US revenue system is under attack. Critics argue that it is inefficient, unfair, and unduly complicated. But when these critics offer proposals for reform, their ideas are generally assailed for the same reasons. How are we to choose? Our goal in this chapter is to establish a set of criteria for evaluating real-world tax systems. We begin by looking at efficiency and distributional considerations that fit squarely within the framework of conventional welfare economics. We then turn to other criteria that do not fit so neatly, but nevertheless have considerable importance and appeal.

Optimal Commodity Taxation

In Florida, wireless phone bills are taxed at a rate of 17.8 percent; most other commodities (except for food, which is exempt) are taxed at a rate of 6 percent. Should wireless phone service be taxed at a higher rate than other things? This is just one example of a very general and very important economic policy question: At what rates should various goods and services be taxed? The purpose of the theory of optimal commodity taxation is to provide a framework for answering this question.

Of course, we can't find the "right" set of taxes without knowing the government's goal. At the outset, we assume that the only goal is to finance the state's expenditures with a minimum of excess burden and without using any lump sum taxes. We return later to issues that arise when distribution as well as efficiency matters.

To begin, consider the situation of Stella, a representative citizen who consumes only two commodities, X and Y, as well as leisure, l. The price of X is P_x, the price of Y is P_y, and the wage rate (which is the price of leisure) is w. The maximum number of hours per year that Stella can work—her **time endowment**—is fixed at $\overline{T}$. (Think of $\overline{T}$ as the amount of time left over after sleep.) It follows that hours of work are $(\overline{T} - l)$—all time not spent on leisure is devoted to work. Income is the product of the wage rate and hours of work—$w(\overline{T} - l)$. Assuming that Stella spends her entire income on commodities X and Y (there is no saving), her budget constraint is

$$w(\overline{T} - l) = P_x X + P_y Y \tag{14.1}$$

The left-hand side gives total earnings, and the right-hand side shows how the earnings are spent.

Equation (14.1) can be rewritten as

$$w\overline{T} = P_x X + P_y Y + wl \tag{14.2}$$

The left-hand side of (14.2) is the value of the time endowment. It shows the income that Stella could earn if she worked every waking hour.

Now suppose that it is possible to tax X, Y, and l at the same ad valorem rate, t. The tax raises the effective price of X to $(1 + t)P_x$, of Y to $(1 + t)P_y$, and of l to $(1 + t)w$. Thus, Stella's after-tax budget constraint is

$$w\overline{T} = (1 + t)P_x X + (1 + t)P_y Y + (1 + t)wl \tag{14.3}$$

Dividing through Equation (14.3) by $(1 + t)$, we have

$$\frac{1}{1 + t}w\overline{T} = P_x X + P_y Y + wl \tag{14.4}$$

Comparison of (14.3) and (14.4) points out the following fact: A tax on all commodities *including leisure,* at the same percentage rate, t, is equivalent to reducing the value of the time endowment from $w\overline{T}$ to $[1/(1 + t)] \times w\overline{T}$. For example, a 25 percent tax on X, Y, and l is equivalent to a reduction of the value of the time endowment by 20 percent. However, because w and $\overline{T}$ are fixed, their product, $w\overline{T}$, is also fixed; for any value of the wage rate, an individual cannot change the value of her time endowment. Therefore, a proportional tax on the time endowment is in effect a lump sum tax. From Chapter 13 we know that lump sum taxes have no excess burden. We conclude that a tax at the same rate on all commodities, *including leisure,* is equivalent to a lump sum tax and has no excess burden.

It sounds good, but there is a problem—putting a tax on leisure time is impossible. The only *available* tax instruments are taxes on commodities

FIGURE 14.1

Marginal excess
burden

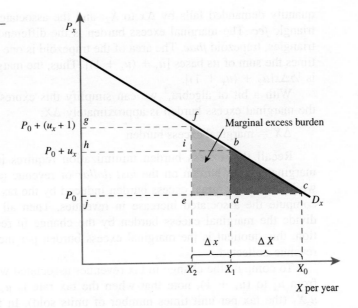

Marginal excess burden

X and Y. Therefore, *some* excess burden generally is inevitable. The goal of optimal commodity taxation is to select tax rates on X and Y in such a way that the excess burden of raising the required tax revenue is as low as possible. It might seem that the solution to this problem is to tax X and Y at the same rate—so-called **neutral taxation.** We will see that, in general, neutral taxation is *not* efficient.

The Ramsey Rule

To raise the revenue with the least excess burden possible, how should the tax rates on X and Y be set? To minimize *overall* excess burden, the *marginal* excess burden of the last dollar of revenue raised from each commodity must be the same. Otherwise, it would be possible to lower overall excess burden by raising the rate on the commodity with the smaller marginal excess burden, and vice versa.

To explore the consequences of this typical example of marginal analysis, suppose for simplicity that for our representative consumer, X and Y are unrelated commodities—they are neither substitutes nor complements for each other. Hence, a change in the price of either commodity affects its own demand and not the demand for the other good. Figure 14.1 shows Stella's compensated demand for X, D_x. Assume that she can buy all the X she wants at the price P_0, so the supply curve of X is horizontal.

Suppose that a unit tax of u_x is levied on X, which lowers quantity demanded from X_0 to X_1, ΔX in the figure. As proven in the last chapter, the excess burden of the tax is the area of triangle abc. Now suppose we raise the tax by 1, so it becomes $(u_x + 1)$. The total price is $P_0 + (u_x + 1)$;

quantity demanded falls by Δx to X_2; and the associated excess burden is triangle *fec*. The marginal excess burden is the difference between the two triangles, trapezoid *fbae*. The area of the trapezoid is one-half its height (Δx) times the sum of its bases [$u_x + (u_x + 1)$]. Thus, the marginal excess burden is $\frac{1}{2}\Delta x[u_x + (u_x + 1)]$.

With a bit of algebra,[1] we can simplify this expression to obtain that the marginal excess burden is approximately ΔX:

$$\Delta X = \text{marginal excess burden} \tag{14.5}$$

Recall that excess burden minimization requires information on the marginal excess burden on the *last dollar* of revenue collected. Now that we know the marginal excess burden induced by the tax increase, we must compute the associated increase in revenues. Then all we have to do is divide the marginal excess burden by the change in revenues. By definition, this quotient is the marginal excess burden per incremental dollar of revenue collected.

To compute the change in tax revenues associated with raising the rate from u_x to ($u_x + 1$), note that when the tax rate is u_x, tax revenues are $u_x X_1$ (the tax per unit times number of units sold). In figure 14.1, this is rectangle *hbaj*. Similarly, when the tax rate is ($u_x + 1$), tax revenues are *gfej*. Comparing these two rectangles, we see that when the tax goes up, the government gains area *gfih* but loses *ibae*. Thus, the change in revenues is *gfih-ibae*. Using algebra, this is $X_2 - (X_1 - X_2)u_x$. A bit of mathematical manipulation[2] leads us to the following approximation to the change in tax revenue:

$$X_1 - \Delta X = \text{marginal tax revenue} \tag{14.6}$$

Marginal excess burden per additional dollar of tax revenue is Equation (14.6) divided by (14.5) or

$$\frac{\Delta X}{X_1 - \Delta X}$$

Exactly the same reasoning indicates that if a unit tax of u_y is levied on Y, the marginal excess burden per last dollar of revenue is

$$\frac{\Delta Y}{Y_1 - \Delta Y}$$

---

[1] The area of the trapezoid is $\frac{1}{2}\Delta x(2u_x + 1)$ or $\Delta x u_x + (\frac{1}{2})\Delta x$, which we can approximate as $\Delta x u_x$ because the second term, which corresponds to triangle *fib* is relatively small and can be ignored. Now note that $1/\Delta x$ and $u_x/\Delta X$ are equal because both measure the slope (in absolute value) of D_x. Hence, $\Delta x u_x = \Delta X$, which is the marginal excess burden.

[2] Note that the expression for marginal tax revenue is equivalent to $X_2(u_x + 1) - X_1 u_x = X_2 + u_x(X_2 - X_1)$. From Figure 14.1, $X_2 = X_1 - \Delta x$. Substituting gives us $X_1 - \Delta x - u_x\Delta x$. But $\Delta x = \Delta X/u_x$ (see previous footnote), giving us $X_1 - \Delta X(1 + u_x)/u_x$. Providing that u_x is large relative to 1, this can be approximated as $X_1 - \Delta X$, the expression in the text for marginal tax revenue.

Because the condition for minimizing overall excess burden is that the marginal excess burden per last dollar of revenue be the same for each commodity, we must set

$$\frac{\Delta X}{X_1 - \Delta X} = \frac{\Delta Y}{Y_1 - \Delta Y}$$

This implies

$$\frac{\Delta X}{X_1} = \frac{\Delta Y}{Y_1} \tag{14.7}$$

To interpret Equation (14.7), note that the *change* in a variable divided by its *total* value is just the percentage change in the variable. Hence, Equation (14.7) says that *to minimize total excess burden, tax rates should be set so that the percentage reduction in the quantity demanded of each commodity is the same.* This result, called the **Ramsey rule** (after its discoverer, Frank Ramsey [1927]), also holds even for cases when X, Y, and l are related goods—substitutes or complements.

But why should efficient taxation induce equiproportional changes in quantities demanded rather than equiproportional changes in prices? Because excess burden is a consequence of distortions in *quantities*. To minimize total excess burden requires that all these changes be in the same proportion.

A Reinterpretation of the Ramsey Rule.   It is useful to explore the relationship between the Ramsey rule and demand elasticities. Let η_x be the compensated elasticity of demand for X. Let t_x be the tax rate on X, this time expressed as an ad valorem rate rather than a unit tax.[3] Now, by definition of an ad valorem tax, t_x is the percentage increase in the price induced by the tax. Hence, $t_x \eta_x$ is the percentage change in the price times the percentage change in quantity demanded when the price increases by 1 percent. This is just the percentage reduction in the demand for X induced by the tax. Defining t_y and η_y analogously, $t_y \eta_y$ is the proportional reduction in Y. The Ramsey rule says that to minimize excess burden, these percentage reductions in quantity demanded must be equal:

$$t_x \eta_x = t_y \eta_y \tag{14.8}$$

Now divide both sides of the equation by $t_y \eta_x$ to obtain

$$\frac{t_x}{t_y} = \frac{\eta_y}{\eta_x} \tag{14.9}$$

---

[3] In a competitive market, any unit tax can be represented by a suitably chosen ad valorem tax, and vice versa. For example, suppose a commodity is subject to a unit tax of 5 cents, and the price paid by consumers is 50 cents. Then the resulting excess burden is the same as that associated with an ad valorem tax equal to 10 percent of the after-tax price.

Equation (14.9) is the **inverse elasticity rule:** As long as goods are unrelated in consumption, tax rates should be inversely proportional to elasticities. That is, the higher is η_y relative to η_x, the lower should be t_y relative to t_x.[4] Efficiency does *not* require that all rates be set uniformly.

The intuition behind the inverse elasticity rule is straightforward. Efficient taxes distort decisions as little as possible. The potential for distortion is greater the more elastic the demand for a commodity. Therefore, efficient taxation requires that relatively high rates of taxation be levied on relatively inelastic goods.

The Corlett-Hague Rule.   Corlett and Hague [1953] proved an interesting implication of the Ramsey rule: When there are two commodities, efficient taxation requires taxing the commodity that is complementary to leisure at a relatively high rate. To understand this result intuitively, recall that *if* it were possible to tax leisure, a "first-best" result would be obtainable—revenues could be raised with no excess burden. Although the tax authorities cannot tax leisure, they *can* tax goods that tend to be consumed jointly *with* leisure, indirectly lowering the demand for leisure. If computer games are taxed at a very high rate, people buy fewer of them and spend less time at leisure. In effect, then, high taxes on complements to leisure provide an indirect way to "get at" leisure, and, hence, move closer to the perfectly efficient outcome that would be possible if leisure were taxable.

Equity Considerations

At this point you may suspect that efficient tax theory has unpleasant policy implications. For example, the inverse elasticity rule says inelastically demanded goods should be taxed at relatively high rates. Is this fair? Do we really want a tax system that collects the bulk of its revenue from taxes on insulin?

Of course not. Efficiency is only one criterion for evaluating a tax system; fairness is also important. In particular, it is widely agreed that a tax system should have **vertical equity:** It should distribute burdens fairly across people with different abilities to pay. The Ramsey rule has been modified to account for the distributional consequences of taxation. Suppose, for example, that the poor spend a greater proportion of their income on

---

[4] A more careful demonstration requires a little calculus. Recall from Equation (13.3) that the excess burdens on commodities X and Y are $\frac{1}{2}\eta_x P_x X t_x^2$ and $\frac{1}{2}\eta_y P_y Y t_y^2$, respectively. Then the total excess burden is $\frac{1}{2}\eta_x P_x X t_x^2 + \frac{1}{2}\eta_y P_y Y t_y^2$. (We can just add up the two expressions because by assumption, X and Y are unrelated.) Now, suppose the required tax revenue is R. Then t_x and t_y must satisfy the relation $P_x X t_x + P_y Y t_y = R$. Our problem is to choose t_x and t_y to minimize $\frac{1}{2}\eta_x P_x X t_x^2 + \frac{1}{2}\eta_y P_y Y t_y^2$ subject to $R - P_x X t_x - P_y Y t_y = 0$. Set up the Lagrangian expression

$$\mathscr{L} = \tfrac{1}{2}\eta_x P_x X t_x^2 + \tfrac{1}{2}\eta_y P_y Y t_y^2 + \lambda[R - P_x X t_x - P_y Y t_y]$$

where λ is the Lagrange multiplier. (The method of Lagrangian multipliers is covered in any intermediate calculus book.) Taking $\partial\mathscr{L}/\partial t_x$ yields $\eta_x t_x = \lambda$ and $\partial\mathscr{L}/\partial t_y$ yields $\eta_y t_y = \lambda$. Hence, $\eta_x t_x = \eta_y t_y$, and Equation (14.9) follows immediately.

commodity X than do the rich, and vice versa for commodity Y. X might be bread, and Y caviar. Suppose further that the social welfare function puts a higher weight on the utilities of the poor than on those of the rich. Then even if X is more inelastically demanded than Y, optimal taxation may require a higher rate of tax on Y than X [Stern, 1987]. True, a high tax rate on Y creates a relatively large excess burden, but it also tends to redistribute income toward the poor. Society may be willing to pay the price of a higher excess burden in return for a more equal distribution of income.

In general, the optimal departure from the Ramsey rule depends on two considerations. First is how much society cares about equality. If society cares only about efficiency—a dollar to one person is the same as a dollar to another, rich or poor—then it may as well strictly follow the Ramsey rule. Second is the extent to which the consumption patterns of the rich and poor differ. If the rich and the poor consume both goods in the same proportion, taxing the goods at different rates cannot affect the distribution of income. Even if society *has* a distributional goal, it cannot be achieved by differential commodity taxation.

Summary

If lump sum taxation were available, taxes could be raised without any excess burden at all. Optimal taxation would need to focus only on distributional issues. Lump sum taxes are not available, however, so the problem is how to raise tax revenue with as small an excess burden as possible. In general, minimizing excess burden requires that taxes be set so that the (compensated) demands for all commodities are reduced in the same proportion. For unrelated goods, this implies that tax rates should be set in inverse proportion to the demand elasticities. However, if society has distributional goals, departures from efficient taxation rules may be appropriate.

Application: Taxation of the Family

Under current federal income tax law, the fundamental unit of income taxation is the family.[5] A husband and wife are taxed on the sum of their incomes. Regardless of whether the wife or the husband earns an extra dollar, it is taxed at the same rate. Is this efficient? In other words, is the family's excess burden minimized by taxing each spouse's income at the same rate?

Imagine the family as a unit whose utility depends on the quantities of three "commodities": total family consumption, husband's hours of work, and wife's hours of work. Family utility increases with family consumption, but decreases with each spouse's hours of work. Each spouse's hours of work depend on his or her wage rate, among other variables. A tax on earnings distorts the work decision, creating an excess burden. (See Chapter 13, Figure 13.7.) How should tax rates be set so the family's excess burden is as small as possible?

---

[5] This section is based on Boskin and Sheshinski [1983].

Assume for simplicity that the husband's and wife's hours of work are approximately "unrelated goods"—an increase in the husband's wage rate has very little impact on the wife's work decision, and vice versa. This assumption is consistent with much empirical research. Then application of the inverse elasticity rule suggests that a higher tax should be levied on the commodity that is relatively inelastically supplied. To enhance efficiency, whoever's labor supply is relatively inelastic should bear a relatively high tax rate. Numerous econometric studies suggest that the husbands' labor supplies are considerably less elastic than wives'. Efficiency could therefore be gained if the current tax law were modified to give husbands higher marginal tax rates than wives.[6]

Again, we emphasize that efficiency is only one consideration in tax design. However, it is interesting that this result is consistent with the claims of some who have argued that on equity grounds, the relative tax rate on the earnings of working wives should be lowered. The next chapter contains a discussion of the actual tax treatment of married couples under US law.

Optimal User Fees

So far we have assumed that all production occurs in the private sector. The government's only problem is to set the tax rates that determine consumer prices. Sometimes, the government itself is the producer of a good or service. In such cases, the government must directly choose a **user fee**—a price paid by users of a good or service provided by the government. As usual, we would like to determine the "best" possible user fee. Analytically, the optimal tax and user fee problems are closely related. In both cases, the government sets the final price paid by consumers. In the optimal tax problem, this is done indirectly by choice of the tax rate, while in the optimal user fee problem, it is done directly.

When should the government choose to produce a good instead of purchasing it from the private sector? In Chapter 4 we argued that government production may be appropriate when the use of some good or service is subject to continually decreasing average costs—the greater the level of output, the lower the cost per unit. Under such circumstances, it is unlikely that the market for the service is competitive. A single firm can take advantage of economies of scale and supply the entire industry output, at least for a sizable region. This phenomenon is often called **natural monopoly.** Examples are bridges, electricity, and cable television. In some cases, these commodities are produced by the private sector and regulated by the government (electricity); and in others they are produced by the public sector (bridges).

---

[6] The important distinction here is not between *husband* and *wife* but between *primary earner* and *secondary earner.* In families where the wife has the lower supply elasticity, efficiency requires that she have the higher tax rate.

FIGURE 14.2

A natural monopoly

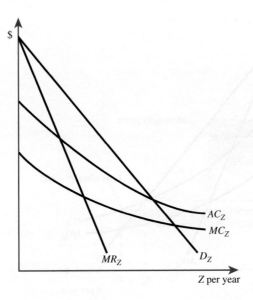

Although we study public production here, many of the important insights apply to regulation of private monopolies.

Figure 14.2 measures the output of the natural monopoly, Z, on the horizontal axis, and dollars on the vertical. The average cost schedule is denoted AC_Z. By assumption, it decreases continuously over all relevant ranges of output. Because average cost is decreasing, marginal cost must be less than average. Therefore, the marginal cost (MC_Z) curve, which shows the incremental cost of providing each unit of Z, lies below AC_Z. The demand curve for Z is represented by D_Z. The associated marginal revenue curve is MR_Z. It shows the incremental revenue associated with each level of output of Z.

To illustrate why decreasing average costs often lead to public sector production or regulated private sector production, consider what would happen if Z were produced by an unregulated monopolist. A monopolist seeking to maximize profits produces up to the point that marginal revenue equals marginal cost, output level Z_m in Figure 14.3. The associated price, P_m, is found by going up to the demand curve, D_Z. Monopoly profits are equal to the product of number of units sold times the profit per unit and are represented geometrically by the light colored rectangle.

Is output Z_m efficient? According to the theory of welfare economics, efficiency requires that price equal marginal cost—the value that people place on the good must equal the incremental cost to society of producing it. At Z_m, price is *greater* than marginal cost. Hence, Z_m is inefficient. This inefficiency plus the fact that society may not approve of the existence of the monopoly profits provide a possible justification for government taking over the production of Z.

FIGURE 14.3

Alternative pricing
schemes for a
natural monopoly

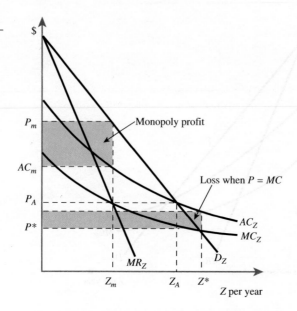

The obvious policy prescription seems to be for the government to produce up to the point where price equals marginal cost. In Figure 14.3, the output at which $P = MC$ is denoted Z^*, and the associated price is P^*. There is a problem, however: at output Z^*, the price is less than the average cost. Price P^* is so low that the operation cannot cover its costs, and it suffers losses. The total loss is equal to the product of the number of units sold, Z^*, times the loss per unit, measured as the vertical distance between the demand curve and AC_Z at Z^*. Geometrically, the loss is the darker colored rectangle in Figure 14.3.

How should the government confront this dilemma? Several solutions have been proposed.

Average Cost Pricing.   By definition, when price equals average cost, there are neither profits nor losses—the enterprise just breaks even. The operation no longer has to worry about a deficit. Geometrically, this corresponds to the intersection of the demand and average cost schedules in Figure 14.3, where output is Z_A and price is P_A. However, note that Z_A is less than Z^*. Although average cost pricing leads to more output than at the profit-maximizing level, it still falls short of the efficient amount.

Marginal Cost Pricing with Lump Sum Taxes.   Charge $P = MC$, and make up the deficit by levying lump sum taxes. Charging $P = MC$ ensures efficiency in the market for Z; financing the deficit with lump sum taxes on the rest of society guarantees that no new inefficiencies are generated by meeting the deficit. However, there are two problems with this solution:

First, as previously noted, lump sum taxes are generally unavailable. The deficit has to be financed by distorting taxes, such as income or commodity taxes. If so, the distortion due to the tax may more than outweigh the efficiency gain in the market for Z.

Second, there is a widespread belief that fairness requires consumers of a publicly provided service to pay for it—the so-called **benefits-received principle.** If this principle is taken seriously, it is unfair to make up the deficit by general taxation. If the coast guard rescues me from a stormy sea, why should you pay for it?

A Ramsey Solution.   So far we have been looking at one government enterprise in isolation. Suppose that the government is running *several* enterprises, and as a group they cannot lose money, but any individual enterprise can. Suppose further that the government wants the financing to come from users of the services produced by the enterprises. By how much should the user fee for each service exceed its marginal cost?

Does this question sound familiar? It should, because it is essentially the same as the optimal tax problem. In effect, the difference between the marginal cost and the user fee is just the "tax" that the government levies on the commodity. And just as in the optimal tax problem, the government has to raise a certain amount of revenue—in this case, enough for the group of enterprises to break even. The Ramsey rule gives the answer—set the user fees so that demands for each commodity are reduced proportionately. This analysis, by the way, illustrates one of the nice features of economic theory. Often a framework that is developed to study one problem can be fruitfully applied to another problem that seems to be quite different.

Overview   Of the various possibilities for dealing with decreasing costs, which has the United States chosen? In most cases, both publicly owned and regulated private enterprises have selected average cost pricing. Although average cost pricing is inefficient, it is probably a reasonable compromise. It has the virtue of being fairly simple and adheres to the popular benefits-received principle. Some economists, however, argue that more reliance on Ramsey pricing would be desirable.

Optimal Income Taxation

Thus far, we have assumed that a government can levy taxes on all commodities and inputs. We now turn to the question of how to design systems in which tax liabilities are based on people's incomes. Specifically, how progressive should the income tax be? There is hardly a more contentious issue in public finance. Nineteenth-century economist John McCulloch, who opposed progressive taxation, argued that once you abandon proportional taxation, "you are at sea without rudder or compass, and there is no amount of injustice and folly you may not commit." The goal of the theory of optimal income taxation is to provide a rudder, that is, to provide a systematic way for thinking about the "right" amount of tax progressivity.

Edgeworth's Model

At the end of the 19th century, Edgeworth [1959/1897] examined the question of optimal income taxation using a simple model based on the following assumptions.

1. Subject to the revenues required, the goal is to make the sum of individuals' utilities as high as possible. Algebraically, if U_i is the utility of the ith individual and W is social welfare, the tax system should maximize

$$W = U_1 + U_2 + \cdots + U_n \tag{4.10}$$

where n is the number of people in the society.

2. Individuals have identical utility functions that depend only on their incomes. These utility functions exhibit diminishing marginal utility of income; as income increases, an individual becomes better off, but at a decreasing rate.

3. The total amount of income available is fixed.

Edgeworth's assumptions are virtually identical to the assumptions behind the optimal income distribution model presented in Chapter 7 under "Rationales for Income Redistribution." There we showed that with these assumptions, maximization of social welfare requires that each person's marginal utility of income be the same. When utility functions are identical, marginal utilities are equal only if incomes are equal. The implications for tax policy are clear: Taxes should be set so that the after-tax distribution of income is as equal as possible. In particular, income should be taken first from the rich because the marginal utility lost is smaller than that of the poor. If the government requires more revenue even after obtaining complete equality, the additional tax burden should be evenly distributed.

Edgeworth's model, then, implies a radically progressive tax structure—incomes are leveled off from the top until complete equality is reached. In effect, marginal tax rates on high income individuals are 100 percent. However, as stressed in Chapter 7, each of the assumptions underlying this analysis is subject to question. In recent decades, economists have investigated how Edgeworth's results change when certain of the assumptions are relaxed.

Modern Studies

One of the most vexing problems with Edgeworth's analysis is the assumption that the total amount of income available to society is fixed. Confiscatory tax rates have no effect on the amount of output produced. More realistically, suppose that individuals' utilities depend not only on income but on leisure as well. Then income taxes distort work decisions and create excess burdens (Chapter 13). A society with a utilitarian social welfare function thus faces an inescapable dilemma. On the one hand, it desires to allocate the tax burden to equalize the after-tax distribution of income. However, in the process of doing so, it reduces the total amount of real

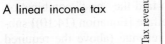

FIGURE 14.4

A linear income tax

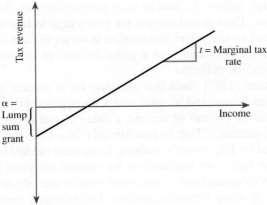

income available. An optimal income tax system must account for the costs (in excess burden) of achieving more equality. In Edgeworth's model, the cost of obtaining more equality is zero, which explains the prescription for a perfectly egalitarian outcome.

How does Edgeworth's result change when work incentives are taken into account? Stern [1987] studied a model similar to Edgeworth's, except that individuals choose between income and leisure. To simplify the analysis, Stern assumed that the tax revenues collected from a person are given by

$$\text{Revenues} = -\alpha + t \times \text{Income} \qquad (14.11)$$

where α and t are positive numbers. For example, suppose that $\alpha = \$3,000$ and $t = .25$. Then a person with income of \$20,000 would have a tax liability of \$2,000 ($= -\$3,000 + .25 \times \$20,000$). A person with an income of \$6,000 would have a tax liability of *minus* \$1,500 ($= -\$3,000 + .25 \times \$6,000$). Such a person would receive a \$1,500 grant from the government.

In Figure 14.4, we graph Equation (14.11) in a diagram with income measured on the horizontal axis and tax revenues on the vertical. When income is zero, the tax burden is negative—the individual receives a lump sum grant from the government of α dollars. Then, for each dollar of income, the individual must pay t dollars to the government. Thus, t is the *marginal* tax rate, the proportion of an additional dollar that must be paid in tax. Because the geometric interpretation of (14.11) is a straight line, it is referred to as a **linear income tax schedule.** In popular discussions, a linear income tax schedule is often called a **flat income tax.** Note that even though the marginal tax rate for a linear tax schedule is constant, the schedule is progressive in the sense that the higher an individual's income, the higher the proportion of income paid in taxes. (See Chapter 12.) Just how progressive depends on the precise values of α and t. Greater values of t are associated with more progressive tax systems. However, at the same time that high values of t lead to more progressiveness, they create larger excess burdens. The optimal income tax problem is to find the "best" combination of α and t—the values that maximize social welfare [Equation (14.10)] subject to the constraint that a given amount of revenue (above the required transfers) be collected.

Stern [1987] finds that allowing for a modest amount of substitution between leisure and income, and with required government revenues equal to about 20 percent of income, a value of t of about 19 percent maximizes social welfare.[7] This is considerably less than the value of 100 percent implied by Edgeworth's analysis. Even quite modest incentive effects appear to have important implications for optimal marginal tax rates. Incidentally, Stern's calculated rate is also much smaller than the actual marginal tax rates found in many Western countries. For example, under the US federal personal income tax, the highest statutory marginal income tax rate in 2003 was 38.6 percent; at times it has been 90 percent.

More generally, Stern showed that the more elastic the supply of labor, the lower the optimal value of t, other things being the same. Intuitively, the cost of redistribution is the excess burden it creates. The more elastic the supply of labor, the greater the excess burden from taxing it. [See Equation (13.4).] More elastic labor supply therefore means a higher cost to redistribution, so that less should be undertaken.

Stern also investigated how alternative social welfare functions affect the results, focusing on the impact of giving different social weights to the utilities of the rich and the poor. In Equation (14.10), more egalitarian preferences are represented by assigning the utilities of poor people higher weights than utilities of the rich. An interesting extreme case is the maximin criterion, according to which the only individual who receives any weight in the social welfare function is the person with the minimum utility (see Chapter 7). Stern found that the maximin criterion calls for a marginal tax rate of about 80 percent. Not surprisingly, if society has extremely egalitarian objectives, high tax rates are called for. Even here, though, the rates fall short of 100 percent.

One limitation of Stern's analysis is that it constrains the income tax system to have only a single marginal tax rate. Gruber and Saez [2000] investigated a more general model that allowed for four marginal tax rates. The most interesting finding to emerge from their analysis is that people in higher-income brackets should face a *lower* marginal tax rate than people in the lower brackets. The intuition behind the result is that, by lowering the marginal tax rate on high-income people, they are induced to supply more labor, and the increased tax revenue can be used to lower the tax burdens on low-income

---

[7] Specifically, the result reported here assumes the elasticity of substitution between leisure and income is 0.6. In Stern's model, this corresponds to a small positive elasticity of labor supply with respect to the net wage, about 0.1.

individuals. Importantly, although marginal tax rates fall with income, average tax rates rise with income, so the optimal tax system is still progressive. This cataloging of results may convey a somewhat false sense of precision as to what economists really know about the optimal tax system. After all, there are many controversial value judgments behind the utilitarian social welfare that the optimal tax system seeks to maximize. Moreover, as explained in Chapter 16, there is substantial uncertainty about the behavioral elasticities that are crucial to analyzing the trade-off between efficiency and equity. Nevertheless, explicit calculations of optimal tax rates under alternative sets of assumptions are extremely informative. The contribution of the literature on optimal taxation is systematically to draw out the implications of alternative ethical and behavioral assumptions, thus facilitating coherent discussions of tax policy.

Politics and the Time Inconsistency Problem

Optimal taxation is a purely normative theory. It does not purport to predict what real-world tax systems look like, or to explain how these tax systems emerge. The theory pays little attention to the institutional and political setting in which tax policy is made. Holcombe [2002] argues that in the presence of real-world political institutions, policy recommendations based on optimal tax logic may actually reduce welfare.

Assume that in a certain society, there are three commodities, X, Y, and leisure. Labor is totally fixed in supply, and therefore, income is fixed. Currently, this society levies a tax on X, but its constitution forbids taxing Y. Viewing this situation, a student of optimal tax theory might say something like: "You are running an inefficient tax system. Because labor is totally fixed in supply, you could have no excess burden if you taxed X and Y at equal rates—an income tax. I recommend that you lower the tax on X and impose a tax at the same rate on Y. Set the rates so that the same amount of revenue is collected as before."

Suppose, however, that the citizens suspect that if they allow taxation of Y, their politicians will not lower the tax rate on X. Rather, they will simply take advantage of the opportunity to tax something new to make tax revenues as large as possible. As we saw in Chapter 6, certain theories of the public sector suggest that those who run the government can and will maximize tax revenues despite the wishes of the citizenry. Therefore, by constitutionally precluding the taxation of Y, the citizens may be rationally protecting themselves against an inefficiently large public sector. In other words, if citizens do not trust the government, what looks inefficient from the point of view of optimal commodity taxation may be efficient in a larger setting.[8] There is, in

---

[8] Holcombe [1998] provides further comparisons between optimal tax theory and an approach that takes politics into account.

fact, some evidence that governments with tax systems that generate large excess burdens tend to grow more slowly than governments with efficient tax systems [Becker and Mulligan, 1998], although research on this matter is at a preliminary stage.

Issues relating to these considerations may help explain, in part, the current controversy over the tax treatment of purchases made on the Internet. Proponents of Internet taxation argue that a good purchased in a store is essentially the same commodity as the same good purchased on the Internet. Taxing the former but not the latter distorts consumers' choices between the two modes of purchase, and hence creates an excess burden. Opponents argue that taxing Internet sales would simply fuel increases in the size of the public sector, which is already inefficiently large.

This discussion is related to a more general phenomenon called the **time inconsistency of optimal policy.** Consider a proposal made by the government of Colombia in 2002. To put down a rebellion, a tax of 1.2 percent of the value of their capital would be levied on all individuals and businesses whose assets exceeded the equivalent of $60,000. Importantly, the tax was to be imposed only one time; it would not be repeated in the future. While capitalists presumably would not be pleased to pay the tax, it would appear to have no impact on their current incentives to save for the future. Such a tax is in effect a lump sum levy and therefore fully efficient.

There is a problem, however. The Colombian government has an incentive to renege on its promise that the tax would only be levied once and pull exactly the same trick next year, raising yet more revenue without an excess burden. Thus, the stated tax policy is inconsistent with the government's incentives over time. Even worse, the capitalists realize the government has an incentive to renege. They will change their saving behavior to reflect the expectation that the more they save now, the more they will be taxed next year. Because the expected tax changes behavior, it introduces an inefficiency.

In short, unless the government can *credibly* promise not to renege, it cannot conduct the fully efficient tax policy. To avoid this time inconsistency problem, the government must be able to commit itself to behave in certain ways in the future. How can this be done? One possible approach is to enact constitutional provisions forbidding the government to go back on its promises. However, as long as the government has an underlying incentive to renege, suspicions will remain, frustrating attempts to run an efficient policy. These considerations suggest that the credibility of the political system must be considered before making recommendations based on optimal tax theory.

Other Criteria for Tax Design

As we have seen, optimal taxation depends on the trade-off between "efficiency" and "fairness." However, the use of these concepts in optimal tax theory does not always correspond closely to lay usage. In the context of optimal tax theory, a fair tax is one that guarantees a socially desirable distribution of the tax burden; an efficient tax is one with a small excess burden. In public discussion, on the other hand, a fair tax is often one that imposes equal liabilities on people who have the same ability to pay, and an efficient tax system is one that keeps down administrative and compliance expenses. These alternative notions of fairness and efficiency in taxation are the subject of this section.

Horizontal Equity

The American humorist Will Rogers once said, "People want *just* taxes more than they want *lower* taxes. They want to know that every man is paying his proportionate share according to his wealth." This criterion for evaluating a tax system is embodied in the economist's notion of **horizontal equity:** People in equal positions should be treated equally. To make horizontal equity an operational idea, one must define "equal positions." Rogers suggests wealth as an index of ability to pay, but income and expenditure might also be used.

Unfortunately, all of these measures represent the *outcomes* of people's decisions and are not really suitable measures of equal position. Consider two individuals, both of whom can earn $10 per hour. Mr. A chooses to work 1,500 hours each year, while Ms. B works 2,200 hours each year. A's income is $15,000 and B's is $22,000, so that in terms of income, A and B are not in "equal positions." In an important sense, however, A and B *are* the same, because their earning capacities are identical—B just happens to work harder. Thus, because work effort is at least to some extent under people's control, two individuals with different incomes may actually be in equal positions. Similar criticism would apply to expenditure or wealth as a criterion for measuring equal positions.

These arguments suggest that the individual's wage *rate* rather than income be considered as a candidate for measuring equal positions, but this idea has problems too. First, investments in human capital—education, on-the-job training, and health care—can influence the wage rate. If Mr. A had to go to college to earn the same wage that Ms. B is able to earn with only a high school degree, is it fair to treat them the same? Second, computing the wage rate requires division of total earnings by hours of work, but the latter is not easy to measure. (How should time spent on coffee breaks be counted?) Indeed, for a given income, it would be worthwhile for a worker to exaggerate hours of work to be able to report a lower wage rate and pay fewer taxes. Presumably, bosses could be induced to collaborate with their employees in return for a share of the tax savings.

As an alternative to measuring equal position either in incomes or wage rates, Feldstein [1976a] suggests it be defined in utilities. Hence, the **utility definition of horizontal equity:** (*a*) if two individuals would be equally well off (have the same utility level) in the absence of taxation, they should also be equally well off if there is taxation; and (*b*) taxes should not alter the utility ordering—if A is better off than B before taxation, he should be better off after.

To assess the implications of Feldstein's definition, first assume all individuals have the same preferences, that is, identical utility functions. In this case, individuals who consume the same commodities (including leisure) should pay the same tax, or, equivalently, all individuals should face the same tax schedule. Otherwise, individuals with equal before-tax utility levels would have different after-tax utilities.

Now assume that people have diverse tastes. For example, let there be two types of individuals, Gourmets and Sunbathers. Both groups consume food (which is purchased using income) and leisure, but Gourmets put a relatively high value on food, as do Sunbathers on leisure time. Assume further that before any taxation, Gourmets and Sunbathers have identical utility levels. If the same proportional income tax is imposed on everybody, Gourmets are necessarily made worse off than Sunbathers, because the former need relatively large amounts of income to support their food habits. Thus, even though this income tax is perfectly fair judged by the traditional definition of horizontal equity, it is not fair according to the utility definition. Indeed, as long as tastes for leisure differ, *any* income tax violates the utility definition of horizontal equity.

Of course, the practical difficulties involved in measuring individuals' utilities preclude the possibility of having a utility tax. Nevertheless, the utility definition of horizontal equity has some provocative policy implications. Assume again that all individuals have the same preferences. Then it can be shown that *any* existing tax structure does not violate the utility definition of horizontal equity *if* individuals are free to choose their activities and expenditures.

To see why, suppose that in one type of job a large part of compensation consists of amenities that are not taxable—pleasant offices, access to a swimming pool, and so forth. In another occupation, compensation is exclusively monetary, all of which is subject to income tax. According to the traditional definition, this situation is a violation of horizontal equity, because a person in the job with a lot of amenities has too small a tax burden. But, if both arrangements coexist and individuals are free to choose, then the net after-tax rewards (including amenities) must be the same in both jobs. Why? Suppose that the net after-tax reward is greater in the jobs with amenities. Then individuals migrate to these jobs to take advantage of them. But the increased supply of workers in these jobs depresses their wages. The process continues until the *net* returns are equal. In short, although people in the different occupations pay unequal taxes, there is no horizontal inequity because of adjustments in the *before-tax* wage.

Some suggest that certain tax advantages available only to the rich are sources of horizontal inequity. According to the utility definition, this notion is wrong. If these advantages are open to everyone with high income, and all high-income people have identical tastes, then the advantages may indeed reduce tax progressiveness, but they have no effect whatsoever on horizontal equity.

We are led to a striking conclusion: Given common tastes, a preexisting tax structure cannot involve horizontal inequity. Rather, all horizontal inequities arise from *changes* in tax laws. This is because individuals make commitments based on the existing tax laws that are difficult or impossible to reverse. For example, people may buy larger houses because of the preferred tax treatment for owner-occupied housing. When the tax laws are changed, their welfare goes down, and horizontal equity is violated. As one congressman put it, "It seems unfair to people who have done something in good faith to change the law on them."[9] These observations give new meaning to the dictum, "The only good tax is an old tax."

The fact that tax changes may generate horizontal inequities does not necessarily imply that they should not be undertaken. After all, tax changes may improve efficiency and/or vertical equity. However, the arguments suggest that it might be appropriate to ease the transition to the new tax system. For example, if it is announced that a given tax reform is not to go into effect until a few years subsequent to its passage, people who have based their behavior on the old tax structure will be able to make at least some adjustments to the new regime. The problem of finding fair processes for changing tax regimes (**transitional equity**) is very difficult, and not many results are available on the subject.

The very conservative implications of the utility definition of horizontal equity should come as no great surprise, because implicit in the definition is the notion that the pretax status quo has special ethical validity. (Otherwise, why be concerned about changes in the ordering of utilities?) However, it is not at all obvious why the status quo deserves to be defended. A more general feature of the utility definition is its focus on the *outcomes* of taxation. In contrast, some have suggested that the essence of horizontal equity is to put constraints on the *rules* that govern the selection of taxes, rather than to provide criteria for judging their effects. Thus, horizontal equity excludes capricious taxes, or taxes based on irrelevant characteristics. For example, we can imagine the government levying special lump sum taxes on people with red hair, or putting very different taxes on angel food and chocolate cakes. The **rule definition of horizontal equity** would presumably exclude such taxes from consideration, even if they had desirable efficiency or distributional effects. In this sense, provisions in the US Constitution that rule out certain kinds of taxes can be interpreted as an attempt to guarantee horizontal equity. (See Chapter 1.)

However, identifying the permissible set of characteristics on which to base taxation is a problem. Most people would agree that religion and race should be irrelevant for purposes of determining tax liability. On the other hand, there is considerable disagreement as to whether or not marital status should influence tax burdens (see Chapter 15). And even with agreement

---

[9] "Changes in Tax Bill Expected," *The New York Times,* May 26, 1986, p. 31.

that certain characteristics are legitimate bases for discrimination, the problem of how much discrimination is appropriate still remains. Everyone agrees that serious physical impairment should be taken into account in determining personal tax liability. But how bad must your vision be to qualify for special tax treatment as blind? And by what amount should your tax bill be reduced?

We are forced to conclude that horizontal equity, however defined, is a rather amorphous concept. Yet it has enormous appeal as a principle of tax design. Notions of fairness among equals, regardless of their vagueness, will continue to play an important role in the development of tax policy.

Costs of Running the Tax System

An implicit assumption in the models we have been studying is that collecting taxes involves no costs. This is clearly false. The tax authorities require resources to do their job. Taxpayers incur costs as well, including outlays for accountants and tax lawyers, as well as the value of time spent filling out tax returns and keeping records.

The costs of administering the income tax in the United States are fairly low. For example, the Internal Revenue Service spends only about 39 cents to raise each $100 in taxes. However, the compliance costs of personal income taxation are quite substantial. On the basis of survey evidence, Slemrod [1996] estimates that, in 1995, US households devoted 2.8 billion hours to federal tax preparation. If the value of time is approximated at $15 per hour, then the time cost of federal tax compliance is $42 billion. Further, Slemrod assesses the monetary expenditures for tax compliance (fees for professional advice, tax preparation manuals, etc.) at about $8 billion, giving a total resource cost of $50 billion, about 8 percent of federal income tax revenue. An updated estimate of compliance costs for the year 2000, including corporate as well as personal taxes, is about $115 billion.

Clearly, the choice of tax and subsidy systems should take account of administrative and compliance costs. Even systems that appear fair and efficient (in the excess burden sense) might be undesirable because they are excessively complicated and expensive to administer. Consider the possibility of taxing output produced in the home—housecleaning, child care, and so on. As suggested in Chapter 13, the fact that market work is taxed but housework is not creates a sizable distortion in the allocation of labor. Moreover, taxing differentially on the basis of choice of workplace violates some notions of horizontal equity. Nevertheless, the difficulties involved in valuing household production would create such huge administrative costs that the idea is infeasible.

Unfortunately, administrative problems often receive insufficient attention. A classic case was the federal luxury tax on new jewelry enacted in 1990. The tax applied only to the portion of the price that exceeded $10,000, and only items worn for adornment were subject to the tax. As one commentator noted, the tax was an administrative nightmare: "loose gems and repairs aren't taxed; market value after a major modification is. Thus, . . . you may be taxed if you have gems from your grandma's brooch put in a new setting. But you won't be if you replace a $30,000 diamond lost from a ring; that's a repair" [Schmedel, 1991, p. A1]. The costs to the Internal Revenue Service of collecting the luxury tax may have exceeded the revenues collected! The tax was finally repealed in 1993.

Obviously, no tax system is costless to administer; the trick is to find the best trade-off between excess burden and administrative costs. For example, administering a sales tax system in which each commodity has its own rate might be very cumbersome, despite the fact that this is the general tack prescribed by the Ramsey rule. Any reductions in excess burden that arise from differentiating the tax rates must be compared to the incremental administrative costs.

Tax Evasion

We now turn to one of the most important problems facing any tax administration—cheating. To begin, one must distinguish between tax avoidance and tax evasion. **Tax avoidance,** which John Maynard Keynes once called "the only intellectual pursuit that carries any reward," is changing your behavior so as to reduce your tax liability. There is nothing illegal about tax avoidance:

> Over and over again courts have said that there is nothing sinister in so arranging one's affairs so as to keep taxes as low as possible. Everybody does so, rich or poor; and all do right, for nobody owes any public duty to pay more than the law demands . . . To demand more in the name of morals is mere cant. [Judge Learned Hand, *Commissioner* v. *Newman,* 1947]

In contrast, **tax evasion** is failing to pay legally due taxes. If a tax on mushrooms is levied and you sell fewer mushrooms, it is tax avoidance. If you fail to report your sales of mushrooms to the government, it is tax evasion. Tax evasion is not a new problem. Centuries ago Plato observed, "When there is an income tax, the just man will pay more and the unjust less on the same amount of income." In recent years, however, tax evasion has received an especially large amount of public attention. A case that received international notice was that of tennis star Steffi Graf. Several years ago, the German authorities accused her of evading as much as $50 million in taxes over a 12-year period. From 1989 to 1992, she did not even file a tax return.

Tax cheating is extremely difficult to measure. The Internal Revenue Service estimates that taxpayers voluntarily pay only about 80 percent of their actual income tax liability. If this estimate is even roughly accurate, it suggests that evasion is a very important issue.

People commit tax fraud in a variety of ways:

- Keep two sets of books to record business transactions. One records the actual business and the other is shown to the tax authorities. Some evaders use two cash registers.

- Moonlight for cash. Of course, working an extra job is perfectly legal. However, the income received on such jobs is often paid in cash rather than by check. Hence, no legal record exists, and the income is not reported to the tax authorities.

- Barter. "I'll fix your car if you bake me five loaves of bread." When you receive payment in kind instead of money, it is legally a taxable transaction. However, such income is seldom reported.
- Deal in cash. Paying for goods and services with cash and checks made out to "cash" makes it very difficult for the Internal Revenue Service to trace transactions.

At one time, tax evasion was associated with millionaires who hid their capital in Swiss bank accounts. The current image of a tax evader may well be a repairer whose income comes from "unofficial" work not reported for tax purposes, or a parent who evades taxes on wages paid to a baby-sitter. Indeed, people who pay maids, nannies, and other household employees more than roughly $1,300 per year are obligated to pay Social Security taxes for them, yet fewer than 0.25 percent of all households pay this "nanny tax" [Herman, 2001, p. A1]. The feeling that "everyone is doing it" is widespread.

We first discuss the positive theory of tax evasion, and then turn to the normative question of how public policy should deal with it.

Positive Analysis of Tax Evasion.   Assume Al cares only about maximizing his expected income. He has a given amount of earnings and is trying to choose R, the amount that he hides from the tax authorities. Suppose Al's marginal income tax rate is 0.3; for each dollar shielded from taxable income, his tax bill falls by 30 cents. This is the marginal benefit to him of hiding a dollar of income from the tax authorities. More generally, when Al faces a marginal income tax rate t, the marginal benefit of each dollar concealed is t.

The tax authority does not know Al's true income, but it randomly audits all taxpayers' returns. As a result, there is some probability, ρ, that Al will be audited. (In the United States, only about 0.49 percent of federal income tax returns are audited.) If he is caught cheating, Al pays a penalty that increases with R at an increasing rate. Note that if it were costless to monitor Al every second of every day, opportunities for evasion would not exist. The fact that such monitoring is infeasible is the fundamental source of the problem.

Assuming that Al knows the value of ρ and the penalty schedule, he makes his decision by comparing the marginal costs and benefits of cheating. In Figure 14.5, the amount of income not reported is measured on the horizontal axis, and dollars on the vertical. The marginal benefit (*MB*) for each dollar not reported is t, the amount of tax saved. The expected marginal cost (*MC*) is the amount by which the penalty goes up for each dollar of cheating (the marginal penalty) times the probability of detection. For example, if the additional penalty for hiding the thousandth dollar is $1.50 and the probability of detection is 1 in 3, then the *expected* marginal penalty is 50 cents. The "optimal" amount of cheating is where the two schedules cross, at R^*. R^* is optimal in the sense that *on average* it is the policy that

FIGURE 14.5

Tax evasion is
positive

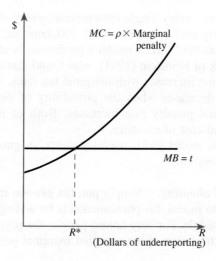

FIGURE 14.6

Tax evasion is zero

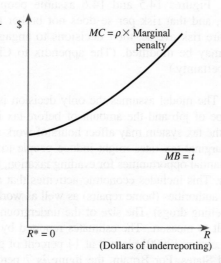

maximizes Al's income. In a world of uncertainty, finding the best policy in this "expected value" sense is a reasonable way to proceed. It is possible, of course, that not cheating at all will be optimal. For the individual in Figure 14.6, the marginal cost of cheating exceeds the marginal benefit for all positive values of R, so the optimum is equal to zero.

The model predicts that cheating increases when marginal tax rates go up. This is because a higher value of t increases the marginal benefit of evasion, shifting up the marginal benefit schedule so the intersection with marginal cost occurs at a higher value of R. This prediction is consistent with anecdotal evidence. Consider, for example, the Russian politician Alexander Lebed's description of the situation in his country: "The Russian tax policy is making everyone, every single entrepreneur, every single businessman, a criminal. On every ruble earned, out of 100 kopecks, if you're lucky you pay 92 kopecks as tax."[10] The model's prediction is also borne out by the econometric work of Feinstein [1991], who found that the amount of under-reporting of income increases with marginal tax rates. A further implication is that cheating decreases when the probability of detection goes up and when the marginal penalty rate increases. Both of these steps raise the expected marginal cost of cheating.

Although this model yields useful insights, it ignores some potentially important considerations.

Psychic costs of cheating.   Simply put, tax evasion may make people feel guilty. One way to model this phenomenon is by adding psychic costs to the marginal cost schedule. For very honest people, the psychic costs are so high they would not cheat even if the expected marginal penalty were zero.

Risk aversion.   Figures 14.5 and 14.6 assume people care only about expected income, and that risk per se does not bother them. To the extent that individuals are risk averse, their decisions to engage in what is essentially a gamble may be modified. (The appendix to Chapter 11 discusses choice under uncertainty.)

Work choices.   The model assumes the only decision is how much income to report. The type of job and the amount of before-tax income are taken as given. In reality, the tax system may affect hours of work and job choices. For example, high marginal tax rates might induce people to choose occupations that provide substantial opportunities for evading taxation, the so-called **underground economy.** This includes economic activities that are legal but easy to hide from the tax authorities (home repairs) as well as work that is criminal per se (prostitution, selling drugs). The size of the underground economy is inherently very difficult to measure. The estimates reported by Friedman, Johnson, Kaufmann, and Lobaton [2000] place it at 14 percent of gross domestic product in the United States. For Britain, the figure is 7 percent, and for Russia 42 percent. One of the few econometric analyses of an underground economy is a study by Fortin, Lemieux, and Frechette [1994] of data from a random survey carried out in the region of Quebec City, Canada. They found that when marginal tax rates increase, so does the probability of participating in the underground sector. This finding is consistent with journalistic reports of what transpired in New York City after cigarette taxes there raised the price per pack to about $7.50. The tax increase fueled a thriving black market in low-tax cigarettes from other states, and the sellers included not only veteran black marketers, "but also amateurs seeking extra income" [Fairclough, 2002, p. B1].

[10] *Wall Street Journal,* November 20, 1996.

Changing probabilities of audit.   In our simple analysis, the probability of an audit is independent of both the amount evaded and the size of income reported. However, in the United States, audit probabilities depend on occupation and the size of reported income. This complicates the model but does not change its essential aspects.

Clearly, cheating is a more complicated phenomenon than Figures 14.5 and 14.6 suggest. Nevertheless, the model provides us with a useful framework for thinking about the factors that influence evasion decisions. As already suggested, it is difficult to do empirical work on tax evasion. Consequently, it is not known whether high fines or frequent audits are more effective ways of deterring cheating. One tentative result that emerges from several econometric studies is that for most groups a heightened threat of audit increases reported income, but the magnitude of the effect is small [Blumenthal, Christian, and Slemrod, 1998].

Normative Analysis of Tax Evasion.   Most public discussions of the underground economy assume that it is a bad thing and that policy should be designed to reduce its size. Although possibly correct, this proposition is worth scrutiny.

An important question in this context is whether or not we care about the welfare of tax evaders. In the jargon of welfare economics, do the utilities of participants in the underground economy belong in the social welfare function? Assume for the moment that they do. Then under certain conditions, the existence of an underground economy raises social welfare. For example, if the supply of labor is more elastic to the underground economy than to the regular economy, optimal tax theory suggests that the former be taxed at a relatively low rate. This is simply an application of the inverse elasticity rule, Equation (14.9). Alternatively, suppose that participants in the underground economy tend to be poorer than those in the regular economy. In fact, many observers believe that the underground economy is a crucial part of life in American inner cities [Templin, 1995]. To the extent society has egalitarian income redistribution objectives, leaving the underground economy intact might be desirable.

Consider now the policy implications when evaders are given no weight in the social welfare function, and the goal is simply to eliminate cheating at the lowest administrative cost possible. Figure 14.5 suggests a straightforward way to accomplish this objective. The expected marginal cost of cheating is the product of the penalty rate and the probability of detection. The probability of detection depends on the amount of resources devoted to tax administration; if the Internal Revenue Service has a big budget, it can catch a lot of cheaters. However, even if the tax authorities have a small budget so that the probability of detection is low, the marginal cost of cheating can still be made arbitrarily high if the penalty is large enough. If only one tax evader were caught each year, but he or she were publicly hanged for the crime, the *expected* cost of tax evasion would deter many people. The fact that such a draconian policy has never been seriously proposed in the United States indicates that existing penalty systems try to incorporate *just retribution*. Contrary to the assumptions of the utilitarian framework, society cares not only about the end result (getting rid of cheaters) but also the processes by which the result is achieved.

Overview

Traditional analysis of tax systems elucidated several "principles" of tax design: taxes should have horizontal and vertical equity, be "neutral" with respect to economic incentives, be administratively easy, and so on. Public finance economists have now integrated these somewhat ad hoc guidelines with the principles of welfare economics. The optimal tax literature *derives* the criteria for a good tax using an underlying social welfare function.

On some occasions, optimal tax analysis has corrected previous errors. For example, it may *not* be efficient for all tax rates to be the same (neutral). Furthermore, optimal tax theory has clarified the trade-offs between efficiency and equity in tax design. As a by-product, the various definitions of "equity" have been scrutinized.

The result of this work is not a blueprint for building a tax system, if for no other reason than the economic theory forming the basis for optimal tax theory has its own problems (see Chapter 3). In this context two comments are cogent: (1) Optimal tax theory generally ignores political and social institutions. An "optimal" tax may easily be ruined by politicians or be overly costly to administer. (2) While the optimal tax approach indicates that the concept of horizontal equity is difficult to make operational, the fact remains that *equal treatment of equals* is an appealing ethical concept. Horizontal equity is difficult to integrate with optimal tax theory because of the latter's focus on outcomes rather than processes.

Thus, optimal tax theory has used the tools of welfare economics to add analytical strength to the traditional discussion of tax design. Nevertheless, it is wedded to the utilitarian welfare approach in economics. As such, it is open to criticisms concerning the adequacy of this ethical system.

Summary

- Efficient commodity tax theory shows how to raise a given amount of revenue with a minimum of excess burden.
- The Ramsey rule stipulates that to minimize excess burden, tax rates should be set so that the proportional reduction in the quantity demanded of each good is the same.

- When goods are unrelated in consumption, the Ramsey rule implies that relative tax rates should be inversely related to compensated demand elasticities.
- Choosing optimal user fees for government-produced services is quite similar to choosing optimal taxes.

- Income taxation is a major source of revenue in developed countries. Edgeworth's early study of optimal income taxes indicated that after-tax incomes should be equal. However, when the excess burden of distorting the leisure-income trade-off is included, marginal tax rates of far less than 100 percent are optimal.

- Tax systems may be evaluated by standards other than those of optimal tax theory. Horizontal equity, the costs of administration, incentives for tax evasion, and political constraints all affect the design of tax systems.

- Traditional definitions of horizontal equity rely on income as a measure of "equal position" in

society. However, income as conventionally measured is inadequate in this context. The utility definition is more precise, but has radically different policy implications and contains an inherent bias toward the pretax status quo. Other definitions of horizontal equity focus on the rules by which taxes are chosen.

- The costs of running a tax system are ignored in most theoretical analyses. However, administrative and compliance costs affect the choice of tax base, tax rates, and the amount of tax evasion.

Discussion Questions

1. According to estimates by Goolsbee and Petrin [2001], the elasticity of demand for basic cable service is -0.51, and the elasticity of demand for direct broadcast satellites is -7.40. Suppose that a community wants to raise a given amount of revenue by taxing cable service and the use of direct broadcast satellites. If the community's goal is to raise the money as efficiently as possible, what should be the ratio of the cable tax to the satellite tax? Discuss briefly the assumptions behind your calculation.

2. In 2002, the US federal government levied a tax of 3 percent on that part of a car's price exceeding $40,000. (For example, the tax liability on a $50,000 car would be $0.03 \times (\$50,000 - \$40,000)$, or $300.) Discuss the efficiency, equity, and administrability of this "luxury car tax."

3. "Peter the Great at one time levied a tax upon beards. He held that the beard was a superfluous and useless ornament. The tax is said to have been proportional according to the length of the beard and progressive according to the social position of its possessor" [Groves, 1946, p. 51]. Evaluate Peter's beard tax from the standpoint of optimal tax theory and from the standpoint of horizontal equity.

4. In recent years, farmers in China have been protesting their tax treatment by the government.

They have many complaints, including a fee that "is collected for production of 'special products' like nuts, even when none are grown" [Eckholm, 1999, p. A10]. Evaluate this nut tax from the viewpoints of both optimal tax theory and horizontal equity.

5. According to Fisman and Wei [2001], importers in China respond to high tariffs by evasive behavior. For example, when they are importing a commodity with a high tariff rate they may lie and claim that it is a different commodity with a lower tariff. They estimate that a 1 percent increase in the tax rate results in a 3 percent increase in evasion. Modify the model from Figure 14.5 to illustrate this phenomenon.

6. Suppose that Sharlene faces a marginal income tax rate of 36 percent, and if she cheats on her taxes, there is a 2 percent chance that she will be caught. Use the logic surrounding Figure 14.5 to compute the smallest fine that will induce Sharlene not to cheat.

7. Real estate magnate Donald Trump once proposed a one-time tax of 14.25 percent on the net wealth of every American with more than $10 million. Would this be an efficient way to raise tax revenue? Include in your answer the concept of the "time inconsistency of optimal policy."

8. Indicate whether each of the following statements is true, false, or uncertain, and explain why:

   a. A proportional tax on all commodities including leisure is equivalent to a lump-sum tax.

   b. Efficiency is maximized when all commodities are taxed at the same rate.

   c. Average cost pricing for a natural monopoly allows the enterprise to break even, but the outcome is inefficient.

   d. Tom's workplace provides free access to a fitness room; Jerry's does not. Horizontal equity requires that Tom be taxed on the value of having access to the fitness room.

Selected References

Holcombe, Randall G. "The Ramsey Rule Reconsidered." *Public Finance Review* 30 (November 2002), pp. 562–78.

Slemrod, Joel, and Shlomo Yitzhaki. "Tax Avoidance, Evasion, and Administration." In *Handbook of Public Economics, Volume 3,* ed. Alan J. Auerbach and Martin Feldstein. New York: Elsevier Science B.V., 2002, pp.1425–70.

Stern, Nicholas. "The Theory of Optimal Commodity and Income Taxation: An Introduction." In *The Theory of Taxation for Developing Countries,* ed. David Newbery and Nicholas Stern. New York: Oxford University Press, 1987, pp. 22–59.

PART 4

The United States Revenue System

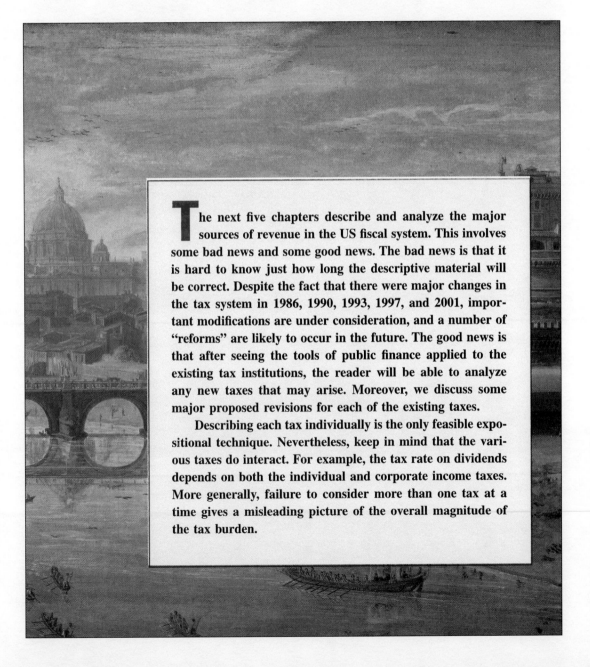

The next five chapters describe and analyze the major sources of revenue in the US fiscal system. This involves some bad news and some good news. The bad news is that it is hard to know just how long the descriptive material will be correct. Despite the fact that there were major changes in the tax system in 1986, 1990, 1993, 1997, and 2001, important modifications are under consideration, and a number of "reforms" are likely to occur in the future. The good news is that after seeing the tools of public finance applied to the existing tax institutions, the reader will be able to analyze any new taxes that may arise. Moreover, we discuss some major proposed revisions for each of the existing taxes.

Describing each tax individually is the only feasible expositional technique. Nevertheless, keep in mind that the various taxes do interact. For example, the tax rate on dividends depends on both the individual and corporate income taxes. More generally, failure to consider more than one tax at a time gives a misleading picture of the overall magnitude of the tax burden.

CHAPTER 15

The Personal Income Tax

It's income tax time again, Americans: time to gather up those receipts, get out those tax forms, sharpen up that pencil, and stab yourself in the aorta.

DAVE BARRY

Several years ago, the chairman of the House Ways and Means Committee, Bill Archer, declared that he wanted to "pull the current income tax code out by its roots and throw it away so it can never grow back." The personal income tax that so vexed Representative Archer (and millions of other Americans) is the workhorse of the federal revenue system. In 2002, almost 130 million tax returns were filed, which generated $858 billion in revenue, about 46 percent of federal revenues.[1] This chapter discusses problems associated with designing a personal income tax system, the efficiency and equity of the US system, and why so many people want to replace it.

Since its inception in 1913, the income tax code has been revised many times. Our discussion devotes special attention to explaining and evaluating the changes that have been made in recent years.

Basic Structure

Americans file an annual tax return that computes their previous year's tax liability. The return is due every April 15. The calculation of tax liability requires a series of steps summarized in Figure 15.1. The first step is to compute **adjusted gross income (AGI),** defined as total income from all taxable sources less certain expenses incurred in earning that income. Taxable

---

[1] Computed from Congressional Budget Office [2003].

FIGURE 15.1

Computation of federal personal income tax liability

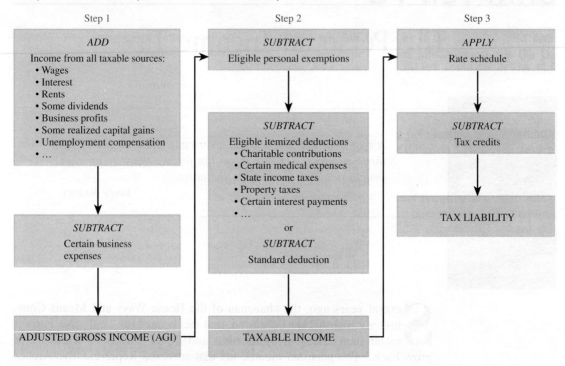

sources include (but are not limited to) wages, dividends, interest, business and farm profits, rents, royalties, prizes, and even the proceeds from embezzlement.

Not all of AGI is taxed. The second step is to convert AGI to **taxable income**—the amount of income subject to tax. This is done by subtracting various amounts called **exemptions** and **deductions** from AGI. Deductions and exemptions are discussed more carefully later.

The final step is to calculate the amount of tax due. A **rate schedule** indicates the tax liability associated with each level of taxable income. Different types of taxpayers face different rate schedules. For example, husbands and wives who file tax returns together—joint returns—have different rates than single people.

For most taxpayers, some tax is withheld out of each paycheck during the year. The amount they actually pay on April 15 is the difference between the tax liability and the accumulated withholding payments. If more has been withheld than is owed, the taxpayer receives a refund.

It sounds pretty straightforward, but in reality, complications arise in every step of the process. We now discuss some of the major problems. If you are interested in the excruciating details of the law, an online searchable version of the tax code is available at http://www.fourmilab.ch/ustax/ustax.html.

Defining Income

Clearly, the ability to identify "income" is necessary to operate an income tax. A natural way to begin this section would be to discuss and evaluate the tax code's definition of income. However, the law provides no definition. The constitutional amendment that introduced the tax merely says, "The Congress shall have power to lay and collect taxes on incomes, from whatever source derived." While the tax law does provide examples of income—wages and salaries, rents, dividends, and so on—the words "from whatever source derived" do not really provide a useful standard for deciding whether or not the exclusion of certain items from taxation is appropriate.

Public finance economists have their own traditional standard, the so-called **Haig-Simons (H-S) definition:** Income is the money value of the net increase in an individual's power to consume during a period.[2] This equals the amount actually consumed during the period plus net additions to wealth. Net additions to wealth—saving—must be included in income because they represent an increase in *potential* consumption.

Importantly, the H-S criterion requires the inclusion of *all* sources of potential increases in consumption, regardless of whether the actual consumption takes place, and regardless of the form in which the consumption occurs. The H-S criterion also implies that any decreases in an individual's potential to consume should be subtracted in determining income. An example is expenses that are incurred to earn income. If the gross revenues from Juliet's cigar store are $100,000, but business expenses (such as rent and the cost of the cigars) are $95,000, then Juliet's potential consumption has only increased by $5,000.

Items Included in H-S Income

The H-S definition encompasses those items ordinarily thought of as income: wages and salaries, business profits, rents, royalties, dividends, and interest. However, it also includes certain unconventional items:

Employer Pension Contributions and Insurance Purchases. Pension contributions, even though not made directly to the recipient, represent an increase in the potential to consume. In the same way, even if compensation is paid to an employee in the form of a certain commodity (such as an insurance policy) instead of cash, it is still income.

Transfer Payments, Including Social Security Retirement Benefits, Unemployment Compensation, and Welfare. Any receipt, be it from the government or an employer, is income.

---

[2] Named after Robert M. Haig and Henry C. Simons, economists who wrote in the first half of the 20th century.

Capital Gains.   Increases in the value of an asset are referred to as **capital gains,** decreases as **capital losses.** Suppose Brutus owns some shares of Microsoft stock that increase in value from $10,000 to $12,500 over the course of a year. Then he has enjoyed a capital gain of $2,500. This $2,500 represents an increase in potential consumption, and hence, belongs in income.[3] If Brutus sells the Microsoft stock at the end of the year, the capital gain is said to be **realized;** otherwise it is **unrealized.** From the H-S point of view, it is absolutely irrelevant whether a capital gain is realized or unrealized. It represents potential to consume and, hence, is income. If Brutus does not sell his Microsoft stock, in effect he chooses to save by reinvesting the capital gain in Microsoft. Because the H-S criterion does not distinguish between different uses of income, the fact that Brutus happens to reinvest is irrelevant. All the arguments for adding in capital gains apply to subtracting capital losses. If Casca's Disney stock decreases in value by $4,200 during a given year, this $4,200 should be subtracted from other sources of income.

Income in Kind.   Some people receive part or all of their incomes in kind—in the form of goods and services rather than cash. For example, in addition to his salary, former General Electric executive Jack Welsh received floor-level seats to the New York Knicks, courtside seats at the US Open, access to a Manhattan apartment, and satellite TV at his four homes, among other things. Less exotically, farmers provide field hands with food; corporations give employees subsidized lunches or access to company fitness centers. One important form of income in kind is the annual rental value of owner-occupied homes. A homeowner receives a stream of services from a dwelling. The net monetary value of these services—**imputed rent**—is equal to the rental payments that would have been received had the owner chosen to rent the house out, after subtracting maintenance expenses, taxes, and so on.

In all these cases, from the H-S point of view, it makes no difference whether benefits are received in monetary form or in the form of goods and services. They are all income.

Some Practical and Conceptual Problems

A number of difficulties arise in attempts to use the Haig-Simons criterion as a basis for constructing a tax system.

- Clearly, only income *net of business expenses* increases potential consumption power. But distinguishing between consumption expenditures and costs of obtaining income can be hard. If Calpurnia buys a desk to use while working at home, but the desk is also a beautiful piece of furniture, to what extent is the desk a business expense? What portion of a "three-martini lunch" designed to woo a

---

[3] Only the real value of capital gains constitutes income, not gains due merely to inflation. This issue is discussed later.

client is consumption and what portion is business? (According to current law, the answer to the latter question is 50 percent is consumption. Fifty percent of business meal expenses are deductible.)

■ Capital gains and losses may be very difficult to measure, particularly when they are unrealized. For assets that are traded in active markets, the problem is fairly manageable. Even if Brutus does not sell his Microsoft shares, it is easy to determine their value at any time by consulting the financial section of the newspaper. It is not nearly as simple to measure the capital gain on a piece of art that has appreciated in value.

■ Imputed income from durables also presents measurement difficulties. For example, it may be hard to estimate the market rent of a particular owner-occupied dwelling. Similarly, measuring the imputed rental streams generated by other durables such as utility vehicles, compact disk players, and motor boats is not feasible.

■ In-kind services are not easy to value. One important example is the income produced by people who do housework rather than participate in the market. These services—housecleaning, cooking, child care, and so forth—are clearly valuable. However, even though markets exist for purchasing these services, it would be difficult to estimate whether a given homemaker's services were equal to the market value.

Evaluating the H-S Criterion

We could list numerous other difficulties involved in implementing the H-S criterion, but the main point is clear. No definition of income can make the administration of an income tax simple and straightforward. Arbitrary decisions about what should be included in income are inevitable. Nevertheless, the Haig-Simons criterion is often regarded as an ideal toward which policymakers should strive: Income should be defined as broadly as is feasible, and all sources of income received by a particular person should be taxed at the same rate.

Why is the H-S criterion so attractive? There are two reasons:

Fairness.   Recall the traditional definition of horizontal equity from Chapter 14—people with equal incomes should pay equal taxes. For this dictum to make any sense, the tax base must include *all* sources of income. Otherwise, two people with identical abilities to pay could end up with different tax liabilities.

On the other hand, one can argue that as long as people's abilities to earn income differ, the H-S criterion cannot produce fair outcomes. Suppose that Popeye is endowed with a lot of brains, and Bluto with a lot of brawn. Suppose further that the work done by brawny people is less pleasant than that available to brainy individuals. In that case, if Bluto and Popeye have the same *income,* then Popeye has more *utility.* Is it fair to tax them as equals?

Efficiency. Defenders of the criterion argue that it has the virtue of *neutrality*—it treats all forms of income the same, and hence, does not distort the pattern of economic activity. Thus, for example, it is argued that the failure to tax imputed rent from owner-occupied housing leads to excessive investment in housing, other things being the same.

It is doubtless true that many departures from the Haig-Simons criterion create inefficiencies. But it does *not* follow that equal tax rates on all income, regardless of source, would be most efficient. Consider income from rent on unimproved land. The supply of such land is perfectly inelastic, and hence, no excess burden would be created by taxing it at a very high rate.[4] An efficient tax system would tax the returns to such land at higher rates than other sources of income, and *not* tax all sources at the same rate, as dictated by the H-S criterion. More generally, the optimal tax literature discussed in Chapter 14 suggests that as long as lump sum taxes are ruled out, efficiency is enhanced when relatively high tax rates are imposed on those activities with relatively inelastic supply. "Neutrality," in the sense of equal tax rates on all types of income, generally does *not* minimize excess burden.

Where does this leave us? McLure [2002] points out that we cannot be sanguine about the possibilities for using optimal tax theory as a framework for designing the tax base, noting that optimal tax rules "generally ignore the administrative difficulty of implementation, as well as the fact that a vast amount of information is required to put them into practice." It would be unwise, therefore, to abandon the Haig-Simons criterion altogether. On the other hand, there is no reason to regard the criterion as sacred. Departures from it should be considered on their merits and should not be viewed prima facie as unfair and inefficient.

Excludable Forms of Money Income

We have seen that some income sources that would be taxable according to the Haig-Simons criterion are omitted from the tax base for practical reasons. In addition, several forms of income that would be administratively relatively easy to tax are partially or altogether excluded from adjusted gross income.

Interest on State and Local Bonds

The interest earned by individuals on bonds issued by states and localities is not subject to federal tax. From the H-S point of view, this exclusion makes no sense—interest from these bonds is as much an addition to potential consumption as is any other form of income. The exclusion originally followed from the view that it would be unconstitutional for one level of government to levy taxes on the securities issued by another level of government. However, many constitutional experts now believe such taxation would be permissible.

---

[4] This fact has long been recognized. See George [1914].

In the absence of legal restrictions, the exclusion of state and local interest might be justified as a powerful tool for helping states and localities to raise revenues. If investors do not have to pay federal tax on interest from state and local bonds, they should be willing to accept a lower before-tax rate of return than they receive on taxable bonds. Suppose Caesar faces a tax rate of 30 percent on additional income, and the rate of return on taxable securities is 15 percent. Then as long as the rate of return on state and local securities exceeds 10.5 percent, Caesar prefers them to taxable securities, other things being the same.[5] More generally, if t is an individual's marginal tax rate and r is the rate of return on taxable securities, he is willing to purchase nontaxable securities as long as their return exceeds $(1 - t)r$. Hence, state and local governments can borrow funds at rates lower than those prevailing on the market. In effect, the revenue forgone by the Treasury subsidizes borrowing by states and localities.

Unfortunately, tax-exempt bonds are an expensive way to help state and local governments. To see why, assume there are two taxpayers, Caesar, who faces a 30 percent tax rate on additional income, and Brutus, who faces a 15 percent rate. If the market rate of return on taxable bonds is 15 percent, Caesar's after-tax return is 10.5 percent and Brutus's is 12.75 percent. To induce *both* Caesar and Brutus to buy something other than taxable bonds, the net rate of return must therefore be at least 12.75 percent. Suppose a town issues tax-exempt bonds yielding just slightly more than 12.75 percent, and both Caesar and Brutus purchase the bonds. Some of the tax break is "wasted" on Caesar—he would have been willing to buy the bond at any yield greater than 10.5 percent, yet he receives 12.75 percent.

What is the net effect on government revenues? Suppose that the town borrows $100 from Brutus at the interest rate of 12.75 percent instead of the market rate of 15 percent. This saves the town $2.25 in interest payments. On the other hand, the US Treasury loses $2.25 (= .15 × $15) in income tax revenue. In effect, the Treasury has provided a $2.25 subsidy to the town. Now, if the town borrows $100 from Caesar it still saves only $2.25. But the Treasury loses $4.50 (= .30 × $15) in tax revenues. Thus, about $2.25 of the tax break is not translated into a gain for the town.

In short, the net effect of tax-exempt bonds is zero only for those investors who are just on the margin of choosing tax-exempt versus taxable securities. For all others, the subsidy to the state and local borrower is outweighed by the revenue lost at the federal level.

Why not eliminate the interest exclusion and subsidize states and localities with direct grants from the federal government? The main reason is political. A direct subsidy to states and localities would be just another item in the federal budget, an item whose existence might be jeopardized by the

---

[5] In particular, it is assumed the two types of securities are perceived as being equally risky. The demand for assets whose risks differ is discussed in the next chapter.

vagaries of the political climate. Indeed, if the subsidy were made explicit, rather than buried in the tax law, voters might decide it was not worthwhile. Hence, state and local officials have lobbied intensively—and successfully—to maintain this exclusion.

Some Dividends

Under legislation passed in 2003, dividend income is not taxed at the same rate as ordinary income. Rather, it is taxed at a maximal rate of 15 percent. To see the justification for the partial exclusion, note that dividends are paid by corporations, and corporations are subject to a separate tax on their incomes. Hence, in the absence of an exclusion, dividends are taxed twice, once at the individual level and once at the corporate level. The idea behind taxing dividends at a lower rate for individuals is to ameliorate this double taxation to some extent. The issues associated with dividend taxation are discussed further in Chapter 17.

Capital Gains

As we will see later in the chapter, statutory marginal tax rates on ordinary income (for example, wages and interest) go as high as 38.6 percent. Under current law, the maximum capital gains rate in 2004 is 15 percent, provided that the asset is held more than one year.[6] Capital gains on assets held less than a year are taxed as ordinary income. Capital losses—decreases in the value of an asset—can be offset against capital gains. Suppose Antony realizes a gain of $6,000 on asset A, but a loss of $2,000 on asset B. Then Antony is treated as if his capital gains are only $4,000. Moreover, capital losses in excess of capital gains (up to a limit of $3,000) can be subtracted from ordinary income. Suppose that in the example just given, asset B had lost $8,200. Then Antony could reduce his capital gains liability to zero and still have $2,200 in losses left over. He could reduce his ordinary taxable income by this amount.

In addition to the fact that capital gains are taxed at preferential rates, their treatment departs from the H-S criterion in several important ways:

Only Realizations Taxed.   Unless a capital gain is actually realized—the asset is sold—no tax is levied. In effect, the tax on a capital gain is deferred until the gain is realized. The mere ability to postpone taxes may not seem all that important, but its consequences are enormous.[7] Consider Cassius, who purchases an asset for $100,000 that increases in value by 12 percent each year. After the first year, it is worth $100,000 \times (1 + .12) = $112,000. After the second year, it is worth $112,000 \times (1 + .12) = $100,000 \times (1 + .12)^2 = $125,440. Similarly, by the end of 20 years, it is worth $100,000 \times (1 + .12)^{20} = $964,629. If the asset is sold at the end of 20 years, Cassius realizes a capital gain of $864,629 (= $964,629 − $100,000). Assume that

---

[6] Individuals in the lowest tax brackets are taxed at 5 percent on capital gains.

[7] At this point, it may be useful to review the discussion of interest compounding from Chapter 11 under "Present Value."

the tax rate applied to *realized* capital gains is 15 percent. Then Cassius' tax liability is $129,694 (= $864,629 × .15), and his net gain (measured in dollars 20 years from now) is $734,935 (= $864,629 − $129,694).

Now assume that the 15 percent capital gains tax is levied *as the capital gains accrue,* regardless of whether they are realized. At the end of the first year, Cassius has $110,200 [= $100,000 × (1 + .102)]. (Remember, $1,800 of the $12,000 gain goes to the tax collector, leaving him with only a 10.2 percent gain.) Assuming that the $10,200 after-tax gain is reinvested in the asset, at the end of two years, Cassius has $110,200 × (1 + .102) = $100,000 × (1.102)^2 = $121,440. Similarly, by the end of 20 years, he has $100,000 × (1.102)^{20} = $697,641. Cassius' after-tax capital gain is $597,641 (= $697,641 − $100,000). Comparing this to the previous amount of $734,935 makes clear that the seemingly innocent device of letting the gains accrue without tax makes a big difference. This is because the deferral allows the investment to grow geometrically at the before-tax rather than the after-tax rate of interest. In effect, the government gives the investor an interest-free loan on taxes due.

It should now be clear why a favorite slogan among tax accountants is "taxes deferred are taxes saved." Many very complicated tax shelter plans are nothing more than devices for deferring payment of taxes.

Because only realized capital gains are subject to tax, taxpayers who are considering switching or selling capital assets must take into account that doing so will create a tax liability. Consequently, they may be less likely to change their portfolios. This phenomenon is referred to as the **lock-in effect,** because the tax system tends to lock investors into their current portfolios.[8] This leads to a misallocation of capital, because it no longer flows to where its return is highest. There have been several econometric studies of the tax treatment of capital gains realizations. Most have found that cuts in capital gains tax rates would significantly increase the realization of long-term capital gains, although the magnitude of the response is controversial [see Burman, 1999].

Gains Not Realized at Death.   Capital gains are not taxed at death. Suppose Octavius purchases an asset for $1,000. During Octavius's lifetime, he never sells the asset, and when he dies, it is worth $1,200. Under US law, the $200 capital gain is not subject to the income tax when Octavius dies. Moreover, when Octavius, Jr. (Octavius's heir) gets around to selling the asset, his computation of capital gains is made as if the purchase price were $1,200, not $1,000. In effect, then, capital gains on assets held to death of the owner are never subject to the income tax. This provision is whimsically referred to as the *Angel of Death loophole.*

---

[8] While the deferral of taxes lowers the effective tax rate on capital gains, this is somewhat offset by the fact that the lock-in effect prevents investors from reallocating their portfolio optimally when economic conditions change. See Kovenock and Rothschild [1983].

Evaluation of Capital Gains Rules.   We conclude that in terms of the Haig-Simons criterion, the tax treatment of capital gains is unsatisfactory. The criterion requires that all capital gains be taxed, whether realized or unrealized. In contrast, the system generally taxes realized gains preferentially, and unrealized capital gains accrue without taxation. If the asset is held until death of the owner, capital gains escape taxation altogether. While the US tax treatment of capital gains may seem light by the standard of the H-S criterion, it is rather heavy compared to several other countries. In the Netherlands and Germany, for example, capital gains on securities are generally totally exempt from taxation.

The optimal tax literature provides no more justification for preferential treatment of capital gains than the Haig-Simons criterion.[9] However, several rationalizations have been proposed for preferential treatment of this form of capital income. Some argue that capital gains are not regular income, but rather windfalls that occur unexpectedly. Fairness requires that such unexpected gains not create a tax liability. Moreover, because investing requires the sacrifice of abstaining from consumption, it is only fair to reward this sacrifice. However, it could just as well be asserted that *labor* income should be treated preferentially, because it involves the unpleasantness of work, while those who receive capital gains need only relax and wait for their money to flow in. Ultimately, it is impossible to argue convincingly that production of one source of income or another requires more sacrifice and should therefore be treated preferentially.

Another justification for preferential taxation of capital gains is that it is needed to stimulate capital accumulation and risk taking: "To tax gains on capital investment at close to the same rate as other income reduces incentives to risk capital, reducing economic growth" [Prizer, 1997, p. A26]. In the next chapter, we deal at some length with the question of how taxation affects saving and risk-taking incentives. For now, we merely note that although there is some preliminary evidence that decreases in capital gains tax rates induce more individuals to become entreprenuers [Gompers and Lerner, 1999], it is not clear that special treatment for capital gains does increase saving and risk taking.

Some promote preferential treatment of capital gains because it helps counterbalance inflation's tendency to increase the effective tax rate on capital gains. As we see later, under existing tax rules, inflation does produce an especially heavy burden on capital income. But arbitrarily taxing capital gains at a different rate is not the best way to deal with this problem.

Finally, we stress that a full picture of the tax treatment of capital income requires taking into account that much of this income is generated by corporations, and corporations are subject to a separate tax system of

---

[9] However, under certain conditions, optimal tax theory suggests that *no* forms of capital income should be taxed. See Chapter 19 under "Personal Consumption Tax."

their own. The overall tax rate on capital income thus depends on the personal *and* corporate rates. We return to this issue in Chapter 17.

Employer Contributions to Benefit Plans

Employers' contributions to their employees' retirement funds are not subject to tax. Neither does the government tax the interest that accrues on the pension contributions over time. Only when the pension is paid out at retirement are the principal and interest subject to taxation. Similarly, employer contributions to medical insurance plans are not included in income.

As already argued, pensions and health insurance should be counted as income according to the Haig-Simons criterion. Similarly, the interest on pension funds should be taxable as it accrues. However, including such items in the tax base appears to be politically infeasible. In 1993, the press reported that the Clinton administration was considering a proposal to tax health insurance benefits. A political furor ensued, and the idea was quickly dropped.

Some Types of Saving

Under certain circumstances, people can save in a variety of tax-favored forms for their retirement or for some other specified purposes. In this section, we list and describe the main plans.

Using an **individual retirement account (IRA),** an individual without a pension at work can deposit up to $3,000 per year (scheduled to increase to $4,000 in 2005) in a *qualified account.* (A qualified account includes most of the usual forms of saving: savings accounts, money market funds, etc.) The money so deposited is deductible from adjusted gross income. In addition, single workers with pensions at work can make fully deductible contributions to IRAs if their AGIs are below $40,000 (for married couples, AGI must be below $60,000).[10] Just as in an employer-managed pension fund, the interest that accrues is untaxed. Tax is due only when the money is paid out at retirement. Penalties are imposed if money is withdrawn early, unless it is spent on certain approved items such as education expenses. In 2000, IRA contributions were $7.5 billion.

Like a conventional IRA, the **Roth IRA** (named after former Senator William Roth) permits a $3,000 per year contribution. The contribution is *not* tax deductible. However, the funds in the account accumulate tax free, and unlike the conventional IRA, there is no tax when the money is withdrawn. The phaseout for the Roth IRA begins at $95,000 for individuals and $150,000 for couples.

With a **401(k) plan,** named for the section of the Internal Revenue Code that authorizes it, an employee can earmark a portion of his or her salary each year, and no income tax liability is incurred on that portion. The limit on contributions is $13,000 in 2004.[11]

---

[10] These figures are for 2003. The beginning of the phaseout will gradually increase to $50,000 for individuals and $80,000 for couples thereafter.

[11] This figure is scheduled to rise to $15,000 in 2006.

A **Self-Employed Retirement plan** is available only to self-employed individuals. Such individuals can exclude from taxation 20 percent of their net business income up to a maximum contribution of $40,000. Again, participants are allowed the powerful advantage of tax-free accrual of interest. In 2000, $11.8 billion was contributed to these plans.

An **Education Savings Account** allows eligible families to make a $2,000 per year nondeductible contribution per child; the funds accumulate tax free, and the phaseouts are the same as for the Roth IRA. When the money is withdrawn, it can be used only to pay for qualified higher education expenses of the child.

An important reason for the existence of the various tax-favored saving options is to stimulate saving. However, it is not clear how aggregate saving is affected. People may merely shuffle around their portfolios, reducing their holdings of some assets and depositing them into retirement accounts. This is a very contentious issue in the literature, although most research favors the view that IRAs stimulate at least some new saving [Hubbard and Skinner, 1996]. In any case, it is clear that the existence of plans for the preferential treatment of retirement saving represents another departure from the H-S criterion. And it is an important departure: About 36 percent of household financial assets are now held in tax-preferred savings accounts.[12]

Even many proponents of tax-favored saving options are dismayed by the complexity associated with the existence of a variety of plans, each with its own eligibility rules, contribution limits, and so on. In 2003, the Bush administration proposed replacing all the existing plans with two new ones. One, a *Lifetime Savings Account,* would essentially be a Roth IRA with a contribution limit of $7,500 per year, but with penalty-free withdrawals at any time and no income limits. The other, an *Employee Retirement Savings Account,* would be like a conventional IRA with a $7,500 limit per year, but could only be used for retirement saving. While advocates of the Bush plan praised its relative simplicity and believed that it would enhance saving, critics argued that it would not increase saving very much, and that only relatively wealthy people would benefit. The legislative fate of the proposal is unclear at the present time.

Gifts and Inheritances

Although gifts and inheritances represent increases in the beneficiaries' potential consumption, these items are not subject to the federal income tax. Instead, separate tax systems cover gifts and estates (see Chapter 19).

Exemptions and Deductions

In terms of Figure 15.1, we have now completed the first step in the computation of income taxes, figuring adjusted gross income. Once AGI is determined, certain subtractions are made to find taxable income. The two principal subtractions are exemptions and deductions, which we discuss in turn.

---

[12] Personal communication from Eric M. Engen and William Gale.

Exemptions

A family is allowed an exemption for each of its members. The exemption—$3,050 in 2003—is adjusted annually for inflation. For example, in 2003 a husband and wife with three dependent children could claim five exemptions and subtract $15,250 from AGI. However, exemptions are phased out for people with AGIs above certain levels. For joint returns, personal exemptions are reduced by 2 percentage points for each $2,500 (or fraction thereof) by which AGI exceeds $209,250.[13] Suppose, for example, that our family of five has an AGI of $250,000. Subtracting $209,250 from $250,000, dividing the result by $2,500, and rounding up to the nearest whole number gives us 17. Hence, the family loses 34 percent (= 17 × 2 percent) of its exemptions. Because 34 percent of $15,250 is $5,185, the family can subtract only $10,065 in determining its taxable income. The phaseout is scheduled to be eliminated gradually beginning in 2006. Yes, there will be a phaseout of the phaseout.

Why are there exemptions? Some argue that they adjust ability to pay for the presence of children. Raising children involves certain nondiscretionary expenses, and taxable income should be adjusted accordingly. However, as most parents can tell you, if the exemption is really there to compensate for the expenses of child rearing, $3,050 is much too little. Moreover, it is not clear why expenses involving children should be considered nondiscretionary in the first place. Given the wide availability of contraceptive methods, many would argue that raising children is the result of conscious choice. If one couple wishes to spend its money on European vacations while another chooses to raise a family, why should the tax system reward the latter?[14] On the other hand, certain people's religions rule out effective birth-control methods, and for them, children are not a *choice* as the term is conventionally defined.

Exemptions can also be viewed as a method of providing tax relief for low-income families. The higher the exemption, the greater adjusted gross income must be before *any* income tax is due. Consider a family of four with an AGI of $12,200 or less. When this family's $12,200 in exemptions is subtracted from AGI, the family is left with zero taxable income, and hence, no income tax liability. More generally, the greater the exemption level, the greater is the progressivity with respect to average tax rates. This effect is reinforced when exemptions are phased out for high-income families.

Deductions

The other subtraction allowed from AGI is a deduction. There are two kinds: **Itemized deductions** are subtractions for specific expenditures cited in the law. The taxpayer must list each item separately on the tax return and be able to prove (at least in principle) that the expenditures have been made. In lieu of itemizing deductions, the taxpayer can take a **standard deduction,**

---

[13] For singles, the beginning of the phaseout range is $139,500. The beginnings for the phaseouts are adjusted annually for inflation.

[14] If there are positive externalities involved in raising children, then a subsidy might be appropriate (see Chapter 5).

which is a fixed amount that requires no documentation. Taxpayers can choose whichever deduction minimizes their tax liability.

Deductibility and Relative Prices.   Before cataloging itemizable expenditures, let us consider the relationship between deductibility of expenditures on an item and its relative price. Suppose that expenditures on commodity Z are tax deductible. The price of Z is $10 per unit. Suppose further that Cleopatra's marginal tax rate is 30 percent. Then, whenever Cleopatra purchases a unit of Z, it only costs her $7.00. Why? Because expenditures on Z are deductible, purchasing a unit lowers Cleopatra's taxable income by $10. Given a 30 percent marginal tax rate, $10 less of taxable income saves Cleopatra $3.00 in taxes. Hence, her effective price of a unit Z is $10 minus $3.00, or $7.00.

More generally, if the price of Z is P_Z and the individual's marginal tax rate is t, allowing deduction of expenses on Z lowers Z's effective price from P_Z to $(1 - t)P_Z$. This analysis brings out two important facts:

- Because deductibility changes the relative price of the commodity involved, in general, we expect the quantity demanded to change.
- The higher the individual's value of t, the greater the value to her of a given dollar amount of deductions and the lower the effective price of the good.[15]

Itemized Deductions.   We now discuss some of the major itemized deductions. The list is far from inclusive; consult any tax guide for further details.

Unreimbursed medical expenses that exceed 7.5 percent of AGI.   The justification is that large medical expenses are nondiscretionary and therefore do not really contribute to an individual's ability to pay. It is hard to say to what extent health care expenditures are under an individual's control. A person suffering a heart attack does not have much in the way of choice. On the other hand, individuals can choose how often to visit their doctors and whether or not to have elective surgery. Moreover, individuals can substitute preventive health care (good diet, exercise, etc.) for formal medical services.

Finally, most people can insure themselves against large medical expenditures (see Chapter 10). Under some insurance plans, the first portion of medical expenses is met entirely by the insured, but after a point, some proportion is paid by the insurance company and the rest by the individual. In effect, by allowing deduction of some medical expenses, the tax system provides a kind of social health care insurance. The terms of this "policy" are

---

[15] Note that these observations apply more generally to expenditures on any items that are excluded from the tax base, not just deductions. For example, the value of excluding interest from municipal bonds increases with the marginal tax rate, other things being the same. So do the values of fringe benefits such as employer-provided health insurance.

that the amount the individual pays entirely on his or her own is 7.5 percent of AGI, and after that the Treasury pays a share equal to the marginal tax rate. The pros and cons of providing social health insurance were discussed in Chapter 10.

State and local income and property taxes.   Under current law, state and local income and property taxes are deductible. In 2000, these deductions amounted to $290 billion. State and local sales taxes are *not* deductible.

Those who support deductibility argue that state and local taxes represent nondiscretionary decreases in ability to pay. An alternative view is that they are simply user fees. A person pays state and local taxes in return for benefits such as public schools, police protection, and so forth. Some people choose to live in jurisdictions that provide a lot of such services, and they pay relatively high amounts of tax; others opt for low-service, low-tax jurisdictions. To the extent this description is accurate, there is no particular reason to allow deductibility of state and local taxes.

On the other hand, if state and local taxes are not user fees, it may be appropriate to regard them as decreases in ability to pay.[16] Unfortunately, it is very difficult to determine what proportion of state and local taxes are user fees for public services.

This deduction can also be considered a way to help state and local governments finance themselves. For people who itemize on their federal tax returns, the deduction lowers the effective cost of state and local tax payments. This may increase political support for tax increases at the state and local levels. Why isn't a more direct method of subsidy used? As was true for the interest exemption for state and local bonds, political considerations are an important part of the explanation. A subsidy hidden in the tax code may be easier to maintain than an explicit subsidy.

Certain interest expenses.   Some payments of interest are deductible and others not:

- Interest paid on consumer debt such as credit card charges and car loans is *not* deductible.
- Certain individuals who have paid interest on qualified education loans may deduct up to $2,500 for such interest expenses.[17] This deduction is available even to taxpayers who do not itemize.
- Deductions for interest on debt incurred to purchase financial assets cannot exceed the amount of income from these assets. Suppose, for example, that your investment income was $10,000, but the

---

[16] But not necessarily! If the taxes are capitalized into the value of property, the current owners may not be bearing any of their burden. See Chapter 12.

[17] The deduction is phased out starting at AGI of $100,000 for couples.

associated interest expenses were $25,000. All you can deduct on your tax return is $10,000. The remaining $15,000 cannot be used to shelter other sources of income from taxation.

■ Interest on home mortgages is subject to special treatment. Mortgage interest for the purchase of up to two residences is deductible, up to a limit of the interest on a $1 million purchase or improvement. Also deductible is interest on a *home equity loan*—a loan for which the home serves as collateral and whose proceeds can be used to finance any purchase (except securities that generate tax-free income). For example, one can obtain a home equity loan and use the money to buy a car. In effect, then, the law allows homeowners to deduct interest on consumer loans, but denies this privilege to renters. There is, in fact, evidence that some consumers shuffle consumer debt into mortgage debt to take advantage of this provision [Maki, 2001]. However, deductible interest on home equity loans is limited to the interest on $100,000 of debt.

Do these rules make sense in terms of the Haig-Simons criterion? For a business investment, it is pretty clear that interest should be deductible. It is a cost of doing business, and hence should not be subject to income tax. There is more controversy with respect to consumer interest. Some argue that it is perfectly appropriate to deduct consumer interest payments because they represent decreases in an individual's potential consumption. Others argue that interest on consumer loans should be regarded merely as a higher price one pays to obtain a commodity sooner than would otherwise be possible. Whatever view is taken, it is hard to justify a system that makes the opportunity to deduct consumer interest depend arbitrarily on one's status as a homeowner.

Tax arbitrage.   The deductibility of interest together with the exemption of certain types of capital income from taxation can lead to lucrative opportunities for smart investors. Assume that Caesar, who has a 30 percent tax rate, can borrow all the money he wants from the bank at a rate of 15 percent. Assuming that Caesar satisfies the criteria for deductibility of interest, for every dollar of interest paid, his tax bill is reduced by 30 cents. Hence, Caesar's effective borrowing rate is only 10.5 percent. Suppose that the going rate of return on tax-exempt state and local bonds is 11 percent. Then Caesar can borrow from the bank at an effective rate of 10.5 percent and lend to states and localities at 11 percent. The tax system appears to have created a "money machine" that can be cranked to generate infinite amounts of income. The process of taking advantage of such opportunities is referred to as *tax arbitrage*.

This example overstates the potential returns to tax arbitrage, because in real-world capital markets, people cannot borrow arbitrarily large sums of money. Moreover, there is a tendency for competition among those who engage in tax arbitrage to reduce the return to that activity. For example, as more and more arbitrageurs buy municipal bonds, their rate of return goes down. If everyone had a 30 percent marginal tax rate, in equilibrium we would expect the return on municipals to fall until it was exactly 70 percent of the rate on taxable bonds. At that point, there would be no net advantage to owning municipals. Still, some opportunities for gain are present. The tax authorities realized this many years ago and made it illegal to deduct interest from loans whose proceeds are used to purchase tax-exempt bonds. But it is not easy to prove that someone is breaking this rule. Given that money can be used for many different purposes, how can it be proved that a given loan was "for" municipal bond purchases rather than for some other purpose? This very simple scam illustrates some important general lessons:

- Interest deductibility in conjunction with preferential treatment of certain capital income can create major money-making opportunities. This is one reason why countries such as Canada do not allow the deductibility of mortgage interest.

- High-income individuals are particularly likely to benefit from these opportunities. This is because they tend to face relatively high tax rates and to have good access to borrowing.

- The tax authorities can certainly declare various tax arbitrage schemes to be illegal, but it is hard to enforce these rules. Moreover, clever lawyers and accountants are always on the lookout for new tax arbitrage opportunities. The Internal Revenue Service is usually right behind them trying to plug the loopholes. In the process, many inefficient investments are made, and a lot of resources are spent on tax avoidance and tax administration.

Charitable contributions.   Individuals can deduct the value of contributions made to religious, charitable, educational, scientific, or literary organizations. Gifts of property are deductible, but personal services are not. In most cases, total charitable deductions cannot exceed 50 percent of adjusted gross income. In 2000, individuals recorded charitable deductions of $134 billion.

Some argue that charitable donations constitute a reduction in taxable capacity and, hence, should be excluded from taxable income. However, as long as the contributions are voluntary, this argument is unconvincing. If people don't receive as much satisfaction from charity as from their own consumption, why make the donations in the first place? Probably the best way to understand the presence of the deduction is as an attempt by the government to encourage charitable giving.

Has the deduction succeeded in doing so? The deductibility provision changes an individual's "price" for a dollar's worth of charity from $1 to $(1 - t)$, where t is the taxpayer's marginal tax rate. The effectiveness of the deduction in encouraging giving therefore depends on the price elasticity of demand for charitable contributions. If the price elasticity is zero, charitable giving is unaffected. The deduction is just a bonus for those who would give anyway. If the price elasticity exceeds zero, then giving is encouraged.

Many econometric studies have estimated the elasticity of charitable giving with respect to its after-tax price. Typically, a regression is estimated in which the dependent variable is the amount of charitable donations, and the explanatory variables are: (1) the "price" of charitable donations (one minus the marginal tax rate); (2) income; and (3) personal characteristics of individuals that might influence their decisions to give, such as age and marital status. Recent studies suggest that the price elasticity of demand for donations is less than one, perhaps around 0.5 [Greene and McClelland, 2001]. If correct, this figure suggests that the deduction has a substantial effect on giving. Consider an individual with a marginal tax rate of 30 percent. The deductibility of charitable donations lowers the price of giving from $1 to 70 cents, a reduction of 30 percent. With an elasticity of 0.5, this increases charitable donations by 15 percent. Note, however, that with an elasticity less than one, the amount that giving increases is less than the revenue that the Treasury loses.

The deduction is controversial apart from its effectiveness in stimulating donations. Whether the government should be subsidizing gifts to private charities can be questioned. Opponents argue that allowing deduction of contributions to churches and synagogues constitutes a violation of the principle of separation of church and state. On the other hand, proponents believe that in the absence of the deduction, many institutions now funded privately would be forced to scale back their activities or close. The current decentralized system stimulates a variety of activities and, hence, promotes the goal of a pluralistic society.

Deductions and Complexity.   Every deduction requires rules to determine which expenditures qualify and which do not. Designing such rules is difficult, even for such apparently straightforward deductions as medical expenditures. Consider the case of a severely obese woman who lost more than 100 pounds and developed "a mass of loose-hanging skin which spanned the width of her abdomen and spilled over onto her upper thighs." She had surgery to correct the problem and deducted the expense. The Internal Revenue Service disallowed the deduction, saying that it was cosmetic. But the Tax Court ruled for the woman, saying that the sagging skin was an aftereffect of the disease [Herman, 2002, p. A1]. Issues also arise in determining allowable charitable deductions. Donations to fraternities and sororities are not deductible. Donations to universities are deductible. What's the proper treatment of a gift to a university that is to be used for constructing a facility for holding sorority meetings? (Under current law, it is deductible.)

The fact that itemized deductions increase complexity does not necessarily mean that they are a bad thing. However, complexity is a factor that needs to be taken into account when assessing the costs and benefits of any particular deduction.

Deductions versus Credits.   As already noted, the higher an individual's marginal tax rate, the greater the value of a deduction of a given dollar amount. In contrast, a **tax credit** is a subtraction from tax liability (*not* taxable income), and hence, its value is independent of the individual's marginal tax rate. A tax credit of $100 reduces tax liability by $100 whether an individual's tax rate is 15 percent or 30 percent. Subtracting tax credits is the last stage in computing one's tax liability. (See Figure 15.1.)

Current law allows a variety of tax credits. A family receives a $600 per child tax credit, sometimes referred to as the *kiddie tax credit*.[18] Credits are also allowed for some college expenses. For example, for the first two years of college, there is a 100 percent credit for the first $1,000 of expenses per year, and a 50 percent credit for the next $1,000. Both the kiddie tax credit and the college expense credit are subject to phaseouts, as is another credit for certain child care expenses. In terms of dollars involved, the most important tax credit is the earned income credit that was described in Chapter 8.

Some argue that deductions and exemptions should be converted into credits. For example, the deduction of mortgage interest payments would be changed to a credit for some percentage of the value of interest paid. With a 20 percent interest credit, individuals could subtract from their tax bills an amount equal to one-fifth of their interest payments. Proponents of credits argue that they are fairer than deductions. Under a regime of tax deductions, a poor person (with a low marginal tax rate) benefits less than a rich person (with a high marginal tax rate) even if they both have identical interest expenses. With a credit, the dollar benefit is the same.

The choice between deductions and credits should depend at least in part on the purpose of the exclusion. If the motivation is to correct for the fact that a given expenditure reduces ability to pay, a deduction is appropriate. If the purpose is mainly to encourage certain behavior, it is unclear whether credits or deductions are superior. A credit reduces the effective price of the favored good by the *same* percentage for all individuals; a deduction decreases the price by *different* percentages for different people. If people differ with respect to their elasticities of demand, it may make sense to present them with different effective prices. For example, it is ineffective to give *any* subsidy to someone whose elasticity of demand for the favored good is zero.

Itemized Deduction Phaseout.   Otherwise allowable itemized deductions are reduced by 3 percent of the amount by which AGI exceeds $139,500. However, the reduction cannot be more than 80 percent of the total of itemized deductions.[19] Consider, for example, a family with AGI of $150,000, mortgage interest of $15,000, and local property taxes of $5,000. In the absence of the phaseout, the family would be allowed to deduct $20,000. Because AGI exceeds $139,500 by $10,500, its itemized deduction must be reduced by $315 (= $10,500 × .03). Hence, only $19,685 of deductions are allowed.

---

[18] This figure is to increase to $1,000 by legislation passed in 2003. The credit is partially refundable, and phased out for high-income taxpayers.

[19] In computing the 80 percent maximum, medical expenses and investment interest are excluded. The threshold is adjusted annually for inflation.

The Standard Deduction.   Itemized deductions are listed separately on the individual's tax return, and in principle each one requires documentation (such as receipts) to prove that the expenditure has indeed been made. All this record-keeping increases the administrative cost of the system. To simplify tax returns, the standard deduction was introduced in 1944. It is a fixed amount available to all taxpayers. Each household can choose between taking the standard deduction or itemizing, depending on which offers the greater advantage. The standard deduction in 2003 was $7,950 for joint filers and $4,750 for singles.[20] The standard deduction is adjusted annually for inflation. About 67 percent of tax returns now use the standard deduction.

Impact on the Tax Base

How does the presence of exemptions and deductions influence the size of the tax base? In 2000, AGI was about $6.3 trillion. After completing all the subtractions from AGI, taxable income was only $4.5 trillion, a reduction of about 29 percent. Hence, deductions and exemptions are quite large relative to the size of the potential tax base.

Tax Expenditures

Failure to include a particular item in the tax base results in a loss to the Treasury. Suppose that as a consequence of not taxing item Z, the Treasury loses $1 billion. Compare this to a situation in which the government simply hands over $1 billion of general revenues to those who purchase item Z. In a sense, these activities are equivalent as both subsidize purchases of Z. It just so happens that one transaction occurs on the expenditure side of the account and the other on the revenue side. The former is a **tax expenditure,** a revenue loss caused by the exclusion of some item from the tax base. The list of tax expenditures has more than 100 items. Estimates of the total revenue loss from tax expenditures for 2004 exceed $600 billion [Joint Committee on Taxation, 2002, Table 1].

The law requires that an annual tax expenditure budget be compiled by the Congressional Budget Office. A major intent of the law is to raise public consciousness of the symmetry between a *direct* subsidy for an activity via an expenditure and an *implicit* subsidy through the tax system. However, the notion of a tax expenditure budget has been subject to several criticisms.

First, a serious technical problem arises in the way the computations are made. It is assumed that in the absence of a deduction for a given item, all the expenditures currently made on it would flow into taxable income. Given that people are quite likely to adjust their behavior in response to changes in the tax system, this is not a good assumption, so the tax expenditure estimates may be quite far off the mark.

Second, the tax expenditure budget is simply a list of items exempt from taxation. However, to characterize an item as exempt, you must first have

---

[20] A joint filer who is elderly (over 65) or blind is entitled to an $900 deduction above the standard deduction.

some kind of criterion for deciding what ought to be included. As we have seen, no rigorous set of principles exists for determining what belongs in income. One person's loophole is someone else's appropriate adjustment of the tax base. Hence, considerable arbitrariness is inevitably involved in deciding what to include in the tax expenditure budget.

Finally, the tax expenditure concept has been attacked on philosophical grounds:

> [L]urking behind the concept of the tax expenditure is a more sinister premise, which is a point not just about national accounting practices but about political philosophy and political economics. It is the subtle disposition to think of all income as virtual state property, and forbearance to tax away every last penny of it as itself a tax expenditure. [Fried, 1995, p. C7]

Defenders of the tax expenditure concept argue that the concept does not really carry this ideological baggage. It is merely an attempt to force recognition of the fact that the tax system is a major method for subsidizing various activities. Moreover, the fact that the estimates are not exact does not mean that they are useless for assessing the implications of tax policy.

Why are tax expenditures so popular? Part of the reason is probably political: "In this age of fiscal austerity, new spending programs are a tough sell in Congress. But if the same initiatives are dressed up as tax cuts they look much more palatable" [Stevenson, 1997, p. E1].

The Simplicity Issue

The income tax law has been complicated for a long time. Franklin Roosevelt did not even bother to read a major piece of his administration's tax legislation, the Revenue Act of 1942. Roosevelt observed that it "might as well have been written in a foreign language" [Samuelson, 1986]. By 1986, the set of instructions for filing the basic personal tax return (Form 1040) was 48 pages long. There were 28 possible schedules to fill out. Many people were enraged by the sheer complexity of the system.

The desire to simplify the tax system was one of the driving forces behind a major piece of legislation passed in 1986, the **Tax Reform Act of 1986 (TRA86).** TRA86 raised the standard deduction, so that fewer families now need to itemize their returns and keep extensive records of various transactions. In addition, TRA86 raised the personal exemption substantially. This simplifies life for the low-income families who now do not have to file at all because they have no tax liability. (However, such families may have to file a relatively simple return if they require a refund on tax withholding.) On the other hand, TRA86 made certain rules, such as those pertaining to the deductibility of interest, more complicated than they were before.

In any case, to the extent that any simplification was achieved in 1986, the gains have been lost since then. Legislation enacted in the early 1990s brought us the exemption and itemized deduction phaseouts and rules that allowed capital gains tax breaks on stock in some types of companies but not in others. But the floodgates really broke in 1997, with provisions that were described as "mind-numbing" and "a nightmare of complexity." The 1997 law introduced several new kinds of IRAs with complicated rules governing who could use them. It also made reporting capital gains more difficult by applying different rates to assets held for different lengths of time. This law introduced a variety of education credits, each with its own complex eligibility rules. And the fact that many of the new provisions were subject to phaseouts made it harder for taxpayers to determine whether they qualified and to what extent.

The **Economic Growth and Tax Relief Reconciliation Act of 2001 (EGTRRA)** introduced a new type of difficulty for taxpayers trying to deal with the system. Among other things EGTRRA mandated phased reductions in rates, increases in the child tax credit,[21] and increases in IRA contributions between 2001 and 2010. But EGTRRA had a "sunset" provision so that it expires on December 31, 2010. That is, in the absence of further legislation, on January 1, 2011, the tax system will revert back to its incarnation in the year 2000! No one believes this will happen, but neither does anyone know how Congress will deal with the situation. Individuals who are trying to do tax planning just have to guess.

In any case, by 2002 the Form 1040 instructions were up to 127 pages, and the Internal Revenue Code contained more than 1,300,000 words. In an article entitled "The Tax Maze Begins Here," a journalist noted that "People with doctoral degrees and even some tax lawyers and accountants say they find themselves stumped" when it comes to filling out today's tax returns [Johnston 2000, p. BU1]. You can see if you agree by checking out the forms and instructions at the Internal Revenue Service's Web site, http://www.irs.ustreas.gov/.

Rate Structure

We have now arrived at the third step in Figure 15.1, calculating the amount of tax that must be paid on a given amount of taxable income. A bracket system is used to define tax rates. The taxable income scale is divided into segments, and the law specifies the marginal tax rate that applies to income in that segment. Actually, there are four different rate schedules, one each for married couples who file together (joint returns), married people who file separately, unmarried people, and single people who are heads of households. (A head of household maintains a home that includes a dependent.)

When the federal income tax was introduced in 1913, the bracket rates ranged from 1 percent to 7 percent. As late as 1939, half the taxpayers faced

---

[21] Some taxpayers with children qualify for both the child credit and the Earned Income Tax Credit, but the two provisions have different definitions of "child."

Table 15.1   **Official statutory tax rate schedule, 2003**

Single Returns		Joint Returns	
Taxable Income	*Marginal Tax Rate*	*Taxable Income*	*Marginal Tax Rate*
$0–$6,000	10%	$0–$12,000	10%
$6,000–$28,400	15	$12,000–$47,450	15
$28,400–$68,800	27	$47,450–$114,650	27
$68,800–$143,500	30	$114,650–$174,700	30
$143,500–$311,950	35	$174,700–$311,950	35
$311,950 and over	38.6	$311,950 and over	38.6

marginal rates below 4 percent. With the advent of World War II, rates went up substantially. In 1945, the lowest bracket rate was 23 percent, and the highest 94 percent. Rates eventually came down after the war. By the mid-1980s, there were 14 brackets, with marginal tax rates ranging from 11 percent to 50 percent. The Tax Reform Act of 1986 was a drastic change in the rate structure. The number of brackets was reduced to two, and the maximum statutory rate was set at only 28 percent. Rates crept back up in the 1990s; this trend was reversed by the 2001 tax act (EGTRRA), which included a phased reduction in rates over the period 2001–2010. For example, prior to EGTRRA, the top marginal tax rate was 39.6 percent; it is currently scheduled to fall to 35 percent. The tax rate schedules for single and joint returns in early 2003 are in Table 15.1.

Unfortunately, these official statutory marginal tax rates do not necessarily correspond to the actual marginal tax rates. The phaseouts of various deductions and credits discussed earlier can lead to higher marginal tax rates than those in the table. Consider, for example, an individual in the itemized deduction phaseout range. When he earns another dollar, there is a direct increase in his tax liability in an amount dictated by the rate for his tax bracket. In addition, there is an indirect effect triggered by the fact that his deductions go down, so his taxable income goes up. The result is an effective marginal tax rate that exceeds the statutory rate. Similar stories apply to the phaseout of personal exemptions, IRA deductions, the kiddie tax credit, the education tax credit, and so on. (See Question 9 at the end of the chapter for further details.) At the bottom of the income scale, marginal tax rates can be negative because the earned income tax credit (EITC) subsidizes wages (see Chapter 8). However, within the EITC phaseout range, actual rates exceed statutory rates substantially.

Figure 15.2 illustrates the actual marginal tax rates for a family of four that takes advantage of various education credits. Compare it to the rates in Table 15.1 to see how phaseouts can lead to dramatic differences between actual and statutory marginal tax rates.

FIGURE 15.2

Effective marginal
tax rates for a
hypothetical family

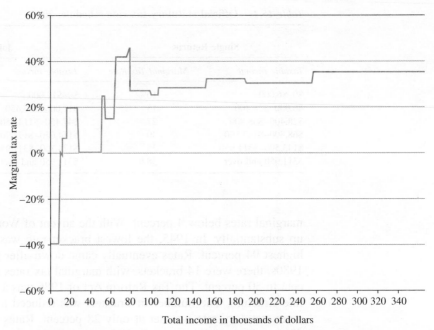

Total income in thousands of dollars

SOURCE: Courtesy of Dr. Kevin Hassett of the American Enterprise Institute. Calculations assume: family of four, one young child, one child in college with tuition of at least $1,500, one adult in school with tuition of at least $1,000, one school loan with deductible interest of at least $2,500, IRA contributions of 10 percent of income up to $5,000, expenditures of 10 percent of income on child care up to $3,000, standard deduction. The calculations are for the year 2003, assuming that the provisions of the 2001 tax law (EGTRRA) are fully phased in.

Effective versus Statutory Rates

Now is a good time to recall the distinction between statutory and effective tax rates. In this section, we have been discussing the former, the legal rates established by the law. In general, these differ from effective tax rates for at least three reasons:

- Because the tax system treats certain types of income preferentially, taxable income may be considerably lower than some more comprehensive measures of income. The fact that tax rates rise rapidly with taxable income does not by itself tell us much about how taxes vary with comprehensive income.

- Even in the absence of loopholes, the link between statutory and effective tax rates is weak. As Chapter 12 emphasized, taxes can be shifted, so that income taxes need not be borne by the people who pay the money to the government. The economic incidence of the income tax is determined by market responses when the tax is levied, and the true pattern of the burden is not known.

- The tax system imposes decreases in utility that exceed revenue collections. Excess burdens arise because taxes distort behavior away from patterns that otherwise would have occurred (see

Income Taxes for an American Family*

Ward and June Cleaver live in a quiet suburb with their two sons, Wallace and Theodore. June stays home and manages the family's investments. Ward works in an office, earning $75,000 per year. Ward's employer contributes $3,000 per year to a pension plan, and also buys him health insurance valued at $10,000. The Cleavers' mortgage interest, property taxes, and charitable donations sum to $9,000. This year, June realized a capital gain of $4,200 on some Amazon.com stock that she had held for 13 months, and $5,500 on some Wal-Mart stock she had held for 11 months.

The employer's $3,000 pension contribution and $10,000 health insurance expenditure are not included in AGI. Hence, the Cleavers' AGI (ignoring capital gains, which we'll get to later) is $75,000. They are entitled to four exemptions worth $12,200 (= 4 × $3,050). Because their itemizable deductions exceed the standard deduction of $7,950, they choose to itemize. Also, because the family's AGI is below $150,000 June is eligible to make a $3,000 deductible contribution into an IRA, and she does so. Hence, the Cleavers' taxable income is $50,800 (= $75,000 − $12,000 − $9,000 − $3,000). From the rate schedule in Table 15.1, we see that the Cleavers are in the 27 percent bracket, and compute their tax liability (exclusive of capital gains) as $7,422. (Only income in excess of $47,450 is taxed at the 27% rate.)

Because the Amazon.com stock was held longer than a year, the associated capital gain is taxed at 20 percent, leading to a tax liability of $840 (= 0.2 × $4,200). The Wal-Mart stock was held less than 12 months, so it is taxed at 27 percent, leading to a liability of $1,485 (= 0.27 × $5,500). Thus, the Cleavers' tentative tax liability is $9,747 (= $7,422 + $840 + $1,485). Subtracting the kiddie tax credit of $600 per child, the Cleavers' final tax bill is $8,547.

*Calculations use the tax law in effect in early 2003. Note that the maximal tax rate on capital gains was then 20 percent.

Chapter 13). Similarly, the costs of compliance with the tax code, in taxpayers' own time as well as explicit payments to accountants and lawyers, must be considered.

In this connection, note that contrary to the impression sometimes received in popular discussions, items like tax-exempt bonds do not, in general, allow the rich to escape entirely the burden of taxation. Consider again Caesar, whose marginal tax rate is 30 percent, and who can buy taxable assets that pay a return of 15 percent. Suppose that the going rate on municipal bonds is 11 percent. We expect that other things being the same, Caesar will buy municipals because their 11 percent return exceeds the after-tax return of 10.5 percent on taxable securities. To be sure, Caesar writes no check to the government. But the tax system nevertheless makes him worse off, because in its absence, he would have been able to make a return of 15 percent. In general, the rate of return on tax-preferred items tends to fall by an amount that reflects the tax advantage. Because of this tendency, high-income individuals face higher tax rates on their capital income than their tax bills would suggest. They are taxed *implicitly* in the form of lower rates of return.

Thus, statutory rates alone probably tell us little about the progressiveness of the current system. Conceivably, a statute with lower marginal tax rates but a broader base would lead to a system with incidence as progressive as that of the current system, and perhaps even more so. At the same time, a system with lower marginal tax rates would reduce excess burden and perhaps lower tax evasion. Such considerations have prompted a number of proposals to restructure the income tax dramatically. One plan that has received a lot of attention is the **flat income tax.**[22] A flat income tax has two attributes:

- It applies the same rate of tax to everyone and to each component of income.
- It allows computation of the tax base with no deductions from total income except personal exemptions and strictly defined business expenses.

Assuming that a certain amount of tax revenue must be collected, the key trade-off under a flat income tax is between the size of the personal exemption and the marginal tax rate. A higher exemption may be desirable to secure relief for those at the bottom of the income schedule and to increase progressiveness (with respect to average tax rates). But a higher exemption means that a higher marginal tax rate must be applied to maintain revenues. A tax rate of roughly 17 percent together with a personal exemption at the current level would satisfy the revenue requirements.[23]

Proponents of the flat income tax claim that lowering marginal tax rates would reduce both the excess burden of the tax system and the incentive to cheat. Moreover, the simplicity gained would lower administrative costs and improve taxpayer morale. And all of this could be achieved without a serious cost in equity because, as just noted, the flat income tax can be made quite progressive by suitable choice of the exemption level.

Opponents of the flat income tax believe that it would probably redistribute more of the tax burden from the rich to the middle classes. It is hard to evaluate this claim because of the usual difficulties involved in doing tax incidence analysis (Chapter 12). Critics also note that the whole range of conceptual and administrative problems involved in defining income will not disappear merely by declaring that business expenses are to be "strictly defined." As pointed out earlier, there will *never* be a simple income tax code.

---

[22] Another, quite different reform, a *flat consumption tax,* has been proposed by several politicians such as former presidential candidate Steve Forbes. It is explained in Chapter 19.

[23] Author's calculation. It does not take into account behavioral responses to the change.

Altig et al.'s [2001] analysis of a flat income tax lends support to the positions of both the proponents and opponents. They studied a very extreme variant—no deductions or exemptions of any kind, just a flat rate on total income—and found that this flat tax would substantially improve efficiency, increasing the long-run level of output by about 5 percent. However, the reform would hurt low-income individuals, who benefit from low effective rates under the status quo.

The notion of a flat income tax enjoyed some popularity in the 1980s, and one way to think of the Tax Reform of 1986 is as a movement in that direction—it lowered the statutory maximum rate from 50 percent to 28 percent and broadened the base by disallowing certain deductions (such as those for state and local sales taxes), and by including all realized capital gains in AGI. However, as noted, high-end rates have increased in recent years; capital gains are again taxed preferentially; and the new IRAs and tax credits have blown new holes in the tax base. The political momentum currently appears to be away from a flat income tax.

Taxes and Inflation

The personal exemption, the standard deduction, the minimum and maximum dollar amounts for each tax rate bracket, the earned income credit, and the thresholds for the deduction and exemption phaseouts are adjusted annually to offset the effects of inflation. The purpose of this process, referred to as **tax indexing,** is to remove automatically the influence of inflation from real tax liabilities. This section discusses motivations for tax indexing and whether the US system of indexing is an adequate response to the problems posed by inflation.

How Inflation Can Affect Taxes

Economists customarily distinguish between "anticipated" and "unanticipated" inflation. The latter is generally viewed as being worse for efficiency, because it does not allow people to adjust their behavior optimally to price level changes. However, with an unindexed income tax system, even perfectly anticipated inflation causes distortions.

The most popularly understood distortion is the phenomenon known as **bracket creep.** Suppose that an individual's earnings and the price level both increase at the same rate over time. Then that person's **real income** (the amount of actual purchasing power) is unchanged. However, an unindexed tax system is based on the individual's **nominal income**—the number of dollars received. As nominal income increases, the individual is pushed into tax brackets with higher marginal tax rates. Hence, the proportion of income that is taxed increases despite the fact that real income stays the same. Even individuals who are not pushed into a higher bracket find more of their incomes taxed at the highest rate to which they are subject. Inflation brings about an automatic increase in real tax burdens without any legislative action.

Another effect of inflation occurs when exemptions and the standard deduction are set in nominal terms. In an unindexed system, increases in the price level decrease their real value. Again, inflation increases the effective tax rate.

It turns out, however, that even with a simple proportional income tax without exemptions or deductions, inflation distorts tax burdens. To be sure, under such a system, general inflation does not affect the real tax burden on wage and salary incomes. If a worker's earnings during a year double, so do his taxes, and there are no real effects. But inflation changes the real tax burden on *capital* income.

Suppose Calpurnia buys an asset for $5,000. Three years later, she sells it for $10,000. Suppose further that during the three years, the general price level doubled. In real terms, selling the asset nets Calpurnia zero. However, capital gains liabilities are based on the difference between the *nominal* selling and buying prices. Hence, Calpurnia incurs a tax liability on $5,000 of illusory capital gains. In short, because the inflationary component of capital gains is subject to tax, the real tax burden depends on the inflation rate.

Those who receive taxable interest income are similarly affected. Suppose that the **nominal interest rate** (the rate observed in the market) is 16 percent. Suppose further that the anticipated rate of inflation is 12 percent. Then for someone who lends at the 16 percent nominal rate, the **real interest rate** is only 4 percent, because that is the percentage by which the lender's real purchasing power is increased. However, taxes are levied on nominal, not real, interest payments. Hence, tax must be paid on receipts that represent no gain in real income.

Let us consider this argument algebraically. Call the nominal interest rate i. Then the after-tax nominal return to lending for an individual with a marginal tax rate of t is $(1 - t)i$. To find the real after-tax rate of return, we must subtract the expected rate of inflation, π. Hence, the real after-tax rate of return r is

$$r = (1 - t)i - \pi \tag{15.1}$$

Suppose $t = .25$, $i = 16$ percent, and $\pi = 10$ percent. Then although the nominal interest rate is 16 percent, the real after-tax return is only 2 percent.

Now suppose for simplicity that any increase in the expected rate of inflation increases the nominal interest rate by the same amount; if inflation increases by four points, the nominal interest rate increases by four points. One might guess that the two increases would cancel out, leaving the real after-tax rate of return unchanged at 2 percent. But Equation (15.1) contradicts this prediction. If π goes from 10 percent to 14 percent and i goes from 16 percent to 20 percent, then with t equal to 0.25, r decreases to 1 percent. Inflation, even though it is perfectly anticipated, is not "neutral." This is a direct consequence of the fact that nominal rather than real interest payments are taxed.

So far we have been considering the issue from the point of view of lenders. Things are just the opposite for borrowers. In the absence of the tax system, the real rate paid by borrowers is the nominal rate minus the anticipated inflation rate. However, assuming the taxpayer satisfies certain criteria, the tax law allows deductibility of nominal interest payments from taxable income. Thus, debtors can subtract from taxable income payments that represent no decrease in their real incomes. Inflation decreases the tax burden on borrowers.

Coping with the Tax/Inflation Problem

As inflation rates began to increase in the late 1960s, people became acutely aware of the fact that inflation leads to unlegislated increases in the real income tax burden. The initial response was to mitigate these effects by a series of ad hoc reductions in statutory rates. Half a dozen such tax cuts were enacted between 1969 and 1981, and they were partially successful in undoing some effects of inflation.

Nevertheless, many people disliked this process. Each tax cut offset inflation only for a short time. After a while, it became necessary to make more changes. The whole business tended to increase public cynicism about the tax-setting process. Many citizens learned that the tax "reductions" about which their legislators boasted were nothing of the kind when measured in *real* terms. Lenin is alleged to have said, "The way to crush the bourgeoisie is to grind them between the millstones of taxation and inflation." Although the interaction of taxes and inflation in the United States had not created quite such drastic effects, there was widespread agreement that it had produced serious distortions.

In 1981, dissatisfaction with the ad hoc approach led to the enactment of legislation requiring indexing of certain parts of the tax code. Currently the personal exemption, standard deduction, bracket widths, and earned income credit are all indexed. These provisions have effectively ended bracket creep. However, no moves have been made in the direction of indexing capital income. This is due in part to the administrative complexity such a statute would entail. For example, as suggested earlier, increases in inflation generate real gains for debtors, because the real value of the amounts they have to repay decreases. In a fully indexed system, such gains would have to be measured and taxed, a task that would certainly be complex.

Should indexing be maintained? Opponents of indexing argue that a system of periodic ad hoc adjustments is a good thing because it allows the legislature to examine and revise other aspects of the tax code that may need changing.[24] Proponents of indexing argue that reducing the opportunities for

---

[24] We have been dealing with this debate from a microeconomic standpoint. People also disagree about the macroeconomic consequences of indexing. Opponents argue that it removes an important tool for conducting macroeconomic policy. For example, if more fiscal restraint is needed during an inflationary period, this is automatically generated by increases in tax revenues. In contrast, voting tax increases and/or expenditure cuts takes time. On the other hand, indexing proponents argue that the automatic rise in federal revenues may simply encourage legislators to spend more, and hence have no stabilizing effect. Indeed, they argue that a nonindexed system creates incentives for legislators to pursue inflationary policies, because these policies tend to increase the real quantity of resources available to the public sector.

revising the tax code may itself be a benefit, because it is desirable to have a stable and predictable tax law. Moreover, fewer opportunities to change the law also mean fewer chances for legislative mischief. Certainly the most important argument of those who favor indexing is that it eliminates unlegislated increases in real tax rates. They believe that allowing the real tax schedule to be changed systematically by a nonlegislative process is antithetical to democratic values.

Proponents of indexing also note that its repeal would have a disproportionately large effect on the tax liabilities of low-income families. For example, high-income families lose some or all of the advantage of personal exemptions because of the exemption phaseout. Hence, if the exemption were no longer indexed, their taxes would not be affected at all, but the real tax liabilities of lower-income individuals would increase. Similarly, higher-income families are more likely to itemize than take the standard deduction, so eliminating its indexation would tend to affect mostly low-income families.

The Alternate Minimum Tax (AMT)

As noted earlier, certain types of income such as interest on state and local bonds are treated preferentially by the tax system. This makes it possible for some high-income households to have little or no tax liability. In 1969 the Secretary of the Treasury set off a political firestorm when he announced that 155 individuals with incomes above $200,000 had paid no federal income tax several years earlier. The **alternative minimum tax (AMT),** enacted in 1969 and modified several times since then, was an attempt to ensure that rich people who benefited from various tax shelters paid at least some tax.

The AMT is essentially a shadow tax system with its own rules for computing the tax base and its own rate schedule. The first step in the computation is to take regular taxable income and add to it items called *AMT preferences.* These items include (but are not limited to) personal exemptions, the standard deduction, and itemized deductions for state taxes. The next step is to subtract the AMT exemption—currently $49,000 for married couples and $35,750 for single individuals. This gives us *alternative minimum tax income (AMTI).* The exemption is the same regardless of the number of dependents, and is phased out for high-income individuals. AMTI is subject to rates of 26 percent on the first $175,000 and 28 percent on the rest. Importantly, unlike the ordinary income tax, neither the exemption nor the brackets are adjusted for inflation.

The tax liability computed by applying this relatively flat rate schedule to AMTI is called *tentative AMT.* To complete the process, compare tentative AMT with tax liability under the regular income tax. If tentative AMT is greater than regular income tax liability, the difference is the taxpayer's AMT, and the taxpayer must pay AMT on top of his regular income tax.

We noted at the outset that the original purpose of the AMT was to catch high-income individuals who were sheltering most or all of their income. It was never intended to be a mass tax. Yet under current law, by 2010 about 35 million taxpayers will be on the AMT, and by 2008 the cost of repealing the AMT will be greater than the cost of repealing the regular income tax! [Tempalski, 2002, p. 342]. Why is this happening? To understand the reason, recall that the AMT kicks in only when tax liability under the AMT is greater than tax liability under the regular income tax. Hence, anything that reduces tax liability under the regular tax relative to the AMT tends to increase the number of AMT taxpayers. In this context, two facts are relevant. First, the AMT is not adjusted for inflation and the ordinary income tax generally is. Hence, the AMT is subject to bracket creep, and over time even moderate rates of inflation raise AMT relative to ordinary tax liabilities. Second, in 2001 EGTRRA cut the regular income tax without making any substantial changes in the AMT. By itself, EGTTRA will account for almost a doubling of the number of AMT taxpayers by 2010.

Should we care that the AMT is becoming a mass tax? The answer is that we should, because it is bad tax policy from virtually every perspective. From the point of view of fairness, the AMT exemption preferences—personal exemptions, standard deduction, and itemized deductions for state taxes—are of greatest importance to middle income taxpayers. As the AMT grows in importance, these are the taxpayers who are adversely affected, not the very rich. From the point of view of efficiency, recall from Chapter 13 that the excess burden of an income tax varies with the square of the marginal tax rate. The minimum rate under the AMT is 26 percent, considerably higher than the regular income tax rates of many families that will be thrown into the AMT. Finally, the AMT is notoriously complicated. One of the main problems is that the only way to find out if you have to pay the AMT is to go through the entire laborious AMT calculation. Thus, even families that ultimately don't have to pay the tax still have to fill out the AMT return, adding substantially to the burden of tax compliance.

In short, the US income tax system is heading for a train wreck by the end of the decade. Most observers believe that Congress will act to avert the wreck, although it is not clear how. There are a number of possibilities: the exemption and brackets could be indexed for inflation, the exemption could be raised, or the AMT could be eliminated altogether. Abstracting from the revenue costs, outright repeal has considerable attraction. If Congress doesn't want people to benefit from certain preferences, doesn't it make more sense simply to eliminate them from the regular income tax than to invent a whole new tax system to get at them? In short, the AMT is another demonstration of the income tax system's lack of coherence. As former Senator Bill Bradley trenchantly put it, "A minimum tax is an admission of failure. It demonstrates not only that the system is broke, but also that Congress doesn't have the guts to fix it."

Choice of Unit and the Marriage Tax

We have discussed at length problems that arise in defining income for taxation purposes. Yet, even very careful definitions of income give little guidance with respect to choosing *who* should be taxed on the income. Should each person be taxed separately on his or her own income? Or should individuals who live together in a family unit be taxed on their joint incomes? Public debate of this question has been intense. In this section, we discuss some of the issues surrounding the controversy.[25]

Background

To begin, consider the following three principles:

1. The income tax should embody increasing marginal tax rates.
2. Families with equal incomes should, other things being the same, pay equal taxes.
3. Two individuals' tax burdens should not change when they marry; the tax system should be **marriage neutral.**

The second and third principles are a bit controversial, but it is probably fair to say they are broadly accepted as desirable features of a tax system. While agreement on the first principle is weaker, increasing marginal tax rates seem to have wide political support.

Despite the appeal of these principles, a problem arises when it comes to implementing them: In general, *no tax system can adhere to all three simultaneously.* This point is made easily with an arithmetic example. Consider the following simple progressive tax schedule: a taxable unit pays in tax 10 percent of all income up to $6,000, and 50 percent of all income in excess of $6,000. The first two columns of Table 15.2 show the incomes and tax liabilities of four individuals, Lucy, Ricky, Fred, and Ethel. (For example, Ricky's tax liability is $12,100 [= .10 × $6,000 + .50 × $23,000].) Now assume that romances develop—Lucy marries Ricky, and Ethel marries Fred. In the absence of joint filing, the tax liability of each individual is unchanged. However, two families with the same income ($30,000) pay

Table 15.2   **Tax liabilities under a hypothetical tax system**

	Individual Income	Individual Tax	Family Tax with Individual Filing	Joint Income	Joint Tax
Lucy	$ 1,000	$ 100 ⎱	$12,200	$30,000	$12,600
Ricky	29,000	12,100 ⎰			
Ethel	15,000	5,100 ⎱	10,200	30,000	12,600
Fred	15,000	5,100 ⎰			

[25] For further details see the references in Carasso and Steuerle [2002].

different amounts of tax. (The Lucy-Rickys pay $12,200 while the Ethel-Freds pay only $10,200, as noted in the third column.) Suppose instead that the law views the family as the taxable unit, so that the tax schedule applies to joint income. In this case, the two families pay equal amounts of tax, but now tax burdens have been changed by marriage. Of course, the actual change in the tax burden depends on the difference between the tax schedules applied to individual and joint returns. This example has assumed for simplicity that the schedule remains unchanged. But it does make the main point: Given increasing marginal tax rates, we cannot have both principles 2 and 3.

What choice has the United States made? Over time, the choice has changed. Before 1948, the taxable unit was the individual, and principle 2 was violated. In 1948, the family became the taxable unit, and simultaneously **income splitting** was introduced. Under income splitting, a family with an income of $50,000 is taxed as if it were two individuals with incomes of $25,000. Clearly, with increasing marginal tax rates, this can be a major advantage. Note also that under such a regime, an unmarried person with a given income finds his or her tax liability reduced substantially if he or she marries a person with little or no income. Indeed, under the 1948 law, it was possible for an individual's tax liability to fall drastically when the person married—a violation of principle 3.

The differential between a single person's tax liability and that of a married couple with the same income was so large that Congress created a new schedule for unmarried people in 1969. Under this schedule, a single person's tax liability could never be more than 20 percent higher than the tax liability of a married couple with the same taxable income. (Under the old regime, differentials of up to 40 percent were possible.)

Unfortunately, this decrease in the single/married differential was purchased at the price of a violation of principle 3 in the opposite direction: it was now possible for persons' tax liabilities to increase when they married. In effect, the personal income tax levied a tax on marriage. In 1981, Congress attempted to reduce the "marriage tax" by introducing a new deduction for two-earner married couples. Two-earner families received a deduction equal to 10 percent of the lower earning spouse's wage income, but no more than $3,000. However, the two-earner deduction was eliminated by TRA86. It was deemed to be unnecessary because lower marginal tax rates reduced the importance of the "marriage tax."

Whatever the merits of this argument, marginal tax rates increased substantially after 1986, and marriage taxes grew along with them. In 2000, both parties pledged to reduce the marriage tax, and the 2001 tax law signed by George W. Bush included several provisions that were designed to do so. Among others, these included expanding the standard deduction for married couples only and increasing the width of the 15 percent bracket, again for married couples only. According to Carasso and Steuerle's [2002] calculations, the 2001 law considerably reduced marriage penalties for most

"And do you promise to love, honor, and cherish each other, and to pay the United States government more in taxes as a married couple than you would have paid if you had just continued living together."

married households. However, marriage penalties still exist, and they tend to be highest when both spouses have similar earnings. Under certain conditions, for example, when two individuals with $25,000 AGIs marry, their joint tax liability can increase by about $1,900. On the other hand, when there are considerable differences in individuals' earnings, the tax code provides a bonus for marriage. If two people with $50,000 and zero AGIs marry, their joint tax liability can decrease by $4,269.[26] In cases like these, the law provides a "tax dowry."

Analyzing the Marriage Tax

The economist surveying this scene is likely to ask the usual two questions—is it equitable and is it efficient? Much of the public debate focuses on the equity issue: is it fairer to tax individuals or families? One argument favoring the family as the choice is that it allows a fairer treatment of non-labor income (dividends, interest, profits). There are fears that with individual filing, high-earnings spouses would transfer property to their mates to

---

[26] These calculations, which are from Carasso and Steuerle [2002], assume that married couples and heads of households have two children.

lower family tax bills (so-called "bedchamber transfers of property"). It is difficult to predict the extent to which this would take place. The view implicit in these fears is that property rights within families are irrelevant. However, given current high rates of divorce, turning property over to a spouse just for tax purposes may be a risky strategy, and there is no strong evidence that such transfers would occur in massive amounts.

The family can also be defended as the appropriate unit of taxation on a more philosophical level:

> [T]he family is . . . the basic economic unit in society . . . Taxation of the individual in . . . disregard of his inevitably close financial and economic ties with the other members of the basic social unit of which he is ordinarily a member, the family, is in our view [a] striking instance of [a] lack of a comprehensive and rational pattern in . . . [a] tax system. [*Report of the Royal Commission,* 1966, pp. 122–23]

Or as the late John Cardinal O'Connor put it, "Marriage matters supremely to every person and every institution in our society" [Allen, 1998, p. A1].

The case for the family unit is less compelling than these quotations suggest, at least to some people. Bittker [1975, p. 1398] argued

> If married couples are taxed on their consolidated income, for example, should the same principle extend to a child who supports an aged parent, two sisters who share an apartment, or a divorced parent who lives with an adolescent child? Should a relationship established by blood or marriage be demanded, to the exclusion, for example, of unmarried persons who live together, homosexual companions, and communes?

Clearly, beliefs concerning the choice of the fairest taxable unit are influenced by value judgments and by attitudes toward the role of the family in society. The debate continues to be lively. Indeed, family-based income taxation has recently been subjected to legal challenge. A man filed a suit in federal Tax Court arguing that he was entitled to file a joint return with another man with whom he had an "economic partnership." The judge ruled that the use of marriage as a criterion for determining tax liability is "constitutionally valid" [Herman, 2000, p. A1].

When we turn to the efficiency aspects of the problem, the question is whether the marriage tax distorts individuals' behavior. The tax system changes the "price of marriage," and anecdotes about postponed marriage, divorce, or separation for tax reasons are common. From a statistical point of view, however, it is hard to make a very strong case that the marriage tax substantially distorts decisions related to marriage. Dickert-Conlin's [1999] econometric analysis of divorce decisions suggests that there is a positive relationship between a couple's marriage penalty and the likelihood that they divorce, but the magnitude of the effect is very small.

An efficiency concern that is easier to document surrounds the impact of joint filing on labor supply decisions. Chapter 14 stated that because married women tend to have more elastic labor supply schedules than their husbands, efficient taxation requires taxing wives at a lower rate. Under joint filing, both spouses face identical marginal tax rates on their last dollars of income. Hence, joint filing is inefficient.

It is hard to imagine Congress implementing separate income tax schedules for wives and husbands. This does not mean, however, that it is impossible to make family taxation more efficient. One possible reform would be simply to eliminate joint filing and have all people file as individuals. This would not only enhance efficiency, but it would also produce more marriage neutrality than the current system. A number of other nations, including Canada, have opted for this approach.[27]

Unfortunately, individual filing would lead to a violation of principle 2: equal taxation of families with equal incomes. This brings us back to where we started. No tax system can satisfy all three criteria, so society must decide which have the highest priority.

Treatment of International Income

We now turn to the tax treatment of individual income that is earned abroad. Such income is potentially of interest to the tax authorities of the citizen's home and host governments. US law recognizes the principle that the host country has the primary right to tax income earned within its borders. At the same time, the United States adheres to the notion that an American citizen, wherever he or she earns money, has a tax obligation to the native land. To avoid double taxation of foreign source income, the United States taxes income earned abroad, but allows a credit for tax paid to foreign governments.[28] Suppose that Ophelia's US tax liability on her income earned in Germany is $7,000, and she had paid $5,500 in German income taxes. Then Ophelia can take a $5,500 credit on her US tax return, so she need pay only $1,500 to the Internal Revenue Service. A US citizen's total tax liability, then, is based on *global* income.

Global versus Territorial Systems.   The philosophical premise of the US system is that equity in taxation is defined on a citizenship basis. If you are a US citizen, your total tax liability should be roughly independent of whether you earn your income at home or abroad. We refer to this as a **global system.** In contrast, virtually every other country adheres to a **territorial system**—a citizen earning income abroad need pay tax only to the host government. Which system is better? It is hard to build a case for the

---

[27] However, in the Canadian system, the primary income earner in a household can receive a nonrefundable tax credit for a spouse who has earned little or no income.

[28] The credit cannot exceed what the US tax on the foreign income would have been. For details, see Joint Committee on Taxation [1999].

superiority of one system over the other on either equity or efficiency grounds. The following paragraphs expand on the problem.

Equity.   John, a citizen of the United Kingdom, and Sam, a US citizen, both work in Hong Kong and have identical incomes. Because the United Kingdom has a territorial system, John pays tax only to Hong Kong. Sam, on the other hand, also owes money to the United States (provided that his US tax bill is higher than his Hong Kong tax payment). Thus, Sam pays more tax than John, even though they have the same income. Although a global system produces equal treatment for citizens of the same country, it can lead to substantially different treatments for citizens of different countries. Should horizontal equity be defined on a national or world basis? Each principle has some merit, but in general, no system of international tax coordination can satisfy both.

Efficiency.   A global system may distort international production decisions. Suppose that American firms operating abroad have to pay the US income tax for their American employees. Dutch firms, which operate under the territorial system, have no analogous obligation. Other things being the same, then, the US companies may end up paying more for their labor, and hence be at a cost disadvantage.[29] Dutch firms could conceivably win more contracts than the American firms, even if the latter are more technologically efficient.

On the other hand, a territorial system can distort a different decision— where people locate. Citizens of a given country may find their decision to work abroad influenced by the fact that their tax liability depends on where they live. Under a global regime, you cannot escape your country's tax collector unless you change citizenship. Hence, there is less incentive to relocate just for tax purposes.

Thus, the global system may distort production decisions, and the territorial system residential decisions. It is hard to know which distortion creates a larger efficiency cost.

State Income Taxes

The role of individual income taxes in state revenue systems has been growing rapidly.[30] In 1960, 12.2 percent of state tax collections were from individual income taxes; by 2000, the figure was 36 percent [US Bureau of the

---

[29] This assumes: (*a*) the incidence of the US tax falls on employers rather than employees, and (*b*) American companies cannot respond simply by hiring foreign workers. The validity of assumption (*a*) depends on the elasticity of supply of US workers to US firms abroad. To the extent the supply curve is not horizontal, employees bear part of the tax. See Chapter 12.

[30] Income taxes are generally not of much importance for local governments, although in some of the larger cities, they play a significant role.

Census, 2002, p. 272]. Presently, 41 states and the District of Columbia have broad-based individual income taxes that include wages. Two additional states tax interest and dividends, but not wages.

State income taxes tend to be similar in structure to the federal tax. The tax base is found by subtracting various deductions and exemptions from gross income, and tax liability is determined by associating a marginal tax rate with each of several income brackets. The marginal rates are much lower than those of the federal system. Among the states that levied income taxes in 2003, the highest bracket rates were mostly in the 6 to 8 percent range. (The maximum was 11 percent in Montana.) The states differ considerably with respect to rules governing deductions and exemptions. Some rule out practically all deductions, while others follow rules similar to the federal system.

It is important not to neglect the effect of state income taxes when assessing overall marginal tax rates. The marginal tax rate facing a Californian in the highest tax bracket is 38.6 percent from the federal tax and then another 9.3 percent from the California income tax, or a total of 47.9 percent. If the individual itemizes her deductions and subtracts state and local taxes, the effect is muted a bit, but the fact is that the cumulative marginal tax rates in high-tax states approach 50 percent.

Politics and Tax Reform

Our discussion of the income tax has revealed a number of features that are hard to justify on the basis of either efficiency or equity. A natural question is why is it so difficult to improve the tax system? One reason is that in many cases, even fairly disinterested experts disagree about what direction reform should take. For example, we noted earlier that despite a consensus among economists that differentially taxing various types of capital income is undesirable, there is dispute about how this should be remedied. What one person views as a reform can be perceived by another as a turn for the worse.

Another difficulty is that attempts to change specific provisions encounter fierce political opposition from those whom the changes will hurt. State government officials, for example, lobby ferociously whenever proposals to limit the deductibility of state income taxes are floated. Chapter 6 discussed some theories suggesting that in the presence of special-interest groups, the political process can lead to expenditure patterns that are suboptimal from society's point of view. The same theories might explain the difficulties involved in attempts to improve the tax system. A member of the House Ways and Means Committee, Andrew Jacobs, once summed it up this way: "If you evade your taxes, you go to the penitentiary. If you want to avoid taxes, you go to the US Congress—and see what they can do for you" [*Tax Policy Guide,* 1982, p. 5].

Organized lobbies are not the only impediments to reform. In many cases, once a tax provision is introduced, ordinary people modify their behavior on its basis and are likely to lose a lot if it is changed. For example, many families purchase larger houses than they otherwise would because of the deductibility of mortgage interest and property taxes. Presumably, if these provisions were eliminated, housing values would fall. Homeowners would not take this lying down. Certain notions of horizontal equity suggest it is unfair to change provisions that have caused people to make decisions that are costly to reverse (see Chapter 14).

Some have argued that attempts to make broad changes in the tax system are likely to be more successful than attempts to modify specific provisions on a piecemeal basis. If *everyone's* ox is being gored, people are less apt to fight for their particular loopholes. The experience with TRA86 lends some support to this viewpoint. One reason it passed was that on certain key votes, its supporters were able to package TRA86 as an all-or-nothing proposition. Accept the whole set of changes, or no changes at all. It is noteworthy, however, that even with a very popular president and extremely powerful congressional leaders behind the bill, it nearly died several times.

In any case, the history since 1986 suggests that a tax system with relatively low rates and a broad base is not stable politically: "Those who argued that a tax system clearly based on a consistent principle would be more likely to endure did not, in TRA86, get the outcome that they desired" [Auerbach and Slemrod, 1997, p. 628].

What are the prospects for a return to the principles of TRA86? Many observers believe that to the extent there are future changes in the tax law, the tendency will be to build additional preferences into the tax code, eroding the tax base and complicating the system further. As Congressman Charles Rangel quipped, critics of the status quo like to "talk about pulling the tax code up by the roots, but every year, they just add more fertilizer to it." This is because a stable and simple tax code is not in the interest of politicians: A major function of the tax system is "enabling legislators (and presidents) to raise campaign funds by inserting or removing loopholes in our present obscenely complicated code" [Friedman, 1998]. We conclude that one cannot be optimistic about the possibilities for improvement.

Summary

- Computing federal individual income tax liability has three major steps: measuring total income (adjusted gross income), converting total income to taxable income, and calculating taxes due.

- A traditional benchmark measure of income is the Haig-Simons definition: Income during a

given period is the net change in the individual's power to consume.

- Implementation of the Haig-Simons criterion is confounded by several difficulties: (1) Income must be measured net of the expenses of earning it. (2) Unrealized capital gains and the imputed income from durable goods are not easily gauged. (3) It is difficult to measure the value of in-kind receipts.

■ Critics of the Haig-Simons criterion argue that it guarantees neither fair nor efficient outcomes.

■ The US income tax base excludes: (1) interest on state and local bonds, (2) employer contributions to pension and medical plans, (3) gifts and inheritances.

■ Exemptions are fixed amounts per family member. Exemptions are subtracted from adjusted gross income (AGI) and phased out at high-income levels.

■ Deductions are either standard or itemized. A standard deduction reduces taxable income by a fixed amount.

■ Itemized deductions are permitted for expenditures on particular goods and services. They are phased out at high-income levels. Itemized deductions change after-tax relative prices, which often affects economic behavior.

■ Major itemized deductions in the US tax code include (1) unreimbursed medical expenses in excess of 7.5 percent of AGI, (2) state and local income and property taxes, (3) certain interest expenses, (4) charitable contributions.

■ Tax expenditures are the revenues forgone due to preferential tax treatment.

■ The final step in determining tax liability is to apply a schedule of rates to taxable income.

Because of various phaseouts, the actual statutory marginal tax rates exceed the official rates.

■ The alternative minimum tax (AMT) was designed to make sure that high-income taxpayers who heavily utilize tax shelters would pay at least some federal income tax. However, due to certain structural flaws, it will soon be the tax system confronting millions of middle-class Americans.

■ Bracket widths, personal exemptions, the standard deduction, and the earned income credit are now indexed against inflation. However, there are no provisions to correct for inflation's effect on the taxation of capital income.

■ No system of family taxation can simultaneously achieve increasing marginal tax rates, marriage neutrality, and equal taxes for families with equal incomes. Under current law, joint tax liabilities may increase or decrease upon marriage, depending on the couple's circumstances.

■ The United States follows a global system with respect to the tax treatment of income earned in other countries. The total amount of tax due is supposed to be roughly independent of whether the income is earned at home or abroad.

■ Income tax systems are important as revenue raisers for the states. State income taxes have lower rates than the federal system and vary widely in their exact provisions.

Discussion Questions

1. Under current law, if your capital losses exceed your capital gains, you can deduct as much as $3,000 of losses against other forms of income. In the wake of massive declines in the stock market, in 2002 several members of Congress suggested that this $3,000 figure be increased to $5,000. Evaluate this proposal from the viewpoint of the Haig-Simons criterion. That is, would the proposal lead to an income tax base that is closer to or farther from the Haig-Simons ideal than the status quo?

2. Under current law, if you buy stock for $5,000 and donate it to charity after it has appreciated to $20,000, you get to take a $20,000 deduction. During his campaign for the presidency in 2000, Senator John McCain proposed a change that, in effect, would allow you to deduct only $5,000. Evaluate McCain's proposal from the point of view of the Haig-Simons criterion. If it were enacted, what effect would you expect the proposal to have on charitable donations. (Relate your answer to the elasticity of donations with respect to the tax price of giving.)

*3. Jones, who has a federal personal income tax rate of 28 percent, holds an oil stock that appreciates in value by 10 percent each year. He bought the stock one year ago. Jones's stockbroker now wants him to switch the oil stock for a gold stock that is equally risky. Jones has decided that if he holds on to the oil stock, he will keep it only one more year and then sell it. If he sells the oil stock now, he will invest all the (after-tax) proceeds of the sale in the gold stock and then sell the gold stock one year from now. What is the minimum rate of return the gold stock must pay for Jones to make the switch? Relate your answer to the *lock-in effect.*

4. In 1997, House Republicans proposed that capital gains be indexed for inflation. *Newsweek*'s Wall Street editor stated that this was unfair to wage earners: "Inflation pushes up salaries, too. But would paychecks get the same generous treatment? Nope. No inflation indexing" [Sloan, 1997, p. 59]. Compose a letter to *Newsweek* in which you comment on this statement.

5. Austin's marginal tax rate is 30 percent and he itemizes his tax deductions. How much is a $500 deduction worth to him? How much is a $500 tax credit worth to him?

6. Suppose that a typical taxpayer has a marginal personal income tax rate of 30 percent. The nominal interest rate is 13 percent, and the expected inflation rate is 8 percent.

   a. What is the real after-tax rate of interest?

   b. Suppose that the expected inflation rate increases by 3 percentage points to 11 percent, and the nominal interest rate increases by the same amount. What happens to the real after-tax rate of return?

   *c. If the inflation rate increases as in part *b,* by how much would the nominal interest rate have to increase to keep the real after-tax interest rate at the same level as in part *a?* Can you generalize your answer using an algebraic formula?

7. Two alternative proposals have been made for dealing with the marriage tax: 1) lower the tax rate on the earnings of the spouse with lower earnings, perhaps by allowing the family to deduct 10 percent of the earnings of that spouse, or 2) increase the standard deduction for married couples. From the point of view of enhancing economic efficiency, which proposal is better? Explain your answer.

8. In 2001 the Bush administration proposed that everyone be allowed to deduct charitable contributions, even people who took the standard deduction. Proponents of the idea, which failed to gain passage, argued that it would stimulate charitable giving. Critics argued that a deduction was not necessary to stimulate giving because part of the standard deduction can be used for a charitable donation. Which side had the better argument? Include in your answer a discussion of how the Bush administration proposal would have changed the price of a dollar of charitable giving.

9. The purpose of this problem is to determine how effective marginal tax rates are affected by the itemized deduction and personal exemption phaseouts.

   a. Consider a family of four whose AGI places it in the exemption phaseout range, and whose taxable income places it in the 30 percent tax bracket.

      i. In the absence of the phaseout, how much are the family's exemptions?

      ii. Now suppose the family's income increases by $2,500. Given a 30 percent bracket, by how much does its tax liability increase?

      iii. By how much does the increase in income reduce the family's exemptions? By how much does this increase the family's taxable income?

      iv. By how much does the increase in taxable income increase their tax liability, given that they are in the 30 percent bracket?

      v. Combine your answers from parts *ii* and *iv* to find the effective marginal tax rate. (Divide the change in tax liability by the $2,500 change in income.)

---

*Difficult.

b. Now consider a different family whose AGI places it in the deduction phaseout range, and the family itemizes its tax deductions. Suppose the family receives another $100 of before-tax income.

   i. Assuming a 30 percent marginal tax rate, what is the change in tax liability?

   ii. What happens to the family's allowable itemized deductions and taxable income?

   iii. How does the change in taxable income affect the family's tax liability?

   iv. What is the family's effective marginal tax rate?

10. You will need a calculator for this problem. Sam earns $4,000 and he wants to save it for retirement, which is 10 years away. He can either save it in a taxable account or put it into a Roth IRA. Suppose that Sam can receive an annual rate of return of 8 percent and his marginal tax rate is 25 percent. By the time he reaches retirement, how much money would he have in either option? [Note: Sam has to pay tax on the $4,000, so he cannot put the full amount either into the taxable account or the Roth IRA.]

Selected References

Burman, Leonard. *The Labyrinth of Capital Gains Tax Policy.* Washington, DC: Brookings Institution, 1999.

Carasso, Adam, and C Eugene Steuerle. "How Marriage Penalties Change under the 2001 Tax Bill." Discussion Paper No. 2, Urban-Brookings Tax Policy Center, May 2002.

Tempalski, Jerry. "The Impact of the 2001 Tax Bill on the Individual AMT." *Proceedings, Ninety-Fourth Annual Conference.* National Tax Association, 2002.

Urban-Brookings Tax Policy Center. URL: http://www.taxpolicycenter.org/.

CHAPTER 16

Personal Taxation and Behavior

If you are out to describe the truth, leave elegance to the tailor.

ALBERT EINSTEIN

During the 1980s, the top statutory marginal income tax rate in the United States fell from 70 percent to 28 percent. During the 1990s, it went back up to 39.6 percent, but a new tax law in 2001 mandated that it be gradually lowered to 35 percent by 2010. We are now in the midst of a debate in which one side says that these reductions should be reversed and the other says that they aren't deep enough. Central to the debate is the question of how taxes affect economic behavior. Those who favor lower taxes argue that high taxes reduce economic activity:

> A fundamental principle of economics is that the more you tax something, the less you get of it. . . . The current confiscatory system begs the questions: Why work harder if each extra dollar earns you less? Why save for tomorrow when spending today is cheaper? . . . The disillusioned answer of many Americans is simply: Why bother? [National Commission on Economic Growth and Tax Reform, 1996, pp. 10, 11]

The proponents of higher taxes respond that such objections are exaggerated. Taxes are like the weather: People talk about them a lot, but don't do anything about them.

Public finance economists are just as interested in this issue as the politicians. The theory of taxation tells us, after all, that both the incidence and efficiency of a tax system depend on how it affects behavior. As shown in Chapter 15, the income tax affects incentives for myriad decisions—everything from the purchase of medical services to the amount of charitable donations. We focus on four particularly important topics that have been studied intensively—the effects of taxation on labor supply, saving, housing consumption, and portfolio decisions.

FIGURE 16.1

Utility-maximizing choice of leisure and income

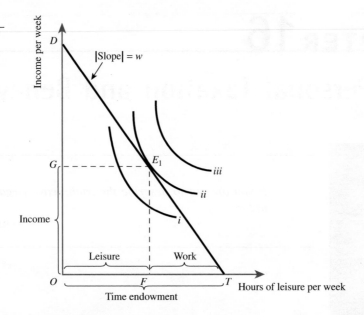

Labor Supply

In 2002, 134 million Americans worked an average of about 34 hours per week and received total compensation of roughly $6 trillion, approximately 72 percent of national income [*Economic Report of the President, 2003*, pp. 308, 319, 332]. How labor supply is determined and whether taxes affect it are the issues to which we now turn.

Theoretical Considerations

Hercules is deciding how much of his time to devote each week to work and how much to leisure. Chapter 8 showed how to analyze this choice graphically. To review the main points in that discussion:

- The number of hours available for market work and nonmarket uses ("leisure") is referred to as the *time endowment*. In Figure 16.1, it is distance *OT* on the horizontal axis. Assuming that all time not spent on leisure is devoted to market work, any point on the horizontal axis simultaneously indicates hours of leisure and hours of work.

- The budget constraint shows the combinations of leisure and income available to an individual given his or her wage rate. If Hercules' wage rate is $w per hour, then his budget constraint is a straight line whose slope in absolute value is w. In Figure 16.1, this is represented by line *TD*.

- The particular point on the budget constraint that is chosen depends on the individual's tastes. Assume that preferences for leisure and income can be represented by normal, convex-to-the-origin indifference

FIGURE 16.2

Proportional income tax decreasing hours of labor supplied

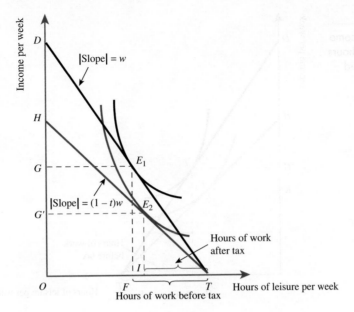

curves. Three such curves are labeled *i*, *ii*, and *iii* in Figure 16.1. Hercules maximizes utility at point E_1, where he devotes *OF* hours to leisure, works *FT* hours, and earns income *OG*.

We are now in a position to analyze the effects of taxation. Suppose that the government levies a tax on earnings at rate *t*. The tax reduces the reward for working an hour from \$w to \$(1 − t)w. When Hercules consumes an hour of leisure, he now gives up only \$(1 − t)w, not \$w. In effect, the tax reduces the opportunity cost of an hour of leisure. In Figure 16.2, the budget constraint facing Hercules is no longer *TD*. Rather, it is the flatter line, *TH*, whose slope in absolute value is (1 − t)w. The original income-leisure choice, E_1, is no longer attainable. Hercules must choose a point somewhere along the after-tax budget constraint *TH*. In Figure 16.2, this is E_2, where he consumes *OI* hours of leisure, works *IT* hours, and has an after-tax income of *OG'*. The tax lowers Hercules' labor supply from *FT* hours to *IT* hours.

Can we therefore conclude that a "rational" individual *always* reduces labor supply in response to a proportional tax? To answer this question, consider Poseidon, who faces exactly the same before- and after-tax budget constraints as Hercules, and who chooses to work the same number of hours (*FT*) before imposition of the tax. As indicated in Figure 16.3, when Poseidon is taxed, he *increases* his hours of work from *FT* to *JT*. This is not "irrational." Depending on a person's tastes, he may want to work more, less, or the same amount after a tax is imposed.

The source of the ambiguity is the conflict between two effects generated by the tax, the *substitution effect* and the *income effect*. When the tax reduces

FIGURE 16.3

Proportional income
tax increasing hours
of labor supplied

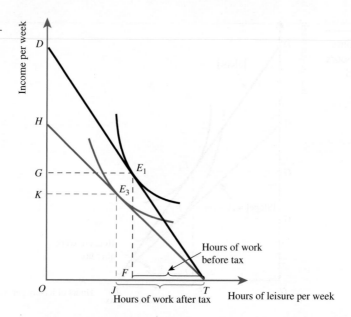

the take-home wage, the opportunity cost of leisure goes down, and there is
a tendency to substitute leisure for work. This is the substitution effect, and
it tends to decrease labor supply. At the same time, for any number of hours
worked, the tax reduces the individual's income. Assuming that leisure is a
normal good, for any number of hours worked, this loss in income leads to
a reduction in consumption of leisure, other things being the same. But a
decrease in leisure means an increase in work. The income effect therefore
tends to induce an individual to work more. Thus, the two effects work in
opposite directions. It is simply impossible to know on the basis of theory
alone whether the income effect or substitution effect dominates. For Hercules,
shown in Figure 16.2, the substitution effect dominates. For Poseidon, shown
in Figure 16.3, the income effect is more important. For a more general discussion of income and substitution effects, see the appendix to the book.

The analysis of a progressive tax is very similar to that of a proportional
tax. Suppose that Hercules is now confronted with increasing marginal tax
rates: t_1 on his first $5,000 of earnings, t_2 on his second $5,000 of earnings,
and t_3 on all income above $10,000. (Note the similarity to the US income
tax, which assigns a marginal tax rate to each income bracket.) Again, the
before-tax budget line is TD, which is depicted in Figure 16.4. After tax, the
budget constraint is the kinked line $TLMN$. Up to $5,000 of before-tax income,
the opportunity cost of an hour of leisure is $(1 - t_1)w$, which is the slope (in
absolute value) of segment TL. At point L, Hercules' income is $(1 - t_1) \times$
$5,000. On segment ML the absolute value of the slope is $(1 - t_2)w$. ML
is flatter than TL because t_2 is greater than t_1. At point M, after-tax income is
$(1 - t_1) \times \$5,000 + (1 - t_2) \times \$5,000$; this is after-tax income at point L
plus the increment to income after receiving an additional $5,000 that is taxed

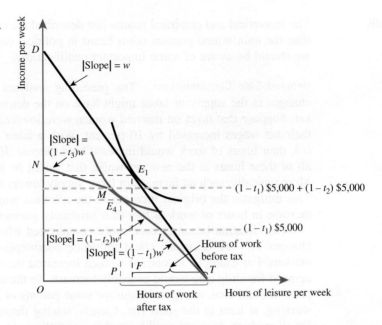

FIGURE 16.4

Leisure–income choice under a progressive income tax

at rate t_2. Finally, on segment MN the slope is $(1 - t_3)w$, which is even flatter. Depending on his preferences, Hercules can end up anywhere on $TLMN$. In Figure 16.4, he maximizes utility at E_4 where he works PT hours.

Empirical Findings

Our theory suggests that an individual's labor supply decision depends on: (a) variables that affect the position of the budget constraint, especially the after-tax wage[1] and (b) variables that affect the individual's indifference curves for leisure and income, such as age, sex, and marital status. Econometricians have estimated regression equations in which annual hours of work is a function of such variables. Although considerable differences in estimates arise due to inevitable differences in samples, time periods, and statistical techniques, the following two important general tendencies have been observed:

- For males between the ages of roughly 20 and 60, the effect of changes in the net wage on hours of work is small in absolute value and is often statistically insignificant. An elasticity of about 0.05 seems a reasonable estimate.

- Although estimated labor supply elasticities for women vary widely, the hours of work and labor force participation decisions of married women seem to be quite sensitive to changes in the net wage. A conservative estimate of the elasticity would be about 0.4 [Hyslop, 2001].

---

[1] Another important determinant of the budget constraint is nonlabor income: dividends, interest, transfer payments, and so forth. Nonlabor income causes a parallel shift in the budget constraint; there is a constant addition to income at every level of hours worked.

Some Caveats

The theoretical and empirical results just described are certainly more useful than the uninformed guesses often heard in political debates. Nevertheless, we should be aware of some important qualifications.

Demand-Side Considerations.　The preceding analyses ignore effects that changes in the supply of labor might have on the demand side of the market. Suppose that taxes on married women were lowered in such a way that their net wages increased by 10 percent. With a labor supply elasticity of 0.4, their hours of work would increase by 4 percent. If firms could absorb all of these hours at the new net wage, that would be the end of the story. More typically, such an increase in labor supply lowers the *before*-tax wage. This mitigates the original increase in the *after*-tax wage, so that the final increase in hours of work is less than originally guessed.

The situation becomes even more complicated when we realize major changes in work decisions could influence consumption patterns in other markets. For example, if married women increased their hours of work, the demand for child care would probably increase. To the extent this raised the price of child care, it might discourage some parents of small children from working, at least in the short run. Clearly, tracing through the implications for all markets, "general equilibrium" is a complicated business. Most investigators are willing to assume that the first-round effects are a reasonable approximation to the final result.

Individual versus Group Effects.　Our focus has been on how much an individual works under alternative tax regimes. It is difficult to use such results to predict how the total hours of work supplied by a *group* of workers will change. When the tax schedule changes, incentives change differently for different people. For example, in a move from a proportional to a progressive tax, low-income workers may find themselves facing lower marginal tax rates while just the opposite is true for those with high incomes. The labor supplies of the two groups might move in opposite directions, making the overall outcome difficult to predict.

Other Dimensions of Labor Supply.　The number of hours worked annually is an important and interesting indicator of labor supply. But the effective amount of labor supplied by an individual depends on more than the number of hours elapsed at the workplace. A highly educated, healthy, well-motivated worker presumably is more productive than a counterpart who lacks these qualities and works the same number of hours. Some have expressed fears that taxes induce people to invest too little in the acquisition of skills. Economic theory yields surprising insights into how taxes might affect the accumulation of *human capital*—investments that people make in themselves to increase their productivity.

Consider Hera, who is contemplating entering an on-the-job training program. Suppose that over her lifetime, the program increases Hera's earnings by an amount whose present value is B. However, participation in the program reduces the amount of time currently available to Hera for income-producing activity, which costs her C in forgone wages. If she is sensible, Hera makes her decision using the investment criterion described in Chapter 11 and enters the program only if the benefits exceed the costs:

$$B - C > 0 \tag{16.1}$$

Now suppose that Hera's earnings are taxed at a proportional rate t. The tax takes away some of the higher wages earned by virtue of participation in the training program. One might guess that the tax therefore lowers the likelihood of her participation. This reasoning is misleading. To see why, assume for the moment that after the tax Hera continues to work the same number of hours as she did before. The tax does indeed reduce the training program's benefits from B to $(1 - t)B$. But at the same time, it reduces the costs. Recall that the costs of the program are the forgone wages. Because these wages would have been taxed, Hera gives up nôt C, but only $(1 - t)C$. The decision to enter the program is based on whether after-tax benefits exceed after-tax costs:

$$(1 - t)B - (1 - t)C = (1 - t)(B - C) > 0 \tag{16.2}$$

A glance at Expression (16.2) indicates that it is exactly equivalent to (16.1). Any combination of benefits and costs that was acceptable before the earnings tax is acceptable afterward. In this model, a proportional earnings tax reduces benefits and cost in the same proportion and therefore has no effect on human capital investment.

A key assumption here is that labor supply is constant after the tax is imposed. Suppose instead that Hera increases her supply of labor. (The income effect predominates.) In this case, the tax leads to an increase in human capital accumulation. In effect, labor supply is the utilization rate of the human capital investment. The more hours a person works, the greater the payoff to an increase in the wage rate from a given human capital investment. Therefore, if the tax induces more work, it makes human capital investments more attractive, other things being the same. Conversely, if the substitution effect predominates so that labor supply decreases, human capital accumulation is discouraged.

This simple model ignores several considerations:

- The returns to a human capital investment cannot be known with certainty. As shown later in this chapter, risky returns complicate the analysis of taxation.
- Some human capital investments involve costs other than forgone earnings. College tuition, which is not tax deductible, is an obvious example.
- Other aspects of the tax system can affect human capital investments. For example, increased taxes on the returns to physical

investments (for example, interest and dividends) tend to increase human capital investment. In effect, one can view physical and human capital as two alternative investment vehicles; increasing the tax on one enhances the relative attractiveness of the other.

■ Unlike the case in Expression (16.2), when the tax system is progressive, the benefits and costs of human capital investments may be taxed at different rates.

However, complicating the model by taking such considerations into account just confirms the basic result—from a theoretical point of view, the effect of earnings taxation on human capital accumulation is ambiguous. Unfortunately, little empirical work on this important question is available.

The Compensation Package.   The basic theory of labor supply assumes that the hourly wage is the only reward for working. In reality, employers often offer employees a compensation *package* that includes not only wages but also health benefits, pensions, "perks" such as access to a company car, in-house sports facilities, and so on. As we noted in the last chapter, most of the nonwage component of compensation is not taxed. When marginal tax rates fall, the relative attractiveness of untaxed forms of income declines, and vice versa. Hence, changes in taxes might affect the composition of the compensation package. Some evidence exists that this is the case. For example, according to Gruber and Lettau [2000], for each 10 percent rise in the tax subsidy to health insurance, the number of firms offering insurance coverage increases by about 3 percent.

The Expenditure Side.   The standard analysis of labor supply and taxation ignores the disposition of the tax receipts. However, at least some of the revenues are used to purchase public goods, the availability of which can affect work decisions. If the tax money is used to provide recreational facilities such as national parks, we expect the demand for leisure to increase, *ceteris paribus*. On the other hand, expenditure on child care facilities for working parents might increase labor supply. Ideally, we should examine the labor supply consequences of the entire budget, not just the tax side. In practice, empirical investigators have not learned much about how public expenditures affect work decisions. This is because of the difficulties involved in determining how individuals value public good consumption, a problem that we have already discussed in several different contexts.

Labor Supply and Tax Revenues

So far, our emphasis has been on finding the labor supply associated with any given tax regime. We now explore the related issue of how tax collections vary with the tax rate.

Consider the supply curve of labor S_L depicted in Figure 16.5. It shows the optimal amount of work for each after-tax wage, other things being the same. As it is drawn, hours of work increase with the net wage—the

FIGURE 16.5

Tax rates, hours of
work, and tax
revenue

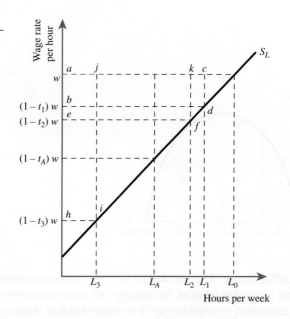

substitution effect dominates. The before-tax wage, w, is associated with
L_0 hours of work. Obviously, since the tax rate is zero, no revenue is collected. Now suppose a proportional tax at rate t_1 is imposed. The net wage
is $(1 - t_1)w$, and labor supply is L_1 hours. Tax collections are equal to the
tax per hour worked (ab) times the number of hours worked (ac), or rectangle, $abdc$. Similar reasoning indicates that if the tax rate were raised to
t_2, tax revenues would be $eakf$. Area $eakf$ exceeds $abdc$—a higher tax rate
leads to greater revenue collections. Do government revenues always
increase when the tax rate goes up? No. For example, at tax rate t_3, revenues $haji$ are less than those at the lower rate t_2. Although the tax collected *per hour* is very high at t_3, the number of hours falls so much that
the product of the tax rate and hours is fairly low. Indeed, as the tax rate
approaches 100 percent, people stop working altogether and tax revenues
fall to zero.

All of this is summarized compactly in Figure 16.6, which shows the
tax rate on the horizontal axis and tax revenue on the vertical. At very low
tax rates, revenue collections are low. As tax rates increase, revenues
increase, reaching a maximum at rate t_A. For rates exceeding t_A, revenues
begin to fall, eventually diminishing to zero. Note that it would be absurd
for the government to impose any tax rate exceeding t_A, because tax rates
could be reduced without the government losing any revenue.

Hard as it may be to believe, Figure 16.6 is at the center of an ongoing
political controversy. This is largely due to the well-publicized assertion by
economist Arthur B. Laffer [1979] that the United States operates to the right
of t_A. In the popular press, the tax rate–tax revenue relationship is known as

FIGURE 16.6

Tax rates versus tax revenue

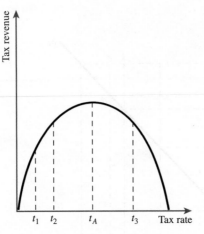

the **Laffer curve.** The notion that tax rate reductions create no revenue losses was an important tenet of the supply-side economics espoused by the Reagan administration; it continues to be a potent force in Washington policy debates.

The popular debate surrounding the Laffer curve has been confused and confusing. A few points are worth making:

- In our simple model, whether tax revenues rise or fall when the tax rate changes is determined by the extent to which changes in hours worked offset the change in the tax rate. This is precisely the issue of the elasticity of labor supply investigated by public finance economists. Hence, the shape of a Laffer curve is determined by the elasticity of labor with respect to the net wage.

- Some critics of supply-side economics argue that the very idea that tax rate reductions can lead to increased revenue is absurd. However, the discussion surrounding Figure 16.6 suggests that in principle, lower tax rates can indeed lead to higher revenue collections.

- It is therefore an empirical question whether or not the economy is actually operating to the right of t_A. As noted earlier, the consensus among economists who have studied taxes and labor supply is that the overall elasticities are modest in size. It is safe to conclude that the economy is not operating to the right of t_A. General tax rate reductions are unlikely to be self-financing in the sense of unleashing so much labor supply that tax revenues do not fall.

- Changes in labor supply are not the only way in which increased tax rates can affect tax revenues. As noted, people can substitute nontaxable forms of income for wages when tax rates go up, so that even with a fixed supply of labor, tax revenues can fall. In the same way, people (especially those with high incomes) can substitute nontaxable forms of capital income such as municipal bond interest for taxable forms of capital income. Or individuals may cheat more when tax rates increase. On the basis of an examination of tax return data, Gruber and Saez [2002] conclude that particularly for high-income individuals, tax rates have a substantial impact on taxable income. Their estimates imply, for example, that reducing the marginal tax rate on a typical high-income individual from 40 percent to 30 percent would increase her taxable income by more than 9 percent. Thus, the decrease in revenue would be less than if there were no behavioral response. On the other hand, the tax decrease would not be self-financing. Some investigators have found more responsiveness than Gruber and Saez, and others less. However, the literature as a whole suggests a claim that is undoubtedly correct and important for policy: The revenue-maximizing tax rate is not the same for all income groups or the same for all types of income.

- Even if tax revenues fail to increase when tax rates fall, it does not mean that tax rate reduction is necessarily undesirable. As emphasized in previous chapters, determination of the optimal tax system depends on a wide array of social and economic considerations. Those who believe that the government sector is too large should presumably be quite happy to see tax revenues reduced.

Overview

The economic theory of taxes and labor supply tells us which variables to examine but provides no firm answers. Econometric work indicates that for prime age males, hours of work are not much affected by taxes. For married women, on the other hand, taxes probably reduce labor force participation rates and hours of work. An important qualification is that the effect of taxes on other dimensions of labor supply, such as educational and job-training decisions, is not well understood. Neither is much known about how tax systems affect the development of attitudes, work habits, and social norms of workers.

Some politicians have suggested that if tax rates were cut, people would work so much more that the Treasury would suffer no revenue loss. On the basis of what is known about labor supply, such an effect is unlikely. However, the notion that tax cuts are partially self-financing is plausible when one considers other ways in which taxpayers can substitute nontaxable for taxable forms of income.

Saving

A second type of behavior that may be affected by taxation is saving. Most modern analysis of saving decisions is based on the **life-cycle model,** which says that individuals' consumption and saving decisions during a given year are the result of a planning process that considers their lifetime economic circumstances [Browning and Crossley, 2001]. The amount you save each year depends not only on your income that year but also on the income that you

FIGURE 16.7

Budget constraint for present and future consumption

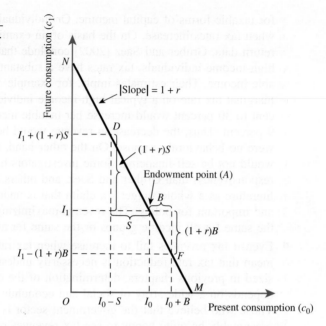

expect in the future and the income you received in the past. This section uses a life-cycle model to explore the impact of taxes on saving decisions.

Consider Scrooge, who expects to live two periods: "now" (period 0) and the "future" (period 1). Scrooge has an income of I_0 dollars now and knows that his income will be I_1 dollars in the future. (Think of "now" as "working years," when I_0 is labor earnings; and the "future" as retirement years, when I_1 is fixed pension income.) His problem is to decide how much to consume in each period. When Scrooge decides how much to consume, he simultaneously decides how much to save or borrow. If his consumption this period exceeds his current income, he must borrow. If his consumption is less than current income, he saves.

The first step in analyzing the saving decision is to depict the possible combinations of present and future consumption available to Scrooge—his budget constraint. In Figure 16.7, the amount of current consumption, c_0, is measured on the horizontal axis, and future consumption, c_1, is measured on the vertical axis. One option available to Scrooge is to consume all his income just as it comes in—to consume I_0 in the present and I_1 in the future. This bundle, called the **endowment point,** is denoted by A in Figure 16.7. At the endowment point, Scrooge neither saves nor borrows.

Another option is to save out of current income in order to consume more in the future. Suppose that Scrooge decides to save S dollars this period. If he invests his savings in an asset with a rate of return of r, he can increase his future consumption by $(1 + r)S$—the principal S plus the interest rS. By decreasing present consumption by S, Scrooge can increase his future consumption by $(1 + r)S$. Graphically, this possibility is represented by moving S dollars to the left of the endowment point A, and $(1 + r)S$ dollars above it—point D in Figure 16.7.

Alternatively, Scrooge can consume more than I_0 in the present if he can borrow against his future income. Assume that Scrooge can borrow money at the same rate of interest, r, at which he can lend. If he borrows B dollars to add to his present consumption, by how much must he reduce his future consumption? When the future arrives, Scrooge must pay back B *plus* interest of rB. Hence, Scrooge can increase present consumption by B only if he is willing to reduce future consumption by $B + rB = (1 + r)B$. Graphically, this process involves moving B dollars to the right of the endowment point, and then $(1 + r)B$ dollars below it—point F in Figure 16.7.

By repeating this procedure for various values of S and B, we can determine how much future consumption is feasible given any amount of current consumption. In the process of doing so, we trace out budget line MN, which passes through the endowment point A, and has a slope in absolute value of $1 + r$. As always, the slope of a budget line represents the opportunity cost of one good in terms of the other. Its slope of $1 + r$ indicates that the cost of \$1 of consumption in the present is $1 + r$ dollars of forgone consumption in the future.[2] Because MN shows the trade-off between consumption across time, it is called the **intertemporal budget constraint.**

To determine the choice along MN, we introduce Scrooge's preferences between future and present consumption, which are represented by conventionally shaped indifference curves. In Figure 16.8 we reproduce Scrooge's budget constraint, MN, and superimpose a few indifference curves labeled *i, ii,* and *iii.* Under the reasonable assumption that more consumption is preferred to less consumption, curves further to the northeast represent higher levels of utility.

Subject to budget constraint MN, Scrooge maximizes utility at point E_1, where he consumes c_0^* in the present and c_1^* in the future. With this information, it is easy to find how much Scrooge saves. Because present income, I_0, exceeds present consumption, c_0^*, then by definition the difference, $I_0 - c_0^*$, is saving.

Of course, this does not prove that it is always rational to save. If the highest feasible indifference curve had been tangent to the budget line below point A, present consumption would have exceeded I_0, and Scrooge would have borrowed. Although the following analysis of taxation assumes Scrooge is a saver, the same techniques can be applied if he is a borrower.

---

[2] To represent the budget line algebraically, note that the fundamental constraint facing Scrooge is that the present value of his consumption equals the present value of his income. (See Chapter 11 for an explanation of present value.) The present value of his consumption is $c_0 + c_1/(1 + r)$, while the present value of his income stream is $I_0 + I_1/(1 + r)$. Thus, his selection of c_0 and c_1 must satisfy $c_0 + c_1/(1 + r) = I_0 + I_1/(1 + r)$. The reader can verify that viewed as a function of c_0 and c_1, this is a straight line whose slope is $-(1 + r)$ and that passes through the point (I_0, I_1).

FIGURE 16.8

Utility-maximizing
choice of present
and future
consumption

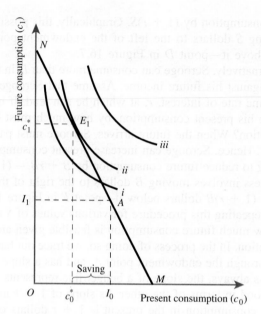

We now consider how the amount of saving changes when a proportional tax on interest income is introduced.[3] In this context, it is important to specify whether payments of interest by borrowers are deductible from taxable income. Before the Tax Reform Act of 1986, interest payments generally were deductible. Under current law, however, it is not safe to assume that a particular taxpayer is allowed to deduct interest payments. It depends, among other things, on whether he or she is a homeowner. (See the previous chapter for details.) We therefore analyze the effect on saving both with and without deductibility.

Case I: Deductible Interest Payments and Taxable Interest Receipts. How does the budget line in Figure 16.8 change when interest is subject to a proportional tax at rate t, and interest payments by borrowers are deductible? Figure 16.9 reproduces the before-tax constraint MN from Figure 16.7. The first thing to note is that the after-tax budget constraint must also pass through the endowment point (I_0, I_1), because interest tax or no interest tax, Scrooge always has the option of neither borrowing nor lending.

The next relevant observation is that the tax reduces the rate of interest received by savers from r to $(1 - t)r$. Therefore, the opportunity cost of consuming a dollar in the present is only $[1 + (1 - t)r]$ dollars in the future. At the same time, for each dollar of interest Scrooge pays, he can deduct

---

[3] We could consider an *income* tax that includes wages as well as interest, but this would complicate matters without adding any important insights.

FIGURE 16.9

Interest receipts taxed and interest payments deductible: saving decreases

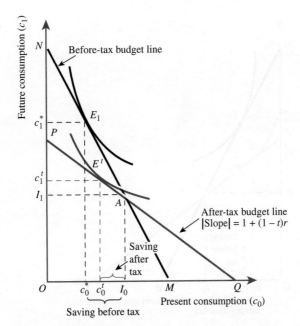

$1 from taxable income. This is worth t to him in lower taxes. Hence, the effective rate that has to be paid for borrowing is $(1 - t)r$. Therefore, the cost of increasing current consumption by one dollar, in terms of future consumption, is only $[1 + (1 - t)r]$ dollars. Together, these facts imply that the after-tax budget line has a slope (in absolute value) of $[1 + (1 - t)r]$.

The budget line that passes through (I_0, I_1) and has a slope of $[1 + (1 - t)r]$ is PAQ in Figure 16.9. As long as the tax rate is positive, it is necessarily flatter than the pretax budget line MAN.

To complete the analysis, we draw in indifference curves. The new optimum is at E^t, where present consumption is c_0^t, and future consumption is c_1^t. As before, saving is the difference between present consumption and present income, distance $c_0^t I_0$. Note that $c_0^t I_0$ is less than $c_0^* I_0$, the before-tax amount that was saved. The interest tax thus lowers saving by distance $c_0^* c_0^t$.

However, saving does not always fall. For a counterexample, consider Figure 16.10. The before- and after-tax budget lines are identical to their counterparts in Figure 16.9, as is the before-tax equilibrium at point E_1. But the new tangency occurs at point $\widetilde{E}$, to the left of E_1. Consumption in the present is $\widetilde{c}_0$, and in the future, $\widetilde{c}_1$. In this case, a tax on interest actually increases saving, from $c_0^* I_0$ to $\widetilde{c}_0^* I_0$. Thus, depending on the individual's preferences, taxing interest can either increase or decrease saving.

The ambiguity arises because of the conflict between two different effects. On one hand, taxing interest reduces the opportunity cost of present consumption, which tends to increase c_0 and lower saving. This is the substitution effect, which comes about because the tax changes the price of c_0

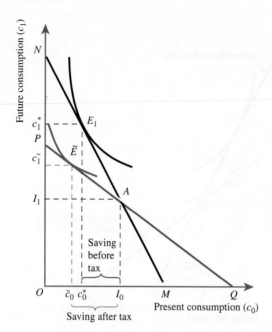

FIGURE 16.10

Interest receipts taxed and interest payments deductible: saving increases

in terms of c_1. On the other hand, the fact that interest is being taxed makes it harder for a lender to achieve any future consumption goal. This is the income effect, which arises because the tax lowers real income. If present consumption is a normal good, a decrease in income lowers c_0, and hence raises saving. Just as in the case of labor supply, whether the substitution or income effect dominates cannot be known on the basis of theory alone.

If the notion that a rational person might actually increase her saving in response to an increased tax on interest seems bizarre to you, consider the extreme case of a "target saver," whose only goal is to have a given amount of consumption in the future—no more and no less. (Perhaps she wants to save just enough to pay her children's future college tuition.) If the tax rate goes up, then the only way for her to reach her target is to increase saving, and vice versa. Thus, for the target saver, saving and the after-tax interest rate move in opposite directions.

Case II: Nondeductible Interest Payments and Taxable Interest Receipts.   We now consider how the budget constraint changes when interest is taxed at rate t, but borrowers cannot deduct interest payments from taxable income. Figure 16.11 reproduces the before-tax budget constraint NM from Figure 16.7. As was true for Case I, the after-tax budget constraint must include the endowment point (I_0, I_1). Now, starting at the endowment point, suppose Scrooge decides to save \$1, that is, move \$1 to the left of point A. Because interest is taxed, this allows him to increase his consumption next period by $[1 + (1 - t)r]$ dollars. *To the left of point A,* then, the opportunity cost of

FIGURE 16.11

Interest receipts taxed and interest payments nondeductible

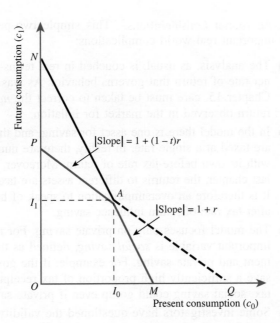

Future consumption (c_1)

$|Slope| = 1 + (1 - t)r$

$|Slope| = 1 + r$

Present consumption (c_0)

increasing present consumption by \$1 is $[1 + (1 - t)r]$ dollars of future consumption. Therefore, the absolute value of the slope of the budget constraint to the left of point A is $[1 + (1 - t)r]$. This coincides with segment PA of the after-tax budget constraint in Figure 16.9.

Now suppose that starting at the endowment point, Scrooge decides to borrow \$1, that is, move \$1 to the right of point A. Because interest is nondeductible, the tax system does not affect the cost of borrowing. Thus, the cost to Scrooge of borrowing the \$1 now is $(1 + r)$ dollars of future consumption, just as it was before the interest tax. Hence, *to the right of point A* the opportunity cost of increasing present consumption by a dollar is $(1 + r)$ dollars. This coincides with segment AM of the before-tax budget constraint NM.

Putting all this together, we see that when interest receipts are taxable but interest payments are nondeductible, the intertemporal budget constraint has a kink at the endowment point. To the left of the endowment point, the absolute value of the slope is $[1 + (1 - t)r]$; to the right, it is $(1 + r)$. What is the impact on saving? If Scrooge was a borrower before the tax was imposed, the system does not affect him. That is, if Scrooge maximized utility along segment AM before the tax was imposed, he also does so after. On the other hand, if Scrooge was a saver before the tax, his choice between present and future consumption must change, because points on segment NA are no longer available to him. However, just as in the discussion surrounding Figures 16.9 and 16.10, we cannot predict a priori whether Scrooge will save more or less. It depends on the relative strengths of the income and substitution effects.

Some Additional Considerations.   This simple two-period model ignores some important real-world complications:

- The analysis, as usual, is couched in real terms—it is the *real* net rate of return that governs behavior. As was emphasized in Chapter 15, care must be taken to correct the *nominal* rates of return observed in the market for inflation.

- In the model there is one asset for saving, and the returns to saving are taxed at a single rate. In reality, there are numerous assets, each with its own before-tax rate of return. Moreover, as observed in the last chapter, the returns to different assets are taxed at different rates. It is therefore an oversimplification to speak of how changes in "the" after-tax rate of return influence saving.

- The model focuses only on private saving. For many purposes, the important variable is *social saving,* defined as the sum of government and private saving. For example, if the government were to save a sufficiently high proportion of tax receipts from an interest tax, social saving could go up even if private saving decreased.

- Some investigators have questioned the validity of the life-cycle model itself. The life-cycle hypothesis posits that people are forward looking; critics argue that a more realistic assumption is that people are myopic. The life-cycle model also assumes that people can borrow and lend freely at the going rate of interest; critics point out that many people are not able to borrow. Of course, neither the proponents of the life-cycle view nor its detractors need be 100 percent correct. At any given time, some families' saving behavior may be explained by the model, while others' saving behavior may be myopic or constrained. In a recent study of US data, King [1993] concluded that most consumers—perhaps 90 percent—behave according to the life-cycle hypothesis.

Despite the controversies surrounding the life-cycle hypothesis, most economists are willing to accept it as a pretty good approximation to reality. In any case, the basic result of our theoretical analysis still holds: the effect of taxation on saving cannot be predicted without empirical work.

Econometric Studies of Saving

Several econometric studies have estimated the effect of taxation on saving. In a typical study, the quantity of saving is the left-hand variable and the explanatory variables are the rate of return to saving, disposable income, and other variables that might plausibly affect saving. If the coefficient on the rate of return is positive, the conclusion is that increases in taxes (which decrease the rate of return) depress saving, and vice versa.

Implementing this framework is difficult. One reason is that computing real market returns requires subtracting the *expected* inflation rate from the observed market rate. Presumably, people's expectations are based on past experience plus anticipation of the future, but no one knows exactly how expectations are formed. Studies using alternative methods for computing expected inflation rates can come to different conclusions.

This problem and others have defied the efforts of economists to reach a firm consensus on how taxes affect saving. The research surveyed by Bernheim [1999] suggests that the impact on saving of changes in the after-tax rate of return is very small or zero. That is, for the population as a whole, the income and substitution effects more or less cancel each other out.

Tax-Preferred Savings Accounts

As noted in the previous chapter, certain taxpayers are allowed to save in a variety of tax-preferred savings accounts. Although Keogh accounts, 401(k) plans, and the various Individual Retirement Accounts (IRAs) differ in their details, they share certain key attributes: The funds deposited into them accumulate at the before-tax rate of interest, and the maximum amounts that can be deposited in any given year are limited by law. A perennial issue in tax policy debates is whether the contribution limits should be increased: Should people be allowed to save more in tax-preferred accounts? The question took on special cogency in 2003, when President Bush proposed expanding IRAs both by increasing the amount that could be contributed annually (from $3,000 to $7,000) and by allowing all families to set up IRA accounts, regardless of income. (Under current law, high-income families are not eligible.)

The central question in debates over such proposals is whether contributions to these accounts represent new saving, or whether people simply deposit money that otherwise would have been saved in some other form. Different investigators have come to very different conclusions on this issue. The basic problem is that it is hard to determine whether differences in people's saving behavior are due to differences in tastes or due to the presence of tax-preferred saving accounts. Suppose, for example, that over time we observe that some people increase both their tax-preferred assets and their other assets. One investigator might say, "This proves that tax-preferred accounts represent new saving, because tax preferred assets grew without diminishing other assets." Another investigator could respond, "Nope. All that is going on is that these people have a strong taste for saving, and over time they increase their holdings of all kinds of assets." On the basis of a survey of the literature on IRAs, Hubbard and Skinner [1996] conclude that a good guess is that 26 cents per dollar of IRA contribution is new saving.

The discussion so far has assumed that the administrative details of tax-preferred savings accounts are irrelevant. Consider two possible scenarios. In the first, your boss says that she will set up a 401(k) account for you. (Recall from Chapter 15 that a 401(k) plan is a kind of tax-preferred savings account similar to a traditional IRA.) All you have to do is fill out a form requesting her to do so. In the second scenario, your boss says that she will set up a 401(k) account for you unless you fill out a form requesting her not to do so. Conventional economic theory suggests that the outcomes in the two scenarios should be identical—you figure out whether or not you want the

401(k) and make your decision. The default option is irrelevant. However, work by Choi *et al.* [2001] suggests that the way in which the options are presented has a major effect. In one company, for example, when eligible employees had to ask to be enrolled in a 401(k) plan, the percentage participating after 12 months was 42 percent. When the company switched to a setup in which employees were automatically enrolled unless they opted out, the participation rate after 12 months was 85.3 percent. Thus, defaults appear to exert an important effect on saving behavior, and this should be taken into account in the design of saving incentives. More generally, these results suggest that to understand saving behavior, it may be necessary to go beyond conventional economic models and take into account insights from psychology that are often ignored by economists. A good deal of research along these lines is currently in progress. (See Choi *et al.* for citations.)

Taxes and the Capital Shortage

The taxation of capital income is a major political issue. Much of the debate centers on the proposition that by discouraging saving, the tax system has led to a *capital shortage*—insufficient capital to meet our national "needs."

A major problem with this line of reasoning is that, as we have just shown, it is not at all obvious that taxation reduces the supply of saving. Let us assume, for the sake of argument, that saving indeed declines because of taxes. Nevertheless, as long as the capital market is competitive, a decrease in saving does not create a gap between the demand for investment funds and their supply. Instead, the interest rate adjusts to equate quantities supplied and demanded. However, it is true that the new equilibrium will, other things being equal, involve a lower rate of investment, possibly leading to lower productivity growth.

But to look only at these issues is unfair. Taxation of *any* factor may reduce the equilibrium quantity. The important efficiency question is whether taxation of capital income leads to larger excess burdens than other ways of raising tax revenues. We defer to Chapter 19 a discussion of whether economic efficiency would be enhanced if taxes on capital were eliminated. In the meantime, we note that there is no reason a high rate of investment alone is a desirable objective. In a utilitarian framework, at least, capital accumulation is a means of enhancing individual welfare, not an end in itself.

Finally, the entire argument that saving incentives can increase the capital stock rests on the premise that investment in the economy depends on its own rate of saving: all national saving is channeled into national investment. This is true in an economy that is closed to international trade. In an open economy, however, domestic saving can be invested abroad. This means that tax policy designed to stimulate saving may not lead to more domestic investment. To the extent that saving flows freely across national boundaries to whatever investment opportunities seem most attractive, the ability of tax policy to stimulate investment through saving is greatly diminished.

A number of econometric studies have found that countries with high domestic saving tend to have high domestic investment, and vice versa. While the data are open to other interpretations, this suggests that saving may not flow into and out of the economy as freely as one would expect in a completely integrated world capital market (Obstfeld and Rogoff [1996, Chap. 3]). As long as saving and domestic investment are correlated, tax policy that affects saving can generally be expected to affect investment. The size of the effect, however, is smaller than one would find in a totally closed economy.

Housing Decisions

When people talk of a capital shortage, they are usually concerned with the amount of capital available to businesses for producing goods. Another very important form of capital is owner-occupied housing. A tax code can have little impact on the overall level of saving yet still significantly affect the allocation of saving across different types of investment. This section discusses how the tax code favors investment in housing.

The effects of the income tax on housing investment can best be illustrated with an example. Macbeth owns a house and decides to rent it out. What is his net income? He receives rent from his tenants, but also has to incur some operating expenses such as making repairs. Call R his rent less these operating expenses. Suppose that Macbeth took out a mortgage to buy the house, and his yearly interest payments are MI. These interest payments are a business expense, and need to be subtracted from R to find net income. Finally, suppose that the house increases in value during the course of the year by ΔV. This is a capital gain, which is also a component of income. (If the house goes down in value, then ΔV is negative; i.e., a capital loss reduces income.) Putting all of this together, Macbeth's net income as a landlord, R_{net}, is

$$R_{net} = R - MI + \Delta V.$$

Under a tax system based on conventional Haig-Simons principles, R_{net} is added into Macbeth's taxable income.

Now suppose that instead of renting the house, Macbeth and his wife move into it themselves. By virtue of living in the house, they receive a benefit equal to the market rental value of the house, while still incurring the operating expenses and mortgage interest payments and getting the capital gain. That is, they receive an *imputed* net rent on the home equal to R_{net}. Whether they live in the house or not, they receive a net benefit of R_{net}; the only difference is that when they rent out the house they explicitly receive the rent in cash, while if they live in the house they effectively pay it to themselves. But implicit or not, it is still income, and under a Haig-Simons income tax, it should be taxed. However, under US law, the implicit rent that people receive on their homes is not included in the tax base, and for most households, housing capital gains are exempt from taxation.[4] By excluding imputed rent from homeownership from the tax base, the tax system in effect subsidizes owner-occupied housing.

Recall from Chapter 15 that homeowners who itemize their deductions can deduct mortgage interest and property tax payments on their tax returns. These deductions lowered tax revenues by about $93 billion in fiscal year 2004 [Joint Committee on Taxation, 2002, p. 22]. However, the deductibility of mortgage interest and property taxes is not the fundamental source of the subsidy to homeownership. Indeed, if imputed rent were included in the tax base, then mortgage interest and property taxes would be legitimate deductions, because they would be construed as expenses of earning this rental income. The basic issue is the failure to include imputed rent in the tax base in the first place.

By excluding net imputed rent from taxation, in effect the tax code lowers the price of owning a home and increases the demand for owner-occupied housing. The precise size of the increase depends on the price elasticity of demand for such housing. Poterba [1992] argues that the price elasticity is about -1.0, and on this basis estimates that, for a family with a $50,000 income, removal of the favorable tax provisions for housing would in the long run reduce the quantity consumed by about 23 percent.

The implicit subsidy affects not only how much housing people purchase but also whether they become owners or renters in the first place. At the end of World War II, 48 percent of US households resided in owner-occupied housing; the figure is now about 65 percent. Over this period, many taxpayers were moving into higher tax brackets, enhancing the attractiveness of the implicit subsidy to owner occupation. Of course, other factors were changing that might have influenced housing patterns; for example, incomes rose considerably. However, a variety of econometric studies indicate that tax considerations have played an important part in the growth of homeownership [Green and Vandell, 1999].

Proposals for Change   In Chapter 5 under "Positive Externalities," we discussed the pros and cons of providing a subsidy for owner-occupied housing. The point made there was that from an externality point of view, the subsidy does not have strong support. Although there is some evidence that homeowners are more likely than renters to take care of their property, to garden, and so on, the exernalities from living around homeowners are not large enough to justify the subsidy [Glaeser and Shapiro, 2002]. Further, the subsidy's value increases with income—62 percent of the tax expenditures associated with the deduction of mortgage interest go to households whose incomes exceed

---

[4] The law provides a $250,000 exclusion on the capital gain on the sale of a principal residence ($500,000 in the case of a joint return).

$100,000 [Joint Committee on Taxation, 2002, p. 34]. Hence, one can hardly claim that it equalizes the income distribution. In light of these facts, a number of proposals have been made to reform the federal tax treatment of housing. Probably the most radical change would be to include net imputed rent in taxable income. Such a move might create administrative problems, because the authorities would have to determine the potential market rental value of each house. Nevertheless, imputed rental income is taxed in several European countries such as Sweden and The Netherlands [Ault, 1997].

Moreover, taxing imputed rent does not appear politically feasible. Homeowners are more likely to perceive their houses as endless drains on their financial resources than as revenue producers. It would not be easy to convince homeowners—who comprise more than half the electorate—that taxing imputed rental income is a good idea.

Several reform proposals have focused on reducing the value of mortgage interest and property tax deductions to upper-income individuals. One possibility would be simply to disallow these deductions. In 1984, the US Treasury suggested the property tax deduction be eliminated. The proposal created a storm and was soon abandoned. And no serious politician has even whispered about removing the mortgage interest deduction. As noted in the previous chapter, the interest expense associated with indebtedness on a principal residence is one of the few types of interest deductible by households.

An alternative to eliminating the property tax and mortgage interest deductions would be to put upper limits on the dollar amounts that can be deducted. Another would be to convert these deductions into credits: each homeowner would be allowed to subtract the *same* proportion of interest and property tax payments from tax liability. In contrast, a deduction has a greater value to a household the higher its marginal tax rate. With a credit—say 25 percent of mortgage and property tax payments—those with higher marginal tax rates would not enjoy an advantage, other things being the same.

Evaluating these proposals is difficult because it is not clear what their objectives are and what other policy instruments are assumed to be available. For example, if a more equal income distribution is the goal, why bother with changing from deductions to credits? It would make more sense just to adjust the rate schedule appropriately.

Finally, we note that much of the debate over the tax treatment of housing implicitly assumes that full taxation of imputed rent would be the most efficient solution. Recall from the theory of optimal taxation (Chapter 14) that if lump sum taxes are excluded, the efficiency-maximizing set of tax rates is generally a function of the elasticities of demand and supply for all commodities. Only in very special cases do we expect efficiency to require equal rates for all sources of income. On the other hand, it is also highly improbable that the efficient tax rate on imputed rental income is zero. Determining the appropriate rate is an important topic for further research.

Portfolio Composition

Taxes may affect not only the total amount of wealth that people accumulate but the assets in which that wealth is held as well. A popular argument is that low taxes (especially on capital gains) encourage investment in risky assets. As an editorial in the *Wall Street Journal* argued, "high marginal tax rates . . . discourage incentives . . . to take risks" (April 19, 2001, p. A18). This proposition seems plausible. Why take a chance on a risky investment if your gains are going to be grabbed by the tax collector? However, the problem is considerably more complicated than this line of argument suggests.

Most modern theoretical work on the relationship between taxes and portfolio composition is based on the path-breaking analysis of Tobin [1958]. In Tobin's model, individuals make their decisions about whether to invest in an asset on the basis of two characteristics—the expected return on the asset, and how risky that return is. Other things being the same, investors prefer assets that are expected to yield high returns. At the same time, investors dislike risk; other things being the same, investors prefer safer assets.

Suppose there are two assets. The first is perfectly safe but it yields a zero rate of return. (Imagine holding money in a world with no inflation.) The second is a bond that *on average* yields a positive rate of return, but it is risky—there is some chance that the price will go down, so the investor incurs a loss.

The investor can adjust the return and risk on the entire portfolio by holding different combinations of the two assets. In one extreme case he or she could hold only the safe asset—there is no return, but no risk. On the other hand, the investor could hold only the risky asset—his or her expected return rises, but so does the risk involved. The typical investor holds a combination of both the risky and safe assets to suit tastes concerning risk and return.

Now assume a proportional tax is levied on the return to capital assets. Assume also the tax allows for **full loss offset**—individuals can deduct all losses from taxable income. (To some extent, this reflects actual practice in the United States; see Chapter 15.) Because the safe asset has a yield of zero, the tax has no effect on its rate of return—the return is still zero. In contrast, the risky asset has a positive expected rate of return, which is lowered by the presence of the tax. The tax seems to reduce the attractiveness of the risky asset compared to the safe asset.

However, at the same time that the tax lowers the return to the risky asset, it lowers its riskiness as well. Why? In effect, introduction of the tax turns the government into the investor's silent partner. If the investor wins (in the sense of receiving a positive return), the government shares in the gain. But because of the loss-offset provision, if the individual loses, the government also shares in the loss. Suppose, for example, that an individual loses $100 on an investment. If the tax rate is 30 percent, by subtracting $100 from taxable income, she lowers her tax bill by $30. Even though the investment lost $100, the investor loses only $70. In short, introduction of the tax tightens the dispersion of returns—the highs are less high and the lows are less low—and hence, reduces the risk. Thus, although the tax makes the risky asset *less* attractive by reducing its expected return, it simultaneously makes it *more* attractive by decreasing its risk. If the second effect dominates, taxation can on balance make the risky asset more desirable.

An important assumption behind this discussion is the existence of a perfectly riskless asset. This is not a very realistic assumption. In a world where no one is sure exactly what the inflation rate will be, even the return on money is risky. But the basic reasoning still holds. Because taxes decrease risk as well as returns, the effect of taxes on portfolio choice is ambiguous.

Resolving this ambiguity econometrically is very difficult. A major problem is that it is hard to obtain reliable information on just which assets people hold. Individuals may not accurately report their holdings to survey takers because they are not sure of the true values at any point in time. Alternatively, people might purposely misrepresent their asset positions because of fears that the information will be reported to the tax authorities. In one study using a fairly reliable data set, Poterba and Samwick [1999] found that other things (including total wealth) being the same, people in higher tax brackets have a higher probability of holding common stock, which is quite risky. This finding lends at least tentative support to the notion that taxation increases risk taking. But the issue is far from being resolved.

A Note on Politics and Elasticities

Despite much investigation, the effect of income taxation on several important kinds of behavior is not known for sure. Different "experts" are therefore likely to give policymakers different pieces of advice. In this situation, it is almost inevitable that policymakers will adopt those behavioral assumptions that are most consistent with their goals. Although it is dangerous to generalize, liberals tend to believe that behavior is not very responsive to the tax system, while conservatives take the opposite view. Liberals prefer low elasticities because they can raise large amounts of money for public sector activity without having to worry too much about charges that they are "killing the goose that laid the golden egg." In contrast, conservatives like to assume high elasticities because this limits the volume of taxes that can be collected before serious efficiency costs are imposed on the economy. Thus, when journalists, politicians, and economists make assertions about how taxes affect incentives, one should evaluate their claims in light of what their hidden agendas might be.

Summary

- The US personal income tax affects many economic decisions, including labor supply, saving, residential housing consumption, and portfolio choice. Analysis of the behavioral effects of taxation is among the most contentious of all areas of public policy.

- Econometric studies of labor supply indicate prime age males vary their hours only slightly in response to tax changes, while hours of married women are quite sensitive to variations in the after-tax wage rate.

- Earnings taxes can increase, decrease, or leave unchanged the amount of human capital investments. The outcome depends in part on how taxes affect hours of work.

- The effect of tax rates on tax revenues depends on the responsiveness of labor supply to changes in tax rates and on the extent of substitution between taxable and nontaxable forms of income.

- The effect of taxes on saving may be analyzed using the life-cycle model, which assumes that people's annual consumption and saving decisions are influenced by their lifetime resources. Taxing interest income lowers the opportunity cost of present consumption and thereby creates incentives to lower saving. However, such a tax reduces total lifetime resources, which tends to reduce present consumption, that is, increase saving. The net effect on saving is an empirical question.

- Econometric studies of saving behavior have foundered on both conceptual and practical difficulties. As a result, there is no firm consensus of opinion on the effects of taxation on saving.

- The personal income tax excludes the imputed rent from owner-occupied housing from taxation. This increases both the percentage of those choosing to own their homes and the quantity of owner-occupied housing.

- The theoretical effects of taxation on portfolio composition are ambiguous. Taxes reduce the expected return on a risky asset but also lessen its riskiness. The net effect of these conflicting tendencies has not been empirically resolved.

Discussion Questions

1. "I promise to lower income tax rates. And I won't have to cut spending, because the lower rates will induce so much economic activity that tax revenues will rise." Would this promise be more credible coming from a candidate for president or a candidate for governor of your state?

2. Suppose that individuals view their loss of income from income taxes as offset by the benefits of public services purchased with the revenues. How are their labor supply decisions affected? (Hint: Decompose the change in hours worked into income and substitution effects.)

3. Under current law, employer-provided health care benefits are excluded from taxation. Use an indifference curve analysis to model the impact of eliminating the exclusion upon the amount of health care benefits. (Hint: Think of an individual as consuming two commodities, "health care benefits" and "all other goods.")

4. The tax law passed in 2001 will eventually lower the top marginal income tax rate from 39.6 percent to 35 percent. What impact do you expect this law to have on labor supply, saving, and tax revenues?

5. In 2003, Senate Democrats proposed that all workers receive a one-time tax rebate check of $300 for each adult in a family, and $300 for each of the first two children. The goal of the program was to stimulate consumer spending. On the basis of the life-cycle model of consumption behavior, would you expect this proposal to be successful? If the life-cycle model is correct and the US government wishes to stimulate consumption, what advice would you give it?

6. An editorial in the *Wall Street Journal* (April 19, 2001) argued that "high marginal tax rates discourage incentives . . . to invest in one's own human capital with additional training or education."

Discuss the circumstances under which this statement is likely to be correct, focusing on the nature of the costs of the human capital investment.

7. The tax act passed in 2001 increased the contribution limit on IRAs from $2,000 to $5,000 by 2008. What impact would you expect this provision to have on personal saving?

8. According to Bartlett [2002], "economic theory is quite clear that full deductibility of (capital) losses is extremely important to risk-taking." Explain the basis for this contention. Under US law, capital losses are only partially deductible against other forms of income. How does this affect incentives to take risk?

9. In an economy, the supply curve of labor, S, is given by

$$S = -100 + 200 \, w_n,$$

where w_n is the after-tax wage rate. Assume that the before-tax wage rate is fixed at 10.

a. Write a formula for tax revenues as a function of the tax rate, and sketch the function in a diagram with the tax rate on the horizontal axis and tax revenues on the vertical axis. (Hint: Note that $w_n = (1 - t)10$, where t is the tax rate, and that tax revenues are the product of hours worked, the gross wage and the tax rate.) Suppose that the government currently imposes a tax rate of 70 percent. What advice would you give it?

b. Try this problem if you know some calculus: At what tax rate are tax revenues maximized in this economy?

Selected References

Choi, James J; David Laibson; Brigitte C Madrian; and Andrew Metrick. "Defined Contribution Pensions: Plan Rules, Participant Decisions, and the Path of Least Resistance." Working Paper No. 8655. Cambridge, MA: National Bureau of Economic Research, December 2001.

Engen, Eric, and Jonathan Skinner. "Taxation and Economic Growth." *National Tax Journal* 49 (December 1996), pp. 617–42.

Gruber, Jonathan, and Emmanuel Saez. "The Elasticity of Taxable Income: Evidence and Implications." *Journal of Public Economics* 84 (April 2002), pp. 1–33.

Hendershott, Patric M, and Michael White. "The Rise and Fall of Housing's Favored Investment Status." *Journal of Housing Research* 11, no. 2, 2000, pp. 257–75.

CHAPTER 17

The Corporation Tax

> *I'll probably kick myself for having said this, but when are we going to have the courage to point out that in our tax structure, the corporation tax is very hard to justify?*
> RONALD W. REAGAN

In 2002, about $5.5 trillion—or 55 percent of the gross domestic product—originated in nonfinancial corporations.[1] A **corporation** is a form of business organization in which ownership is usually represented by transferable stock certificates. The stockholders have *limited liability* for the acts of the corporation. This means that their liability to the creditors of the corporation is limited to the amount they have invested.

Corporations are independent legal entities and as such are often referred to as artificial legal persons. A corporation may make contracts, hold property, incur debt, sue, and be sued. And just like any other person, a corporation must pay tax on its income. Corporation income tax revenues account for about 8 percent of federal tax collections [Congressional Budget Office, 2003, p. 150]. This chapter explains the structure of the federal corporation income tax and analyzes its effects on the allocation of resources.

Why Tax Corporations?

Let's begin by addressing the question raised in the Ronald Reagan quotation above: Does it make sense to have a special tax system for corporations in the first place? To be sure, from a *legal* point of view, corporations are people. But from an economic standpoint, this notion makes no sense. As we stressed in Chapter 12, only real people can pay a tax. If so, why

---

[1] *Economic Report of the President, 2003*, pp. 292, 294.

should corporate activity be subject to a special tax? Why not just tax the incomes of the corporation *owners* via the personal income tax?

A number of justifications for a separate corporation tax have been proposed: First, contrary to the view just stated, corporations—especially very big ones—really are distinct entities. Large corporations have thousands of stockholders, and the managers of such corporations are controlled only very loosely, if at all, by the stockholder/owners. Most economists would certainly agree that ownership and control are separated in large corporations, and this creates important problems for understanding just how corporations function. Nevertheless, it does not follow that the corporation should be taxed as a separate entity.

A second justification for corporate taxation is that the corporation receives a number of special privileges from society, the most important of which is limited liability of the stockholders. The corporation tax can be viewed as a user fee for this benefit. However, there is no reason to believe that the revenues paid approximate the benefits received. In any case, why should we view laws that permit an efficient way for individuals to aggregate their capital as being a benefit that requires a payment? Laws that allow other kinds of contracts are not viewed in this way.

Finally, the corporation tax protects the integrity of the personal income tax. Suppose that Karl's share of the earnings of a corporation during a given year is $10,000. According to the economist's standard convention for defining income, this $10,000 is income whether the money happens to be retained by the corporation or paid out to Karl. If the $10,000 is paid out, it is taxed in an amount that depends on his personal income tax rate. In the absence of a corporation tax, the $10,000 creates no tax liability if it is retained by the corporation. Hence, unless corporation income is taxed, Karl can reduce his tax liability by accumulating income within the corporation. Of course, the money will be taxed when it is eventually paid out, but in the meantime, the full $10,000 grows at the before-tax rate of interest. Remember from Chapter 15, taxes deferred are taxes saved.

It is certainly true that not taxing corporate income creates opportunities for personal tax avoidance. But a special tax on corporations is not the only way to include earnings accumulated in corporations. We discuss an alternative method many economists view as superior at the end of this chapter.

Structure

The corporate tax rate structure is graduated. The lowest bracket is 15 percent, and the highest bracket, which begins at $10 million of taxable income, is 35 percent.[2] Most corporate income is taxed at the 35 percent rate, so for our purposes, the system can safely be presented as a flat rate of 35 percent.

---

[2] In certain ranges, the effective marginal tax rate may exceed 35 percent.

This rate is low by historical standards. Before the Tax Reform Act of 1986, it was 46 percent. The act lowered the rate to 34 percent, and it was raised a point in 1993.

However, as in the case of the personal income tax, the statutory rate by itself gives relatively little information about the effective burden. We must know exactly which deductions from before-tax corporate income are allowed. Accordingly, we now discuss the rules for defining taxable corporate income.[3]

Employee Compensation Deducted

As we saw in Chapter 15, a fundamental principle in defining personal income is that income should be measured net of the expenses incurred in earning it. The same logic applies to the measurement of corporate income. One important business expense is labor, and compensation paid to workers (wages and benefits) is excluded from taxable income.

Interest, but Not Dividends, Deducted

When corporations borrow, interest payments to lenders are excluded from taxable income. Again, the justification is that business costs should be deductible. However, when firms finance their activities by issuing stock, the dividends paid to the stockholders are *not* deductible from corporate earnings. We discuss the consequences of this asymmetry later.

Depreciation Deducted

Suppose that during a given year the XYZ Corporation makes two purchases: (1) $1,000 worth of stationery, which is used up within the year; and (2) a $1,000 drill press, which will last for 10 years. How should these two items be treated for purposes of determining XYZ's taxable income? The stationery case is fairly straightforward. Because it is entirely consumed within the year of its purchase, its entire value should be deductible from that year's corporate income, and the tax law does in fact allow such a deduction. The drill press is more complicated because it is a durable good. When the drill press is purchased, the transaction is merely an exchange of assets—the firm gives up cash in exchange for the drill press. The purchase of the asset *per se* is not an economic cost. However, as the drill press is used, it is subject to wear and tear, which decreases its value. This decrease in value, called **economic depreciation,** is an economic cost to the firm.

It follows that during the first year of the drill press's life, a consistent definition of income requires that only the economic depreciation experienced that year be subtracted from the firm's before-tax income. Similarly, the economic depreciation of the machine during its second year of use should be deductible from that year's gross income, and so on for as long as the machine is in service.

It is a lot easier to state this principle than to apply it. In practice, the tax authorities do not know exactly how much a given investment asset depreciates each year, or even what the useful life of the machine is. The

---

[3] Note also that many of these rules apply to noncorporate businesses. Also, a corporate alternative minimum tax applies in certain cases.

tax law has rules that indicate for each type of asset what proportion of its acquisition value can be depreciated each year, and over how many years depreciation can be taken—the **tax life** of the asset. Next, we discuss these rules, which often fail to reflect true economic depreciation.

Calculating the Value of Depreciation Allowances.   Assume that the tax life of the $1,000 drill press is 10 years, and a firm is allowed to depreciate ¹⁄₁₀th the machine's value each year. How much is this stream of depreciation allowances worth to the XYZ Corporation?

At the end of the first year, XYZ is permitted to subtract ¹⁄₁₀th the acquisition value, or $100, from its taxable income. With a corporation income tax rate of 35 percent, this $100 deduction saves the firm $35. Note, however, that XYZ receives this benefit a year after the machine is purchased. The present value of the $35 is found by dividing it by $(1 + r)$, where r is the opportunity cost of funds to the firm. (See Chapter 11 if you need to review present value.)

At the end of the second year, XYZ is again entitled to subtract $100 from taxable income, which generates a saving of $35 that year. Because this saving comes two years in the future, its present value is $\$35/(1 + r)^2$. Similarly, the present value of depreciation taken during the third year is $\$35/(1 + r)^3$, during the fourth year, $\$35/(1 + r)^4$, and so on. The present value of the entire stream of depreciation allowances is

$$\frac{\$35}{1 + r} + \frac{\$35}{(1 + r)^2} + \frac{\$35}{(1 + r)^3} + \cdots + \frac{\$35}{(1 + r)^{10}}$$

For example, if $r = 10$ percent, this expression is equal to $215.10. In effect, then, the depreciation allowances lower the price of the drill press after taxes from $1,000 to $784.90 (= $1,000 − $215.10). Intuitively, the effective price is below the acquisition price because the purchase leads to a stream of tax savings in the future.

More generally, suppose that the tax law allows a firm to depreciate a given asset over T years, and the proportion of the asset that can be written off against taxable income in the nth year is $D(n)$. The $D(n)$ terms sum to one, meaning that the tax law eventually allows the entire purchase price of the asset to be written off. (In the preceding example, T was 10, and $D(n)$ was equal to ¹⁄₁₀th every year. Some depreciation schemes, however, allow $D(n)$ to vary by year.) Consider the purchase of an investment asset that costs $1. The amount that can be depreciated at the end of the first year is $D(1)$ dollars, the value of which to the firm is $\theta \times D(1)$ dollars, where θ is the corporation tax rate. (Because the asset costs $1, $D(1)$ is a fraction.) Similarly, the value to the firm of the allowances in the second year is $\theta \times D(2)$. The present value of all the tax savings generated by the depreciation allowances from a $1 purchase, which we denote ψ, is

$$\psi = \frac{\theta \times D(1)}{1 + r} + \frac{\theta \times D(2)}{(1 + r)^2} + \cdots + \frac{\theta \times D(T)}{(1 + r)^T} \tag{17.1}$$

Because ψ is the tax saving for one dollar of expenditure, it follows that if the acquisition price of an asset is $\$q$, the presence of depreciation allowances lowers the effective price to $(1- \psi)q$. For example, a value of $\psi = 0.25$ indicates that for each dollar spent on an asset, 25 cents worth of tax savings are produced. Hence, if the machine cost $\$1,000$ ($q = \$1,000$), the effective price is only 75 percent of the purchase price, or $\$750$.

Equation (17.1) suggests that the tax savings from depreciation depend critically on the value of T and the function $D(n)$. In particular, the tax benefits are greater: (1) the shorter the time period over which the machine is written off—the lower is T; and (2) the greater the proportion of the machine's value that is written off at the beginning of its life—the larger the value of $D(n)$ when n is small. Schemes that allow firms to write off assets faster than true economic depreciation are referred to as **accelerated depreciation.** An extreme possibility is to allow the firm to deduct from taxable income the asset's full cost at the time of acquisition. This is referred to as **expensing.**

Under current law, every depreciable asset is assigned one of eight possible tax lives (that is, values of T). The tax lives vary from 3 to 39 years. For example, certain racehorses are 3-year property; most computers and business equipment are in the 5-year class, while most nonresidential structures have a tax life of $31\frac{1}{2}$ years. Generally, tax lives are shorter than actual useful lives. This has potential consequences for corporate investment behavior, which we discuss later.

Intangible Assets: Take Me Out to the Ballgame.   Our discussion of depreciation has assumed that the asset involved is tangible like a machine. Similar issues arise in the context of intangible assets. Suppose that a company spends money on an advertising campaign. The campaign is expected to increase sales over a period of years. One can think of the advertising as an asset that is producing a stream of revenues over time, just like a machine. By analogy, then, the firm should be allowed to deduct only the depreciation of the advertising "asset" each year. Determining the appropriate depreciation schedules for such assets is a major headache for tax administrators.

A good example relates to the acquisition of baseball franchises. If you buy a baseball team, part of what you are buying is the contracts of the players. The tax authorities have ruled that the component of the acquisition cost that is attributable to player contracts is a depreciable asset, and can be depreciated (straight-line) over a five-year period. On the other hand, other components of the value of the franchise, such as television contracts, are not depreciable. Predictably, club owners are locked in perpetual battle with the Internal Revenue Service over the value of the player-component of acquisition costs—the owners want a large proportion of the cost allocated to player contracts while the IRS wants a small proportion. In addition, the IRS notes that most other intangibles are depreciated over a 15-year period rather than the five years for player contracts, and wants baseball treated like other businesses. All of these disputes take place in an environment in which it is very difficult to determine the merits of the various arguments. In short, intractable complexities are involved in administering depreciation rules. However, dealing with depreciation is unavoidable with a tax based on income.

No Investment Tax Credit

Before 1986, the tax code included an **investment tax credit (ITC),** which permitted a firm to subtract some portion of the purchase price of an asset from its tax liability at the time the asset was acquired. If a drill press cost $1,000, and if the XYZ firm was allowed an investment tax credit of 10 percent, the purchase of a drill press lowered XYZ's tax bill by $100. The effective price of the drill press (before depreciation allowances) was thus $900. More generally, if the investment tax credit was k and the acquisition price was q, the effective price of the asset was $(1 - k)q$. In contrast to depreciation allowances, the value to the firm of an ITC did not depend on the corporate income tax rate. This was because the credit was subtracted from tax liability rather than taxable income. In the early 1980s, the credit for equipment was 6 or 10 percent (depending on its tax life).

The Tax Reform Act of 1986 eliminated the investment tax credit. Thus, k is now equal to zero. Nevertheless, the ITC remains popular among policymakers. The Clinton administration proposed reintroducing a version of the ITC, but Congress rejected the proposal. The idea is likely to surface again in future debates over tax policy.

Treatment of Dividends versus Retained Earnings

So far we have been focusing on taxes directly payable by the corporation. For many purposes, however, the important issue is not the corporation's tax liability per se, but rather the total tax rate on income generated in the corporate sector. Understanding how the corporate and personal tax structures interact is important.

Corporate profits may either be retained by the firm or paid to stockholders in the form of dividends. Dividends paid are *not* deductible from corporation income and hence are subject to the corporation income tax. Further, until recently, dividends received by stockholders were treated as ordinary income and taxed at the individual's marginal income tax rate. In effect, then, such payments were taxed twice—once at the corporation level and again when distributed to the shareholder. Some movement in the direction of removing this **double taxation** of dividends was included in legislation passed in 2003, which set a maximal rate of 15 percent on dividends received at the individual level.

To assess the tax consequences to the stockholder of retained earnings is a bit more complicated. Suppose that XYZ retains $1 of earnings. To the extent that the stock market accurately values firms, the fact that the firm now has one more dollar causes the value of XYZ stock to increase by $1. But as we saw in Chapter 15, income generated by increases in the value of stock—capital gain—is treated preferentially for tax purposes. This is because the gain received by a typical XYZ stockholder is not taxed until it is realized, and even then the rate is relatively low. The tax system thus creates incentives for firms to retain earnings rather than pay them out as dividends.

Effective Tax Rate on Corporate Capital

We began this section by noting the statutory tax rate on capital income in the corporate sector is currently 35 percent. Clearly, it would be most surprising if this were the effective rate as well. At the corporate level, computing the effective rate requires considering the effects of interest deductibility, depreciation allowances, and inflation. Moreover, as just noted, corporate income in the form of dividends and realized capital gains is also taxed at the personal level. Allowing for all these considerations, Jorgenson and Yun [2001, p. 275] estimates the effective overall marginal tax rate on corporate capital income to be 46 percent. The noncorporate rate is only 37 percent.[4]

Of course, any such calculation requires assumptions on items such as the appropriate choice of discount rate [r of Equation (17.1)], the expected rate of inflation, the extent of true economic depreciation, and so forth. Moreover, as we will see in the next section, the effective burden of the corporate tax depends in part on how investments are financed—by borrowing, issuing stock, or using internal funds. Investigators using other assumptions might generate somewhat different effective tax rates. It is unlikely, however, that alternative methods would much modify the difference between statutory and effective marginal tax rates.

Incidence and Excess Burden

Understanding tax rules and computing effective tax rates is only the first step in analyzing the corporation tax. We still must determine who ultimately bears the burden of the tax and measure the costs of any inefficiencies it induces. The economic consequences of the corporation tax are among the most controversial subjects in public finance. An important reason for the controversy is disagreement with respect to just what kind of tax it is. We can identify several views.

A Tax on Corporate Capital

Recall from our discussion of the structure of the corporation tax that the firm is not allowed to deduct from taxable income the opportunity cost of capital supplied by shareholders. Since the opportunity cost of capital is included in the tax base, it appears reasonable to view the corporation tax as a tax on capital used in the corporate sector. In the classification scheme developed in Chapter 12, the corporation tax is a partial factor tax. This is the view that predominates in most writing on the subject.

---

[4] These figures are for income generated by long-lived assets.

In a model that examines effects in all markets ("general equilibrium"), the tax on corporate capital leads to a migration of capital from the corporate sector until after-tax rates of return are equal throughout the economy. Evidence that the corporation tax does indeed lead to less economic activity being undertaken by corporations is provided by Goolsbee [2002], who notes that in states with relatively high corporation income tax rates, the number of firms doing business as corporations is relatively low, other things being the same. As capital moves to the noncorporate sector, the rate of return to capital there is depressed so that ultimately *all* owners of capital, not just those in the corporate sector, are affected. The reallocation of capital between the two sectors also affects the return to labor. The extent to which capital and labor bear the ultimate burden of the tax depends on the technologies used in production in each of the sectors, as well as the structure of consumers' demands for corporate and noncorporate goods. In their survey of public finance economists, Fuchs, Krueger, and Poterba [1997, p. 12] found that virtually all of them believe that the burden of the corporate income tax is shared by both capital and labor, "but there is significant disagreement about the precise division."

Turning now to efficiency aspects of the problem, we discussed computation of the excess burden of a partial factor tax in Chapter 13. By inducing less capital accumulation in the corporate sector than otherwise would have been the case, the corporation tax diverts capital from its most productive uses and creates an excess burden. According to the estimates of Jorgenson and Yun [2001, p. 302], the excess burden of the corporation tax is very high, about 24 percent of the revenues collected.

A Tax on Economic Profits

An alternative view is that the corporation tax is a tax on economic profits. This view is based on the observation that the tax base is determined by subtracting costs of production from gross corporate income, leaving only "profits." As we explained in Chapter 12, analyzing the incidence of a tax on economic profits is straightforward. As long as a firm maximizes economic profits, a tax on them induces no adjustments in firm behavior—all decisions regarding prices and production are unchanged. Hence, there is no way to shift the tax, and it is borne by the owners of the firm at the time the tax is levied. Moreover, by virtue of the fact that the tax leaves behavior unchanged, it generates no misallocation of resources. Hence, the excess burden is zero.

Modeling the corporation tax as a simple tax on economic profits is almost certainly wrong. The base of a pure profits tax is computed by subtracting from gross earnings the value of *all* inputs *including* the opportunity cost of the inputs supplied by the owners. As noted earlier, no such deduction for the capital supplied by shareholders is allowed, so the base of the tax includes elements other than economic profits.

Nevertheless, there are circumstances under which the corporation tax is *equivalent* to an economic profits tax. Stiglitz [1973] showed that under certain conditions, as long as the corporation is allowed to deduct interest payments made to its creditors, the corporation tax amounts to a tax on economic profits.

To understand the reasoning behind Stiglitz's result, consider a firm that is contemplating the purchase of a machine costing $1. Suppose the before-tax value of the output produced by the machine is known with certainty to be G dollars. Suppose also that the firm finances the purchase with debt—it borrows $1 and must pay an interest charge of r dollars. In the absence of any taxes, the firm buys the machine if the net return (total revenue minus depreciation minus interest) is positive. Algebraically, the firm purchases the machine if

$$G - r > 0 \tag{17.2}$$

Now assume that a corporation tax with the following features is levied: (1) net income is taxed at rate θ; and (2) net income is computed by subtracting interest costs from total revenue. How does such a tax influence the firm's decision about whether to undertake the project? Clearly, the firm must make its decision on the basis of the *after*-tax profitability of the project. In light of feature 2, the firm's taxable income is $G - r$. Given feature 1, the project therefore creates a tax liability of $\theta(G - r)$, so the after-tax profit on the project is $(1 - \theta)(G - r)$. The firm undertakes the project only if the after-tax profit is positive; that is, if

$$(1 - \theta)(G - r) > 0 \tag{17.3}$$

Now note that any project that passes the after-tax criterion (17.3) also satisfies the before-tax criterion (17.2). [Just divide Equation (17.3) through by $(1 - \theta)$ to get Equation (17.2).] Hence, imposition of the tax leaves the firm's investment decision unchanged—anything it would have done before the tax, it will do after. The owners of the firm continue to behave exactly as they did before the tax; they simply lose some of their profit on the investment to the government. In this sense the tax is equivalent to an economic profits tax. And like an economic profits tax, its incidence is on the owners of the firm, and it creates no excess burden.

This conclusion depends critically on the underlying assumptions, and these can easily be called into question. Recall that the argument assumes that firms finance their additional projects by borrowing. There are several reasons why they might instead raise money by selling shares or using retained earnings. For example, firms may face constraints in the capital market and be unable to borrow all they want. Alternatively, if a firm is uncertain about the project's return, it might be reluctant to finance the project by borrowing. If things go wrong, the greater a firm's debt, the higher the probability of bankruptcy, other things being the same.

Hence, Stiglitz's main contribution is not the conclusion that the corporate tax has no excess burden. Rather, the key insight is that the impact of the corporation tax depends in an important way on the structure of corporate finance.

Effects on Behavior

The corporation tax influences a wide range of corporate decisions. In this section we discuss three important types: (1) the total amount of physical investment (equipment and structures) to undertake; (2) the types of physical assets to purchase; and (3) the way to finance these investments. In a sense, it is artificial to discuss these decisions separately because presumably the firm makes them simultaneously. However, we discuss them separately for expositional ease.

Total Physical Investment

A firm's net investment during a given period is the increase in physical assets during that time. The main policy question is whether features such as accelerated depreciation and the investment tax credit stimulate investment demand. The question is important. For example, when some congressional Republicans proposed making depreciation allowances more generous in 2002, they argued that it would increase investment substantially. Their opponents asserted that it would not have much effect. Who was right?

The answer depends in part on your view of how corporations make their investment decisions. Many different models have been proposed, and there is no agreement on which is the best.[5] We discuss three investment models that have received substantial attention.

Accelerator Model. Suppose the ratio of capital to output in production is fixed. For example, production of every unit of output requires three units of capital. Then for each unit increase in output, the firm must increase its capital stock—invest—three units of capital. Thus, the main determinant of the amount of investment is changes in the level of output demanded.

This theory, sometimes referred to as the accelerator model, implies that depreciation allowances and ITCs are basically *irrelevant* when it comes to influencing physical investment. It is only the quantity of output that influences the amount of investment, because technology dictates the ratio in which capital and output must be used. In other words, tax benefits for capital may make capital cheaper, but in the accelerator model this does not matter, because the demand for capital does not depend on its price.

Neoclassical Model. A less extreme view of the investment process is that the ratio of capital to output is not technologically fixed. Rather, the firm can choose among alternative technologies. But how does it choose? According to Jorgenson's [1963] neoclassical model, a key variable is the firm's **user cost of capital**—the cost the firm incurs as a consequence of owning an asset. As we show later, the user cost of capital includes both the opportunity cost of forgoing other investments and direct costs such

---

[5] See Chirinko [2002] for a discussion of various models.

as depreciation and taxes. The user cost of capital indicates the rate of return a project must attain to be profitable. For example, if the user cost of capital on a project is 15 percent, a firm undertakes the project only if its rate of return exceeds 15 percent. The higher the user cost of capital, the lower is the number of profitable projects, and the lower the firm's desired stock of capital. In the neoclassical model, when the cost of capital increases, firms choose less capital-intensive technologies, and vice versa. To the extent that tax policy reduces the cost of capital, it can increase the amount of capital that firms desire and, hence, increase investment.

All of this leaves open two important questions: (1) How do changes in the tax system affect the user cost of capital? and (2) Just how sensitive is investment to changes in the user cost of capital? We discuss these questions in turn.

The user cost of capital.   Consider Leona, an entrepreneur who can lend her money and receive an after-tax rate of return of 10 percent. Leona is the sole stockholder in a corporation that runs a chain of hotels. Because she can always earn 10 percent simply by lending in the capital market, she will not make any investment in the hotel that yields less than that amount. Assume that Leona is considering the acquisition of a vacuum cleaner that would experience economic depreciation of 2 percent annually. Ignoring taxes for the moment, the user cost of capital for the vacuum cleaner would be 12 percent, because the vacuum cleaner would have to generate a 12 percent return to earn Leona the 10 percent return that she could receive simply by lending her money. Algebraically, if r is the after-tax rate of return and δ is the economic rate of depreciation, the user cost of capital is $(r + \delta)$. If the vacuum cleaner cannot earn $(r + \delta)$ (or 12 percent) after taxes, there is no reason for the firm to purchase it.

Now assume that the corporate tax rate is 35 percent, that Leona's marginal tax rate on dividends is 15 percent, and that all of the corporation's earnings are paid out to Leona as dividends. Then if the corporation earns $1, a corporation tax of $0.35 (= 0.35 × $1) is due, leaving $0.65 available to distribute to Leona. When Leona receives the $0.65 as dividends, she pays individual tax at a rate of 15 percent, leading to a tax liability of $0.098 (= 0.15 × $0.65), which leaves her with $0.552. Algebraically, if θ is the corporate tax rate and t is the individual tax rate on dividend income, the after-tax return from $1 of corporate profits is $(1 - \theta) \times (1 - t)$.

How do these taxes affect the cost of capital? We have to find a before-tax return such that, after the corporate and individual income taxes, Leona receives 12 percent. Calling the user cost of capital C, then C must be the solution to the equation $(1 - 0.35) \times (1 - 0.15) \times C = 12$ percent, or $C = 21.7$ percent. Thus, Leona is unwilling to purchase the vacuum cleaner unless its before-tax return is 21.7 percent or greater. Using our algebraic notation, the user cost of capital is the value of C that solves the equation $(1 - \theta) \times (1 - t) \times C = (r + \delta)$, or

$$C = \frac{(r + \delta)}{(1 - \theta) \times (1 - t)} \tag{17.4}$$

So far, we have shown how corporate and individual tax rates increase the user cost of capital. However, other provisions in the tax code such as accelerated depreciation lower the cost of capital. In Equation (17.1), we defined ψ as the present value of the depreciation allowances that flow from a \$1 investment. Suppose that ψ for the vacuum cleaner is 0.25. In effect, then, depreciation allowances reduce the cost of acquiring the vacuum cleaner by one-fourth, and hence lower by one-fourth the before-tax return that the firm has to earn to attain any given after-tax return. In our example, instead of having to earn 21.7 percent, the vacuum cleaner now only has to earn 16.3 percent [= 21.7 × (1 − 0.25)]. Algebraically, depreciation allowances lower the cost of capital by a factor of $(1 - \psi)$. Similarly, we showed that an investment tax credit at rate k reduces the cost of a \$1 acquisition to $(1 - k)$ dollars. In the presence of both depreciation allowances and an investment tax credit, the cost of capital is reduced by a factor of $(1 - \psi - k)$.[6] Thus, the expression for C in Equation (17.4) must be multiplied by $(1 - \psi - k)$ to adjust for accelerated depreciation and investment tax credits:

$$C = \frac{(r + \delta) \times (1 - \psi - k)}{(1 - \theta) \times (1 - t)} \tag{17.5}$$

Equation (17.5) summarizes how the corporate tax system influences the firm's user cost of capital. By taxing corporate income, the tax makes capital investment more expensive, other things being the same. However, depreciation allowances and ITCs tend to lower the user cost. Any change in the corporation tax system influences some combination of θ, ψ, and k, and hence changes the user cost of capital.

Effect of user cost on investment.   Once we know how the tax system affects the user cost of capital, the next step is to ascertain how changes in the user cost influence investment. If the accelerator model is correct, even drastic reductions in the user cost have no impact on investment. On the other hand, if investment responds to the user cost of capital, depreciation allowances and ITCs can be powerful tools for influencing investment.

Dealing with this issue econometrically is very difficult. The main reason is the critical role of expectations in the investment process. Suppose, for example, that firms expect the investment tax credit to be hiked *next* year. Presumably, this has a major effect on their decisions *this* year. Specifically, they

---

[6] This assumes the basis used to compute depreciation allowances is not reduced when the firm takes the ITC.

put off at least some of the investments they would have made this year in order to take advantage of the credit next year. More generally, current investment depends on expectations of future values of the user cost of capital. But as we noted in our discussion of saving behavior in Chapter 16, we have no really satisfactory model of expectations formation. A variety of studies have been done using different assumptions. Taken together, these studies suggest that an elasticity of investment with respect to the user cost of about 0.4 is plausible [Chirinko, 2002]. This lends support to the neoclassical model—investment does respond to changes in the tax system.

An important implicit assumption in this discussion is that the before-tax price of capital goods is not affected by tax-induced changes in the user cost of capital. If, for example, firms start purchasing more capital goods in response to the introduction of an investment tax credit, this does not increase the price of capital goods. In more technical terms, the supply curve of capital goods is perfectly horizontal. However, Goolsbee [1998b] found that the introduction of an investment tax credit increases the relative wages of workers who produce capital goods, which would tend to increase the price of capital goods. Hence, some of the increase in investment induced by the credit is dampened by an increase in the before-tax price of capital goods.

Finally, we must remember that the United States is, to a large extent, an open economy. If the tax code makes investment in the United States more attractive to foreigners, saving from abroad can finance investment in this country. The consequence for tax policy toward investment is the flip side of the relationship we saw in Chapter 16 between tax policy and saving: The possibility of domestic saving flowing out of the country makes it harder to stimulate domestic investment indirectly by manipulating saving, but the possibility of attracting foreign capital makes it easier to stimulate investment through direct manipulation of the user cost of capital.

Cash Flow Model.   If you ask people in business what determines their investment decisions, they likely will mention **cash flow**—the difference between revenues and expenditures for inputs. The more money that is on hand, the greater the capacity for investment. In contrast, cash flow is irrelevant in the neoclassical investment model. In that model, internal funds and borrowed money both have the same opportunity cost—the going rate of return in the economy. Further, the firm can borrow as much money at the going rate of return as it wishes. Under these conditions, if the return on producing a new kind of computer chip exceeds the opportunity cost, the firm will make the chip, whether it has to borrow the money or use internal sources.

A critical assumption behind the neoclassical story is that the cost to the firm of internal and external funds is the same. Many economists believe that this is a bad assumption. To see why, suppose that the managers of the firm have better information about the prospects for the computer chip than the potential lenders do. In particular, the lenders may view the project as being more uncertain than management and so charge a very high interest rate on

Table 17.1   **Effective marginal tax rates by asset type**

	Before TRA86	Current Law
Equipment	14.7%	37.1%
Structures	32.3%	40.5%

SOURCE: Jorgenson and Yun [2001, p. 140].

the loan. Or they might not be willing to lend any money at all. Thus, the cost of internal funds is lower than the cost of external funds, so the amount of investment depends on the flow of these internal funds, the cash flow.

There does indeed seem to be a statistical relationship between cash flow and investment [Hubbard, 1998]. However, the interpretation of this finding is not quite clear—do firms invest because their cash flow is high, or do successful firms have both high cash flow and investment? In any case, if the cash flow theory is correct, it has major implications for the impact of taxes on investment behavior. For example, in the neoclassical model, a lump sum tax on the corporation has no effect on investment. In contrast, in a cash flow model, investment falls. Currently, cash flow models are an active subject of research.

Types of Asset

The tax system affects the types of assets purchased by firms as well as the total volume of investment. For example, the system encourages the purchase of assets that receive relatively generous depreciation allowances.

Jorgenson and Yun [2001] computed the effective marginal tax rates on various assets both before TRA86 and under current law. Some of their results are reported in Table 17.1. The table indicates that both before and after the Tax Reform Act of 1986, structures were taxed more heavily than equipment. But TRA86 dramatically reduced the difference between the tax rates on these two types of assets. The system is now more nearly neutral. As a consequence, excess burdens associated with tax-induced distortions in investment patterns are now smaller than previously.

Corporate Finance

In addition to "real" decisions concerning physical investment, the owners of a firm must determine how to finance the firm's operations and whether to distribute or retain profits. We discuss the effects of taxes on these financial decisions in this section.

Why Do Firms Pay Dividends?   Profits earned by a corporation may be either distributed to shareholders in the form of dividends or retained by the company. If we assume that (1) outcomes of all investments are known in advance with certainty and (2) there are no taxes, then the owners of a firm are indifferent between a dollar of dividends and a dollar of retained earnings. Provided that the stock market accurately reflects the firm's value, $1 of retained earnings increases the value of the firm's stock by $1. This $1 capital gain is as much income as a $1 dividend receipt. Under the previous assumptions, then, stockholders do not care whether profits are distributed.

Of course, in reality, considerable uncertainty surrounds the outcomes of economic decisions, and corporate income *is* subject to a variety of taxes. As already noted, when dividends are paid out, the shareholder incurs a tax liability, while retained earnings generate no concurrent tax liability. True, the retention creates a capital gain for the stockholder, but no tax is due until the gain is realized.

On the basis of these observations, it appears that paying dividends is more or less equivalent to giving away money to the tax collector, and we would expect firms to retain virtually all of their earnings. Surprise! In a typical year, almost 79 percent of after-tax corporate profits are paid out as dividends on average [*Economic Report of the President, 2003,* p. 381]. This phenomenon is a puzzle for students of corporate finance.

One possible explanation is that dividend payments signal the firm's financial strength. If investors perceive firms that regularly pay dividends as "solid," then paying dividends enhances the value of the firms' shares. In the same way, a firm that reduces its dividend payments may be perceived as being in financial straits. However, although it is conceivable that the owners of a firm would be willing to pay some extra taxes to provide a positive signal to potential shareholders, it is hard to imagine that the benefits gained are worth the huge sums sacrificed.

Another explanation centers on the fact that not all investors have the same marginal tax rate. In particular, untaxed institutions (such as pension funds and universities) face a rate of zero. Those with low marginal tax rates would tend to put a relatively high valuation on dividends, and it may be that some firms "specialize" in attracting these investors by paying out dividends. This is referred to as a **clientele effect,** because firms set their financial policies to cater to different clienteles. Econometric studies of the clientele effect are hindered by the lack of data on just who owns shares in what firms. However, there is some evidence that mutual funds, whose shareholders are taxable, tend to hold stocks with low-dividend yields, while untaxed institutions show no preference between low- and high-dividend stocks [Graham, 2001].

Effect of Taxes on Dividend Policy. Because the tax system appears to bias firms against paying dividends (although it by no means discourages them completely), the natural question is how corporate financial policy would change if the tax treatment of dividends vis-à-vis retained earnings were modified. Suppose that for whatever reasons, firms want to pay some dividends as well as retain earnings. One factor that determines the desired amount of retained earnings is the opportunity cost in terms of after-tax dividends paid to stockholders. For example, if there were no taxes, the opportunity cost of $1 of retained earnings would be $1 of dividends. On the other hand, if the stockholder faces a 15 percent marginal income tax rate on dividends, the opportunity cost of retaining a dollar in the firm is only 85 cents of dividends.[7] In effect, then, the current tax system lowers the opportunity cost of retained earnings.

Several econometric studies have found that when the opportunity cost of retained earnings decreases, dividend payments go down [see US Department of the Treasury, 1992, p. 117]. It appears, then, that the tax system increases the amount of earnings retained by corporations. Some argue that this is desirable because increasing retained earnings makes more money available for investment. Now, it is true that retained earnings represent saving. However, it may be that shareholders take corporate saving into consideration when making their personal financial decisions. Specifically, if owners of the firm perceive that the corporation is saving a dollar on their behalf, they may simply reduce their personal saving by that amount. Thus, although the composition of overall saving has changed, its total amount is just the same as before the retention. There is indeed some econometric evidence that personal and corporate saving are somewhat offsetting [Poterba 1991]. This analysis illustrates once again the pitfalls of viewing the corporation as a separate person with an existence apart from the stockholders.

Debt versus Equity Finance.   Another important financial decision for a corporation is how to raise money. The firm has basically two options. It can borrow money (issue debt). The firm must pay interest on its debt, and inability to meet the interest payments or repay the principal may have serious consequences. A firm can also issue shares of stock (equity) and stockholders may receive dividends on their shares.

Recall that under the US tax system, corporations are permitted to deduct payments of interest from taxable income, but are not allowed to deduct dividends. The tax law therefore builds in a bias toward debt financing. Indeed, we might wonder why firms do not use debt financing exclusively. Part of the answer lies in the uncertainty that firms face. There is always some possibility of a very bad outcome and bankruptcy. The more a firm borrows, the higher its debt payments, and the greater the probability of bankruptcy, other things being the same. Heavy reliance on debt finance has in fact led some major corporations to declare bankruptcy, including K-Mart, Enron, and WorldCom. Some argue that by encouraging the use of debt, the tax system has the undesirable effect of increasing probabilities of bankruptcy above levels that otherwise would have prevailed.

That said, it is difficult to estimate precisely the impact that the tax system has on the debt–equity choice. In one econometric study, Gordon and Lee [2001] note that if taxes affect debt-equity ratios, then corporations

---

[7] A more careful calculation would take into account the effective capital gains tax liability that is eventually generated by the retention. This is ignored for purposes of illustration.

with lower tax rates should use less debt, other things being the same. This is because the advantage of being able to deduct interest from corporate taxable income is less when the tax rate is lower. Gordon and Lee's analysis of US firms is consistent with this hypothesis. They find that lowering the corporate rate by 10 percentage points lowers the percentage of the firm's assets financed by debt by 4 percent.

Did the Tax System Cause the Corporate Accounting Scandals?   The United States was recently rocked by a wave of corporate accounting scandals. A number of major firms, most notably Enron, used deceptive and fraudulent practices to inflate their reported earnings and thereby increase the value of their stock. The wake of the scandal brought calls for a variety of reforms in corporate governance and accounting procedures, such as making chief executive officers personally responsible for misleading financial statements. However, some observers argued that a root cause of the problem was the US tax system, and that meaningful improvements in corporate behavior will not occur without appropriate reform.

Why blame the tax system? Siegel [2002] notes that in the 19th century, years before any government regulatory involvement in the securities industry, corporate management could release any information about their firms without having to worry about being prosecuted if it were somehow misleading. But if there were no standards for corporate financial statements, how could the public know if the earnings that the corporations claimed were real? Siegel responds, "The old-fashioned way, by paying dividends, an action that gave tangible evidence of the firm's profitability and proof that the firms' earnings were authentic." This is the dividends-as-signal theory that was discussed above—reported earnings are relatively easy to manipulate, but dividends are tangible cash, and therefore impossible to fake. The argument is that by discouraging the payment of dividends, the tax system has led to increased reliance on other methods for signaling a firm's status that are more susceptible to manipulation. While it is difficult to know how much credence to give this argument, it is a fascinating example of the unintended consequences that taxes may have.

State Corporation Taxes

Almost all the states levy their own corporation income taxes, and corporate tax revenues account for about 2.3 percent of total state and local revenues [*Economic Report of the President, 2003*, p. 377]. Like state personal income taxes, state corporate tax systems differ substantially with respect to rate structures and rules for defining taxable income.

All of the complications that arise in analyzing the incidence and efficiency effects of the federal corporation income tax also bedevil attempts to understand the state systems. The variation in rates across state lines gives rise to a set of even more intractable questions. If a given state levies a corporation tax, how much of the burden is exported to citizens of other states? How is the portion that is not exported shared by the residents of the state?

Preliminary answers to these questions may be obtained by applying the theory of tax incidence (Chapter 12). Recall the general intuitive proposition that immobile factors of production are more likely to end up bearing a tax than mobile factors, other things being the same. This means, for example, that if capital is easier to move to another state than labor, the incidence of a state corporation tax tends to fall on labor. Thus, analyzing a system of varying corporate tax rates requires that the effects of interstate mobility be added to the already formidable list of factors that come into play when studying the federal corporation tax. Research on this issue is at a formative stage.

Taxation of Multinational Corporations

American firms do a substantial amount of investment abroad. In 2001, the value of the stock of assets directly invested in foreign countries was $6 trillion. The tax treatment of foreign source income is of increasing importance.

US multinational corporations are subject to tax at the standard rate on their global taxable income, including income earned abroad. A credit is then allowed for foreign taxes paid. The credit cannot exceed the amount that would have been owed under US tax law. Suppose, for example, that a US corporation earns $100 in a foreign country with a 15 percent tax rate. The corporation pays $15 to the foreign country. In the absence of the foreign tax credit, it would owe $35 to the US Treasury (because the US corporate tax rate is 35 percent). However, the firm can take a $15 credit against the $35 liability, and needs to pay the United States only $20.

In 1999, corporations' US income tax liability before the foreign tax credit was $242 billion; the foreign tax credit reduced that figure by $49 billion [Internal Revenue Service, 2002, p. 233].

A number of considerations complicate the taxation of foreign-source corporate income.

Subsidiary Status. Taxation of the income from a foreign enterprise can be deferred if the operation is a **subsidiary.** (A foreign subsidiary is a company owned by a US corporation but incorporated abroad and, hence, a separate corporation from a legal point of view.) Profits earned by a subsidiary are taxed only if returned (**repatriated**) to the parent company as dividends. Thus, for as long as the subsidiary exists, earnings retained abroad can be kept out of reach of the US tax system. It is hard to say how much tax revenue is lost because of deferral. Given the credit system, the answer depends on the tax rate levied abroad. If all foreign countries have tax rates greater than that of the United States, no additional tax revenue is gained by this country. However, to the extent that a foreign country taxes corporate income less heavily than does the United States, deferral makes the country attractive to US firms as a "tax haven."[8]

Income Allocation. It is often difficult to know how much of a multinational firm's total income to allocate to its operations in a given country. The procedure now used for allocating income between domestic and foreign operations is the **arm's length system.** Essentially the domestic and foreign operations are treated as separate enterprises doing business independently ("at arm's length"). The taxable profits of each entity are computed as its own sales minus its own costs.

The problem is that it is not always clear how to allocate costs to various locations, and this can lead to major opportunities for tax avoidance. To see why, consider a multinational firm that owns a patent for a gene-splicing process. One of the subsidiaries owns the patent, and the other subsidiaries pay royalties to it for the privilege of using the process. The company has an incentive to assign the patent to one of its subsidiaries in a low-tax country, so that the royalties received from the other subsidiaries will be taxed at a relatively low rate. At the same time, it wants the subsidiaries that use the patent to be in relatively high-tax countries—high tax rates mean that the value of the deductions associated with the royalty payments is maximized. Indeed, since the transaction is entirely internal to the company, it will set the royalty payment to be as large as possible in order to maximize the tax benefit of this arrangement. And if there is no active market for the rights to the patent outside the company, then the tax authorities have little basis for deciding whether or not the royalty payment is excessive.

This is called the **transfer-pricing** problem, because it refers to the price that one part of the company uses for transferring resources to another. Given that it is essentially arbitrary how costs for many items are assigned to various subsidiaries, multinational corporations and the tax authorities are constantly at odds over whether the companies have done their transfer pricing appropriately. This is rapidly becoming one of the most complicated areas of tax law. Indeed, multinational corporations have been complaining about the expense and complexity of complying with it. An extreme case is the tax return filed by the financial firm Citigroup several years ago. The return included computations for subsidiaries located in about 100 countries, exceeded 30,000 pages, and required the work of more than 200 tax professionals both in the United States and abroad [Herman, 1999].

Evaluation

An evaluation of the US tax treatment of multinational firms requires a careful statement of the policy goal. One possible objective is to maximize

---

[8] A few countries such as the Bahamas have intentionally structured their laws to allow US firms to abuse the tax system. There are some provisions to limit the tax savings from these true tax havens, but they have not had much impact.

worldwide income; another is to maximize national income. A system that is optimal given one goal may not be optimal given another.

Maximization of World Income. The maximization of world income requires that the before-tax rate of return on the last dollar invested in each country—the marginal rate of return—be the same.[9] To see why, imagine a situation in which marginal returns are not equal. Then one can increase world income simply by taking capital from a country where its marginal return is low and moving it to one where the marginal return is high.[10] Algebraically, if r_{US} is the marginal rate of return in the United States and r_f is the marginal rate of return in a given foreign country, then worldwide efficiency requires

$$r_f = r_{US} \tag{17.6}$$

What kind of tax system induces profit-maximizing firms to allocate their capital so that the outcome is consistent with Equation (17.6)? The answer hinges on the fact that investors make their decisions on the basis of after-tax returns. They therefore allocate their capital across countries so that the after-tax marginal return in each country is equal. If t_{US} is the US tax rate and t_f is the foreign tax rate, a firm allocates its capital so that

$$(1 - t_f)r_f = (1 - t_{US})r_{US} \tag{17.7}$$

Condition (17.7) tells us that efficiency is attained if and only if t_f equals t_{US}. Intuitively, if we want capital allocated efficiently from a global point of view, capital must be taxed at the same rate wherever it is located.

The policy implication seems to be that if the United States cares about maximizing world income, it should devise a system that makes its firms' tax liabilities independent of their location. A *full* credit against foreign taxes paid would do the trick. However, as already noted, the US system allows a tax credit *only* up to the amount that US tax on the foreign earnings would have been.

Why is the credit limited? Our model implicitly assumes the behavior of foreign governments is independent of US government actions. Suppose the United States announces it will pursue a policy of allowing a full foreign tax credit to its multinational firms. Then foreign governments have an incentive to raise their own tax rates on US corporations virtually without limit. Doing so will not drive out the foreign countries' American firms, because the tax liability for their domestic operations is reduced by a dollar for every dollar foreign taxes are increased.[11] Essentially, the program turns into a transfer

---

[9] As usual, we refer here to rates of return after differences in risk are taken into account.

[10] For further discussion of this principle, see the appendix at the end of the book.

[11] The amount the foreign government can extract in this way is limited to the firm's tax liability to the United States on its domestic operations. Suppose the firm's tax liability on its US operations is $1,000. If the foreign government levies a tax of $1,000, under a full credit, the firm's US tax liability is zero. If the foreign government raises the tax to $1,001, the firm's domestic tax liability cannot be reduced any further (because there is no negative income tax for corporations).

from the United States to foreign treasuries. Limiting the credit is an obvious way to prevent this from happening.

Maximization of National Income.   At the outset, we noted the importance of defining the objectives of tax policy on foreign source corporate income. Some argue that tax policy should maximize not world income, but national income. We must exercise care in defining national income here. It is the sum of *before*-tax domestically produced income and foreign-source income *after* foreign taxes are paid. This is because taxes paid by US firms to the US government, although not available to the firms themselves, are still part of US income. Thus, domestic income is counted before tax. However, taxes paid to foreign governments are not available to US citizens, so foreign income is counted after tax.

National income maximization requires a different condition than Equation (17.6). The difference arises because marginal rates of return must now be measured from the US point of view. According to the US perspective, the marginal rate of return abroad is $(1 - t_f)r_f$—foreign taxes represent a cost from the US point of view and hence are excluded in valuing the rate of return. The marginal return on investments in the United States is measured at the before-tax rate, r_{US}. Hence, maximization of national income requires

$$(1 - t_f)r_f = r_{US} \tag{17.8}$$

A comparison with Equation (17.6) suggests that under a regime of world income maximization, investments are made abroad until $r_f = r_{US}$, while if national income maximization is the goal, foreign investment is carried to the point where $r_f = r_{US}/(1 - t_f)$. In words, if national income maximization is the goal, the before-tax marginal rate of return on foreign investment is higher than it would be if global income maximization were the goal. [As long as t_f is less than one, $r_{US} < r_{US}/(1 - t_f)$.] But under the reasonable assumption that the marginal return to investment decreases with the amount of investment, a higher before-tax rate of return means less investment. In short, from a national point of view, world income maximization results in "too much" investment abroad.

What kind of tax system induces American firms to allocate their capital so that Equation (17.8) is satisfied? Suppose that, contrary to the US system, multinational firms are allowed to *deduct* foreign tax payments from their US taxable income. (For example, a firm with domestic income of $1,000 and foreign taxes of $200 would have a US taxable income of $800.) Given that foreign tax payments are deductible, a firm's overseas return of r_f increases its taxable US income by $r_f(1 - t_f)$. Therefore, after US taxes, the return on the foreign investment is $r_f(1 - t_f)(1 - t_{US})$. At the same time, the after-tax return on investments in the United States is $r_{US}(1 - t_{US})$. Assuming that the investors equalize after-tax marginal returns at home and abroad,

$$r_f(1 - t_f)(1 - t_{US}) = r_{US}(1 - t_{US}) \tag{17.9}$$

Clearly, Equations (17.8) and (17.9) are equivalent. [Just divide both sides of (17.9) by $(1 - t_{US})$.] Because Equation (17.8) is the condition for national income maximization, this implies that deduction of foreign tax payments leads to a pattern of investment that maximizes US income.

Such reasoning has led to some political support for replacing the foreign-tax credit with a deduction. One important problem with the case for deductions is that the analysis assumes the capital-exporting country can impose the tax rate that maximizes its income, while the capital-importing foreign countries passively keep their own tax rates constant. Suppose, to the contrary, that the capital-exporting country takes into account the possibility that changes in its tax rate may induce changes in the host countries' tax rates. The United States might believe, for example, that if it lowers its tax rate on capital invested abroad, host governments will do the same. In this case, it may be worthwhile for the United States to tax preferentially income earned abroad. Of course, host governments might choose to raise their tax rates when the US rate goes down. The point is that when interdependent behavior is allowed, the national income-maximizing tax system generally does not consist of a simple deduction for foreign taxes paid. The effective tax rate on foreign-source income can be either larger or smaller than that associated with deductibility. Just as in the strictly domestic context, optimal tax theory shows that simple rules of thumb for tax policy do not necessarily achieve a given goal.

Finally, we note that our normative analysis of international taxation rests on the positive assumption that firms take into account after-tax rates of return when deciding in which countries to invest. Desai, Foley, and Hines [2002] examined the amount of foreign direct investment in European countries, and estimated that a 10 percent higher tax rate is associated with 7.7 percent less investment from abroad, other things being the same. This evidence suggests that the assumption that firms respond to after-tax rates of return is reasonable.

Corporation Tax Reform

We observed earlier that if corporate income were untaxed, individuals could avoid personal income taxes by accumulating income within corporations. Evidently, this would lead to serious equity and efficiency problems. The US response has been to construct a system that taxes corporate income twice: first at the corporate level, where the statutory tax rate is 35 percent, and again at the personal level, where distributions of dividends are taxed as ordinary income (at a maximum statutory rate of 38.6 percent in 2003).

A number of proposals have been made to integrate personal and corporate income taxes into a single system. We now discuss two of them, full integration and dividend relief.

Full Integration

The most radical approach is the **partnership method,** sometimes referred to as **full integration.** Under this approach, all earnings of the corporation during a given year, whether they are distributed or not, are attributed to stockholders just as if the corporation were a partnership. Each shareholder is then liable for personal income tax on his share of the earnings. Thus, if Karl owns 2 percent of the shares of Time Warner, each year his taxable income includes 2 percent of Time Warner's taxable earnings. The corporation tax as a separate entity is eliminated.

The debate in the United States with respect to the desirability of adopting the partnership method has focused on several issues:

Nature of the Corporation.   Those who favor full integration emphasize that a corporation is, in effect, merely a conduit for transmitting earnings to shareholders. It makes more sense to tax the people who receive the income than the institution that happens to pass it along. Those who oppose full integration argue that in large modern corporations, it is ridiculous to think of the shareholders as partners, and that the corporation is best regarded as a separate entity.

Administrative Feasibility.   Opponents of full integration stress the administrative difficulties that it would create. How are corporate earnings imputed to individuals who hold stock for less than a year? Would shareholders be allowed to deduct the firm's operating losses from their personal taxable income? Proponents of full integration argue that a certain number of fairly arbitrary decisions must be made to administer any complicated tax system. The administrative problems here are no worse than those that have arisen in other parts of the tax code and can probably be dealt with satisfactorily.

Effects on Efficiency.   Those who favor integration point out that the current corporate tax system imposes large excess burdens on the economy, many of which would be eliminated or at least lessened under full integration. The economy would benefit from four types of efficiency gains:

- The misallocation of resources between the corporate and noncorporate sectors would be eliminated.
- To the extent that integration lowered the rate of taxation on the return to capital, tax-induced distortions in savings decisions would be reduced.
- Integration would remove the incentives for "excessive" retained earnings that characterize the current system. Firms with substantial retained earnings are not forced to convince investors to finance new projects. Without the discipline that comes from having to persuade outsiders that projects are worthwhile, such firms may invest inefficiently. For example, some observers believe that Microsoft's ill-advised entry into cable television would not have occurred if it had not had huge amounts of cash (about $40 billion!) on hand [*The Economist*, 2003].

- Integration would remove the present system's bias toward debt financing because there would be no separate corporate tax base from which to deduct payments of interest. High ratios of debt to equity increase the probability of bankruptcy. This increased risk and the actual bankruptcies that do occur lower welfare without any concomitant gain to society.

Although it is difficult to determine the value of all these efficiency gains, some estimates suggest that they are quite high. Jorgenson and Yun [2001] found that the present value of the lifetime efficiency gain from full integration would be more than $250 billion.

Opponents of full integration point out that given all the uncertainties concerning the operation of the corporation tax, the supposed efficiency gains may not exist at all. For example, as discussed earlier, to the extent that Stiglitz's view of the tax as equivalent to a levy on pure profits is correct, the tax induces no distortion between the corporate and noncorporate sectors. Similarly, there is no solid evidence that corporations invest internal funds less efficiently than those raised externally.

Effects on Saving.   Some argue that full integration would lower the effective tax rate on capital and therefore lead to more saving. As we saw in Chapter 16, this is a non sequitur. From a theoretical point of view, the volume of saving may increase, decrease, or stay the same when the tax rate on capital income decreases. Econometric work has not yet provided a definitive answer.

Effect on the Distribution of Income.   If the efficiency arguments in favor of full integration are correct, then in principle, all taxpayers could benefit if it were instituted. Still, people in different groups would be affected differently. For example, stockholders with relatively high personal income tax rates would tend to gain less from integration than those with low personal income tax rates. At the same time, integration would tend to benefit those individuals who receive a relatively large share of their incomes from capital. Taking these effects together, Fullerton and Rogers [1993] find a roughly U-shaped pattern to the distribution of benefits of integration—people at the high and low ends of the income distribution gain somewhat more than those in the middle. The usual caveat is required in interpreting this result. It depends on the values of a number of parameters such as the elasticity of saving with respect to the tax rate. There is much uncertainty about their magnitudes.

Overview.   Clearly, there is considerable uncertainty surrounding the likely impact of full integration. This simply reflects our imperfect knowledge of the workings of the current system of corporate taxation. There is by no means unanimous agreement that introducing the partnership method would be a good thing. However, on the basis of the existing and admittedly imperfect evidence, many economists have concluded that both efficiency and equity would be enhanced if the personal and corporate taxes were integrated.

Dividend Relief

A less extreme approach to integration has at its starting point the notion that the source of many of the problems with the status quo is that dividends are taxed twice, once at the corporation level and again at the individual level. The idea of dividend relief is to eliminate double taxation while still maintaining the corporation tax as a separate system. There are basically two approaches. One is to allow the corporation to deduct dividends paid to stockholders just as it now deducts interest payments to bondholders. The advantage of this scheme is that it removes the asymmetric tax treatment of debt and equity. Further, dividends end up getting taxed at the individual's marginal tax rate, which makes sense from the standpoint of the Haig-Simons definition of income. However, it turns out that a corporate dividend deduction is rather cumbersome from an administrative standpoint [US Department of the Treasury, 1992].

An alternative approach is simply to exclude dividends from taxation at the individual level. Under this approach, dividends are taxed only once, but at the corporation rate rather than the individual rate. From an efficiency point of view, this approach is probably less satisfactory than a corporate dividend deduction—there remains some non-neutrality in the treatment of debt and equity. But it likely enhances efficiency relative to the status quo, and is relatively easy to administer. Legislation passed in 2003 moved in the direction of a dividend exclusion, by lowering to 15 percent the maximal tax rate applied to dividends at the individual level.

Summary

- Corporations are subject to a separate federal income tax. The tax accounts for about 8 percent of all federal revenues.

- Before applying the 35 percent tax rate, firms may deduct employee compensation, interest payments, and depreciation allowances. These are meant to measure the cost of producing revenue. Dividends, the cost of acquiring equity funds, are not deductible. However, dividends are taxed preferentially at the individual level.

- Investment tax credits (ITCs) are deducted from the firm's tax bill when particular physical capital assets are purchased. The Tax Reform Act of 1986 repealed ITCs, but they often surface in policy debates.

- The corporate tax has been viewed either as an economic profits tax or as a partial factor tax. In the former case, the tax is borne entirely by owners of firms, while in the latter the incidence

- depends on capital mobility between sectors, substitutability of factors of production, the structure of consumer demand, and the sensitivity of capital accumulation to the net rate of return.

- The effect of the corporate tax system on physical investment depends on (1) its effect on the user cost of capital, and (2) the sensitivity of investment to changes in the user cost.

- In the accelerator model, investment depends only on output, making the user cost irrelevant. The neoclassical model assumes that capital demand depends on the user cost. In the cash flow model, internal funds play a key role in determining investment.

- In the neoclassical investment model, the user cost of capital (C) is

$$C = \frac{(r + \delta) \times (1 - \psi - k)}{(1 - \theta) \times (1 - t)}$$

where r is the after-tax interest rate, δ the economic depreciation rate, θ the corporation tax rate, k the ITC, and ψ the present value of depreciation allowances per dollar.

■ Estimates of the effect of the user cost on investment vary greatly, but most recent research suggests that there is some responsiveness.

■ Due to the double taxation of dividends, it is puzzling that firms pay them. Dividends may serve as a signal of the firm's financial strength, or be used to cater to particular clienteles.

■ Interest deductibility provides a strong incentive for debt finance. However, increasing the proportion of debt may lead to larger bankruptcy costs.

■ Most states have corporate income taxes. The possibilities for tax exporting and interstate

mobility of factors of production complicate analysis of these taxes.

■ US multinational corporations are allowed tax credits for taxes paid to foreign governments. Complications arise due to tax deferral using foreign subsidiaries and opportunities for tax avoidance via transfer pricing.

■ One possible corporate tax reform is full integration of the corporate and personal income taxes. Owners of stock would be taxed on their share of corporate income as if they were partners. The corporation tax as a separate entity would cease to exist.

■ Another approach to integration is dividend relief, in which dividends are taxed only once, either by allowing a deduction at the corporate level or an exclusion at the individual level.

Discussion Questions

1. "Small corporations should face lower tax rates than large businesses, just as individuals with low incomes should face lower income tax rates than those with high incomes." What view of the corporation is implicit in this statement? Contrast this view with the view of conventional economics.

2. Under US law, depreciation allowances are based on the original cost of acquiring the asset. No account is taken for the effects of inflation on the price level over time.

    a. How does inflation affect the real value of depreciation allowances? Organize your answer around Equation (17.1).

    b. When inflation increases, what is the impact on the user cost of capital? Organize your answer around Equation (17.5).

    c. Suggest a policy that could undo the effects of inflation from part b.

3. Several years ago, RJR Nabisco incurred $2 million in costs for package design—the physical construction of a package and its graphic design. Nabisco wanted to deduct the entire $2 million in the year it was spent; the Internal Revenue Service insisted that the $2 million be treated like a capital expenditure and depreciated over time. Eventually, the Tax Court sided with Nabisco.

    a. Explain carefully why Nabisco would prefer to have the $2 million treated as a current expense rather than a capital expenditure.

    b. Do you agree with the ruling of the Tax Court?

4. In 2000, Germany introduced a major tax reform. Under the new law, corporations pay a rate of 25 percent on retained earnings and 30 percent on earnings that are distributed to shareholders. Further, under the personal income tax, dividends are taxed at half the rate of ordinary income. Does this law make sense from the standpoint of the Haig-Simons definition of income?

5. The following suggestion for reforming the corporation tax was made on the editorial page of the *Wall Street Journal:* "First, make dividends tax deductible for corporations and, second, eliminate them entirely for shareholders. Abolishing the tax in both places not only ends the double taxation of dividends but creates the same incentives for equity and dividends as for debt and interest. *Voila!* A level playing field." (August 6, 2002, p. A20). Discuss whether this proposal would, in fact, lead to a "level playing field" between corporate debt and equity.

6. Corporations, like individuals, face an alternative minimum tax (AMT). (See the discussion in Chapter 15.) In 2001, the House of Representatives

passed a bill abolishing the corporate AMT *retroactively*. This meant that rebate checks would be sent to corporations for past payments of the AMT. The intention of the bill was to stimulate investment. Use the neoclassical theory of investment to assess whether a retroactive tax cut can be an effective way to stimulate investment. (Hint: How does such a tax cut affect the user cost of capital?)

7. Before former Treasury Secretary Paul H. O'Neill had that job in the government, he was the chief executive of Alcoa, the leading manufacturer of aluminum. He said, "As a businessman I never made an investment decision based on the tax code." If O'Neill meant what he said, how would you react to it if you had owned stock in Alcoa while he was in charge?

8. During the wave of corporate accounting scandals in 2001, it was revealed that Enron had raised money using a special financial instrument that had been developed by the investment banking firm of Goldman Sachs & Company. The financial instrument, called a MIPS (Monthly Income Preferred Shares), "was designed in such a way that it could be called debt or equity, as needed. For the tax man, it resembled a loan. . . . For shareholders and rating agencies . . . it resembled equity" [McKinnon and Hitt, 2002]. Explain why using such a financial instrument would be attractive to a corporation (or at least a corporation managed by people who weren't overly concerned with ethical issues).

9. The ABC corporation is contemplating purchasing a new computer system that would yield a before-tax return of 30 percent. The system would depreciate at a rate of 1 percent a year. The after-tax interest rate is 8 percent, the corporation tax rate is 35 percent, and a typical shareholder of ABC has a marginal tax rate of 30 percent. Assume for simplicity that there are no depreciation allowances or investment tax credits. Do you expect ABC to buy the new computer system? Explain your answer. (Hint: Use Equation 17.4.)

Selected References

Chirinko, Robert S. "Corporate Taxation, Capital Formation, and the Substitution Elasticity between Labor and Capital." *National Tax Journal* 55 (June 2002), pp. 339–55.

Goolsbee, Austan. "The Impact and Efficiency of the Corporate Income Tax: Evidence from State Organizational Form Data." Working Paper No. 9141. Cambridge, MA: National Bureau of Economic Research, September 2002.

US Department of the Treasury. *Integration of the Individual and Corporate Tax Systems.* Washington, DC: US Government Printing Office, 1992.

CHAPTER 18

Deficit Finance

As a very important source of strength and security, cherish public credit.

GEORGE WASHINGTON

Having discussed the federal government's major taxes in previous chapters, we now turn to its other major revenue source: borrowing. The issue of debt finance has dominated discussions of economic policy for years; it is constantly debated in political campaigns and on editorial pages. As the cartoon on the next page indicates, it is hard to avoid the subject. This chapter discusses problems in measuring the size of the debt, who bears its burden, and the circumstances under which debt is a suitable way to finance government expenditures.

How Big Is the Debt?

We need a few definitions to begin our discussion. The **deficit** during a time period is the excess of spending over revenues; if revenues exceed expenditures, there is a **surplus.** That seems simple enough until we recall from Chapter 1 that the federal government does not include all its activities in its official budget. Under current rules, for example, revenues and expenditures associated with Social Security are off-budget. Despite this legal distinction, a proper measure of the extent of government borrowing requires that all revenues and expenditures be taken into account. Hence, it is useful to consider the sum of the **on-budget deficit (or surplus)** (which considers only on-budget activity) and the **off-budget deficit (or surplus)** (which takes into account only off-budget activity) to arrive at the total deficit or surplus. For example, in 2002, the on-budget deficit was $317.5 billion, but adding in a $159.6 billion off-budget surplus gave a total deficit of $157.8 billion [Congressional Budget Office, 2003, p. 148].

*"You might ask, 'Can two people who love each other find
happiness in an era of skyrocketing deficits?' I think they can."*

• • •

Table 18.1 shows total federal deficits (i.e., including off-budget revenues and expenditures) for selected years from 1970 to 2005. To put these figures in perspective, we also show their size relative to gross domestic product. The budget was in surplus from 1998 to 2001, but deficits have generally been the rule.

One must distinguish between the concepts of deficit and debt. The **debt** at a given time is the sum of all past budget deficits. That is, the debt is the cumulative excess of past spending over past receipts. Thus, in a year with a deficit the debt goes up; in a year with a surplus, the debt goes down. In the jargon of economics, the debt is a "stock variable" (measured at a point in time), while deficits and surpluses are "flow variables" (measured during a period of time). As reported in official government statistics, the federal debt at the end of 2002 was about $3.5 *trillion,* a number so large that it is hard to comprehend. As the humorist Russell Baker [1985] observed, "Like the light year, the trillion is an abstruse philosophical idea that can interest only persons with a morbid interest in mathematics. This explains why most people go limp with boredom when told that the national debt will soon be

Table 18.1   **Federal government deficits, 1970–2005**

Fiscal Year	Total Deficit (−) or Surplus ($ billions)	Total Deficit (−) or Surplus Percent of GDP
1970	−2.8	−0.3
1980	−73.8	−2.9
1985	−212.3	−5.4
1990	−221.4	−4.0
2000	236.4	2.4
2002	−157.8	−1.5
2005*	−73.0	−0.6

*Projections.

Source: Congressional Budget Office, *The Economic and Budget Outlook: Fiscal Years 2004–2013*, January 2003, pp. xvi, 148.

Table 18.2   **Federal government debt held by the public, 1970–2005**

Fiscal Year	Debt Held by the Public ($ billions)	Debt Held by the Public as a Percent of GDP
1970	283	29.4
1980	709	27.8
1985	1,499	38.4
1990	2,410	44.6
2000	3,410	35.1
2002	3,540	34.3
2005*	4,013	33.6

*Projections.

Source: Congressional Budget Office, *The Economic and Budget Outlook: Fiscal Years 2004–2013*, January 2003, pp. xvi, 149.

$2 trillion, or $20 trillion, or $200 trillion. The incomprehensible is incomprehensible, no matter how you number it."

Despite Baker's warning, let us try to put the debt in perspective, again by comparing it to GDP. The 2002 federal debt of $3.5 trillion was about 34 percent of that year's GDP—34 cents of every dollar produced would have been required to liquidate the debt. Table 18.2 reports comparable figures for other years as well.

Just like a private borrower, the government must pay interest to its lenders. In 2002, interest payments were $171 billion, or 8.5 percent of federal outlays [Congressional Budget Office, 2003, p. 152].

Interpreting Deficit, Surplus, and Debt Numbers

It is hard to overestimate the political importance of numbers of the sort reported in Tables 18.1 and 18.2. Public officials and journalists focus on them almost exclusively when assessing the state of public finance. In 2003, for example, there were fierce debates over the possible consequences of anticipated deficits. It is quite likely, though, that the figures that formed the basis for this and other debates about deficits and surpluses are not economically meaningful. In this section we explain why.

Government Debt Held by the Federal Reserve Bank.   In the course of conducting its monetary operations, the Federal Reserve Bank purchases US government securities.[1] Its holdings in 2002 were $604 billion [*Economic*

---

[1] Some agencies of the federal government lend to the Treasury, but unlike the Federal Reserve Bank, their holdings are not included in figures on debt held by the public.

Report of the President, 2003, p. 372]. Because statutorily the Federal Reserve Bank is an independent agency, its holdings are counted as debt held by the public; it would seem that the amount of debt held by nongovernmental agencies is more relevant for most purposes.

State and Local Government Debt.   Although we often think of debt as a federal government issue, state and local governments borrow as well. In 1999, state and local debt outstanding was $1.37 trillion [US Bureau of the Census, 2002, p. 269]. The federal figure for that year was $3.6 trillion; the sum of the two numbers is relevant if we wish to assess the pressure that government as a whole has exerted on credit markets.

Effects of Inflation.   In standard calculations of the deficit, taxes are viewed as the only source of government revenue. However, when the government is a debtor and the price level changes, changes in the real value of the debt may be an important source of revenue. To see why, suppose that at the beginning of the year you owe a creditor $1,000, and the sum does not have to be repaid until the end of the year. Suppose further that over the course of the year, prices rise by 10 percent. Then the dollars you use to repay your creditor are worth 10 percent less than those you borrowed. In effect, inflation has reduced the real value of your debt by $100 (10 percent of $1,000). Alternatively, your real income has increased by $100 as a consequence of inflation. Of course, at the same time, your creditor's real income has fallen by $100.[2]

Let us apply this logic to an analysis of the federal deficit in 2002. At the beginning of fiscal year 2002, the federal government's outstanding debt was about $3.5 trillion. During 2002, the rate of inflation was about 1.4 percent. Hence, inflation reduced the real value of the federal debt by $49 billion (= $3.5 trillion × 0.014). In effect, this is as much a receipt for the government as any conventional tax. If we take this "inflation tax" into account, the conventionally measured deficit of $158 billion is reduced to $109 billion. However, the government's accounting procedures do not allow the inclusion of gains due to inflationary erosion of the debt. This induces a tendency to overestimate the size of the real deficit.

Capital versus Current Accounting.   The federal government lumps together all expenditures that are legally required to be included in the budget. There is no attempt to distinguish between *current spending* and *capital spending*. Current spending refers to expenditures for services that are consumed within the year—upkeep at the Washington Monument or salaries for marines, for example. Capital spending, in contrast, refers to expenditures for durable

---

[2] If the inflation is anticipated by borrowers and lenders, one expects the interest rate charged to be increased to take inflation into account. This phenomenon was discussed in Chapter 15.

items that yield services over a long time, such as dams, radar stations, and aircraft carriers. The stock of federally financed physical capital is about $2.1 trillion, of which $643 billion is related to national defense and the remainder to nondefense [Office of Management and Budget 2003, p. 153].

In contrast to federal government practice, the standard accounting procedure for both US businesses and many state and local governments is to keep separate budgets for current and capital expenditure. Maintaining a separate capital budget can provide a more accurate picture of an organization's financial status. Why? Purchase of a durable does not generally represent a "loss." It is only the trade of one asset (money) for another (the durable). Hence, acquisition of the asset does not contribute to an organization's deficit. Of course, as the capital asset is used, it wears out (depreciation), and this *does* constitute a loss. Thus, standard accounting procedures require that only the annual depreciation of durable assets be included in the current budget, not their entire purchase price.

The idea of the federal government adopting capital budgeting is controversial. Proponents of capital budgeting note that its absence leads to some bizarre governmental decisions. In particular, politicians can hold "yard sales" in which they sell off government assets to the private sector and claim that they are reducing the deficit. Part of the Bush administration's deficit reduction plan in 2002, for example, was to sell a large number of nondefense federal buildings. Now, as we pointed out in Chapter 4, there may be good reasons for transferring such assets to private individuals, but such transactions have nothing to do with reducing the real budget deficit. They simply represent the government trading one asset for the other. However, under the current accounting system, the proceeds of such sales are treated as equivalent to tax revenues, and so count toward reducing the deficit.

A final argument in favor of capital budgeting is simply that it reminds people that borrowing is not necessarily a bad thing. Just as a prudent household may go into debt to purchase capital assets like a house or a car, a prudent government can borrow to finance the purchase of long-lived assets.

Opponents of capital budgeting point out that, for governments, it is particularly difficult to distinguish between current and capital expenditure. Are educational and job-training programs a current expense, or an investment in human capital that will yield future returns? Is a missile an investment (because it will last a long time), or a current expenditure (because it is not reusable)? Such ambiguities could lead to political mischief, with every proponent of a new spending program claiming it was an investment and therefore belonged in the capital budget. In fact, advocates of transfer programs such as food stamps often promote them as "investments," because enhancing the diets of the poor today makes them more productive tomorrow. Critics assert that classifying transfer payments as investments renders meaningless the distinction between capital and current spending.

Tangible Assets.   Suppose that a family owns tangible assets (yachts, houses, Rembrandts) worth $15 million, owes the local bank $25,000 for credit card charges, and has no other assets or liabilities. It would be pretty silly to characterize the family's overall position as being $25,000 in debt. All assets and liabilities must be considered to assess overall financial position.

The federal government has not only massive financial liabilities (as depicted in Table 18.2), but vast tangible assets as well. These include residential and nonresidential buildings, equipment, gold, and mineral rights. However, public discussion has focused almost entirely on the government's financial liabilities, and not its tangible assets. Some have argued that the omission of tangibles leads to a highly misleading picture of the government's financial position.

Implicit Obligations.   A bond is simply a promise to make certain payments of money in the future. The present value of these payments is the amount by which the bond contributes to the debt. But bonds are not the only method that the federal government uses to promise money in the future. It can do so by legislation. The most important example is Social Security, which promises benefits to future retirees that must be paid out of future tax revenues. The precise value is hard to calculate, but estimates of Social Security's unfunded future liability range around $9 trillion. Medicare similarly imposes future obligations on the government; their present value is about $6 trillion. In addition, federal legislation promises retirement benefits to civilian and military employees. Federal pension liabilities are about $1.75 trillion [Office of Management and Budget, 2003, p. 24].

Of course, legislative promises and official debt are not exactly equivalent. Their legal status is quite different; explicit forms of debt represent legal commitments, while Social Security and Medicare payments can be reduced by legislative action, at least in principle. Nevertheless, political support for these programs is strong, and it would be surprising to see the government substantially renege on these promises. On this basis, a number of economists have argued that the present value of promised Social Security, Medicare, and other entitlement benefits should be included in the national debt.

Summing Up

How big is the national debt? The answer depends on which assets and liabilities are included in the calculation, and how they are valued. As in other similar situations, the "correct" answer depends on your purposes. For example, if the goal is to obtain some sense of all the obligations that have to be met by future taxpayers, then measures including implicit obligations like Social Security might be appropriate. But if the purpose is to assess the effect of fiscal policy on credit markets (discussed later), then more conventional deficit or surplus measures including only official liabilities might be more useful. Our discussion certainly shows that considerable caution must be exercised in interpreting figures on debts, deficits, and surpluses.

The Burden of the Debt

There is widespread agreement that reducing the nationl debt would be a good thing. But why should we care about the national debt, and whether it is increasing or decreasing? It's a tough question, and answering it requires hard thinking about the costs of debt finance and who bears them.

We begin by noting that future generations either have to retire the debt, or else refinance it. (Refinancing simply means borrowing new money to pay existing creditors.) In either case, there is a transfer from future taxpayers to bondholders because even if the debt is refinanced, interest payments must be made to the new bondholders. It would appear, then, that future generations must bear the burden of the debt. But the theory of incidence (Chapter 12) tells us to be suspicious of this line of reasoning. Merely because the legal burden is on future generations does not mean that they bear a real burden. Just as in the case of tax incidence, the chain of events set in motion when borrowing occurs can make the economic incidence quite different from the statutory incidence. As with other incidence problems, the answer depends on the assumptions made about economic behavior.

Lerner's View

Assume the government borrows from its own citizens—the obligation is an **internal debt.** According to Lerner [1948], an internal debt creates no burden for the future generation. Members of the future generation simply owe it to each other. When the debt is paid off, there is a transfer of income from one group of citizens (those who do not hold bonds) to another (bondholders). However, the future generation as a whole is no worse off in the sense that its consumption level is the same as it would have been. As an 18th-century writer named Melon put it, the "right hand owes to the left" [Musgrave, 1985, p. 49].

The story is quite different when a country borrows from abroad to finance current expenditure. This is referred to as an **external debt.** (In the United States, about 39 percent of the privately held federal debt is held by foreign investors [*Economic Report of the President 2003,* p. 380].) Suppose that the money borrowed from overseas is used to finance current consumption. In this case, the future generation certainly bears a burden, because its consumption level is reduced by an amount equal to the loan plus the accrued interest that must be sent to foreign lenders.[3] If, on the other hand, the loan is used to finance capital accumulation, the outcome depends on the project's productivity. If the marginal return on the investment is greater than the marginal cost of funds obtained abroad, the combination of the debt and capital expenditure actually makes the future generation better off. To the extent that the project's return is less than the marginal cost, the future generation is worse off.

---

[3] If the loan is refinanced, only the interest must be paid.

Table 18.3 **Overlapping generations model**

	Young	Middle-Aged	Old
The Period 2004–2024			
(1) Income	$ 12,000	$ 12,000	$12,000
(2) Government borrowing	−6,000	−6,000	
(3) Government-provided consumption	4,000	4,000	4,000
The Year 2024			
	Young	Middle-Aged	Old
(4) Government raises taxes to pay back the debt	$−4,000	$−4,000	$−4,000
(5) Government pays back the debt		+6,000	+6,000

The view that an internally held debt does not burden future generations dominated the economics profession in the 1940s and 1950s. Economists now believe that things are considerably more complicated.

An Overlapping Generations Model

In Lerner's model, a "generation" consists of everyone who is alive at a given time. A more sensible way to define a generation is everyone who was born at about the same time. Using this definition, at any given time several generations coexist simultaneously, a phenomenon that is central to an **overlapping generations model.** Analysis of a simple overlapping generations model shows how the burden of a debt can be transferred across generations.

Assume that the population consists of equal numbers of young, middle-aged, and old people. Each generation is 20 years long, and each person has a fixed income of $12,000 over the 20-year period. There is no private saving—everyone consumes their entire income. This situation is expected to continue forever. Income levels for three representative people for the period 2004 to 2024 are depicted in row 1 of Table 18.3.

Now assume that the government decides to borrow $12,000 to finance public consumption. The loan is to be repaid in the year 2024. Only the young and the middle-aged are willing to lend to the government—the old are unwilling because they will not be around in 20 years to obtain repayment. Assume that half the lending is done by the young and half by the middle-aged, so that consumption of each person is reduced by $6,000 during the period 2004 to 2024. This fact is recorded in row 2 of Table 18.3. However, with the money obtained from the loan, the government provides an equal amount of consumption for all—each person receives $4,000. This is noted in line 3.

Time passes, and the year 2024 arrives. The generation that was old in 2004 has departed from the scene. The formerly middle-aged are now old, the young are now middle-aged, and a new young generation has been born. The government has to raise $12,000 to pay off the debt. It does so by levying a tax of $4,000 on each person. This is recorded in line 4. With the tax receipts in hand, the government can pay back its debt holders, the now middle-aged and old (row 5). (We assume for simplicity that the rate of interest is zero, so all the government has to pay back is the principal. Introducing a positive rate of interest would not change the substantive result and means there is no need to discount future consumption to find its present value.)

The following results now emerge from Table 18.3:

1. As a consequence of the debt and accompanying tax policies, the generation that was old in 2004 to 2024 has a lifetime consumption level $4,000 higher than it otherwise would have had.

2. Those who were young and middle-aged in 2004 to 2024 are no better or worse off from the point of view of lifetime consumption.

3. The young generation in 2024 has a lifetime consumption stream that is $4,000 lower than it would have been in the absence of the debt and accompanying fiscal policies.

In effect, $4,000 has been transferred from the young of 2024 to the old of 2004. To be sure, the debt repayment in 2024 involves a transfer between people who are alive at the time, but the young are at the short end of the transfer because they have to contribute to repaying a debt from which they never benefited. Note also that the internal-external distinction that was key in Lerner's model is irrelevant here; even though the debt is all internal, it creates a burden for the future generation.

The model in Table 18.3 suggests a natural framework for comparing across generations the burdens (and benefits) of government fiscal policies. This framework, called **generational accounting,** involves the following steps. First, take a representative person in each generation and compute the present value of all taxes she pays to the government. Next, compute the present value of all transfers received from the government, including Social Security, Medicare, and so on. The difference between the present value of the taxes and the transfers is the "net tax" paid by a member of that generation. By comparing the net taxes paid by different generations, one can get a sense of how government policy redistributes income across generations.

Most calculations using this framework suggest that current generations benefit at the expense of future generations. Gokhale, Page, and Sturrock [1999, p. 497] estimate that if current policies are maintained, the net tax rate as a percent of lifetime income for people born in 1980 will be 31 percent,

29 percent for those born in 1995, and 49.2 percent for future generations. Of course, such calculations rest heavily on assumptions about future tax rates, interest rates, and so on. Further, they do not allow for the possibility that individuals in a given generation may care about their descendants as well as themselves (see below). Thus, the main contribution of the generational accounts framework is to focus our attention on the lifetime (rather than annual) consequences of government fiscal policies. Like conventional deficit figures, the specific net tax rates must be taken with a grain of salt.

Neoclassical Model

The intergenerational models discussed so far do not allow for the fact that economic decisions can be affected by government debt policy, and changes in these decisions have consequences for who bears the burden of the debt. Instead, it has been assumed that the taxes levied to pay off the debt affect neither work nor savings behavior. If taxes distort these decisions, real costs are imposed on the economy.

More importantly, we have ignored the potentially important effect of debt finance on capital formation. The neoclassical model of the debt stresses that when the government initiates a project, whether financed by taxes or borrowing, resources are removed from the private sector. One usually assumes that when tax finance is used, most of the resources removed come at the expense of consumption. On the other hand, when the government borrows, it competes for funds with individuals and firms who want the money for their own investment projects. If so, debt has most of its effect on private investment. To the extent that these assumptions are correct, debt finance leaves the future generation with a smaller capital stock, *ceteris paribus*. Its members therefore are less productive and have smaller real incomes than otherwise would have been the case. Thus, the debt imposes a burden on future generations through its impact on capital formation. (Note, however, that one of the things that is held equal here is the public sector capital stock. As suggested earlier, to the extent that the public sector undertakes productive investment with the resources it extracts from the private sector, the total capital stock increases.)

The assumption that government borrowing reduces private investment plays a key role in the neoclassical analysis. It is sometimes referred to as the **crowding out hypothesis**—when the public sector draws on the pool of resources available for investment, private investment gets crowded out. Crowding out is induced by changes in the interest rate. When the government increases its demand for credit, the interest rate, which is just the price of credit, goes up. But if the interest rate increases, private investment becomes more expensive and less of it is undertaken.[4]

---

[4] When capital is internationally mobile, the debt-induced increase in the interest rate leads to an inflow of funds from abroad. This increases the demand for dollars, causing the dollar to appreciate, which increases the relative price of American exports. Hence, net exports are crowded out rather than domestic investment. In the US economy, some of both domestic investment and exports are likely to be crowded out.

Expressed this way, it would appear relatively straightforward to test the crowding out hypothesis. Just examine the historical relationship between the interest rate and government deficits (as a proportion of gross domestic product). A positive correlation between the two variables tends to support the crowding out hypothesis, and vice versa. The question of how deficits affect interest rates actually became a hot political topic in 2003. Proponents of the Bush administration's budget proposals, which included substantial deficits, argued that there would be little effect on interest rates, while the opponents argued that interest rates would rise.

Unfortunately, resolving this controversy is complicated by the fact that other variables can also probably affect interest rates. For example, during a recession, investment decreases and hence the interest rate falls. At the same time, slack business conditions lead to smaller tax collections, which increases the deficit, *ceteris paribus*. Hence, the data may show an inverse relationship between interest rates and deficits, although this says nothing one way or the other about crowding out. As usual, the problem is to sort out the *independent* effect of deficits on interest rates, and as we showed in Chapter 2, this kind of problem can be quite difficult. Several decades of intensive econometric work on this issue have failed to lead to conclusive results.[5]

Despite the murkiness of the econometric evidence, the theoretical case for at least some crowding out is so strong that most economists agree that large deficits cause some reduction in the capital stock.[6] However, the precise size of this reduction, and hence the reduction in welfare for future generations, is not known with any precision. One rough guess is that as a consequence of past deficits, US national income today is about 6 percent lower than otherwise would have been the case [Ball and Mankiw, 1995, p. 106]. If this estimate is correct, it suggests that deficit spending has had a negative, but not disastrous, impact on the economy.

Ricardian Model

Our discussion so far has ignored the potential importance of individuals' intentional transfers across generations. Barro [1974] has argued that when the government borrows, members of the "old" generation realize that their heirs will be made worse off. Suppose further that the old care about the welfare of their descendants and therefore do not want their descendants' consumption levels reduced. What can the old do about this? One possibility is simply to increase their bequests by an amount sufficient to pay the extra taxes that will be due in the future. The result is that nothing really changes. Each generation consumes exactly the same amount as before the government borrowed. In terms of the model in Table 18.3, the old generation in

---

[5] For two different perspectives, see Gale and Potter [2002] and Calomiris and Hassett [2002].

[6] To the extent that higher interest rates attract foreign investment, less crowding out occurs. However, the burden on future generations is roughly unchanged because of the interest they must pay to foreigners.

2004 saves $4,000 to give to the young of 2024 so that the consumption of each generation is unchanged.

In effect, then, private individuals undo the intergenerational effects of government debt policy so that tax and debt finance are essentially equivalent. This view, that the form of government finance is irrelevant, is often referred to as the Ricardian model because its antecedents appeared in the work of the 19th-century British economist David Ricardo. (However, Ricardo was skeptical about the theory that now bears his name.)

Barro's provocative hypothesis on the irrelevance of government fiscal policy has been the subject of much debate. Some reject the idea as being based on incredible assumptions. Information on the implications of current deficits for future tax burdens is not easy to obtain; indeed, as emphasized earlier in this chapter, it isn't even clear how big the debt is! Another criticism is that people are not as farsighted as supposed in the model.

On the other hand, one could argue that the ultimate test of the theory is not the plausibility of its assumptions, but whether or not its predictions are confirmed by the data. Skeptics note that in the early 1980s, there was a huge increase in federal deficits. If the Ricardian model were correct, one would have expected private saving to increase commensurately. However, private saving (relative to net national product) actually fell. While this finding is suggestive, it is not conclusive because factors other than the deficit affect the saving rate. A number of econometric studies have analyzed the relationship between budget deficits and saving. (See Smetters [1999].) The evidence is rather mixed, and the Ricardian model has both critics and adherents among professional economists.

Overview

The burden of the debt is essentially a tax incidence problem in an intergenerational setting. Like many other incidence problems, the burden of the debt is hard to pin down. First, it is not even obvious how burden should be defined. One possibility is to measure it in terms of the lifetime consumption possibilities of a group of people about the same age. Another is in terms of the consumption available to all people alive at a given time. Even when we settle on a definition, the existence of a burden depends on the answers to several questions: Is the debt internal or external? How are various economic decisions affected by debt policy? What kind of projects are financed by the debt? Empirical examination of some of these decisions has been attempted, but so far no consensus has emerged.

To Tax or to Borrow?

At the outset of the war in Iraq in 2003, President Bush announced that $75 billion would be needed to pay for it. A debate immediately began over whether the war should be financed by raising taxes or increasing borrowing. How to choose between debt and taxes is one of the most fundamental questions in the field of public finance. Armed with the results of our discussion of the burden of the debt, we are in a good position to evaluate several approaches to answering the question.

Benefits-Received Principle

This independent normative principle states that the beneficiaries of a particular government spending program should have to pay for it. Thus, to the extent that the program creates benefits for future generations, it is appropriate to shift the burden to future generations via loan finance. A possible example is borrowing to pay for schools that benefit students by increasing their future earnings.

Intergenerational Equity

Suppose that due to technological progress, our grandchildren will be richer than we are. If it makes sense to transfer income from rich to poor people within a generation, why shouldn't we transfer income from rich to poor generations? Of course, if future generations are expected to be poorer than we are (due, say, to the exhaustion of irreplaceable resources) then this logic leads to just the opposite conclusion.

Efficiency Considerations

From an efficiency standpoint, the question is whether debt or tax finance generates a higher excess burden. The key to analyzing this question is to realize that *every* increase in government spending must ultimately be financed by an increase in taxes. The choice between tax and debt finance is just a choice between the timing of the taxes. With tax finance, one large payment is made at the time the expenditure is undertaken. With debt finance, many small payments are made over time to finance the interest due on the debt. The present values of the tax collections must be the same in both cases.

If the present values of tax collections for the two methods are the same, is there any reason to prefer one or the other on efficiency grounds? Assume for simplicity that all revenues to finance the debt are raised by taxes on labor income. As shown in Chapter 13 [Equation (13.4)], such a tax distorts the labor supply decision, resulting in an excess burden of

$$\tfrac{1}{2}\varepsilon w L t^2$$

where ε is the compensated elasticity of hours of work with respect to the wage, w is the before-tax wage, L is hours worked, and t is the ad valorem tax rate. Note that excess burden increases with the *square* of the tax rate—when the tax rate doubles, the excess burden quadruples. Thus, from the excess burden point of view, two small taxes are not equivalent to one big tax. Two small taxes are preferred.

This point is made graphically in Figure 18.1, which depicts the quadratic relationship between excess burden and the tax rate. The excess burden associated with the low tax rate, t_1, is χ_1, and the excess burden associated with the higher rate, t_2, is χ_2. From an efficiency point of view, it is better to be taxed twice at rate t_1, than once at rate t_2. The implication is that debt finance, which results in a series of relatively small tax rates, is superior to tax finance on efficiency grounds.

FIGURE 18.1

The relationship
between tax rate
and excess burden

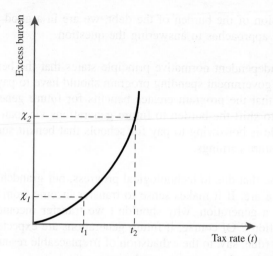

This argument is correct as far as it goes. However, it ignores another important consideration—to the extent the increase in debt reduces the capital stock, it creates an additional excess burden.[7] Thus, while debt finance may be more efficient from the point of view of labor supply choices, it will be less efficient from the point of view of capital allocation decisions. A priori it is unclear which effect is more important, so we cannot know whether debt or tax finance is more efficient.

Thus, the "crowding out" issue, which was so important in our discussion of the intergenerational burden of the debt, is also central to the efficiency issue. Recall that according to the Ricardian model, there is no crowding out. Thus, taxes distort only labor supply choices, and debt finance is unambiguously superior on efficiency grounds. However, to the extent that crowding out occurs, tax finance becomes more attractive. Clearly, as long as the empirical evidence on crowding out is inconclusive, we cannot know for sure the relative efficiency merits of debt versus tax finance.

Macroeconomic Considerations

Thus far, we have made our usual assumption that all resources are fully employed. This is appropriate for characterizing long-run tendencies in the economy. How does one choose between tax and deficit finance in the short run when unemployment is possible? In the standard Keynesian macroeconomic model, the choice depends on the level of unemployment. When unemployment is very low, extra government spending might lead to inflation, so it is necessary to siphon off some spending power from

---

[7] More precisely, an additional excess burden is created if the capital stock starts out below the optimal level because of, for example, capital income taxes [see Feldstein, 1985, p. 234].

the private sector—increase taxes. Conversely, when unemployment is high, running a deficit is a sensible way to stimulate demand. This approach is sometimes referred to as **functional finance**—use taxes and deficits to keep aggregate demand at the right level, and don't worry about balancing the budget per se.

When the Keynesian consensus collapsed in the 1970s, so did the almost universal belief in functional finance. While a thorough discussion of the relevant developments in macroeconomic theory would take us much too far afield, a couple of points are worth making:

- If Barro's intergenerational altruism model is correct, people can undo the effects of government debt policy. Government cannot stabilize the economy.[8]
- Even in the context of the Keynesian model, there is a lot of uncertainty regarding just how long it takes for changes in fiscal policy to become translated into changes in employment. But successful unemployment policy requires that the timing be right. Otherwise, one might end up stimulating the economy when it is no longer required, perhaps contributing to inflation.

Moral and Political Considerations

Some commentators have suggested that the decision between tax and debt finance is a moral issue. Too much reliance on deficits "is not merely, or even primarily, an economic matter. It reflects moral failing, a defect in the formation of the public's character and conservatisms" [Will, 1985a]. Morality requires self-restraint; deficits are indicative of a lack of restraint; therefore, deficits are immoral. The implicit assumption that debt is immoral is a feature of many political discussions of the topic.

As emphasized throughout this text, ethical issues are critical in the formulation of public policy, so arguments that deficits are immoral deserve serious consideration. One should note, however, that this *normative* view seems to rest heavily on the unproven *positive* hypothesis that the burden of the debt is shifted to future generations. Moreover, it is not clear why this particular normative view is superior to, for example, the benefits-received principle, which implies that sometimes borrowing is the morally right thing to do.

A perhaps more compelling noneconomic argument against deficit spending is a political one. As noted in Chapter 6, some have argued that the political process tends to underestimate the costs of government spending and to overestimate the benefits. The discipline of a balanced budget may produce a more careful weighing of benefits and costs, thus preventing the public sector from growing beyond its optimal size.

---

[8] More precisely, *anticipated* changes in policy have no impact. Unanticipated changes may have an effect, because by definition, people cannot change their behavior to counteract them.

However, some who believe that government spends too much have a different viewpoint, arguing that deficits may serve as an effective brake on government spending. According to Nobel laureate Milton Friedman [2003, p. A10], the conventional view is that the level of government spending is fixed, regardless of whether there is a deficit or not. If that is true, then raising taxes can eliminate the deficit. But Friedman argues that a better model is that spending is not fixed—if the government gets more money in taxes, it will simply spend the money. "What is predetermined is not spending but the politically tolerable deficit. Raise taxes by enough to eliminate the existing deficit and spending will go up to restore the tolerable deficit." A better strategy for restraining government is cutting taxes. "Resulting deficits will be an effective . . . restraint on the spending propensities of the executive branch and the legislature." As emphasized in Chapter 6, it is very difficult to assess the validity of theories of government spending. Thus, while we must view Friedman's approach as a conjecture, it reminds us of the importance of considering the political environment when making policy recommendations.

Overview

The national debt is an emotional and difficult subject. The analysis of this chapter brings the following perspectives to bear on the debate:

- The size of the deficit during a given year depends on one's accounting conventions. This fact underscores the arbitrariness of any number that purports to be *the* deficit, *the* surplus, or *the* debt.

- The consequences of deficits and surpluses, while potentially important, are hard to measure. And even if we knew exactly what the effects were, the implications for the conduct of debt policy would still depend on ethical views concerning the intergenerational distribution of income.

In light of all these considerations, it makes little sense to evaluate the economic operation of the public sector solely on the basis of the size of the official deficit or surplus. A deficit is not necessarily bad and a surplus is not necessarily good. More important is whether the levels of government services are optimal, particularly considering the costs of securing the resources required to provide these services. A lively debate over the spending and financing activities of government is important in a democracy. The consequences of deficit versus other forms of finance are important and worthy of public consideration. Nevertheless, the tendency of both liberals and conservatives to evaluate the state of public finance solely on the basis of the deficit tends to obscure and confuse the debate.

Summary

- Borrowing is an important method of government finance. The deficit during a period of time is the excess of spending over revenues; the surplus is the excess of revenues over spending; the debt as of a given point in time is the algebraic sum of past deficits and surpluses.

- Official figures regarding the size of federal government deficits, surpluses, and debts must be viewed with caution for several reasons:

  State and local governments also have large amounts of debt outstanding.

  Inflation erodes the real value of the debt; the official deficit or surplus does not reflect this fact.

  The federal government does not distinguish between capital and current expenditure. However, attempts to design a capital budget for the federal government could founder on both conceptual and political problems.

  Tangible assets owned by the government should be taken into account, as should the government's implicit obligations (such as promises to pay Social Security and Medicare benefits).

- Whether or not the burden of debt is borne by future generations is controversial. One view is that an internal debt creates no net burden for the future generation because it is simply an intragenerational transfer. However, in an overlapping generations model, debt finance can produce a real burden on future generations.

- The burden of the debt also depends on whether debt finance crowds out private investment. If it does, future generations have a smaller capital stock and, hence, lower real incomes, *ceteris paribus*. In a Ricardian model, voluntary transfers across generations undo the effects of debt policy, so that crowding out does not occur.

- Several factors influence whether a given government expenditure should be financed by taxes or debt. The benefits-received principle suggests that if the project will benefit future generations, then having them pay for it via loan finance is appropriate. Also, if future generations are expected to be richer than the present one, some principles of equity suggest that it is fair to burden them.

- From an efficiency standpoint, one must compare the excess burdens of tax and debt finance. If there is no crowding out, debt finance has less of an excess burden, because a series of small tax increases generates a smaller excess burden than one large tax increase. However, if crowding out occurs, this conclusion may be reversed.

Discussion Questions

1. How would each of the following events affect the national debt as it is currently measured?

   a. The government borrows to finance a Memorial Day parade.

   b. The Statue of Liberty is sold to a group of private entrepreneurs.

   c. A law is passed promising free medical care to every child under 5 years of age.

   d. The government levies a tax of $100 on Lynne this year, and promises to pay her $105 next year.

   e. The government borrows $100 from Lynne this year, and pays back the $100 with 5 percent interest next year.

   If you were designing an accounting system for the government, how would you treat each of these items?

2. In the 1770s, a French civil servant named Montyon observed that "Great Britain finances by taxation neither all nor part of the costs of war, it finances them by loans . . . In wartime it is our habit to increase taxes" [Sargent and Velde, 1995]. Montyon thought that the British policy was superior. Do you agree? Explain why it is relevant to your answer whether the Ricardian model holds.

3. According to Schick [2002, p. 46], "The arrival of a surplus [in the late 1990s] triggered a spending frenzy that vitiated the discretionary

spending caps established by the 1990 Budget Enforcement Act and made a mockery of the BEA requirement that increased spending be offset by cuts in other spending or by revenue increases." Discuss the relationship of this episode to Milton Friedman's approach to thinking about the relationship between deficits and government spending.

4. Suppose that the compensated elasticity of labor supply with respect to the wage is zero. On efficiency grounds, what are the consequences for the optimal choice between debt and tax finance?

5. In 2000, Ohio Senator George Voinovich said, "Common sense says that our first priority should be to use our budget surplus to pay down our huge national debt." Evaluate this statement.

6. In his State of the Union address in 2002, President Bush said, "To achieve these great national objectives—to win the war, protect the homeland, and revitalize our economy—our budget will run a deficit that will be small and short-term." Under what conditions is it sensible to use a deficit to finance a war?

Selected References

Elmendorf, Douglas W, and N Gregory Mankiw. "Government Debt." In *Handbook of Macroeconomics,* volume 1C, eds. John B. Taylor and Michael Woodford. Amsterdam: North-Hollard, 1999.

Kotlikoff, Laurence J. "Generational Policy." Working Paper No. 8163. Cambridge, MA: National Bureau of Economic Research, March 2001.

CHAPTER 19

Taxes on Consumption and Wealth

But when the impositions are laid upon those things which men consume, every man payeth equally for what he useth: nor is the common wealth defrauded by the luxurious waste of private men.

THOMAS HOBBES

There is substantial dissatisfaction with the federal personal and corporate income tax systems. Some reformers wish to move the system away from the use of income and toward other bases. One much discussed idea is to adopt some kind of consumption tax, whose base is the value (or quantity) of commodities sold to a person for *actual* consumption (as opposed to an income tax, whose base is the change in *potential* consumption). Another possibility is a tax on wealth, whose base is accumulated saving, that is, the accumulated difference between potential and actual consumption. This chapter discusses the current roles of consumption and wealth taxes in the US fiscal system and how those roles might be expanded.

Retail Sales Tax

In the United States today, the most important consumption taxes are retail sales taxes levied on purchases of a wide variety of commodities (see Table 19.1). A **general sales tax** imposes the same tax rate on the purchase of all commodities. In the United States, state sales taxes that cover a wide variety of goods are often given the label *general*. This is something of a misnomer, however, because even states that tax most goods exempt the sales of virtually all services from taxation.

Table 19.1   **State and local sales tax revenues by source**   *($ billions)*

Source	State	Local
General sales tax	$164	$29.7
Motor fuel	29.2	0.8
Alcoholic beverages	3.9	0.3
Tobacco	8.2	0.2
Public utilities	8.9	7.3
Percent of own-source revenue from sales taxes	36.7%	10.0%

SOURCE: US Bureau of the Census [2002, p. 270]. Figures are for 1999.

A **selective sales tax,** also referred to as an **excise tax,** or a **differential commodity tax,** is levied at different rates on the purchase of different commodities. (Some of those rates can be zero.)[1]

Sales taxes generally take one of two forms: A **unit tax** is a given amount for each unit purchased. For example, most states levy a tax on motor fuel that is a certain number of cents per gallon; a typical rate is 16 cents. In contrast, an **ad valorem tax** is computed as a percentage of the value of the purchase. For example, the federal excise tax rate on bows and arrows is 11 percent.

The federal government levies no general sales tax. It does tax motor fuel, alcoholic beverages, tobacco, and a few other commodities, but these taxes account for less than 10 percent of federal revenues. As Table 19.1 indicates, sales taxes are particularly important in the revenue systems of state governments. Forty-five states plus the District of Columbia have general sales taxes, with rates that vary from 2.9 to 7.25 percent. Most of the states exempt food from tax, and virtually all exempt prescription drugs. In about half the states, municipalities and counties levy their own general sales taxes.

Rationalizations

Administrative Considerations.   Perhaps the main attraction of sales taxes is ease of administration. The sales tax is collected from sellers at the retail level. Relative to an income tax, there are fewer individuals whose behavior has to be monitored by the tax authorities. This is not to say that administration of a sales tax is without complications. Many difficulties arise because it is unclear whether a given transaction creates a tax liability. In California, "snacks" are subject to a special sales tax while "food" is not. What is a snack and what is food? Under the law, Ritz crackers and wrapped slices of pie are subject to the snack tax, while soda crackers and a slice of pie served

---

[1] Another type of sales tax is a **use tax**—a sales tax that residents of a given state must pay on purchases made in other states. The purpose of a use tax is to prevent individuals from avoiding sales taxes by making purchases out of state. Historically, use taxes have yielded very little revenue. However, some states are becoming more aggressive in their collection techniques, so use taxes may become more important in the future.

on a plate are not. Some states determine whether a juice is a nontaxable food by a formula based on the amount of actual fruit in the juice. The point is that defining the base for a sales tax requires arbitrary distinctions, just like the personal and corporate income taxes. Moreover, as is true for other taxes, tax evasion can be a real problem. A case that received a lot of attention recently was that of the former Chairman of Tyco International, Dennis Kozlowski, who was indicted for evading 8.25 percent New York City sales taxes on millions of dollars on artwork that he purchased there. (He pretended that the art was being shipped to his office in New Hampshire, which has no sales tax.) A less exotic but more significant example is provided by Canada, which several years ago cut its high taxes on cigarettes after concluding that smuggling was creating unacceptable demands on law enforcement agencies.

Despite such horror stories, most observers believe that, at present levels, compliance with state-level retail taxes is quite good. We return later to the issue of administrative problems that might be encountered with a national retail sales tax.

Optimal Tax Considerations.   When thinking about retail sales taxes in an optimal tax framework, the key question is what role can differential commodity taxes play given that an income tax is already in place? It can be shown that if the income tax schedule is chosen optimally, then under fairly reasonable conditions, social welfare cannot be improved by levying differential commodity taxes.[2] However, if for some reason the income tax is not optimal, differential commodity taxes can improve welfare. For example, if society has egalitarian goals, social welfare can be improved by taxing luxury goods at relatively high rates.

A related question is how to set the rates, given a decision to have differential commodity taxes. Obviously, the answer depends on the government's objectives. If the goal is to collect a specified amount of revenue as efficiently as possible, tax rates should be set so that the compensated demand for each commodity is reduced in the same proportion (see Chapter 14). When the demand for each good depends only on its own price, this is equivalent to the rule that tax rates be inversely related to compensated price elasticities of demand. Tax goods with inelastic demands at relatively high rates, and vice versa. Efficiency does not require a general sales tax with the same tax rate for each commodity.

If the government cares about equity as well as efficiency, optimal tax theory requires departures from the inverse elasticity rule. As noted in Chapter 14, if price-inelastic commodities make up a high proportion of the

[2] See Atkinson and Stiglitz [1980]. Suppose the utility function of each individual is a function of his or her consumption of leisure and a set of other commodities. Then as long as the marginal rate of substitution between any two commodities is independent of the amount of leisure, differential commodity taxation cannot improve social welfare in the presence of an optimal earnings tax.

budgets of the poor, governments with egalitarian objectives should tax such goods lightly or not at all. This may help explain why so many states exempt food from sales taxation.

Within the conventional welfare economics framework, another justification for a sales tax is the presence of externalities. If consumption of a commodity generates costs not included in its price, then efficiency requires a tax on the use of that good (see Chapter 6). High tax rates on tobacco—state plus federal rates now average about $1 per pack—are sometimes rationalized in this way. Smokers impose costs on others by polluting the atmosphere, so a tax on tobacco may enhance economic efficiency.

In some cases, sales taxes can be viewed as substitutes for user fees. With current technology, it is infeasible to charge motorists a fee for every mile driven, even though the process of driving creates costs in terms of road damage, congestion, and so on. Because the amount of road use is related to gasoline consumption, road use can be taxed indirectly by putting a tax on gasoline. Of course, the correspondence is far from perfect: Some cars are more fuel efficient than others, and some do more damage than others. Still, an approximately correct user fee may be more efficient than none at all.

Other Considerations.   Several rationalizations for differential commodity taxation lie outside the framework of conventional economics. Certain excises can be regarded as taxes on "sin." A particular commodity, such as tobacco or alcohol, is deemed to be bad per se, and its consumption is therefore discouraged by the state. Such commodities are just the opposite of "merit goods" (see Chapter 3), which are viewed as being good per se. In both cases, the government is essentially imposing its preferences on those of the citizenry.

Some argue that politicians like sales taxes because they are included in the final price of the commodity and so are relatively easy to hide. However, it is hard to determine whether citizens really are less sensitive to sales taxes than to other types of taxes.

Efficiency and Distributional Implications

From an efficiency point of view, the fundamental question is whether the pattern of sales tax rates minimizes excess burden. As pointed out in Chapter 13, when a group of commodities is being taxed, the overall excess burden depends not only on the elasticities of each good but also on the degree to which the goods are complementary and substitutable. At this time, values of all the relevant elasticities are not known with any degree of certainty. Therefore, no definitive judgment as to the efficiency of the existing set of sales taxes is available.

As noted earlier, setting all rates equal is almost certainly not efficient. On the other hand, given that the information required to determine fully efficient taxes is not presently available (and perhaps never will be), uniform tax rates may not be a bad approach. This is particularly likely if departures from uniformity open the door to tax rate differentiation based on political rather than equity or efficiency considerations.

The conventional view of the distributional effects of retail sales taxes is that they are regressive. As the Washington organization Citizens for Tax Justice put it, "Wealthy people are taxed at a far lower rate than middle-income families. Why? Because higher-income people spend a smaller proportion of their income."[3]

This line of reasoning has two problems. First, it looks at the tax as a proportion of *annual* income. In the absence of severe credit market restrictions, *lifetime* income is more relevant, and there is reasonably strong evidence that the proportion of lifetime income devoted to consumption is about the same at all levels. Indeed, computations by Metcalf [1993] suggest general sales taxes are somewhat progressive when measured with respect to lifetime (rather than annual) income. Second, and perhaps more fundamentally, the conventional view totally ignores the theory of tax incidence. Implicitly, it is assumed that the taxes on a good are borne entirely by the consumers of that good. As emphasized in Chapter 12, however, a commodity tax generally is shifted in a complicated fashion that depends on the supply and demand responses when the tax is imposed. The effect of sales taxes on the distribution of income is still an open question.[4]

The incidence of selective sales tax systems depends crucially on which goods are taxed at low rates or exempted altogether. By exempting those goods consumed intensively by the poor, the after-tax income distribution can be made more equal, other things being the same. But achieving equality this way is difficult. Even if it is true that food expenditures on average play an especially important role in the budgets of the poor, there are still many upper-income families whose food consumption is proportionately very high. Moreover, exempting certain commodities creates administrative complexities, because it is not always clear whether certain goods belong in the favored category. Just recall the California snack tax described earlier.

We conclude that the use of selective sales taxation is a fairly clumsy way to achieve egalitarian goals, particularly if a progressive income tax system is already in place.

A National Retail Sales Tax?

Recently, several legislators have proposed replacing the existing federal tax system with a national retail sales tax. To its proponents, the key advantages of a national retail sales tax are simplicity and ease of compliance. The tax is collected by businesses when they sell commodities, so the Internal Revenue Service stays out of the lives of most citizens.

---

[3] Citizens for Tax Justice, "The Loophole Lobbyists vs. The People," Washington, DC, undated.

[4] In the United States, analyzing the incidence of sales taxes is further complicated by the fact that the rate on a given good varies from jurisdiction to jurisdiction. This may induce citizens from one jurisdiction to make purchases in another, so it is hard to tell just who is paying the tax. In New York, clothing is taxed; in New Jersey, it is not. Not surprisingly, many New Yorkers who live near New Jersey do their clothes shopping across the border. Similarly, it is not unknown for Massachusetts citizens to buy their alcohol in New Hampshire, where the tax rate on liquor is relatively low.

As already noted, compliance is in fact not much of a problem with current state sales taxes. But as also noted, the rates associated with those systems are relatively low, in the range of 3 to 7 percent. In order to raise as much revenue as the federal personal income, payroll, and estate taxes, a federal retail tax rate of about *35* percent would be required [Gale and Holtzblatt, 2002, p. 198]. And at high rates, a retail sales tax becomes extremely difficult to enforce since it "collects all the money from what is, for compliance purposes, the weakest link in the production and distribution chain—retail. Consumers have no incentive to make sure retailers are paying their sales tax, and retailers have no incentive to pay aside from the threat of audit" [Slemrod and Bakija, 2000, p. 213]. We know from the theory of tax evasion (Chapter 14) that the benefit to cheating depends on the size of the tax rate. With the relatively low sales tax rates now in existence, the benefit is apparently not high enough to make it worthwhile to cheat extensively. But most authorities believe that once the rate goes above 10 percent, compliance becomes a serious issue. Hence, a national retail sales tax loses some of its allure as a tax reform option.

Transitional Issues

Introduction of a national sales tax would create serious transitional problems. Individuals who had accumulated wealth under the existing income tax system would suffer during the transition period. During their working years, they accumulated wealth for future consumption. The interest, dividends, and realized capital gains that they received along the way were subject to the personal income tax. A reasonable expectation for such people is that when they decided to consume their wealth (say, at retirement), their consumption would not be subject to new taxes. If a national sales tax were suddenly introduced, however, these expectations would be disappointed.

This observation, by the way, puts the distributional consequences of moving to a national retail sales tax in a new light. Introduction of such a tax would be accompanied, in effect, by a one-time tax on existing wealth. Because wealth is unequally distributed, this would have a progressive impact on the distribution of income [Gentry and Hubbard, 1997]. This result holds for any broad-based consumption tax, not just the retail sales tax.

Value-Added Tax

Can one structure a sales tax that has better compliance properties than a retail sales tax? To think about this issue, we begin by noting that typically, goods are produced in several stages. Consider a simple model of bread production.[5] The farmer grows wheat and sells it to a miller who turns it into flour. The miller sells the flour to a baker who transforms it into bread. The

---

[5] For a detailed description of how value-added taxes work, see Cnossen [2001].

Table 19.2 **Implementation of a value-added tax (VAT)**

Producer	Purchases	Sales	Value Added	VAT at 20 Percent Rate
Farmer	$ 0	$ 400	$ 400	$ 80
Miller	400	700	300	60
Baker	700	950	250	50
Grocer	950	1,000	50	10
Total	$2,050	$3,050	$1,000	$200

bread is purchased by a grocer who sells it to consumers. A hypothetical numerical example is provided in Table 19.2. Column 1 shows the purchases made by the producer at each stage of production, and column 2 shows the sales value at each stage. For example, the miller pays $400 to the farmer for wheat, and sells the processed wheat to the baker for $700. The **value added** at each stage of production is the difference between the firm's sales and the purchased material inputs used in production. The baker paid $700 for the wheat and sold the bread for $950, so his value added is $250. The value added at each stage of production is computed by subtracting purchases from sales, shown in column 3.[6]

A **value-added tax (VAT)** is a percentage tax on value added applied at each stage of production. For example, if the rate of the VAT is 20 percent, the grocer would pay $10, which is 20 percent of $50. Column 4 shows the amount of VAT liability at each stage of production. The total revenue created by the VAT is found by summing the amounts paid at each stage, and equals $200.

The identical result could have been generated by levying a 20 percent tax at the retail level, that is, by a tax of 20 percent on the value of sales made to consumers by the grocer. *In essence, then, a VAT is just an alternative method for collecting a retail sales tax.*

Implementation Issues

Although the United States has never had a national VAT, this tax is popular in Europe. The European experience indicates that certain administrative decisions have a major impact on a VAT's ultimate economic effects.

The first is how purchases of investment assets by firms are treated in the computation of value added. The practice in Europe is to treat an investment good like any other material input. Its full value is subtracted from sales in the computation, despite the fact that it is durable. This is referred to as a **consumption-type VAT** because the tax base excludes investment and involves only consumption.

[6] By definition, value added must equal the sum of factor payments made by the producer: wages, interest, rent, and economic profits.

Second, a collection procedure must be devised. European countries use the **invoice method,** which can be illustrated in the hypothetical example in Table 19.2. Each firm is liable for tax on the basis of its total sales, but it can claim the taxes already paid by its suppliers as a credit against this liability. For example, the baker is liable for taxes on his $950 in sales, giving him a tax obligation of $190 (= .20 × $950). However, he can claim a credit of $140 (the sum of taxes paid by the farmer and the miller), leaving him a net obligation of $50. The catch is that the credit is allowed only if supported by invoices provided by the baker and the miller. This system provides an incentive for the producers to police themselves against tax evasion. Whatever taxes the farmer and miller evade must be paid by the baker, so the baker will only do business with firms that provide proper invoices. The invoice method cannot eliminate evasion completely. For example, producers can collude to falsify invoices. Nevertheless, compliance is better than it would be under a national retail sales tax.

Finally, a rate structure is needed. In our simple example, all commodities are taxed at the same rate. In Europe, commodities are taxed differentially. Food and health care products are taxed at low rates, presumably because of equity considerations. For reasons of administrative feasibility, some countries exempt very small firms. Similarly, banking and finance institutions escape taxation because they tend to provide services in kind; therefore, it is difficult to compute value added. The consumption of services generated by owner-occupied housing is exempt from tax for the same reasons that it is usually exempted from income taxation (see Chapter 16).

Nonuniform taxation increases administrative complexity, especially when firms produce multiple outputs, some of which are taxable and some of which are not. But the system can work, as evidenced by the European experience. For the United States, then, the question is not whether a national VAT is feasible, but whether it would be better than the status quo.

A VAT for the United States?

The VATs suggested for the United States are usually of the European consumption type, and hence essentially general sales taxes. Therefore, the arguments regarding the efficiency and equity of sales taxes made earlier in this chapter are applicable, and we need not repeat them. The fundamental problem is the same: Attempts to obtain additional equity by exempting various goods may increase the excess burden of the tax system as a whole and lead to greater administrative complexity.

More generally, the desirability of a national VAT can be determined only if we know what tax (or taxes) it would replace, how the revenues would be spent, and so forth. For example, many public finance economists believe that the corporation income tax is undesirable in practically all respects and would be happy to see a VAT replace it, other things being the same. However, they would probably not be as well disposed toward replacing the personal income tax with a VAT. Altig *et al.* [2001] analyzed the impact of replacing the existing US tax system with a comprehensive proportional consumption tax like a VAT, and found that in the long run, it would increase income by about 9 percent. This result, however, depends importantly on assumptions about the responsiveness of saving to changes in the income tax. As noted in Chapter 16, this is a controversial issue, so this particular figure must be regarded with some caution.

In addition, we must consider the political implications of introducing a VAT. Once it is in place, each percentage point increase in a comprehensive VAT would yield roughly $40 billion in tax revenues.[7] In a world where political institutions accurately reflect citizens' wishes, this observation may not be of much significance. But for those who believe that the government's interests can differ from those of the public (see Chapter 6), the revenue potential of a VAT is frightening. Some fear that the VAT might be used to sneak by an increase in the size of the government sector:

> Because it would be collected by business enterprises, VAT would be concealed in the total price the consumer paid and hence not perceived as a direct tax burden. That is its advantage to legislators—and its major defect to the taxpayers. [Friedman, 1980, p. 90]

Indeed, in virtually all countries with a VAT, the rate has increased over time. For example, in the nations of the European Union, when the VAT was introduced, the average rate was 13.9 percent; it is now 19.4 percent, an increase of almost 40 percent [Cnossen, 2001, p. 485]. At the same time, the share of gross domestic product devoted to taxes in these countries has increased. Indeed, Becker and Mulligan [1998] show that the greater the number of years a country has had a VAT, the larger its government. Of course, this does not prove that the VAT was responsible for a larger government sector. On the other hand, one would not expect to be successful in assuaging the fears just expressed by appealing to the experience of other countries with the VAT.

Finally, it is important to consider the international implications of a VAT, because some VAT proponents have argued that the tax would enhance America's trade position vis-à-vis its competitors. This notion rests on the fact that according to the World Trade Organization (WTO), which regulates international trade practices, a VAT can be rebated on a country's exports and levied on imports. In contrast, personal and corporate income taxes cannot be rebated. Since a VAT can be rebated while income taxes cannot, some have argued that US international competitiveness would be enhanced if the US adopted a VAT and simultaneously reduced the role of income taxation. Former Congressman Bill Archer [1996] argued that such a scheme would "give us a fair trade advantage in the global marketplace."

To analyze this plan, consider each part separately: introduction of a VAT, and then reduction in personal and corporate income taxes. Imposing

---

[7] This is a projection based on Congressional Budget Office [1997a, p. 390].

a VAT would tend to increase the relative prices of the taxed goods by an amount determined by the relevant supply and demand elasticities. However, all that rebating the VAT at the border does is undo the price increase generated by the tax. If you put an extra weight on a horse and then remove it, the horse does not run any faster.

Turning now to the second part of the plan, would reducing corporate and personal income taxes reduce the relative prices of American exports? Again, the answer depends on the incidence of these taxes, and it is not at all obvious. For example, if the market for labor is competitive and its supply is perfectly inelastic, producers' wage costs are unchanged when personal income taxes are reduced. The entire benefit of the tax reduction goes to workers. (See Chapter 12.) In this case, prices may not change at all. More generally, of course, prices might fall, but no evidence suggests that the reduction would be very large.

In short, there is no reason to believe that adoption of a VAT would dramatically improve the US trade position. Of course, this fact by itself does not mean that a VAT would be a bad thing. As noted already, VATs have both advantages and disadvantages. But they are not a panacea for US trade problems.

Hall–Rabushka Flat Tax

A distinguishing feature of both the retail sales tax and the VAT is that the legal incidence falls upon businesses. Consumers make no explicit payments to the government (although they likely bear a share of the economic incidence). However, much of the current interest in consumption taxes has centered on *personal* consumption taxes that require individuals to file tax returns and write checks to the government. Unlike the retail sales tax or the VAT, these systems allow individuals' tax liabilities to depend on their personal circumstances.

The best known of these proposals is the one put forward by Hall and Rabushka (H&R) [1995], which they call a *flat tax*. The H&R proposal, a version of which was the centerpiece of 2000 presidential candidate Steve Forbes' campaign, has two tax-collecting vehicles, a business tax and an individual compensation tax. The coordinated use of these two instruments allows the government to levy a progressive tax.

The calculation of the business tax base begins with a computation like that of a consumption-type VAT—sales less purchases from other firms. The key difference is that the firm also deducts payments to its workers. Firms then pay a flat rate of tax on the final amount.

The base for the individual tax is the payments received by individuals for their labor services. No capital income is taxed at the individual level. In principle, any tax schedule could be applied to this base—the tax rate could be flat or increasing, and an exemption might or might not be allowed. H&R propose only one rate (19 percent), and it is the same as the rate that applies to cash flow at the business level. H&R build progressivity into the system by allowing an exemption of $25,000 (for a family of four). No other deductions are allowed. This is what permits the rate to be so low.

At this point you might be wondering why the H&R tax is a consumption tax. To see why, consider a VAT that taxes all goods and services at the same rate, say, 19 percent. As shown above, this is economically equivalent to a 19 percent retail sales tax. Now consider an H&R-type flat tax that taxes both individuals and firms at 19 percent and that has no exemptions or deductions at the personal level. Recall that under the VAT, the firm's tax base is sales minus purchases from other firms. Wage payments are not deductible. In effect, then, wage payments are subject to a 19 percent tax. Under the H&R tax, wage payments are deductible at the firm level, but they are taxed at the individual level. The amount of tax is exactly the same as under a VAT; all that changes is the point of collection for part of the tax. The personal exemption simply builds some progressivity into the system. In short, except for the exemption, the H&R flat tax is essentially equivalent to a VAT or a retail sales tax. Hence, for all intents and purposes, any results pertaining to the economic effects of one apply to all.

Cash–Flow Tax	Another personal consumption tax is the cash-flow tax. Under this variant, each household files a return reporting its consumption expenditures during the year. Just as under the personal income tax, various exemptions and deductions can be taken to allow for special circumstances such as extraordinary medical expenses. Each individual's tax bill is then determined by applying a rate schedule to the adjusted amount of consumption.

From an administrative point of view, the big question is how does the taxpayer compute his or her annual consumption? The most sensible approach is to measure consumption on a *cash-flow basis,* meaning that it would be calculated simply as the difference between all cash receipts and saving. To keep track of saving, qualified accounts would be established at savings banks, security brokerage houses, and other types of financial institutions. Funds that were certified by these institutions as having been deposited in qualified accounts would be exempt from tax. Most of the record-keeping responsibility would be met by these institutions and would not involve more paperwork than exists already. As long as capital gains and interest from such accounts were retained, they would not be taxed. For some taxpayers, such qualified accounts already exist in the forms of 401(k) plans and conventional individual retirement accounts (see Chapter 15). One way to look at a cash-flow tax is simply as an expansion of the opportunities to invest in such accounts. However, many analysts believe that the record-keeping requirements associated with a cash-flow tax would make it very difficult administratively.

Efficiency and Fairness of Personal Consumption Taxes

Some argue that if the income tax were replaced by a personal consumption tax such as the H&R flat tax or the cash-flow tax, efficiency, equity, and administrative simplicity would be enhanced. The defenders of the income tax have argued that the case for personal consumption taxation is seriously flawed. We now discuss the controversy.

Efficiency Issues

The efficiency implications of personal consumption versus income taxation can be examined using the life-cycle model of consumption and saving introduced in Chapter 16. In that model, the individual's labor supply each period is fixed. The two commodities she purchases are present consumption, c_0, and future consumption, c_1. If r is the interest rate, every additional dollar of consumption today means that the individual's future consumption is reduced by $(1 + r)$. Hence, the relative price of c_0—its opportunity cost—is $(1 + r)$.

Consider now the case of Juliet, on whom a 30 percent income tax is levied. Assuming that the tax allows for the deductibility of interest payments, how does this affect the relative price of c_0?[8] If Juliet saves a dollar and it earns a return of r, the government taxes away 30 percent of the return, leaving her only $0.70 \times r$. If she borrows a dollar, the interest payments are deductible, so the cost of borrowing is reduced to $0.70 \times r$. In short, the income tax induces a reduction in the relative price of present consumption from $(1 + r)$ to $(1 + 0.70r)$. A wedge is inserted between the amount a borrower pays and a lender receives. As we showed in Chapter 13, tax wedges create excess burdens. We conclude that an income tax generates an excess burden.

Now consider a consumption tax that raises the same amount of revenue as the income tax. The key thing to note in this context is that the consumption tax leaves unchanged the market rate of return available to Juliet. This is because the receipt of interest income by itself does not create a tax liability. Hence, after the consumption tax, the relative price of c_0 is still $(1 + r)$. Unlike the income tax, there is no tax wedge and, hence, no excess burden. Apparently, consumption taxation is superior to income taxation on efficiency grounds.

Is this result general, or is it a consequence of some special assumptions? Recall that in Chapter 13 a similar argument was used to "prove" that taxes at equal rates on all commodities are always more efficient than differential rates. We showed the fallacy in that argument. Because even an equiproportional tax distorts the choice between leisure and each of the taxed commodities, it is not clear that taxing all commodities at the same rate is efficient. The same logic applies here. The argument in the preceding

---

[8] As stressed in Chapters 15 and 16, not all taxpayers can deduct payments of interest. As an exercise, discuss how the following analysis is modified when interest is not deductible.

paragraphs was built on the *assumption* that the supply of labor is fixed. Once we recognize that labor-supply decisions are choices, it is no longer true that the consumption tax is *necessarily* more efficient than an income tax.

True, unlike the income tax, the consumption tax leaves unchanged the rate at which Juliet can trade off consumption between the two periods. However, in general, the consumption tax *does* distort the rate at which she can trade off leisure against consumption. Suppose Juliet's wage rate is w. Before the consumption tax, she can trade off one hour of leisure for w dollars' worth of consumption. If consumption is taxed at rate tc, however, surrendering one hour of leisure allows her only $w/(1 + t_c)$ dollars' worth of consumption. Thus, the consumption tax distorts the decision between leisure and consumption.

In short, provided that labor supply is a matter of choice, both income and consumption taxes distort some decisions. Therefore, both systems induce an efficiency cost, and only empirical work can determine which tax's cost is smaller. Several studies indicate that given what is known about labor supply and saving behavior, a consumption tax creates a smaller excess burden than an income tax, even when labor supply distortions created by both taxes are taken into account. (See, for example, Altig *et al.* [2001].)

Equity Issues

Progressiveness. Earlier we noted the widespread assumption that sales taxes are regressive. Whatever the merits of this view, there is an unfortunate tendency to assume that it applies to any tax with consumption as a base. This is simply wrong. A personal consumption tax proposal can be made as progressive as desired by suitable adjustments to the exemption level and rate schedule.

Ability to Pay. Those who favor the income base argue that *actual* consumption is merely one component of *potential* consumption. It is the power to consume, not necessarily its exercise, that is relevant. They point out that under a consumption tax, a miserly millionaire might have a smaller tax liability than a much poorer person. A possible response is that it is fairer to tax an individual according to what he or she "takes out" of the economic system, in the form of consumption, than what he or she "contributes" to society, as measured by income. As Thomas Hobbes said in the 17th century:

> For what reason is there, that he which laboureth much, and sparing the fruit of his labour, consumeth little, should be more charged, than he that liveth idly, getteth little, and spendeth all he gets; seeing the one hath no more protection from the commonwealth than the other. [1651/1963, p. 303]

From this point of view, if the miserly millionaire chooses not to consume very much, that is all to the good, because the resources he or she saves become available to society for capital accumulation.

A related question is whether or not an income tax results in double taxation of interest income. Some argue that an income tax is unfair because it taxes capital income twice: once when the original income is earned, and again when the investment produces a return. However, the logic of income taxation impels that the return to saving be taxed. Whether or not this is fair depends, as usual, on value judgments.

Annual versus Lifetime Equity. Events that influence a person's economic position for only a very short time do not provide an adequate basis for determining ability to pay. Indeed, some have argued that ideally tax liabilities should be related to lifetime income. Proponents of consumption taxation point out that an annual income tax leads to tax burdens that can differ quite substantially even for people who have the same lifetime wealth.

To see why, consider Mr. Grasshopper and Ms. Ant, both of whom live for two periods. In the present, they have identical fixed labor incomes of I_0, and in the future, they both have labor incomes of zero. (The assumption of zero second-period income is made solely for convenience.) Grasshopper chooses to consume heavily early in life because he is not very concerned about his retirement years. Ant chooses to consume most of her wealth later in life, because she wants a lavish retirement.

Define Ant's present consumption in the presence of a proportional income tax as c_0^A, and Grasshopper's as c_0^G. By assumption, $c_0^G > c_0^A$. Ant's future income before tax is the interest she earns on her savings: $r(I_0 - c_0^A)$. Similarly, Grasshopper's future income before tax is $r(I_0 - c_0^G)$.

Now, if the proportional income tax rate is t, in the present Ant and Grasshopper have identical tax liabilities of tI_0. However, in the future, Ant's tax liability is $tr(I_0 - c_0^A)$, while Grasshopper's is $tr(I_0 - c_0^G)$. Because $c_0^G > c_0^A$, Ant's future tax liability is higher. Solely because Ant has a greater taste for saving than Grasshopper, her lifetime tax burden (the discounted sum of taxes in the two periods) is greater than Grasshopper's.

In contrast, under a proportional consumption tax, lifetime tax burdens are *independent* of tastes for saving, other things being the same.[9] To prove this, all we need to do is write down the equation for each taxpayer's budget constraint. Because all of Ant's noncapital income (I_0) comes in the present, its present value is simply I_0. Now, the present value of lifetime consumption must equal the present value of lifetime income. Hence, Ant's consumption pattern must satisfy the relation

$$I_0 = c_0^A + \frac{c_1^A}{1 + r} \tag{19.1}$$

Similarly, Grasshopper is constrained by

$$I_0 = c_0^G + \frac{c_1^G}{1 + r} \tag{19.2}$$

---

[9] However, when marginal tax rates depend on the level of consumption, this may not be the case.

Equations (19.1) and (19.2) say simply that the lifetime value of income must equal the lifetime value of consumption.

If the proportional consumption tax rate is t_c, Ant's tax liability in the first period is $t_c c_0^A$; her tax liability in the second period is $t_c c_1^A$; and the present value of her lifetime consumption tax liability, R_c^A, is

$$R_c^A = t_c c_0^A + \frac{t_c c_1^A}{1 + r} \tag{19.3}$$

Similarly, Grasshopper's lifetime tax liability is

$$R_c^G = t_c c_0^G + \frac{t_c c_1^G}{1 + r} \tag{19.4}$$

By comparing Equations (19.3) and (19.1), we see that Ant's lifetime tax liability is equal to $t_c I_0$. [Just multiply Equation (19.1) through by t_c.] Similarly, Equations (19.2) and (19.4) indicate that Grasshopper's lifetime tax liability is also $t_c I_0$. We conclude that under a proportional consumption tax, two people with identical lifetime incomes always pay identical lifetime taxes (where lifetime is interpreted in the present value sense). This stands in stark contrast to a proportional income tax, where the pattern of lifetime consumption influences lifetime tax burdens.

A related argument in favor of the consumption tax centers on the fact that income tends to fluctuate more than consumption. In years when income is unusually low, individuals may draw on their savings or borrow to smooth out fluctuations in their consumption levels. Annual consumption is likely to be a better reflection of lifetime circumstances than annual income.

Opponents of consumption taxation question whether a lifetime point of view is really appropriate. There is too much uncertainty in both the political and economic environments for a lifetime perspective to be very realistic. Moreover, the consumption smoothing described in the lifetime arguments requires that individuals be able to save and borrow freely at the going rate of interest. Given that individuals often face constraints on the amounts they can borrow, it is not clear how relevant the lifetime arguments are. Although a considerable body of empirical work suggests the life-cycle model is a useful analytical framework (Browning and Crossley [2001]), this argument still deserves some consideration.

Income versus Consumption Taxation

We have now discussed four prototypes for a broad-based consumption tax: a retail sales tax, a VAT, the Hall-Rabushka flat tax, and the cash-flow tax. They differ substantially in how they are administered, but their economic effects are basically the same, because they are just different ways of taxing the same base, consumption. We now catalog some advantages and disadvantages of consumption taxation relative to income taxation and also note a few problems that are common to both.

Advantages of a Consumption Tax.   Proponents of consumption taxation point to several advantages of these systems.

No need to measure capital gains and depreciation.

Some of the most vexing problems with taxing income arise from difficulties in measuring additions to wealth. For example, it requires calculation of capital gains and losses even on those assets not sold during the year, a task so difficult that it is not even attempted under the current system. Similarly, for those who have income produced by capital equipment, additions to wealth must be lowered by the amount the equipment depreciates during the year. As noted in Chapter 17, we know very little about actual depreciation patterns. Andrews [1983, p. 282] views the inability of real-world income tax systems to measure and tax additions to wealth as their fatal flaw: "A comprehensive income tax ideal with an immediate concession that taxation is not to be based on actual value is like a blueprint for constructing a building in which part of the foundation is required to be located in quicksand. If the terrain cannot be changed, the blueprint had better be amended." Under a consumption tax, all such problems disappear because additions to wealth per se are no longer part of the tax base.

Fewer problems with inflation.

In the presence of a nonindexed income tax, inflation creates important distortions. Some of these are caused by a progressive rate structure, but some would occur even if the tax were proportional. These distortions occur because computing capital income requires the use of figures from years that have different price levels. For example, if an asset is sold, calculation of the capital gain or loss requires subtracting the value in the year of purchase from its value in the current year. In general, part of the change in value is due to inflation, so individuals are taxed on gains that do not reflect increases in real income. As noted in Chapter 15, setting up an appropriate scheme for indexing income generated by investments is very complicated and has not been attempted in the United States.

In contrast, under a consumption tax, calculation of the tax base involves only current-year transactions. Therefore, distortions associated with inflation are much less of a problem.

No need for separate corporation tax.

Some consumption tax variants would allow removal of the corporation income tax, at least in theory. Recall from Chapter 17 that one of the main justifications of the corporation tax is to get at income that people accumulate in corporations. If accumulation per se were no longer part of the personal income tax base, this would not be necessary. Elimination of the corporation tax would probably enhance efficiency.

Advocates of consumption taxation point out that adoption would not be as radical a move as first appearances might suggest. In some respects, the present system *already* looks very much like a consumption tax:

- For some taxpayers, income is exempt from taxation when it is saved in certain forms such as 401(k) plans and IRAs.
- Unrealized capital gains on financial assets are untaxed, as are virtually all capital gains on housing.
- Realized capital gains are free of all taxation at the death of the owner.
- Accelerated depreciation reduces the amount of investment purchases included in the tax base.

In light of these considerations, characterizing the status quo as an income tax is a serious misnomer; it is more a hybrid between income and consumption taxation.

Disadvantages of a Consumption Tax.   Critics of personal consumption taxation note a number of disadvantages:

Administrative problems.   Opponents believe that it would lead to increased monitoring and accounting costs. Consider, for example, the business level tax of the H&R proposal. The tax base excludes investment expenditures. However, distinguishing consumption commodities from investment expenditures is not always simple, particularly for small businesses. (Is a desk purchased for use at home consumption or investment?) Of course, a similar problem exists under the income tax. But the incentives for avoidance and evasion are stronger under the H&R tax, because firms deduct the entire value of the investment item, while under the income tax, generally only a portion can be deducted. (Recall the discussion of depreciation allowances from Chapter 17.)

Transitional problems.   Critics also argue that despite already existing elements of consumption taxation in the present system, the switch to a consumption tax would be accompanied by enormous transitional problems. In particular, the elderly generation would be subject to double jeopardy—in their working years, when they were accumulating wealth for retirement, their capital income was subject to tax. Then, when they reach retirement, they are taxed on the consumption itself. This type of problem arises in any major tax reform—people who have made commitments on the basis of the existing system are likely to be hurt when it changes. Fairness would seem to require that the elderly be compensated for the losses they incur during the transition. Consumption tax advocates have proposed a number of rules for alleviating transitional problems [see Sakar and Zodrow, 1993]. But the more special rules there are, the more complicated the system becomes.

Gifts and bequests.   The discussion surrounding Equations (19.1) through (19.4) demonstrated that in a simple life-cycle model, a proportional consumption tax is equivalent to a tax on lifetime income. Contrary to the assumptions of the life-cycle model, some people set aside part of their lifetime income for gifts and bequests. How should such transfers be treated under a consumption tax? One view is that there is no need to tax gifts and bequests until they are consumed by their recipients. An alternative position is that gifts and bequests should be treated as consumption on the part of the donor. Hence, gifts and bequests should be taxed at the time the transfer is made. Proponents of this view point out that it would not be politically viable to institute a tax system that allowed substantial amounts of wealth to accumulate free of tax, and then failed to tax it on transfer. However, as explained later, major conceptual and practical problems are involved in taxing transfers of wealth.

Problems with Both Systems.   Even the most enthusiastic proponents of the consumption tax recognize that its adoption would not usher in an era of tax nirvana. Several of the most intractable problems inherent in the income tax system would also plague any consumption tax. These include, but are not limited to:

- Defining consumption itself. (Are health care expenditures part of consumption, or should they be deductible?)
- Choosing the unit of taxation and determining an appropriate rate structure.
- Valuing fringe benefits of various occupations. (If a job gives a person access to the company swimming pool, should the consumption benefits be taxed? If so, how can they be valued?)
- Determining a method for averaging across time if the schedule has increasing marginal tax rates.
- Taxing production that occurs in the home.
- Discouraging incentives to avoid taxes by participating in the underground economy.

Finally, we emphasize that it is not quite fair to compare an *ideal* consumption tax to the *actual* income tax. Historically, special interests have persuaded politicians to tax certain types of income preferentially. Adoption of a consumption tax could hardly be expected to eliminate political corruption of the tax structure. One pessimistic economist suggested, "I find the choice between the consumption base and the income base an almost sterile debate; we do not tax all income now, and were we to adopt a consumption tax system, we would end up exempting as much consumption from the tax base as we do income now."[10] It is hard to predict whether a real-world consumption tax would be better than the current system.

---

[10] Emil Sunley quoted in Makin [1985, p. 20].

Wealth Taxes

The taxes we have discussed so far are levied on items such as income, consumption, and sales. In the jargon of economics, these are called **flow variables,** and are associated with a time dimension. For instance, income is a flow, because the concept is meaningful only when put in the context of some time interval. If you say "My income is $10,000," it means nothing unless one knows whether it is over a week, month, or year. A **stock variable,** on the other hand, has no time dimension. It is a quantity at a point in time, not a rate per unit of time. Wealth is a stock, because it refers to the value of the assets an individual has accumulated as of a given time. This section discusses issues related to the taxation of wealth.

Why Tax Wealth?

Before turning to the specifics of each tax, we might ask what justifications there are for using wealth as a tax base. Several answers have been proposed:

Wealth taxes help to correct certain (inevitable) problems that arise in the administration of an income tax. Recall that *all* capital gains, realized or not, belong in the tax base of a comprehensive income tax. In practice, it is often impossible to tax unrealized capital gains. By taxing the wealth of which these gains become a part, perhaps this situation can be remedied. Now, it is true that wealth at a given point in time includes the sum of capital gains and losses from all earlier years. However, there is no reason to believe that the yield from an annual wealth tax approximates the revenues that would have been generated by full annual taxation of unrealized capital gains.

The higher an individual's wealth, the greater his or her ability to pay, other things—including income—being the same. Therefore, wealthy individuals should pay higher taxes. Suppose that a miser has accumulated a huge hoard of gold that yields no income. Should she be taxed on the value of the hoard? Some believe that as long as the miser was subject to the income tax while the hoard was accumulating, it should not be taxed again. Others would argue that the gold per se generates utility and should be subject to tax. Perhaps the major problem in the ability-to-pay argument is that even rich people have a substantial component of their wealth in *human* capital—their stock of education, skills, and so on. However, there is no way to value human capital except by reference to the income it yields. This logic points us back to income as the appropriate base.

Wealth taxation reduces the concentration of wealth, which is desirable socially and politically. As we saw in Chapter 7, although it is difficult to measure income precisely, the best estimates suggest the distribution of income in the United States is quite unequal. The quality of data on wealth is even lower. What information there is suggests that the distribution of wealth is very unequal. One survey indicated that the top 1 percent of the wealth distribution owned 38 percent of the total [Wolff, 2000]. The desirability of such inequality turns on a complicated set of ethical issues quite similar to those discussed in Chapter 7 in connection with the distribution of income. A related concern is that a highly concentrated distribution of wealth leads to corruption of democratic political processes. Skeptics respond that if concentration of power is the issue, then there is no justification for taxing accretions of wealth of $1 million, $10 million, or even $50 million. As Stein [1997] notes, "It takes a lot more money than that to generate power in the U.S. today." Stein further observes that there are sources of influence other than money: "Oprah Winfrey ha[s] more power than any megarich person today." Should Oprah face a special tax because she is powerful?

Wealth taxes are payments for benefits that wealth holders receive from government. As President Theodore Roosevelt said, "The man of great wealth owes a peculiar obligation to the State because he derives special advantages from the mere existence of government." One might argue, for example, that a major goal of defense spending is to protect (from foreign enemies) our existing wealth. If so, perhaps a wealth tax is a just method for financing defense. In addition, government makes certain expenditures that are likely to benefit wealth holders especially. If the state builds and maintains a road that goes by my store, then it confers a benefit on me for which I should pay. Although the notion of basing taxes on benefits has some appeal, it is not clear that any feasible wealth tax can achieve this goal. A lawyer arguing the case for taxing property asked rhetorically, "[I]sn't it true that one with twice as much house receives twice as much benefit from . . . police and fire services rendered to property?" [Hagman, 1978, p. 42]. Contrary to what he apparently believed, the answer is "probably not." The value to a given household of most services provided by local government depends on factors other than house size. For example, the value of education depends on the number of children. Even the value of fire and police services depends on how much furniture is in the house and how much insurance protection has been purchased. If benefit taxation is the goal, a system of user fees for public services would be more appropriate than a wealth tax.

To summarize, wealth taxes have been rationalized on both ability-to-pay and benefit grounds. Both sets of arguments are very controversial.

By far the most important wealth tax in the United States is the property tax, which is particularly crucial to the operations of local governments. Accordingly, we postpone our discussion of the property tax until the next chapter, in which we discuss subnational units of government.

Estate and Gift Taxes

The federal government levies wealth taxes against estates and gifts. These taxes are levied at irregular intervals on the occurrence of certain events—the estate tax on the death of the wealth holder **(decedent),** and the gift tax when property is transferred between the living **(*inter vivos*).** Both federal and some state governments levy taxes on gifts and estates. At neither level are the taxes very important as revenue raisers. Estate and gift taxes account for only about 1.4 percent of federal tax revenues. The federal tax does not touch the lives of most citizens. Fewer than 2 percent of all decedents have estates that are subject to the tax [McCaffery and Wagner, 2000]. Some have suggested that the role of estate and gift taxes should be expanded. However, the political momentum appears to be going the other way. As noted below, in 2001 opponents of the tax—who refer to it as the *death tax*—managed to pass legislation that schedules its phased reduction over the decade, until it is eliminated in 2010. The arguments pro and con estate and gift taxes are explored in this section.

Rationales

The following issues have been raised in the debate over the desirability of estate taxes:

Payment for Services.   Some argue that the government protects property rights and oversees the transfer of property from the decedent to his or her heirs. As compensation for providing these services, the state is entitled to a share of the estate. Those who oppose the estate tax believe that provision of such services is a fundamental right that does not have to be paid for. As former Congressman Bill Archer put it, "Death by itself should not trigger a tax." Moreover, it seems arbitrary to pick out property transfers as special objects of taxation. If Moe spends $10,000 on a trip to Europe, Curly spends $10,000 on his daughter's college education, and Larry leaves $10,000 to his son, why should Larry face a special tax?

Reversion of Property to Society.   Estate tax proponents claim that ultimately, all property belongs to society as a whole. During an individual's lifetime, society permits her to dispose of the property she has managed to accumulate as she wishes. But at death, the property reverts to society, which can dispose of it at will. In this view, although people may be entitled to what they earn, their descendants hold no compelling ethical claim to it. Recall from Chapter 7 that many controversial value judgments lie behind such assertions. Opponents believe that it is fundamentally wrong to argue that a person holds wealth only at the pleasure of "society," or that "society" ever has any valid claim on personal wealth.

Incentives.   The most famous statement of the theme that estate taxes are good for incentives is Andrew Carnegie's: "The parent who leaves his son enormous wealth generally deadens the talents and energies of the son, and tempts him to lead a less useful and less worthy life than he otherwise would." By taxing away estates, the government can prevent this from happening. There is some evidence that Carnegie's conjecture about the labor supply effects of inheritances is correct. In their econometric study of the behavior of a group of individuals who received large inheritances,

Holtz-Eakin, Joulfaian, and Rosen [1993] found that the higher the inheritance, the less likely that the recipient continued to work after receiving it.

Nevertheless, the incentive problem is much more complicated than suggested by Carnegie, because we must take into account the donor's behavior, not just the recipient's. Consider Lear, an individual who is motivated to work hard during his lifetime to leave a big estate to his daughters. The presence of an estate tax might discourage Lear's work effort. ("Why should I work hard if my wealth is going to the tax collector instead of my daughters?") On the other hand, with an estate tax, a greater amount of wealth has to be accumulated to leave a given after-tax bequest. Thus, the presence of an estate tax might induce Lear to work harder to maintain the net value of his estate. Consequently, whether or not an estate tax induces a donor to work more or less is logically indeterminate.[11] Even if Carnegie were right and estate taxation induces potential heirs to work more, it might also generate incentives for donors to work less. Theory alone does not tell us which tendency dominates.

Similarly, we cannot predict how an estate tax affects the donor's saving behavior. It is easy to describe scenarios in which he saves less and in which he saves more.

In this context, observe that the presence of an estate tax can affect not only the amount of wealth transferred across generations but also the form in which the transfers occur. A tax on bequests of physical capital creates incentives to transmit wealth in the form of human capital. Thus, instead of giving each daughter $80,000 worth of stocks and bonds, Lear might spend $80,000 on each of their college educations. An estate tax could thus lead to overinvestment in human capital.

Empirical research on the incentive effects of the estate tax is in its formative stages. In one study, Slemrod and Kopczuk [2000] examined estate tax returns filed between 1916 and 1996 to assess the effect of estate tax rates on reported estates. They found a negative relationship between the magnitude of the tax rate that prevailed 10 years before death and the size of the estate, which suggests that increases in the tax rate reduce wealth accumulation. A rough calculation based on their estimates suggests that overall wealth accumulation would rise by 1.5 percent if the tax were eliminated. While this finding is provocative, Slemrod and Kopczuk emphasize that it must be regarded with caution, if for no other reason than it is not clear how best to calculate the lifetime estate tax rate that is relevant. Presumably, the rate is determined in part by expectations of what the rate will be when the individual dies, but it is not clear how such expectations are formed. Nevertheless, this result suggests that the incentive effects of the estate tax may be substantial and that this is an important topic for future research.

---

[11] The ambiguity arises because of the familiar conflict between substitution and income effects. See Chapter 16.

Relation to Personal Income Tax. Estate and gift taxation is necessary, it can be argued, because receipts of gifts and inheritances are excluded from the recipient's personal income tax base. A natural response to this observation is to ask why gifts and estates are not included in adjusted gross income. After all, they constitute additions to potential consumption, and by the conventional definition are therefore income to the recipient. However, there has always been a strong aversion to including inheritances and gifts in the income tax base. Such receipts simply are not perceived as being in the same class as those from wages and interest. It is not necessarily the case, though, that the estate and gift tax is the best remedy for this omission. We discuss a possible alternative later.

Income Distribution. An estate tax is a valuable tool for creating a more equal distribution of income. As William Gates Sr. (the father of the Microsoft billionaire) argued, an estate tax is needed for "protecting our democracy from a further buildup of hereditary wealth" [Gates and Collins, 2002]. Let us leave aside the normative question of whether or not the government ought to pursue a more equal income distribution and consider the positive issue of whether or not an effective system of estate taxation is likely to achieve this goal. Certainly the prevailing assumption is that it would: "From its beginning the estate tax was viewed as a counterweight to an undue concentration of wealth" [Gale and Slemrod, 2000, p. 931]. However, there are several reasons why taxing bequests might backfire and create a less equal distribution of income.

- If the estate tax reduces saving, there will be less capital. This leads to a lower real wage for labor, and under certain conditions, a smaller share of income going to labor.[12] To the extent that capital income is more unequally distributed than labor income, the effect is to increase inequality.

- *Within* a generation, it is likely that most individuals transfer wealth only to others who are worse off than they are. Such transfers clearly tend to enhance equality. Reducing such voluntary transfers could well lead to more inequality.

- Suppose that parents whose earnings capacities are much higher than average produce children whose earnings capacities are closer to the average level. (This phenomenon is known as *regression toward the mean.*) Well-off parents, who wish to compensate their children for their lesser earnings capacity by making bequests, tend to decrease inequality *across* generations. Conversely, reducing such transfers increases intergenerational inequality.

---

[12] See Stiglitz [1978]. When the wage rate decreases, the quantity of labor demanded increases. Thus, what happens to labor income—the product of the wage and the quantity demanded—depends on the elasticity of demand for labor. This in turn depends on the ease with which capital may be substituted for labor (the elasticity of substitution of capital for labor).

A related concern is that the focus of policy should be the inequality of consumption rather than the inequality of wealth. To the extent the estate tax encourages rich people to spend more money while they are alive, then it worsens consumption inequality. We conclude that, from a theoretical point of view, the effect of estate taxation on inequality is ambiguous. Empirical research has not settled whether the equality-increasing or equality-decreasing effect dominates.

Provisions

Gift taxation and estate taxation are inextricably bound. Suppose that estates are taxed and gifts are not. If Lear desires to pass his wealth on to his daughters and knows it will be taxed at his death, then he can avoid tax by making the transfer as a gift *inter vivos*. Similar opportunities would arise if there were a gift tax but no estate tax. Since 1976, the gift and estate taxes in the United States have been integrated and are officially referred to as the **unified transfer tax.**

The unified transfer tax is similar in basic structure to the personal income tax. After the gross estate is calculated, various deductions and exemptions are subtracted, leaving the taxable estate. The tax liability is determined by applying a progressive rate schedule to the taxable estate.

Computing the Taxable Base.   The **gross estate** consists of all property owned by the decedent at the time of death, including real property, stocks, bonds, and insurance policies. It also includes gifts made during the decedent's lifetime. To find the **taxable estate,** deductions are allowed for funeral expenses, costs of settling the estate (lawyers' fees), and any outstanding debts of the estate. Gifts to charity are deductible without limit. The following deductions are available:

- Each estate is allowed a lifetime exemption of $1.5 million in 2004. No federal estate tax is levied on estates that are less than the lifetime exemption. The exemption is not indexed for inflation.
- All qualified transfers to spouses—by gift or bequest—are deductible in arriving at the taxable base. Thus, the estate of a multimillionaire who leaves $1.5 million to her children and the rest to her husband bears no tax liability. Because of the spousal deduction, most married couples do not pay any estate tax until both spouses have died.
- Each individual is qualified for an annual gift exclusion of $11,000 per recipient in 2003 that is indexed for inflation. (The recipient need not be a relative.) Consider a family with three children. Each year Mom can give $11,000 to each child, as can Dad. Together, then, the couple can give their three children annually $66,000 tax-free. Interestingly, there is some evidence that wealthy people do not fully exploit the tax advantages of distributing wealth before death. Why? There is a story about a rich man who gave

each of his children $1 million when they reached the age of 21. When asked why he did so, the millionaire explained that he wanted his children to be able to tell him to "go to hell"—to have total financial independence. It appears that most people would just as soon *not* have their children be able to tell them to go to hell. These people therefore keep control of their wealth as long as possible, even at the cost of a larger-than-necessary tax liability.

Rate Structure.   The taxable base is subject to increasing marginal tax rates. The maximal rate in 2004 is 48 percent. Whether or not this rate is efficient in the sense of optimal tax theory is hard to say. As usual, the answer depends on the responsiveness of behavior to changes in the tax rate. But as indicated earlier, little is known about how economic decisions are affected by estate and gift taxes.

Death of the death tax?   Under legislation passed in 2001, the exemption is set to rise gradually to $3.5 million in 2009, and the highest rate is scheduled to fall to 45 percent by 2009. Then, in 2010, the estate tax is scheduled for repeal altogether. However, like other provisions of the 2001 tax law, the estate tax provisions expire at the end of 2010. This means that unless legislation to the contrary is enacted at some point, in 2011 the estate tax will revert to its 2001 incarnation. In other words, if your great-aunt dies on December 31, 2010, no tax will be levied on her estate, but if she dies on January 1, 2011, after an exemption of $675,000, her estate will be subject to marginal rates up to 55 percent. This is clearly an untenable situation, and Congress is expected to deal with it sometime during the next decade. One possibility is that they will make repeal permanent; another is that the tax will be reinstated in some form or another. At this time, no one knows whether the estate tax will survive into the next decade or not.

Special Problems.   A number of difficulties arise in the administration of an estate and gift tax.

Jointly held property.   Suppose a husband and wife own property together. For purposes of estate taxation, should this be considered one estate or two? We discussed the philosophical problems concerning whether the family or the individual should be the unit of taxation in Chapter 15 under "Choice of Unit," and there is no need to do so again here. Under current federal law, half of the value of jointly held property is now included in the gross estate of the first spouse to die, regardless of the relative extent to which the spouses contributed to the accumulation of the property.[13]

---

[13] More precisely, this rule holds for joint property owned with **right of survivorship,** meaning that on the death of one owner, the property automatically passes to the other owner.

Closely held businesses.   Suppose Lear wants to bequeath his business, which is the only asset he owns, to his daughters. Because there is no cash in Lear's estate, the daughters may have to sell the business to pay the estate tax due. To reduce the likelihood of such an event, the law allows the estate taxes on closely held businesses to be paid off over as long as 14 years, at favorable rates of interest. Moreover, in computing the gross estate, qualified family farms and businesses are valued at less than their fair market value. Such provisions reflect a value judgment that it is socially desirable per se to have the same family control a given business for several generations. They also reflect the political power of the owners of small businesses.

Avoidance strategies.   An implicit goal of the estate tax is to tax wealth at least once a generation. However, people can avoid the tax in a number of ways. Many of them involve setting up *trusts,* which are arrangements whereby a person or institution known as a trustee holds legal title to assets with the obligation to use them for the benefit of another party. As an example of the use of trusts for estate tax avoidance, consider the problem facing parents who own life insurance policies naming their children as beneficiaries. The proceeds from insurance policies are included in the parents' gross estate. However, parents can establish an **insurance trust** and assign the insurance policy to the trust. Since the parents no longer own the policy, it is out of their estate, and their children receive the full benefit of the life insurance.

Another relatively simple and popular technique involves granting one's heirs shares of stock in a closely held corporation. Specifically, suppose that Mickey incorporates his business and owns all the stock. During his lifetime, Mickey makes gifts of a substantial portion of the stock—but less than half—to his heirs, Morty and Ferdy. If the transfers occur relatively early in the life of the business, the shares are not worth very much, so little if any gift tax liability is incurred. Because Mickey owns the majority of the firm's stock, he stays in charge of the company and effectively controls the value of the transferred shares. If Mickey's firm prospers, by the time he dies, Morty and Ferdy's shares may be extremely valuable. Mickey has thus managed to transfer substantial wealth to his heirs and shield the transfer from the gift and estate tax. What about the shares that Mickey still owns at death? Other more complicated techniques are available to shelter them.

In short, many methods are available for making intergenerational transfers of wealth without bearing any taxes and without losing effective control of the property during your life. Many of these avoidance techniques are complicated and expensive. As McCaffery and Wagner [2000, p. 804] note, the estate tax "has fueled a well-paid cottage industry of death tax lawyers and planners." In effect, the only people who pay the tax are those who neglect to do the appropriate planning. However, even in cases where the tax generates no revenues, it may create excess burdens and/or compliance costs for people who modify their behavior to avoid it.

Reforming Estate and Gift Taxes

For those who wish to expand the role of estate and gift taxes, the most straightforward approach would be to lower the lifetime exemption. However, if the estate tax is ever to play an important part in the revenue system, methods for dealing with avoidance via trusts and other such instruments must be devised.

Some tax theorists propose integrating the estate- and gift-tax system into the personal income tax. Gifts and inheritances would be taxed as income to the recipients. As noted earlier, such receipts are income, and according to the Haig-Simons definition of income, should therefore be included in adjusted gross income. To account for the fact that income in this form tends to be "lumpy," some form of averaging would have to be devised.

There is, however, popular resistance to taxing gifts and inheritances as ordinary income. A different method of moving the focus of estate and gift taxation from the donor to the recipient is an **accessions tax,** under which each individual is taxed on total lifetime acquisitions from inheritances and gifts. The rate schedule could be made progressive and include an exemption, if so desired. The attraction of such a scheme is that it relates tax liabilities to the recipient's ability to pay rather than to the estate. Administrative difficulties would arise from the need for taxpayers to keep records of all sizable gifts and estates. But if it is ever decided to tax wealth transfers more aggressively, an accessions tax deserves serious consideration. On the other hand, for those who object to the taxation of wealth transfers on philosophical or economic grounds, the best reform of the estate tax is the one scheduled for 2010: Abolish it.

Summary

- General sales and excise taxes are important revenue sources at the state and local levels.

- A major attraction of sales taxes is ease of administration, at least when the rates are not too high. Some sales taxes can be justified as correctives for externalities or as substitutes for user fees.

- Sales taxes are typically viewed as regressive. However, this view is based on calculations involving annual rather than lifetime income, and assumes that the incidence of the tax lies with the purchaser.

- The value-added tax (VAT) is popular in Europe but is not used in the United States. The VAT is levied on the difference between sales revenue and cost of purchased commodity inputs.

- Personal consumption taxes allow an individual's tax liability to depend upon his or her personal circumstances. One example is the Hall-Rabushka flat tax, which taxes the difference between firms' revenues and expenditures for inputs at a flat rate and applies the same rate to individuals' wages. Progressivity is built into the system by means of a personal exemption. Another example is the cash-flow tax, which taxes each individual on his or her annual consumption expenditures.

- Proponents of personal consumption taxes argue that they eliminate double taxation of interest income, promote lifetime equity, tax individuals on the basis of the amount of economic resources they use, may be adjusted to achieve any desired level of progressiveness, and are administratively superior to an income tax.

- Opponents of consumption taxes point out difficult transition problems, argue that income better

- measures ability to pay, feel that they are administratively burdensome, and argue that in the absence of appropriate taxes on gifts and bequests, they would lead to excessive concentration of wealth.
- Wealth taxes are assessed on a stock of assets instead of a flow such as income or sales.
- Proponents of wealth taxes believe that they permit the taxation of unrealized capital gains that escape the income tax, reduce the concentration of wealth, and compensate for benefits received by wealth holders. Some also argue that wealth is a good index of ability to pay and should, therefore, be subject to tax.

- Estate and gift taxes are levied on the value of wealth transfers, either from a decedent or from another living individual. Neither is a major revenue source at any level of government. Little is known about the incentive effects or incidence of estate and gift taxes.
- Major proposals for reform of estate and gift taxes are either to incorporate these transfers in the personal income tax system or to institute an accessions tax (a tax based on total lifetime gifts and bequests received). Opponents of the estate tax argue for abolishing it. The tax is scheduled for repeal in 2010, but it is not clear that this will actually happen.

Discussion Questions

1. An important distinction in this chapter is between *stocks* and *flows*. Use this distinction to explain what is misleading about the following statement: "Microsoft has a market value of $500 billion. If Microsoft were a nation, its gross national product would rank right behind Spain's, the ninth largest economy in the world."

2. Evaluate the following critique of the Hall-Rabushka flat tax: "The flat tax does not treat all income the same. It taxes only salaries and leaves investment income untouched" [Chait, 1996, p. A17].

3. Discuss carefully the following quotation: "It is reasonable to assume . . . that business can pass along the full value of the [value-added] tax to final consumers. But if [it is assumed that] businesses have the power to raise prices a dollar for each dollar they pay in value-added taxes, then it should also [be] assume[d] businesses can similarly raise prices against every dollar they now pay in payroll and corporate income taxes" [Cockburn and Pollin, 1992, p. A15].

4. An interesting set of tax questions came up in 1998 when baseball stars Mark McGwire and Sammy Sosa were getting close to breaking the record for the number of home runs during a single season. Assume for this discussion that the home run ball that broke the record would be worth $1 million. In each case below, what are the tax consequences for the fan who catches the ball?

   a. The fan gives the ball back to the player who hit it.

   b. The fan keeps the ball and holds onto it until he dies.

   c. The fan gives the ball to a charity and the charity sells the ball for a profit.

   d. The fan sells the ball immediately.

   e. The fan sells the ball after holding it a year.

5. In 2001, two members of Congress submitted the *Fairtax Act,* which would replace the income, estate, payroll, and corporation taxes with a flat retail sales tax on goods and services. According to a supporter of this idea [Vessalla, 2001], the proposal has the following virtues:

   a. "What you earn is what you keep."

   b. "Investment and savings would soar."

   c. "There is no evading the Fairtax."

   Evaluate each of these claims.

6. In January 2003, my colleague Professor David Bradford told a *New York Times* reporter that a consumption tax discourages work effort. Shortly thereafter, he received the following e-mail: "Since when is a tax on consumption a disincentive to work? This sort of specious reasoning ran amok in this article. I laughed as I saw it was

labeled 'Economic Analysis.'" Who was correct, Professor Bradford or his correspondent? Justify your answer using either an arithmetic or algebraic argument. (Hint: Bradford was right.)

7. Rich lives two periods. His earnings in the present are 100, in the future they are 75.6. The interest rate is 8 percent.

   a. If his consumption in the future is 108, what is the most that he can consume in the present?

   b. Suppose that Rich's earnings are subject to a 25 percent tax. Find a consumption tax rate that will yield the same tax revenue (in present value) to the government.

8. Amy and Shirley both live two periods. Both have earnings of 1,000 in the present and zero in the future. The interest rate is 8 percent. Suppose that they are each subject to an income tax, and Amy's first period consumption is 200 while Shirley's is 300. Who has the higher lifetime tax burden? Under a proportional consumption tax, how would their lifetime tax burdens compare?

Selected References

Gale, William G, and Joel B Slemrod. "Death Watch for the Estate Tax." *Journal of Economic Perspectives* 15 (Winter 2001), pp. 205–18.

Hall, Robert E, and Alvin Rabushka. *The Flat Tax,* 2d ed. Stanford, CA: Hoover Institution Press, 1995.

McCaffery, Edward J. "A Voluntary Tax? Revisited." *National Tax Association—Proceedings of the Ninety-third Annual Conference,* 2001, pp. 268–74

Slemrod, Joel, and Jon Bakija. *Taxing Ourselves,* 2d ed. Cambridge, MA: MIT Press, 2000, chap. 7.

PART 5

Multigovernment Public Finance

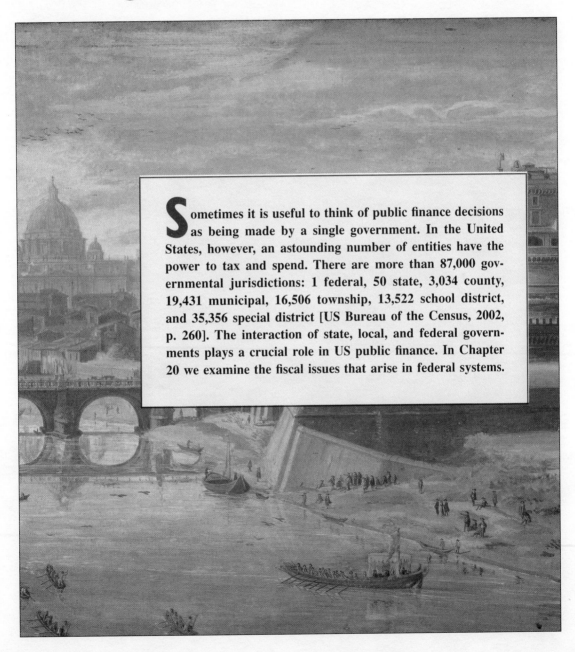

Sometimes it is useful to think of public finance decisions as being made by a single government. In the United States, however, an astounding number of entities have the power to tax and spend. There are more than 87,000 governmental jurisdictions: 1 federal, 50 state, 3,034 county, 19,431 municipal, 16,506 township, 13,522 school district, and 35,356 special district [US Bureau of the Census, 2002, p. 260]. The interaction of state, local, and federal governments plays a crucial role in US public finance. In Chapter 20 we examine the fiscal issues that arise in federal systems.

PART 5

Multigovernment Public Finance

Public Finance in a Federal System

Texans can run Texas.

GEORGE W. BUSH

In 1996, a sweeping change in the US welfare system was introduced. Among its more important and controversial provisions was a shift in responsibility for welfare from the national government to the states.[1] Under the old regime, the federal government guaranteed a minimal stipend to welfare recipients. There was no statutory limit to federal spending, but states had to match federal dollars with their own. Under the new regime, states have much more latitude in determining welfare benefits. Further, each state receives a fixed amount of federal money without any matching requirement.

The law's passage led to an acrimonious debate that is still going on. Opponents believe that only the national government should be responsible for welfare. They argue further that because of the elimination of matching grants, states and localities spend less on welfare, in part because their tax systems are inadequate to the task of raising sufficient money.

This debate highlights several enduring questions that surround the operation of the US system of public finance:

■ How should various responsibilities be allocated to different levels of government?

■ Is decentralized governmental decision making desirable?

■ Are locally raised taxes a good way to pay for the services provided by state and local governments? Or should the money come from the federal government?

---

[1] For a discussion of other aspects of the reform, see Chapter 8.

These are important issues in the United States, where the appropriate division of power among the various levels of government has been a matter of controversy since the nation's founding. The issues are of equal consequence to China, which is considering whether or not to devolve power to provincial governments, and to European nations, which are currently deciding which economic policymaking functions will be surrendered to the European Union. This chapter examines the normative and positive aspects of public finance in a federal system.

Background

A **federal system** consists of different levels of government that provide public goods and services and have some scope for making decisions. The subject of **fiscal federalism** explores "the roles of the different levels of government and the ways in which they relate to one another" [Oates, 1999, p. 1120]. One federal system is more centralized than another when more of its decision-making powers are in the hands of authorities with a larger jurisdiction. The most common measure of the extent to which a system is centralized is the **centralization ratio,** the proportion of total direct government expenditures made by the central government. ("Direct" government expenditure comprises all expenditure except transfers made to other governmental units.) Centralization ratios vary widely across nations. In France, it is 81 percent; in Canada, 43 percent; and in the United States, 51 percent.[2]

Table 20.1 shows that during the last century, the US centralization ratio has increased, although the movement upward has not been steady. However, the centralization ratio is by no means a foolproof indicator. For example, states and localities make expenditures for computers in public libraries, but some of the money comes in the form of grants from the federal government. The Child Online Protection Act requires that libraries install software to screen against obscene materials; libraries that do not comply lose their grants. Most libraries comply. Who is really in charge? The point is that if local and state government spending behavior is constrained by the central government, the centralization ratio underestimates the true extent of centralization in the system. In fact, a substantial amount of state and local spending is dictated by the federal government. The federal government simply mandates that the subfederal government provide certain services, but without a corresponding increase in financial support. These unfunded mandates, which cover areas as diverse as handicapped rights, hazardous waste disposal, and motor vehicle safety, are estimated to cost the states and localities $40 billion annually [Cullen, 1996, p. 1].

A number of important activities are mostly in the hands of state and local governments, including education and public safety. On the other hand,

---

[2] Computed from Fisman and Gatti [2002, p. 340], except see Table 20.1 for the United States.

Table 20.1 **Distribution of all US government expenditure by level of government** *(selected years)*

	Federal	State	Local
1900	34.1%	8.2%	57.7%
1910	30.1	9.0	60.9
1920	39.7	9.8	50.5
1930	32.5	16.3	51.2
1950	59.3	15.2	26.5
1960	57.6	13.8	28.6
1971	48.4	18.6	33.0
1980	54.9	18.1	27.0
1990	56.2	17.9	25.9
1999	51.2	20.9	27.9

SOURCE: Werner Pommerehne, "Quantitative Aspects of Federalism: A Study of Six Countries," in *The Political Economy of Fiscal Federalism*, ed. W. Oates (Lexington, MA: D.C. Heath, 1977), p. 311, except for figures after 1980, which are computed from various editions of US Bureau of the Census, *Statistical Abstract of the United States*.

the federal government has the entire responsibility for defense and Social Security. And all three levels of government spend substantial amounts of money on public welfare. Is this division of powers in the US fiscal system sensible? Before providing an answer, we need to discuss the special features associated with local government.

Community Formation

To understand the appropriate fiscal roles for local jurisdictions, we examine why communities are formed. In this context, it is useful to think of a community as a **club**—a voluntary association of people who band together to share some kind of benefit. This section develops a theory of clubs and uses it to explain how the size of a community and its provision of public goods are determined.

Consider a group of people who wish to band together to purchase land for a public park. For simplicity, assume that all members of the group have identical tastes and that they intend to share equally the use of the park and its costs. The "community" can costlessly exclude all nonmembers, and it operates with no transaction costs. Given the assumption of identical tastes, we need consider only the desires of a representative member. Two decisions must be made: how large a park to acquire and how many members to have in the community.

Assuming that it wants to maximize the welfare of its citizens, how does the community decide? Consider first the relationship between the total cost per member and the number of members, *given* that a certain size park is selected. Clearly, the larger the community, the more people there are to shoulder the expense of the park, and the smaller the required contribution per member. If the per capita cost continually decreases with membership size, why not simply invite as many people as possible to join? The problem is that as more people join the community, the park becomes congested. The marginal congestion cost measures the dollar cost of the incremental congestion created by each new member. We assume that marginal congestion cost increases with the number of members. *The community should expand its membership until the marginal decrease in the membership fee just equals the per person marginal increase in congestion costs.*

Now turn to the flip side of the problem: For any given number of members in the community, how big should the park be? A bigger park yields greater benefits, although like most goods, we assume it is subject to diminishing marginal utility. The per member marginal cost of increased park acreage is just the price of the extra land divided by the number of members sharing its cost. *Acreage should be increased to the point where each member's marginal benefit just equals the per member marginal cost.*

We can now put together these two pieces of the picture to describe an optimal community or club. The optimal community is one in which the number of members and the level of services simultaneously satisfy the condition that the marginal cost equal the corresponding marginal benefit. Although this club model is very simple, it highlights the crucial aspects of the community-formation process. Specifically, it suggests how community size depends on the type of public goods the people want to consume, the extent to which these goods are subject to crowding, and the costs of obtaining them, among other things.

How close is the analogy between a club and a real-world community? In many cases, it is closer than you might think. About 28 million Americans live in areas governed by private community associations. These "gated communities" decide how many members they will have, how many security guards to hire, whether to construct golf courses and communal swimming pools, etc. Nevertheless, in most cases, viewing communities as clubs leaves unanswered several important questions that are relevant for understanding local public finance:

- How are the public services to be financed? A country club can charge a membership fee, but a town normally levies taxes to pay for public goods.
- A club (or gated community) can exclude nonmembers and so eliminate the free rider problem. How can towns achieve this end?
- When people throughout the country organize themselves into many different clubs (communities), is the overall allocation of public goods equitable and efficient?

These questions are taken up in the next section.

The Tiebout Model

"Love it or leave it." When people who oppose US federal government policy are given this advice, it is generally about as constructive as telling them to "drop dead." Only in extreme cases do we expect people to leave their country because of government policy.[3] Because of the large pecuniary and psychic costs of emigrating, a more realistic option is to stay home and try to change the policy. On the other hand, most citizens are not as strongly attached to their local communities. If you dislike the policies being followed in Skokie, Illinois, the easiest thing to do may be to move a few miles away to Evanston. This section discusses the relationship among intercommunity mobility, voluntary community formation, and the efficient provision of public goods.

Chapter 4 examined the idea that markets generally fail to provide public goods efficiently. The root of the problem is that the market does not force individuals to reveal their true preferences for public goods. Everyone has an incentive to be a free rider. The usual conclusion is that some kind of government intervention is required.

In an important article, Tiebout [1956] (rhymes with "me too") argued that the ability of individuals to move among jurisdictions produces a market-like solution to the local public goods problem. As the cartoon on the next page suggests, individuals vote with their feet and locate in the community that offers the bundle of public services and taxes they like best. Much as Jones satisfies her demand for private goods by purchasing them on the market, she satisfies her demand for public services by the appropriate selection of a community in which to live, and pays taxes for the services. In equilibrium, people distribute themselves across communities on the basis of their demands for public services. Each individual receives her desired level of public services and cannot be made better off by moving (or else she would). Hence, the equilibrium is Pareto efficient, and government action is not required to achieve efficiency.

Tiebout's Assumptions

Tiebout's provocative assertion that a quasi-market process can solve the public goods problem has stimulated a lot of research. Much of it has been directed toward finding a precise set of sufficient conditions under which the ability of citizens to vote with their feet leads to efficient public goods provision. The key conditions follow.[4]

Government activities generate no externalities. As noted later, spillover effects among communities can lead to inefficiencies.

Individuals are completely mobile. Each person can travel costlessly to a jurisdiction whose public services are best for him. The location of his

---

[3] For example, in the 1960s, some young men left the country to evade military service in Vietnam.

[4] Not all of these conditions were included in Tiebout's original article.

place of employment puts no restriction on where he resides and does not affect his income.

People have perfect information with respect to each community's public services and taxes.

There are enough different communities so that each individual can find one with public services meeting her demands.

The cost per unit of public services is constant, so that if the quantity of public services doubles, the total cost also doubles. In addition, the technology of public service provision is such that if the number of residents doubles, the quantity of the public service provided must double. To see why these conditions are required for a Tiebout equilibrium to be efficient, imagine instead that the cost per unit of public services fell as the scale of provision increased. In that case, there would be scale economies of which independently operating communities might fail to take advantage.

This assumption makes the public service essentially a publicly provided private good. "Pure" public goods (such as national defense) do not satisfy this assumption. However, many local public services such as education and garbage collection fit this description reasonably well.

Public services are financed by a proportional property tax. The tax rate can vary across communities.[5]

---

[5] Tiebout [1956] assumed finance by head taxes. The more realistic assumption of property taxation is from Hamilton [1975].

*Communities can enact **exclusionary zoning laws**—statutes that prohibit certain uses of land.* Specifically, they can require that all houses be of some minimum size. To see why this assumption is crucial, recall that in Tiebout equilibrium, communities are segregated on the basis of their members' demands for public goods. If income is positively correlated with the demand for public services, community segregation by income results. In high-income communities, the *level* of property values tends to be high, and, hence, the community can finance a given amount of public spending with a relatively low property tax *rate*. Low-income families have an incentive to move into rich communities and build relatively small houses. Because of the low tax rate, low-income families have relatively small tax liabilities, but nevertheless enjoy the high level of public service provision. As more low-income families get the idea and move in, the tax base per family in the community falls. Tax rates must be increased to finance the expanded level of public services required to serve the increased population.

Since we assume perfect mobility, the rich have no reason to put up with this. They can just move to another community. But what stops the poor from following them? In the absence of constraints on mobility, nothing. Clearly, a game of musical suburbs can develop in a Tiebout model. Exclusionary zoning prevents this phenomenon and thus maintains a stable Pareto efficient equilibrium.

Tiebout and the Real World

The Tiebout model is clearly not a perfect description of the real world. People are not perfectly mobile; there are not enough communities to provide each family with a bundle of services that suits it perfectly; and so on. Moreover, contrary to the model's implication, we observe many communities with massive income differences and, hence, presumably different desired levels of public service provision. Just consider any major city.

However, we should not dismiss the Tiebout mechanism too hastily. There is a lot of mobility in the American economy. A persistent pattern is that in any given year, about 16 percent of Americans have different residences than they had the year before [US Bureau of the Census, 2002, p. 29]. Moreover, most metropolitan areas allow a wide range of choice with respect to type of community. Within a 20-mile radius of a large American city, one can often choose to locate among several hundred suburbs. Certainly, casual observation suggests that across suburbs there is considerable residential segregation by income, that exclusionary zoning is practiced widely, and that service levels differ (even when incomes are similar).

There have been several formal empirical tests of the Tiebout hypothesis. One type of study looks at whether the values of local public services and taxes are capitalized into local property values. The idea is that if people move in response to local packages of taxes and public services, differences in these packages should be reflected in property values. A community with better public services should have higher property values, other things (including taxes) being the same. These capitalization studies are discussed later in this chapter in the context of property taxation. As noted there, capitalization does appear to be a widespread phenomenon. This result suggests that, at least in some settings, the Tiebout model is a good depiction of reality.

Optimal Federalism

Now that we have an idea of how to characterize local governments, we return to our earlier question. What is the optimal allocation of economic responsibilities among levels of government in a federal system? Let us first briefly consider macroeconomic functions. Most economists agree that spending and taxing decisions intended to affect the levels of unemployment and inflation should be made by the central government. No state or local government is large enough to affect the overall level of economic activity. It would not make sense, for example, for each locality to issue its own money supply and pursue an independent monetary policy.

With respect to the microeconomic activities of enhancing efficiency and equity, there is considerably more controversy. Posed within the framework of welfare economics, the question is whether a centralized or decentralized system is more likely to maximize social welfare. For simplicity, most of our discussion assumes just two levels of government, "central" and "local." No important insights are lost with this assumption.

Disadvantages of a Decentralized System

Consider a country composed of a group of small communities. Each community government makes decisions to maximize a social welfare function depending only on the utilities of its members—outsiders do not count.[6] How do the results compare to those that would emerge from maximizing a national social welfare function that took into account all citizens' utilities? We consider efficiency and then equity issues.

Efficiency Issues.   A system of decentralized governments might lead to an inefficient allocation of resources for several reasons.

Externalities.   A public good with benefits that accrue only to members of a particular community is called a **local public good.** For example, the public library in Austin, Texas, has little effect on the welfare of people in Ann Arbor, Michigan. However, the activities undertaken by one community can sometimes affect the well-being of people in other communities. If one town provides good public education for its children and some of them eventually emigrate, then other communities may benefit from having a better-educated work force. Towns can affect each other negatively as well. Victoria, British Columbia, dumps its raw sewage into the sea; some of the

---

[6] We ignore for now the questions of how the social welfare function is determined and whether the people who run the government actually try to maximize it. (See Chapters 3 and 6.)

waste makes its way to Seattle, Washington, whose citizens don't like it one bit. In short, communities impose externalities (both positive and negative) on each other. If each community cares only about its own members, these externalities are overlooked. Hence, according to the standard argument (see Chapter 5), resources are allocated inefficiently.

Scale economies in provision of public goods.   For certain public services, the cost per person falls as the number of users increases. For example, the more people who use a public library, the lower the cost per user. If each community sets up its own library, costs per user are higher than necessary. A central jurisdiction, on the other hand, could build one library, allowing people to benefit from the scale economies.

Of course, various activities are subject to different scale economies. The optimal scale for library services might differ from that for fire protection. And both surely differ from the optimal scale for national defense. This observation, incidentally, helps rationalize a system of overlapping jurisdictions— each jurisdiction can handle those services with scale economies that are appropriate for the jurisdiction's size.

On the other hand, consolidation is not the only way for communities to take advantage of scale economies. Some New Jersey communities jointly run their school systems and libraries, taking advantage of scale economies yet still retaining their independence. Alternatively, in California, some towns contract out to other governments or to the private sector for the provision of certain public goods and services. These arrangements weaken the link between the jurisdiction's decisions over how much of a publicly provided good to consume and how much to produce.

Inefficient tax systems.   Roughly speaking, efficient taxation requires that inelastically demanded or supplied goods be taxed at relatively high rates, and vice versa. (See Chapter 14.) Suppose that the supply of capital to the entire country is fixed, but capital is highly mobile across subfederal jurisdictions. Each jurisdiction realizes that if it levies a substantial tax on capital, the capital will simply move elsewhere, thus making the jurisdiction worse off. In such a situation, a rational jurisdiction taxes capital very lightly, or even subsidizes it. One prominent example is Alabama, which over a nine-year period provided almost $700 million in tax breaks to induce firms such as Mercedes-Benz, Honda, and Hyundai to locate factories there [Brooks, 2002]. More generally, Tannenwald [2002] notes that between 1986 and 2002, the ratio of state corporate taxes to corporate profits fell from 7.6 percent to 3.9 percent, and suggests that this was due in part to state competition to attract capital. However, to the extent that the national supply of capital is inelastic, low rates on capital are not efficient.

In reality, of course, the total capital stock is not fixed in supply. Nor is it known just how responsive firms' locational decisions are to differences in local tax rates, although there is some statistical evidence that employment growth in a jurisdiction is inversely correlated with its tax rates on businesses [Mark, McGuire, and Papke, 2000]. But the basic point remains: Taxes levied by decentralized communities are unlikely to be efficient from a national standpoint. Instead, communities are likely to select taxes on the basis of whether they can be exported to outsiders. For example, if a community has the only coal mine in the country, we expect that the incidence of a locally imposed tax on coal will fall largely on coal users outside the community.[7] A coal tax would be a good idea from the community's point of view, but not necessarily from the nation's.[8]

An important implication of tax shifting is that communities may purchase too many local public goods. Efficiency requires that local public goods be purchased up to the point where their marginal social benefit equals marginal social cost. If communities can shift some of the burden to other jurisdictions, the community's perceived marginal cost is less than marginal social cost. When communities set marginal social benefit equal to the perceived marginal cost, the result is an inefficiently large amount of local public goods.

Scale economies in tax collection.   Individual communities may not be able to take advantage of scale economies in the collection of taxes. Each community has to devote resources to tax administration, and savings may be obtained by having a joint taxing authority. Why not split the costs of a single computer to keep track of tax returns, rather than have each community purchase its own? Of course, some of these economies might be achieved just by cooperation among the jurisdictions, without actual consolidation taking place. In some states, for example, taxes levied by cities are collected by state revenue departments.

Equity Issues.   In a utilitarian philosophical framework, the maximization of social welfare may require income transfers to the poor. Suppose that the pattern of taxes and expenditures in a particular community is favorable to its low-income members. If there are no barriers to movement between communities, we expect an in-migration of the poor from the rest of the country. As the poor population increases, so does the cost of the redistributive fiscal policy. At the same time, the town's upper-income people may decide to exit. Why should they pay high taxes for the poor when they can move to another community with a more advantageous fiscal structure? Thus, the demands on the community's tax base increase while its size decreases. Eventually the redistributive program has to be abandoned.

---

[7] As usual, a precise answer to the incidence question requires information on market structure, elasticity of demand, and the structure of costs. See Chapter 12.

[8] Coal-producing states such as Montana have tried to export their tax burdens to the rest of the country.

This argument relies heavily on the notion that people's decisions to locate in a given jurisdiction are influenced by the available tax-welfare package. There is some casual support for this proposition. In the 1990s, California lawmakers were sufficiently concerned about welfare-induced migration to their state that they restricted new migrants, for their first year in the state, to the welfare benefits of the states from which they had moved. However, the Supreme Court declared such laws to be unconstitutional in 1999.

Some evidence along these lines is provided by Feldstein and Wrobel [1998] who note that if high-income individuals can avoid unfavorable tax conditions by migrating to states with lower tax rates, then employers in high-tax states will have to pay higher before-tax wages in order to keep their workers. The net effect is no change in the distribution of income. Feldstein and Wrobel find that, in fact, when states raise their tax rates, before-tax wages soon increase. The interpretation of this finding is a bit tricky; it might be the case that causation runs in the other direction— states whose citizens have experienced wage increases vote for more progressive tax systems. In any case, the result suggests that caution is required when decentralized jurisdictions attempt to undertake income redistribution.

Advantages of a Decentralized System

Tailoring Outputs to Local Tastes.   Some people want their children's high schools to have extensive athletic programs; others believe this is unnecessary. Some people enjoy parks; others do not. A centralized government tends to provide the same level of public services throughout the country, regardless of the fact that people's tastes differ. As de Tocqueville observed, "In great centralized nations the legislator is obliged to give a character of uniformity to the laws, which does not always suit the diversity of customs and of districts." Clearly, it is inefficient to provide individuals with more or less of a public good than they desire if the quantity they receive can be more closely tailored to their preferences. Under a decentralized system, individuals with similar tastes for public goods group together, so communities provide the types and quantities of public goods desired by their inhabitants. (Remember the "club" view of communities.)

A closely related notion is that local government's greater proximity to the people makes it more responsive to citizens' preferences than central government.[9] This is especially likely to be the case in a large country where the costs of obtaining and processing information on everybody's tastes are substantial. The chief executive of McDonald's once said, "You can't manage 25,000 restaurants in a centralized way. Many decisions need to be

---

[9] However, if one believes that the preferences of members of some communities are wrong, this advantage turns into a disadvantage. For example, a community might decide to legalize slavery. Determining the circumstances under which the central government should be able to overrule state and local governments is a difficult political and ethical issue.

decided closer to the marketplace" [Barboza 1999]. A federal system applies the same principle to government decision making.

This logic suggests that the more that preferences vary within an area, the greater the benefits to decentralized decision-making within that area. To examine whether this notion has any predictive power, Strumpf and Ober-holzer-Gee [2002] examined differences across states as to which level of government controls the regulation of the sale of liquor. People of different religious backgrounds differ about whether liquor should be prohibited. Therefore, the theory of federalism suggests that states with more religious diversity should be more likely to decentralize control over regulatory policy toward alcohol, other things being the same. They found support for this hypothesis—local control increases with variation of preferences within the state.

The logic of federalism also suggests that economic regulations enacted at the national level may not make sense in every community. For example, we showed in Chapter 5 that it does not make sense for environmental regulations to be uniform throughout the country. The marginal costs and benefits of pollution abatement depend on population density, weather patterns, and so on. To the extent that officials in a given jurisdiction have better information about specific issues relating to their area than the federal government, it makes sense to give them some latitude in determining regulatory policy. In the United States, the states can opt to take responsibility for implementing and enforcing federal environmental policy, which gives the states substantial power in determining the ultimate effects of the regulations. There is some evidence that states that take advantage of this option are more stringent than the federal government in enforcing the regulations [Sigman, 2003].

Fostering Intergovernment Competition. In many contexts, government managers lack incentives to produce at minimum feasible cost (see Chapter 6). Managers of private firms who fail to minimize costs are eventually driven out of business. In contrast, government managers can continue to muddle along. However, if citizens can choose among communities, then substantial mismanagement may cause citizens simply to choose to live elsewhere. This threat may create incentives for government managers to produce more efficiently and be more responsive to their citizens. In this context, it is interesting to note that there is some evidence that the more decentralized a country's fiscal system, the less corrupt its government is likely to be, other things being the same [Fisman and Gatti, 2002].

Experimentation and Innovation in Locally Provided Goods and Services. For many policy questions, no one knows what the right answer is, or even whether a single solution is best in all situations. One way to find out is to let each community choose its own way, and then compare the results. A system of diverse governments enhances the chances that new solutions to problems will be sought. As Supreme Court Justice Louis Brandeis once observed, "It

is one of the happy incidents of the Federal system that a single courageous state may, if its citizens choose, serve as a laboratory, and try moral, social, and economic experiments without risk to the rest of the country."

From all appearances, Brandeis's laboratories are busily at work:

- Item: Sunnyvale, California, has adopted performance-based budgeting, under which budget laws contain clear and precise goals for various programs. For example, in return for its appropriation, the city parks department is obligated to repair all reported vandalism within three working days 90 percent of the time. Other towns are watching to see if the system leads to better performance.

- Item: A panel charged with improving public schools in Philadelphia recently voted to transfer control of over 40 failing schools to 7 outside managers, in "what is believed to be the largest experiment in privatization mounted by an American school district" [Steinberg, 2002, p. A3].

- Item: Florida offers tax exemptions on equipment purchases to employers that hire and retain former welfare recipients.

In the past, some programs that began as experiments at the state level eventually became federal policy. During the Great Depression, for example, the designers of Social Security took advantage of the experience of several states that had earlier instituted social insurance programs.

Implications

The foregoing discussion makes it clear that a purely decentralized system cannot be expected to maximize social welfare. Efficiency requires that commodities with spillovers that affect the entire country—national public goods like defense—be provided at the national level. On the other hand, local public goods should be provided locally.

This leaves us with the in-between case of community activities that create spillover effects that are not national in scope. One possible solution is to put all the communities that affect each other under a single regional government. In theory, this government would take into account the welfare of all its citizens, and so internalize the externalities. However, a larger governmental jurisdiction may be less responsive to local differences in tastes.

An alternative method for dealing with externalities is a system of Pigouvian taxes and subsidies. Chapter 5 shows that the government can enhance efficiency by taxing activities that create negative externalities and subsidizing activities that create positive externalities. We can imagine the central government using similar devices to influence the decisions of local governments. For example, if primary and secondary education create benefits that go beyond the boundaries of a jurisdiction, the central government can provide communities with educational subsidies. Local autonomy is maintained, yet the externality is corrected. We see later that some federal grants to communities roughly follow this model.

Our theory suggests a fairly clean division of responsibility for public good provision—local public goods by localities, and national public goods by the central government. In practice, there is considerable interplay between levels of government. For example, most law enforcement agents are state and local officials. Yet many of their actions are governed by federal criminal law, which "has grown explosively as Congress has taken stands against such offenses as carjacking and church burning, disrupting a rodeo and damaging a livestock facility" [Derthick, 2000, p. 27]. Given that localities might act inappropriately in the absence of such regulations, their presence may improve welfare. However, some believe the system of federal regulation over subfederal governmental units has become so complicated that it may be difficult to determine which level of government has responsibility for what. Proposals have been made to reform the US federal system along the lines suggested by the theory of optimal federalism, but they have not been enacted. The political failure of such proposals is probably well explained by Representative Barney Frank of Massachusetts, who observed, "99.9 percent of Congress clearly prefer that the issue be decided at that level of government which will decide the issue the way they like" [Clymer, 1997, p. 6].

If a division of responsibilities is appropriate from an efficiency point of view, does the same hold for income distribution? Most economists believe the mobility considerations discussed earlier rule out relying heavily on local governments to achieve distributional aims. An individual jurisdiction that attempts to do so is likely to find itself in financial trouble. This may be one of the reasons why New York City often is under fiscal stress. In fact, the great bulk of spending for income maintenance in the United States is done at the federal level. Social Security, Supplemental Security Income, food stamps, and the earned income credit are all federal programs. Although the 1996 welfare reform (discussed in Chapter 8) gave the states some new responsibilities in this area, the amount of money involved is relatively minor compared to that spent by the federal programs.

Public Education in a Federal System

A useful way to apply the theory of optimal federalism is to employ it to analyze education, one of the most important items in the budgets of state and local governments.[10] Total government spending on education in 1999 was $566 billion. Of this, the federal government spent 14.6 percent, state governments 22 percent, and other governments the rest. Education accounts for about 18 percent of direct expenditures at the state level and about 38 percent of local spending [US Census Bureau, 2002, pp. 135, 270]. Nine out of 10 American children are educated in public schools.

Does this pattern of spending on education by the different levels of government conform to our views of optimal federalism? One argument for the

---

[10] The more fundamental question of whether government should be involved in providing education in the first place is discussed in Chapter 4.

decentralized provision of a good is that it can be tailored to local tastes. Because many parents hold strong views about their children's education and these views differ across communities, the leading role played by local governments in providing education makes sense. One could, of course, allow local discretion over school policy while providing funding from state or federal levels of government. Politically, however, it may be difficult to maintain control of the schools if the financing comes from some other level of government— he who pays the piper, calls the tune. In California, for example, a substantial amount of public funding comes from the state government. The public schools are subject to a 9,000-page state education code, which tells them which textbooks to buy, how to teach phonics, and that their cafeterias must have full-service kitchens, among other things [Kronholz, 2000, p. A10].

Local governments raise money for education primarily through property taxation; there are wide variations in the amount of property wealth available to school districts. Variations in the property tax base can be associated with huge differences in funding for school districts. In the 2001–2002 school year, for example, the wealthiest district in Texas spent $12,600 per student, while the poorest district spent $4,500. An egalitarian view of educational spending would call for funding from a level of government that could redistribute resources across local boundaries, regardless of its possible effects on local autonomy. As we see later in this chapter, intergovernmental grants are an important part of education finance.

Federal funding for education is centered in two areas: At the elementary and secondary levels, Department of Education funding goes primarily to programs serving educationally disadvantaged ($8.5 billion in 2001) and disabled ($5.8 billion) populations [US Census Bureau, 2002, p. 135]. This is consistent with the observation that redistribution is hard to carry out at the local level. In higher education, a great deal of federal spending is directed toward research. The information forthcoming from research is a public good, and we have seen that centralized provision or subsidization of public goods can avoid the free rider problem that might arise at the local level.

One should note, however, that the federal role in education does not stop with funding. A vast body of federal law and regulation governs public education. Federal legislation covers such diverse topics as teacher training, libraries, standards for handicapped students, and sex education. States whose practices do not follow the rules may lose federal funds. Thus, although the system of American education finance seems broadly consistent with the basic tenets of optimal federalism, the division of decision-making is not as clear as the theory would suggest.

Federalism and the Urban Crisis

Many American cities are experiencing major social and economic difficulties. The urban problem has many dimensions: loss of population, physically decaying neighborhoods, inability to pay for public services, and a high proportion of residents on public assistance, among others. There is no dearth of theories to explain the cities' difficulties; see Mills and Lubuele [1997]

for a survey. Our purpose is to discuss how the US system of local public finance may have contributed to the urban crisis.

Imagine a situation where low-income households in a city gain political power and use this power to establish a pro-poor pattern of expenditures and taxes. Provided that they are sufficiently mobile, high-income individuals who do not like this policy can leave for the suburbs. The poor are unable to follow them, either because they are less mobile, or because of exclusionary zoning in the suburbs. As a consequence, the proportion of low-income families in the city increases. At the same time, the city's income- and property-tax bases fall because of the exit of the middle and upper classes.

In this extremely simple model of urban decline, the villain is the fragmented system of local public finance. If an entire metropolitan area had a unified government, fiscal decisions would apply uniformly to the entire jurisdiction. As a consequence, those with relatively high incomes would have less incentive to leave the central city behind. However, it is surprisingly hard to predict the distributional consequences of moving to a unified system. Changes in both the patterns of taxation and expenditure must be considered.[11]

Imposing uniform property tax rates throughout the metropolitan area would create capital losses for those property owners whose tax rates were formerly lower than average, and vice versa (other things being the same). Would these changes make the distribution of wealth more or less equal? To answer this question, we need information on the initial wealth positions of city landlords, among other things. If the move to a unified system ended up lowering tax rates in the city, and urban landlords were wealthy to begin with, the distribution of wealth would tend to become more unequal. If urban landlords were less wealthy than their suburban counterparts, just the opposite conclusion would emerge. Unfortunately, little information on the wealth of inner-city landlords is available.

On the expenditure side of the account, guaranteeing equal school expenditures for each pupil in the metropolitan area would tend to redistribute real income from high- to low-income people. This is because under the current system, communities with more income tend to spend greater amounts on education than do those communities with less. However, if expenditures on *all* public services were equalized throughout the metropolitan area, it might hurt poorer central city residents, because smaller suburban communities often provide fewer public sector services than the cities. A small suburb, for example, may have a volunteer fire department and leave garbage collection to private firms. Requiring equal expenditure everywhere would benefit such communities, other things being the same.

An important assumption in this analysis is that urban problems have relatively little negative effect on the suburbs. In contrast, Haughwout and

---

[11] This discussion is based on Bradford and Oates [1974].

Inman [2002] argue that poorly managed city finances lead to an exodus of people and firms from the entire metropolitan area, which ultimately causes poor suburban economic health. In principle, then, suburban residents should be willing to pay to enhance the finances of the center cities. Again, one mechanism for accomplishing this end would be a unified system of public finance for the metropolitan area.

A major problem with a unified system is that community autonomy would be severely limited. As noted earlier, the ability of communities to make their own decisions has certain efficiency advantages. On balance, then, there is simply not enough information to say which system is superior. In any case, metropolitan consolidation has received very little political support in the United States. In practice, the main method for dealing with urban fiscal problems has been to use grants-in-aid from federal and state governments to supplement local property-tax revenues. These two major revenue sources for local governments, property taxes and intergovernmental grants, are examined in turn.

Property Tax

In 1999, property taxes in the United States were $240 billion, about $12 billion of which were collected by the states and $228 billion by localities [US Census Bureau, 2002, p. 270]. There is no federal property tax. Although it is not as important as many other taxes when viewed from a national perspective, the property tax plays a key role in local public finance—it accounts for about 72 percent of local governments' tax revenues.

An individual's property tax liability is the product of the tax rate and the property's **assessed value**—the value the jurisdiction assigns to the property. In most cases, jurisdictions attempt to make assessed values correspond to market values.[12] However, if a piece of property has not been sold recently, the tax collector does not know its market value and must therefore make an estimate, perhaps based on the market values of comparable properties that have been sold recently.

Market and assessed values diverge to an extent that depends on the accuracy of the jurisdiction's estimating procedure. The ratio of the assessed value to market value is called the **assessment ratio.** If all properties have the same statutory rate and the same assessment ratio, their effective tax rates are the same. Suppose, however, that assessment ratios differ across properties. Ophelia and Hamlet both own properties worth $100,000. Ophelia's property is assessed at $100,000 and Hamlet's at $80,000. Clearly, even if they face the same statutory rate (say, 2 percent), Ophelia's effective rate of 2 percent (= $2,000/$100,000) is higher than Hamlet's 1.6 percent

---

[12] However, sometimes certain types of property are systematically assessed at lower rates than others. For example, many states have special assessment rates for farm property.

Table 20.2   Residential property tax rates in selected cities

City	Effective Tax Rate*
Newark	3.34%
Atlanta	1.87
Detroit	1.81
New Orleans	1.70
Charlotte	1.13
Los Angeles	1.07
Chicago	0.93
New York	0.80

*Figures are for 2000.

SOURCE: US Census Bureau, *Statistical Abstract of the United States: 2002* (Washington, DC: US Government Printing Office, 2002), p. 290.

(= $1,600/$100,000). In fact, many communities do a very poor job of assessing values so that properties with the same statutory rate face drastically different effective rates.

To analyze the property tax, at the outset one must realize that in the United States, literally thousands of jurisdictions operate their property tax systems more or less independently. No jurisdiction includes a comprehensive measure of wealth in its tax base, but there are major differences with respect to just what types of property are excludable and what rates are applied. Religious and nonprofit institutions make "voluntary" contributions in lieu of taxes for property owned. Some communities tax new business plants preferentially, presumably to attract more commercial activity. Few areas tax personal wealth other than homes so that items such as cars, jewels, and stocks and bonds are usually exempt. Typically, structures and the land on which they are built are subject to tax. But, as Table 20.2 demonstrates, the effective rates differ substantially across jurisdictions.

Thus, although we continue to describe the subject matter of this section as "the" property tax, it should now be clear that there is no such thing. The variety of property taxes is crucial to assessing the economic effects of the system as a whole.

Incidence and Efficiency Effects

The question of who ultimately bears the burden of the property tax is controversial. We discuss three different views and then try to reconcile them.

Traditional View: Property Tax as an Excise Tax. The traditional view is that the property tax is an excise tax that falls on land and structures. Incidence of the tax is determined by the shapes of the relevant supply and demand schedules as explained in Chapter 12. The shapes of the schedules are different for land and structures.

FIGURE 20.1

Incidence of a tax on land

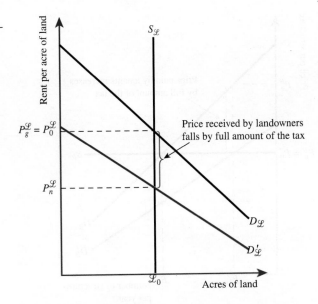

Price received by landowners falls by full amount of the tax

Land. As long as the amount of land is fixed, its supply curve is perfectly vertical, and landowners bear the entire burden of a tax levied on it. Intuitively, because its quantity is fixed, land cannot "escape" the tax. This is illustrated in Figure 20.1. $S_{\mathscr{L}}$ is the supply of land. Before the tax, the demand curve is $D_{\mathscr{L}}$, and the equilibrium rental value of land is $P_0^{\mathscr{L}}$ The imposition of an ad valorem tax on land pivots the demand curve. The after-tax demand curve is $D_{\mathscr{L}}'$. The rent received by suppliers of land (landowners), $P_n^{\mathscr{L}}$, is found at the intersection of the supply curve with $D_{\mathscr{L}}'$. We find the rent paid by the users of land by adding the tax per acre of land to $P_n^{\mathscr{L}}$, giving $P_g^{\mathscr{L}}$. As expected, the rent paid by the users of the land is unchanged ($P_0^{\mathscr{L}} = P_g^{\mathscr{L}}$); the rent received by landowners falls by the full amount of the tax. Landowners bear the entire burden of the tax.

As discussed in Chapter 12, under certain circumstances the tax is capitalized into the value of the land. Prospective land purchasers take into account the fact that if they buy the land, they also buy a future stream of tax liabilities. This lowers the amount they are willing to pay for the land. Therefore, the landlord, when the tax is levied, bears the tax for all time. To be sure, future landlords write checks to the tax authorities, but such payments are not really a burden because they just balance the lower price paid at purchase. Capitalization complicates attempts to assess the incidence of the land tax. Knowing the identities of current owners is not sufficient; we must know who the landlords *were* at the time the tax was imposed.

To the extent that land is *not* fixed in supply, the preceding analysis requires modification. For example, the supply of urban land can be extended at the fringes of urban areas that are adjacent to farmland. Similarly, the supply can be increased if landfills or reclamation of wasteland is feasible. In

FIGURE 20.2

Incidence of a tax
on structures

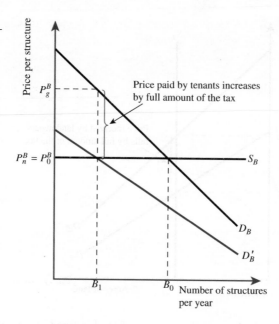

such cases, the tax on land is borne both by landlords and the users of land, in proportions that depend on the elasticities of demand and supply. But a vertical supply curve for land is usually a good approximation of reality.

Structures. To understand the traditional view of the tax on structures, we begin by considering the national market for capital. Capital can be used for many purposes: construction of structures, equipment for manufacturing, public sector projects like dams, and so forth. At any given time, capital has some price that rations it among alternative uses. According to the traditional view, in the long run, the construction industry can obtain all the capital it demands at the market price. Thus, the supply curve of structures is perfectly horizontal.

The market for structures under these conditions is depicted in Figure 20.2. Before the tax, the demand for structures by tenants is D_B, and the supply curve, S_B, is horizontal at the going price, P_0^B. At price P_0^B the quantity exchanged is B_0. On imposition of the tax, the demand curve pivots to D_B', just as the demand for land pivoted in Figure 20.1. But the outcome is totally different. The price received by the suppliers of structures, P_n^B, is the same as the price before the tax was imposed ($P_n^B = P_0^B$). Demanders of structures pay a price, P_g^B, which exceeds the original price, P_0^B, by precisely the amount of the tax. Hence, the burden is shifted entirely to tenants. This result, of course, follows from the assumption that the supply curve is horizontal. Intuitively, the horizontal supply curve means capital will leave the housing sector if it does not receive a return of at least P_0^B. But if the price received by the suppliers of capital cannot fall, tenants must bear the entire tax.

Summary and implications of the traditional view. The part of the tax on land falls on landowners (or at least the landowners at the time the tax is levied); the tax on structures is passed on to tenants. Therefore, the land part of the property tax is borne by people in proportion to the amount of rental income they receive, and the structures part of the tax is borne by people in proportion to the amount of housing they consume. It follows that the impact of the land part of the tax on progressiveness hinges on whether or not the share of income from land ownership tends to rise with income. There is fairly widespread agreement that it does, so this part of the tax is progressive. Similarly, the progressiveness of the tax on structures depends critically on whether the proportion of income devoted to housing rises or falls as income increases. If it falls, then the structures part of the tax is regressive, and vice versa.

An enormous amount of econometric work has focused on how housing expenditures actually do respond to changes in income. The ability to reach a consensus has been impeded by disagreement over which concept of income to use. Some investigators use *yearly* income. They tend to find that the proportion of income devoted to housing falls as income increases, suggesting that the tax is regressive. Other investigators believe that some measure of *permanent* income is more relevant to understanding housing decisions. According to this view, the fact that a family's annual income in a given year happens to be higher or lower than its permanent income has little impact on that year's housing consumption. Housing decisions are made in the context of the family's long-run prospects, not yearly variations.

Of course, those who believe that permanent income is the appropriate variable must find some way to estimate it. One approach is to define permanent income as the average of several years' annual incomes. Housing expenditures turn out to be more responsive to changes in permanent income than to changes in annual income. Indeed, although the evidence is mixed, it is reasonable to say that housing consumption is roughly proportional to permanent income. Hence, the structures part of the tax is probably neither regressive nor progressive. Unfortunately, analyses based on annual income, which suggest the tax is regressive, generally dominate public discussions of the tax.

The New View: Property Tax as a Capital Tax. The traditional view uses a standard partial equilibrium framework. As we noted in Chapter 12, although partial equilibrium analysis is often useful, it may produce misleading results for taxes that are large relative to the economy. The so-called new view of the property tax takes a general equilibrium perspective and leads to some surprising conclusions.[13]

According to the new view, it is best to think of the property tax as a general wealth tax with some assets taxed below the average rate and some

---

[13] See Zodrow [2001] for details.

taxed above. Both the average level of the tax and the deviations from that average have to be analyzed.

General tax effect.   Assume for the moment that the property tax can be approximated as a uniform tax on all capital. Then the property tax is just a general factor tax on capital. Assume further that the supply of capital to the economy is fixed. As shown in Chapter 12, when a factor is fixed in supply, it bears the full burden of a general tax levied on it. Hence, the property tax falls entirely on owners of capital. And since the proportion of income from capital tends to rise with income, a tax on capital tends to be progressive. Thus, the property tax is progressive, a conclusion that turns the traditional view exactly on its head!

Excise tax effects.   As noted earlier, the property tax is emphatically not a uniform tax. Rates vary according to the type of property and the jurisdiction in which it is located. Hence, the property tax is a set of excise taxes on capital. According to the new view, capital tends to migrate from areas where it faces a high tax rate to those where the rate is low. In a process reminiscent of the Harberger model presented in Chapter 12, as capital migrates into low-tax-rate areas, its before-tax rate of return there is bid down. At the same time, the before-tax rate of return in high-tax areas increases as capital leaves. The process continues until after-tax rates of return are equal throughout the economy. In general, as capital moves, returns to other factors of production also change. The impact on the other factors depends in part on their mobility. Land, which is perfectly immobile, cannot shift the tax. (In this conclusion, at least, the new and old views agree.) Similarly, the least-mobile types of capital are most likely to bear the tax. The ultimate incidence depends on how production is organized, the structure of consumer demand, and the extent to which various factors are mobile.

Long-run effects.   Our discussion of the general tax effect of the property tax assumed the amount of capital available to the economy is fixed. However, in the long run, the supply of capital may depend on the tax rate. If the property tax decreases the supply of capital, the productivity of labor, and hence the real wage, falls. If the tax increases capital accumulation, just the opposite occurs.

Summary of the new view.   The property tax is a general tax on capital with some types of capital taxed at rates above the average, others below. The general effect of the tax is to lower the return to capital, which tends to be progressive in its impact on the income distribution. The differentials in tax rates create excise effects, which tend to hurt immobile factors in highly taxed jurisdictions. The adjustment process set in motion by these excise effects is very complicated, and not much is known about their effects on progressiveness. Neither can much be said concerning the importance of long-term effects created by changes in the size of the capital stock. If the excise and long-run effects do not counter the general effect too strongly, the overall impact of the property tax is progressive.

Property Tax as a User Fee. The discussion so far has ignored the fact that communities use property taxes to purchase public services such as education and police protection. In the Tiebout model, the property tax is just the cost of purchasing public services, and each individual buys exactly the amount he or she desires. Thus, the property tax is really not a tax at all; it is more like a user fee for public services. This view has three important implications:

- The notion of the *incidence of the property tax* is meaningless because the levy is not a tax in the normal sense of the word.
- The property tax creates no excess burden. Because it is merely the fee for public services, it does not distort the housing market any more than the price of any other commodity.
- By allowing the deduction of property tax payments, the federal income tax in effect subsidizes the consumption of local public services for individuals who itemize on their tax returns. As long as the demand for local public services slopes downward, the deduction increases the size of the local public sector desired by itemizers, other things being the same.

As noted earlier, the link between property taxes and services received is often tenuous, so we should not take the notion of the property tax as a user fee too literally. Nevertheless, this line of reasoning has interesting implications. For example, if people care about the public services they receive, we expect the depressing effects of high property taxes on housing values to be counteracted by the public services financed by these taxes. In a classic paper, Oates [1969] constructed an econometric model of property value determination. In his model, the value of homes in a community depends positively on the quality of public services in the community and negatively on the tax rate, other things being the same. Of course, across communities, factors that influence house prices do differ. These include physical characteristics of the houses, such as number of rooms, and characteristics of the communities themselves, such as distance from an urban center. These factors must be considered when trying to sort out the effects of property taxes and local public goods on property values. Oates used multiple regression analysis to do so.

Oates's regression results suggest that increases in the property tax rate decrease housing values, while increases in per pupil expenditures increase housing values. Moreover, the parameter values implied that the increase in property values created by expanding school expenditures approximately offset the decrease generated by the property taxes raised to finance them. These results need to be interpreted with caution. For one thing, expenditure per pupil may not be an adequate measure of local public services. Localities provide many public services other than education, such as police protection, parks, and libraries. Furthermore, even if education were the only local public good, expenditure per pupil might not be a good measure of educational quality. It is possible, for example, that expenditures in a given community are high because the community has to pay a lot for its teachers, its schools are not administered efficiently, or its students are particularly difficult to educate.

Subsequent to Oates's study, many other investigators have examined the relationships among property values, property taxes, and local public goods using data from different geographical areas and employing different sets of explanatory variables. Although the results are a bit mixed, Oates's general conclusion seems to be valid—property taxes and the value of local public services are capitalized into housing prices. (See, for example, Weimer and Wolkoff [2001].) Thus, if two communities have the same level of public services, but the first has higher taxes than the second (perhaps because its cost of providing the services is greater), we expect the first to have lower property values, other things being the same. More generally, these results imply that to understand how well off members of a community are, we cannot look at property tax rates in isolation. Government services and property values must also be considered.

Reconciling the Three Views.   The three views of the property tax are not mutually exclusive. Each may be valid in different contexts. If, for example, we want to find the consequences of eliminating all property taxes and replacing them with a national sales tax, the "new view" is appropriate because a change that affects all communities requires a general equilibrium framework. On the other hand, if a given community is considering lowering its property tax rate and making up the revenue loss from a local sales tax, the "traditional view" offers the most insight. This is because a single community is so small relative to the economy that its supply of capital is essentially perfectly horizontal, and Figure 20.2 applies. Finally, when taxes and benefits are jointly changed and people are sufficiently mobile to be able to pick and choose communities, the "user fee view" is useful.

Why Do People Hate the Property Tax So Much?

On June 7, 1978, the voters of California approved a statewide property tax limitation initiative known as Proposition 13. Its key provisions were (1) to put a 1 percent ceiling on the property tax rate that any locality could impose, (2) to limit the assessed value of property to its 1975 value,[14] and

---

[14] For property transferred after 1975, the assessed value was defined as the market value at which the transaction took place.

(3) to forbid state and local governments to impose any additional property taxes without approval by a two-thirds majority local vote. Proposition 13 began a movement to limit the property tax that is still going strong today. Public opinion polls regularly indicate that people dislike the property tax even more than the federal income tax.

Why is the property tax so unpopular? Several explanations have been advanced:

Because housing market transactions typically occur infrequently, the property tax must be levied on an estimated value. To the extent that this valuation is done incompetently (or corruptly), the tax is perceived as unfair.

The property tax is highly visible. Under the federal income and payroll taxes, payments are withheld from workers' paychecks, and the employer sends the proceeds to the government. In contrast, the property tax is often paid directly by the taxpayer. Moreover, the payments are due on a quarterly or an annual basis, so each payment comes as a large shock. It is hard to know how seriously to take this argument. Even those citizens who are somehow oblivious to the fact that federal income and payroll taxes are withheld during the year receive a pointed reminder of how much they have paid every April. There may be enough rage in that one month to last a whole year.

The property tax is perceived as being regressive. This perception is due partly to the continued dominance of the "traditional view" of the property tax in public debate. It is reinforced by the fact that some property owners, particularly the elderly, do not have enough cash to make property tax payments and may therefore be forced to sell their homes. Some states have responded to this phenomenon by introducing **circuit breakers** that provide benefits to taxpayers (usually in the form of a refund on state income taxes) that depend on the excess of residential property tax payments over some specified proportion of income. A better solution would be to defer tax payments until the time when the property is transferred.

Taxpayers may dislike other taxes as much as the property tax, but they feel powerless to do anything about the others. It is relatively easy to take aim at the property tax, which is levied locally. In contrast, mounting a drive against the federal income tax is very difficult, if for no other reason than a national campaign would be necessary and hence involve large coordination costs.

In light of the widespread hostility toward the tax, it is natural to ask whether it can be improved. A very modest proposal is to improve assessment procedures. The use of computers and modern valuation techniques can make assessments more uniform. Compared to the current system of differing effective tax rates within a jurisdiction, uniform tax rates would probably enhance efficiency. The equity issues are more complicated. Superficially, it seems a violation of horizontal equity for two people with identical properties to pay different taxes on them. However, the phenomenon of capitalization requires that we distinguish carefully between the owners at the time the tax is levied and the current owners. A property with an unduly high tax rate will sell for a lower price, other things being the same. Thus, a high tax rate does not necessarily make an individual who buys the property *after* the tax is imposed worse off. Indeed, equalizing assessment ratios could generate a whole new set of horizontal inequities.

A more ambitious reform of the property tax would be to convert it into a **personal net worth tax,** whose base is the difference between the market value of all the taxpayer's assets and liabilities. An advantage of such a system over a property tax is that by allowing for deduction of liabilities, it provides a better index of ability to pay. Moreover, because it is a personal tax, exemptions can be built into the system and the rates can be varied to attain the desired degree of progressivity.

A personal net worth tax is a kind of general wealth tax, and we discussed the administrative and economic issues associated with wealth taxation in the last chapter. In the context of property tax reform, it is particularly important to note that because individuals can have assets and liabilities in different jurisdictions, a net worth tax would undoubtedly have to be administered by the federal government. This brings us to what many people consider to be the main justification for the current system of property taxation. Whatever its flaws, the property tax can be administered locally without any help from the federal or state governments. Hence, it provides local government with considerable fiscal autonomy: "Property taxation offers people in different localities an instrument by which they can make local choices significant" [Harris, 1978, p. 38]. According to this view, elimination of the property tax would ultimately destroy the economic independence of local units of government.

California's experience after Proposition 13 is consistent with this notion. Because Proposition 13 limited the ability of communities to raise money via property taxes, that measure "concentrated power to raise revenue in the State Legislature, and with it the right to determine policies and priorities once set locally" [Lindsey, 1986]. Thus, the political role of the property tax needs to be taken seriously in any discussion of its reform.

Intergovernmental Grants

As already noted, federal grants are a very important source of revenue to states and localities. Grants from one level of government to another are the main method for changing fiscal resources within a federal system. Table 20.3 indicates that between 1960 and 2001, grants from the federal government increased both in real terms and as a proportion of

Table 20.3   **Relation of federal grants-in-aid to federal and state–local expenditures** *(selected fiscal years)*

Year	Total Grants (billions of 2001 dollars)*	Grants as a Percent of Total Federal Outlays	Grants as a Percent of State and Local Expenditures
1960	$ 20	4.3%	10.5%
1970	73	9.8	18.0
1980	139	12.2	23.5
1990	141	8.9	16.9
2001	277	14.9	21.4

*Amounts are converted to 2001 dollars using the GDP deflator.

SOURCE: Computed from *Economic Report of the President 2003* (Washington, DC: US Government Printing Office, 2003), pp. 369, 373.

total federal outlays.[15] Grants as a percentage of state and local expenditures have also increased. The importance of grants as an element in local public finance is particularly striking. Grants from federal and state government are about 34 percent of total local general revenues [US Census Bureau, 2002, p. 270]. Grants help finance activities that run practically the entire gamut of government functions, everything from food inspection to rural community fire protection.

Why have intergovernmental transfers grown so much over the long run? This question is closely related to why government spending in general has increased. As we saw in Chapter 6, the answer is far from clear. One explanation for the growth of grants emphasizes that over the last several decades, the demand for the types of services traditionally provided by the state and local sector—education, transportation, and police protection—has been growing rapidly. However, the state and local revenue structures, which are based mainly on sales and property taxes, have not provided the means to keep pace with the growth of desired expenditures. In contrast, federal tax revenues have grown automatically over time, largely due to the progressive nature of the federal personal income tax and, until the advent of indexing in the mid-1980s, inflation. Hence, there is a "mismatch" between where tax money is collected and where it is demanded. Grants from the central government to states and localities provide a way of correcting this mismatch.

The mismatch theory is unsatisfying because it fails to explain why states and localities cannot raise their tax *rates* to keep up with increases in the demand for local public goods and services. As noted in the next section, we

---

[15] In addition to explicit grants, the federal government subsidizes states and localities by exempting from taxation the interest on state and local bonds and allowing the deductibility of state/local income and property taxes. In 2002, tax expenditures for the interest exclusion were $16 billion; for tax deductibility, $66 billion [Joint Committee on Taxation, 2002, pp. 22, 27].

FIGURE 20.3

A matching grant

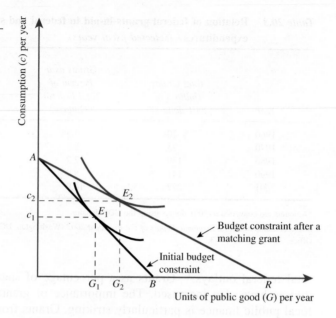

probably have to turn to political considerations to explain the pattern of intergovernmental grants.

Types of Grants

A grant's structure influences its economic impact. There are basically two types, conditional and unconditional, which we discuss in turn.

Conditional Grants.   These are sometimes called **categorical grants.** The donor specifies, to some extent, the purposes for which the recipient can use the funds. The vast majority of federal grants are earmarked for specific purposes, and the rules for spending the money are often spelled out in minute detail. For example, the federal government gives grants to states to establish anti–drunk driving programs. The terms of the law specify everything from the percent of blood-alcohol concentration that constitutes intoxication to how soon an offender's driver's license must be taken away after he or she is convicted. Such restrictions are not atypical.

There are several types of conditional grants.

Matching grants.   For every dollar given by the donor to support a particular activity, a certain sum must be expended by the recipient. For example, a grant might stipulate that whenever a community spends a dollar on education, the federal government will contribute a dollar as well.

The standard theory of rational choice can help us analyze matching grants. In Figure 20.3, the horizontal axis measures the quantity of local government output, G, consumed by the residents of the town of Smallville. The vertical axis measures Smallville's total consumption, c. Assume for simplicity that units of G and c are defined so the price of one unit of each is \$1. Hence, assuming no saving, c is equal to after-tax income. With these assumptions, Smallville's budget constraint between c and G is a straight line whose slope in absolute value is one.[16] The unitary slope indicates that for each dollar Smallville is willing to spend, it can obtain one unit of public good. The budget constraint is denoted AB in Figure 20.3.

Suppose that Smallville's preferences for G and c can be represented by a set of conventionally shaped indifference curves.[17] Then if the town seeks to maximize its utility subject to the budget constraint, it chooses point E_1, where public good consumption is G_1 and community after-tax income is c_1.

Now suppose that a one-for-one matching grant regime is instituted. When Smallville gives up \$1 of income, it can obtain *\$2* worth of G—one of its own dollars and one from the federal government. The slope (in absolute value) of Smallville's budget line therefore becomes one-half. In effect, the matching grant halves the price of G. It is an ad valorem subsidy on consumption of the public good. The new budget line is drawn in Figure 20.3 as AR.

Smallville now consumes G_2 public goods and has c_2 available for private consumption. Note that not only is G_2 greater than G_1 but c_2 is also greater than c_1. Smallville uses part of the grant to buy more of the public good and part to reduce its tax burden. It would be possible, of course, to draw the indifference curves so that c_2 equals c_1, or even so that c_2 is less than c_1. Nevertheless, it is a distinct possibility that part of the grant meant to stimulate public consumption will be used not to buy more G but to obtain tax relief. In an extreme case, the community's indifference curves might be such that $G_2 = G_1$—the community consumes the same amount of the public good and uses the entire grant to reduce taxes. Thus, theory alone cannot indicate how a matching grant affects a community's expenditure on a public good. It depends on the responsiveness of demand to changes in price. Economists have therefore conducted statistical studies of how the demands for various public goods vary with their prices. According to the literature surveyed by Fisher and Papke [2000], the price elasticity of demand for education lies between 0.15 and 0.50.

A matching grant is a sensible way to correct for the presence of a positive externality. As explained in Chapter 5, when an individual or a firm generates a positive externality at the margin, an appropriate subsidy can enhance efficiency. The same logic applies to a community. Of course, all the problems that arise in implementing the subsidy scheme are still present. In particular, the central government has to be able to measure the actual size of the externality. In this context, it is interesting to note that many federal

---

[16] Details on the construction of budget constraints are provided in the appendix at the end of the book. This model ignores the deduction of state and local property taxes in the federal income tax system. If taxpayers itemize deductions and the marginal federal income tax rate is t, the absolute value of the slope of AB is $(1 - t)$.

[17] Of course, this supposition ignores all the problems—and perhaps the impossibility—of preference aggregation raised in Chapter 6. We return to this issue later.

FIGURE 20.4

A closed-ended
matching grant

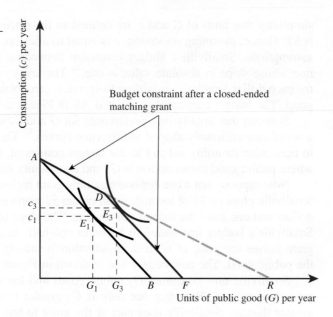

grant programs are very difficult to rationalize using efficiency criteria. The high matching rates (often 80 to 90 percent) are much greater than reasonable estimates of the externalities generated by the subsidized state and local activities [Oates, 1999, p. 1129]. In fact, the literature surveyed by Borck and Owings [2003] suggests that political rather than efficiency considerations predominate in the distribution of governmental grants. For example, more money tends to go to states that have representatives on important congressional committees.

Matching closed-ended grant.   The cost to the donor of a matching grant ultimately depends on the recipient's behavior. If Smallville increases its consumption of G substantially, the central government's contributions will be quite large, and vice versa. To put a ceiling on the cost, the donor may specify some maximum amount that it will contribute. Such a closed-ended matching grant is illustrated in Figure 20.4. As before, prior to the grant, Smallville's budget line is AB, and the equilibrium is at point E_1. With the closed-ended matching grant, the budget constraint is the kinked line segment ADF. Segment AD's slope is minus one-half, reflecting the one-for-one matching provision. But after some point D, the donor no longer matches dollar for dollar. Smallville's opportunity cost of a unit of government spending again becomes \$1, which is reflected in the slope of segment DF.

The new equilibrium at E_3 involves more consumption of G than under the status quo, but less than under the open-ended matching grant. The fact that the grant runs out limits its ability to stimulate expenditure on

FIGURE 20.5

A nonmatching grant

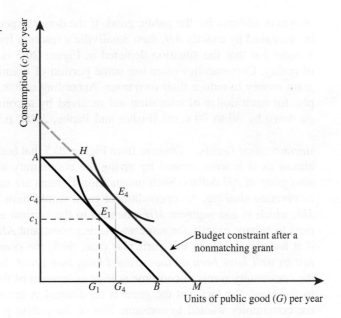

the public good. However, in some cases the closed-endedness can be irrelevant. If desired community consumption of G involves an expenditure below the ceiling, the presence of the ceiling simply does not matter. In graphical terms, if the new tangency had been along segment AD of Figure 20.4, it would be irrelevant that points along DR were not available. Baker, Payne, and Smart [1999] conducted an interesting study of the impact of moving from an open-ended to a closed-ended matching grant system in Canada. Before the 1990s, for every dollar a Canadian province spent on welfare programs, the central government matched the dollar. In order to contain costs, in 1990 the central government converted the program to a closed-ended system in three of the ten provinces. Consistent with the story in Figure 20.4, spending in the three affected provinces fell relative to the others.

Nonmatching grant. Here the donor gives a fixed sum of money with the stipulation that it be spent on the public good. Figure 20.5 depicts a nonmatching grant to buy AH units of G. At each level of community income, Smallville can now buy AH more units of the public good than it did before. Thus, the new budget constraint is found by adding a horizontal distance AH to the original budget constraint AB. The result is the kinked line AHM.

Smallville maximizes utility at point E_4. Note that although public good consumption goes up from G_1 to G_4, the difference between the two is less than the amount of the grant, AH. Smallville has followed the stipulation that it spend the entire grant on G, *but* at the same time, it has reduced its own expenditures for the public good. If the donor expected expenditures to be increased by exactly *AH*, then Smallville's reaction frustrates these hopes. It turns out that the situation depicted in Figure 20.5 is a good description of reality. Communities often use some portion of nonmatching conditional grant money to reduce their own taxes. According to one estimate, for example, for each dollar of education aid received by a community, local taxes go down by 30 to 70 cents [Fisher and Papke, 2000, p. 157].

Unconditional Grants.   Observe from Figure 20.5 that budget line *AHM* looks almost as if it were created by giving the community an unrestricted lump sum grant of *AH* dollars. Such unconditional grants are sometimes referred to as **revenue sharing.** An unconditional grant would have led to a budget line *JM*, which is just segment *MH* extended to the vertical axis. Smallville happens to behave exactly the same way facing constraint *AHM* as it would have if it had faced *JM*. In this particular case, then, *the conditional grant could just as well have been an unrestricted lump sum grant.* Intuitively, as long as the community wants to consume at least an amount of the public good equal to the grant, the fact that the grant is conditional is irrelevant. In contrast, if the community wanted to consume less of the public good than *AH* (if the indifference curves were such that the optimum along *JM* is to the left of *H*), then the conditional nature of the grant would actually affect behavior.

Why should the central government be in the business of giving unconditional grants to states and localities? The usual response is that such grants can equalize the income distribution. It is not clear that this argument is compelling. Even if a goal of public policy is to help poor people, it does not follow that the best way to do so is to help poor communities. After all, the chances are that a community with a low average income has some relatively rich members and vice versa. If the goal is to help the poor, why not give them the money directly?

One possible explanation is that the central government is particularly concerned that the poor consume a greater quantity of the publicly provided good. An important example is education. This is a kind of commodity egalitarianism (Chapter 7) applied to the output of the public sector. However, as we just demonstrated, with unconditional grants we cannot know for sure that all the money will ultimately be spent on the favored good. (Indeed, the same is also true for conditional grants.)

Measuring need.   In any case, a redistributive grant program requires the donor to determine which communities "need" money and in what amounts. Federal allocations are based on complicated formulas established by Congress. The amount of grant money received by a state depends on such factors as per capita income, the size of its urban population, and the amount of its state income tax collections. The allocations to localities are functions of such conventional economic factors and may also depend on items such as the ethnicity of the population.

An important factor in determining how much a community receives from the federal government is its **tax effort,** normally defined as the ratio of tax collections to tax capacity. The idea is that communities that try hard to raise taxes but still cannot finance a very high level of public services are worthy of receiving a grant. Unfortunately, this and related measures may yield little or no information about a community's true effort. Suppose that Smallville is in a position to export its tax burden in the sense that the incidence of any taxes it levies falls on outsiders. Then a high tax rate tells us nothing about how much the members of the community are sacrificing.

More fundamentally, the tax effort approach may be rendered totally meaningless because of the phenomenon of capitalization. Consider two towns, Sodom and Gomorrah. They are identical except for the fact that Sodom has a brook providing water at essentially zero cost. In Gomorrah, on the other hand, it is necessary to dig a well and pump the water.

Gomorrah levies a property tax to finance the water pump. If there is a tax in Gomorrah and none in Sodom, and the communities are otherwise identical, why should anyone live in Gomorrah? As people migrate to Sodom, property values increase there (and decrease in Gomorrah) until there is no net advantage to living in either community. In short, property values are higher in Sodom to reflect the presence of the brook.

For reasons discussed previously, we do not expect the advantage to be necessarily 100 percent capitalized into Sodom's property values. Nevertheless, capitalization compensates at least partially for the differences between the towns. Just because Gomorrah levies a tax does *not* mean it is "trying harder" than Sodom, because the Sodomites have already paid for their water by a higher price for living there. We conclude that conventional measures of tax effort may not be very meaningful.

The Flypaper Effect

Our community indifference curve analysis begs a fundamental question: *Whose* indifference curves are they? According to median voter theory (Chapter 6), the preferences are those of the community's median voter. Bureaucrats and elected officials play a passive role in implementing the median voter's wishes.

A straightforward implication of the median voter rule is that a $1 increase in community income has exactly the same impact on public spending as receipt of a $1 unconditional grant. In terms of Figure 20.5, both events generate identical parallel outward shifts of the initial budget line. If the budget line changes are identical, the changes in public spending must also be identical.

A considerable amount of econometric work has been done on the determinants of local public spending. (See Oates [1999] for a survey.) Contrary to what one might expect, virtually all studies conclude that a dollar received by the community in the form of a grant results in *greater* public spending than a dollar increase in community income. Roughly speaking, the estimates suggest that a dollar received as a grant generates 40 cents of public spending, while an additional dollar of private income increases public spending by only 10 cents. This phenomenon has been dubbed the **flypaper effect,** because the money seems to stick in the sector where it initially hits.

Some explanations of the flypaper effect focus on the role of bureaucrats. Filimon, Romer, and Rosenthal [1982] argue that bureaucrats seek to maximize the sizes of their budgets. As budget maximizers, the bureaucrats have no incentive to inform citizens about the community's true level of grant funding. By concealing this information, the bureaucrats may trick citizens into voting for a higher level of funding than would otherwise have been the case. According to this view, the flypaper effect occurs because citizens are unaware of the true budget constraint. To support their theory, Filimon, Romer, and Rosenthal noted that in states with direct referenda on spending questions, ballots often contain information about the tax base but rarely have data on grants.

Intergovernmental Grants for Education

In 1971, the court case of *Serrano* v. *Priest* ushered in a new era in education finance. The California Supreme Court ruled that disparities in property wealth across school districts led to unconstitutionally disparate school quality when local property taxation was exclusively relied on for school finance. Since then, courts have struck down similar financing schemes in more than a dozen states. In response, states have assumed an increasingly large role in financing elementary and secondary education. States use two basic kinds of grants to support local schools: **Foundation aid** seeks to assure a minimum level of expenditure per pupil, regardless of local property wealth. **District power equalization (DPE) grants** assure that the revenue raised by the local property tax rate corresponds to what would be raised if the district's property wealth per pupil did not fall below a guaranteed level.

From our standpoint, the key thing about these grants is that they represent a centralization of school finance. Instead of a system in which each locality funds its own schools via the property tax, the state raises the money via an income tax, and transfers resources to poorer districts through one mechanism or another.

Is this a sensible way to improve the educational attainment of children from disadvantaged backgrounds? The threshold question is whether higher expenditures lead to better education. After all, we are ultimately concerned with educational outcomes for students, not educational expenditures per se. We discussed this issue in Chapter 4 and concluded that, according to the econometric evidence, it is not at all clear that more spending leads to better outcomes.

A second issue relates to the impact of centralized financing on voters' support for public education. Recall that in the Tiebout model, people choose their communities on the basis of their demands for education (and other public services) and pay for this education via the property tax. Centralized finance eliminates the link between what people pay for their children's education and what they receive, perhaps weakening voter support for public education as a whole. On this basis, some have argued that reforming the finance of education might actually lead to a drop in spending on education. However, Murray, Evans, and Schwab [1998] find that in states with court-mandated reform, spending in low-income districts increased while spending in high-income districts remained the same, leading to an overall increase in education expenditures.

Overview

At the beginning of this chapter we posed some questions concerning federal systems: Is decentralized decision making desirable? How should responsibilities be allocated? How should local governments finance themselves? Our answers suggest that federalism is a sensible system. Allowing local communities to make their own decisions very likely enhances efficiency in the provision of local public goods. However, efficiency and equity are also likely to require a significant economic role for a central government. In particular, a system in which only local resources are used to finance local public goods is viewed by many as inequitable.

While our focus has naturally been on economic issues, questions of power and politics are never far beneath the surface in discussions of federalism. The dispersion of economic power is generally associated with the dispersion of political power. How should power be allocated? Is your image of subfederal government a racist governor keeping black students out of the state university, or a town hall meeting in which citizens democratically make collective decisions? When you think of the central government, do you picture an uncaring and remote bureaucrat imposing bothersome regulations, or a justice department lawyer working to guarantee the civil rights of all citizens? The different images coexist in our minds, creating conflicting feelings about the proper distribution of governmental power.

Summary

- In a federal system, different governments provide different services to overlapping jurisdictions.
- The club model of community formation indicates that community size and quantity of public goods depend on tastes for public goods, costs of providing public services, and the costs of crowding.
- The Tiebout model emphasizes the key roles of mobility, property taxes, and zoning rules in local public finance. Under certain conditions, "voting

with the feet"—moving to one's preferred community—results in a Pareto efficient allocation of public goods.

- Disadvantages of decentralization are intercommunity externalities, forgone scale economies in the provision of public goods, inefficient taxation, and lack of ability to redistribute income.
- Advantages of decentralization are the ability to alter the mix of public services to suit local tastes, the beneficial effects of competition among local governments, and the potential for

low-cost experimentation at the subfederal level.

■ Local responsibility for education can be justified on the basis of different tastes across communities. However, some federal involvement in the distribution of resources available for education may be appropriate.

■ Property taxes are an important revenue source for state and local governments. The "traditional view" of the property tax is that it is an excise tax on land and structures. The "new view" is that the property tax is a general tax on all capital with rates that vary across jurisdictions and different types of capital. The "user-fee view" regards property taxes as payment for local public services.

■ The property tax is very unpopular. Perhaps its main advantage in the context of a federal system is that it can be administered locally.

■ Grants may be either conditional (categorical) or unconditional (lump sum). Each type of grant embodies different incentives for local governments. The final mix of increased expenditure versus lower local taxes depends on the preferences dictating local choices.

■ Empirical studies of intergovernmental grants indicate a *flypaper effect*—an increase in grant money induces greater spending on public goods than does an equivalent increase in local income. One possible explanation is that bureaucrats exploit citizens' incomplete information about the community budget constraint.

Discussion Questions

1. State whether each activity should be under the control of the federal, state, or local government, and explain why.

   a. Air pollution control regulations.

   b. Regulating solid waste landfills.

   c. Provision of weather satellites.

   d. Public refuse collection.

   e. Airport security.

2. David and Jonathan own identical homes. David has owned his home for many years and paid $100,000 for it. Jonathan purchased his home after a recent property tax increase and paid $80,000. Should the local assessor change the assessed value of Jonathan's home to maintain horizontal equity? (Assume there has been no inflation in housing prices since David purchased his home and that David and Jonathan value equally all public services provided in the local community.) In your answer, carefully define all key concepts.

3. Illustrate the following circumstances using community indifference curves and the local government budget constraint:

   a. An unconditional grant increases both the quantity of public goods purchased and local taxes.

   b. A matching grant leaves provision of the public good unchanged.

   c. A closed-ended matching grant has the same impact as a conditional nonmatching grant.

   d. A closed-ended matching grant leaves local taxes unchanged.

4. An econometric study found that the more ethnically diverse a country, the more decentralized its public sector is likely to be, other things being the same [Panizza, 1999]. Is this finding consistent with our theory of fiscal federalism?

5. A number of states have debated whether to institute lotteries. One argument used to great effect by lottery proponents is that lottery revenues will be devoted to education.

   Sketch a state's budget constraint between "education" and "expenditures on all other commodities." Show how the introduction of revenues from a lottery affects the budget constraint. Draw an indifference map and show how education expenditures compare before and after the lottery. According to your diagram, do education expenditures increase by the full amount of the lottery revenues? Why would it be difficult to determine whether the government was keeping its promise to spend all the lottery revenues on education?

6. Assume that the towns of Belmont and Lexington have different demand curves for firefighters and can hire firefighters at the same constant marginal cost. Suppose that historically their state government has required the two towns to hire the same number of firefighters, but the state has recently decentralized decision making. Show that the gain in welfare from decentralization is greater the more inelastic the communities' demand curves, other things being the same.

7. Heal [2001, p. 1] notes that when Frederick Law Olmsted, the designer of New York City's Central Park, was asked how the city could pay for the park, "he responded that its presence would raise property values and the extra tax revenues would easily repay the construction costs. History shows that was correct." This episode illustrates best which of the three views of the nature of the local property tax?

8. The federal government subsidizes state spending on welfare, thus changing the effective price to states of welfare spending. According to Baicker [2001], the elasticity of state spending on benefits per recipient is 0.38. Suppose that the federal government matches state welfare spending on a one-for-one basis, and then changes to a two-for-one basis. How would you expect state welfare spending to change?

Selected References

Fisher, Ronald C, and Leslie E Papke. "Local Government Responses to Education Grants." *National Tax Journal* 53 (March 2000), pp. 153–68.

Oates, Wallace E. "An Essay on Fiscal Federalism." *Journal of Economic Literature* 37 (September 1999), pp. 1120–49.

Tannenwald, Robert. "Are State and Local Revenue Systems Becoming Obsolete?" *National Tax Journal* 55 (September 2002), pp. 467–90.

Some Basic Microeconomics

We are living in a material world.

MADONNA

Certain tools of microeconomics are used throughout the text. We briefly review them in this appendix. Readers who have taken an introductory course in microeconomics will likely find this review sufficient to refresh their memories. Those confronting the material for the first time may want to consult one of the standard introductory texts. The subjects covered are demand and supply, consumer choice, marginal analysis, and consumer and producer surplus.

Demand and Supply

Within a recent two-year period, the price per pound of coffee beans dropped from 95 cents to 45 cents. Coffee producers were distressed but coffee consumers were pleased. Why did the price fall so much? The demand and supply model provides a framework for thinking about how the price and output of a commodity are determined in a competitive market. We discuss in turn the determinants of demand, supply, and their interaction.

Demand

Which factors influence people's decisions to consume certain goods? Continuing with our coffee example, a bit of introspection suggests that the following factors affect the amount that people want to consume during a given time period:

1. **Price.** We expect that as the price goes up, the quantity demanded goes down.

2. **Income.** Changes in income affect people's consumption opportunities. It is hard to say a priori, however, what effect such changes have on consumption of a given good. Perhaps people purchase more coffee when their incomes go up. On the other hand, it may

be that as incomes increase, people consume less coffee, perhaps spending their money on cognac instead. If an increase in income increases the demand (other things being the same), the good is called a **normal good.** If an increase in income decreases demand (other things being the same), the good is called an **inferior good.**

3. **Prices of related goods.** Suppose the price of tea goes up. If people can substitute coffee for tea, this increase in the price of tea increases the amount of coffee people wish to consume. Now suppose the price of cream goes up. If people consume coffee and cream together, this tends to decrease the amount of coffee consumed. Goods like tea and coffee are called **substitutes;** goods like coffee and cream are called **complements.**

4. **Tastes.** The extent to which people "like" a good affects the amount they demand. Not much coffee is demanded by Mormons because their religion prohibits it. Often, it is realistic to assume that consumers' tastes stay the same over time, but not always. For example, when some scientists claimed that coffee might cause birth defects, many pregnant women dropped the beverage.

We see, then, that a wide variety of things can affect demand. However, it is often useful to focus on the relationship between the quantity of a commodity demanded and its price. Suppose that we fix income, the prices of related goods, and tastes. We can imagine varying the price of coffee and seeing how the quantity demanded changes under the assumption that the other relevant variables stay at their fixed values. A **demand schedule** (or **demand curve**) is the relation between the market price of a good and its quantity demanded during a given time period, other things being the same. (Economists often use the Latin for "other things being the same," *ceteris paribus.*)

A hypothetical demand schedule for coffee is represented graphically by curve D_c in Figure A.1. The horizontal axis measures pounds of coffee per year in a particular market, and the price per pound is measured on the vertical. Thus, for example, if the price is $2.29 per pound, people are willing to consume 750 pounds; when the price is only $1.38, they are willing to consume 1,225 pounds. The downward slope of the demand schedule reflects the reasonable assumption that when the price goes up, the quantity demanded goes down.

The demand curve can also be interpreted as an approximate schedule of "willingness to pay," because it shows the maximum price that people would pay for a given quantity. For example, when people purchase 750 pounds per year, they value it at $2.29 per pound. At any price more than $2.29, they would not willingly consume 750 pounds per year. If for some reason people were able to obtain 750 pounds at a price less than $2.29, this would in some sense be a "bargain."

FIGURE A.1

Hypothetical demand curve for coffee

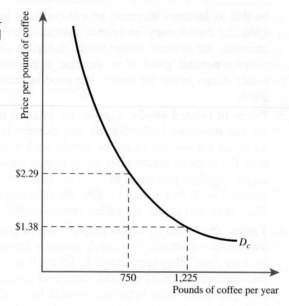

FIGURE A.2

Effect of an increase in the price of tea on the demand for coffee

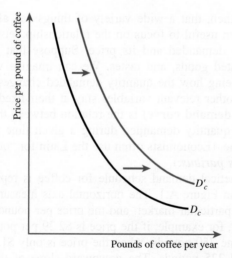

As already stressed, the demand curve is drawn on the assumption that all other variables that might affect quantity demanded do not change. What happens if one of them does? Suppose, for example, that the price of tea increases, and as a consequence, people want to buy more coffee. In Figure A.2, we reproduce schedule D_c from Figure A.1 (before the increase). Due to the increase in the price of tea, at *each price* of coffee people are willing to purchase more coffee than they did previously. In effect, then, an increase in the price of tea shifts each point on D_c to the right. The collection of new points is D_c'. Because D_c' shows how much people are willing to consume at each price (*ceteris paribus*), it is by definition the demand curve.

More generally, a change in any variable that influences the demand for a good—except its own price—shifts the demand curve.[1] (A change in a good's own price induces a movement *along* the demand curve.)

Supply

Now consider the factors that determine the quantity of a commodity that firms supply to the market. We will continue using coffee as our example.

1. **Price.** It is often reasonable to assume that the higher the price per pound of coffee, the greater the quantity profit-maximizing firms are willing to supply.

2. **Price of inputs.** Coffee producers employ inputs to produce coffee—labor, land, and fertilizer. If their input costs go up, the amount of coffee that they can profitably supply at any given price goes down.

3. **Conditions of production.** The most important factor here is the state of technology. If there is a technological improvement in coffee production, the supply increases. Other variables also affect production conditions. For agricultural goods, weather is important. Several years ago, for example, flooding in Latin America seriously reduced the coffee crop.

As with the demand curve, we focus on the relationship between the quantity of a commodity supplied and its price, holding the other variables at fixed levels. The **supply schedule** is the relation between market prices and the amount of a good that producers are willing to supply during a given time period, *ceteris paribus*. A supply schedule for coffee is depicted as S_c in Figure A.3. Its upward slope reflects the assumption that the higher the price, the greater the quantity supplied, *ceteris paribus*.

When any variable that influences supply (other than the commodity's own price) changes, the supply schedule shifts. Suppose, for example, that the wage rate for coffee-bean pickers increases. This increase reduces the amount of coffee that firms are willing to supply at any given price. The supply curve therefore shifts to the left. As depicted in Figure A.4, the new supply curve is S_c'. More generally, when any variable other than the commodity's own price changes, the supply curve shifts. (A change in the commodity's price induces a movement along the supply curve.)

Equilibrium

The demand and supply curves provide answers to a set of hypothetical questions: *If* the price of coffee is $2 per pound, how much are consumers willing to purchase? *If* the price is $1.75 per pound, how much are firms

---

[1] There is no need, incidentally, for D_c' to be parallel to D_c. In general, this will not be the case.

FIGURE A.3

Hypothetical supply curve for coffee

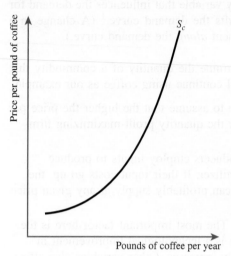

FIGURE A.4

Effect of an increase in the wages of coffee-bean pickers on the supply of coffee

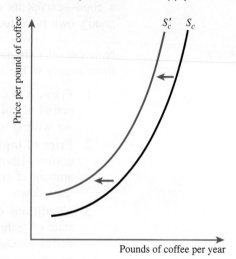

willing to supply? Neither schedule by itself tells us the actual price and quantity. But taken together, they do.

In Figure A.5 we superimpose demand schedule D_c from Figure A.1 on supply schedule S_c from Figure A.3. We want to find the price and output at which there is an **equilibrium**—a situation that tends to be maintained unless there is an underlying change in the system. Suppose the price is P_1 dollars per pound. At this price, the quantity demanded is Q_1^D and the quantity supplied is Q_1^S. Price P_1 cannot be maintained, because firms want to supply more coffee than consumers are willing to purchase. This excess supply tends to push the price down, as suggested by the arrows.

Now consider price P_2. At this price, the quantity of coffee demanded, Q_2^D, exceeds the quantity supplied, Q_2^S. Because there is excess demand for coffee, we expect the price to rise.

Similar reasoning suggests that any price at which the quantity supplied and quantity demanded are unequal cannot be an equilibrium. In Figure A.5, quantity demanded equals quantity supplied at price P_e. The associated output level is Q_e pounds per year. Unless something else in the system changes, this price and output combination continues year after year. It is an equilibrium.

Suppose something else does change. For example, the weather turns bad, ruining a considerable portion of the coffee crop. In Figure A.6, D_c and S_c are reproduced from Figure A.5, and as before, the equilibrium price and output are P_e and Q_e, respectively. Because of the weather change, the supply curve

FIGURE A.5

Equilibrium in the
coffee market

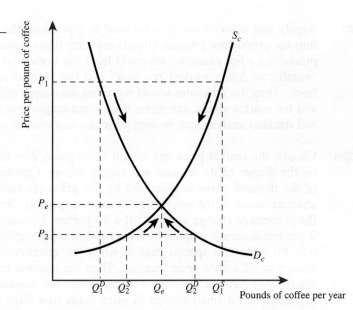

FIGURE A.6

Effect of bad
weather on the
coffee market

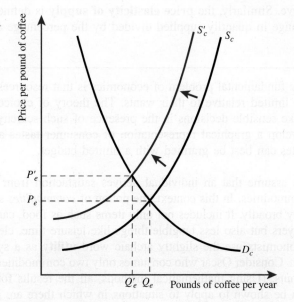

shifts to the left, say, to S_c'. Given the new supply curve, P_e is no longer the
equilibrium price. Rather, equilibrium is at the intersection of D_c and S_c', at
price P_e' and output Q_e'. Note that, as one might expect, the crop disaster
leads to a higher price and smaller output—$P_e' > P_e$ and $Q_e' < Q_e$. More
generally, a change in any variable that affects supply or demand creates a
new equilibrium combination of price and quantity.

Supply and Demand for Inputs

Supply and demand can also be used to investigate the markets for inputs into the production process. (Inputs are sometimes referred to as *factors of production*.) For example, we could label the horizontal axis in Figure A.5 "number of hours worked per year" and the vertical axis "wage rate per hour." Then the schedules would represent the supply and demand for labor, and the market would determine wages and employment. Similarly, supply and demand analysis can be applied to the markets for capital and for land.

Measuring the Shapes of Supply and Demand Curves

Clearly, the market price and output for a given item depend substantially on the shapes of its demand and supply curves. Conventionally, the shape of the demand curve is measured by the **price elasticity of demand:** the absolute value of the percentage change in quantity demanded divided by the percentage change in price.[2] If a 10 percent increase in price leads to a 2 percent decrease in quantity demanded, the price elasticity of demand is 0.2. An important special case is when the quantity demanded does not change at all with a price increase. Then the demand curve is vertical and elasticity is zero. At the other extreme, when the demand curve is horizontal, then even a small change in price leads to a huge change in quantity demanded. By convention, this is referred to as an infinitely elastic demand curve. Similarly, the **price elasticity of supply** is defined as the percentage change in quantity supplied divided by the percentage change in price.

Theory of Choice

The fundamental problem of economics is that resources available to people are limited relative to their wants. The theory of choice shows how people make sensible decisions in the presence of such scarcity. In this section we develop a graphical representation of consumer tastes and show how these tastes can best be gratified with a limited budget.

Tastes

We assume that an individual derives satisfaction from the consumption of commodities. In this context, the notion of *commodities* should be interpreted very broadly. It includes not only items such as food, cars, and compact disk players but also less tangible things like leisure time, clean air, and so forth. Economists use the slightly archaic word **utility** as a synonym for satisfaction. Consider Oscar who consumes only two commodities, marshmallows and donuts. (Using mathematical methods, all the results for the two-good case can be shown to apply to situations in which there are many commodities.) Assume further that for all feasible quantities of marshmallows and donuts, Oscar is never satiated—more consumption of either commodity always produces some increase in his utility. Like the father in the cartoon, economists believe that under most circumstances, this assumption is pretty realistic.

---

[2] The elasticity need not be constant all along the demand curve.

*"It's true that more is not necessarily better, Edward, but it
frequently is."*

• •

In Figure A.7, the horizontal axis measures the number of donuts consumed each day, and the vertical axis shows daily marshmallow consumption. Thus, each point in the quadrant represents some bundle of marshmallows and donuts. For example, point *a* represents a bundle with seven marshmallows and five donuts.

Because Oscar's utility depends only on his consumption of marshmallows and donuts, we can also associate with each point in the quadrant a certain level of utility. For example, if seven marshmallows and five donuts create 100 "utils" of happiness, then point *a* is associated with 100 "utils."

Some commodity bundles create more utility than point *a*, and others less. Consider point *b* in Figure A.7, which has both more marshmallows and donuts than point *a*. Since satiation is ruled out, *b* must yield higher utility than *a*. Bundle *f* has more donuts than *a* and no fewer marshmallows, and is also preferred to *a*. Indeed, any point to the northeast of *a* is preferred to *a*.

Similar reasoning suggests that bundle *a* is preferred to bundle *g*, because *g* has fewer marshmallows and donuts than *a*. Point *h* is also less desirable than *a*, because although it has the same number of marshmallows as *a*, it has fewer donuts. Point *a* is preferred to any point southwest of it.

FIGURE A.7

Ranking alternative
bundles

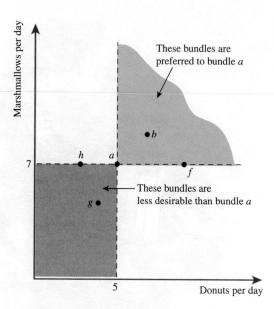

FIGURE A.8

Derivation of an
indifference curve

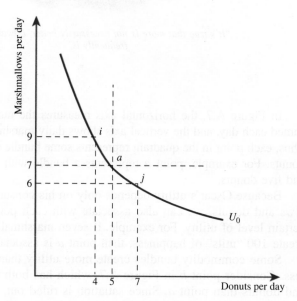

We have identified some bundles that yield more utility than *a* and some
that yield less. Can we find some bundles that produce just the same amount
of utility? Presumably there are such bundles, but we need more information
about the individual to find out which they are. Consider Figure A.8, which
reproduces point *a* from Figure A.7. Imagine that we pose the following
question to Oscar: "You are now consuming seven marshmallows and five
donuts. If I take away one of your donuts, how many marshmallows do I

FIGURE A.9

An indifference curve with a diminishing marginal rate of substitution

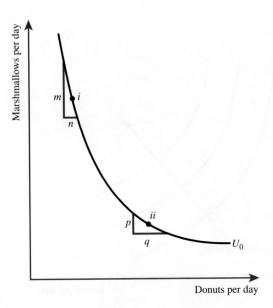

need to give you to make you just as satisfied as you were initially?" Suppose that after thinking a while, Oscar (honestly) answers that he would require two more marshmallows. Then by definition, the bundle consisting of four donuts and nine marshmallows yields the same amount of utility as a. This bundle is denoted i in Figure A.8.

We could find another bundle of equal utility by asking: "Starting again at point a, suppose I take away one marshmallow. How many more donuts must I give you to keep you as well off as you originally were?" Assume the answer is two donuts. Then the bundle with six marshmallows and seven donuts, denoted j in Figure A.8, must also yield the same amount of utility as bundle a.

We could go on like this indefinitely—start at point a, take away various amounts of one commodity, find out the amount of the other commodity required for compensation, and record the results on Figure A.8. The outcome is curve U_0, which shows all points that yield the same amount of utility. U_0 is referred to as an **indifference curve,** because it shows all consumption bundles among which the individual is indifferent.

By definition, the *slope* of a curve is the change in the value of the variable measured on the vertical axis divided by the change in the variable measured on the horizontal—the "rise over the run." The slope of an indifference curve has an important economic interpretation. It shows the rate at which the individual is willing to trade one good for another. For example, in Figure A.9, around point i, the slope of the indifference curve is $-m/n$. But by definition of an indifference curve, n is just the amount of donuts that Oscar is willing to substitute for sacrificing m marshmallows. For this reason, the absolute value of the slope of the indifference curve is referred

FIGURE A.10

An indifference map

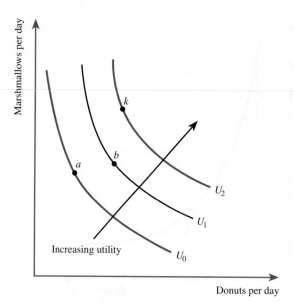

to as the **marginal rate of substitution** of donuts for marshmallows, abbreviated MRS_{dm}. As noted later, *marginal* means *additional* or *incremental*. The indifference curve's slope shows the *marginal* rate of substitution because it indicates the rate at which the individual would be willing to substitute marshmallows for an *additional* donut.

The marginal rate of substitution in Figure A.9 declines as we move down along the indifference curve. For example, around point *ii*, MRS_{dm} is p/q, which is clearly smaller than m/n. This makes intuitive sense. Around point *i*, Oscar has a lot of marshmallows relative to donuts and is therefore willing to give up quite a few marshmallows in return for an additional donut—hence a high MRS_{dm}. On the other hand, around point *ii*, Oscar has a lot of donuts relative to marshmallows, so he is unwilling to sacrifice a lot of marshmallows in return for yet another donut. The decline of MRS_{dm} as we move down along the indifference curve is called a **diminishing marginal rate of substitution.**

Recall that our construction of indifference curve U_0 used bundle *a* as a starting point. But point *a* was chosen arbitrarily, and we could just as well have started at any other point in the quadrant. In Figure A.10, if we start with point *b* and proceed in the same way, we generate indifference curve U_1. Or starting at point *k*, we generate indifference curve U_2. Note that any point on U_2 represents a higher level of utility than any point on U_1, which in turn, is preferred to any point on U_0. If Oscar wants to maximize his utility, he tries to reach the highest indifference curve that he can.

The entire collection of indifference curves is referred to as the **indifference map.** The indifference map tells us everything there is to know about the individual's preferences.

FIGURE A.11

Budget constraint

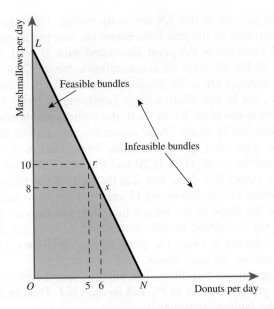

Feasible bundles

Infeasible bundles

Budget Constraint

Basic Setup.   Suppose that marshmallows (M) cost 3 cents apiece, donuts (D) cost 6 cents, and Oscar's weekly income is 60 cents. What options does Oscar have? His purchases must satisfy the equation

$$3 \times M + 6 \times D = 60 \tag{A.1}$$

In words, expenditures on marshmallows ($3 \times M$) plus expenditures on donuts ($6 \times D$) must equal income (60).[3] Thus, for example, if $M = 10$, then to satisfy Equation (A.1), D must equal 5 ($3 \times 10 + 6 \times 5 = 60$). Alternatively, if $M = 8$, then D must equal 6 ($3 \times 8 + 6 \times 6 = 60$).

Let us represent Equation (A.1) graphically. The usual way is to graph a number of points that satisfy the equation. This is straightforward once we recall from basic algebra that (A.1) is just the equation of a straight line. Given two points on the line, the rest of the line is determined by connecting them. In Figure A.11, point r represents 10 marshmallows and 5 donuts, and point s represents 8 marshmallows and 6 donuts. Therefore, the line associated with Equation (A.1) is LN, which passes through these points. By construction, *any* combination of marshmallows and donuts that lies along LN satisfies Equation (A.1). Line LN is known as the **budget constraint** or the **budget line.** Any point on or below LN (the shaded area) is feasible because it involves an expenditure less than or equal to income. Any point above LN is impossible because it involves an expenditure greater than income.

---

[3] If Oscar is a utility maximizer, he will not throw away any of his income.

Two aspects of line *LN* are worth noting. First, the horizontal and vertical intercepts of the line have economic interpretations. By definition, the vertical intercept is the point associated with $D = 0$. At this point, Oscar spends all his 60 cents on marshmallows, buying 20 ($= 60 \div 3$) of them. Hence, distance *OL* is 20. Similarly, at point *N*, Oscar consumes zero marshmallows, but he can afford a binge consisting of 10 ($= 60 \div 6$) donuts. Distance *ON* is therefore 10. In short, the vertical and horizontal intercepts represent bundles in which Oscar consumes only one of the commodities.

The slope also has an economic interpretation. To calculate the slope, recall that the "rise" (*OL*) is 20 and the "run" (*ON*) is 10, so the slope (in absolute value) is 2. Note that 2 is the ratio of the price of donuts (6 cents) to the price of marshmallows (3 cents). This is no accident. The absolute value of the slope of the budget line indicates the rate at which the market permits an individual to substitute marshmallows for donuts. Because the price of donuts is twice the price of marshmallows, Oscar can trade two marshmallows for each donut.

To generalize this discussion, suppose that the price per marshmallow is P_m, the price per donut is P_d, and income is I. Then in analogy to Equation (A.1), the budget constraint is

$$P_m M + P_d D = I \tag{A.2}$$

If M is measured on the vertical axis and D on the horizontal, the vertical intercept is I/P_m and the horizontal intercept is I/P_d. The slope of the budget constraint, in absolute value, is P_d/P_m. A common mistake is to assume that because M is measured on the vertical axis, the absolute value of the slope of the budget constraint is P_m/P_d. To see that this is wrong just divide the rise (I/P_m) by the run (I/P_d): (I/P_m) $\div$ (I/P_d) $= P_d/P_m$. Intuitively, P_d must be in the numerator because its ratio to P_m shows the rate at which the market permits one to trade M for D.

Changes in Prices and Income.　The budget line shows Oscar's consumption opportunities given his current income and the prevailing prices. What if any of these change? Return to the case where $P_m = 3$, $P_d = 6$, and $I = 60$. The associated budget line, $3M + 6D = 60$, is drawn as *LN* in Figure A.12. Now suppose that Oscar's income falls to 30. Substituting into Equation (A.2), the new budget line is $3M + 6D = 30$. To graph this equation, note that the vertical intercept is 10 and the horizontal intercept is 5. Denoting these two points in Figure A.12 as *R* and *S*, respectively, and recalling that two points determine a line, we find that the new budget constraint is *RS*. The slope of *RS* in absolute value is 2, just like that of *LN*. This is because the relative prices of donuts and marshmallows have not changed. A change in income, *ceteris paribus*, induces a parallel shift in the budget line. If income decreases, the constraint shifts in; if income increases, it shifts out.

Return again to the original constraint, $3M + 6D = 60$, which is reproduced in Figure A.13 as *LN*. Suppose that the price of *D* increases to 12, but everything else stays the same. Then, by Equation (A.2), the budget

FIGURE A.12

Effect on the budget
constraint of a
decrease in income

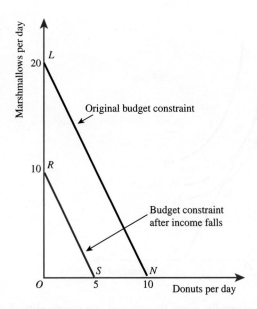

FIGURE A.13

Effect on the budget
constraint of a
change in relative
prices

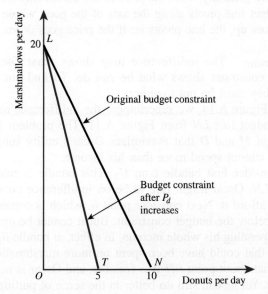

constraint is $3M + 12D = 60$. To graph this new constraint, we begin by
noting that it has a vertical intercept of 20, which is the same as that of LN.
Because the price of M has stayed the same, if Oscar spends all his money
only on M, then he can buy just as much as he did before. The horizontal
intercept, however, is changed. It is now at five donuts ($= 60 \div 12$), a point
denoted T in Figure A.13. The new budget constraint is then LT. The slope
of LT in absolute value is 4 ($= 20 \div 5$), reflecting the fact that the market
now allows each individual to trade four marshmallows per donut.

FIGURE A.14

Utility maximization subject to a budget constraint

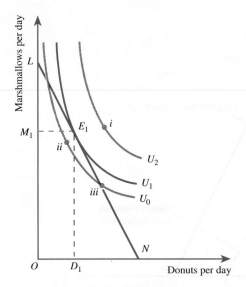

More generally, when the price of one commodity changes, *ceteris paribus,* the budget line pivots along the axis of the good whose price changes. If the price goes up, the line pivots in; if the price goes down, the line pivots out.

Equilibrium.   The indifference map shows what Oscar *wants* to do; the budget constraint shows what he *can* do. To find out what Oscar *actually* does, they must be put together.

In Figure A.14, we superimpose the indifference map from Figure A.10 onto budget line *LN* from Figure A.11. The problem is to find the combination of *M* and *D* that maximizes Oscar's utility subject to the constraint that he cannot spend more than his income.

Consider first bundle *i* on U_2. This bundle is ruled out, because it is above *LN*. Oscar might like to be on indifference curve U_2, but he simply cannot afford it. Next consider point *ii*, which is certainly feasible, because it lies below the budget constraint. But it cannot be optimal, because Oscar is not spending his whole income. In effect, at bundle *ii*, he just throws away money that could have been spent on more marshmallows and/or donuts.

What about point *iii*? It is feasible, and Oscar is not throwing away any income. Yet he can still do better in the sense of putting himself on a higher indifference curve. Consider point E_1, where Oscar consumes D_1 donuts and M_1 marshmallows. Because it lies on *LN*, it is feasible. Moreover, it is more desirable than bundle *iii*, because E_1 lies on U_1, which is above U_0. Indeed, no point on *LN* touches an indifference curve that is higher than U_1. Therefore, the bundle consisting of M_1 and D_1 maximizes Oscar's utility subject to budget constraint *LN*. E_1 is an equilibrium because unless something else changes, Oscar continues to consume M_1 marshmallows and D_1 donuts day after day.

FIGURE A.15

Effect on equilibrium
of a change in
relative prices

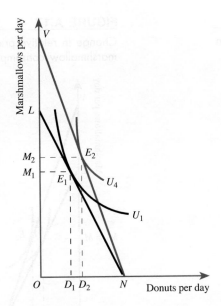

Note that at the equilibrium, indifference curve U_1 just barely touches the budget line. Intuitively, this is because Oscar is trying to achieve the very highest indifference curve he can while still keeping on LN. In more technical language, line LN is *tangent* to curve U_1 at point E_1. This means that at point E_1 the slope of U_1 is equal to the slope of LN.

This observation suggests an equation to characterize the utility-maximizing bundle. Recall that by definition, the slope of the indifference curve (in absolute value) is the marginal rate of substitution of donuts for marshmallows, MRS_{dm}. The slope of the budget line (in absolute value) is P_d/P_m. But we just showed that at equilibrium, the two slopes are equal, or

$$MRS_{dm} = P_d/P_m \qquad\qquad\qquad\qquad (A.3)$$

Equation (A.3) is a necessary condition for utility maximization.[4] That is, if the consumption bundle is not consistent with Equation (A.3), then Oscar could do better by reallocating his income between the two commodities. Intuitively, MRS_{dm} is the rate at which Oscar is willing to trade M for D, while P_d/P_m is the rate at which the market allows Oscar to trade M for D. At equilibrium, these two rates must be equal.

Now suppose that the price of marshmallows falls. Figure A.15 reproduces the equilibrium point E_1 from Figure A.14. As we showed earlier, when a price changes (*ceteris paribus*) the budget line pivots along the axis of the good whose price has changed. Because P_m falls, the budget

---

[4] The equation holds only if some of each commodity is consumed. If the consumption of some commodity is zero, then a related inequality needs to be satisfied.

FIGURE A.16

Change in relative prices with no effect on donut consumption

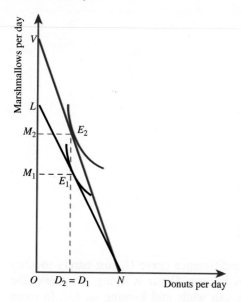

FIGURE A.17

Change in relative prices with no effect on marshmallow consumption

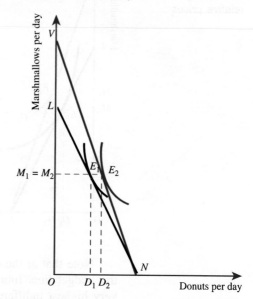

line LN pivots around N to a higher point on the vertical axis. The new budget line is VN. Given that Oscar now faces budget line VN, E_1 is no longer an equilibrium. The fall in P_m creates new opportunities for Oscar, and as a utility-maximizer, he takes advantage of them. Specifically, subject to budget line VN, Oscar maximizes utility at point E_2, where he consumes M_2 marshmallows and D_2 donuts.

At the new equilibrium, more of both D and M are consumed than at the old equilibrium ($D_2 > D_1$ and $M_2 > M_1$). The price decrease in marshmallows allows Oscar to purchase more marshmallows and still have money left to purchase more donuts. While this is common, it need not always be the case. The change depends on the tastes of the particular individual. Suppose that Bert faces exactly the same prices as Oscar and also has the same income. Bert's indifference map and budget constraints are depicted in Figure A.16. Bert's donut consumption is totally unchanged by the decrease in the price of marshmallows. On the other hand, Ernie's preferences, depicted in Figure A.17, are such that a fall in P_m leaves the amount of marshmallows the same, and only the amount of donuts increases. Thus, we require information about the individual's indifference map to predict just how he or she will respond to a change in relative prices.

More generally, a change in prices and/or income leads to a new budget constraint. The individual then *reoptimizes*—finds the point that maximizes

FIGURE A.18

Demand curve for marshmallows derived from an indifference map

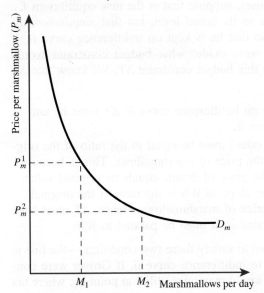

FIGURE A.19

Substitution and income effects of a price change

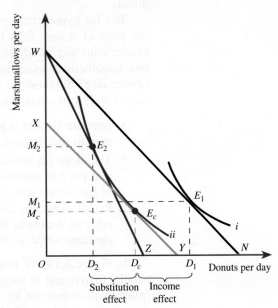

utility subject to the new budget constraint. This usually involves the selection of a new commodity bundle, but without information on the individual's tastes, one cannot know for sure exactly what the new bundle looks like. We do know, however, that as long as the individual is a utility maximizer, the new bundle satisfies the condition that the price ratio equal the marginal rate of substitution.

Derivation of Demand Curves

There is a simple connection between the theory of consumer choice and individual demand curves. Recall from Figure A.15 that at the original price of marshmallows—call it P_m^1—Oscar consumed M_1 marshmallows. When the price fell to P_m^2, Oscar increased his marshmallow consumption to M_2. This pair of points may be plotted as in Figure A.18.

Repeating this experiment for various prices of marshmallows, we find the quantity of marshmallows demanded at each price, holding fixed money income, the price of donuts, and tastes. By definition, this is the demand curve for marshmallows, shown as Dm in Figure A.18. Thus, we can derive the demand curve from the underlying indifference map.

Substitution and Income Effects

Figure A.19 depicts the situation of Grover, who initially faces budget constraint WN, and maximizes utility at point E_1 on indifference curve i, where he consumes D_1 donuts. Suppose now that the price of donuts increases. Grover's budget constraint pivots from *WN* to *WZ*, and at the new equilibrium, point E_2 on indifference curve *ii*, he consumes D_2 donuts.

Just for hypothetical purposes, suppose that at the new equilibrium E_2, the price of donuts falls back to its initial level, but that *simultaneously,* Grover's income is adjusted so that he is kept on indifference curve *ii*. If this hypothetical adjustment were made, what budget constraint would Grover face? Suppose we call this budget constraint *XY*. We know that *XY* must satisfy two conditions:

- Because Grover is kept on indifference curve *ii*, *XY* must be tangent to indifference curve *ii*.
- The slope (in absolute value) must be equal to the ratio of the original price of donuts to the price of marshmallows. This is because of the stipulation that the price of donuts equals its original value. Recall, however, that the slope of *WN* is the ratio of the original price of donuts to the price of marshmallows. Hence, *XY* must have the same slope as *WN*; that is, it must be parallel to *WN*.

In Figure A.19, *XY* is drawn to satisfy these two conditions—the line is parallel to *WN* and is tangent to indifference curve *ii*. If Grover were confronted with constraint *XY*, he would maximize utility at point E_c, where his consumption of donuts is D_c.

Why is this hypothetical budget line of any interest? Because drawing line *XY* helps us break down the effect of the change in the price of donuts into two components, the first from E_1 to E_c and the second from E_c to E_2.

1. The movement from E_1 to E_c is generated by the parallel shift of *WN* down to *XY*. But recall from Figure A.12 that such parallel movements are associated with changes in income, holding relative prices constant. Hence, the movement from E_1 to E_c is essentially induced by a change in income and is called the **income effect** of the price change.

2. The movement from E_c to E_2 is a consequence purely of the change in the relative price of donuts to marshmallows. This movement shows that Grover substitutes marshmallows for donuts when donuts become more expensive. Hence, the movement from E_c to E_2 is called the **substitution effect.** Because the movement from E_c to E_2 involves compensating income (in the sense of changing income to stay on the same indifference curve), the movement from E_c to E_2 is sometimes called the compensated response to a change in price. If we wish to keep utility at the level represented by indifference curve *ii*, we measure the substitution effect by moving along *ii*. If, alternatively, we had wanted to keep utility at the level enjoyed along indifference curve *i*, we

could have measured the substitution effect along indifference curve *i* instead. In any case, the compensated response to a price change shows how the price change affects quantity demanded when income is simultaneously altered so that the level of utility is constant.

Intuitively, when the price of donuts increases two things happen:

■ The increase in price reduces the individual's real income—his or her ability to afford commodities. When income goes down, the quantity purchased generally changes, even without any change in relative prices. This is the income effect.

■ The increase in the price of donuts makes donuts less attractive relative to marshmallows, inducing the substitution effect.

Any change in prices can be broken down into an income effect and a substitution effect.

We could repeat the exercise depicted in Figure A.19 for any change in the price of marshmallows. Suppose that for each price, we find the compensated quantity of donuts demanded and make a plot with price on the vertical axis and donuts on the horizontal. This plot is called the **compensated demand curve** for donuts. The ordinary demand curve discussed at the beginning of this appendix shows how quantity demanded varies with price, holding the level of *money income* fixed. In contrast, the compensated demand shows how quantity demanded varies with price, holding the level of *utility* fixed.

Marginal Analysis	In economics, the word **marginal** usually means *additional* or *incremental*. Suppose, for example, the annual total benefit per citizen of a 50-mile road is \$42, and the annual total benefit of a 51-mile road is \$43.50. Then the marginal benefit of the 51st mile is \$1.50 (\$43.50 − \$42.00). Similarly, if the annual total cost per person of maintaining a 50-mile road is \$38, and the total cost of a 51-mile road is \$40, then the marginal cost of the 51st mile is \$2.

Economists focus a lot of attention on marginal quantities because they usually convey the information required for rational decision making. Suppose that the government is deciding whether to construct the 51st mile. The key question is whether the *marginal* benefit is at least as great as the *marginal* cost. In our example, the marginal cost is \$2 while the marginal benefit is only \$1.50. Does it make sense to spend \$2 to create \$1.50 worth of benefits? The answer is no, and the extra mile should not be built. Note that basing the decision on total benefits and costs would have led to the wrong answer. The total cost per person of the 51-mile road (\$40) is less than the total benefit (\$43.50). Still, it is not sensible to build the 51st mile. An

Table A.1   **Total profit**

Tons of Fertilizer	Wheat	Corn
0	$ 0	$ 0
1	100	325
2	150	385
3	170	415
4	175	435
5	177	441
6	178	444

Table A.2   **Marginal profit**

Tons of Fertilizer	Wheat	Corn
1	$100	$325
2	50	60
3	20	30
4	5	20
5	2	6
6	1	3

activity should be pursued only if its marginal benefit is at least as large as its marginal cost.[5]

Another example of marginal analysis: Farmer McGregor has two fields. The first is planted in wheat and the second in corn. McGregor has seven tons of fertilizer to distribute between the two fields and wants to allocate the fertilizer so that his total profits are as high as possible. The relationship between the amount of fertilizer and *total* profitability for each crop is depicted in Table A.1. For example, if six tons of fertilizer were devoted to wheat and one ton to corn, total profits would be $503 (= $178 + $325).

To find the optimal allocation of fertilizer between the fields, it helps to compute the marginal contribution to profits made by each ton of fertilizer. The first ton in the wheat field increases profits from $0 to $100, so the marginal contribution is $100. The second ton increases profits from $100 to $150, so its marginal contribution is $50. The complete set of computations for both crops is recorded in Table A.2.

Suppose that McGregor puts two tons of fertilizer on the wheat field and five tons on the cornfield. Is he maximizing profits? To answer this question, we must determine whether any other allocation would lead to higher total profits. Suppose that one ton of fertilizer were removed from the cornfield and devoted instead to wheat. Removing the fertilizer from the cornfield lowers profits there by $6. But at the same time, profits from the wheat field increase by $20 (the marginal profit associated with the third ton of fertilizer in the wheat field). Farmer McGregor would therefore be $14 richer on balance. Clearly, it is not sensible for McGregor to put two tons of fertilizer on the wheat field and five tons on the corn, because he can do better (by $14) with three tons devoted to wheat and four to corn.

Is this latter allocation optimal? To answer, note that at this allocation, the marginal profit of fertilizer in each field is equal to $20. When the marginal profitability of fertilizer is the same in each field, there is *no way* that

---

[5] If the marginal cost of an action just equals its marginal benefit, one is indifferent between taking the action and not taking it.

fertilizer can be reallocated between fields to increase total profit. In other words, total profits are maximized when the marginal profit in each field is the same. If you don't believe it, try to find an allocation of the seven tons of fertilizer that leads to a total profit higher than the $605 ($170 + $435) associated with the allocation at which the marginal profits are equal.

In general, if resources are distributed across several activities, maximization of *total* returns requires that *marginal* returns in each activity be equal.[6]

Consumer and Producer Surplus

Our supply and demand model tells us how prices change in response to changes in the underlying economic environment. It is often useful to be able to put a dollar value on how such price changes affect people's welfare. Suppose, for example, that initially the price of apples is 40¢ per apple, but then it falls to 25¢. Clearly, apple consumers are better off because of the change. But by just how much are they better off? *Consumer surplus* is a tool for obtaining a dollar measure.

Consumer Surplus

To begin our discussion of consumer surplus, consider the demand curve for apples, D_a, depicted in Figure A.20. Assume consumers can obtain all the apples they demand at the going market price, 40¢. Then the supply curve for apples, S_a, is a horizontal line at this price. According to the diagram, the associated quantity demanded is 65 tons.

Suppose now that more land is brought into apple production, and the supply curve shifts to S_a'. At the new equilibrium, the price falls to 25¢, and apple consumption increases to 100 tons. How much better off are consumers? Another way of stating this question is, "How much would consumers be willing to pay for the privilege of consuming 100 tons of apples at 25¢ per apple rather than 65 tons of apples at 40¢?"

To provide an answer, begin by recalling that the demand curve shows the *maximum* amount that individuals *would* be willing to pay for each apple they consume. Consider some arbitrary quantity of apples, say, 20 tons. The most people would be willing to pay for the 20th ton is the vertical distance up to the demand curve, 62¢. Initially, consumers in fact had to pay only 40¢ per apple. In a sense then, on their purchase of the 20th ton, consumers enjoyed a surplus of 22¢. The amount by which the sum that individuals would have been *willing* to pay exceeds the sum they *actually* have to pay is called the **consumer surplus.**

Of course, the same exercise could be repeated at any quantity, not just at 20 tons. When the price is 40¢ per apple, the consumer surplus at each output level equals the distance between the demand curve and the horizontal line at 40¢. Summing the surpluses for each apple purchased, we find that

---

[6] More precisely, this result requires that the marginal returns be diminishing, as they are in Table A.2. In most applications, this is a reasonable assumption.

FIGURE A.20

Measuring consumer
surplus

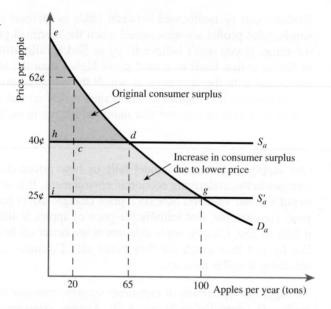

the total consumer surplus when the price is 40¢ is the area *ehd*. More generally, *consumer surplus is measured by the area under the demand curve
and above a horizontal line at the market price.*

When the price falls to 25¢, consumer surplus is still the area under the
demand curve and above a horizontal line at the going price; because the price
is now 25¢, the relevant area is *eig*. Consumer surplus therefore increases by
the difference between areas *eig* and *ehd*, area *higd*. Thus, the area behind the
demand curve between the two prices measures the value to consumers of
being able to purchase apples at the lower price.

To implement this procedure for a real-world problem, an investigator
needs to know the shape of the demand curve. Generally, this can be
obtained by using one or more of the tools of positive analysis discussed in
Chapter 2. Hence, consumer surplus is a very practical tool for measuring
the changes in welfare induced by changes in the economic environment.

A caveat that may be important under some circumstances: The area
under an ordinary demand curve provides only an approximation to the true
value of the change in consumer welfare. This is because as price changes,
so do people's real incomes, and this may change the value that they place
on additions to their income (the marginal utility of income). However,
Willig [1976] has shown that measuring consumer surplus by the area under
the ordinary demand curve is likely to be a pretty good approximation in
most cases, and this approach is used widely in applied work.[7]

---

[7] Alternatively, one can compute welfare changes using areas under a *compensated demand curve*, which
is defined earlier in this appendix.

FIGURE A.21

Measuring producer surplus

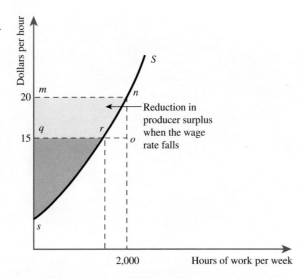

Producer Surplus

In analogy to consumer surplus, we can define *producer surplus* as the amount of income individuals receive in excess of what they would require to supply a given number of units of a factor. To measure producer surplus, consider Jacob's labor supply curve (*S*), which is represented in Figure A.21. Each point on the labor supply curve shows the wage rate required to coax Jacob into supplying the associated number of hours of work. Hence, the distance between any point on the labor supply curve and the wage rate is the difference between the minimum payment that Jacob needs to receive for that hour of work and the amount he actually receives (the wage rate). Thus, *the area above the supply curve and below the wage rate is the producer surplus.*

To strengthen your understanding of producer surplus, imagine that initially Jacob works 2,000 hours per year at a wage of $20 per hour, but then his wage falls to $15 per hour. How much worse off is he? One possible answer is: "He was working 2,000 hours and is now earning $5 less per hour, so he is worse off by $10,000." This corresponds to area *mqon* in Figure A.21. However, producer surplus analysis tells us that this answer is incorrect. Before the wage cut, Jacob's surplus is area *msn*. When the wage rate falls to $15, his surplus falls to *qsr*. Hence, Jacob's loss from the wage cut is area *mqrn*. This is less than the naive answer of *mqon*. Intuitively, the naive answer overstates the loss in welfare because it ignores the fact that when a person's wage falls, he can substitute leisure for consumption. While the increased consumption of leisure certainly does not fully compensate for the wage decrease, it does have some value.

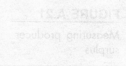

Glossary

Ability to Pay Capacity to pay a tax, which may be measured by income, consumption, or wealth.

Absolute Tax Incidence The effect of a tax on the distribution of income when there is no change in either other taxes or government spending.

Accelerated Depreciation Allowing firms to take depreciation allowances faster than true economic depreciation.

Accessions Tax A tax levied on an individual's total lifetime acquisitions from inheritances and gifts.

Ad Valorem Tax A tax computed as a percentage of the purchase value.

Additive Social Welfare Function An equation defining social welfare as the sum of individuals' utilities.

Adjusted Gross Income (AGI) Total income from all taxable sources less certain expenses incurred in earning that income.

Adverse Selection The situation that occurs when the people who are most likely to receive benefits from a certain type of insurance are the ones who are most likely to purchase it.

Agenda Manipulation The process of organizing the order in which votes are taken to assure a favorable outcome.

Aid to Families with Dependent Children (AFDC) Program of cash transfers from 1935 to 1996. Anyone whose income was below a particular level and met certain other conditions was entitled to a cash benefit indefinitely.

Alternative Minimum Tax (AMT) The tax liability calculated by an alternative set of rules designed to force individuals with high levels of preference income to incur at least some tax liability.

Annuity A sum of money payable yearly or at some other regular interval.

Arm's Length System A method of calculating taxes for multinational corporations by treating transactions between domestic and foreign operations as if they were separate enterprises.

Arrow's Impossibility Theorem It is impossible to translate individual preferences into collective preferences without violating at least one of a specified list of ethically reasonable conditions.

Assessed Value The value a jurisdiction assigns to a property for tax purposes.

Assessment Ratio The ratio of a property's assessed value to its market value.

Asymmetric Information A situation in which one side of an economic relationship has better information than the other.

Average Indexed Monthly Earnings (AIME) The average wages in covered employment over the length of an individual's working life. The AIME is used in the computation of an individual's Social Security benefit.

Average Tax Rate Ratio of taxes paid to income.

Benefit-Cost Ratio The ratio of the present value of a stream of benefits to the present value of a stream of costs for a project.

Benefits-Received Principle Consumers of a publicly provided service should be the ones who pay for it.

Bequest Effect   Individuals save more to counteract the redistribution of income from children to parents implicit in the Social Security system. The increased saving is used to finance a larger bequest to children.

Bracket Creep   When an increase in an individual's nominal income pushes her into a higher tax bracket despite the fact that her real income is unchanged. See also **tax indexing.**

Budget Constraint   The representation of the bundles among which a consumer may choose, given his income and the prices he faces.

Budget Enforcement Act (BEA)   Legislation passed in 1990 that sets annual spending and revenue targets for the federal budget.

Budget Line   See **budget constraint.**

Capital Gain (Loss)   An increase (decrease) in the value of an asset.

Capital Intensive   An industry in which the ratio of capital to labor inputs is relatively high.

Capitalization   The process by which a stream of tax liabilities becomes incorporated into the price of an asset.

Capitation-Based Reimbursement   Health care providers receive annual payments for each patient in their care, regardless of the services actually used by that patient.

Capitation Fee   A system under which medical care is provided for a particular individual or set of individuals for a fixed monthly fee.

Cash Flow   The difference between revenues and expenditures.

Catastrophic Cap   An upper limit to the amount of an individual's out-of-pocket costs for an illness.

Categorical Grants   Grants for which the donor specifies how the funds can be used.

Centralization Ratio   The proportion of total direct government expenditures made by the central government.

Certainty Equivalent   The value of an uncertain project measured in terms of how much certain income an individual would be willing to give up for the set of uncertain outcomes generated by the project.

Ceteris Paribus   Other things being the same.

Circuit Breakers   Transfers to individuals based on the excess of residential property tax payments over some specified portion of income.

Clientele Effect   Firms structure their financial policies to meet different clienteles' needs. Those with low dividend payments attract shareholders with high marginal tax rates, and vice versa.

Club   A voluntary association of people who band together to finance and share some kind of benefit.

Coase Theorem   Provided that transactions costs are negligible, an efficient solution to an externality problem is achieved as long as someone is assigned property rights, independent of who is assigned those rights.

Coinsurance Rate   Proportion of the bill which the insured individual pays.

Commodity Egalitarianism   The idea that some commodities ought to be made available to everybody.

Compensated Demand Curve   A demand curve that shows how quantity demanded varies with price, holding utility constant.

Complements   Two goods are complements if an increase in the price of one good leads to decreased consumption of the other good.

Conditional Grants   See **categorical grants.**

Consumer Surplus   The amount by which consumers' willingness to pay for a commodity exceeds the sum they actually have to pay.

Consumption-Type VAT   Capital investments are subtracted from sales in the computation of the value added.

Contract Curve   The locus of all Pareto-efficient points.

Corlett-Hague Rule   Efficient taxation requires taxing commodities that are complementary to leisure at relatively high rates.

Corporation   A state-chartered form of business organization, usually with limited liability for shareholders (owners) and an independent legal status.

Cost-Based Reimbursements   A system under which health care providers report their costs to the government and receive payment in that amount.

Cost-Benefit Analysis   A set of procedures based on welfare economics for guiding public expenditure decisions.

Cost-Effectiveness Analysis   Comparing the costs of the various alternatives that attain similar benefits to determine which one is the cheapest.

Cost-Plus Contract   A contract specifying that a firm is paid a certain fee plus all costs it incurs in completing a project.

Credit Budget   An annual statement that estimates the volume of new direct loans and loan guarantees made by the federal government for the fiscal year.

Crowding Out Hypothesis   Government borrowing decreases private investment by raising the market interest rate.

Cycling   When paired majority voting on more than two possibilities goes on indefinitely without a conclusion ever being reached.

Debt   The total amount owed at a given point in time; the sum of all past deficits.

Decedent   A deceased person.

Deductible   The expenses an individual must pay out of pocket before an insurance policy makes any contribution.

Deductions   Certain expenses that may be subtracted from adjusted gross income in the computation of taxable income.

Deficit   The excess of expenditures over revenues during a period of time.

Demand Curve   A graph of the demand schedule.

Demand Schedule   The relation between the price of a good and the quantity demanded, *ceteris paribus.*

Diagnostic Related Groups (DRGs)   Categories of illnesses and treatment types defined by the Medicare system; they determine how much a hospital will be paid for an individual's treatment under a prospective reimbursement system.

Differential Commodity Tax   See **excise tax.**

Differential Tax Incidence   The effect on the income distribution of a change in taxes, with government expenditures held constant.

Diminishing Marginal Rate of Substitution   The marginal rate of substitution falls as we move down along an indifference curve.

Direct Loans   Loans from the federal government made directly to individuals, businesses, nonprofit institutions, and local governments.

Director's Law   Government expenditures tend to benefit the middle class, while taxes are borne also by the rich and the poor.

Discount Factor   The number by which an amount of future income must be divided to compute its present value. If the interest rate is r and the income is receivable T periods in the future, the discount factor is $(1 + r)^T$.

Discount Rate   The rate of interest used to compute present value.

District Power Equalization (DPE) Grant   Grant to local government to raise local revenue to a level that would be achieved if the local property tax base were at a certain hypothetical level.

Dividend Relief Approach   Relieving double taxation by allowing the corporation to deduct dividends paid to the stockholders.

Double-Dividend Hypothesis   If the proceeds from a Pigouvian tax are used to reduce income tax rates, then efficiency increases in both markets. The logic may not hold because the Pigouvian tax exacerbates pre-existing distortions in the labor market.

Double-Peaked Preferences   If, as a voter moves away from his most preferred outcome, utility goes down, but then goes back up again.

Double Taxation   Taxing corporate income first at the corporate level, and again when it is distributed to shareholders.

Earned Income Tax Credit (EITC)   A tax credit for low-income individuals.

Econometrics   The statistical tools for analyzing economic data.

Economic Depreciation   The extent to which an asset decreases in value during a period of time.

Economic Incidence   The change in the distribution of real income induced by a tax.

Economic Profit   The return to owners of a firm above the opportunity costs of all the factors used in production. Also called supranormal or excess profit.

Edgeworth Box   A device used to depict the distribution of goods in a two good–two person world.

Education Savings Account   A tax-preferred savings vehicle. Contributions are not tax deductible, but funds accumulate tax free. Funds may be withdrawn to pay for higher education expenses of a child.

Efficient   See **Pareto efficient.**

Effluent Fee   A fee paid for permission to produce some amount of pollution.

Elasticity of Substitution   A measure of the ease with which one factor of production can be substituted for another.

Empirical Work   Analysis based on observation and experience as opposed to theory.

Endowment Point   The consumption bundle that is available if there are no exchanges with the market.

Entitlement Programs   Programs whose expenditures are determined by the number of people who qualify, rather than preset budget allocations.

Equilibrium   A situation that tends to be maintained unless there is an underlying change in the system.

Equivalent Variation   A change in income that has the same effect on utility as a change in the price of a commodity.

Excess Burden   A loss of welfare above and beyond taxes collected. Also called welfare cost or dead-weight loss.

Excise Tax   A tax levied on the purchase of a particular commodity.

Exclusionary Zoning Laws   Statutes that prohibit certain uses of land.

Exemption   When calculating taxable income, an amount per family member that can be subtracted from adjusted gross income.

Expenditure Incidence   The impact of government expenditures on the distribution of real income.

Expensing   Deducting the entire value of an asset in the computation of taxable income.

Experience Rated   A method of determining what unemployment insurance tax rate a firm should pay based on the firm's past layoff experience.

External Debt   The amount a government owes to foreigners.

Externality   An activity of one entity affects the welfare of another entity in a way that is outside the market.

Federal System   Consists of different levels of government that provide public goods and services and have some scope for making decisions.

Fee-For Service   See **cost-based reimbursements.**

Fiscal Federalism   The field that examines the roles of different levels of government and the ways in which they interact with each other.

Fixed Price Contract   A contract stipulating that the firm will complete a project in return for a price independent of its costs.

Flat Income Tax   A tax schedule for which the marginal tax rate is constant throughout the entire range of incomes.

Flow Variable   A variable that is measured over a period of time. See also **stock variable.**

Flypaper Effect   A dollar received by the community in the form of a grant to its government results in greater public spending than a dollar increase in community income.

Foreign Subsidiary   A company incorporated abroad but owned by a US corporation.

Foundation Aid   Grant designed to assure a minimum level of expenditure.

401(k) Plan   A savings plan under which an employee can earmark a portion of her salary each year, with no income tax liability incurred on that portion.

Free Rider   The incentive to let other people pay for a public good while you enjoy the benefits.

Full Integration   See **partnership method.**

Full Loss Offset   Allowing individuals to deduct from taxable income all losses on capital assets.

Fully Funded   A pension system in which an individual's benefits are paid out of deposits which have been made during his or her working life, plus accumulated interest.

Functional Distribution of Income   The way income is distributed among people when they are classified according to the inputs they supply to the production process (for example, landlords, capitalists, laborers).

Functional Finance   Using fiscal policy to keep aggregate demand at the desired level, regardless of the impact on deficits.

General Agreement on Tariffs and Trade (GATT)   A multinational pact that regulates international trade practices. GATT allows a country to grant an export rebate on certain taxes.

General Equilibrium Analysis   The study of how various markets are interrelated.

General Sales Tax   A tax levied at the same rate on the purchase of all commodities.

Generational Accounting   Method for measuring the state of government fiscal policy that takes into account the present value of all taxes and benefits received by members of each generation.

Global System   A system under which an individual is taxed on income whether it is earned in the home country or abroad.

Gross Estate   All property owned by the decedent at the time of death.

Gross Income–Type VAT   No deductions are allowed for capital investments when calculating value added.

Gross Replacement Rate   The proportion of pretax earnings replaced by unemployment insurance.

Haig-Simons (H-S) Definition of Income   Money value of the net increase in an individual's power to consume during a period.

Health Maintenance Organization (HMO)   Offers comprehensive health care from an established panel of providers, often using capitation-based reimbursement.

Hicks-Kaldor Criterion   A project should be undertaken if it has a positive net present value, regardless of the distributional consequences.

Horizontal Equity   People in equal positions should be treated equally.

Horizontal Summation   The process of creating a market demand curve by summing the quantities demanded by each individual at every price.

Hospital Insurance (HI)   A provision of Medicare that covers specified amounts of inpatient medical care and care in a nursing facility.

Impure Public Good   A good that is rival to some extent. See **public good.**

Imputed Rent   The net monetary value of the services a homeowner receives from a dwelling.

Incentive Contract   A contract specifying that the contracting firm receives a fixed fee plus some fraction of the costs of the project.

Income Effect   The effect of a price change on the quantity demanded due exclusively to the fact that the consumer's real income has changed.

Income Splitting   Using the arithmetic average of family income to determine each family member's taxable income, regardless of whose income it is.

Independence of Irrelevant Alternatives   Society's ranking of two different projects depends only on individuals' rankings of the two projects, not on how individuals rank the two projects relative to other alternatives.

Indifference Curve   The locus of consumption bundles that yields the same total utility.

Indifference Map   The collection of all indifference curves.

Individual Retirement Account (IRA)   For qualified individuals, a savings account in which the contributions are tax deductible and the interest accrues tax free, provided the funds are held until retirement. On withdrawal, both contributions and accrued interest are subject to tax.

Inferior Good   A good whose demand decreases as income increases.

Inheritance Tax   Tax levied on an individual receiving an inheritance.

In-Kind Transfers   Payments from the government to individuals in the form of commodities or services rather than cash.

Insurance Trust   A trust that is the legal owner of a life insurance policy. It allows the beneficiaries of the policy to avoid the estate tax.

***Inter Vivos* Transfers**   Transfers of wealth between living people.

Internal Debt   The amount that a government owes to its own citizens.

Internal Rate of Return   The discount rate that would make a project's net present value zero.

Intertemporal Budget Constraint   The schedule showing all feasible consumption levels across time.

Inverse Elasticity Rule   For goods that are unrelated in consumption, efficiency requires that tax rates be inversely proportional to elasticities.

Investment Tax Credit (ITC)   A reduction in tax liability equal to some portion of the purchase price of an asset. The Tax Reform Act of 1986 eliminated ITCs in the United States.

Invoice Method   Each firm is liable for taxes on total sales but can claim the taxes already paid by suppliers as a credit against this liability, provided this tax payment is verified by invoices from suppliers.

Iron Triangle   The cooperation of three groups—the legislators who authorize a program, the bureaucrats who administer it, and the special-interest groups that benefit from it—to obtain mutually beneficial outcomes.

Itemized Deduction   A specific type of expenditure that can be subtracted from adjusted gross income in the computation of taxable income.

Kennedy-Kassenbaum Act   1996 legislation designed to help people who change jobs hold onto their health insurance.

Labor Intensive   An industry in which the ratio of capital to labor inputs is relatively low.

Laffer Curve   A graph of the tax rate–tax revenue relationship.

Life-Cycle Model   Individuals' consumption and saving behavior during a given year is the result of a planning process that considers their lifetime economic circumstances.

Lindahl Prices   The tax share an individual must pay per unit of public good.

Linear Income Tax Schedule   See **flat income tax.**

Local Public Good   A public good that benefits only the members of a particular community.

Lock-In Effect   The disincentive to change portfolios that arises because an individual incurs a tax on realized capital gains.

Logrolling   The trading of votes to obtain passage of a package of legislative proposals.

Lump Sum Tax   A tax whose value is independent of the individual's behavior.

Majority Voting Rule   One more than half of the voters must favor a measure for it to be approved.

Managed Care   Any of a variety of health care arrangements in which the patient faces little or no cost sharing and costs are kept down through supply-side incentives and constraints.

Marginal   Incremental, additional.

Marginal Cost   The incremental cost of producing one more unit of output.

Marginal Rate of Substitution   The rate at which an individual is willing to trade one good for another; it is the slope of an indifference curve.

Marginal Rate of Transformation   The rate at which the economy can transform one good into another good; it is the slope of the production possibilities frontier.

Marginal Tax Rate   The proportion of the last dollar of income taxed by the government.

Marriage Neutral   Individuals' tax liabilities are independent of their marital status.

Maximin Criterion   Social welfare depends on the utility of the individual who has the minimum utility in the society.

Means-Tested   A spending program whose benefits flow only to those whose financial resources fall below a certain level.

Mechanistic View of Government   Government is a creation of individuals to better achieve their individual goals.

Median Voter   The voter whose preferences lie in the middle of the set of all voters' preferences; half the voters want more of the item selected and half want less.

Median Voter Theorem   As long as all preferences are single-peaked and several other conditions are satisfied, the outcome of majority voting reflects the preferences of the median voter.

Medicare Part C (Medicare+Choice)   Medicare program that allows eligible individuals to enroll in coordinated care plans, such as Health Maintenance Organizations.

Merit Good   A commodity that ought to be provided even if people do not demand it.

Monopoly   A market with only one seller of a good.

Moral Hazard   When an individual's behavior is affected by the fact that he is insured.

Multiple Regression Analysis   An econometric technique for estimating the parameters of an equation involving a dependent variable and more than one explanatory variable.

Natural Monopoly   A situation in which factors inherent to the production process lead to a single firm supplying the entire industry's output.

Neoclassical Model   A model in which the cost of capital is the primary determinant of the amount of capital investment.

Net Income–Type VAT   The tax base for the VAT is based on net income so that depreciation is excluded from the base.

Net Replacement Rate   The proportion of after-tax income replaced by unemployment insurance.

Net Wage   The wage after taxes.

Neutral Taxation   Taxing each good at the same rate.

Nominal Amounts   Amounts of money that are valued according to the price levels that exist in the year that the amount is received.

Nominal Income   Income measured in terms of current prices.

Nominal Interest Rate   The interest rate observed in the market.

Noncategorical Welfare Program   A program in which an individual's benefit depends only on income, not on whether he or she has a particular personal characteristic (such as being a single parent).

Normal Good   A good whose demand increases as income increases.

Normative Economics   The study of whether or not the economy produces socially desirable results.

Off-Budget Deficit   The deficit resulting from off-budget expenditures and revenues.

Off-Budget Federal Agencies   Federally owned and controlled agencies whose fiscal activities are excluded by law from budget totals.

On-Budget Deficit   The deficit resulting from on-budget expenditures and revenues.

Organic View of Government   The political philosophy that views society as a natural organism with the government as its heart.

Original Position   An imaginary situation in which people have no knowledge of what their economic status in society will be.

Overlapping Generations Model   A model that takes into account the fact that several different generations may coexist simultaneously.

Parameters   In econometrics, the coefficients of the explanatory variables that define the relationship between a change in an explanatory variable and a change in the dependent variable.

Pareto Efficient   An allocation of resources such that no person can be made better off without making another person worse off.

Pareto Improvement   A reallocation of resources that makes at least one person better off without making anyone else worse off.

Partial Equilibrium Models   Models that study only one market and ignore possible spillover effects in other markets.

Partial Factor Tax   Tax levied on an input in only some of its uses.

Partnership Method   Each stockholder incurs a tax liability on her share of the earnings of a corporation, whether or not the earnings are distributed.

Pay-As-You-Go   A Social Security system under which benefits paid to current retirees come from payments made by current workers.

Peak   A point on the graph of an individual's preferences at which all the neighboring points have lower utility.

Pecuniary Externality   Effects on welfare that are transmitted via the price system.

Perfect Price Discrimination   When a producer charges each person the maximum he is willing to pay for the good.

Personal Net Worth Tax   A tax based on the difference between the market value of all the taxpayer's assets and liabilities.

Pigouvian Tax   A tax levied on each unit of a polluter's output in an amount equal to the marginal damage that it inflicts at the efficient level of pollution.

Political Economy   The field that applies economic principles to the analysis of political decision making.

Positive Economics   The study of how the economy actually functions (as opposed to how it ought to function).

Poverty Gap   The amount of money that would be required to raise the incomes of all poor households to the poverty line, assuming that the transfers would induce no changes in behavior.

Poverty Line   A fixed level of real income considered enough to provide a minimally adequate standard of living.

Present Value   The value today of a given amount of money to be paid or received in the future.

Present Value Criteria   Rules for evaluating projects stating that (1) only projects with positive net present value should be carried out; and (2) of two mutually exclusive projects, the preferred project is the one with the higher net present value.

Price Elasticity of Demand   The absolute value of the percentage change in quantity demanded divided by the percentage change in price.

Price Elasticity of Supply   The absolute value of the percentage change in quantity supplied divided by the percentage change in price.

Price Taker   An agent unable to affect the price of a good.

Primary Insurance Amount (PIA)   The basic Social Security benefit payable to a worker who retires at age 65 or who becomes disabled.

Principal-Agent Problem   When one person (the principal) wants another person (the agent) to perform a task, the principal has to design the agent's incentives so that the principal's expected gain is maximized.

Private Good   A commodity that is rival in consumption.

Privatization   The process of changing ownership or control of an enterprise from the public to the private sector.

Production Possibilities Curve   A graph that shows the maximum quantity of one output that can be produced, given the amount of the other output.

Production Possibilities Frontier   The set of all the feasible combinations of goods that can be produced with a given quantity of efficiently employed inputs.

Progressive   A tax system under which an individual's average tax rate increases with income.

Proportional   A tax system under which an individual's average tax rate is the same at each level of income.

Public Economics   See **public finance.**

Public Finance   The field of economics that analyzes government taxation and spending policies.

Public Good   A good that is not rival in consumption; the fact that one person benefits from this good does not prevent another person from doing the same simultaneously.

Public Sector Economics   See **public finance.**

Pure Public Good   See **public good.**

Ramsey Rule   To minimize total excess burden, tax rates should be set so that the tax-induced percentage reduction in the quantity demanded of each commodity is the same.

Random Error   The term of a regression equation representing the unexplained difference between the dependent variable and its value as predicted by the model.

Rate Schedule   A list of the tax liabilities associated with each level of taxable income.

Real Amounts   Amounts of money adjusted for changes in the general price level.

Real Income   A measure of income taking into account changes in the general price level.

Real Interest Rate   The nominal interest rate corrected for changes in the level of prices by subtracting the expected inflation rate.

Realized Capital Gain   A capital gain resulting from the sale of an asset.

Regression Coefficient   See **parameters.**

Regression Line   The line that provides the best fit through a scatter of points.

Regressive   A tax system under which an individual's average tax rate decreases with income.

Regulatory Budget   An annual statement of the costs imposed on the economy by government regulations. (Currently, there is no such budget.)

Rent-Seeking   Using the government to obtain higher than normal returns ("rents").

Repatriate   To return the earnings of a subsidiary to its parent company.

Retirement Effect   Social Security may induce an individual to retire earlier, which means that, *ceteris paribus,* she has to save more to finance a longer retirement period.

Revenue Sharing   A grant from the federal government to a state or locality that places no restrictions on the use of funds.

Right of Survivorship   For jointly owned property, on the death of one owner, the property is automatically passed on to the other owner.

Roth IRA   A tax-preferred savings vehicle. Contributions are not tax deductible, but funds accumulate tax free.

Rule Definition of Horizontal Equity   The rules that govern the selection of taxes are more important for judging fairness than the outcomes themselves.

Selective Sales Tax   See **excise tax.**

Self-Employed Retirement Plan   A savings plan that allows self-employed individuals to exclude some percentage of their net business income from taxation if the money is deposited into a qualified account.

Shadow Price   The underlying social cost of an input.

Single-Peaked Preferences   Utility consistently falls as a voter moves away from his most preferred outcome.

Size Distribution of Income   The way that total income is distributed across income classes.

Social Insurance   Government programs that allow individuals to smooth their consumption in the presence of uncertainty.

Social Rate of Discount   The rate at which society is willing to trade off present consumption for future consumption.

Social Security Trust Fund   A fund in which Social Security payroll taxes are accumulated for the purpose of paying out benefits in the future.

Social Security Wealth   The present value of expected future Social Security benefits.

Social Welfare Function   A function reflecting society's views on how the utilities of its members affect the well-being of society as a whole.

Standard Deduction   Subtraction of a fixed amount from adjusted gross income that does not require documentation.

Standard Error   A statistical measure of how much an estimated parameter might vary from its true value.

Statistically Significant   When the standard error of a regression coefficient is low in relation to the size of the estimated parameter.

Statutory Incidence   Indicates who is legally responsible for a tax.

Stock Variable   Variable that is measured as of a given point in time. See also **flow variable.**

Subsidiary   A company owned by one corporation but chartered separately from the parent corporation.

Substitutes   Two goods are substitutes if an increase in the price of one good leads to increased consumption of the other good.

Substitution Effect   The tendency of an individual to consume more of one good and less of another because of a change in the two goods' relative prices.

Supplementary Medical Insurance (SMI)   The portion of Medicare that pays for physicians, supplies ordered by physicians, and medical services rendered outside a hospital.

Supplementary Security Income (SSI)   A welfare program that provides a minimum income guarantee for the aged and disabled.

Supply Schedule   The relation between market price of a good and the quantity that producers are willing to supply, *ceteris paribus.*

Surplus   The excess of revenues over spending.

Tax Arbitrage   Producing a risk-free profit by exploiting inconsistencies in the tax code.

Tax Avoidance   Altering behavior in such a way as to reduce your legal tax liability.

Tax Credit   A subtraction from tax liability (as opposed to a subtraction from taxable income).

Tax Effort   The ratio of tax collections to tax capacity.

Tax Evasion   Not paying taxes legally due.

Tax Expenditure   A loss of tax revenue because some item is excluded from the tax base.

Tax Indexing   Automatically adjusting the tax schedule to compensate for inflation so that an individual's real tax burden is independent of inflation.

Tax Life   The number of years an asset can be depreciated.

Tax Reform Act of 1986 (TRA86)   Tax legislation that eliminated a number of itemized deductions and other tax preferences, and lowered marginal tax rates for many taxpayers.

Tax Shifting   The difference between statutory incidence and economic incidence.

Tax Wedge   The tax-induced difference between the price paid by consumers and the price received by producers.

Taxable Estate   The gross estate less deductions for costs of settling the estate, outstanding debts of the estate, and charitable contributions.

Taxable Income   The amount of income subject to tax.

Taxpayer Relief Act of 1997   Tax legislation that introduced substantial preferences for realized capital gains, several new forms of tax-preferred savings accounts, and tax credits for certain educational expenditures, among other items.

Temporary Assistance for Needy Families (TANF)   Welfare program passed in 1996 under which payments to recipients are available only on a temporary and provisional basis.

Territorial System   A system under which an individual earning income in a foreign country owes taxes only to the host government.

Theory of the Second Best   In the presence of existing distortions, policies that in isolation would increase efficiency can decrease it, and vice versa.

Third-Party Payment   Payment for services by someone other than the provider or the consumer.

Time Endowment   The maximum number of hours per year an individual can work.

Time Inconsistency of Optimal Policy   A situation in which the government cannot implement an optimal tax policy because the stated policy is inconsistent with the government's incentives over time, and taxpayers realize this fact.

Transfer Price   The price that one subsidiary charges another for some input.

Transitional Equity   Fairness in changing tax regimes.

Turnover Tax   A tax whose base is the total value of sales at each level of production.

Underground Economy   Those economic activities that are either illegal, or legal but hidden from tax authorities.

Unearned Income   Income, such as dividends and interest, that is not directly gained through supplying labor.

Unified Budget   The document which itemizes all the federal government's expenditures and revenues.

Unified Transfer Tax   A tax in which amounts transferred as gifts and bequests are jointly taken into account.

Unit Tax   A tax levied as a fixed amount per unit of commodity purchased.

Unrealized Capital Gain   A capital gain on an asset not yet sold.

Use Tax   A sales tax that residents of a given state must pay to that state even if the commodity was purchased in another state.

User Cost of Capital   The opportunity cost to a firm of owning a piece of capital.

User Fee   A price paid by users of a government-provided good or service.

Utilitarian Social Welfare Function   An equation stating that social welfare is some function of individuals' utilities.

Utility   The amount of satisfaction a person derives from consuming a particular bundle of commodities.

Utility Definition of Horizontal Equity   A method of classifying people of "equal positions" in terms of their utility levels.

Utility Possibilities Curve   A graph showing the maximum amount of one person's utility given each level of utility attained by the other person.

Value Added   The difference between sales and the cost of purchased material inputs.

Value-Added Tax (VAT)   A percentage tax on value added at each stage of production.

Vertical Equity   Distributing tax burdens fairly across people with different abilities to pay.

Vertical Summation   The process of creating an aggregate demand curve for a public good by adding the prices each individual is willing to pay for a given quantity of the good.

Voting Paradox   With majority voting, community preferences can be inconsistent even though each individual's preferences are consistent.

Vouchers   Grants earmarked for particular commodities, such as medical care or education, given to individuals.

Wagner's Law   Government expenditures rise faster than incomes.

Wealth Substitution Effect   Individuals save less in anticipation of the fact that they will receive Social Security benefits after retirement, *ceteris paribus*.

Welfare Economics   The branch of economic theory concerned with the social desirability of alternative economic states.

Workfare   Able-bodied individuals who qualify for income support receive it only if they agree to participate in a work-related activity.

References

Aaron, Henry J. *Shelters and Subsidies.* Washington, DC: Brookings Institution, 1972.

Aaron, Henry J. "Six Welfare Questions Still Searching for Answers." *Brookings Review* 3, no. 1 (Fall 1984), pp. 12–17.

Aaron, Henry J. *Can America Afford to Grow Old? Financing Social Security.* Washington, DC: . . Brookings Institution, 1989.

Aaron, Henry J. "The Myths of Social Security Crisis: Behind the Privatization Push." *NTA Forum* 26 (Summer 1996), pp. 1, 6, 7.

Alesina, Alberto, and Eliana La Ferrara. "Preferences for Redistribution in the Land of Opportunities." Working Paper No. 8267. Cambridge, MA: National Bureau of Economic Research, May 2001.

Allen, Mike. "Cardinal Sees Marriage Harm in Partners Bill." *New York Times* (May 25, 1998), p. A1.

Altig, David; Alan J Auerbach; Laurence J Kotlikoff; Kent A Smetters; and Jan Walliser. "Simulating Fundamental Tax Reform in the United States." *American Economic Review* 91 (June 2001), pp. 574–95.

"America's Poor Showing." *Newsweek* (October 18, 1993), p. 44.

Andrews, William D. "A Consumption-Type or Cash Flow Personal Income Tax." *Harvard Law Review* 87 (April 1974), pp. 1113–188.

Andrews, William D. "The Achilles' Heel of the Comprehensive Income Tax." In *New Directions in Federal Tax Policy for the 1980s,* ed. Charles E Walker and Mark A Bloomfield. Cambridge, MA: Ballinger, 1983, pp. 278–84.

Archer, Bill. "VAT's Arch Enemy." *Wall Street Journal* (August 27, 1996), p. A11.

Armitage-Smith, George. *Principles and Methods of Taxation.* London: John Murray, 1907.

Arrow, Kenneth J. *Social Choice and Individual Values.* New York: Wiley, 1951.

Arrow, Kenneth J. *The Limits of Organization.* New York: W W Norton, 1974.

Atkinson, Anthony B. *The Economics of Inequality.* Oxford: Oxford University Press, 1983.

Atkinson, Anthony B, and Nicholas H Stern. "Pigou, Taxation and Public Goods." *Review of Economic Studies* 41 (1974), pp. 119–28.

Atkinson, Anthony B, and Joseph E Stiglitz. *Lectures on Public Economics.* New York: McGraw-Hill, 1980.

Auerbach, Alan J. "The Theory of Excess Burden and Optimal Taxation." In *Handbook of Public Economics,* Vol. 1, ed. Alan J Auerbach and Martin S Feldstein. Amsterdam: North-Holland, 1985, pp. 61–128.

Auerbach, Alan J, and Joel Slemrod. "The Economic Effects of the Tax Reform Act of 1986." *Journal of Economic Literature* 35 (June 1997), pp. 589–632.

Ault, Hugh J. *Comparative Income Taxation—A Structural Analysis.* The Hague: Kluwer Law International, 1997.

Auten, Gerald, and Robert Carroll. "The Effect of Income Taxes on Household Behavior." Working Paper. Washington, DC: Office of Tax Analysis, US Department of the Treasury, 1997.

Ayres, Ian, and Steven D Levitt. "Measuring Positive Externalities from Unobservable Victim Precaution: An Empirical Analysis of Lojack." Working Paper No. 5928. Cambridge, MA: National Bureau of Economic Research, 1997.

Baicker, Katherine. "Extensive or Intensive Generosity? The Price and Income Effects of Federal Grants." Working Paper No. 8384. Cambridge, MA: National Bureau of Economic Research, July 2001.

Baker, Michael, A; Abigail Payne; and Michael Smart. "An Empirical Study of Matching Grants: The 'Cap on CPA'." *Journal of Public Economics* 72 (May 1999), pp. 269–88.

Baker, Russell. "Reagan Revises Dirksen." *New York Times* (October 2, 1985), p. A27.

Ball, Laurence, and N Gregory Mankiw. "What Do Budget Deficits Do?" In *Budget Deficits and Debt: Issues and Options.* Kansas City, MO: Federal Reserve Bank of Kansas City, 1995, pp. 95–119.

Ballard, Charles L, and John H Goddeeris. "The Efficiency Cost of Redistribution: A Review Analysis." *Public Economics Review* 1 (December 1996), pp. 32–67.

Barboza, David. "Pluralism under Golden Arches." *New York Times* (February 12, 1999), p. C1.

Barlow, Robin; Harvey E Brazer; and James N Morgan. *Economic Behavior of the Affluent.* Washington, DC: Brookings Institution, 1966.

Barro, Robert J. "Are Government Bonds Net Wealth?" *Journal of Political Economy* 82 (1974), pp. 1095–117.

Bartlett, Bruce. "Bush's Tax Cuts for Investors Will Boost Market." *Wall Street Journal* (August 26, 2002), p. A10.

Bauman, Kurt. "Shifting Family Definitions: The Effect of Cohabitation and Other Household Relationships on Measures of Poverty." WWW Document. [URL: http://www.census.gov/hhes/poverty/povmeas/papers/shft_cen.html], January 1997.

Baumol, William J. "Book Reviews—Economics and Clean Water." *Yale Law Journal* 85, no. 3 (January 1976), pp. 441–46.

Baumol, William J, and Hilda Baumol. "Book Review." *Journal of Political Economy* 89, no. 2 (April 1981), pp. 425–28.

Baxter, Marianne. "Social Security as a Financial Asset: Gender-Specific Risks and Returns." Working Paper No. 8329. Cambridge, MA: National Bureau of Economic Research, June 2001.

Bazelon, Coleman, and Kent Smetters. "Discounting Inside the Washington, D.C., Beltway." *Journal of Economic Perspectives* (Fall 1999), pp. 213–28.

Becker, Gary, and Casey Mulligan. "Deadweight Costs and the Size of Government." Working Paper No. 6789. Cambridge, MA: National Bureau of Economic Research, November 1998.

Bernheim, B Douglas. "Taxation and Saving." Working Paper No. 7061. Cambridge, MA: National Bureau of Economic Research, March 1999.

Bittker, Boris. "Federal Income Taxation and the Family." *Stanford Law Review* 27 (July 1975), pp. 1392–1463.

Blair, Douglas H, and Robert A Pollak. "Rational Collective Choice." *Scientific American* 249, no. 2 (August 1983), pp. 88–95.

Blank, Rebecca. "Evaluating Welfare Reform in the United States." *Journal of Economic Literature* 40 (December 2002), pp. 1105–166.

Bloom, Alan. *The Closing of the American Mind.* New York: Simon & Schuster, 1987.

Blumenthal, Marsha; Charles Christian; and Joel Slemrod. "The Determinants of Income Tax Compliance: Evidence from a Controlled Experiment in Minnesota." Working Paper No. 6575. Cambridge, MA: National Bureau of Economic Research, May 1998.

Blumstein, James F. "Why the GOP's Constitutional Amendments Are a Bad Idea." *Wall Street Journal* (January 4, 1995), p. A13.

Boardman, Anthony E; David H Greenberg; Aidan R Vining; and David L Weimer. *Cost Benefit Analysis: Concepts and Practice.* New York: Prentice Hall, 1996.

Borcherding, Thomas E. "The Causes of Government Expenditure Growth: A Survey of the US Evidence." *Journal of Public Economics* 28, no. 3 (December 1985), pp. 359–82.

Borck, Rainald, and Stephanie Owings. "The Political Economy of Intergovernmental Grants." *Regional Science and Urban Economics* 33 (March 2003), pp. 139–56.

Boskin, Michael J. "Efficiency Aspects of the Differential Tax Treatment of Market and Household

Economic Activities." *Journal of Public Economics* 4 (1975), pp. 1–25.

Boskin, Michael, and Eytan Sheshinski. "Optimal Treatment of the Family: Married Couples." *Journal of Public Economics* 20 (August 1983), pp. 281–97.

Bovard, James. "This Farm Program Is Just Plain Nuts." *Wall Street Journal* (August 30, 1995), p. A10.

Bradford, David, and Wallace Oates. "Suburban Exploitation of Central Cities and Government Structure." In *Redistribution through Public Choice*, ed. Harold Hochman and George Peterson. New York: Columbia University Press, 1974.

Break, George F. "Income Taxes and Incentives to Work." *American Economic Review* 47 (1957), pp. 529–49.

Breitbard, Stanley H. "Capital Gains Taxpayers Get No Free Loan." *New York Times* (March 13, 1997), p. A26.

Brooks, Rick. "How Big Incentives Won Alabama a Piece of the Auto Industry." *Wall Street Journal* (April 3, 2002), p. A1.

Broome, J. "Trying to Value a Life." *Journal of Public Economics* (February 1978), pp. 91–100.

Browning, Edgar K. "The Case Against Income Redistribution." *Public Finance Review* 30 (November 2002), pp. 509–30.

Browning, Martin, and Thomas F Crossley. "The Life-Cycle Model of Consumption and Saving." *Journal of Economic Perspectives* 15 (Summer 2001), pp. 3–22.

Buchanan, James M. "Social Choice, Democracy, and Free Markets." In *Fiscal Theory and Political Economy—Selected Essays*, ed. James M Buchanan. Chapel Hill: University of North Carolina Press, 1960, pp. 75–89.

Buchanan, James M. "Clarifying Confusion about the Balanced Budget Amendment." *National Tax Journal* 48 (September 1995), pp. 347–56.

Burke, Vee. *Cash and Noncash Benefits for Persons with Limited Income: Eligibility Rules, Recipient and Expenditure Data, FY 1998–2000.* Washington, DC: Congressional Research Service, 2001.

Burman, Leonard. *The Labyrinth of Capital Gains Tax Policy.* Washington, DC: Brookings Institution, 1999.

Burtless, Gary. "The Case for Randomized Field Trials in Economic and Policy Research." *Journal of*

Economic Perspectives 9, no. 2 (Spring 1995), pp. 63–84.

Burtraw, Dallas. "Book Review." *Regional Science and Urban Economics* 32 (January 2002), pp. 139–44.

Butler, Stuart M. "Creating a National Health System through Tax Reform." *National Tax Association—Proceedings of the Eighty-fifth Annual Conference*, 1992.

Calomiris, Charles W, and Kevin A Hassett. "Marginal Tax Rates Cuts and the Public Tax Debate." *National Tax Journal* 40 (March 2002), pp. 119–31.

Cameron, Stephen V, and James J Heckman. "The Dynamics of Educational Attainment for Blacks, Hispanics, and Whites." Working Paper. Chicago: University of Chicago, March 1997.

Cameron, Stephen V, and James J Heckman. "The Dynamics of Educational Attainment for Blacks, Hispanics, and Whites." Working Paper No. 7249. Cambridge, MA: National Bureau of Economic Research, July 1999.

Carasso, Adam, and C Eugene Steuerle. "How Marriage Penalties Change under the 2001 Tax Bill." Discussion Paper No. 2. Washington, DC: Urban-Brookings Tax Policy Center, May 2002.

Card, David, and Alan B Krueger. "School Resources and Student Outcomes: An Overview of the Literature and New Evidence from North and South Carolina." *Journal of Economic Perspectives* (Fall 1996), pp. 31–50.

Caves, Douglas W, and Laurits R Christensen. "The Relative Efficiency of Public and Private Firms in a Competitive Environment: The Case of Canadian Railroads." *Journal of Political Economy* 88, no. 5 (October 1980), pp. 958–76.

Centers for Disease Control and Prevention. "Health Statistics." WWW Document. [URL: http://www.cdc.gov/scientific.htm], 2003.

Centers for Medicare and Medicaid Services. "Managed Care Trends." WWW Document. [URL: http://cms.hhs.gov/medicaid/managedcare/trends02.pdf], 2002.

Chay, Kenneth Y, and Michael Greenstone. "Does Air Quality Matter? Evidence from the Housing Market." Working Paper No. 6826. Cambridge, MA: National Bureau of Economic Research, December 1998.

Chen, David W. "A Sip of Wine, a Rustic View, and Hog Waste." *New York Times* (August 12, 2001), p. L1.

Chiappori, Pierre-André, and Bernard Salanié. "Testing for Asymmetric Information in Insurance Markets." *Journal of Political Economy* (February 2000), pp. 56–78.

Chirinko, Robert S. "Corporate Taxation, Capital Formation, and the Substitution Elasticity between Labor and Capital." *National Tax Journal* 40 (June 2002), pp. 339–55.

Choi, James J; David Laibson; Brigitte C Madrian; and Andrew Metrick. "Defined Contribution Pensions: Plan Rules, Participant Decisions, and the Path of Least Resistance." Working Paper No. 8655. Cambridge, MA: National Bureau of Economic Research, December 2001.

Chubb, John E, and Terry M Moe. *Politics, Markets, and America's Schools.* Washington, DC: Brookings Institution, 1990.

Citizens for Tax Justice. "The Loophole Lobbyists vs. the People." Washington, DC, nd.

City of Clinton v. Cedar Rapids and Missouri River RR. Co., 24 Iowa 475 (1868).

Clotfelter, Charles T. *Federal Tax Policy and Charitable Giving.* Chicago: University of Chicago Press, 1985.

Clymer, Adam. "Switching Sides on States' Rights." *New York Times* (June 1, 1997), section 4, pp. 1, 6.

Cnossen, Sijbren. "Tax Policy in the European Union—A Review of Issues and Options," *FinanzArchiv* 58 (November 2001), pp. 466–558.

Coase, Ronald H. "The Problem of Social Cost." *Journal of Law and Economics* (October 1960).

Coase, Ronald H. "The Lighthouse in Economics." *Journal of Law and Economics* (October 1974).

Cockburn, Alexander, and Robert Pollin. "Why the Left Should Support the Flat Tax." *Wall Street Journal* (April 2, 1992), p. A15.

Coe, Norma B; Gregory Acs; Robert I Lerman; and Keith Watson. "Does Work Pay? A Summary of the Work Incentives under TANF." Paper No. A-28. Washington, DC: The Urban Institute, December 1998.

Committee on Ways and Means. *Overview of Entitlement Programs: 2000 Green Book.* Washington, DC: US Government Printing Office, 2000.

Conda, Cesar V. "An Environment for Reform." *Wall Street Journal* (January 23, 1995), p. A18.

Congressional Budget Office. *Reducing the Deficit: Spending and Revenue Options.* Washington, DC: US Government Printing Office, 1997a.

Congressional Budget Office. *The Economic Effects of Comprehensive Tax Reform.* Washington, DC: US Government Printing Office, July 1997b.

Congressional Budget Office. *The Economic and Budget Outlook: Fiscal Years 2002–2011.* Washington, DC: US Government Printing Office, January 2001.

Congressional Budget Office. *Social Security: A Primer.* Washington, DC: US Government Printing Office, September 2001.

Congressional Budget Office. *Issues in Designing a Prescription Drug Benefit for Medicare.* Washington, DC: US Government Printing Office, October 2002.

Congressional Budget Office. *The Budget and Economic Outlook: Fiscal Years 2004–2013.* Washington, DC: US Government Printing Office, January 2003.

Cooper, Michael. "Cigarette Tax, Highest in Nation, Cuts Sales by Half." *New York Times* (August 6, 2002), pp. B1, B7.

Cooper, Philip F, and Barbara Steinberg Schone. "More Offers, Fewer Takers for Employment-Based Health Insurance: 1987 and 1996." *Health Affairs* 16, November/December 1997.

Corlett, W J, and D C Hague. "Complementarity and the Excess Burden of Taxation." *Review of Economic Studies* 21 (1953), pp. 21–30.

Cornes, Richard, and Todd Sandler. *The Theory of Externalities, Public Goods and Club Goods,* 2d ed. Cambridge, England: Cambridge University Press, 1996.

Crandall, Robert W. "Policy Watch: Corporate Average Fuel Economy Standards." *Journal of Economic Perspectives* 6 (Spring 1992), pp. 171–80.

Crews, Amy D. "Do Housing Programs for Low-Income Households Improve Their Housing?" Working Paper. Syracuse, NY: Syracuse University (March 1995).

Cropper, Maureen L, and Wallace E Oates. "Environmental Economics: A Survey." *Journal of Economic Literature* 30 (June 1992), pp. 675–740.

Cullen, Julie Berry. "The Incidence of Special Education Mandates: Does the Mainstream Pay?" Working Paper. Cambridge, MA: MIT, 1996.

Currie, Janet, and Jonathan Gruber. "Health Insurance Eligibility, Utilization of Medical Care, and Child Health." *The Quarterly Journal of Economics* 111 (May 1996), pp. 431–66.

Currie, Janet, and Duncan Thomas. "Does Head Start Make a Difference?" *American Economic Review* 85 (June 1995), pp. 341–64.

Cushman, John H Jr. "E.P.A. Head Adamant on Clean Air Rules." *New York Times* (June 1, 1997), pp. 1, 28.

Cutler, David M. "Health Care and the Public Sector." Working Paper No. 8802. Cambridge, MA: National Bureau of Economic Research, February 2002.

Cutler, David M, and Mark McClellan. "Is Technological Change in Medicine Worth It?" *Health Affairs* 20 (October 2001), pp. 11–29.

Danziger, Sheldon H; Robert H Haveman; and Robert D Plotnick. "Anti-Poverty Policy: Effects on the Poor and the Non-Poor." In *Fighting Poverty: What Works and What Doesn't,* ed. Sheldon H Danziger and Daniel H Weinberg. Cambridge, MA: Harvard University Press, 1986.

Deaton, Angus, and Christina Paxson. "Mortality, Income, and Income Inequality Over Time in Britain and the United States." Working Paper No. 8354. Cambridge, MA: National Bureau of Economic Research, October 2001.

Delipalla, Sofia, and Michael Keen. "The Comparison between Ad Valorem and Specific Taxation under Imperfect Competition." *Journal of Public Economics* 49 (December 1992), pp. 351–68.

Derthick, Martha. "American Federalism—Half-Full or Half-Empty." *Brookings Review* (Winter 2000), pp. 24–28.

Desai, Mihir, C Fritz Foley, and James Hines Jr. "Chains of Ownership, Regional Tax Competition, and Foreign Direct Investment." Working Paper No. 9224. Cambridge, MA: National Bureau of Economic Research, September 2002.

Dewenter, Kathryn, and Paul H Malatesta. "State-Owned and Privately Owned Firms: An Empirical Analysis of Profitability, Leverage, and Labor Intensity." *American Economic Review* 91 (March 2001), pp. 320–34.

Diamond, Peter A. "A Framework for Social Security Analysis." *Journal of Public Economics* 8, no. 3 (December 1977), pp. 275–98.

Diamond, Peter, and Jonathan Gruber. "Social Security and Retirement in the United States." In *Social Security and Retirement Around the World,* eds. Jonathan Gruber and David A. Wise. Chicago: University of Chicago Press, 1999, pp. 437–73.

Dickert-Conlin, Stacy. "Taxes and Transfers: Their Effects on the Decision to End a Marriage." *Journal of Public Economics* (August 1999), pp. 217–40.

Downs, Anthony. *An Economic Theory of Democracy.* New York: Harper & Row, 1957.

Duggan, Mark. "Does Contracting Out Increase the Efficiency of Government Programs? Evidence from Medicaid HMOs." Working Paper No. 9091. Cambridge, MA: National Bureau of Economic Research, August 2002.

Dugger, Celia W. "In India's Capital, a Prayer for the Belching Buses." *New York Times* (September 28, 2001), p. A3.

Eckholm, Erik. "Rising Farmers' Protests Meet Violence in China." *New York Times* (February 1, 1999), p. A10.

Economic Report of the President, 1986. Washington, DC: US Government Printing Office, 1986.

Economic Report of the President, 1992. Washington, DC: US Government Printing Office, 1992.

Economic Report of the President, 1994. Washington, DC: US Government Printing Office, 1994.

Economic Report of the President, 1998. Washington, DC: US Government Printing Office, 1998.

Economic Report of the President, 2000. Washington, DC: US Government Printing Office, 2000.

Economic Report of the President, 2003. Washington, DC: US Government Printing Office, 2003.

Economist. "Suffer Little Children" (December 7, 1996), p. 28.

Economist. "The Dividend Puzzle" (January 11, 2003), pp. 53–54.

Edgeworth, F Y. "The Pure Theory of Taxation." Reprinted in *Readings in the Economics of Taxation,* ed. Richard A Musgrave and Carl S Shoup. Homewood, IL: Irwin, 1959, pp. 258–96.

Edwards, Sebastian. "The Chilean Pension Reform: A Pioneering Program." In *Privatizing Social Security,* ed. Martin Feldstein. Chicago: University of Chicago Press, 1998.

Egan, Timothy. "Adapting to Fees for Enjoying Public Lands." *New York Times* (August 21, 1997), p. A1.

Eissa, Nada, and Jeffrey B Liebman. "Labor Supply Response to the Earned Income Tax Credit." Working Paper No. 5158. Cambridge, MA: National Bureau of Economic Research, June 1995.

Ellwood, David T. *Poor Support: Poverty and the American Family.* New York: Basic Books, 1988.

Engen, Eric, and Jonathan Skinner. "Taxation and Economic Growth." *National Tax Journal* 49 (December 1996), pp. 617–42.

Epstein, Richard A. "Through the Smog: What the Court Actually Ruled." *Wall Street Journal* (March 1, 2001), p. A22.

Fair, Ray C. "The Optimal Distribution of Income." *Quarterly Journal of Economics* 85 (1971), pp. 551–79.

Fairclough, Gordon. "Pssst! Wanna Cheap Smoke?" *Wall Street Journal* (December 27, 2002), p. B1.

Farney, Dennis. "Ask Teddy Roosevelt Why Gore and Bush Sound So Much Alike." *Wall Street Journal* (March 10, 2000), p. A1.

Feinstein, Jonathan S. "An Econometric Analysis of Tax Evasion and Its Detection." *Rand Journal of Economics* 22 (Spring 1991), pp. 14–35.

Feldstein, Martin. "Social Security, Induced Retirement, and Aggregate Capital Accumulation." *Journal of Political Economy* 82, no. 5 (September–October 1974), pp. 905–26.

Feldstein, Martin. "On the Theory of Tax Reform." *Journal of Public Economics* 6 (1976a), pp. 77–104.

Feldstein, Martin. "Social Insurance." Discussion Paper 477. Cambridge, MA: Harvard Institute of Economic Research, 1976b.

Feldstein, Martin. "Inflation, Tax Rules, and Investment: Some Econometric Evidence." *Econometrica* 50, no. 4 (July 1982), pp. 825–62.

Feldstein, Martin. "Debt and Taxes in the Theory of Public Finance." *Journal of Public Economics* 28, no. 2 (November 1985), pp. 233–46.

Feldstein, Martin. "The Economics of Health and Health Care: What Have We Learned? What Have I Learned." *American Economic Review* 85 (May 1995), pp. 28–31.

Feldstein, Martin. "Social Security and Saving: New Time Series Evidence." *National Tax Journal* 49 (June 1996), pp. 151–64.

Feldstein, Martin. "Vouchers Can Free Us from Foreign Oil." *Wall Street Journal* (December 31, 2001), p. A12.

Feldstein, Martin, and Andrew Samwick. "Potential Paths of Social Security Reform." Working Paper No. 8592. Cambridge, MA: National Bureau of Economic Research, November 2001.

Feldstein, Martin, and Marian Vaillant Wrobel. "Can State Taxes Redistribute Income?" *Journal of Public Economics* 68 (June 1998), pp. 369–96.

Filimon, R; T Romer; and H Rosenthal. "Asymmetric Information and Agenda Control: The Bases of Monopoly Power and Public Spending." *Journal of Public Economics* 17 (1982), pp. 51–70.

Finkelstein, Amy. "Minimum Standards and Insurance Regulation: Evidence from the Medigap Market." Working Paper No. 8917. Cambridge, MA: National Bureau of Economic Research, May 2002.

Finkelstein, Amy. "Health Policy and Technological Change: Evidence from the Vaccine Industry." Working Paper No. 9460. Cambridge, MA: National Bureau of Economic Research, January 2003.

Fisher Ronald C, and Leslie E Papke. "Local Government Responses to Education Grants." *National Tax Journal* 53 (March 2000), pp. 153–68.

Fisman, Raymond, and Roberta Gatti. "Decentralization and Corruption: Evidence across Countries." *Journal of Public Economics* 83 (March 2002), pp. 325–46.

Fisman, Raymond, and Shang-Jin Wei. "Tax Rates and Tax Evasion: Evidence from Missing Imports in China." Working Paper No. 8551. Cambridge, MA: National Bureau of Economic Research, October 2001.

Formby, John P; W James Smith; and David Sykes. "Intersecting Tax Concentration Curves and the Measurement of Tax Progressivity: A Comment."

National Tax Journal 39, no. 1 (March 1986), pp. 115–18.

Fortin, Bernard; Thomas Lemieux; and Pierre Frechette. "The Effect of Taxes on Labor Supply in the Underground Economy." *American Economic Review* 84 (March 1994), pp. 231–54.

Freeman, A Myrick III. "Environmental Policy Since Earth Day I: What Have We Gained?" *Journal of Economic Perspectives* 16 (Winter 2002), pp. 125–46.

Fried, Charles. "Whose Money Is It?" *Washington Post* (January 1, 1995), p. C7.

Friedman, Eric; Simon Johnson; Daniel Kaufmann; and Pablo Zoido-Lobaton. "Dodging the Grabbing Hand: The Determinants of Unofficial Activity in 69 Countries." *Journal of Public Economics* 76 (June 2000), pp. 495–520.

Friedman, Milton. "Our New Hidden Taxes." *Newsweek* (April 14, 1980), p. 90.

Friedman, Milton. "Let's Revamp the Tax Code— But How?" *Wall Street Journal* (April 15, 1998), p. A22.

Friedman, Milton. "Social Security Chimeras." *New York Times* (January 11, 1999), p. A17.

Friedman, Milton. "What Every American Wants." *Wall Street Journal* (January 15, 2003), p. A10.

Fuchs, Victor. "An Economist's View of Health Care Reform." *New York Times* (May 2, 2000), pp. F6–F7.

Fuchs, Victor R; Alan B Krueger; and James M Poterba. "Why Do Economists Disagree about Policy? The Roles of Beliefs about Parameters and Values." Mimeo. Stanford, CA: Stanford University, August 1997.

Fullerton, Don, and Diane Lim Rogers. "Neglected Effects on the Uses Side: Even a Uniform Tax Would Change Relative Goods Prices." *American Economic Review* 87 (May 1997), pp. 120–25.

Gale, William G. "The Required Tax Rate in a National Retail Sales." *National Tax Journal* 52 (September 1999), pp. 443–57.

Gale, William G, and Janet Holtzblatt. "The Role of Administrative Issues in Tax Reform: Simplicity, Compliance, and Administration." In *United States Tax Reform in the 21st Century,* eds. George R Zodrow and Peter Mieszkowski. New York: Cambridge University Press, 2002, pp. 179–214.

Gale, William G, and Samara R Potter. "An Economic Evaluation of the Economic Growth and Tax Relief Reconciliation Act of 2001." *National Tax Journal* 40 (March 2002), pp. 133–86.

Gale, William G, and Joel B Slemrod. "A Matter of Life and Death: Reassessing the Estate and Gift Tax." *Tax Notes* (August 14, 2000), pp. 927–32.

Garber, Alan M; Thomas MaCurdy; and Mark McClellan. "Medical Care at the End of Life: Diseases, Treatment Patterns, and Costs." In *Frontiers in Health Policy Research* 2, ed. Alan M Garber. Cambridge, MA: MIT Press, 1999.

Garces, Eliana; Duncan Thomas; and Janet Currie. "Longer Term Effects of Head Start." Working Paper No. 8054. Cambridge, MA: National Bureau of Economic Research, December 2000.

Garen, J. "Compensating Wage Differentials and the Endogeneity of Job Riskiness." *Review of Economics and Statistics* 70, no. 1 (February 1988).

Gargan, Edward A. "A Student's Prayer: Let Me Join the Ruling Class." *New York Times* (December 6, 1993), p. A4.

"Gas Tax Rise Likely to Show Up at Pump." *New York Times* (April 1, 1983), p. D1.

Gates, William H, Sr, and Chuck Collins. "Tax the Wealthy." *The American Prospect* 13 (June 17, 2002), [URL: http://www.prospect.org/print/V13/11/index.html].

Gentry, William M, and R Glenn Hubbard. *Distributional Implications of a Consumption Tax.* Washington, DC: American Enterprise Institute, 1997.

George, Henry. *Progress and Poverty,* Book VII. New York: Doubleday, 1914.

Gillis, Malcolm, and Charles E McLure. "Excess Profits Taxation: Post-Mortem on the Mexican Experience." *National Tax Journal* 32, no. 4 (December 1979), pp. 501–11.

Glaeser, Edward L, and Jesse M Shapiro. "The Benefits of the Home Mortgage Interest Deduction." Working Paper No. 9284. Cambridge, MA: National Bureau of Economic Research, October 2002.

Glaeser, Edward L, and Andrei Shleifer. "The Curley Effect." Working Paper No. 8942. Cambridge, MA: National Bureau of Economic Research, May 2002a.

Glaeser Edward L, and Andrei Shleifer. "The Injustice of Inequality." Working Paper No. 9150.

Cambridge, MA: National Bureau of Economic Research, September 2002b.

Gokhale, Jadadeesh; Benjamin R Page; and John R Sturrock. "Generational Accounts for the United States: An Update." In *Generational Accounting Around the World*, eds. Alan J Auerbach, Laurence J Kotlikoff, and Willi Leibfritz. Chicago: University of Chicago Press, 1999, pp. 489–517.

Gompers, Paul A, and Josh Lerner. "What Drives Venture Capital Fundraising?" Working Paper No. 6906. Cambridge, MA: National Bureau of Economic Research, January 1999.

Goolsbee, Austan. "Does Government R&D Policy Mainly Benefit Scientists and Engineers?" *American Economic Review* 88 (May 1998a), pp. 298–302.

Goolsbee, Austan. "Investment Subsidies and Wages in Capital Goods Industries: To the Workers Go the Spoils?" Working Paper 6526. Cambridge, MA: National Bureau of Economic Research, April 1998b.

Goolsbee, Austan. "The Impact and Efficiency of the Corporate Income Tax: Evidence from State Organizational Form Data." Working Paper No. 9141. Cambridge, MA: National Bureau of Economic Research, September 2002.

Goolsbee, Austan, and Amil Petrin. "The Consumer Gains from Direct Broadcast Satellites and the Competition with Cable Television." Working Paper No. 8317. Cambridge, MA: National Bureau of Economic Research, June 2001.

Gordon, Roger H, and Young Lee. "Do Taxes Affect Corporate Debt Policy? Evidence from US Corporate Tax Return Data." *Journal of Public Economics* 82 (November 2001), pp. 195–224.

Gottschalk, Peter. "Inequality, Income Growth, and Mobility: The Basic Facts." *Journal of Economic Perspectives* 11 (Spring 1997), pp. 21–40.

Gottschalk, Peter, and Timothy Smeeding. "Cross National Comparisons of Earnings and Income Inequality." *Journal of Economic Literature* 35 (June, 1997), pp. 633–87.

Graham, John R. "Taxes and Corporate Finance: A Review." Working Paper. Durham, NC: Duke University, 2001.

Green, Richard K, and Kerry D Vandell. "Giving Households Credit: How Changes in the US Tax Code Could Promote Homeownership." *Regional Science and Urban Economics* 29 (July 1999), pp. 419–44.

Greene, Pamela, and Robert McClelland. "Taxes and Charitable Giving." *National Tax Journal* 55 (September 2001), pp. 433–54.

Grogger, Jeffrey. "The Effects of Time Limits and Other Policy Changes on Welfare Use, Work, and Income among Female-Headed Families." Working Paper No. 8153. Cambridge, MA: National Bureau of Economic Research, March 2001.

Groves, Harold M. *Financing Government.* New York: Henry Holt, 1946.

Groves, Theodore, and Martin Loeb. "Incentives and Public Inputs." *Journal of Public Economics* 4, no. 3 (August 1975), pp. 211–26.

Gruber, Jonathan, and Michael Lettau. "How Elastic Is the Firm's Demand for Health Insurance?" Working Paper No. 8021. Cambridge, MA: National Bureau of Economic Research, November 2000.

Gruber, Jonathan, and James Poterba. "Tax Subsidies to Employer-Provided Health Insurance." In *Empirical Foundations of Household Taxation,* ed. Martin Feldstein and James Poterba. Chicago: University of Chicago Press, pp. 135–64.

Gruber, Jonathan, and Emmanuel Saez. "The Elasticity of Taxable Income: Evidence and Implications." *Journal of Public Economics* 84 (April 2002), pp. 1–33.

Gruber, Jonathan, and David Wise. "Social Security and Retirement: An International Comparison." *American Economic Review* 88 (May 1998), pp. 158–63.

Gruber, Jonathan, and David A Wise. "Introduction and Summary." In *Social Security and Retirement Around the World,* eds. Jonathan Gruber and David A Wise. Chicago: University of Chicago Press, 1999, pp. 1–36.

Hadley, Jack, and John Holahan. "How Much Medical Care Do the Uninsured Use and Who Pays for It?" Washington, DC: The Urban Institute, February 2003 [URL: http://www.kaisernetwork.org/health_cast/uploaded_files/ACF532.pdf].

Hagman, Donald C. "Proposition 13: A Prostitution of Conservative Principles." *Tax Review* 39, no. 9 (September 1978), pp. 39–42.

Hahn, Robert W; Jason K Burnett; Yee-Ho I Chan; Elizabeth A Mader; and Petrea R Moyle.

"Assessing the Quality of Regulatory Impact Analyses." Working Paper 00-1. Washington, DC: AEI-Brookings Joint Center for Regulatory Studies, January 2000.

Hall, Robert E, and Alvin Rabushka. *The Flat Tax,* 2d ed. Stanford, CA: Hoover Institution Press, 1995.

Hamilton, Bruce. "Zoning and Property Taxation in a System of Local Governments." *Urban Studies* 12 (June 1975), pp. 205–11.

Harberger, Arnold C. *Project Evaluation: Collected Papers.* Chicago: Markham, 1974.

Harberger, Arnold C. "Taxation, Resource Allocation, and Welfare." In *Taxation and Welfare,* ed. Arnold C Harberger. Boston: Little, Brown, 1974a, pp. 25–62.

Harberger, Arnold C. "Efficiency Effects of Taxes on Income from Capital." In *Taxation and Welfare,* ed. Arnold C Harberger. Boston: Little, Brown, 1974b, pp. 163–70.

Harberger, Arnold C. "The Incidence of the Corporation Income Tax." In *Taxation and Welfare,* ed. Arnold C Harberger. Boston: Little, Brown, 1974c, pp. 135–62.

Harris, C Lowell. "Property Taxation after the California Vote." *Tax Review* 39, no. 8 (August 1978), pp. 35–38.

Hart, Oliver; Andrei Shleifer; and Robert W Vishny. "The Proper Scope of Government: Theory and an Application to Prisons." *Quarterly Journal of Economics* 112:4 (1997), pp. 1127–161.

Haughwout, Andrew F, and Robert P Inman. "Should Suburbs Help Their Central City?" In *Brookings-Wharton Papers on Urban Affairs 2002,* eds. William G Gale and Janet Rothenberg Pack. Washington, DC: Brookings Institution Press, 2002.

Heal, Geoffrey. "Bundling Public and Private Goods: Are Development and Conservation Necessarily in Conflict?" Working Paper. New York: Columbia Business School, June 2001.

Heckman, James J. "What Has Been Learned about Labor Supply in the United States in the Past Twenty Years?" *American Economic Review* 83 (May 1993), pp. 116–21.

Heckman, James J. "Policies to Foster Human Capital." Working Paper No. 7288. Cambridge, MA: National Bureau of Economic Research, August 1999.

Hendel, Igal, and Alessandro Lizzeri. "The Role of Commitment in Dynamic Contracts: Evidence from Life Insurance." Working Paper No. 7470. Cambridge, MA: National Bureau of Economic Research, January 2000.

Henriques, Diana B. "In Death's Shadow, Valuing Each Life." *New York Times* (December 30, 2001), p. WK10.

Herbert, Bob. "Safety? Too Costly." *New York Times* (April 19, 1995), p. A23.

Herman, Tom. "Tax Report." *Wall Street Journal* (January 12, 1994), p. A1.

Herman, Tom. "Tax Report." *Wall Street Journal* (July 22, 1999), p. A1.

Herman, Tom. "Tax Report." *Wall Street Journal* (July 19, 2000), p. A1.

Herman, Tom. "Tax Report." *Wall Street Journal* (October 31, 2001), p. A1.

Herman, Tom. "Tax Report." *Wall Street Journal* (February 20, 2002), p. A1.

"A High Court Win for OSHA." *Newsweek* (June 29, 1981), p. 59.

Hines, James R. "Review of U.S. Taxation of International Income: Blueprint for Reform." *National Tax Journal* 46 (March 1993), pp. 69–71.

Hines, James R, Jr. "Three Sides of Harberger Triangles." *Journal of Economic Perspectives* (Spring 1999), pp. 167–88.

Hitler, Adolf. *Mein Kampf.* Trans. Ralph Manheim. Boston: Houghton Mifflin, 1971 (1925).

Hobbes, Thomas. *Leviathan.* New York: Meridian Books, 1963 (1651).

Holcombe, Randall G. "Tax Policy from a Public Choice Perspective." *National Tax Journal* 51 (June 1998), pp. 359–71.

Holcombe, Randall G. "The Ramsey Rule Reconsidered." *Public Finance Review* 30 (November 2002), pp. 562–78.

Holtz-Eakin, Douglas. "Unobserved Tastes and the Determination of Municipal Services." *National Tax Journal* (December 1986), pp. 527–32.

Holtz-Eakin, Douglas. "Health Insurance Provision and Labor Market Efficiency in the United States and Germany." In *Social Protection versus Economic Flexibility: Is There a Tradeoff?* ed. Rebecca Blank and Richard Freeman. Chicago: University of Chicago Press, 1994.

Holtz-Eakin, Douglas; David Joulfaian; and Harvey S Rosen. "The Carnegie Conjecture: Some Empirical Evidence." *Quarterly Journal of Economics* (May 1993), pp. 413–35.

Hoxby, Caroline Minter. "Do Private Schools Provide Competition for Public Schools." Working Paper No. 4978. Cambridge, MA: National Bureau of Economic Research, 1994.

Hoxby, Caroline M. "School Choice and School Productivity (Or Could School Choice Be a Tide That Lifts All Boats?)" Working Paper No. 8873. Cambridge, MA: National Bureau of Economic Research, April 2002a.

Hoxby, Caroline M. "The Cost of Accountability." Working Paper No. 8855. Cambridge, MA: National Bureau of Economic Research, April 2002b.

Hubbard, R Glenn. "Capital-Market Imperfections and Investment." *Journal of Economic Literature* 36 (March 1998), pp. 193–225.

Hubbard, R Glenn, and Jonathan S Skinner. "Assessing the Effectiveness of Saving Incentives." *Journal of Economic Perspectives* 10 (Fall 1996), pp. 73–90.

Hurd, Michael. "Research on the Elderly: Economic Status, Retirement, and Consumption and Saving." *Journal of Economic Literature* 28 (June 1990), pp. 565–637.

Husted, Thomas A, and Lawrence W Kenny. "The Effect of the Expansion of the Voting Franchise on the Size of Government." *Journal of Political Economy* 105 (February 1997), pp. 54–82.

Hyslop, Dean R. "Rising US Earnings Inequality and Family Labor Supply: The Covariance Structure of Intrafamily Earnings." *American Economic Review* 91 (September 2001), pp. 755–77.

Ingram, Gregory K. "Comment." In *Social Experimentation,* ed. Jerry A Hausman and David A Wise. Chicago: University of Chicago Press, 1985, pp. 87–94.

Inman, Robert P. "The Fiscal Performance of Local Governments: An Interpretative Review." In *Current Issues in Urban Economics,* ed. Peter Mieszkowski and Mahlon Straszheim. Baltimore: Johns Hopkins University Press, 1979, pp. 270–321.

Internal Revenue Service. *Statistics of Income Bulletin* 22 (Summer 2002), Washington, DC, 2002.

Isaac, R Mark; Kenneth F McCue; and Charles R Plott. "Public Goods Provision in an Experimental Environment." *Journal of Public Economics* 26, no. 1 (February 1985), pp. 51–74.

Johansen, Leif. "The Theory of Public Goods: Misplaced Emphasis?" *Journal of Public Economics* 7, no. 1 (February 1977), pp. 147–52.

Johnson, Kirk. "The Economics of Recycling." *New York Times* (August 19, 2001), p. L23.

Johnson, Paul. *Modern Times.* New York: Harper & Row, 1983.

Johnston, David Cay. "The Tax Maze Begins Here. No, Here. No . . ." *New York Times* (February 27, 2000), p. BU1.

Joint Committee on Taxation. *Estimates of Federal Tax Expenditures for Fiscal Years 2002–2006.* Washington, DC: US Government Printing Office, January 2002.

Jorgenson, Dale W. "Capital Theory and Investment Behavior." *American Economic Review* 53, no. 2 (May 1963), pp. 247–59.

Jorgenson, Dale W. "Did We Lose the War on Poverty?" *Journal of Economic Perspectives* 12 (Winter 1998), pp. 79–96.

Jorgenson, Dale W, and Kun-Young Yun. *Investment, Volume 3, Lifting the Burden: Tax Reform, the Cost of Capital, and US Economic Growth.* Cambridge, MA: MIT Press, 2001.

Kaestner, Robert; Neeraj Kaushal; and Garrett Van Ryzin. "Migration Consequences of Welfare Reform." Working Paper No. 8560. Cambridge, MA: National Bureau of Economic Research, October 2001.

Kahn, Joseph. "Equality at Trade Talks: No Country Gets a Vote." *New York Times* (November 12, 2001), p. A3.

Kane, Thomas J. *The Price of Admission—Rethinking How Americans Pay for College.* Washington, DC: Brookings Institution Press, 1998.

Katz, Lawrence; Jeffrey R Kling; and Jeffrey B Liebman. "The Early Impacts of Moving to Opportunity in Boston: Final Report to the US Department of Housing and Urban Development." Working Paper. Cambridge, MA: Harvard University, February 2000.

Katz, Lawrence; Jeffrey R Kling; and Jeffrey B Liebman. "Moving to Opportunity in Boston: Early Results of a Randomized Mobility Experiment." *Quarterly Journal of Economics* 116 (May 2001), pp. 607–54.

Keller, Bill. "Same Old Bureaucracy Serves New South Africa." *New York Times* (June 4, 1994), p. A1.

Keynes, John Maynard. *The General Theory of Employment, Interest, and Money.* New York: Harcourt Brace and World, 1965 (1936).

Kinzer, Stephen. "At 25, the Hippies' 'Free City' Isn't So Carefree." *New York Times* (May 16, 1996), p. A3.

Kneller, Richard; Michael F Bleaney; and Norman Gemmell. "Fiscal Policy and Growth: Evidence from OECD Countries." *Journal of Public Economics* (November 1999), pp. 171–90.

Kotlikoff, Laurence J, and Lawrence Summers. "The Role of Intergenerational Transfers in Aggregate Capital Accumulation." *Journal of Political Economy* 89, no. 4 (August 1981), pp. 706–32.

Kotlikoff, Laurence, and Lawrence Summers. "Tax Incidence." In *Handbook of Public Economics,* Vol. II, ed. Alan J Auerbach and Martin S Feldstein. Amsterdam: North-Holland, 1987, chap. 16.

Kovenock, Daniel J, and Michael Rothschild. "Notes on the Effect of Capital Gains Taxation on Non-Austrian Assets." *Journal of Public Economics* 21 (July 1983), pp. 215–56.

Krauss, Clifford. "Long Lines Mar Canada's Low-Cost Health Care." *New York Times* (February 13, 2003), p. A3.

Kristol, Irving. "Income Inequality Without Class Conflict." *Wall Street Journal* (December 18, 1997), p. A22.

Kronholz, Jane. "A Superintendent Is Entrepreneurial about Charters." *Wall Street Journal* (April 11, 2000), p. A10.

Krueger, Alan B, and Mikael Lindahl. "Education for Growth in Sweden and the World." Working Paper No. 7190. Cambridge, MA: National Bureau of Economic Research, June 1999.

Laffer, Arthur B. "Statement Prepared for the Joint Economic Committee, May 20." Reprinted in *The Economics of the Tax Revolt: A Reader,* ed. Arthur B Laffer and Jan P Seymour. New York: Harcourt Brace Jovanovich, 1979, pp. 75–79.

Lenin, Vladimir. "The Marxist Theory of the State and the Tasks of the Proletariat in the Revolution." In *Lenin on Politics and Revolution,* ed. James E Connor. Indianapolis, IN: Bobbs-Merrill, 1968 (1917), pp. 184–232.

Lerman, Allen H. "Average and Marginal Income Tax and Social Security (FICA) Tax Rates for Four-Person Families at the Same Relative Positions in the Income Distribution, 1955–1998." Mimeo. Washington, DC: Office of Tax Analysis, US Department of the Treasury, 1998.

Lerner, A P. "The Burden of the National Debt." In *Income, Employment, and Public Policy: Essays in Honor of Alvin H Hansen,* ed. L A Metzler et al. New York: W W Norton, 1948.

Levin, Jonathan, and Barry Nalebuff. "An Introduction to Vote-Counting Schemes." *Journal of Economic Perspectives* 9 (Winter 1995), pp. 3–26.

Lichtenberg, Frank. "Benefits and Costs of Newer Drugs: An Update." Working Paper No. 8996. Cambridge, MA: National Bureau of Economic Research, June 2002.

Liebman, Jeffrey. "The Optimal Design of the Earned Income Tax Credit." In *Making Work Pay: The Earned Income Tax Credit and its Impact on America's Families,* eds. Bruce D Meyer and Douglas Holtz-Eakin. New York: Russell Sage Foundation Press, 2001a, pp. 196–233.

Liebman, Jeffrey. "Redistribution in the Current US Social Security System." Working Paper No. 8625. Cambridge, MA: National Bureau of Economic Research, December 2001b.

Lindahl, E. "Just Taxation—A Positive Solution." In *Classics in the Theory of Public Finance,* ed. R A Musgrave and A T Peacock. New York: St. Martin's Press, 1958.

Lindsey, Robert. "California Agencies Begin to Feel Tax Revolt." *New York Times* (April 21, 1986), p. A13.

Lipton, James. *An Exaltation of Larks.* New York: Penguin, 1977.

Lopez-de-Silanes, Florencio; Andrei Shleifer; and Robert W Vishny. "Privatization in the United States." *Rand Journal of Economics* 28 (August 1997).

Lott, John R. "Public Schooling, Indoctrination, and Totalitarianism." *Journal of Political Economy* Part II (December 1999), pp. S127–S157.

Lyall, Sarah. "British College Students Face a New Test: Tuition." *New York Times* (July 24, 1997), p. A7.

MacAvoy, Paul. *Industry Regulation and the Performance of the American Economy.* New York: W W Norton, 1992.

Maki, Dean M. "Household Debt and the Tax Reform Act of 1986." *American Economic Review* 91 (March 2001), pp. 305–19.

Makin, John H, ed. *Real Tax Reform—Replacing the Income Tax.* Washington, DC: American Enterprise Institute for Public Policy Research, 1985.

Mark, Stephen T; Therese J McGuire; and Leslie E Papke. "The Influence of Taxes on Employment and Population Growth: Evidence from the Washington, D.C. Metropolitan Area." *National Tax Journal* 53 (March 2000), pp. 105–24.

Martinez-Vazquez, Jorge. "Tax Systems in Transition Economies." Working Paper. Atlanta: Georgia State University, 1997.

McCaffery, Edward J, and Richard E Wagner. "A Bipartisan Declaration of Independence from Death Taxation." *Tax Notes* (August 7, 2000), p. 801–14.

McGarry, Kathleen. "Guaranteed Income: SSI and the Well-Being of the Elderly Poor." Working Paper No. 7574. Cambridge, MA: National Bureau of Economic Research, March 2000.

McGinley, Laurie. "As Nursing Homes Say 'No,' Hospitals Feel Pain." *Wall Street Journal* (May 26, 1999), p. B1.

McHale, John. "The Risk of Social Security Benefit Rule Changes: Some International Evidence." Working Paper No. 7031. Cambridge, MA: National Bureau of Economic Research, March 1999.

McKinnon, John D. "IRS Weighs Using Debt Collectors to Get Back Taxes." *Wall Street Journal* (October 15, 2002), p. A1.

McKinnon, John D, and Greg Hit. "How Treasury Lost in Battle to Quash a Dubious Security." *Wall Street Journal* (February 4, 2002), p. A1.

McLure, Charles. "Thinking Straight about the Taxation of Electronic Commerce: Tax Principles, Compliance Problems, and Nexus." In *Tax Policy and the Economy, Volume 16,* ed. James M Poterba. Cambridge, MA: MIT Press, 2002.

Meer, Jonathan, and Harvey S Rosen. "Insurance and the Utilization of Medical Services." Working Paper No. 9812. Cambridge, MA: National Bureau of Economic Research, 2003.

Menchik, Paul L. "The Distribution of Federal Expenditures." *National Tax Journal* 44 (September 1991), pp. 269–76.

Metcalf, Gilbert E. "The Lifetime Incidence of State and Local Taxes: Measuring Changes during the 1980s." Working Paper No. 4252. Cambridge, MA: National Bureau of Economic Research, January 1993.

Meyer, Bruce D. "Lessons from the U.S. Unemployment Insurance Experiments." *Journal of Economic Literature* 33 (March 1995), pp. 91–131.

Meyer, Bruce D. "Comparing In-Work Benefits and the Reward to Work for Families with Children in the US and UK." *Fiscal Studies* 23 (March 2002), pp. 1–49.

Meyer, Bruce D, and Dan T Rosenbaum. "Welfare, the Earned Income Tax Credit, and the Labor Supply of Single Mothers." *Quarterly Journal of Economics* 116 (August 2001), pp. 1063–114.

Milbank, Dana. "Old Flaws Undermine New Poverty-Level Data." *Wall Street Journal* (October 10, 1995), pp. B1, B8.

Miller, Henry J. "Gore Remakes Economics in His Own Image." *Wall Street Journal* (May 13, 1997), p. A22.

Mills, Edwin S, and Luan S Lubuele. "Inner Cities." *Journal of Economic Literature* 35 (June 1997), pp. 727–56.

Mishan, E J. "The Post-War Literature on Externalities: An Interpretative Essay." *Journal of Economic Literature* 9 (1971), pp. 1–28.

Moffitt, Robert A. "The Effect of Welfare on Marriage and Fertility" In *Welfare, the Family, and Reproductive Behavior: Research Perspectives,* ed. Robert Moffitt. Washington, DC: National Academies Press, 1998, pp. 50–97.

Moffitt, Robert A. "The Temporary Assistance for Needy Families Program." Working Paper No. 8749. Cambridge, MA: National Bureau of Economic Research, February 2002.

Munnell, Alicia H. "Reforming Social Security: The Case against Individual Accounts." *National Tax Journal* 52 (December 1999), pp. 783–802.

Murphy, Kevin M, and Robert Topel. "Medical Research—What's It Worth?" *The Milken Institute Review* (First Quarter, 2000), pp. 23–30.

Murray, Sheila E; William N Evans; and Robert M Schwab. "Education-Finance Reform and the Distribution of Education Resources." *American Economic Review* 88 (September 1998), pp. 789–812.

Musgrave, Richard A. *The Theory of Public Finance.* New York: McGraw-Hill, 1959.

Musgrave, Richard A. "Theories of Fiscal Crises: An Essay in Fiscal Sociology." In *The Economics of Taxation,* ed. Henry J Aaron and Michael J Boskin. Washington, DC: Brookings Institution, 1980.

Musgrave, Richard A. "A Brief History of Fiscal Doctrine." In *Handbook of Public Economics,* Vol. 1, ed. Alan Auerbach and Martin S Feldstein. Amsterdam: North-Holland, 1985.

National Commission on Economic Growth and Tax Reform. *Unleashing America's Potential.* New York: St. Martin's/Griffin, 1996.

Newhouse, Joseph P. "Medical Care Costs: How Much Welfare Loss?" *Journal of Economic Perspectives* 6, no. 3 (Summer 1992a), pp. 3–22.

Newhouse, Joseph P. "Distinguished Fellow: In Honor of Victor Fuchs." *Journal of Economic Perspectives* 6, no. 3 (Summer 1992b), pp. 179–90.

Newhouse, Joseph P. "Medicare." *Journal of Economic Perspectives* 10 (Summer 1996), pp. 159–68.

Newhouse, Joseph P. "Medical Care Price Indices: Problems and Opportunities." Working Paper No. 8168. Cambridge, MA: National Bureau of Economic Research, March 2001.

Newhouse, Joseph P, and the Insurance Experiment Group. *Free for All? Lessons from the RAND Health Insurance Experiment.* Cambridge, MA: Harvard University Press, 1993.

Niskanen, William A, Jr. *Bureaucracy and Representative Government.* Chicago: Aldine, 1971.

Nivola, Pietro S. "The New Pork Barrel." *The Brookings Review* (Winter 1998), pp. 6–9.

Norris, Floyd. "Using Phony Numbers to Push for Tax Cuts." *New York Times* (February 14, 1999), p. 12WK.

Nozick, Robert. *Anarchy, State, and Utopia.* Oxford: Basil Blackwell, 1974.

Oates, Wallace E. "The Effects of Property Taxes and Local Spending on Property Values: An Empirical Study of Tax Capitalization and the Tiebout Hypothesis." *Journal of Political Economy* 77 (1969), pp. 957–71.

Oates, Wallace E. "An Essay on Fiscal Federalism." *Journal of Economic Literature* 37 (September 1999), pp. 1120–149.

Obstfeld, Maurice, and Kenneth Rogoff. *Foundations of International Macroeconomics.* Cambridge, MA: MIT Press, 1996.

OECD. Department of Economics and Statistics. *National Accounts of OECD Countries 1964–1981,* Vol. II. Paris, 1983.

OECD. Department of Economics and Statistics. *National Accounts of OECD Countries 1975–1987,* Vol. II. Paris, 1990.

Office of Management and Budget. *Analytical Perspectives. Budget of the United States Government, Fiscal Year 2004.* Washington, DC: US Government Printing Office, 2003.

Olsen, Edgar O. "Housing Programs for Low-Income Households." Working Paper No. 8208. Cambridge, MA: National Bureau of Economic Research, April 2001.

Oum, Tae Hoon; W G Waters; and Jong-Say Yong. "Concepts of Price Elasticities of Transport Demand and Recent Empirical Estimates: An Interpretative Survey." *Journal of Transport Economics and Policy* 26 (May 1992), pp. 139–54.

Palfrey, Thomas R, and Jeffrey E Prisbrey. "Anomalous Behavior in Public Goods Experiments: How Much and Why?" *American Economic Review* 87 (5) (December 1997), pp. 829–46.

Palmer, Karen; Wallace E Oates; and Paul R Portney. "Tightening Environmental Standards: The Benefit-Cost of the No-Cost Paradigm?" *Journal of Economic Perspectives* 9 (Fall 1995), pp. 119–32.

Panizza, Ugo. "On the Determinants of Fiscal Centralization: Theory and Evidence." *Journal of Public Economics* 74 (October 1999), pp. 97–140.

Papke, Leslie E. "Interstate Business Tax Differentials and New Firm Location: Evidence from Panel Data." *Journal of Public Economics* 45, no. 1 (June 1991), pp. 47–68.

Parry, Ian W H, and Wallace E Oates. "Policy Analysis in the Presence of Distorting Taxes." *Journal of Policy Analysis and Management* 19 (2000), pp. 603–13.

Passell, Peter. "Lend to Any Student." *New York Times* (April 1, 1985), p. A20.

Peacock, A T, and J Wiseman. *The Growth of Public Expenditure in the United Kingdom,* 2d ed. London: Allen & Unwin, 1967.

Pear, Robert. "Congress Weighs More Regulation on Managed Care." *New York Times* (March 10, 1997), p. A1.

Peltzman, Sam. "Class Size and Earnings." *Journal of Economic Perspectives* (Fall 1997), pp. 225–26.

Persson, Torsten, and Guida Tabellini. "Political Economics and Public Finance." Working Paper No. 7097. Cambridge, MA: National Bureau of Economic Research, April 1999.

Pigou, A C. *The Economics of Welfare.* New York: Macmillan, 1932.

Pollock, Ellen Joan. "Mediation Firms Alter the Legal Landscape." *Wall Street Journal* (March 22, 1993), p. B1.

Pommerehne, Werner. "Quantitative Aspects of Federalism: A Study of Six Countries." In *The Political Economy of Fiscal Federalism,* ed. Wallace Oates. Lexington, MA: DC Heath, 1977, pp. 275–355.

Portney, Paul R. "Policy Watch: Economics and the Clean Air Act." *Journal of Economic Perspectives* (Fall 1990), pp. 178–82.

Poterba, James M. "Dividends, Capital Gains, and the Corporate Veil: Evidence from Britain, Canada, and the United States." In *National Saving and Economic Performance,* ed. Douglas B Bernheim and John B Shoven. Chicago: University of Chicago Press, 1991, pp. 49–71.

Poterba, James M. "Taxation and Housing: Old Questions, New Answers." *American Economic Review* 82, no. 2 (May 1992), pp. 237–42.

Poterba, James M. "Do Budget Rules Work?" In *Fiscal Policy: Lessons from Economic Research*, ed. Alan J Auerbach. Cambridge, MA: MIT Press, 1997.

Poterba, James M, and Andrew Samwick. "Taxation and Household Portfolio Composition: US Evidence from the 1980s and 1990s." Working Paper No. 7392. Cambridge, MA: National Bureau of Economic Research, October 1999.

Power, Stephen. "War on Terror Has Lawmakers Battling for Deals." *Wall Street Journal* (January 24, 2003), p. A9.

Prizer, Charles J. "Risk Deserves Reward." *New York Times* (March 13, 1997), p. A26.

Raab, Selwyn. "12% of Stores Inspected Evaded Tax, Study Says." *New York Times* (November 2, 1986), p. 42.

Ramsey, Frank P. "A Contribution to the Theory of Taxation." *Economic Journal* 37 (1927), pp. 47–61.

Rawls, John. *A Theory of Justice.* Cambridge, MA: Harvard University Press, 1971.

Ricks, Thomas E. "Senate Clears $252 Billion Defense Bill That Underscores Industrial Policy." *Wall Street Journal* (July 5, 1994), p. A14.

Rosenberg, Debra. "Medicare's Foundation Is Crumbling." *Newsweek* (December 9, 2002), p. 11.

Ross, Gilbert L. "Price of Alarmism." *New York Times* (September 2, 1999), p. A26.

Rouse, Cecilia E. "Private School Vouchers and Student Achievement: An Evaluation of the Milwaukee Parental Choice Program." *Quarterly Journal of Economics* 113 (2) (May 1998), pp. 553–602.

Royal Commission on Taxation. *Report of the Royal Commission on Taxation,* Vol. 3. *Taxation of Income.* Ottawa, Canada: Queen's Printer and Controller of Stationery, 1966.

Rundle, Rhonda L. "The Outlook—Can Managed Care Manage Costs?" *Wall Street Journal* (August 9, 1999), p. A1.

Sakar, Shounak, and George R Zodrow. "Transitional Issues in Moving to a Direct Consumption Tax." *National Tax Journal* 46, no. 3 (September 1993), pp. 359–76.

Salins, Peter D. "Jump-Starting New York." *New York Times Magazine* (November 3, 1991), pp. 52–54.

Samuelson, Paul A. "The Pure Theory of Public Expenditure." *Review of Economics and Statistics* 36 (1954), pp. 387–89.

Samuelson, Paul A. "Diagrammatic Exposition of a Theory of Public Expenditure." *Review of Economics and Statistics* 37 (1955), pp. 350–56.

Samuelson, Robert J. "The True Tax Burden." *Newsweek* (April 21, 1986), p. 68.

Sander, William. "Expenditures and Student Achievement in Illinois: New Evidence." *Journal of Public Economics* 52 (October 1993), pp. 403–16.

Sargent, Thomas J, and Francois R Velde. "Macroeconomic Features of the French Revolution." *Journal of Political Economy* (1995), pp. 474–518.

Schick, Allen. "The Deficit That Didn't Just Happen." *The Brookings Review* (Spring 2002), pp. 45–46.

Schmedel, Scott R. "Tax Report." *Wall Street Journal* (January 9, 1991), p. A1.

Schultze, Charles L. "The Balanced Budget Amendment: Needed? Effective? Efficient?" *National Tax Journal* 48 (September 1995), pp. 317–28.

Sen, Amartya. "The Possibility of Social Choice." *American Economic Review* 89 (June 1999), pp. 349–78.

Shaviro, Daniel. "Effective Marginal Tax Rates on Low-Income Households." Washington, DC: Employment Policies Institute, 1999 [URL: http://www.epionline.org/study_shaviro_02-1999_charts.html].

Sheshinski, Eytan, and Luis Felipe Lopez-Calva. "Privatization and Its Benefits: Theory and Evidence." Working Paper. Cambridge, MA: Harvard Institute for International Development, January 1999.

Shleifer, Andrei. "State versus Private Ownership." *Journal of Economic Perspectives,* vol. 12, no. 4 (Fall 1998), pp. 133–50.

Shoven, John B. *Administrative Aspects of Investment-Based Social Security Reform.* Chicago: University of Chicago Press, 2000.

Siegel, Jeremy J. "The Dividend Deficit." *Wall Street Journal* (February 13, 2002).

Sigman, Hilary. "Letting States Do the Dirty Work: State Responsibility for Federal Environmental Regulation." Working Paper No. 9451. Cambridge, MA: National Bureau of Economic Research, January 2003.

Sinai, Todd, and Joel Waldfogel. "Do Low-Income Housing Subsidies Increase Housing Consumption?" Working Paper No. 8709. Cambridge, MA: National Bureau of Economic Research, January 2002.

Slemrod, Joel. "Do We Know How Progressive the Income Tax System Should Be?" *National Tax Journal* 36, no. 3 (September 1983), pp. 361–70.

Slemrod, Joel. *Do Taxes Matter? The Impact of the Tax Reform Act of 1986.* Cambridge, MA: MIT Press, 1991.

Slemrod, Joel. "Which Is the Simplest Tax System of Them All?" In *The Economic Effects of Fundamental Tax Reform,* ed. Henry Aaron and William Gale. Washington, DC: Brookings Institution, 1996.

Slemrod, Joel, and Jon Bakija. *Taxing Ourselves,* 2d ed. Cambridge, MA: MIT Press, 2000.

Slemrod, Joel, and Wojciech Kopczuk. "The Impact of the Estate Tax on the Wealth Accumulation and Avoidance Behavior of Donors." Working Paper No. 7960. Cambridge, MA: National Bureau of Economic Research, October 2000.

Sloan, Allan. "Fat Tax, Skinny Tax." *Newsweek* (June 13, 1997), p. 59.

Small, Kenneth A. "Urban Transportation Economics." *Fundamentals of Pure and Applied Economics.* Chur, Switzerland: Harwood Academic Publishers, 1992, pp. 43–45.

Smetters, Kent. "Ricardian Equivalence: Long-Run Leviathan." *Journal of Public Economics* 73 (September 1999), pp. 395–422.

Smith, Adam. *The Wealth of Nations.* London: J M Dent and Sons, 1977 (1776).

Social Security Administration, Office of the Chief Actuary [URL: http://www.ssa.gov], November 29, 2000.

Stavins, Robert N. "Experience with Market-Based Environmental Policy Instruments." Working Paper. Cambridge, MA: John F. Kennedy School of Government, Harvard University, December 1999.

Stein, Herbert. "The Income Inequality Debate." *Wall Street Journal* (May 1, 1996), p. A14.

Stein, Herbert. "Death *and* Taxes." *Wall Street Journal* (July 3, 1997), p. A10.

Steinberg, Jacques. "Private Groups Get 42 Schools in Philadelphia." *New York Times* (April 18, 2002), p. A3.

Stevenson, Richard W. "The Secret Language of Social Engineering." *New York Times* (July 6, 1997), pp. E1, E7.

Stigler, George J. "Director's Law of Public Income Distribution." *Journal of Law and Economics* 13 (April 1970), pp. 1–10.

Stiglitz, Joseph E. "Taxation, Corporate Financial Policy, and the Cost of Capital." *Journal of Public Economics* 2 (1973), pp. 1–34.

Stiglitz, Joseph E. "Notes on Estate Taxes, Redistribution, and the Concept of Balanced Growth Path Incidence." *Journal of Political Economy* 86 (1978), pp. S137–50.

Stone, Lawrence. *The Family, Sex, and Marriage in England, 1500–1800.* New York: Harper & Row, 1977.

Strumpf, Koleman S, and Felix Oberholzer-Gee. "Endogenous Policy Decentralization: Testing the Central Tenet of Economic Federalism." *Journal of Political Economy* 110 (February 2002), pp. 1–36.

Stuckart, Wilhelm, and Hans Globke. "Civil Rights and the Natural Inequality of Man." In *Nazi Culture,* ed. George L Morse. New York: Universal Library, 1968.

Sugg, Ike C. "Selling Hunting Rights Saves Animals." *Wall Street Journal* (July 23, 1996), p. A22.

Tannenwald, Robert. "Are State and Local Revenue Systems Becoming Obsolete?" *National Tax Journal* 55 (September 2002), pp. 467–90.

Tax Policy Guide. Washington, DC: Citizens for Tax Justice, June 1982.

Tempalski, Jerry. "The Impact of the 2001 Tax Bill on the Individual AMT." Washington, DC: National Tax Association, *Proceedings, Ninety-Fourth Annual Conference,* 2002.

Tideman, T Nicolaus, and Gordon Tullock. "A New and Superior Process for Making Social Choices." *Journal of Political Economy* 84 (December 1976), pp. 1145–1160.

Tiebout, Charles. "A Pure Theory of Local Expenditures." *Journal of Political Economy* 64 (1956), pp. 416–24.

Tobin, James. "Liquidity Preference as Attitude toward Risk." *Review of Economic Studies* 25 (February 1958), pp. 65–86.

Tomsho, Robert. "Fund-Raising Drive for Schools Leaves Manchester Disunited." *Wall Street Journal* (February 7, 2001), p. A1.

Topel, Robert H. "Factor Proportions and Relative Wages: The Supply-Side Determinants of Wage Inequality." *Journal of Economic Perspectives* 11 (Spring 1997), pp. 55–74.

Tresch, Richard W. *Public Finance: A Normative Theory,* 2d ed. New York: Academic Press, 2002.

Tucker, Robert C, ed. *The Marx-Engels Reader,* 2d ed. New York: W W Norton, 1978.

Uchitelle, Louis. "Now, Uncle Sam Wants You." *New York Times* (November 25, 2001), p. WK3.

US Bureau of the Census. *Historical Statistics of the United States, Colonial Times to 1970.* Washington, DC: US Government Printing Office, 1975.

US Bureau of the Census. *Statistical Abstract of the United States: 2002,* 122nd ed. Washington, DC: US Government Printing Office, 2002.

US Bureau of the Census. *Health Insurance Coverage: 2001* [URL: http://landview.census.gov/prod/2002pubs/p60-220.pdf], September 2002b.

US Department of Agriculture. *Food Stamp Program* [URL: http://www.fns.usda.gov/fsp/rules/Memo/Support/03/2001-characteristics.htm], 2003a.

US Department of Agriculture. *Characteristics of Food Stamp Recipients, Fiscal Year 2001.* Report No. FSP -03-CHAR, January 2003b.

US Department of the Treasury. *Integration of the Individual and Corporate Tax Systems.* Washington, DC: US Government Printing Office, 1992.

Vessella, Tom. "How about This for a Tax Plan: Eliminate the IRS." *The Princeton Tory* (March 2001), pp. 17–18.

Viscusi, W Kip. "Carcinogen Regulation: Risk Characteristics and the Synthetic Risk Bias." *American Economic Review* 85 (May 1995), pp. 50–54.

Viscusi, W Kip, and Joseph E Aldy. "The Value of a Statistical Life: A Critical Review of Market Estimates throughout the World." Working Paper No. 9487. Cambridge, MA: National Bureau of Economic Research, February 2003.

Walls, Margaret, and Jean Hanson. "Distributional Aspects of an Environmental Tax Shift: The Case of Motor Vehicle Emissions Taxes." *National Tax Journal* LII, no. 1 (March 1999), pp. 53–66.

Watanabe, Katsunori; Takayuki Watanabe; and Tsutomu Watanabe. "Tax Policy and Consumer Spending: Evidence from Japanese Fiscal Experiements." Working Paper No. 7252. Cambridge, MA: National Bureau of Economic Research, July 1999.

Weicher, John C. "Urban Housing Policy." In *Current Issues in Economics,* ed. Peter Mieszkowski and Mahlon R Straszheim. Baltimore: Johns Hopkins University Press, 1979, pp. 469–508.

Weimer, David L, and Michael J Wolkoff. "School Performance and Housing Values: Using Non-Contiguous District and Incorporation Boundaries to Identify School Effects." *National Tax Journal* 54 (June 2001), pp. 231–54.

Weinstein, Michael M. "Rewriting the Book on Capitalism." *New York Times* (June 5, 1999), p. B7.

Wetstone, Gregory S. "And Now, Regulatory Reform (See Above)." *New York Times* (February 23, 1995), p. A23.

Whitmore, Diane. "What Are Food Stamps Worth?" Industrial Relations Section Working Paper No. 468. Princeton, NJ: Princeton University, July 2002.

Will, George F. "The Soul of Conservatism." *Newsweek* (November 11, 1985a).

Will, George F. "You Ain't Seen Nothing Yet!" *Newsweek* (December 23, 1985b), p. 84.

Willig, Robert. "Consumer's Surplus without Apology." *American Economic Review* 66 (September 1976), pp. 589–97.

Wilson, James Q. "A New Approach to Welfare Reform: Humility." *Wall Street Journal* (December 29, 1994), p. A10.

Wilson, James Q. "Pork Is Kosher under Our Constitution." *Wall Street Journal* (February 15, 2000), p. A26.

Winston, Clifford, and Chad Shirley. *Alternate Route—Toward Efficient Urban Transportation.* Washington, DC: Brookings Institution Press, 1998.

Wolff, Edward N. "Recent Trends in Wealth Ownership, 1983–1998." Working Paper No. 300. Annadale-on-Hudson, NY: Jerome Levy Economics Institute, May 2000.

Wooldridge, Jeffrey M. *Introductory Econometrics,* 2d ed. Cincinnati, OH: South-Western College Publishing, 2003.

Yellen, Janet. "The Job's Not Done Yet." *New York Times* (July 18, 1997), p. A29.

Yelowitz, Aaron. "The Medicaid Notch, Labor Supply, and Welfare Participation: Evidence from Eligibility Expansions." *Quarterly Journal of Economics* 110 (1995), pp. 909–40.

"Your Stake in the Fight over Social Security." *Consumer Reports* (September 1981), pp. 503–10.

Zodrow, George R. "The Property Tax as a Capital Tax: A Room with Three Views." *National Tax Journal* 54 (March 2001), pp. 139–56.

Author Index

Subject Index

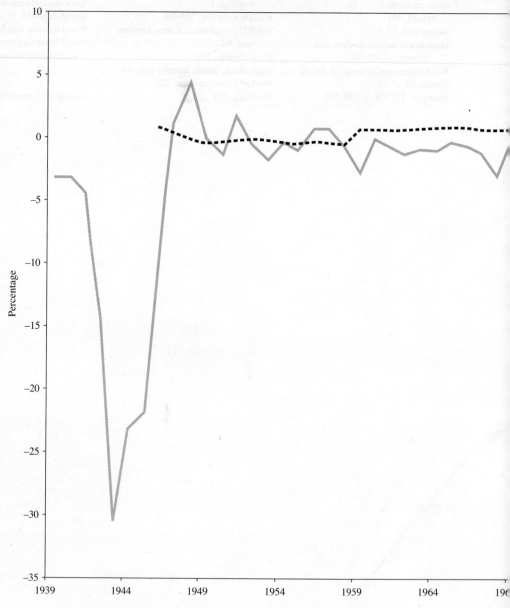

* Positive numbers are surpluses; negative numbers are deficits